Biko's Ghost

Brett Hilton-Barber,
Shadow, circa 1979.

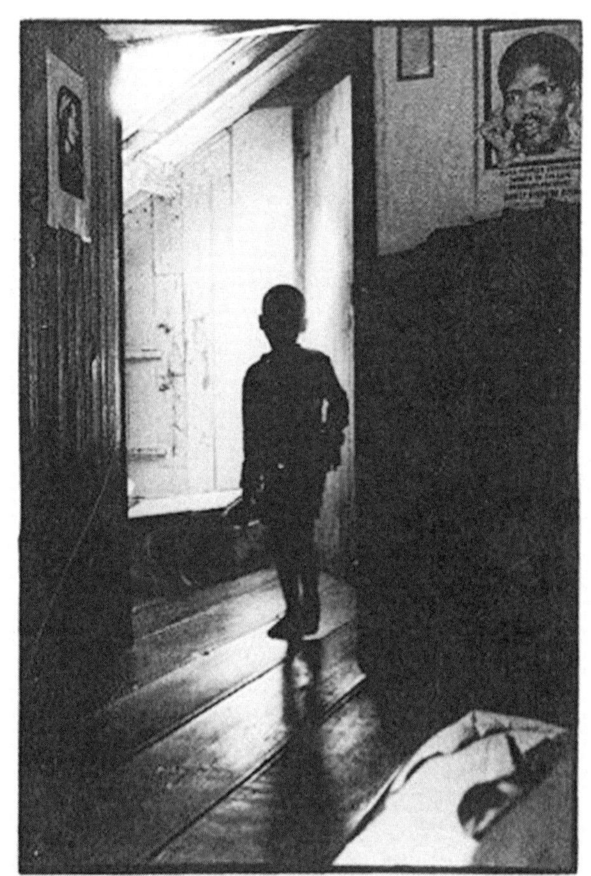

Biko's Ghost

The Iconography of Black Consciousness

SHANNEN L. HILL

University of Minnesota Press
Minneapolis | London

The University of Minnesota Press gratefully acknowledges the generous contribution made to the publication of this book from the Margaret S. Harding Memorial Endowment, honoring the first director of the University of Minnesota Press.

The frontispiece photograph on page ii by Brett Hilton-Barber is from *Staffrider* 2, no. 4 (November/December 1979): 40.

Published by the University of Minnesota Press
111 Third Avenue South, Suite 290
Minneapolis, MN 55401–2520
http://www.upress.umn.edu

Library of Congress Cataloging-in-Publication Data
Hill, Shannen L.
    Biko's ghost : the iconography of Black Consciousness / Shannen L. Hill.
    Includes bibliographical references and index.
    ISBN 978-0-8166-7636-1 (hc)
    ISBN 978-0-8166-7637-8 (pb)
    1. Biko, Steve, 1946–1977—Portraits. 2. Blacks in art. 3. Blacks in popular
culture—South Africa. 4. Black Consciousness Movement of South Africa.
    5. Art and social action—South Africa. 6. South Africa—Race relations. I. Title.
    N7628.B55H55 2015
    704.9'49305896—dc23
                                                    2015000052

Printed in the United States of America on acid-free paper

The University of Minnesota is an equal-opportunity educator and employer.

20 19 18 17 16 15   10 9 8 7 6 5 4 3 2 1

For Peter, Jonah, and Linus,
to no end

When I was very young . . . something in me wondered,
What will happen to all that beauty?

— James Baldwin, *The Fire Next Time*

Contents

Abbreviations

NP National Party
NUSAS National Union of South African Students
PAC Pan Africanist Congress
PCB Publications Control Board (of Parliament)
SAAWU South African Allied Workers Union
SACP South African Communist Party
SADE South African Department of Education
SANG South African National Gallery
SASM South African Students' Movement
SASO South African Students' Organization
SPRO-CAS Study Project on Christianity in Apartheid South Africa
STP Screen Training Project (in Johannesburg)
SWAPO South West Africa Peoples' Organization
TRC Truth and Reconciliation Commission
UDF United Democratic Front
USSALEP United States–South Africa Leadership Exchange Program

Introduction
Let's Talk about Consciousness

APPROACHING HISTORY THROUGH THE LENS OF VISUAL CULTURE ENABLES us to see how meaning is made through intersecting paths of analysis. South African visual culture in and around Black Consciousness and its foremost spokesman, Bantu Stephen Biko (1948–1977), begs our consideration from multiple vantage points. This is a book that interweaves their histories by combining the fields of art history, political science, media studies, and post/anticolonial theory to uncover how these two entities—an ideology on the one hand and the man popularly honored as its "father" on the other—have held influence these past forty years. These disciplinary paths led me to conclude that Mr. Biko, the famed martyr whose death in detention came to stand for the horrors of apartheid writ large, and Black Consciousness, popularly expressed as BC, are both entities that have mightily influenced race discourse in South Africa and, indeed, worldwide.

Regrettably, neither Biko nor the ideology he espoused has been properly credited with expanding our vision of this important topic. Their rejection of race and difference continues to be read as a promotion of these very things because too much emphasis is placed on the color that consciousness names. So let's talk about consciousness, place our emphasis here, and understand that black in this context is a unifying tool that enlivens opposition to (neo)colonial geopolitics but rejects the ideology of difference that drives it. Ben Khoapa, a BC leader of the 1970s, said that Black Consciousness meets its "cruel responsibility of going to the very gate of racism in order to destroy racism—to the gate, not further."[1] With this I agree.

In titling this introduction, I borrow from Biko's 1972 essay "Let's Talk about Bantustans," an often quoted critique of ethnic (neé racial) divisions manufactured by the state when it created ten "Homelands" within its own borders and ten more in Southwest Africa (now Namibia).[2] This legislation was driven by a belief in something called separateness (apartheid), or an essence of the body (race) that demanded that people live divided and apart from one another. It effectively stripped black South Africans of citizenship, a process called "denaturalization" coded in the nation's visual culture of the twentieth century. Biko's rejection of ethnicity in this essay is in keeping with BC's rejection of race as it welcomed all people commonly oppressed by colonial powers into what its founders called "the undivided house" of Black Consciousness.[3] Unlike their local predecessors who worked to end apartheid, the BC-minded did not adopt an alliance of parts that struggled in concert (what we might call a multicultural approach today) because it did not accept the racial divisions legislated under the Population Registration Act (1950, amended to include Indians in 1962). People divided once as Bantu, Coloured, and Indian were BC's audience. When BC leaders originally asked sympathetic liberals (then a white identifier) to work outside its network, it rejected neither them nor their efforts. Instead, BC advocated that its audience turn inward to generate a threefold sensibility: common unity against oppression, pride in an ancestry of resistance, and the call to act on the consciousness these create, to liberate oneself from racism's grip. BC leadership called individuals to actively insist on liberation across the board and in doing so express their own black consciousness.[4]

Let us pause here to consider visual culture in these previous paragraphs. Images are conjured through varied text. That text may be written or spoken; it may be drawn, photographed, or otherwise re-presented. Bantu translates as "people," and it names a family of languages that share common roots across a wide stretch of central Africa, from its western to eastern shores and down to its southern tip. As such, Bantu embodies being and its most profound effect: language, the hinge to heritage, home, and with these the will to resist denaturalization, or the stripping of one's rights in the land of their birth. "Let's Talk about Bantustans" was first published under the delightful pen name Biko necessarily chose after the state banned him in 1972 to King William's Town and Ginsberg, a township nearby.[5] Known as Frank Talk, Steve Biko and his defiance of the banning order became legendary. This essay is like so much of the literature that came from BC's initial hosts, the South African Students' Organization (SASO; Biko was its first president) and the Black Peoples' Convention (BPC; ditto), in that it borrowed from and contributed to the visual cultures of Pan Africanism and Negritude already circulating in the Atlantic world. This tricontinental awareness registers in all sorts of documents, from minutes of meetings in regional districts to policy manifestos signed by agents nationwide.[6] Thus the visual culture of Black Consciousness moves us well beyond the notion of race as worn on the body to the acceptance of race as a concept, an idea, something of the mind.

At Home in the World

Black Consciousness is an idea that means many things to people worldwide, but consistent among them is the belief that self-realization, a liberation of the mind, is enhanced by identification with a particular history. Although commonly associated with skin color, this history is named black not for any identification with race; rather, black codes the profound personal agency that drove people of African descent to liberate themselves and others from enslavement. In the 420 years of what is disappointingly known as the Atlantic Slave Trade (1450–1870), nearly the whole of what we now call the Global South fed the economies that ushered in our modern era. Its tricontinental ancestry includes people in South America, Africa, and Southeast Asia, with large populations in the West Indies, parts of Europe and North America. So, too, does Black Consciousness speak to and from those bodies once suppressed by an entity that, despite its variants, is both hegemonic and colonial. This entity wields power to divide the world's people into units of being (this thing called "race" or, in other contexts, "ethnicity") much as it once divided them into units of labor.[7] In concert with anticolonial movements expressed elsewhere in the Atlantic world, Black Consciousness sprung from South Africa in the early 1970s and was aligned with ideological and cultural movements that went before—Pan Africanism from North America and West Africa, and Negritude, to some extent, by way of the West Indies, France, and Senegal. Like these predecessors, Black Consciousness names a manner of thought with political and cultural consequence, and as such it cannot be claimed by any political or cultural organization. Thus we see its diverse expression in Brazil, the United States, Britain, and South Africa, among other places, as individuals join organizations named for Black Consciousness. In doing so, people proclaim their own roles in a transnational, anticolonial fight more than two centuries in the making. Black Consciousness is thought and expression, identification and agency. It cannot be pinned down.

As independent agents, people who adopt BC's core values of community, pride, and self-determination (or unity, ancestry, and agency/action) promote these from varied political bases. Since Black Consciousness is an ideology—an idea rooted in mindfulness toward the common objective of liberation—it is fluidly adopted and adapted by individuals who claim membership in different political parties. This is extremely important to our understanding of how race is framed in the world of visual culture wherein images received (be they in any form) greatly sway how we position ourselves in relation to one another.

In narrating the varied tracts of Black Consciousness in South Africa, I emphasize that the BC-minded are driven not by "being" black. They are driven by their personal claim to a history of self-liberation and, most important, the need to promote emancipation from what Biko called a multifaceted "situation of oppression."[8]

Black includes many hues. It is not positioned in relation to white. It is an identifier that indicates awareness of one's own ability to challenge neocolonialist practice wherever it may be in the world.

How Black Consciousness Changed Notions of Race in South Africa

"Apartheid" is an Afrikaans word that means "separateness," indicative of belief in inner (or essence/essential) difference based on the appearance of physical (or external/superficial) features and, with them, sociocultural practices. Built on a racist foundation, apartheid has come to stand for an entire structure of legalized racism rooted in South Africa but evidenced elsewhere in the world. Indeed, Jacques Derrida convinces us that apartheid is so commonly understood as such that it need not be italicized; few would find it foreign.[9] Although the nation's history hardly begins in 1948, this is the year that the National Party, a heavy favorite among Afrikaners, won legislative majorities in all branches of governance, after which a veritable flood of laws were passed built on the idea that separation of "races" was natural, thus Godly. Studying apartheid law and its enforcement surely takes one to troubling places, but the acts most relevant to a discussion of taxonomy include that which divided and classified people by skin color (Population Registration Act, 1950) and then divided the largest of these, Bantu, into eight ethnicities and ended parliamentary representation for "natives" (Bantu Self-Government Act, 1959). Finally, this same populace was compelled to become citizens of a proscribed area called a Bantustan, and they were stripped of South African citizenship (Bantu Homelands Citizens Act, 1970).

Of course, other forms of legalized racism preceded apartheid law. For the purposes of this study, we can begin in 1902 when British and Afrikaner, long at war, signed a treaty at Vereeniging, which in 1910 constituted the Union of South Africa and a disenfranchised majority. Varied opposition ran throughout, with the best known among them, the South African Native National Congress formed in 1912, changing its name to the African National Congress (ANC) eleven years later. At this time, the ANC accepted only black members, but it worked collaboratively with other political parties that were also segregated. Only the Communist Party of South Africa (later renamed the South African Communist Party, or SACP) welcomed all people regardless of race.[10] In 1959, the Pan Africanist Congress (PAC) formed after some ANC leaders objected to their party's alliance with the SACP and with those who formed the Congress Alliance when, in 1955, they signed the Freedom Charter, a historic demand for individual rights inherent to democracy. Other signatories also segregated themselves according to the units assigned by the state: the Coloured Peoples' Congress, the South African Indian Congress, and the South African Congress of Democrats (for white people). Until 1960, passive resistance was the preferred mode of expression for parties that organized opposition to laws that left the vast majority with few rights. This changed when, in March of that year, police fired on demonstrators who gathered in Sharpeville to protest pass laws, a debased system that monitored the movement of those called Bantu by the state. Despite their peaceful march, 69 people were killed and 180 wounded in what became known as the Sharpeville Massacre.

Now convinced that passive resistance would not work, parties in the Congress Alliance chose to take up arms against their nation rather than lose it through gross disenfranchisement. The PAC and the SACP advocated the same. Banned less than one month later under the Unlawful Organizations Act of 1960, the ANC and PAC continued operations in exile and concentrated energies on equipping and training recruits for armed struggle within South Africa. They also substantially aided liberation from colonial rule elsewhere in southern Africa. But in 1962 many ANC and PAC leaders were captured and charged with sabotage and conspiring to overthrow the government. As their leaders began long internments on Robben Island and elsewhere, a lull is said to have spread over organized resistance to apartheid in that decade. Meanwhile, members in exile continued their work.

The South African Students' Organization (SASO) was founded in Durban in 1969 under the principles of BC. SASO and its cousin, the Black Peoples' Convention (BPC, established in 1972), which spread BC beyond university campuses, unified by refusing to segregate by race as opposition parties once did, located ancestry in resistance to colonialism, and advocated action or self-determination. These principles—unity, ancestry, and action—formed the basis of what Biko called "modern black culture," and as such they underscored a truth seldom recognized: black labor created the modern era and black culture enabled modernity, or a conception of being modern. Borrowing from

Negritude philosophy, SASO promoted BC's cultural components (which, in the South African context, also masked its political intentions), which centered on the pride, beauty, strength, and humanity of black cultures. For instance, the phrase "Black Is Beautiful" was adopted, as was James Brown's anthem "Say It Loud: I'm Black and I'm Proud." Further, Pan African modes of community building were favored in BC's promotion of communalism, a socioeconomic structure called "African" in organization.[11] This was favored over capitalism and communism, both of which were seen as foreign imports. Naïve as such nativist conceits may be, nonetheless they were tools that dismantled racist stereotypes of a tribal Africa in need of civilization/colonization.

To overcome the formidable apparatus of apartheid, BC advocates called on millions to stand together beneath the common banner of black.[12] The tenor of resistance politics in the late 1960s prompted a break from liberals (effectively a white identifier) so the BC-minded could develop a plan of action that best reflected their concerns. (These men and women still called themselves nonwhite in SASO's early documents, suggesting how much a new self-awareness was needed.) Black brought strength in numbers, since in the 1970s nearly 90 percent of South Africans could self-identify with it.[13] By 1978, more than 8.5 million in the nation did so.[14] No doubt BC appealed for several reasons, but among them is the fact that it offered South Africans something rarely offered before: the chance to reject racial divisions assigned by the state in a way that only one political party, the South African Communist Party, had done prior. Through BC, the majority, constituted by varied hues, could "close their ranks . . . to work out their new direction clearly [in their own voice, free of liberal interruption] and bargain from a position of strength."[15]

South Africa's unique history of race and political expression includes something called *nonracialism,* which had, by the 1980s, become a rejection of racialist ideas (and their consequences) in all forms. Nonracialism proved persuasive in that dozens of antiapartheid organizations eventually adopted it; indeed, it formed the bedrock of the nation's new constitution in 1994. Enshrined there as a "founding value" of the nation, nonracialism remains profoundly ambiguous because, in Michael MacDonald's words, "'nonracialism' means a number of things, some developed by the ANC [which dominates liberation narratives], and others not, some consistent with alternate definitions and others not."[16] He locates the term's origins in the Cape Colony of the mid- to late nineteenth century and writes of its reinterpretation by political parties in the century that followed. In the liberal ethos of the Cape at this time, in 1872 nonracialism became law for a period when African and so-called Coloured men could vote once they passed the muster of European standards: they needed to own property and, after 1892, pass educational exams.[17] Thus race was conceived in cultural terms here, and this distinguished Cape Colony liberals from voters in Natal and the two Boer Republics, who understood race as biological difference.[18] In its first decades, the African National Congress, with national ambitions, accepted the latter by calling all "tribes" and "races" to combine efforts to ensure "*racial* equality," which MacDonald finds is "not the same as seeking full equality under the law."[19] In effect, the ANC interpreted race as conservatively as did legislators in the Boer Republics and Natal. MacDonald assesses its "commitment to non-racialism sincere and abiding," but reminds that the term was fluid and the "substance of the ANC's non-racialism was contingent on other forces."[20] I contend that Black Consciousness was just such a force. Until its influence began to spread, the ANC found identity in South Africa's multiracial, multicultural interaction. Although leaders like Albert Luthuli described the ANC's mission as realizing "a non-racial democracy," he meant it not as a denial of difference but as a need to ensure liberties for all despite these. Black Consciousness rejected the notion of difference and caused nonracialists to think hard about their position and how they came to it. Having done so, they were "welcome at the African table." Here the old adage rang true: where you sit determines where you stand.

Scholarly narratives of Black Consciousness frequently begin with mention of the National Union of South African Students (NUSAS), since Biko and others originally belonged to this body but left it to form the South African Students' Organization. Their rejection of NUSAS appeared to be a rejection of nonracialism, but this was not the case. Minutes from SASO and BPC meetings show that the question of uniform inclusion was debated throughout their existence.[21] Although BC's originators did not disfavor nonracialism, they disliked its inevitable consequence in South Africa's unique political system—a situation in which whites could speak only for people and realities they knew little about. (NUSAS membership was overwhelmingly white since university education was mostly for whites.) Thus in 1970 the BC-minded discontinued their work with NUSAS and created SASO.

At the time of SASO's creation, banned political parties of the previous decade continued their opposition in exile. The African National Congress (ANC) remained the best known among them, and it continued to promote a multiracialist approach until the early 1970s when it adopted nonracialism as its ideological home. The distinction is important. While multiracialism sought to unite members of different parties (and "tribes"), nonracialism sought to dissolve these distinctions; both are fervently antiracist.[22] The confluence of events—liberals now facing exclusion, and the dominant exiled resistance party adopting new terminology—caused Black Consciousness to be miscast as racial by the nonracialist camp. This troubling misinterpretation has persisted in liberation narratives that represent 1980s' nonracialism as the driving force behind what was called, post-1994, the "rainbow nation," when in fact that force remains centered in whiteness.

Rainbows dissolve. In this book I encourage us to rethink the dominance of nonracialist narratives and contest their power to name history's actors and influences. For instance, Black Consciousness is said to have been properly "abandoned" when, in the last quarter of 1977, the state killed Steve Biko, banned nineteen BC organizations and jailed their leaders, and caused hundreds to flee north to join armed militias in exile (mostly the ANC). Scholars condescend that BC "evolved" toward less "racially exclusive" ideologies and ultimately became "obsolete."[23] Others persuade that a "culture of resistance" emanated from nonracialist quarters in the 1980s, when in fact its origins are a decade earlier and located in Black Consciousness. As the histories addressed in this book evidence, BC remained highly influential despite the censoring of its expression by both the state and antiapartheid activists. As an ideology, BC always had the flexibility to mean and be different things, thus the adoption of its principles (and its iconography) by people of varied politics is expected.

Contrary to the perception of Black Consciousness as an ideology mired in intellectualism and devoid of practice, BC proponents have always advocated action and produced it.[24] Whether realized through the grassroots tactics employed by members of early BC organizations or through the images examined in a central stream of this book, BC positively effected change on a mass scale before its leading advocates were banned, detained, and in some cases killed between 1971 and 1977.[25] These same tactics were used by more people in the 1980s, but scholars of visual culture have located the roots of the decade's prolific poster production, for instance, in nonracialist history.[26] I recover the central influence of BC in creating a "culture of resistance" from which people of extremely different families could unite to advance apartheid's end. Whiteness still frames this history, and we would do well to reconsider its centrality.

So, too, has whiteness crucially informed global response to Steve Biko in the years since his death when he became the best-known martyr to a monolithic (thus mythical) antiapartheid cause. Many people know him only because of the state's hand in his death, which, by virtue of its reasons, lasted an agonizing five days. Cast in this light, he remains imprisoned in the last month of his life. I analyze this interest in the pages that follow, but more important is the BC prevalence for staging the continued life of Biko's ideas, or the ongoing influence of Black Consciousness despite the state's massive suppression of it. Given that this control from above began in 1971, one wonders why the efficacy of BC was questioned since it was under attack before its second year of existence. That one can steadily locate Black Consciousness over more than four decades of South African visual culture thoroughly discredits the notion that it was ineffectual after 1977. As the visuals reproduced here show, BC has in fact proved meaningful to millions despite decades of censored voice and vision.

Who Was Steve Biko?

The third child of four born to Mzingaye and Alice Nokuzole "Mamcethe" Biko, Steve was known as Bantu to his family, a name meaning "people" that Steve translated to "son of man" when he felt mischievous.[27] Known for his quick wit even as a boy, Biko was well loved by the Ginsberg community in which he was raised after having been born on December 18, 1946, at his grandmother's home in Tarkastad, all within the Eastern Cape. Indeed, it was this town of eight hundred families that raised the funds Biko needed, at sixteen years of age, to attend the Lovedale Institution in Alice, also home to Fort Hare University, both famed venues for black education. Within three months of study, Biko was caught up in a sweep of suspected activists with presumed links to Poqo, a Cape-based organization with links to the then-banned thus exiled Pan Africanist Congress. Interrogated by seven police officers at once, he was not charged, but Lovedale expelled him just the same. His brother Khaya, also detained, was arrested and held for ten months before winning acquittal. The entire episode stung. Biko later described it as a political awakening, "a bitter experience. I was terribly young."[28]

Raised in a Christian home where politics leaned toward a PAC platform, Biko found the party's exclusivist Africanism unappealing, though it seems he did appreciate its rejection of Marxism due to its race-blinded vision.[29] Thus when he arrived at the Mariannhill-based St. Francis College outside Durban in 1964, at age eighteen, he was well prepared for debates of both a political and theological bent. With classmates he listened to news of African liberations elsewhere and engaged in long discussions with both an unnamed Catholic nun at Mariannhill and, through correspondence, Father Aelred Stubbs, an Anglican whom he met in Alice when he was arrested. Although religion was not central to his life, Biko sought these discussions and was thus drawn to and comfortable with religion's potential to activate meaningful social change. He desired a law degree like his father, but as this was associated with political activism and thus discouraged, he chose medicine instead and won a scholarship to the University of Natal in Durban where in 1966 he enrolled in the Non-European Section together with other "nonwhite" students. Here he joined the National Union of South African Students, and through the limitations of this experience combined with empowering discussions at Mariannhill, Natal, and the University Christian Movement (founded 1968) he developed both the ideological basis for Black Consciousness and the methods to put it into action (see chapter 1).

Biko's father and maternal grandfather were policemen; the former studied for a law degree at the University of South Africa but died of an illness before completing it when Biko was four years old. His mother raised four children on the salary she earned first as a domestic laborer in Ginsberg for twenty-three years, then as a cook at Grey Hospital in King William's Town, a white city nearby. Surely Biko's experience of his mother's life held profound influence. Biographer Lindy Wilson writes that he was "deeply committed to her well-being. It made a profound impression on him that she labored for such long hours in such unrewarding jobs, for very little pay."[30] Such was the strain of his advocacy when as president of the South African Students' Organization (1970) he advanced its programs beyond university campuses into communities and eventually helped found the Black Peoples' Convention and Black Community Programmes.

Biko is said to have been a physically large person whose personality was equal in size. Many favorably recall his interest in listening, even drawing out the opinions of others through a kind of vigorous dialogue he enjoyed. He is remembered as someone who stood back and put others forward, so that despite his appealing manner "he managed not to be dominant. It was an infusion of ideas which he encouraged."[31] He is credited for getting people to raise issues instead of simply respond to them. Wilson's vision of the man, and our incapacity to fully translate it, fills the picture most clearly for me:

His arrival in a doorway, his large physical frame relaxed into a chair, were essential elements of who he was. The welcome he gave, the sound of his laughter and his immediate questioning curiosity are glaringly missing here. He is not easily packaged. Biko was by no means a paragon of virtue. Though he could hold his drink, he often drank too much; he earned a reputation of being a "womaniser"; and he could not always judge for himself his own emotional and psychological capacity. He was essentially human, but also exceptional.[32]

In writing the book I know this: it is not responsible to write separately about Biko or Black Consciousness or the visual cultures to which they have given rise (as an anonymous reader of a shorter draft once suggested I must do), lest their histories remain woefully unconnected and the story falls short of its potential. One must present them together, in one space, in order to best comprehend the lasting presence of their message today.

The Look of This Book

A study of this kind demands attention to art history, visual culture, and political theory and practice. This particular history of an ideology invested in tri-continental empowerment is but one of many worldwide that beg our attention. A visual history of Steve Biko and Black Consciousness in South Africa takes us through three streams of analysis that require varied approaches or different (but sometimes related) theories of representation. Further, my essential argument requires a chronological narrative, thus I weave these stories and theories across chapters, sometimes focusing on the man, other times on the ideology, but always on the visual culture that creates them anew through history.

We begin when Black Consciousness does, in 1967, in a chapter that first develops its history of BC aesthetics from the voices registered in its central organs, SASO and the BPC. Through all matter of material culture—manifestos, newsletters, press statements, public letters and lectures, cultural journals, and records of demonstration (in music, poetry, literature, and art)—I have located an aesthetics of Black Consciousness that promotes unity, ancestry, and action. Such materials offer some pictures, but the richness of vision they create comes mostly from word. Thus the material of visual culture: both pictures and text (printed, spoken, heard) combine to forge ideas, some gaining greater sway than others through repetition. As repetition and representation require a gap (re-), there is always fresh space for translation. It is not surprising that in the chapter's second half we find that BC ideals are expressed in different ways in the lives and works of artists in the Johannesburg–Pretoria nexus. But whether located in figural (thus potentially narratable) studies, or in non-figural (frequently called abstract) ones, their makers advanced BC's vision of Steve Biko's "modern black culture," and in this vision was fundamental. Gavin Jantjes, whose explicit support of BC has circulated for more than four decades, described the need for "black art . . . to create a new visual language—a new voice . . . that is addressing the realities of the present."[33] The visual language may vary, but the voice, Black Consciousness, is the same.

Whereas the first chapter establishes a language of aesthetics, BC iconography dominates chapter 2. Iconography differs from aesthetics in that whereas the latter can convey a sensibility or outlook, icons are (once exclusively religious) images that come to embody an ideal. They personify potential. Whether they include the representation of a face or not, icons are portraits just the same. Chapter 2 analyzes varied portraits of Biko and Black Consciousness that circulated in South Africa's press in the last quarter of 1977 when his murder, BC's banning, and the state's inquest into the cause(s) of Biko's death transpired. Four types of portraits are studied: Biko as Statesman, as Everyman, as Fist, and the many Bikos that follow what I call his Iconic Autopsy.[34] Because his death was torturous in fact and in length (after three weeks of detention, he suffered greatly in the five days before the brain hemorrhage he sustained proved fatal), the enormous volume of visual culture created in this period is violent in nearly every facet. This is true whether Biko's likeness displays overt injury or not. Given that his living likeness was printed alongside narratives of a long death, the two become one in the language of visual culture. In these weeks icons battled. In the state's portrayal/portrait, Biko is weak and apt to naturally decline, as his is a body in duress, dead, ultimately forced to yield to the state's pathology. Yet these same state portraits embodied strength and conviction when illustrated in the popular press. Thus theories of spectacle and trauma fuel and feed this history, one that is actively remade annually in the days surrounding that of Biko's death, September 12.[35]

Chapter 3 compares works of the late seventies and early eighties that remain the best-known works about Biko today. Those by Ezrom Legae are abstract compositions with hybrid creatures in varied states of strain. They are united in their common plight: a struggle for freedom (of flight, of person) and the transformative states these invariably bring. Others by Paul Stopforth include the iconic autopsy variety in chapter 2, thus they are intimate renderings of one person's well-known decline and demise. But unlike their predecessors they cannot sit as spectacle and process; working through the images is central to dislodging them from the torment of superficial wonder. Rendering art when the wounds of Biko's death were fresh, artists Legae and Stopforth meaningfully delved into his traumatized remains by asking questions of their practice. What is the call of a visual culture devoted to a death of this kind? How were artists to respond to the dramatic death narrated (sometimes performed, literally "staged") in chapter 2? What might we gain from time spent with these works, investing ourselves in their layers? Julia Kristeva's well-known theories about "the power of horror" resonate meaningfully in this study because they encourage process as a means to control abjection. By giving themselves over to the visual culture of Biko's death, Legae and Stopforth translated it for others, made it comprehensible in ways that artistry can. Their attention to the effective detail of the wound rather than the spectacular arena of the press enables pain to register within us. Indeed, so operational is that detail that devotional icons have emphasized it since before the early modern era, which is to say the wound has been starkly imag(in)ed for this effect since medieval times. Rendered realistically by Stopforth, or abstractly by Legae, these famed works "about Biko's death" are ultimately so much more.

Chapters 4 and 5 are the heart of the book in that they respond to scholarship that has sidelined BC's history (at best) and vilified it (at worst), by presenting visual evidence of its efficacy over a period of intensified silencing. Chapter 4 explores print media of two kinds to show the pervasiveness of both BC aesthetics and iconography in popular graphics. Newsletters and literary journals are studied first for signs of BC aesthetics that resonate, often loudly, in pictures and poems, drawings and short stories, and in explicit opinion columns and news reporting. Next we explore posters issued by political organizations that discredit Black Consciousness as outdated and ineffectual, but borrow SASO and BPC iconography to advance their cause. They include the raised clenched fist icon of BC, most particularly of the hands-breaking-chains variety, which chapter 2 has established as a portrait of Biko and BC at once (for he embodies it like no other). I reject the high/low divides that some may find in an analysis of a literary journal on the one hand and a popular, streetworn graphic on the other. Both fix "the people" as audience as they endlessly feed one another, and their tangled shifts constitute a vital organ of visual culture. They are even subject to the same forces of history and its inquiry: for instance, both *Staffrider* (a journal with limited subscription) and the United Democratic Front (umbrella for more than six hundred political organizations with millions of members) are understood to be the achievements of nonracialists, yet the visual culture of Black Consciousness pops up in the print matter of both.

This critique of BC's neglect is followed by one devoted to censorship within other realms: the state's heavy-handed, even iconoclastic response to works about Biko and the assault that self-described "cultural workers" made on fellow South Africans who invested themselves in art making (elsewhere framed as a *debate,* I find that word too polite for the assumptions embedded in the argument). In notes to this chapter and the next, readers will find discussion of the proposed censure of "the Biko doctors" by the national professional organizations to which they belonged, cases that lasted six years and secured Biko's importance to the question of medical ethics in South African history. So, too, did these cases against district surgeons inform the visual culture of Biko because the press reported on them with some regularity until they were resolved mid-1985, just after the first state of emergency was declared on July 21.

A period of transitions and truths of the most heart-wrenching kind consumed the nation in the 1990s as it climbed out of civil war, waded through years of violent conflict among factions seeking to establish their place (entirely common to nations that battled within borders), held its first democratic election, and established a new constitution deemed the most progressive in the world at the time, all within a bit more than five years. Chapter 6 historicizes Biko's legacy during this uncertain period when hope and worry intertwined daily. In cases large (mass-produced works) and small (singular pieces), Biko is cast as a saint of sorts, someone who laid down his life to realize a more humane and just world, thereby assuring peaceful transition from governance with "separateness" (apartheid) at its core to one of togetherness, or ubuntu.

Trauma and representation return to anchor the second half of chapter 6. In 1997, the Truth and Reconciliation Commission began hearing testimony from five police officers implicated in Biko's death. Viewed on television and in print, the hearings enabled Fiona Rankin-Smith to muse that the figures in Paul Stopforth's famed triptych *The Interrogators* (Figure 3.2) had "come to life."[36] Since the figures are based on press imagery circulated during the state's 1977 inquest, at that moment a network of visual culture stumbled forth—from event to photograph to mass circulation into the hands of an artist, his intervention and its display; audience reception; then, twenty years on, back to mass circulation and an artwork recalled, or imagined, in conversation. In real time, the length of that circuit was accompanied by all sorts of collisions, breaks, and fusions, each of which brought new experiences to the artists and other authors who examined trauma through Biko's death. Thus chapter 6 also engages recent theories centered on memory's relation to violence, the centrality of a translator (be they artist, as Kristeva would have it, or audience, as Veena Das prefers), and those that explore "truth" in its varied manifestations.

To end this book, as one reader suggested, with the Biko case before the Truth and Reconciliation Commission would be to end with a story based in trauma and recovery from it postapartheid. It would also suggest that the story of Biko and BC ends here, with the nation's scrutiny of the past, when in fact I mean to emphasize the ongoing mobility of these two "beings," both of which embody ideals that we value and contest today. Artists and activists continue to rely on Biko and BC to represent their interests in the fraught terrains that are at once political and cultural: heritage, identity, access to markets, and, with those, access to a more comfortable life. Chapter 7 offers three case studies in how Biko and BC are envisioned, and thus useful, in our time: as contested by political parties who claim his legacy as their own; as base point for a collective of artists who used it to reinvigorate listening among arts arbiters in and around Cape Town; and in intersections of picture and word, private and public, high and low, in which activists and artists invest in BC's visual culture to make meaning of identity today.

I leave you with a consideration of Brett Hilton-Barber's photograph published here as the frontispiece. I like this image because it captures so many of the tensions and beauty that arise from this book's subject. The maker aimed for artistry, a quest that the makers of the posters within the photograph would have discredited. Further, the histories this image contains are multifold. (Untitled when published in *Staffrider,* Hilton-Barber asked that it be called "Shadow" in this book.) One is aware of a child in a room we take to be home. Two portraits, both posters, hang prominently, their subjects (Amina Cachalia on the left and Steve Biko on the right) pointing to one another with hands and eyes. Their common gesture and gaze form a bridge over the boy who has joined us here, in this intimate space, from the entrance behind his shoulder, stage right. Daylight saturates the foyer and backlights the boy to cast him in silhouette. Unlike shadows, silhouettes have no ghostly features. Born from an act that cuts a likeness from black paper, silhouettes affirm a presence in the world in that they are individuated and have mass. This boy's being—his sense of self—is affirmed daily by the heroes' presence in this space, a family home. Their methods took different forms but their mission was the same: ending the racist government of apartheid and with it the racism it supported. To do this one took risks (one could be arrested for displaying such posters anywhere, even at home),[37] but the future, signaled here through the presence of youth, demands our action. Once *conscientized*, as Biko originally put it (a term adopted by many nonracialists in subsequent years), we must act to secure justice, the message that confronts us through the boy.

This boy's message is my own. Once aware of the historic and varied visual culture that expresses the ongoing value of Black Consciousness, we can no longer leave it out of the picture.

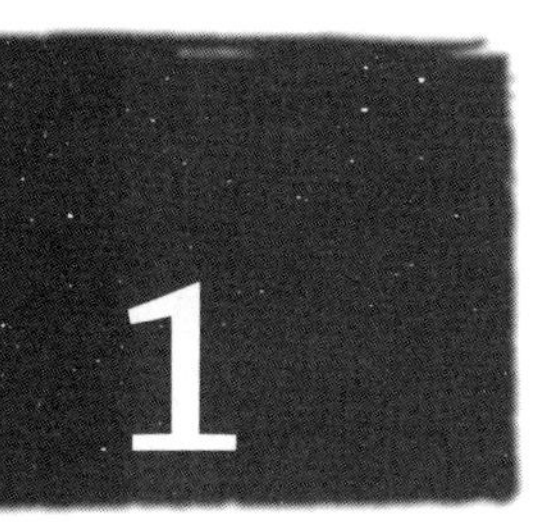

Shaping Modern Black Culture in the 1970s

When you say, "Black Is Beautiful," what in fact you are saying . . . is: Man, you are okay as you are; begin to look upon yourself as a human being.

— Steve Biko, 1976

THE MEN WHO FIRST FORMULATED THE IDEOLOGY OF BLACK CONSCIOUSNESS did so in the period leading up to July 1967.[1] Soon before, in the eastern half of a large territory then called the Cape Province, students at tertiary schools eagerly consumed and discussed news of liberation movements elsewhere in the world. At Fort Hare, the nation's most famed black university, talks were frequent about anticolonial and anti-imperialist struggles in Angola, Mozambique, Guinea-Bissau, the United States through the Black Power and civil rights movements, and, above all, Vietnam, where "the battering of the American giant in the jungles" satisfied.[2] At St. Francis College in Mariannhill, Steve Biko's alma mater, classmates also debated the tactics of African liberation movements and eagerly awaited news of Hastings Banda, Ahmed Ben Bella, and Oginga Odinga in nations later named Malawi, Algeria, and Kenya.[3] An array of banned material was exchanged on black campuses and in townships across the country.[4] These included the works of African leaders and writers who promoted Pan Africanism, like Chinua Achebe, Amilcar Cabral, Frantz Fanon, Kenneth Kaunda, Patrice Lumumba, Ngũgĩ wa Thiong'o, Kwame Nkrumah, Julius Nyerere, and Sékou Touré; writers and activists from the United States who did the same, like Amiri Baraka (then named Imamu Baraka), Eldridge Cleaver, Ralph Ellison, Charles Hamilton, Martin Luther King Jr., Kwame Touré (then named Stokely Carmichael), Richard Wright, and Malcolm X; Negritude writers, such as Aimé Césaire and Léopold Sédar Senghor; and revolutionaries from other parts of the tricontinental world, like Fidel Castro, Ernesto Che Guevara, Paulo Freire, Mao Tse-Tung, and Võ Nguyên.[5] Of these, Black Consciousness is said to have been particularly influenced by Fanon and Cabral,[6] and Carmichael and Hamilton's *Black Power: The Politics of Liberation in America* is called "a seminal work" to BC's evolution within South Africa.[7]

Student-led sit-ins and other demonstrations worldwide also affected the development of BC activism in the late 1960s and early 1970s.[8] Students at Fort Hare staged their own response to the appointment of yet another Afrikaner to a top administrative post (Figure 1.1).[9] Twenty-one students, the well-known BC leader Barney Pityana among them, were expelled and Operation Catwalk was born. Extending on the poster arts issued by a campus organization called Ndikubheilkile and plastered at Fort Hare, mostly in the form of political satire and commentary in text rather than image, those involved with Operation Catwalk painted graffiti across campus one night in late October 1968. Caught by surprise, the university had no ready response, so the graffiti was not erased until three weeks later. Students at Rhodes University in nearby Grahamstown showed solidarity through mimicry.[10]

The sentiments expressed at Fort Hare were akin to that expressed by James Brown when he sang "Sing it loud! I'm black and I'm proud!"—powerful words that resonated across the tricontinental world in which Black Consciousness flourishes. Words that testify and demand that we witness, this phrase was scrawled on South African walls and declared as a fundamentally "African Cultural Concept" by Biko in an essay of the same title.[11] Biko saw the vitality of Brown's message as imparting "our modern culture(:) A culture of defiance, self-assertion and group pride, and solidarity. This is a culture that emanates from a situation of the common experience of oppression."[12] Music and song, he wrote, have long been used by oppressed people to reassure troubled souls in troubled times. And they bear an important message: "Our songs (have) made much more urgent the need to settle the score."[13]

Enrolled in segregated universities around Durban, the founders of Black Consciousness gave organization to their beliefs by forming the South African Students' Organization (SASO) in 1969. As students, SASO members were intellectually inclined, even gifted, given that they thrived despite the limits of the Bantu Education Act (1953), which diminished facilities and faculty, and restricted learning so as "to equip [students subjected to it] to meet the demands which the economic life of South Africa will impose upon him," that is, a life of service to white interests.[14] For SASO members, nearly four thousand in number, the writers who held their attention urged action.[15] From the beginning SASO took a grassroots approach to positively effecting change. Their newsletters always

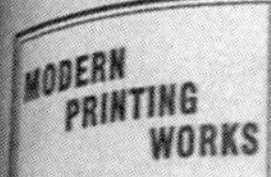
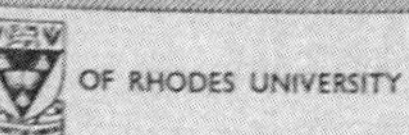
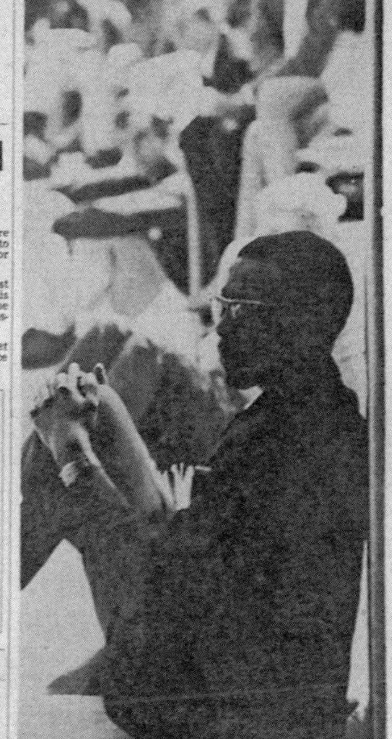
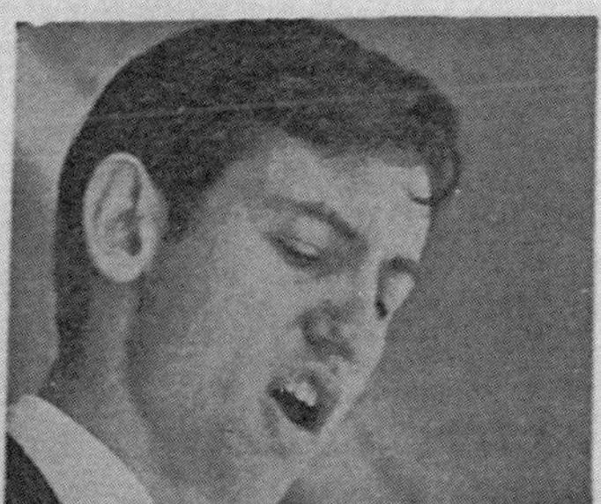

FIGURE 1.1. Student at a sit-in, Fort Hare University, 1968. Printed in *Rhodeo,* the student newspaper of Rhodes University, September 19, 1968. Reprinted by permission of *Activate,* formerly *Rhodeo.*

represented blackness as strength, a calling of historic African heroes, and this blackness as strength emphasized power of unity in concert.

Understanding the value that culture holds to convey BC ideals, SASO organized a Cultural Committee (CulCom) that began to solicit and field proposals from artists, and it hired them to perform at SASO events large and small. Lefifi Tladi appreciated the CulCom members who visited him and others outside Pretoria because they were "not vertical invaders," that is, they were there to listen and learn and share and promote.[16] David Koloane worked with CulCom to build financial support for The Gallery, a project put on hold when SASO was banned mid-October 1977. Until then, SASO's Cultural Committee was at work realizing BC's vision in the arts. From quite early on, the ideology's aesthetics were expressed through varied forms, political and artistic, with all kinds of cross-pollination.

In their earliest form, Black Consciousness aesthetics embraced the rhetoric of the ideology by challenging the very notion of difference (first racial, later ethnic) at the heart of apartheid and, indeed, at the core of colonial and imperial interests elsewhere in the world. Proponents celebrated Africa's past, emphasizing the essential humanness of all people. Heroes were honored, both well known and unnamed, who showed fearlessness in the face of a formidable enemy that denied them fundamental human rights. By unifying as black, and glorifying Africa's past, BC adherents experienced a shift in awareness from *less-able,* as cast by apartheid's makers, to *self-able.* Action depended on one thing: a belief in oneself as agent of change.

In word and image, music and fashion, this aesthetic of conviction made headway among the BC-minded at this time, as all were seen as politically pertinent. As Biko once put it, "A country in Africa, in which the majority of the people are African, must inevitably exhibit African values and be African in style."[17] Black Power culture from the United States particularly inflected meaning within Black Consciousness.[18] Some students dropped the "slave names" they had once gone by and chose their African names for daily use.[19] The slogan "Black Is Beautiful" was exchanged. Steve Biko commented on it at the SASO-BPC trial in May 1976:

> I think that slogan has been meant to serve and I think is serving a very important aspect of our attempt to get at humanity. You are challenging the very deep roots of the Black man's belief about himself. When you say, "Black is Beautiful," what in fact you are saying to him is: Man, you are okay as you are; begin to look upon yourself as a human being.[20]

More men were wearing dashikis, but a young Willie Bester, whose work appears in chapter 6, wore an army jacket with "Black Is Beautiful" stitched on the back along with a peace sign.[21] Women within SASO in particular recall the hairstyles and hot pants they favored to complement their new sense of beauty. Some chose an Afro for its global currency. Mamphela Ramphele tossed out wigs, once worn for a "respectable" look, and opted to show her shorn locks.[22] Sales of products used to straighten and bleach black hair dropped in Natal, a sign that women in this province enjoyed the personal aesthetics of Black Consciousness.[23] Transgression of expectations was important, particularly to BC women, many of whom also smoked and drank along with their male counterparts. As Ramphele put it, "As a woman, an African woman at that, one had to be outrageous to be heard, let alone to be taken seriously."[24]

Steve Biko credited tricontinental solidarity with the rise of Black Consciousness and found both inspiration and comfort in this extended family. He described his own time and place as participant in "a surge towards black consciousness . . . a phenomenon that has manifested itself throughout the so-called Third World. . . . This is the modern black culture that is responsible for the restoration of our faith in ourselves and therefore offers a hope, the direction we are taking from here."[25] Black Consciousness adherents argued that black culture values humanity above all (is "Man-centered" in the language of the day) and that this is visible in many ways: in the ready welcome given upon entering the home, in the sense of extended family experienced by a whole community, in the intimacy shared with and concern given to one's neighbors. Keen to experience, modern black culture understands suffering and, through it, shares a spiritual response that is fundamentally, deeply centered on the betterment of life for all. Having shared oppression, tricontinental peoples share a survivor instinct that manifests itself first in the ability to adjust and adapt, borrowing and lending cultural elements as desired. But ultimately they share the decision to oppose their oppressors' values, both cultural and political. Localizing this tricontinental culture, Biko described how BC's audience should respond: "Being an historically dispossessed group, they have the strongest foundation from which to operate. The philosophy of BC, therefore, expresses group pride and determination of blacks to rise and attain the envisaged self."[26]

Demonstrating agency through unity was always central to BC's method and mission. And in more personal ways, identifying with Black Consciousness and living its creed projected pride, one that they hoped would inspire. As Temba Sono, then president of SASO, put it in 1971:

> We can be what we want to be only if we stand up and BE what we want to be. We *can* be black, with black face and black faith and our deeds the epitome of that which is noble—Blackness. We do not have to prove our humanity in spite of our blackness. Our blackness is an aspect of humanity. This is what the student in the black community teaches the people. He does this through self-help schemes.[27]

Black Consciousness thus views humanity as implicit to an awareness that fundamentally constituted the self as much as it was realized outside the self. Popularly embraced as ubuntu today, humanity is the realization that "a person is a person through other people." To be black is to be noble (ancestral) and to be noble is to promote modern black culture, an ethos that swells from a common experience of oppression. In SASO's literature, the representation of Black Consciousness is fundamentally one of struggle, and both sides of that equation are represented: one of personal despair and one of communal triumph with emphasis on the latter.

In the first year of its existence, SASO executive officers identified a number of dates on the calendar to emphasize their message. March 21 was Heroes' Day, so named to make clear that the sixty-nine peaceful protesters gunned down at Sharpeville that day in 1960 were not victims of apartheid but heroes of the struggle against it. Called "biblical," the sacrifices of common people were commemorated on this day to offer blacks "a sense of achievement, a sense of security in being united over a particular aspect of our history."[28] Persons of historical import were also newly celebrated by SASO as a corrective to the lessons taught at school and to inspire black pride. As Biko wrote:

> We have to rewrite our history and produce in it the heroes that formed the core of our resistance to the white invaders. More has to be revealed, and stress has to be laid on the successful nation-building attempts of men such as Shaka, Moshoeshoe and Hintsa. . . . Our culture must be defined in concrete terms. We must relate the past to the present and demonstrate a historical evolution of the modern black man.[29]

Living leaders of the Pan Africanist Congress and the African National Congress were also honored, despite laws that banned reproducing their words or image. Robert Sobukwe, Nelson Mandela, and Govan Mbeke were all called "our true leaders" by BC advocates, regardless of their approach to dismantling apartheid. As Biko put it, with membership in a Black Consciousness organi-

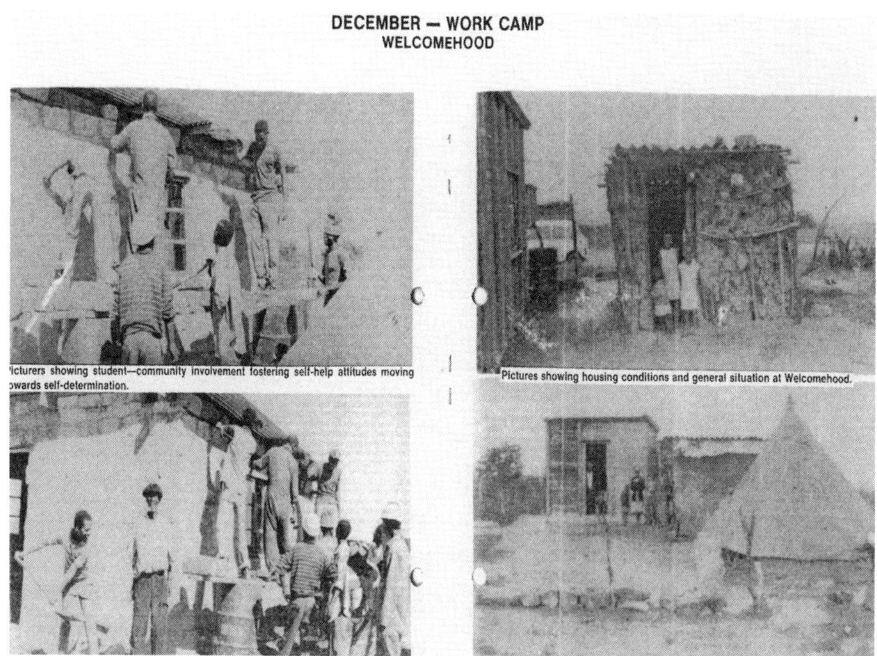

FIGURE 1.2. *December—Work Camp, Welcomehood.* Unattributed photographs within *SASO Newsletter* (March/April 1976): 8–9. University of South Africa Archive.

zation, "you develop a hope, you develop a view of history, you begin to know where you are going."[30]

The SASO calendar marked May 10 as Suffer Day and August 17 as Compassion Day so that student members would be prompted to focus energy on solving problems common to those whom they sought to help. As in Black Theology, these celebratory dates appealed to adherents' sense of humanity in their call to improve the lives of individuals in the present. Though BC graphics largely emphasized black agency, the BC-minded understood that "very colorful language" about the realities of poverty could "touch the mothers . . . [and] touch the men" in an audience. Articulating the effects of poverty on children was deemed particularly persuasive.[31]

Published in the March/April 1976 issue of SASO's newsletter, the photo essay *December—Work Camp, Welcomehood* (Figure 1.2) elicits interest in that it depicts SASO members at left alleviating the poverty represented at right.

This single-page essay, composed of a title, four photographs, and two captions, represented one of SASO's expectations of its members: they were to work within communities during periods of university recess. Photographic essays are fundamentally political in nature and, though captioned, give prominent weight to the visual.[32] In this way, this comparative essay structures its argument in pairs, with teams in opposing columns. At right, "Pictures showing housing conditions and general situation at Welcomehood." Four types of homes are shown, with their occupants looking at us through the camera. The home at top is in significant disrepair; its mud-based walls need resurfacing. The children in its doorway are more prominent than any other in this column, so they embody the poverty of their neighborhood and, being so young, elicit great sympathy. At left we see SASO members hard at work, which the caption describes succinctly: "Pictures showing student–community involvement fostering self-help attitudes moving towards self-determination." Clusters of SASO members work to either build or repair a building that suggests its modernity by way of size, clay brick and mortar, glass windows, and what appears to be a higher-pitched tin roof. These hard-working SASO members enjoy themselves: every face smiles.

In 1972, the Study Project on Christianity in Apartheid South Africa (SPRO-CAS) worked in concert with Black Community Programmes to initiate "a project for social change" that included a series of posters aimed at a white audience.[33] The poster in Figure 1.3 was part of this series; it was printed by Joe Setlabogo, a man who shared BC convictions with his coworker at another locale, the now well-known artist Thami Mnyele.[34] Each work in the series sets a black-and-white photograph on a black field captioned in white below. The contrast of colors and use of familiar phrases capture our attention. This example recalls Matthew 25:35; it intones "I was hungry" beneath a picture of a child with pleading eyes and worried brow. Another in the series suggests that children, surrounded by makeshift fences and walls, are condemned to a "life sentence." Yet one more poster reminds, "Home is where the heart is," a phrase offset by an image of a miner in his cramped living quarters.[35] In Figure 1.3, a thin child sits on a field of debris; the place may be urban or rural, so the ground may be covered in trash or fallen plant stalks. The youngster holds an empty bowl. Although the speaker in Matthew 25:35 has his needs met, this child's hunger goes unanswered. A worn tin cup substitutes for hands. They will sit empty while a committee, made up of the viewer's world, examines the case.

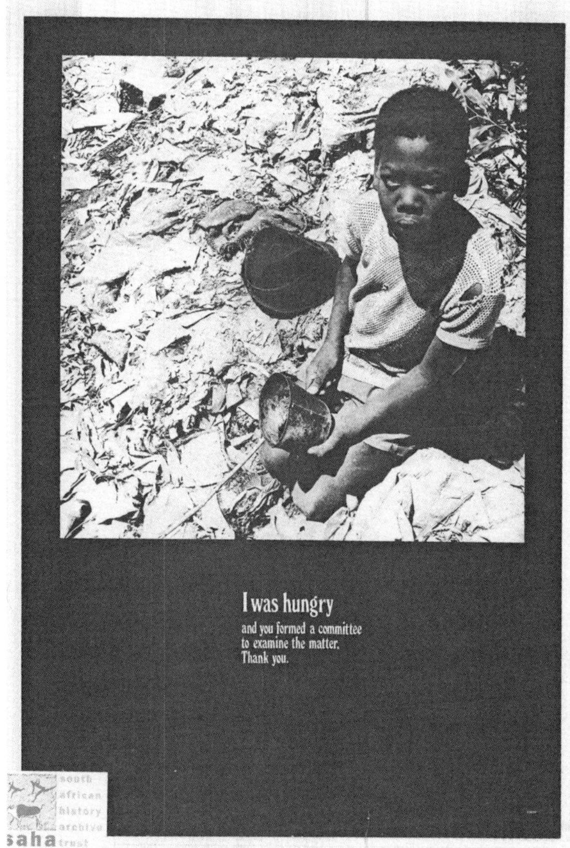

FIGURE 1.3. *I was hungry.* Unattributed poster made for the Study Project on Christianity in Apartheid South Africa (SPRO-CAS). Printed at the Christian Institute by Joseph Setlabogo, 1972. South African History Archive, University of the Witwatersrand.

A Word about Fists

Hands and fingers, with their distinctive prints, mark our individuality. As instruments of labor, they facilitate our productivity. Like no other part of the body, hands signify both who we are and who we can potentially be. A gesture associated with workers' solidarity worldwide, the raised clenched fist took on a double meaning when it became the most prominent visual script of Black Consciousness. SASO's logo bore the motif in red or black encased in a circle. The BPC logo, rendered in black, later dramatized its self-agency by arranging two clenched fists actively breaking a chain that once bound them. In South

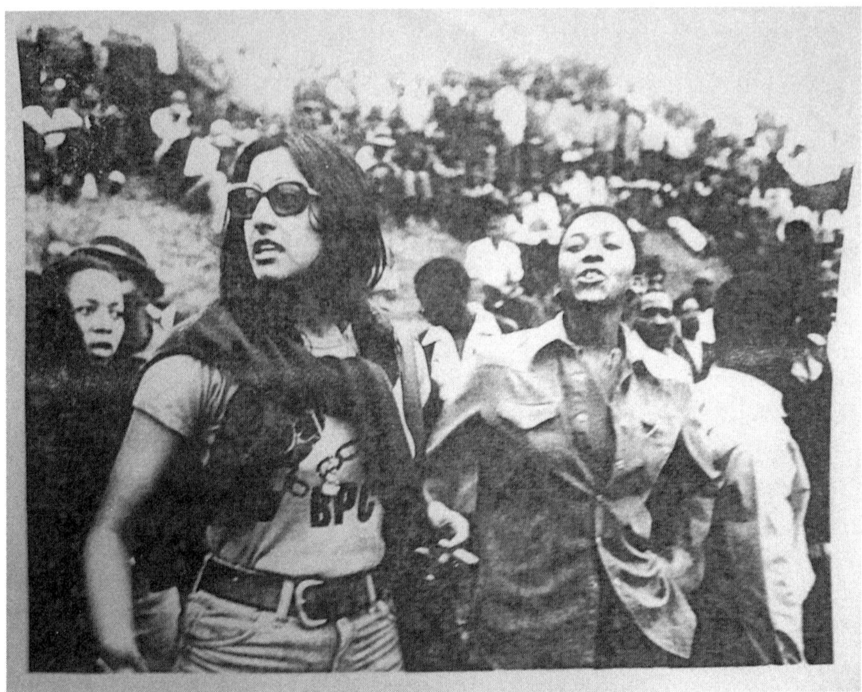

FIGURE 1.4. In defiance of a government ban on pro-FRELIMO rallies, a woman wearing a Black Peoples' Convention T-shirt celebrates the liberation of Mozambique at Currie's Fountain in Durban, 1974. Mayibuye Center Archive.

Africa, the raised fist was a salute that distinguished BC proponents from affiliation with political parties of earlier decades, namely the Pan Africanist Congress (PAC), whose members raised an open palm, and the African National Congress (ANC), identified by a salute that folded four fingers and extended the thumb outward. Determinedly unaligned, BC adherents chose a salute different from those adopted before. BC organizations showed their strength through the solid clenched fist.[36]

The fist motif has long conveyed solidarity among laborers, and the adoption of it by BC leaders does not diminish that reading but expands it. As Vuyile Voyiya rightly said, "BC *is* workerist."[37] Its widespread use in tricontinental liberation movements in the 1960s conveyed likemindedness and a newly realized sense of self-agency that was driven by racial unity. SASO's manifesto of

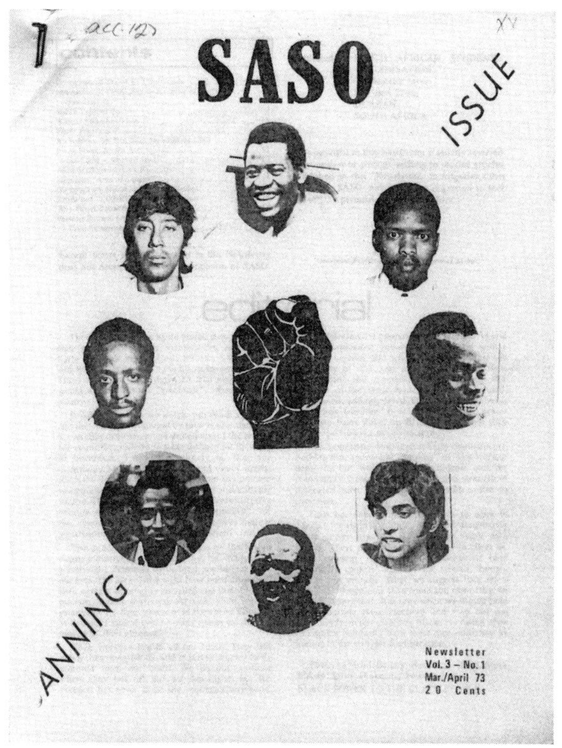

FIGURE 1.5. "SASO: Banning Issue," cover of the *SASO Newsletter* (March/April 1973). SASO and BPC Collection, Acc. 127, Documentation Centre for African Studies, UNISA Archives.

1970 translates consciousness to fist: "SASO upholds the concept of BC and the drive towards Black *awareness* as the most logical and significant *means* of ridding ourselves of the shackles that bind us to perpetual servitude."[38] For BC adherents, the fist embodied the fearlessness that leaders long advocated. It also provoked fear in others. In 1972, the Publications Control Board denied SASO permission to print its logo on T-shirts.[39] Still, T-shirts with the logo were made, establishing BC organs as perhaps the first in South Africa to produce protest graphics as wearable art, a fashion choice that gained significant popularity in the 1980s (Figure 1.4). And the raised clenched fist of Black Consciousness—not the curled fingers with extended thumb of the ANC or the open-palm salute of the PAC—was widely used by liberation activists from all sorts of organizations post-1977, when the last of the BC bodies was banned and its leaders were silenced (Figure 1.5). A close analysis of this iconography in graphics of anti-apartheid organizations in the 1980s forms the heart of chapter 4.

A visual culture of fists was commonly evoked within internal memos issued by both SASO and the BPC. "People's Power" and "Breaking the Chains" were customarily used, set off in quotation marks and capital letters. Although the American term *Black Power* had gained popular use among South African youth by the mid-1970s, it was never adopted by BC organizations at the time. Indeed, leaders' insistence on maintaining a distinction between Black Power and Black Consciousness was made plain in a number of public venues, most prominently during the SASO–BPC trial in May 1976.[40] Modern black culture had helped renew a sense of rebellion within South Africa, but BC leaders cautioned that Americans were at a different stage in their struggle. Like most of its tricontinental counterparts, BC's rhetorical imaging of audience included diverse people united against an oppressor offstage. In the next decade these were given visual form in the graphics of many organizations, political, cultural, and otherwise (for example, see Plate 5). "People's Power" popularly became "Black Power" by 1976, then cycled around again in the 1980s, altered in audience but visually rendered the same.

Black Consciousness in Art from the 1970s

Black Consciousness affected the aesthetic and professional choices of artists within South Africa in profound ways. Those who responded to its call reveled in technical experimentation, which they saw as fundamentally African in origin. They gave shape to the sense of modern black culture described by Black Consciousness; its message of unity, ancestry, and action was often translated as black, African, and revolutionary. Typically and problematically cast as "African surrealists," BC's earliest artists quite purposefully sought and created an aesthetic that saw liberation as more than a dream. Women were usually represented as mothers, strong and purposeful in their embodiment of BC ideals. Diana Wylie writes that they represented a "pregnant mood in the 1970s," but really these women bore liberation itself.[41] As the history of Black Consciousness within South African art is written, we must not divorce, as John Peffer does, the "essential combination of elements" witnessed in the early 1970s, what he calls "a linked set of signifiers of racial tribulation but also the seeds of liberation," from that which followed 1976, what he sees as "an art of contemplation and revolution."[42] I must emphasize that the core of BC aesthetics carried on despite the fracture of its movement by the state. Indeed, Peffer's leap from black centeredness (1976) to nonracialism (1983) without a word about the years in between is troublingly common in scholarship about South Africa.[43] As I see it, the problem resides in the persistent branding of BC as "racially exclusive," and in a rather timid interpretation of its lasting effects.[44]

Further, BC artists in the 1970s openly rejected restrictions based on race that dominated trade in art by black hands among white patrons. (See chapter 5 for a continuance of this stance in the 1980s.) As BC spread, artists challenged the sentimentalized visions of poverty that dominated the market for their work. Instead, they chose subjects of interest to a black audience and had little to do with white businesses. Most of the artists discussed here launched their own exhibitions within townships, developed and led workshops in art making for youth, ran their own galleries, and developed international ties with artists and curators. In the face of a nation-state and business world that did not listen, these artists developed their own markets in which to create.

Consider, for instance, *A South African Colouring Book*, which Gavin Jantjes (b. 1948) made at the height of BC's founding era, 1974–75 (Figure 1.6 and Plate 1). Living in London for much of the 1970s and 1980s, Jantjes created art in this period that was invested in South African liberation and repeatedly calls up BC through its content and popular imagery.[45] Indeed, in 1982 he delivered a paper called "Art and Black Consciousness" at the First National Black Art Convention at Wolverhampton Polytechnic in England. This same year Rasheed Araeen had come to call British art of Jantjes's ilk expressive of Black Consciousness both for its aesthetic aims and content, and for the artists' radical, highly vocal positioning in modernism.[46] At work in Britain since the early 1970s, "black art," as they called it, has always been a contemporary art, thus it is unbound to tradition or location. Araeen identifies the particularity is its direct emergence

> from the joint struggle of Asian, African, and the Caribbean people against racism, and the art work itself explicitly refers to that struggle. It specifically deals with and expresses a human condition, the condition of AfroAsian people resulting from their existence or predicament in a racist society or/and, in global terms, from Western cultural imperialism.[47]

Although the eleven-part series is more remarked on than any other piece in this chapter, neither Jantjes's BC convictions nor their transmission through the work have been considered.[48] Most analyses of *A South African Colouring Book* read it as a nod to child's play. A few aspects prompt this interpretation, including the outlined watercolor palette on each work with instructions nearby; the sense that some are left undone, as a child might leave a drawing; and the series title. Although a coloring book induces nostalgia for some, it also refers to the passbooks that people of "colour" were required to carry.[49] But unlike a child's toy, these works are directed at adults. The instructions beside each color palette are pointedly political ("Colour this labor dirt cheap" or "Colour these workers sold out") and not for a child's eyes ("Colour these people dead"). Further, the quotations affixed to some individual works record the words that Frantz Fanon and B. J. Vorster wrote for adult audiences. Accountants' paper serves as the base for all eleven works in the series. Its neat squares thinly bleed through every image and word.

The Population Registration Act of 1950 is Jantjes's target here. In "Classify This Coloured" (Figure 1.6), third in the series, a copy of Jantjes's father's passbook fills the top half. The artist's handwritten memo fills the lower half; it critiques the act and the subsequent subdivision of people into ethnicities. A photograph of the artist in his midtwenties is affixed at bottom and it casts a slight shadow on the ledger. His face bears the trace of his father's, and, through the direction of his gaze, he responds to this man's history. His father's passbook was like others in that it identified him as a subject/target population. Classified here: Mr. G. P. Jantjes, number 022 561735. His son's memo is a personalized accounting of the act's effects on a child. We read of the sense of inferiority that attends a "non-white" designation, and the real limits in education, work, and representation that result.[50] Jantjes, whose Afro, beads, and dark shirt register his own sense of black consciousness, focused here on opportunity denied.

Jantjes left South Africa soon after Black Consciousness took root there. His ready adoption of BC while living elsewhere reflects South Africa's sway in tricontinental struggles, artistic and otherwise. As Jantjes described it, black art synthesized artists' roots and current concerns. From these emerged what the artist called "a new voice—a new set of conventions within visual art that articulates, expresses, and creates consciousness, Black consciousness."[51] Black art, he believes,

> is an innovative expression of a particular reality—a reality set in the framework of specific cultural and historic forces. These are: cultural domination by Western Eurocentrism and marginality to it; the experience of exploitation, appropriation, slavery, inequality, and racism; and the long abominable history of colonialism. A black art emerges from this framework and is vitalized by these forces. They give it its libratory character—make it a creation for liberation.

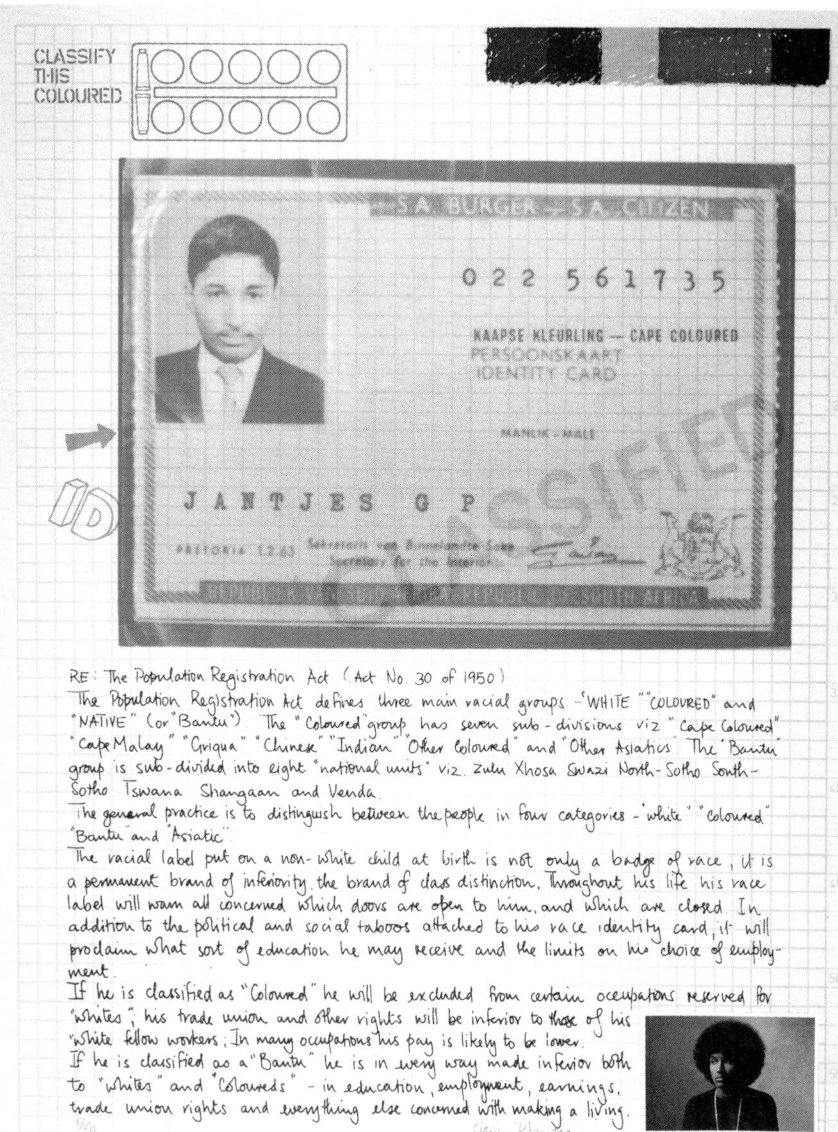

FIGURE 1.6. Gavin Jantjes, "Classify This Coloured," in *A South African Colouring Book* (a suite of eleven prints), 1974–75. Screen print on paper with mixed media, 60 x 45 cm (23⅝ x 17¹¹⁄₁₆ inches). Museum purchase, 2003-16-1.2. Photograph by Franko Khoury. Courtesy of Gavin Jantjes and the National Museum of African Art, Smithsonian Institution.

Just like the tight constricting mantle around gunpowder turns it into an explosive, the constricting framework confining black visual expression activates the energies for its liberation.[52]

All eleven works in *A South African Colouring Book* invest in and advance Black Consciousness. One likens South Africa's Christian Nationalism to Nazism. Three critique black subjects who partake in white worlds as "desperate" and "sold out" and, in the last case, what BC folks would dismiss as "nonwhite" in the extreme by virtue of being "Black policemen." Three works in the series honor heroes who fell to state violence while peacefully protesting the Population Registration Act and its mandate to carry identity passbooks. "Colour These People Dead" (Plate 1) includes Sharpeville's iconic photograph of murdered activists paired with one of living policemen surveying their kill. The deceased are stamped DEAD in the same blue hue used elsewhere to denote violence by white hands. This work and another that records a burial procession honor the 69 killed and 180 wounded at Sharpeville on March 21, 1960. The text affixed to "Colour These People Dead" does exactly as BC proscribes: it magnifies their courage and the event's lasting effects. Styled like a reporter's Teletype, an excerpt reads:

JET AIRCRAFT WHICH SCREAMED DOWN ON THE NATIVESIN AN ATTEMPT TO FRIGHTEN THEM***ONLY MADE THEM MORE ANGRY***THE SHOOTING OF THE AFRICANS HAS CREATED STRONG PROTESTS FROM ALL PARTS OF THE WORLD**** KEYSTONE****

Finally, three works in the series critique apartheid industry and disclose the reason behind population registration within South Africa: "Colour This Labor Dirt Cheap," "Colour This Slavery Golden," and "Gold Market Industrials Foreign Exchanges" exemplify both the heart of the matter and the verve to name it. Two laws in particular conspired to keep the majority subservient, the Bantu Education Act of 1953 and the Jobs Reservation Act of 1956. The first prepared black youth for a labor market and the second restricted their advancement once in it. As Steve Biko wrote, these laws eroded the spirit and caused "a certain state of alienation [within] the black man . . . [who] rejects himself, precisely because he attaches the meaning white to all that is good, in other words he associates good and he equates good with white."[53] Black Consciousness targeted this false construct and aimed to reverse it. As Biko explained, "Hence thinking along lines of Black Consciousness makes the black man see himself as a being, entire in himself, and not an extension of a broom or additional leverage to some machine. At the end of it all, he cannot tolerate attempts by anybody to dwarf the significance of his manhood. Once this happens, we shall know that the real man in the black person is beginning to shine through."[54]

A South African Colouring Book shines on in history for reasons beyond what have been emphasized elsewhere. Its efficacy registers in the details, like Jantjes's personal preference for Afro, black T-shirt, and necklace juxtaposed to the style choice of his father, with neatly trimmed hair, suit, and tie. We sense it through the heat and sweat that emanates from miners in "Colour This Slavery Golden," a public space used only by white women but never cleaned by them, the distanced stamp DEAD across Sharpeville's fallen. These elements give us pause. So, too, do the undercurrents of Black Consciousness within the suite. In 1983, Jantjes said that those committed to making black art, itself implicitly modern,

> have not lost sight of the essential social role of their traditional art and mirror this role in their art. [It is therefore] frustrating that the words about us have failed to grasp this reflection; failed to put into perspective the crumbling social fabric in which this art was made; failed to recognize the lack of opportunity; failed to perceive the humanity and the human beings; and finally, how upsetting that we have allowed this to happen. . . . Our forefathers were as aware of social, political, and economic problems as we are. They were as aware of aesthetic, poetic, philosophical, [and] historical problems as we should be, and I think that if we can get that from tradition then we can go somewhere and take the definition out of the hands of the dominant culture and redefine it ourselves. Our definitions could become, should become the foundations to build a contemporary art.[55]

In this Jantjes calls up BC's core values of unity, ancestry, and action, and, importantly, shapes them for this moment in time.

Steven Sack's landmark exhibition and catalog *The Neglected Tradition: Towards a New History of South African Art (1930–1988)* characterized black art in the 1960s and 1970s as divided into one of two stylistic camps, problematic designations that remain largely unchallenged.[56] In Sack's synthesis, subject matter in the first style focuses on apartheid's negative effects: the realities of poverty, hard labor, imprisonment, pollution, and illness exemplify this type. Works in this genre are emotive and often spark sentimentality; as I've indicated, white collectors were its principle market. To a very limited extent, some Black

Consciousness artists, like Thami Mnyele, borrowed from this style in realizing figures (though not the context in which they were placed), but the pictorial content of such works ran counter to BC ideals. In her welcomed biography about Mnyele, Diana Wylie incorrectly reports that "tortured figures—those big-footed, round-eyed creatures" were of a type that "Black Consciousness artists commonly used to express their disenchantment."[57] Let the record state that such figuration was not common among BC artists. Fikile Magadlela captured the sentiment best when he dismissed such work as wrapped up in "self-pity."[58] BC leaders likewise condemned imagery that cast their people as victims, devoid of agency. In describing BC's "quest for a true humanity," Biko described its visual opposite: "We do not want to be reminded that it is we, the indigenous people, who are poor and exploited in the land of our birth. These are concepts which the Black Consciousness approach wishes to eradicate from the black man's minds."[59] Artist Motlhabane Mashiangwako described such art as "trapped in the oppressor's context. Its inferiority is based on the fact that it is subscribed to a debased human situation."[60]

In Sack's assessment, the second style of black art in this period "celebrated the beautiful and the mystical," a reading that conforms to other writing on the subject, which regularly mislabels early BC artists as "African surrealists."[61] Instead, these artists actually visualized Black Consciousness—they re-presented it for our contemplation. Sack came close to this conclusion when he described this style as "an art inspired by music, literature, poetry, and an affirmative view of the political struggle: as a site of hope rather than despair."[62] In keeping with BC, black art honors origins. Figures often blossom from barren landscapes; sometimes they float free, liberated from context altogether. They are figured in dignified poses, often in communal groupings.

Fikile Magadlela (1954–2003) most famously exemplifies Black Consciousness in art of the 1970s as it resolutely informed his being. He once said, "There's one thing I believe in: if you draw a black man, he must be beautiful, handsome; the woman must be heavenly. Drape them with the most beautiful clothes."[63] He made pointed remarks about Black Consciousness—"Black art is an important facet of Black Consciousness and Black artists are very conscious of their heritage," for example—but these have barely filtered through critical response to his work.[64] Instead, critics stress "the mystical" or religious aspects of his art. Although he described his work as spiritual, BC clearly drove Magadlela's sense of the word. In contrast, critics emphasize a "prophetic quality" within his work and even locate a comfortably benign "religious art" as his source of inspiration.[65]

Magadlela was a superb draftsman, and his greatest legacy is the evocative visualization of Black Consciousness ideals. His works are poetic and political. In an untitled drawing from 1971 (Figure 1.7), a statuesque man has risen from the earth and broken a hole through a second terrain, a rocky solid layer with mountains of its own. Our hero, whose fist remains clenched midbody, looks fixedly on a hazy sun nestled at upper right. His determined action has caused thunderous clouds to gather all around him; the darkened terrain below churns with trauma. A pillar of strength, he has ruptured a world thickly hostile to his growth. Typically Magadlela's treatment of landscape suggests a kind ancestral protection, either through faces that form on the rock surface or through long-stemmed plants that impossibly blossom out of fissures in the landscape. But that landscape, rooted as it is in African ancestry, is sometimes threatening. *Untitled* of about 1974 (Figure 1.8) is a bloody work, but not a violent one. Nature's spire is cast here as a weapon that pierces the skull of a black man. He remains at peace nonetheless. Only his forehead reveals tension, and this is the site of thought. Framed by a halo or basking in the sun, the deceased is a martyr for the cause of liberation. At Magadlela's death in 2003, it was said, "Patriotic death is a concept that he played over in his works, believed at some point in his life, but lately it knotted his spirit with balls of tension."[66] In the early 1970s, the cost and cause were clearer.

The "new order of awareness" that surfaced in Magadlela's art is not, as E. J. de Jager once called it, the combination of "irrational and rational" common to "many surrealists."[67] The form compels wonder, but the intellectual approach was pointedly influenced. The new order of the day was also reflected in the artist's determination to control his creations and their sale. Celebrating the history, cultural richness, and beauty of blackness, Magadlela was among a group of artists living in townships along the Johannesburg–Pretoria nexus that curated and exhibited within shows of black art, for black audiences, at black venues. They also sold works to black patrons at affordable rates and on payment plans, if necessary.[68] They were entrepreneurs, examples of self-determination. Magadlela's figures may appear fixed in stone or given to the wind, but make no mistake: they are agents of change. Organic matter, be it human or plant, rejuvenates against the odds. Bodies may become celestial beings, their minds bearing the fruit of new worlds.[69]

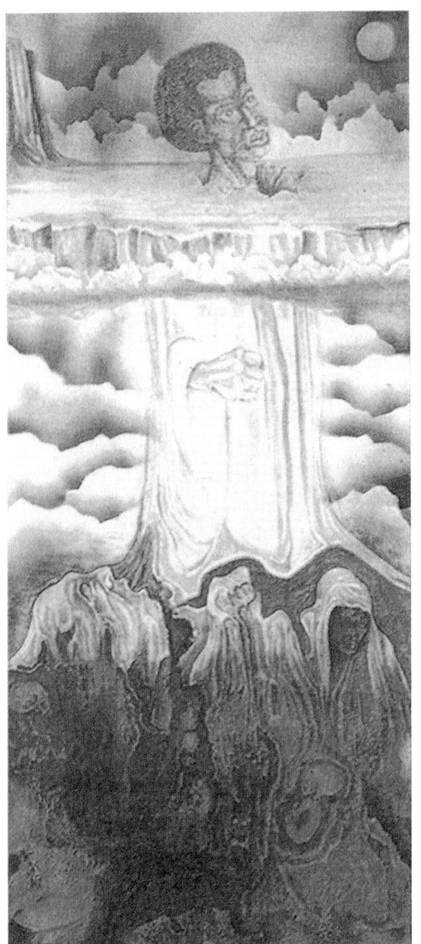

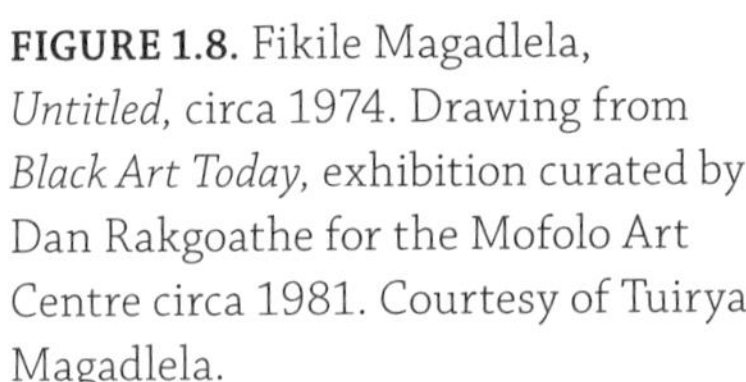

FIGURE 1.8. Fikile Magadlela, *Untitled*, circa 1974. Drawing from *Black Art Today*, exhibition curated by Dan Rakgoathe for the Mofolo Art Centre circa 1981. Courtesy of Tuirya Magadlela.

FIGURE 1.7. Fikile Magadlela, *Untitled*, 1971. Drawing. Fort Hare University. Courtesy of Tuirya Magadlela.

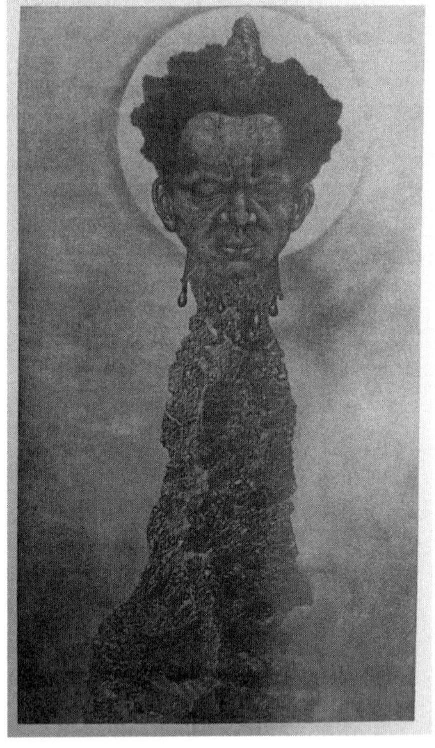

Magadlela was part of a collective that shared studio space at the home of Geoff and Maokaneng Mphakati in Mamelodi West near Pretoria; also included were Cyril Kumalo, Gilbert Mabale, Dikobé Martins, Motlhabane Mashiangwako, Winston Saoli, and Lefifi Tladi. Here they shared ideas, materials, and techniques, which causes us to question the designation of "self-trained" ascribed to each. They felt a common sense of purpose in Black Consciousness and, together with artists in nearby Ga-Rankuwa (Anthony Molongwana Makou, Mike Mmutle, Harry Moyaga, Matsemela Nkoana, David Phoshoko, Ranko Pudi, and Johnny Ribeiro), they aimed to impart BC's essence through their work.[70] In this pursuit, the Mphakatis shared more than their home; their collection of music, poetry, and literature was also freely available, and Geoff shared his considered knowledge of African history. Despite the banning of several titles, the Mphakatis' library included many books popular in tricontinental liberation struggles of which BC was part.[71] What arose in this time and place was a rich exchange with transnational blackness at its core.

Geoff Mphakati (1940–2004) nurtured the careers of many artists, writers, and musicians from a region that reached south from townships around Pretoria to those near Johannesburg. Tributes at his passing praised this energetic, deeply effectual man devoted to black arts. His Jazz Appreciation Society in Pretoria enabled a forum wherein "countless . . . important jazz artists got their first taste of the advanced avant-garde sounds of freedom."[72] He managed Dashiki, which was among the first BC-oriented ensembles of poets, actors, musicians, and visual artists. Established in 1969, Dashiki begat "a cultural renaissance" of Black Consciousness that drew from African traditions to spawn a new approach to the making of art and its promotion. Other BC collectives included Mihloti, People's Experimental Theatre (PET), and the Theatre Council of Natal (TECON).[73] The Culture Committee of SASO was among BC organs that hired Mihloti and Dashiki to perform during its weeklong July 1972 General Students Council meeting in Hammanskraal.[74] This meeting proved historic for its formation of the Black Peoples' Convention.[75] Artists within Mphakati's network performed and displayed their work at this meeting in which Black Consciousness adherents organized to expand beyond university and college campuses.

Geoff Mphakati extended the reach of artists within his community into other nations. He transported art between South Africa and Botswana in the late 1970s after the state's final suppressive measures caused the exile of some artists and the end of BC-organizations and affiliates. He established the Association for the Advancement of Creative Artists in the early 1980s and curated exhibitions of BC-inflected art that traveled to Norway, Holland, Russia, and the United States.[76] He helped realize public exhibition venues within South Africa, notably a museum that Lefifi Tladi created and ran in Ga-Rankuwa from 1970–74, but more often than not art was seen at the foreign embassies and homes of diplomats around Pretoria.[77] Artists ran workshops at high schools and black colleges near and far; Tladi and Motlhabane Mashiangwako devoted great energy to these initiatives. In fact, as early as 1966 Tladi ran workshops for a youth club with the witty name DeOlympia, a delightful decentering of pedagogy.[78] Together with Mphakati, their chief promoter, BC artists in this region formed organizations within townships that advanced black arts for black audiences. Two of these, Mamelodi's Music Poetry Art and Drama Organization (MPANDO) and Johannesburg's Music Drama Art and Literature (MDALI), organized a major cultural event in Mamelodi in 1975, which SASO's Cultural Committee supported.[79] The renowned Malangatana Valente Ngwenya of Mozambique contributed works and attended the opening, with Ben Arnold, Mashiangwako, and Zakes Mokae (a poet and actor) representing South Africa.[80] All of these cultural initiatives were driven by their makers' investment in the ideology of Black Consciousness. Agency, ownership, voice, and unity are everywhere present in this history. (Notably, the well-known Medu Art Ensemble is an offspring of these very BC initiatives. See chapter 4 for this history.)

Among the great talents of this period is Motlhabane Mashiangwako (1945–2010). His artistic vision and professional decisions evidence black centeredness ever since he first took up drawing at the Mphakati residence in 1974. Most urgent for this study is Mashiangwako's own memory of how his awareness of art and of Black Consciousness coalesced, each driving the other from the start. After a frustrated youth in Potegietersrust, he found, around the age of twenty-three, "when Black Consciousness came in, it was like the answer. It gave me direction. That was a time that I put everything into my art. . . . I now know who I am, I know where I came from and where I am heading."[81] He further infused budding artists of the early 1980s with BC objectives and ideals when he taught at the Mamelodi Association for the Advancement of Creative Artists (MAACA).

Mashiangwako was always a keen follower of the news. An avid interest in current events and a commitment to social justice caused him to attend every political trial of the Pretoria Central Magistrates' Court; he almost certainly attended the Biko Inquest of November and December 1977.[82] He translated the visual culture of these hearings into a set of technically interesting and beautiful works he made to honor heroes in 1979 and 1980. These include *Soul of a Dying Black Man*, for Solomon Mahlangu, a martyr born out of Black Consciousness who was executed for his work in Umkhonto we Sizwe (MK), the armed wing of the ANC; *Dedication to the People of Biafra: Four Meditations on the Biafran War*, a statement on Nigerian independence (Plate 9); and *Leokotsane: For Steve Biko* (Plate 8).[83] These and other reasons prompt my interest in Mashiangwako.

Time Past, Present, and Future of 1974 (Figure 1.9) is among his first works. Black Consciousness seeps through the drawing, enlivening its trilateral elements toward liberation. Three hands—Black, Coloured, and Indian, one each for those "races" united by Black Consciousness—grasp the spear on the central axis, with overlapping sun and moon at its top. To either side are two figures, male and female. The male figure actively charges to the right, one fist held high while another clasps an inspiring document. The female figure drifts leftward, inwardly focused and well toned. Mashiangwako describes her as emblematic of women's physical and spiritual strength.[84] These figures rise out of the spear, weapon of choice for the once-divided hands that now join to raise it. Steve Biko's often-quoted words come to mind:

> Being an historically dispossessed group, they have the strongest foundation from which to operate. The philosophy of Black Consciousness, therefore, expresses group pride and the determination of blacks to rise and attain the envisaged self. At the heart of this kind of thinking is the realization by the Blacks that the most potent weapon in the hands of the oppressor is the mind of the oppressed.[85]

Black Consciousness is ultimately in charge here having chosen its weapon in response.

The life of Mashiangwako's friend Lefifi Tladi (b. 1949) bears Black Consciousness in its deepest expression, but this is easily missed because his experiments in poetry, music, and art (an example of which is discussed in chapter 5) layer so many influences that scholars initially view them as abstractions, thus apolitical. But Tladi's creations demand our time and effort; what's more, they require our flexibility, and in this they represent some of the best of Black Consciousness. Tladi was there at the beginning and among those who crucially shaped the forms that BC aesthetics would take. Among these forms is the choice to create as one envisions, free of dictates about what "African art(ists)" should look like, for this is an exercise in self-determination. His 1966 creation of an artistic youth club, DeOlympia (a delightful feminist-turned-postcolonial

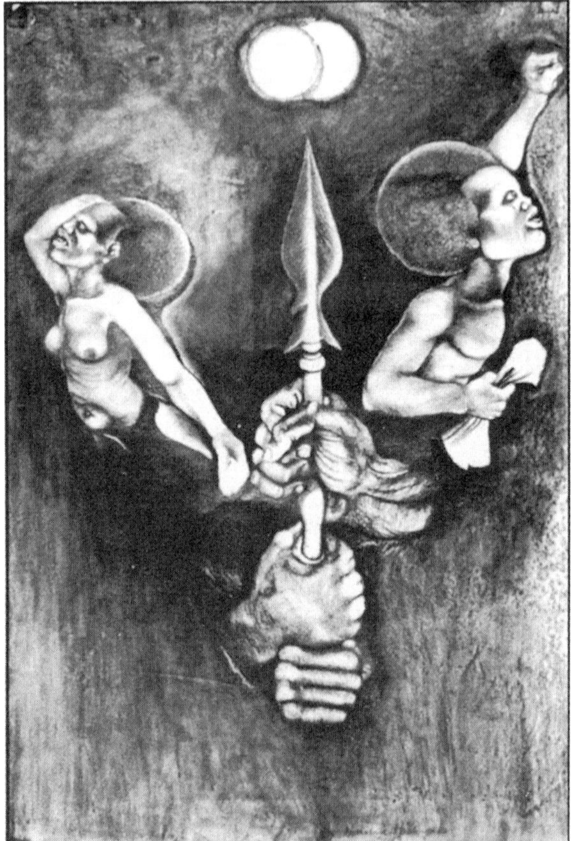

FIGURE 1.9. Motlhabane Mashiangwako, *Time Past, Present, and Future,* 1974. Pencil on paper, 86 x 61 cm. Collection of A. P. Malakalaka. Courtesy of Mashiangwako Estate.

deconstruction of Édouard Manet's famed 1863 painting *Olympia*), precedes the widespread articulation of BC, as does his 1970 creation of a Museum for African Art, a four-roomed home in Ga-Rankuwa for the display of contemporary work and the preservation of books and archives.[86] These initiatives brought SASO's attention and soon the workshops that Tladi and Mashiangwako conducted were "in the spirit of BC."[87] Tladi recalled, "Those were the days when being was meaningful." A founder of and drummer within Dashiki, Tladi expressed his BC beliefs in an entrepreneurial spirit that always led him to push boundaries. Forced into exile along with thousands in 1976, he took this BC with him to Gaborone, Botswana, where he and Rantobeng Mokou started the Dashiki Art Ensemble.[88] It later merged with the Pelindaba Cultural Ensemble to form TUKA Art Unit. Many of TUKA's members joined the now well-known Medu Art Ensemble, but Tladi was not among them. He chose exile in Sweden and returned to South Africa in 1994.

Dikobé Ben Martins (b. 1956) was also among those who worked out of the Mphakati home for a time during the 1970s.[89] Today a member of parliament and of the South African Communist Party, for nearly two decades Martins was the best-known artist to ascribe to Black Consciousness because he designed a commemorative poster (see Figure 2.6) and (with Robin Holmes) a T-shirt for Steve Biko's funeral. His legacy within South African visual culture includes the ready adoption of these popular graphic forms by protest organizations in the 1980s when both posters and T-shirts became prominent vehicles of political expression. The Biko T-shirt, which was banned in 1978 and is difficult (if not impossible) to locate, may well be the first within an important genre of visual culture that regularly appeared at funerals of political activists in the 1980s: that of the martyr's portrait alongside inspirational text. Following the historic 1982 Culture and Resistance Festival in Gaborone, Botswana (see chapter 4), Martins established one of the earliest poster-making collectives in the South African city of Pietermaritzburg. Here he taught workshops wherein Black Con-sciousness guided his method. At the Gaborone festival, he said, "As politics must teach people the ways and give them the means to take control over their own lives, art must teach people, in the most vivid and imaginative ways pos-sible, how to take control over their own experience and observations, how to link these with the struggle for liberation and a just society free of race, class and exploitation."[90] His work at the collective was cut short in November 1983 when he was sentenced to ten years in prison for his work as an MK soldier.[91]

Born and raised in Alexandra, Martins first identified with Black Conscious-ness while in high school in the early seventies. There authors like Eldridge Cleaver, Malcolm X, and Karl Marx were discussed, although Martins says he was "very dismissive" of the latter's class-based orientation at this time.[92] He came to know and exhibited with Fikile Magadlela, who is credited as the primary link among artists along the Johannesburg–Pretoria corridor in this period.[93] By 1974, Martins also studied with Bill Ainslie in Parktown, a Johannesburg suburb where Ainslie lived and many artists worked. Here Ainslie encouraged artists "to get on with the job of discovering ourselves," free of labels, expecta-tions, and restrictions.[94] Martins continued his work in this area until 1977, when he moved to Pietermaritzburg. *The World according to Serote* (Figure 1.10) was drawn at this time.

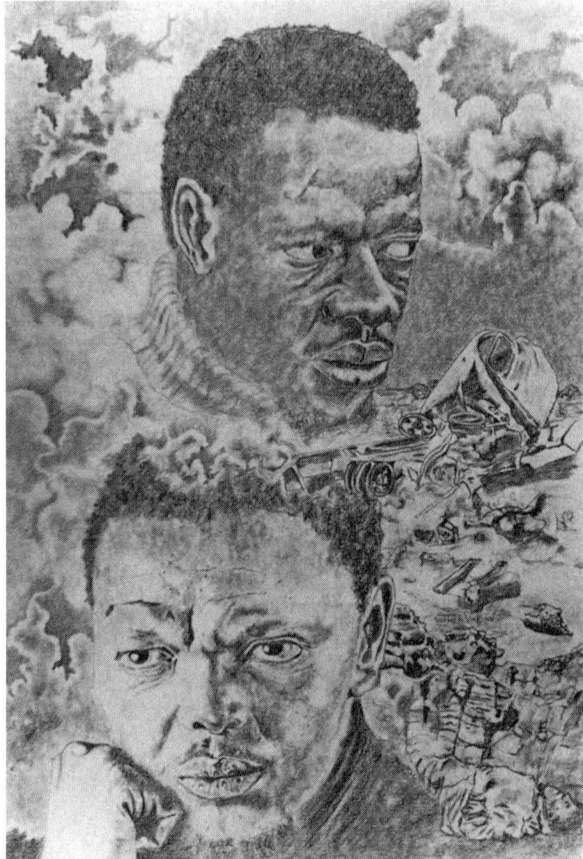

FIGURE 1.10. Dikobé Martins, *The World according to Serote,* 1977. Pencil on paper, 54.4 x 37.3 cm. Campbell Collections of the University of Natal.

Beautifully rendered in pencil are two portraits of the esteemed poet and novelist Mongane Wally Serote.[95] Martins, it must be said, is a noted poet in his own right. Like Martins, Serote grew up in Alexandra, a township that borders Johannesburg's white suburbs to the northeast. Serote's brilliance is conveyed here through his depiction as a thinker who is mindful of what happens in the real world, beyond the frame. In the portrait above, he looks rightward across a landscape that represents Alexandra. We see the shell of an automobile at right, twisted metal, and scattered debris, and below the body of a man emerges from a rocky ledge. He seems to be formed from its rough contours. Clouds surround them. Sharing a common home and mind-set, this work likely stems from the poem "Alexandra" (1972) in which a son of the beloved township left it, found an unwelcoming world beyond its borders, then "waded back" home again to find himself "simple and black," sustained by the body of a loving but violent place. Cast as mother, Alexandra is a home he seeks to find even as he is tied to it.

> Were it possible to say,
> Mother, I have seen more beautiful mothers
> A most loving mother,
> And tell her there I will go,
> Alexandra, I would have long gone from you.
>
> But we have only one mother, none can replace,
> Just as we have no choice to be born,
> We can't choose our mothers;
> We fall out of them like we fall out of life to death.
>
> And Alexandra,
> My beginning was knotted to you,
> Just like you knot my destiny.
> You throb in my inside silences
> You are silent in my heart-beat that's loud to me.
> Alexandra often I've cried.
> When I was thirsty my tongue tasted dust,
> Dust burdening your nipples.
> I cry Alexandra when I am thirsty.
> Your breasts ooze the dirty waters of your dongas,
>
> Waters diluted with the blood of my brothers, your children,
> Who once chose dongas for death-beds.
> Do you love me Alexandra, or what are you doing to me?
>
> You frighten me, Mama,
> You wear expressions like you would be nasty to me,
> You frighten me, Mama,
> When I lie on your breast to rest, something tells me
> You are bloody cruel.
> Alexandra, hell
> What have you done to me?

> I have seen people but I feel like I'm not one,
> Alexandra what are you doing to me?
>
> I feel I have sunk to such meekness!
> I lie flat while others walk on me to far places.
> I have gone from you, many times,
> I come back.
> Alexandra, I love you;
> I know
> When all these worlds become funny to me
> I silently waded back to you
> And amid the rubble I lay,
> Simple and black.[96]

The world imagined here is one of transition and longing, where we "fall out" of our mothers, our home, into contradictory contexts and uncertain futures. We yearn for comfort, resolution, the ability to "feel like" people. The speaker finds it in Alexandra, this most beautiful mother who also sparks fear, because here he can be who he is in simple silence: he can be black.

Serote's *Yakhal'inkomo* (1972), an award-winning collection of poems, included "Alexandra." The volume inspired Martins because it epitomizes Black Consciousness by its insistence that blackness be defined as a statement from within. In this book and in *Tsetlo* (1974), Serote conjured images of revolt and resistance in forceful yet compassionate words and aimed to mobilize readers to act on their own behalf. In 1977, Martins did just that by moving from Alexandra to Pietermaritzburg to begin community work.[97] Serote links the two locales in his poem: Alexandra, whose "dirty waters" remain "diluted with the blood of my brothers, your children, / Who once chose dongas for deathbeds," near Pietermaritzburg. Here Serote links Alexandrans to Zulus who died by the thousands at war with Afrikaners near Ncome River on December 16, 1838. The river was said to have turned red with the blood of Zulus who fought there. Serote reminds us that transitions cause difficulty, but these could not dissuade the BC-minded from their "destiny," a "throb" felt deep within, a "heartbeat that's loud to me."

It is not unusual that Serote's *Selected Poems* of 1982, echoed as pivotal voices in the creation of BC aesthetics, would feature his portrait by Martins on the cover (Figure 1.11).[98] Expertly realized by Martins, the portrait registers the same questioning stare published on the 1973 cover of *Black Review,* a SASO

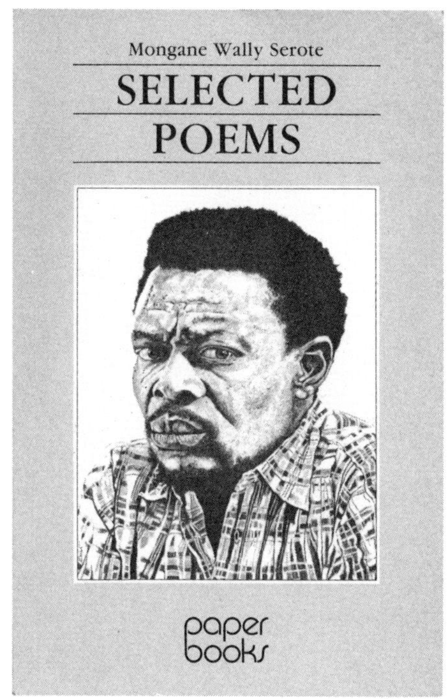

FIGURE 1.11. Dikobé Martins, cover of *Selected Poems,* by Mongane Wally Serote (Houghton: A. D. Donker, 1982).

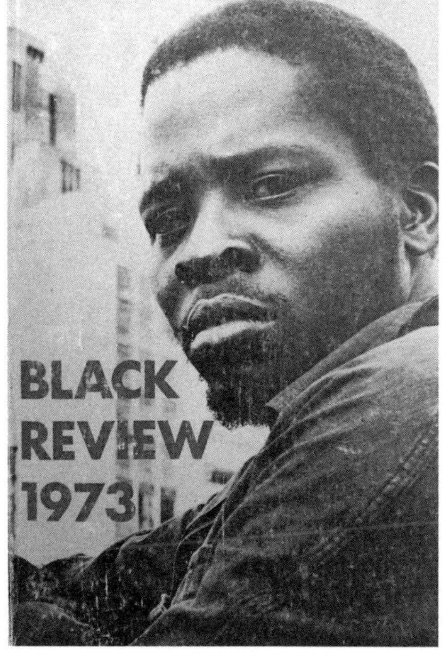

FIGURE 1.12. Cover of *Black Review,* 1973, literary journal of the Black Peoples' Convention.

literary publication that included their work (Figure 1.12).[99] The combination of a bust portrait that fills the field, an open-collared shirt, a male with black features, and a steady gaze that locks with our own expresses Black Consciousness in no uncertain terms. Fraser MacLean's portrait of Steve Biko, who once edited *Black Review,* relies on these same elements, the composite of which supplants the iconographic representation of Black Consciousness by 1997 (see Figures 6.1 and 6.4).

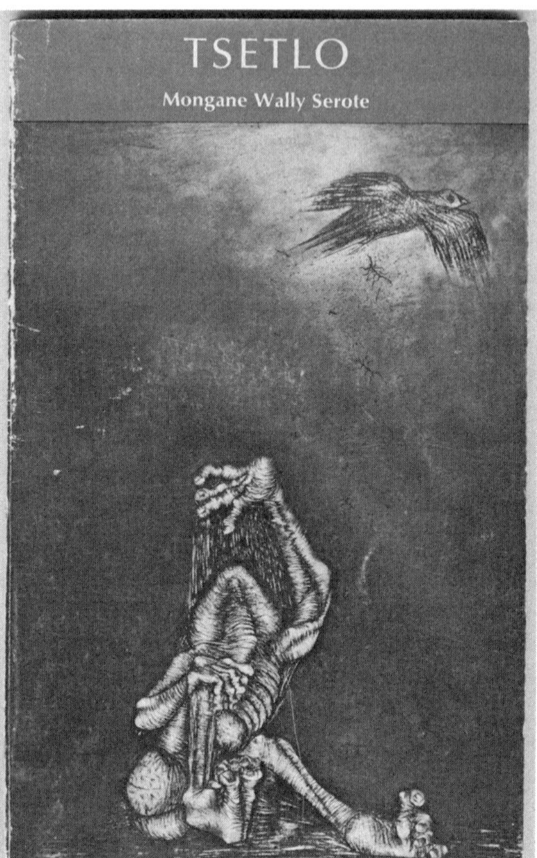

FIGURE 1.13. Thami Mnyele, cover of *Tsetlo*, by Mongane Wally Serote, 1974.

Thamsanqa (Thami) Harry Mnyele (1948–1985) was another Alexandra-born draftsman and printmaker whose BC roots are now well known.[100] So, too, was his ready friendship with Serote, who was variously called Mnyele's brother, father figure, and guru.[101] Among Mnyele's earliest works are the covers he illustrated for Serote's first two volumes of poetry, *Yakhal'inkomo* and *Tsetlo*.[102] For the first cover, maternity, poverty, and modernity are all conjured through a nude, feminized, globular form with swollen eyes; she carries on her back a smaller figure with a rather detailed ear. The two are presented in profile. One might imagine the mother's head as a fist raised high. Her child looks upward, ear tilted to better hear her message. For the cover of *Tsetlo*, Mnyele drew a fully

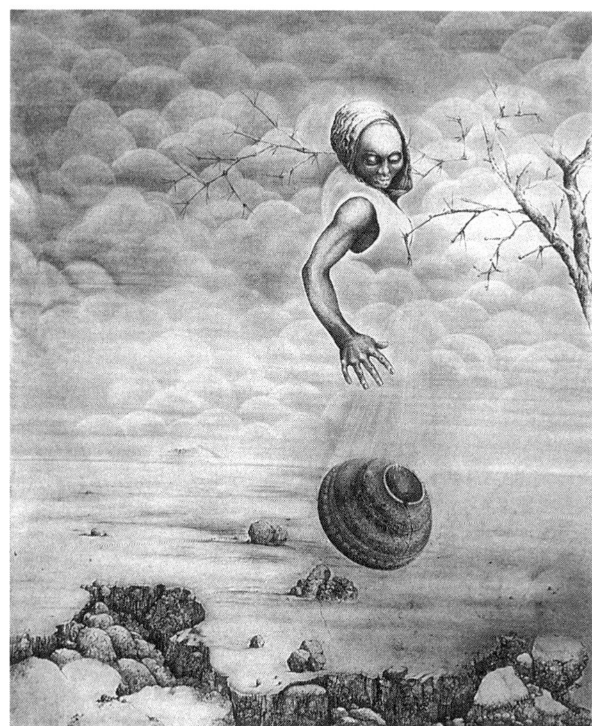

FIGURE 1.14. Thami Mnyele, *Things Fall Apart*, 1976. Charcoal, pen, and ink on paper, 108.5 x 88.5 cm. Botswana National Museum and Art Gallery. Photograph by Mark Henningsen.

figured person, rare for him in this period, who recalls Dumile Feni's influence like no other (Figure 1.13). The figure faces forward but twists in several directions at once. His head is thrown back so that a strong neck and jaw stand in for a face. Voice is represented here. It is carried from the throat, along an arm that stretches upward and beyond the large gnarled hand at its end. A bird at upper right carries the voice beyond our sight, up into a lightening sky.

Black Consciousness brought Mnyele his own artistic voice.[103] His most compelling works date to the mid- to late 1970s: finely drafted pictures of tradition amid transition, mindful excursions into worlds where past and future mix, where figures frequently direct our attention to change. His *Things Fall Apart* (Figure 1.14) is a praise poem to Chinua Achebe, whose classic tale of cultural and religious collision is realized anew within a BC view. Achebe set his novel of 1958 at the turn of the nineteenth century in what is today southeastern Nigeria. In 1976, Mnyele made sense of the story for South Africans and, more immediately, township residents who in June of that year joined forces nationwide to support Soweto's youth in their demands for justice in education. In fact, Soweto would be the venue for this work one year later when, on September 15, 1977, Mnyele, Magadlela, and Ben Arnold opened a joint exhibition called *A New Day* at the Dube YWCA in Soweto. Thousands attended.[104]

Mnyele made two works with the title *Things Fall Apart* in 1976.[105] That in the collection of the Botswana National Museum and Art Gallery shows a strong woman in headscarf figured from above her ribs. She floats in a sky of uniform shape, a modernist cloudscape that fills more than half of the space. She has dropped a large clay water pot from her shoulder; faint streaks of light give speed to its fall across an impossibly vast distance. The vessel is neatly patterned, but it is already cracked. It will eventually meet a wide canyon that is deeply carved from the base of an otherwise sparse and flat landscape. The water pot, keeper of tradition, is at a temporal counterpoint to the viewer. It appears fixed at the center of the drawing as space rapidly rises above and falls away from it. Where, and when, even how, will it land? The woman glances back at her falling vessel. She is ensnared by thorns from a tree that sprouts buds, promise of new life. Like the students of Soweto, her peaceful gait has been violently interrupted. A tradition of nonviolent protest will give way to armed defense.

Heralded as the first African modern novel, Achebe's *Things Fall Apart* is alive with tensions, both inside the book (between Igbo and British colonialists) and outside it (between a Nigerian writer reflecting on colonialism and the staff bearers of modernism). Both kinds of tensions arose for Mnyele and fellow artists in South Africa at this time. We see it here in Mnyele's chosen subject matter: a battle not between Igbo and British but between BC-infused youth of the Soweto-born uprisings and the governing National Party and its apartheid apparatus. Professional tension—a kind that names and conditions modernism and its participants—arose in Mnyele's decision to create as he did, experimenting with texture and form and multiple styles when the mainstream market wanted something else from black artists. His "surrealist" leanings, or what John Peffer calls his "emotionally expressive style," in this period were complemented by figural "realism" evidenced more readily in his later works.[106] Aesthetics aside, I draw attention to the personal meaning Mnyele must have found in Achebe's investment in his own subject and in himself as a writer. In turn, Black Consciousness prompted Mnyele to make sense of this key modernist text within his own history and through his art.

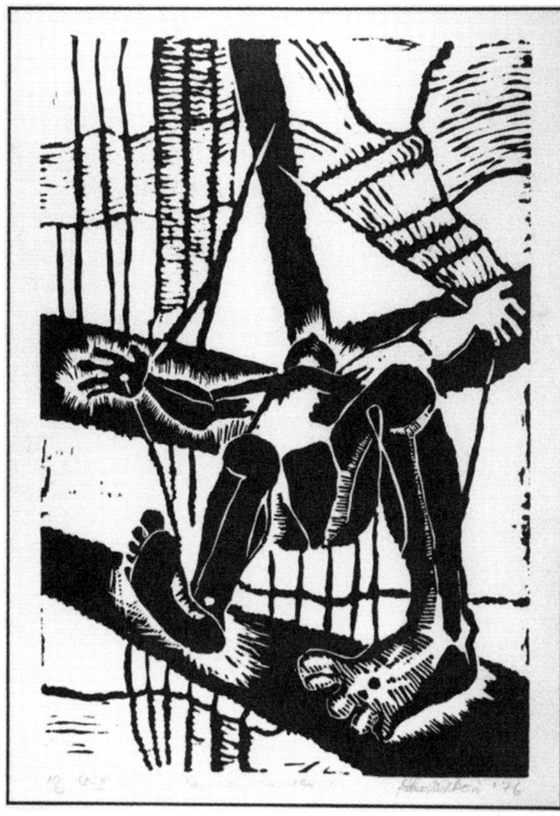

FIGURE 1.15. Sokhaya Charles Nkosi, *Pain on the Cross I,* from the series *Black Crucifixion,* 1976. Linocut, 52 x 40.5 cm. Private collection.

An important series of prints called *Black Crucifixion* also appeared in 1976.[107] At the time, Sokhaya Charles Nkosi (b. 1949) was finishing a two-year residency at Rorke's Drift in Natal, an art center devoted to black education that Swedish Lutheran missionaries founded in 1962. Black Theology, a socioreligious ideology that shares numerous tenets with Black Consciousness, held sway with several artists who trained there, and by the mid-1970s "New Testament themes were energetically employed in the re-picturing of Christ as an oppressed victim struggling to free himself."[108] Christ is a black man in this series, which conflates the traditional rendering of his Passions with the manacles and jail cells familiar to black South Africans at this time. One work in the series, *Pain on the Cross I* (Figure 1.15), combines his agony upon execution with the bars of a prison.[109] Three of his four limbs are colored black; a nail punctures each one.

The sharp white lines that radiate from the black hand and black feet reveal the pain he suffers. The arm and hand at right are rendered in white, remain whole, and lack any register of suffering. The figure is dramatically foreshortened with his knees jutting outward midcomposition, an abstraction that lends itself to the sense that we view his agony from below. Yet we share his space inside the bars and might reach out to alleviate his anguish since the bar at his feet seems within reach. He appears to be winning the struggle to free himself (that is, to act as Black Consciousness proscribed), since the bars are spread overhead and his escape looks imminent.

Nkosi's series, like so many works by black artists of this period, evidence the place of BC within its maker. Thus far, studies of Black Consciousness in theater and poetry have received more attention than other arts and their expressions of BC. No doubt there were a good many artists, visual and otherwise, who found meaning in its message during the 1970s. Those discussed here are but a few.

1976: Black Consciousness Speaks

As an ideology, Black Consciousness has its method. As lived experience and as projected image, Black Consciousness embodies the dignity, aspiration, and beauty that is blackness, and in this sense it is a tool. To be sure, BC is foremost a personal realization, the importance of which I mean to emphasize rather than diminish, but BC is also a tool in a larger sense, one that ultimately drives the agency that liberation requires. In the first half of 1976, South Africans enacted their own black consciousness loudly and clearly; they were heard and seen around the world. Over five days in early May, BC's best-known proponent stood in a Pretoria courthouse and delivered what amounted to a treatise on the subject, at the trial of a collective popularly known as the SASO Nine. It was billed as the SASO–BPC trial, and the *Rand Daily Mail* rightly called it a trial of Black Consciousness.[110]

More than rhetorical speech, Biko's strategy and performance over these days portrayed BC in action, and he became "the toast of the Soweto shebeens" nearby,[111] where BC had already flourished through organizations like the Soweto Students' Representative Council and the Black Parents' Association.[112] As Biko's image and text were printed in the press nationwide, a portrait of Black Consciousness took shape with a person banned three years now called by the state to articulate his politics on a very public stage. The link between the "trial of Black Consciousness" in early May and its most historic expression, the Soweto Student Uprising just five weeks later, was driven by visual culture at its most widespread span.

The sense of personal empowerment demonstrated among Soweto youth on June 16, 1976, was born of Black Consciousness. The demonstrations nationwide in the weeks that followed exhibited BC's reach and are credited with launching a new period of active resistance to apartheid that accelerated its demise. The trial's outcome, given December 15, 1976, was likewise influenced by the surge of Black Consciousness witnessed during the last weeks of June. The trial and the uprising are intertwined in history and image. I conclude this chapter with analysis of their impact registered through pictures and words during this pivotal period in history.

The Trial

Initially, the National Party regarded Black Consciousness as supportive of its own segregationist policy, so in the first years advocates spoke and wrote freely about their cause. But by 1971 some BC advocates began to face restrictions, and by 1973 several were banned (see Figure 1.5).[113] By this time the state looked for reasons to ban BC organizations entirely. It found a way to do so on September 25, 1974. On SASO and BPC calendars, this date marked rallies organized in Johannesburg, Port Elizabeth, Cape Town, East London, and Durban to celebrate the black-led liberation of Mozambique to the north. September 25 coincided with their neighbor's introduction of a transitional government to manage the state's full independence from Portugal, to occur on June 25, 1975. Samora Machel's Front for the Liberation of Mozambique (FRELIMO) had led the charge, so the rallies in South Africa were called Pro-FRELIMO.[114] Already nervous about liberation at its borders, the state banned all pro-FRELIMO rallies just before they were to take place.[115] Large crowds gathered nonetheless, notably at the University of the North–Turfloop and at Currie's Fountain in Durban, where five thousand people refused the government's ban.[116] The state responded with on-site beatings and arrests, followed by a raid on SASO and BPC offices, and the detention of twelve SASO and BPC leaders; nine were charged with terrorism and faced the possibility of death by hanging.[117]

The nine leaders charged had committed no physical act of violence or recruited anyone to do such, but the words they wrote and distributed between 1971 and 1974 were said to promote revolution and "a course of preparation . . .

[to form a] black power bloc" that would overthrow the state.[118] The real issue was whether Black Consciousness constituted terrorism. Though it is rightly said that "the very concept and theory of Black Consciousness" was on trial, for the nine men accused, the result was sentences of three to six years of imprisonment.[119] Zithulele Cindi, Saths Cooper, Patrick Lekota, Aubrey Mokoape, Strini Moodley, Muntu Myeza, Pandelani Nefolovhodwe, Nkwenkwe Nkomo, and Kaborane Sedibe spent sixteen months in a Pretoria prison before being sentenced. They had the misfortune of being subjected to the longest trial then yet heard under the Terrorism Act of 1950: 136 days.[120]

Biko had not been charged because at the time he was banned to the magisterial district of King William's Town, so he did not take part in planning the pro-FRELIMO rallies. He was the principal witness for the accused, however, and his testimony from May 3–7 was a forceful speech on the strength and necessity of Black Consciousness.[121] Both defense and prosecution counsel spent considerable time on BC's approach to whiteness, but Biko repeatedly managed to swing the exchange back toward the central concerns of Black Consciousness. He created a vivid picture of black life under apartheid. Bleak in every way, BC offered a positive response to the self-negation that racism fosters. As Biko put it,

> we do make reference to the conditions of the black man and the conditions in which the black man lives. We try to get blacks in conscientization to grapple realistically with their problems, to attempt to find solutions to their problems, to develop what one might call an awareness, a physical awareness of their situation, to be able to analyze it, and to provide answers for themselves. The purpose behind it really being to provide some kind of hope; I think the central theme about black society is that it has got elements of a defeated society, people often look like they have given up the struggle. . . . Now this sense of defeat is basically what we are fighting against; people must not just give in to the hardship of life, people must develop a hope, people must develop some form of security to be together to look at their problems, and people must in this way build up their humanity. This is the point about conscientization and Black Consciousness.[122]

Discussion of South Africa's economic and political state arose over two days in three lengthy discussions. In order that people might "provide answers for themselves," BC proponents advocated that blacks unionize, restrict business to black proprietors, keep their reading to the black press, and invest in their communities through educational and religious centers. Biko explained that the "totality of power," propagated and controlled by whites, would only change once blacks adopted the "totality of involvement" that is Black Consciousness.[123] The ultimate goal was a society free of racial distinctions, but this could only be realized once equality was seen as a human right. This required BC's audience to see their own humanity while living in a society that denied it. It must be said that stating this goal was not an endorsement of the ANC, as Diana Wylie has read it, but an objective of those committed to Black Consciousness.[124] Indeed, over two days the prosecutor tried to align BC organizations with the ANC and the Pan Africanist Congress, both banned parties, but Biko resisted these efforts and remained focused on BC itself. He described the Black Peoples' Convention as "a political party in the making."[125]

The state accused the nine men on trial of "endangering the maintenance of law and order" by conspiring to "transform the state by unconstitutional, revolutionary and/or violent means." They were said to "create and foster feelings of racial hatred, hostility and antipathy by the Blacks toward the White population group of the Republic . . . [and] to discourage, hamper, deter or prevent foreign investment in the economy of the Republic."[126] Since their words formed the body of evidence put forth, language and its representation (the makings of visual culture) were discussed at length. The debate turned on cultural differences in the use and reception of language: the prosecutor insisted on defining specific words as inflammatory, while Biko held that meaning can only be found in the context of their delivery and in the culture of the audience that receives them. Nuances matter, particularly when the words used are not in the language that listeners use at home. In a brilliant exchange on the third day, Millard Arnold imparts that Biko, "by sheer force of personality reverse[ed] roles and actually cross examine[d] his interrogator."[127] The following was one of the more delight-inducing rallies:

> K. ATTWELL: Do you think there are still lots of people who understand [the words] . . . freedom fighter?
>
> STEVE BIKO: Freedom Fighter is again . . . . There is an intellectual interpretation of the term, and the historical interpretation of the term. The intellectual interpretation of the term means anybody who fights for freedom. Now, I would describe and I have described myself to people who ask as a freedom fighter, but at the same time I do know that there is this historical

interpretation of the term which relates to the movements that have been operating on the borders [north of South Africa] as well.

ATTWELL: When you used the term to describe yourself, to whom have you been addressing yourself?

BIKO: Oh, other folk.

ATTWELL: Not other intellectuals?

BIKO: Certainly with intellectuals but with ordinary folk as well. . . .

ATTWELL: And if somebody did not know you, and you met them for the first time, or you met a group of people for the first time, and there were not intellectuals, would you describe yourself as a freedom fighter?

BIKO: No, I did not define it but I did use it once with the Special Branch, who were being introduced to me, who wanted to know what my profession was, and I said I was a freedom fighter.

ATTWELL: I think that was a bit of tongue-in-cheek, not so?

BIKO: He laughed.

ATTWELL: It was a bit of tongue-in-cheek, not so?

BIKO: Well, it was making conversation, and if you have got to live with the Security Police on your neck all the time you have got to devise a way of talking to them, you know, and this is one of the ways.

ATTWELL: They understand only one language. [Laughter.] The point I want to make is that. . . . Would you describe yourself as a freedom fighter to people you did not know and who were not intellectuals without defining the term?

BIKO: No, I do not think so. It depends of course how it crops up in conversation.

ATTWELL: Why would you not?

BIKO: It depends, as I say, how it crops up in conversation. I mean, if my intention is to perhaps deal with what I am doing fully, then I would go straight into the hub of the matter and talk about what I am doing, but if a person— and this depends on how it crops up—wants to know what you do, right? Now, I am not working right now, for instance. I am not working. I am persecuted for my political beliefs or mental beliefs. I have not done anything which is against the law, and I have got no profession as such. So if a guy in a round table is asking, What is your profession, and someone says, I am a doctor. What is your profession, I am a lawyer. They come to me, I always say freedom fighter—precisely because this is what the State wants me to do, to sit at home and think about my freedom rather than be involved in creative work.

ATTWELL: But there you were talking to other people who were a doctor and a lawyer—they were intellectuals?

BIKO: Right. Common people do not normally ask you for a profession.[128]

On May 6, the court examined two publications that Biko had written under the pseudonym Frank Talk: "The Definition of Black Consciousness" and "Fear— An Important Determinant in South African Politics," both of which had been published in SASO newsletters. (In retrospect, the exchange about them at the SASO–BPC trial foreshadowed the events of June 16 in compelling ways.)[129] From the first article, Attwell highlighted two sentences: "Blacks are out to completely transform the System and make of it what they wish," and "Blacks no longer seek to reform the System, because so doing implies acceptance of the major points around which the System revolves." He again made "White values" the major concern. Where were they in BC's vision of a new South Africa? Biko had answered this question several times over the preceding days for both defense and prosecution counsel. This time he deferred: "I think you will have to wait for a definition of that future society, and this is what I am saying BPC has finally given. You must examine that, and perhaps you will get an indication within that of what shall be retained." Though Attwell tried to show that the first article intended to incite racial violence, Biko insisted that the excerpts chosen for cross-examination falsely represented his argument. Taken in full, the article underscored how fear drives racism. Biko said that he sought to "eradicate the thinking that is prevalent in White society, so to speak, which makes them operate from fear as a basis." This fear caused the state's heavy hand, witnessed daily in townships as police aggression. Their actions had "inculcated fear in Blacks, you know, fear against authority, and I am saying this is an unhealthy fear because it is the kind of fear which, if it goes unchecked, generates an uncontrollable response, some kind of blowup." Attwell drew attention to the article's end: "The stage is therefore set for a very interesting turn of events." He queried Biko's meaning. Blacks should no longer "accept crumbs from the White table. . . . As soon as Blacks demonstrate beyond any doubt [their willingness to work within the system] . . . we would like to see what Mr. Vorster will have to offer."

Black Consciousness, which Attwell summarized as a "diabolical plan,"[130] drove the Soweto uprisings that began on June 16 and fanned across the nation in the weeks that followed. Like the trial, Soweto was about "Black Consciousness itself." And just as the trial influenced the uprisings, the reverse is likely true, too. The judge's final verdict was given on December 15, 1976. All nine SASO and BPC leaders were found guilty on at least one of two counts under the Terrorism Act: Count One alleged conspiracy to cause or promote hostile relations between people of different races; Count Two declared that the accused had organized a banned rally.[131] Just as Soweto brought significant change, so did the verdict in the SASO–BPC trial. Thereafter, Hilda Bernstein writes, "Terrorism could be committed not only through physical violence, but also through the expression of thoughts, ideas and desires for liberation."[132]

The Uprisings

By the mid-1970s, Black Consciousness had proven so effective that Anthony Marx says it provided "the only terms (for liberation) then current in townships."[133] Exiled political organizations claimed no real credibility for mobilizing township youth within South Africa; indeed, by late 1977, young activists called Steve Biko a greater influence on their lives than Nelson Mandela.[134] In Soweto, BC spread through varied channels, with the South African Students' Movement (SASM) providing the most direct tie to SASO as a secondary-school counterpart to SASO's university-based membership.[135] A famous artist today, Patrick Mautloa designed a T-shirt for SASM members in Soweto, his childhood home; it represented BC's union of Bantu, Coloured, and Indian activists, a denial of race and racism rather than its promotion.[136] BC spread through informal means, too. Gail Gerhart adds that the expulsion of SASO activists from universities around the country in mid-1972 influenced younger siblings, who protested in 1976.[137] Early that year, SASM members at three Soweto high schools organized to march against the state's decision to use Afrikaans as the language of instruction in several disciplines. In January, the Department of Bantu Education took up the plan anyway, even though teachers did not always speak Afrikaans well enough to use it in the classroom. Several Soweto teachers refused to use the language and were fired in March as a result. SASM undertook different measures of protest, including the boycott of midyear exams.

Calling themselves the Soweto Students' Representative Council, these SASM members planned a peaceful protest for June 16 at which students from twelve assembly points would converge at a single place and march en masse to the stadium in Orlando, a neighborhood within the township's border. In what Marx calls "the single most impressive organizational feat associated with Black

Consciousness," an estimated ten thousand students took part in this demonstration to demand that English and indigenous languages be used in the classroom.[138] Several sang freedom songs and carried signs with slogans such as Viva Azania and Down with Afrikaans. En route to the stadium they encountered fifty policemen who had set up a roadblock to prevent them from reaching their destination. Shots were fired, then stones were thrown and chaos broke out.

Soweto was not alone. In the following weeks, the uprising had spread to more than one hundred urban and rural areas nationwide.[139] Within one week, 130 people had been killed in townships. A little more than a year later, just before Biko was murdered, a quarter-million students had boycotted classes, a thousand were killed while protesting, and twenty-one thousand had been prosecuted for offenses related to the uprising that began June 16.[140] "In retrospect," writes Marx, "the shootings by police had provided a very useful weapon in merging the young and the old, with the resulting unrest having proved that countrywide unity was possible." Black Consciousness had reached its founders' goal.

Many photographers captured examples of Black Consciousness in action in the weeks that followed June 16. The photographs of Peter Magubane are among the best known. He photographed the men seen in Figure 1.16 somewhere in the Eastern Cape soon after that first day. At least nine BC adherents raise their fists high; one person extends his palm to show preference for the Pan Africanist Congress. Right of center, two men wear dashikis, one of gold fabric edged in black, the colors of the Black Peoples' Convention. He bends his neck to face downward (as does another person in the lower right corner), a gesture that resonates with the solemnity of Olympians Tommie Smith and John Carlos of the United States who, in 1968, saluted a transnational identity centered on blackness when they received their medals. Through the power of photography, their common gesture and posture—raised fist with bowed head—became an icon of tricontinental activism. The men in Magubane's photograph likewise shape their identity.

Another photograph, taken at the funeral of Hector Pieterson, captures the raised clenched fist of a pastor who officiated (Figure 1.17).[141] The fist here was Magubane's focal point: this is a portrait of Black Consciousness. It identifies not the man but the collective of which he is part. Rising forth from a triangular base of two bibles, this symbol of Black solidarity (theology and politics in concert) seems to grab the sunlight and anchor the day, Pieterson's own, in Black Consciousness. This portrait is one of aggressive action, for in the frame

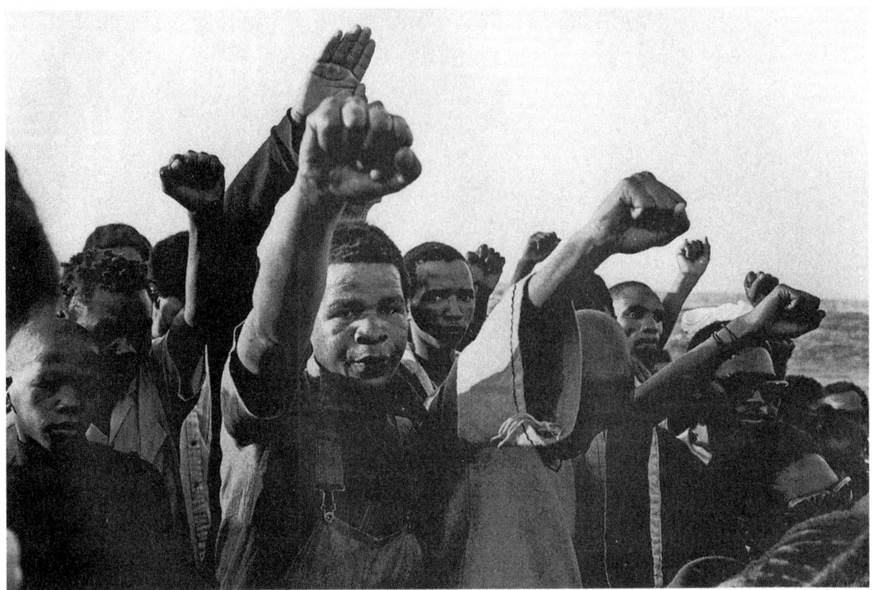

FIGURE 1.16. Peter Magubane, *Supporters of the Soweto Student Uprising, Eastern Cape, June 1976,* 1976. Courtesy of Peter Magubane.

of Black Theology, Biko described "Christ as a fighting God, not a passive God who allows a lie to rest unchallenged. It grapples with existential problems and does not claim to be a theology of absolutes. It seeks to *bring back God* to the black man and to the truth and reality of his situation."[142]

Black Theology has been called "an important aspect of Black Consciousness," and indeed it is, but equally so is BC vital to Black Theology. In 1971, Biko argued that it was "the duty . . . of all black priests and ministers of religion to save Christianity" and Christians from the gross misrepresentation of Africa and Africans in the hands of colonial clergy. Anglican and communalist, Biko promoted a "(hu)man-centered society whose sacred tradition is that of sharing." Africa best embodied this approach. Cast as ubuntu today, the notion that "a person is a person through other people" has always been at the heart of both Black Consciousness and Black Theology. Their mutual reliance is widely known and much studied, especially since apartheid's official end in 1994.[143] This vast literature is necessarily part of another study, but I highlight it here

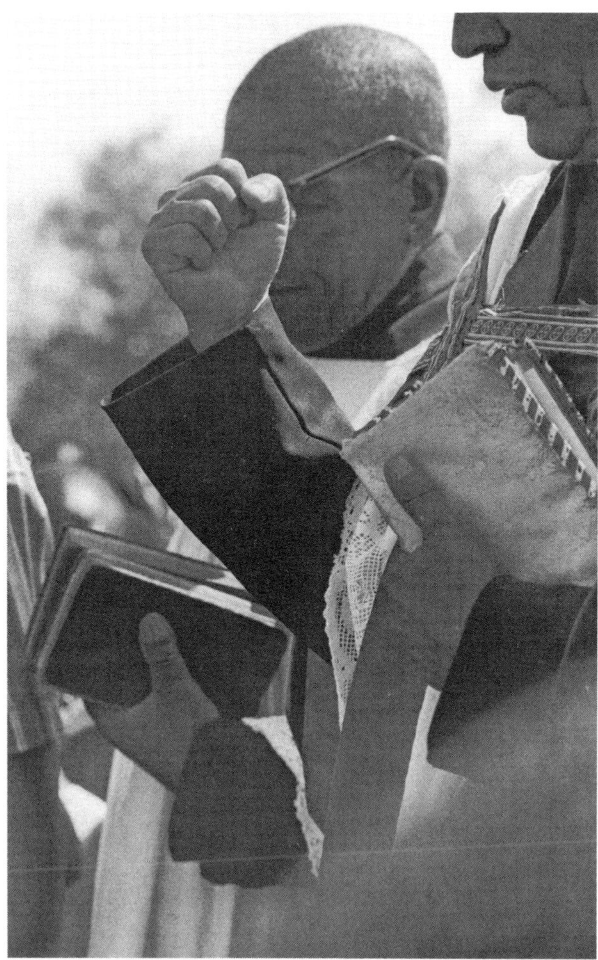

FIGURE 1.17. Peter Magubane, *A Bible and a Clenched Fist at Hector Pieterson's Funeral, June 1976*, 1976. Courtesy of Peter Magubane.

for two reasons. First, its reach and influence are widespread and lasting, as are misrepresentations of its mission. These were evident in the 2008 election of then-Senator Barack Obama to the presidency of the United States through campaigns that sought to smear his candidacy by representing Black Theology as a belief system structured on race rather than liberation. This shows that we must better understand how representations of race condition our response to political action. Second, Steve Biko's death in detention on September 12, 1977, generated a visual response centered on socioreligious martyrdom. Such presentations necessarily engage ideas of sacrifice for the higher cause that Black Theology supports. The immense visual history of Black Theology in South Africa remains to be studied.

Black Consciousness is not about racial awareness; it is about liberating oneself from oppression. BC has always rejected the divisions of race and ethnicity to which its adherents are subjected from without. It started small, among individuals, who organized and fanned outward into communities, mostly urban but also rural. Its most famous mark in history, the Soweto Uprisings, testifies to its popular strength and historic efficacy. Its lasting mark is remarkable in consideration of the regular obstacles the state imposed en route. It first banned select BC proponents from speaking publically and attending meetings in 1971.[144] The next year, when the Black Peoples' Convention (BPC) was launched,[145] the state began its clandestine surveillance of BC organizations on campuses nationwide,[146] and Abram Tiro gave a famous speech that revealed a desire for armed response within BC ranks.[147] At the start of 1973, a series of labor strikes by black workers in Durban warranted worldwide publicity. Two new BPC affiliates, the Black Allied Workers' Union (BAWU) and the Black Workers' Project (BWP), were associated with the strikes, and leaders Drake Kgalushe Koka (from BAWU) and James Bokwe Mafuna (from BWP) were banned.[148] In March 1973, still more leaders were banned: Steve Biko, Barney Pityana, Harry Nengwekhulu, and four others.[149] In 1974, Tiro was assassinated in Botswana by a parcel bomb, and the so-called SASO Nine were arrested and charged under the Terrorism Act.[150] As the visual culture of this book makes clear, BC amassed a significant amount of influence, especially among youth, despite the state's substantial and awful efforts to squelch it. Indeed, Anthony Marx rightly argues that the state's repression further legitimized BC's cause.[151]

Although the form of Black Consciousness that realized the Soweto Uprisings has been described as "an angry desire to tear down rather than to build up," this was more likely the result of violence done to Sowetans (and their supporters elsewhere) rather than its cause.[152] BC was young, still (smartly) taking shape, when 1976 hit. In previous years, division often arose in SASO and BPC meetings over such things as inclusivity, socioeconomic platform, and violence as a means to an end. The minutes of these meetings enable us to see versatility at BC's core, thus it is not surprising that the BC-minded chose to identify with varied political parties in the 1980s. After the events of September and

October 1977 (Steve Biko's death in detention, the banning of nineteen BC organizations, and the detention and banning of many BC supporters), BC's reach branched out and became contested in its diverse influence.

Black Consciousness names an ideology instead of a party, and its beneficiaries from the 1970s took their sense of pride, confidence, and commitment to liberation into varied political affiliations in the 1980s. Condemned by those who emphasize race over awareness, BC has been cast as ineffectual in realizing liberation. But today we see BC's lasting effects as ideological and organizational, and we see them expressed in both popular and professional artistic spheres. Mbulelo Mzamane and his coauthors are among those who recently argued, "Activity, not activism as such, marked BC strategy," as early adherents labored to help meet physical needs in rural and urban communities.[153] For instance, BC organs brought about medical centers, aid for families of political detainees, microprojects on literacy, childcare, auto service, and housing construction, among others. Residents of distant places like Winterveldt, Lenyenye, and Inanda in Transvaal, Welcomehood and Dududu in Natal, and Ginsberg in the Eastern Cape benefited from BC's action-oriented approach. By early 1972 and until at least 1975, students at black high schools were offered leadership training through clubs.[154] And BC organs promoted like-minded artists by hosting their theatrical performances at official gatherings and, in at least one case involving visual art, funding a Johannesburg gallery run by David Koloane, one of South Africa's best-known artists.[155] As stated by Mzamane and others, "The lasting legacy of BC, then, was not only intellectual but it was also organizational. . . . That is, in fact, what the 1980s owe to the 1970s."[156] So, too, do nonracialist organizations of the 1980s owe Black Consciousness credit for creating the conditions in which white activists would listen. Regrettably, whiteness still dominates academic translation of BC, and we would do well to question how it affects discussion of race today.

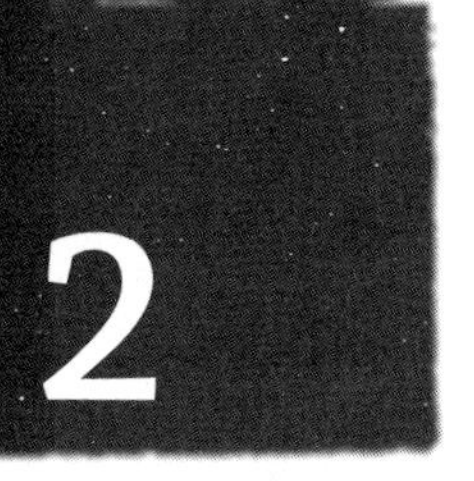

2 Of Icons and Inquests

"Steve Biko,
God Be with You, BPC"

STEPHEN BIKO'S GLOBAL STATURE WAS EVIDENT BUT MODEST BEFORE HIS death. This quickly changed. When he died in police custody on September 12, 1977, his image was printed around the world. In nearly all international reports, Black Consciousness, the philosophy for which he had died, became secondary to the abuses of the South African police, the symbol of which he became. Through his likeness a new spotlight was cast on South Africa's abusive Terrorism Act, portions of which allowed political activists to be held incommunicado, without charge and without access to anyone outside the state. Within South Africa, Biko's prominence as *the* father of Black Consciousness prompted journalists to analyze it almost as forcefully as they did his death. Though already known to South Africans who formed the nucleus of this creed, those outside it were now able to learn about one of the most influential leaders in their nation. All of these readers met Steve Biko through portraiture that appeared in the South African press in the last quarter of 1977. Visual culture is crucial to realizing Biko's legacy because it indicates that the tug of war over his words and likeness, a divide readily seen in the decades ahead, was there right from the start.

Portraiture is the vehicle of study here because it inscribes social identity as much as it describes an individual. When the person imaged is of political importance, that social identity becomes one of national significance. In the immediate aftermath of Biko's death, a visual language developed in the press around three types of portraiture that have effected his legacy ever since. The first type casts him as the embodiment of Black Consciousness. Shown in a work shirt, he is Everyman and promises others that they too can live proudly and "stand tall," as Adam Small repeatedly encouraged in *DRUM* magazine's

November 1977 tribute issue. The second portrait type images Biko as Fallen Statesman, a much-mourned intellectual who was the primary spokesman for South Africa's majority populace. The third portrait type, generated by the state's autopsy of Biko's corpse, became an emblem of state abuse and forceful resistance to it. So, too, did a particular living portrait that appeared at his funeral and has since been reproduced many times over, ultimately becoming what W. J. T. Mitchell calls a "hypericon" (Figure 2.1).[1] Dikobé Ben Martins used the photograph in a poster he designed and mass-produced for Biko's funeral (see Figure 2.6); thus, although it depicts Biko while alive, it remains a potent image of death. With this origin, the otherwise statesmanly portrait became a visual condemnation of a government that ruled by violence. Its iconic currency is captured in a 1994 election poster printed by the African National Congress (see Figure 6.2). Reproduced beneath the words "Never Again!" the funeral image maintains its place twenty years later as a potent symbol of resistance to South Africa's violent history.

The photograph portraits first appeared in the popular press, and afterward they were painted and later set in motion by virtue of being held aloft in protest demonstrations. They served as counterpart to the drawings by dozens of amateur artists who sent their work to the popular press for print. Collected and mass-produced with or without narrative text, these became visual essays, a genre of debate driven by pictures. W. J. T. Mitchell and Carol Shloss agree on the features of visual essays: they presume a common referential reality (rather than a doctored realism), convey the intimacy of personal perspective and compellingly remain unfinished.[2] Like essays, photographs are "always incomplete"—their parameters must be cut to fit a defined space. Mitchell finds the mix of word and image in photographic essays "united by a documentary purpose, often political, journalistic, sometimes scientific . . . [which are] the product of progressive liberal conscience, associated with political reform and leftist causes."[3] Photographic essays were highly critical of the social and legal structure that allowed Biko's death in detention. So effective were these essays in the context of this history that while testifying at the inquest, Colonel Pieter Johannes Goosen, then divisional commander of the Eastern Province Security Police, condemned "the Press and liberalists [which] had created a climate of revolt against [the] Security legislation" under which Biko was held.[4]

The mass-produced portraits of Biko at this time became a kind of composite "death mask" of the kind that Roland Barthes famously used to describe all photographs due to their conjuring of the past, always yesterday.[5] The small

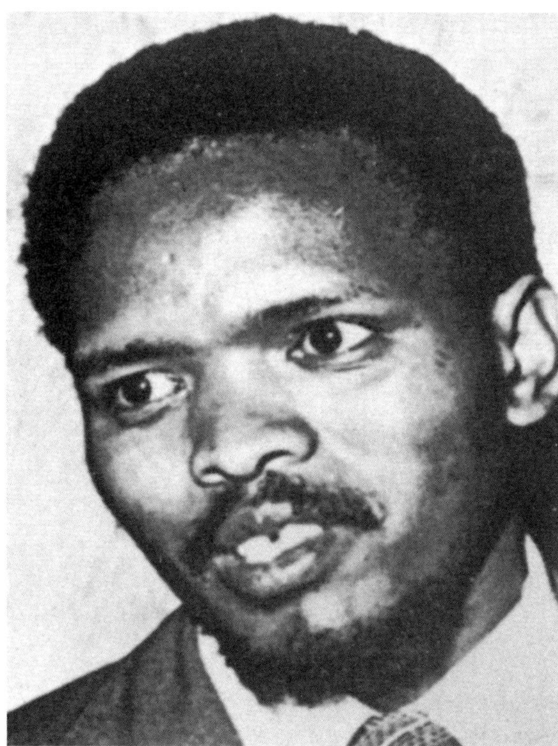

FIGURE 2.1. Iconic photograph of Steve Biko, circa 1970. Photographer unknown.

collection of portrait photographs published after Biko's death always retain a sense of unsupportable loss, thus they generate a desire to make present something that is absent. Biko's death mask (the iconic portrait in Figure 2.1) has been reused to such an extent that it fundamentally informs his legacy. To borrow a phrase from John Tagg, the hypericon is unlike others from this period in that hereafter it works to make Biko "retrospectively real."[6] These images are not merely tokens of nostalgia that invariably conjure loss, as Barthes suggested, but objects that activate. They are used to persuade and affect us. They have generated a history of their own.

The News: Reporting on Biko's Death

The news of Biko's death hit the South African press on September 13, 1977, and within two days papers around the world were questioning its cause on the front page (Figure 2.2). European and American radio covered the story day after day. As the South African government found itself under the spotlight of suspicion by a range of bodies from within its borders and without (e.g., governments, journalists, academics, lawyers, religious and athletic organizations, political activists, medical doctors), it offered conflicting accounts as to how Steve Biko could have died in its care. The official line changed as pressure mounted: first, Biko was said to have died as the result of a hunger strike, then that he succumbed to a preexisting kidney ailment, and finally that he died due to head injuries sustained when he attacked his interrogators. The last of these explanations rode on through the state inquest that was conducted over a three-week period from November 14 to December 2, 1977.[7] It remained the official line for decades to come. In fact, the men involved in Biko's death maintained this version of events as they testified before the Truth and Reconciliation Commission twenty years later.

Minister of Justice James Kruger was notoriously flippant in his early remarks. On September 14, he joked before members of Parliament about Biko's death and received hearty laughter in response. Speaking in his native Afrikaans, he spoke words that gained considerable notice:

> I am not glad and I am not sorry about Mr. Biko. It leaves me cold. I can
> say nothing to you. Any person who dies . . . I shall also be sorry if I die.
> *(Laughter)* . . . . Then [Biko] said he would go on a hunger strike . . . . And
> indeed he began to push his food and water away. . . . Prisoners in South Africa
> hav[e] the "democratic right" to starve themselves to death. It is a democratic
> land. *(Laughter)*
>
> We are now asked, "When you saw he went on a hunger strike why didn't
> you force him to eat?" *(Laughter)*
>
> Mr. Chairman, can you imagine that these same people who smear the
> police day and night because they touched this man—and there's a mark on his
> foot, and there's a mark on his ankle, and here's a mark behind his ear and it
> must be the police—do you think the police must still force that man to eat? . . .
>
> Incidentally, I can just tell congress, the day before yesterday one of my own
> lieutenants in the prison service also committed suicide and we have not yet
> accused a single prisoner. *(Laughter)*[8]

The public quickly condemned such callous humor, and Kruger's explanation was widely contested. Biko was known to be in excellent health when he was detained on August 18, 1977, and eight days was logically too short a time be-

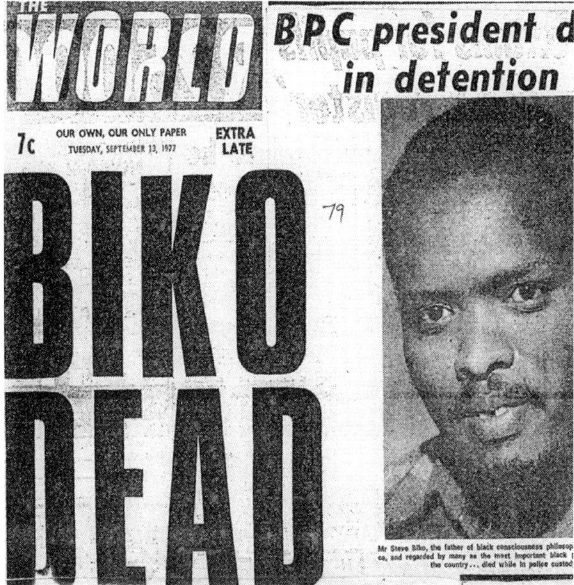

FIGURE 2.2. "BIKO DEAD."
Cover of *The World*,
September 13, 1977, 1.

tween the start of a hunger strike and his death.[9] Kruger had also given conflicting accounts of where Biko had died, first citing the hospital and later his cell. He even attempted to absolve the state of responsibility by stating that Biko was in the "neutral ground" of a hospital when he died and therefore out of the hands of the police.[10] Suspicion of police culpability arose among Nationalist stalwarts after Kruger appeared on national television to say Biko had been fed intravenously.[11] Such blunders furthered international condemnation of apartheid. Biko's death "dealt South Africa a blow as damaging as the Sharpeville shooting in 1960 and the Soweto riots."[12] The world became aware that Biko was the forty-sixth South African to die while in custody since no-trial detention laws were first passed in 1963; twenty others had died in the previous eighteen months alone.[13]

By the time portions of Biko's autopsy report were leaked to the press on September 20, public distrust had caused President B. J. Vorster to agree to an inquest and to censure Minister Kruger for his mismanagement of the state's "crisis." The unofficial autopsy suggested Biko had suffered fatal injuries to his head. Extensive abrasions and bruises were said to be evident elsewhere on his body, principally his rib cage, wrists, ankles, and limbs. On September 25, 1977, the day Biko was buried, headlines read "Biko's Brain Injured."[14] Other injuries came to light when the official sixteen-page autopsy became available to the press on October 26: acute renal failure and uremia; internal chest injuries due to impact to his ribs; lung tissue swollen with fluid; nose broken; at least twelve bruises, burns, and abrasions on his skin; heart dilated; blood clotting and reduced blood circulation due to head injury. With this report, the world learned that both pathologists (Dr. Jonathan Gluckman for the Biko family and Professor Johan Loubser for the state) believed a massive brain hemorrhage was the primary cause of Biko's death.[15] Kruger's response to these findings was as callous as his initial remarks, and he again blamed Biko for self-inflicting his injuries: "A man may damage his brain in many ways. I can tell you that under Press harassment I've often felt like banging my head against a wall, too, but realising now, with the Biko autopsy, that may be fatal, I haven't done it."[16] Kruger's evident lack of humanity ultimately caused a worldwide "wave of revulsion" toward South Africa.[17]

This sense of revulsion was acute for the two thousand South Africans who called for Minister Kruger's resignation, and certainly so for those who knew Biko personally. This magnified as the state slandered him in the following weeks with words that conjure a visual culture of fear. Biko was called a "violent revolutionary" who was said to have authored a pamphlet titled "August 18 Commemoration Day" that encouraged arson and murder. These "secret documents" were said to provide "damning evidence" of his criminal tendencies. (The culture of silence and secrecy that pervaded South Africa in this period is discussed in depth in chapter 5.) Much was made of the pamphlet's inclusion of a black clenched-fist motif as the state co-opted BC iconography in its effort to scare white readers. But many people have speculated the pamphlet was made after Biko's death, thus rendering it a kind of black propaganda akin to that shown in Figure 4.1.[18] The state consistently called Biko a "Black Power" activist, and President Vorster naïvely surmised that Biko would have been known to just one in a hundred people before his death.[19] Although certain press factions did not critically engage such falsehoods, most journalists understood that Black Consciousness and Black Power were (and are) different things, that Biko would only be pulled into an act of aggression if violence were inflicted on him, and that he was widely known within South Africa and without.

Hlaku Kenneth Rachidi, president of the Black Peoples' Convention (BPC) at the time, responded to such falsehoods in short order. Kruger and others in Vorster's cabinet had repeatedly aligned Black Consciousness with communism in order to spark fear among Christians and capitalists alike, and to undermine its persuasiveness among Africans of any religious conviction. To this, Rachidi said,

> Black Consciousness is not a foreign concept. That is, it is neither capitalism, communism, nor western socialism—hence the ease with which the people understand, accept and adapt themselves to it. . . . [Kruger is] frightened by the fact that the message of Black Consciousness will convert even the hard core nationalist by its message of equality and its stress on the value of human dignity regardless of colour, race, or creed.[20]

Rachidi and others who survived Biko became his mouthpiece, because as a person banned when he died Biko could not be quoted in the press.[21] To this journalist Donald Woods wrote, "They think the enemy is words . . . but their enemy is ideas."[22] (Woods and his family were named as government conspirators in other pamphlets distributed in East London townships.) The state permitted at least one quotation, however, when it allowed the conservative daily *The Citizen* to publish an extract from an interview Biko gave to the *New York Times* years prior.[23] The quotation, which can only have been interpreted and/or reported without regard to context, was damning. The point here is not what Biko purportedly said, but that exceptions to the rule were allowed. Further, the interview's existence undercuts Vorster's claim that Biko was not significant until after his death. Why else would an American journalist from "the paper of record" travel to remote King William's Town to interview him? European journalists had done the same.[24]

In various ways the state snuffed out attempts to commemorate Biko and investigate what had happened in his final days. Banning orders were applied against people, BPC-affiliated organizations, newspapers, and other businesses in quick succession from mid-September to mid-October 1977. Numerous student organizations planned commemorative events at universities across South Africa—overnight vigils, daytime protests against deaths in detention—and all were banned under Section Two of the Riotous Assemblies Act. The University of Cape Town managed to have its ban lifted, and Donald Woods gave a significant address there on September 16. Seven hundred students at Fort Hare University were arrested when they went forward with their meeting on September 15. Police and conservative students tore down posters made by the National Union of South African Students (NUSAS) to promote these events. Buses that would ferry thousands of mourners to Biko's funeral on September 25 were denied permission to travel, and many were stopped en route. In early October, Minister Kruger sought "an urgent hearing of national importance" with the South African Press Council to penalize and censure the *Rand Daily Mail* for running a headline that countered his claim that Biko undertook a hunger strike. Kruger received the hearing quickly but failed to attend despite the "national importance" of his claim. The Press Council found in favor of its absentee claimant, and the *Rand Daily Mail* was fined. Within the same week, Kruger sought action against two more newspapers—*The World* and *Pretoria News*—lamenting that South Africa's English press was responsible for the heightened international attention. Ultimately, *The Economist,* in an issue that printed Biko's coffin on its cover, stated that President Vorster "seems to have authorized Mr. Kruger to divert attention from the subject of Mr. Biko's death by harassing the newspapers that are trying to get at the truth."[25] On October 19, nineteen Black Consciousness affiliates were banned, including Black Peoples' Convention, Black Community Programmes, and *The World*. Percy Qoboza, editor of this important Johannesburg-based daily, was detained along with an estimated seven to eight hundred BC adherents under the same provision that had held Biko: Section Six of the Terrorism Act.[26] This act stipulated that people could be detained without trial, without access to family, a lawyer, and medical doctor of choice or the guarantee that a state magistrate would learn anything about their case. Thus the state turned a deaf ear to the many voices from varied sectors that questioned the constitutionality of the law in the wake of Biko's death.

The Press: "He Was a Monument of Man's Decency"

A division is notable among the South African magazines and newspapers that regularly printed portraits of Steve Biko during the last quarter of 1977. Print matter with largely black readership often portrayed him in flannel work shirt and jeans, sometimes enjoying light moments with his family, other times engaging us directly (see Figure 2.2), projecting the embodiment of pride and agency at the heart of Black Consciousness. Pictured thus, he is cast as Everyman and inspires viewers to likewise live the creed. Accompanying him in this light on September 12, 1977, the headline in Figure 2.2 echoes others that were bracingly simple: "BIKO DEAD." All other text affirms that Biko and BC were well known to readers, as were the horrid statistics about abuse in detention. Through visual culture, a combination of pictorial and textual representation circulated popularly, Biko is positioned here as an exalted hero who embodies the ideals of Black Consciousness, yet he is also one with millions of readers. This tactic enabled South Africa's majority to see itself as potentially heroic, capable of living the doctrine of BC and contributing to the social and political changes Biko so vigorously upheld. The motto of *The World,* "Our Own, Our Only Paper," addressed this audience, and their favorable response is evident; Keyan Tomaselli and P. Eric Louw called *The World* "the most widely read and influential black-oriented publication in South Africa."[27]

Alternatively, English presses with mostly white readers favored portraits that cast Biko as Statesman (Figure 2.3). Newspapers in Afrikaans printed his image much less often. Photographed or drawn in suit and tie, books and papers resting comfortably in the crook of his arm, Biko is presented in the small collection of portraits from his diplomatic side. He is shown engaged, humored, and resolute. Photographs of Biko meeting with local and foreign dignitaries who came to call also appear in these pages. Captions often reaffirm his nonviolent approach in a way that would have reassured white readers. For example, the *Daily Dispatch* remembered Biko as "a man of peace [who] should be remembered as he would like to be remembered—a man who wanted love and reconciliation, not bitterness and hatred."[28] Interestingly, there appear to be no pictures of Biko with foreign visitors in the pages of papers owned, operated, and read by black South Africans. This is in line with criticism he received from BPC members for meeting with particular diplomats, notably Americans.

The *Daily Dispatch* led its September 13, 1977, issue with the headline "BIKO DIES IN DETENTION" above a watercolor portrait by staff artist Donald Kenyon (Figure 2.4).[29] Biko is named "Hero of the Nation" in English and Xhosa. His likeness matches that seen in Figure 2.3 on the far right, top row, a look of thoughtful repose. Kenyon represents Biko in three-quarter view, a perspective historically associated with aristocracy and, when the subject is male, brilliance

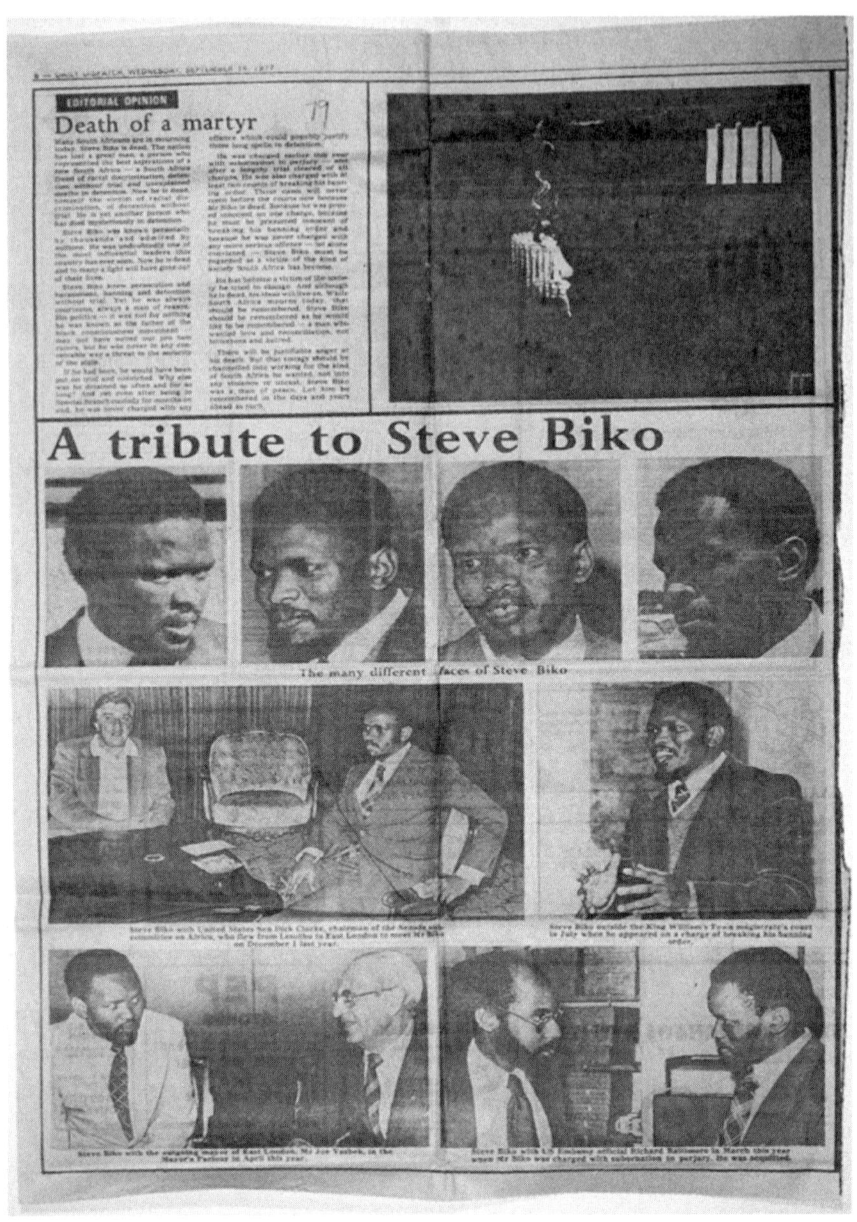

FIGURE 2.3. "A Tribute to Steve Biko." Photo essay in the *Daily Dispatch,* September 14, 1977, 8, 458.

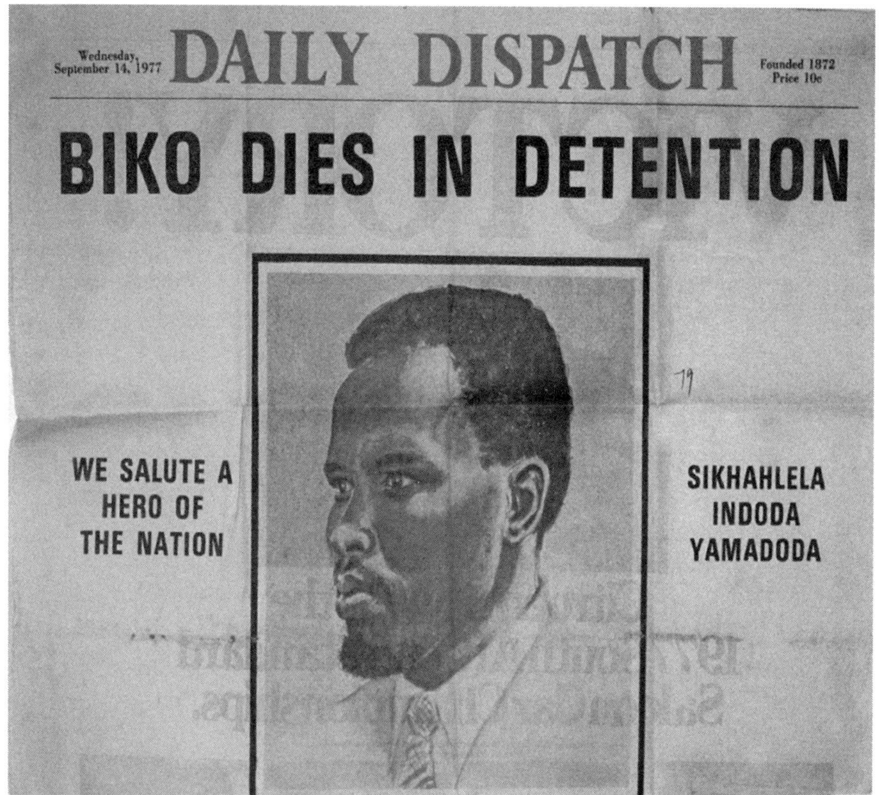

FIGURE 2.4. Donald Kenyon, *We Salute a Hero of the Nation*. Watercolor, printed on the cover of *Daily Dispatch*, September 14, 1977.

or thoughtful purpose.[30] Note the attention Kenyon paid to Biko's facial features, which are more fully realized than the clothing he wears. The suit and tie are drawn so lightly that they look merely sketched and incomplete. The portrait appears against a plain blue backdrop and is framed in black, pictorial devices that lend an aura of worldliness and social importance to the subject.

These visual clues were not lost on editors of *The World*, which reproduced Kenyon's portrait in its September 23, 1977, issue devoted to Biko's funeral, or on readers of these papers who clipped the portrait for use in protests.[31] During commemorations in September 1977, copies of Kenyon's work were hung behind podiums together with posters depicting detainees behind bars. When

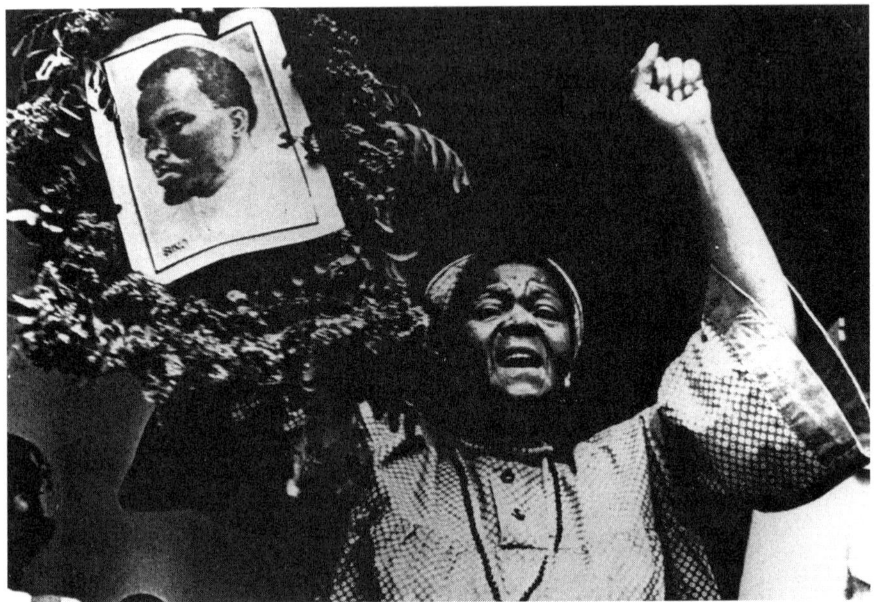

FIGURE 2.5. Peter Magubane, *Winnie Kgware with Wreath,* 1977. Mayibuye Centre, University of Western Cape. Courtesy of Peter Magubane.

the inquest into Biko's death began on November 14, former BPC President Winnie Kgware encircled the Kenyon portrait with a wreath and carried it high through the packed Pretoria courtroom while singing "Senzeni Na" (What have we done?).[32] Those in attendance raised their fists and shouted "Amandla!" (Power!) in response. During the court's recess, she stood on the building's steps, held the wreathed portrait aloft, and led more than a hundred people in a lengthy rendition of the song once more (Figure 2.5). As a witness remembered, they also sang praise songs to Biko and the family's inquest counsel, but "more often . . . spat out . . . contempt and threats to Vorster, Kruger, or one or another of the team of interrogators in the witness box."[33] Soon after, a man took the image from Kgware and ripped it up, presumably to safeguard her from penalty for having displayed a banned image.

These varied portrait types popularized a picture of Biko that was at once idealized and common, a visual history familiar to socialist refrains, which, as David Kunzle reminds, have long blended "the tradition of hero imagery [with] the idea of the individual as representative of, rather than transcending, the mass."[34] Millions of people worldwide regularly identified themselves as being at one with Biko after his death; many have continued to do so ever since. The South African sampling selected for study here is substantive but not complete. Through word and image, the core of visual culture, Biko in death stood for the ongoing life of Black Consciousness. Consider these sentiments shared at a commemorative service for Biko in Soweto's historic Regina Mundi Church. A SASO representative said, "Steve Biko is not dead but reincarnated in the entire black community. He made his voice known against all the atrocities which are perpetuated against the black community."[35] And continuing, the representative said, "Biko was the living soul of black awareness. He was our manhood and he headed our revival. . . . But Biko was something more. He was a monument of man's decency. He upheld the greatest principle—that all people, irrespective of race or colour, were created by God."[36] Today, Biko remains for many the living embodiment of individual will and honor, a martyr for causes that are humanist. As I take you into the decades following Biko's death, you must recall that humanism is at the core of Black Consciousness.

DRUM, a widely popular monthly publication from South Africa with distribution across Anglophone Africa, did something unusual in November 1977: it published a tributary portrait on its cover, timed to correspond with the inquest proceedings (Plate 2); its maker remains unidentified. Like Donald Kenyon, this artist also based his portrait on one of the photos from the *Daily Dispatch* photo essay (far right, top photograph in Figure 2.3), but crucially he dressed Biko in workers' garb, assuring his relevance to the majority. His intellectual might, ancestral pride, and dignity belonged to the majority; Biko wears a thick flannel shirt he favored. The image thus promotes the spirit of BC: the belief that self-worth and self-actualization are vital facets of being that must be internally accepted and outwardly insisted on. The text of the cover story advances this argument. Poet Adam Small identified Biko's "indestructible pride" as a catalyst for nurturing the self-confidence of *DRUM*'s audience. Small summarized BC in a repeated phrase:

> The point is that being original people, we do not like being told. . . . We are the original people, I said, and we do not like being told. Not even by the very worldly-wise. We do not like being told. Was this not at the heart of Steve Biko's thinking, that we shall be we, that we shall not be told?[37]

Small's accompanying text is a veritable drum beat against the liberal response to Biko's death, which he condemns and characterizes as a kind of fanatical, self-glorifying exercise. Thus in this we have a second strand of evidence in the visual culture of the period that advanced the span of how Biko would be remembered and by whom.

DRUM promotes Biko's legacy as the father of Black Consciousness. The photo essay begins with two sepia-toned images: one of a female mourner standing resolute above his open casket during the prefuneral viewing, and another of a woman whose hand shields her grief-stricken face.[38] Their captions urge us to contemplate the meaning of Biko's death for South Africa. The next four pages are largely covered in captioned black-and-white photographs of the funeral procession interspersed with portraits of Biko that emphasize his humanity. They also vilify the South African state by the inclusion of an autopsy portrait photograph and the repeated image of Biko's second child, Samora, in tears at his father's funeral. Here the infant substitutes for women who characteristically give grief a public face at funerals. Following Veena Das, as "witness [to death, they] convert silence into speech."[39] But women who survive political martyrs must fulfill another function—nobility, heroism, sacrifice. In the words of Mamphela Ramphele, they "represent the highest ideals of public service, [which] are not easily associated with a woman's body."[40] Thus at political funerals, the traditional role of grieving women is necessarily cast through the child.

DRUM includes a photograph of four mourners grasping the sides of a single poster that was designed by Dikobé Ben Martins and is now well known (Figure 2.6). This portrait photograph and emblematic attribute became the definitive image of the period as dozens of newspapers illustrated their coverage of the funeral with photographs of the poster held aloft.[41] The photograph in Figure 2.1 gained its hypericonic status in this context of death, but Martins altered the image in fundamental ways. He took away Biko's suit and tie and he drew the BPC symbol beneath Biko's montaged head; two raised fists break a chain that bound the arms cuff to cuff. As Richard Brilliant might have it, this icon of the Black Peoples' Convention came to represent Biko himself, thus expanding his funeral portrait so that it carries all the traits associated with the active emblem: strength in unity, confirmed self-worth, and unwavering determination, to name but a few.[42]

Like the T-shirt that Dikobé Martins designed for Biko's funeral, his poster appears to be the first in a modern, print-based tradition of funeral portraits that steadily grew throughout the 1980s and subsequently became well known.[43] Its currency is magnified in a drawing Martins made one year later: its dimensions

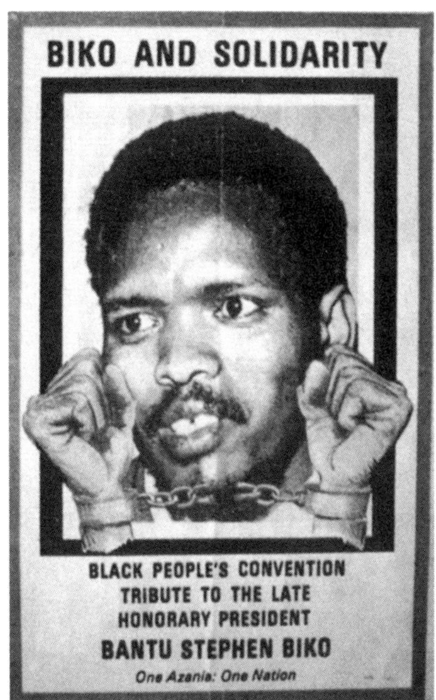

FIGURE 2.6. Dikobé Martins, *Biko and Solidarity*, 1977. South African History Archive, University of the Witwatersrand.

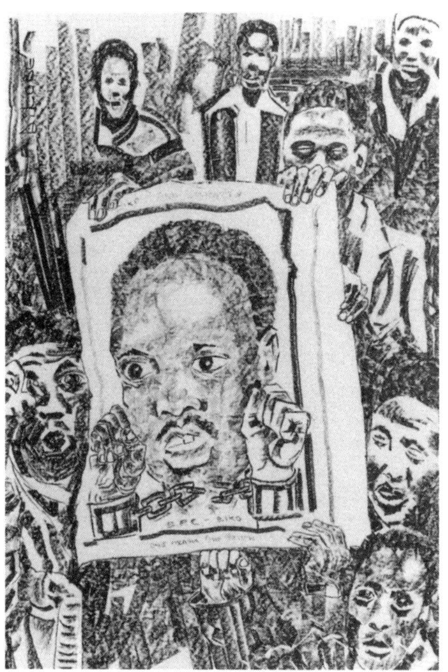

FIGURE 2.7. Dikobé Martins, *Biko and Solidarity—One Nation*, 1978. Campbell Collection, University of Natal.

in *Biko and Solidarity—One Nation* amplify its hypericonic status (Figure 2.7). The artist's decision to strip Biko of the suit and tie certainly drives our reading of him as an idealized Everyman. Martins ultimately made this explicit when he modified this 1978 drawing for the cover of the 1991 book *Bounds of Possibility: The Legacy of Steve Biko and Black Consciousness* (see Figure 6.1). By then he replaced the hypericonic death mask with Fraser MacLean's photograph of Biko in a laborer's heavy workshirt to suggest that Biko remains most significant to South Africa's majority. As I show in chapter 6, it also anticipates the later favoritism given to MacLean's portrait of Biko once the Truth and Reconciliation Commission heard testimony on his case in 1997 (see Figures 6.3 and 6.4). Both in 1978 and 1991, Martins forcefully reclaims Biko's legacy from that emphasized by liberal activists who positioned him first as international statesman and later as martyr for a "rainbow nation."

The Funeral: A Chariot-Born Portrait, an Engine of War

Twenty thousand people gathered in the small and relatively isolated place of King William's Town on September 25, 1977, to collectively mourn and witness the burial of Steve Biko. Thousands more would have attended had policemen not systematically prevented their transport from arriving in King William's Town. And still many more thousands paid tribute in different locations across South Africa and overseas. Foreign diplomats arrived on site from at least thirteen nations, and others sent wreaths and printed condolences.[44] Pope John XXIII sent a statement on human dignity that was read at Victoria Grounds where a four-hour Anglican requiem mass was held. Speeches and prayers were offered, poems and hymns were sung, as was "Nkosi Sikelel' iAfrika," the national anthem promoted by several resistance organizations that was officially adopted as such nearly seventeen years later. Representatives from many groups commemorated Biko that day, and the Anglican clergy counted five in number, headed by then- Bishop Desmond Tutu.[45] This enormous gathering was peaceful, despite the state's projection that it would be otherwise.

The tributes paid and biblical passages selected for the funeral emphasized justice, righteousness, selflessness, generosity, and strength in union. The BPC produced the funeral program, which lists Psalm 23, Matthew 25 (the Judgment of Nations), Isaiah 58 (True Fasting), and Revelation 21 (Apocalypse) as readings. These scriptures spoke directly to Biko's last days insofar as they envisage prisons and pain. Matthew reminds us that God will divide those before him, "all nations" gathered before his throne. The righteous will have cared for those in need and in so doing have cared for the Lord. But to people who do not tend to those among us who are "ahungered, or athirst, or a stranger, or naked, or sick or in prison," God has this to say: "Verily I say unto you, inasmuch as ye did it not to one of the least of these, ye did it not for me." Thus they will suffer "everlasting punishment" while the righteous come into "life eternal" (Matthew 25:44–46).[46] False fasting is the essence of Isaiah. Through Isaiah, men of the cloth critiqued Kruger's claim that Biko had refused food and water. The sons of Jacob make a great show of appearing righteous, but God sees their deceit and asks them:

> Is not this the fast that *I have chosen*? To *loose the bands of wickedness,* to undo the heavy burdens, and to let the oppressed go free, and that *ye break every yoke*? . . . and if thou draw thy soul to the hungry, and satisfy the afflicted soul; then shall thy light rise in obscurity, and thy darkness be as the noonday; and

the LORD shall guide thee continually, and satisfy thy soul in drought, and make fat thy bones: and thou shalt be like a watered garden, and like a spring of water, whose waters fail not. (Isaiah 58:6, 10–11)[47]

The heads of several local and national political organizations spoke.[48] Though Hlaku Kenneth Rachidi's address evoked some biblical referents (he called Biko a "prophet of Black Solidarity" and assured those who joined BPC's ranks that they would "see the light"), he carefully called attention to the many BPC adherents who suffered death, imprisonment, and banishment prior to Biko's death. He upheld BPC's standard of nonviolence, but he acknowledged that "we are convinced that there is no struggle without casualties. We further maintain that nobody on this earth, [is] going to dictate to us except one with selfless and human ethics, as what to say and do and who our true leaders are."[49] Biko as unifier was the dominant theme of Rachidi's speech: "Steve was meant for the nation—he died to unite the Black people in this country." Rachidi spent great energy encouraging supporters of the newly created "Homelands" to see the "stink of naked racism [behind this] Bantustan game." Equally so, he objected to the "empty gaudy colors of a rainbow or mirages in the so-called TRIPETITE government" (the White, Indian, and Coloured political groups, also and more commonly called Tripartite) and encouraged leaders within it to come over to Black Consciousness. There is strength in numbers, and black solidarity was the primary aim. "Many a man," Rachidi assured, "has lost his life along this path [toward emancipation]—many more may be destined to follow—Steve the physical giant is dead but Steve the idea lives and burns brighter than ever."

Following the mass, a procession ferried Biko's coffin, itself an ornate object with carved effigies and gold leaf lettering on multiple sides, from the crowded arena at Victoria Gardens to the cemetery in Ginsberg. Pallbearers were BPC members who wore the uniform, gold dashikis edged in black, that Biko also wore that day. A large BPC banner of red and black with SASO's hands-breaking-chains motif stitched into it was held high above the coffin (Figure 2.8). This motif was rendered also in low relief on wood and affixed to the top of Biko's coffin, as was his portrait likeness (Figure 2.9). Interspersed among these raised images and rendered in gold leaf was the motto "One Azania, One Nation" and the acronym "B.P.C." More imagery and lettering appeared on the sides of the coffin: a raised and clenched fist, the African continent, and the words that title this chapter, "Steve Biko, God be with you, BPC."

Outside of the arena, Biko's coffin sat on a cart that was pulled by oxen for long

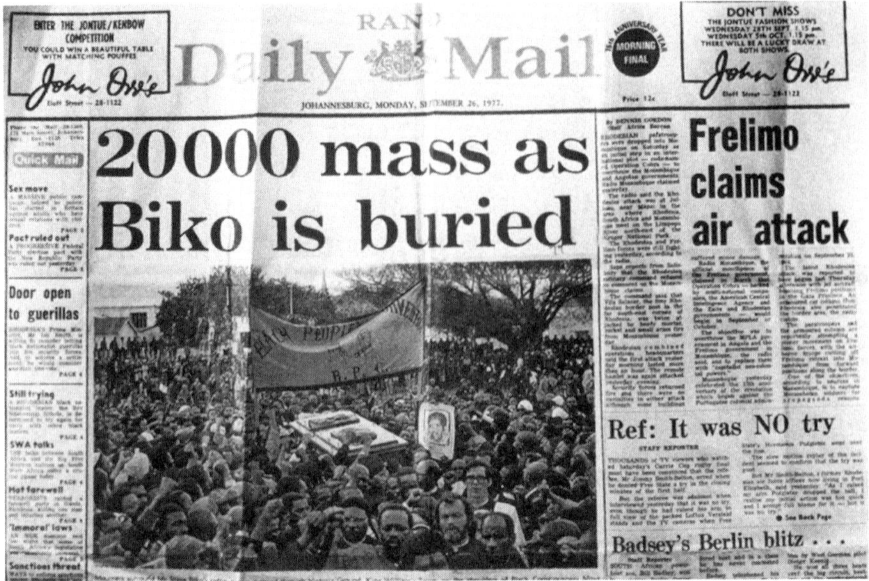

FIGURE 2.8. "20000 Mass as Biko Is Buried." Cover of *Rand Daily Mail,* September 26, 1977.

stretches over open terrain. The liberal press likened this element to the "traditional olden day" of Bantu custom, but this funerary rite has also taken place for centuries outside of Africa. In his famed study of death's social conventions, Philippe Ariés writes that ox-drawn chariots carrying waxen or wooden representations of royalty were customary over many centuries in parts of Europe. By the early sixteenth century, smaller carts were used within Flemish cemeteries. In joining the two—ox-drawn chariot and common cart—used to pull the remains of less distinguished persons as they were moved about, he writes, "But whatever its appearance, the chariot of Death is an engine of war."[50] I understand its presence at Biko's funeral as such, a reading enhanced by the language used this day to ascribe meaning to his life. Make no mistake, despite BC's peaceful nature, an engine of war was building. It drew energy from Biko's coffin and the portrait affixed to it. Surely the agency evidenced there, the hands-breaking-chains motif that hereafter reads as his portrait likeness, counters the atrocities he suffered that were both imagined in visual culture and experienced privately.

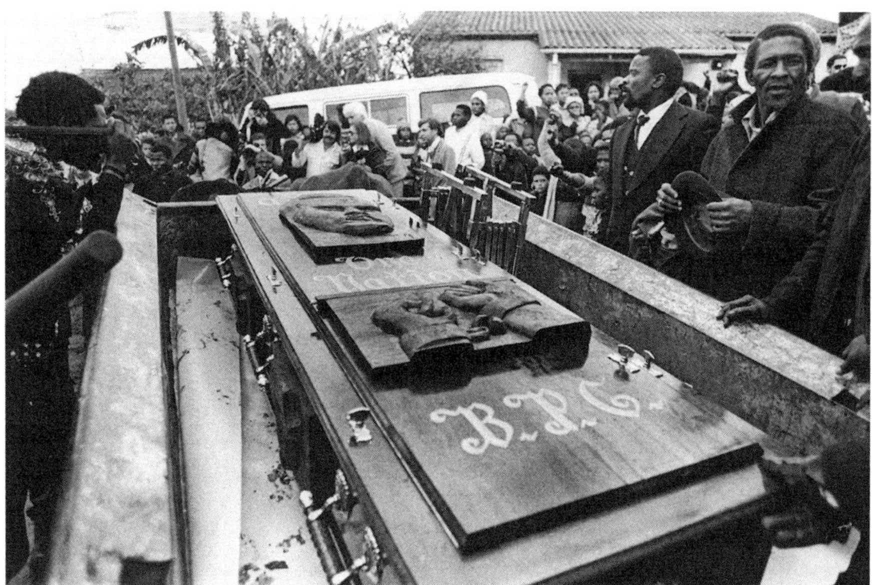

FIGURE 2.9. Mourners gather beside Biko's coffin before burial at a cemetery in Ginsberg, September 20, 1977. Copyright Bailey's African History Archives. Photograph by BAHA Drum Photographer.

Thus the engine of war was sharply visualized through Biko's coffin as it was moved from home to arena to burial place by oxen-drawn cart.

Although the image of Biko in his coffin is among the most difficult and disturbing of that period (Figure 2.10), it vividly reclaims and thus heals the body previously captured first in September as state autopsy archive and again, one month later, when that file was released to the press.[51] In mid-October, photographs of Biko's battered corpse circulated internationally. That which imaged him at rest, among family, dressed in the gown of the Black Peoples' Convention, counters those of the state in no uncertain terms. Only two photographs of mourners in the Biko's Ginsberg home have appeared in print, and they were taken from the same angle, moments apart. In *DRUM* we see that Biko was buried in the gold-and-black-trimmed dashiki also worn by BPC casket bearers. The left side of his forehead, the site of the wound that proved fatal, was covered with a velvet cloth. His body, postautopsy, was not restored as a mortician would favor in order to affect the so-called "last sleep"; rather,

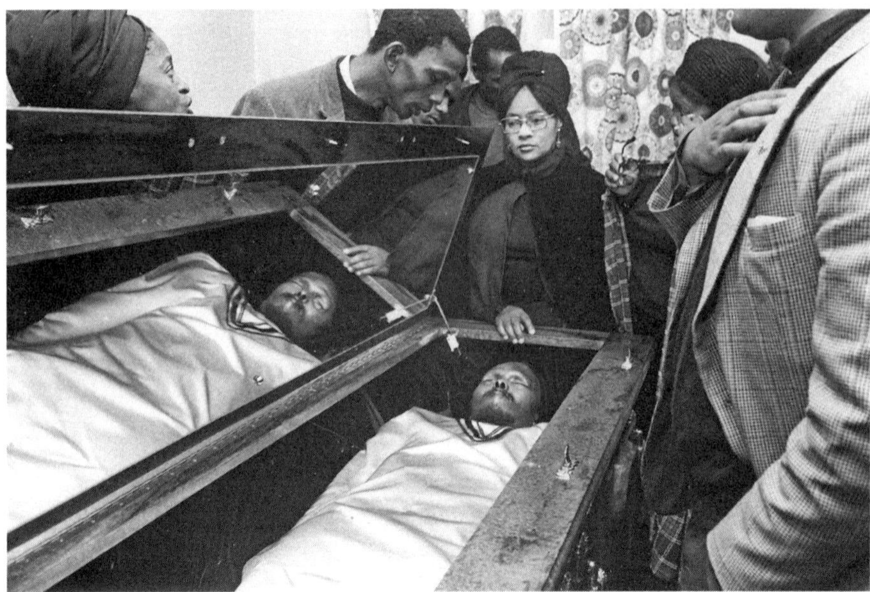

FIGURE 2.10. Viewing of Biko's body at his family's home in Ginsberg, September 20, 1977. Copyright Bailey's African History Archives. Photograph by BAHA Drum Photographer.

the physical abuse he suffered in his last month of life was expressly revealed. The presence of a mirror affixed to the inside of his coffin magnifies this abuse. While it certainly intensified the reading of state violence upon Biko, photographs of this mirrored moment sharpened the self-reflection of viewers who saw it in the press. Like the well-known Mirrors of Mortality rendered by artists over centuries, the mirror here aimed "to shape the inner condition of the living."[52] Printed images of this type were intended to comment on and shape public conduct and morality. They circulated widely and aimed to instruct the spiritual community, both in life and death.[53] Thus the photographs that image Biko in his coffin aim to instruct. They are akin to the photographs taken at the funeral of young Emmett Till, an American lynched by racists in 1955. In both cases, the presentation of the deceased before burial transmitted, as Julia Kristeva would put it, "the disorder, dysfunction and danger" of their respective nations.[54]

A reciprocal relationship exists between the image of death mirrored in Biko's coffin and the image of life that was carved and placed on top of it. The lasting effigy projected to the twenty thousand who attended his funeral was not of his death but of his living likeness. Indeed, in low relief he actively breaks the chains that bind him. Phillipe Ariés reports that the historical function of such effigies has been "to convey a complete sense of the person's role," their place in "the order of the world."[55] In death, Biko continued to live. Often and in many ways during September 1977, it was said that Steve Biko had become something other than human; he became an idea, a saint, a prophet. In this capacity he became incarnate through others. Perhaps most succinctly, at the Regina Mundi commemoration on September 18, Nthatho Motlana said, "Biko has not died in vain. There are hundreds of Bikos around."[56] The effigy that was buried with him captures the essence of the man—determined, active, proud. This is the lasting image of Steve Biko at rest.[57]

The Inquest: "Mr. Steve Biko Is a Picture of the Violent Police State That Is South Africa"

Upon learning of Biko's death, the Black Peoples' Convention issued a press release that imaged Biko as described above.[58] This vision was widely accepted among blacks and leftward-leaning whites long before photographs of Biko's autopsy became available to the press. When these images and other photographs were used as evidence at the November inquest, newspapers and journals throughout the world printed them.

Autopsy images—by-products of "the coroner's court"—record reasons behind a person's end, but they become the starting point for inquiry, "the narrative reconstruction of life."[59] For their original purpose, autopsy photographs are by-products of state discipline.[60] In them, the body is made object; it is forced to yield to the viewers' scrutiny, much as it did to the coroner's knife. Alienation is part of the aesthetic, even a "precondition of meaning."[61] Despite this, autopsy photographs call for personal investiture by their evocation of mystery; we strive to understand the history that led to their making. Thus the meaning of the object imaged is inevitably contested, and in cases like Biko's the arguments extend beyond the physical body and into the social sphere as order and disorder are questioned. The interpretative framework of the autopsy creates two bodies—the medico-legal body and the social body—both of which "define the corpse as a source of knowledge."[62] The social readings of Biko's corpse are of central concern here.

In the state's archive, the image of Biko's corpse represented his utter vulnerability before the law. Symbolically, he was permanently detained.[63] This reading was reversed in popular reproductions of the autopsy photographs where Biko's corpse became a symbol of strength because he was seen to have paid the ultimate sacrifice for a higher purpose. His family readily conveyed this strength in a photograph taken days after his death that has been reproduced often (Figure 2.11). Juxtaposed against his autopsy image, Biko's widow, Nontsikelelo Biko, and sons Samora (left) and Nkosinathi (right) raise their arms to enact the symbol that conveyed the life and pride of their loved one.[64] Autopsy photographs were reproduced in newspapers around the world. *DRUM* included one, too, with text that urged viewers to uphold the principles for which Biko died. It also expresses profound anger over his death.[65] *DRUM* captioned each image as a "Moment" of one sort or another and called the autopsy photograph a "Moment of Reality."[66] In his text, Adam Small claimed Biko for the present: "This is Steve Biko's measure of greatness, realistically, soberly: that he was one of the initiators *in this place and at this time,* of the black man's walking tall upon the streets of South Africa—walking tall, never to be bent again."[67]

Because sudden death is "out of time and out of place," those who grieve experience personal rupture to "their own sense of self."[68] Their narratives about the deceased fulfill a personal need to reconstruct their own identities and establish a meaningful path for the future. The tributes to Biko printed in *DRUM* and *Newsweek* both included images from his autopsy beside living likenesses. The pairing here in these examples illustrates changes that might seem absolute (the living body is now dead) but, rather, suggest that Biko's legacy can live on in readers, that they must live the principles of Black Consciousness for which he died. In this context, Biko is no longer the object of interrogation but retains his personhood as subject, the model around which readers can reconstruct their sense of personal dignity and collective destiny. They continue to gain agency despite this loss; indeed, representation assures it.

At the inquest, the representation of Steve Biko in his last days was contested. An inquest differs from a trial in several ways: there is no one accused, no defendant per se; there is no jury of peers to decide the outcome since a magistrate fills this need. The aim of an inquest is to determine whether a culpable party exists either through act or omission, whereafter a trial may ensue. In South Africa's legal system at that time, only representatives of the state were allowed to question witnesses in a trial. An inquest, however, enabled a privately employed advocate to cross-examine those under oath on the stand.[69] The Biko

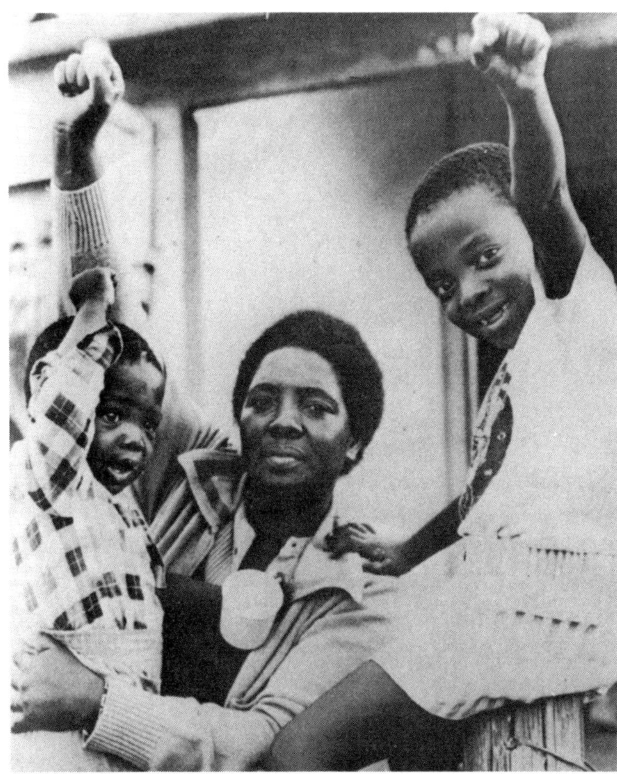

FIGURE 2.11. Biko's widow, Nontsikelelo, and their sons Samora (left) and Nkosinathi (right) outside their home in the days following his death. Hulton Archive/Getty Images.

family favored an inquest since it allowed their lawyers to pose questions that might reveal information otherwise kept secret. The state's inquest into the death of Steve Biko began on November 14, 1977, at the Old Synagogue in Pretoria.[70] Chief Magistrate of Pretoria Marthinus J. Prins presided. The well-known advocate Sydney Kentridge led a team on behalf of the Biko family; Retief van Rooyen was lead counsel for the state; B. De V. Pickard headed up the doctors' counsel.[71]

In the inquest's first week, ten police officers testified and were cross-examined before an audience of "mostly black and young" South Africans. What they heard from the witness stand (and what an international press recorded) "has been humiliating and downright degrading to the image" of Biko.[72] The more significant testimony came from Colonel Pieter Johannes Goosen, Divisional Commander of the Eastern Province Security Police, who oversaw Biko's treatment after September 7; Major Harold Snyman, who led the interrogation of

Biko on September 6 and 7; and Captain Daantjie P. Siebert, a member of the interrogation squad.[73] In their language, all three men revealed their racism by repeatedly using phrases that described Biko as wild or nonhuman. Upon interrogation, Snyman claimed that Biko "went beserk [and threw] wild swinging punches. . . . he charged Warrant Officer J. Beneke, [and] lashed out wildly at him."[74] Snyman maintained that Biko's physical power was so strong that it took five large men to constrain and shackle him once more. Siebert described Biko as "possessed . . . [and] beside himself with fury."[75] Before Biko's head injury, Goosen compared him to "a wild animal [with a] wild expression in his eyes."[76] News sources also evoked bestial imagery but applied it to Biko's keepers, who kept him "like an animal on a pallet on the floor, chained to a grille with handcuffs and leg irons." When these objects were shown in court, the audience "gasped at the monstrousness of them."[77] Kentridge asked Goosen if he would keep a dog chained as long as Biko had been:

> SYDNEY KENTRIDGE: What right did you have to keep a man in chains for 48 hours?
>
> PIETER JOHANNES GOOSEN: I have the full power to do it. Prisoners could attempt suicide or escape.
>
> KENTRIDGE: Let's have an honest answer—where did you get your powers?
>
> GOOSEN: It is my power.
>
> KENRIDGE: Are you people above the law?
>
> GOOSEN: I have full powers to ensure a man's safety.
>
> KENTRIDGE: I am asking for the statute.
>
> GOOSEN: We don't work under statutes.
>
> KENTRIDGE: Thank you very much. That is what we have always suspected.[78]

Biko's preinjury response—this so-called "wild" behavior—was allegedly prompted by sworn statements his colleagues had made that identified him as coauthor, with Peter Jones and Patrick Titi, of the inflammatory pamphlet described at the start of this chapter. Snyman claimed he was "attacked" by Biko, who is said to have responded to his colleagues' purported betrayal by throwing a heavy metal chair. The interrogating team reported that a scuffle ensued thereafter, with much thrashing about onto the floor, over desks, into file cabinets, and so forth. Their collective story was that Biko's head hit a wall in the scuffle. Snyman, the only one who claimed to have seen this event, dramatically demonstrated a frontal fall for the court, then recanted his version of events after a short break saying that Biko hit the back of his head instead. All officers maintained this line, but no one else would say that they witnessed Biko's head hitting the wall. None would admit seeing Biko unconscious after this moment, a fact that three leading pathologists said was an absolute aftereffect of the injury that he had sustained. (Van Rooyen, counsel for the police, later cast such medical knowledge as "dogmatic.")[79] The duration of unconsciousness would have been between twenty minutes and one hour, surely observable.[80] Professor I. Simson, a top pathologist employed by the University of Pretoria, later testified that a patient with Biko's injury would manifest all of the signs that Biko did and might "become violent, occasionally lapse into a stupor, suffer from incontinence of urine and phases of delirium. He would try to put on his clothes and run out of the room." Over the succeeding days, Biko evidenced all of these symptoms. "This is the picture of Biko," Kentridge said. And he continued,

> If one accepted the description of Mr. Biko's scuffle with police on September 7, during which he allegedly went berserk, then on the basis of medical authority it appeared probable that his violence was a symptom of a head injury which he had already received.[81]

At best, the police appeared to have skewed the calendar to make Biko responsible for his own death. Their approach, Kentridge said, indicated a "conspiracy of silence."[82]

The statements that were said to spark this scuffle were presented as evidence *but not admitted* as such after Kentridge noted that they were signed and dated September 13 and 30. As Biko was interrogated September 6 and 7, and died on September 12, he could not have seen them.[83] Interestingly, twenty years later the Truth and Reconciliation Commission revealed that the police became incensed when Biko refused their order to stand up from the chair on which he sat. This "impertinence . . . drove Capt. Siebert to unbridled action against a black man who did not know his place."[84] The significance of the chair also arose in Peter Jones's recount of his interrogation on August 24–25, 1977, by the very same team that confronted Biko. In addition to Snyman, Siebert, and Beneke, both Jones and Biko were interrogated by Warrant Officer Ruben Marx and Detective Sergeant Gideon Nieuwoudt. Jones was also questioned about the pamphlet; he endured torture in between questions about it and about why he and Biko traveled to Cape Town. His interrogation took place at the Sanlam Building in downtown Port Elizabeth; Biko's did, too, in room 619. After being held in solitary confinement for seventeen months without charge, Jones recorded memories of his interrogation in August 1977. One can assume that the techniques used on Jones were also used on Biko. He must be quoted here at length:

> The first [interrogation] session lasted for more than twenty hours. . . . We drove at high speed to Sanlam Building. . . . immediately I entered the room I was held by several police while one of my hands . . . [was] freed and my clothes were taken off. I was made to sit naked on a chair with my left hand chained with the handcuff to the chair. Snyman and Siebert occupied chairs at desks respectively to the left and right of me.
>
> On the desk in front of Siebert was a length of green hosepipe. I was able to look right into the hole of the pipe and noticed that the hole was filled—with what, I cannot say, but it was something metallic. . . . [After some resistance, Jones was forced to stand on two small pieces of brick.] Two chairs [heavy steel ones] were placed one on top of the other [the one upside down], and both Beneke and Nieuwoudt had to lift these until I could hold them high above my head. Siebert told me that should the chairs lower or fall I would "get it." I told him it was impossible to hold. I was already experiencing cramps in my legs. . . . Snyman started calling me names and calling me a liar. He got up from his chair and kicked me on the left leg. I stumbled and the chairs came tumbling down, one hitting him on the head and the other landing on Siebert's desk. . . . I was taken from the bricks, on which I had by now spent several hours, and both hands were handcuffed. Siebert got up and asked me when I was going to stop lying, and started to deliver heavy blows with both hands to my face. I grabbed both his hands and pulled him down towards me. I told him that the treatment was unnecessary as I was answering their questions. Siebert, who is smaller than me, told me to let go of him, and did I want to fight? Two fist blows followed delivered by Nieuwoudt and Beneke. . . . These two grabbed my arms and held them firmly.
>
> Siebert removed his watch and rolled up his sleeves. For a very long time he slapped my face with both hands continuously and without pause. I remained silent, felt my senses dimming gradually to the stage where I could with a detachedness just feel the blows going through my head while I looked straight into Siebert's eyes. . . .
>
> Just behind Siebert was a mirror hanging on the wall and I could see my face in it. As the blows continued I would from time to time look into the mirror, amazed that my face could assume such dimensions. Another "lip" was forming, blood from my mouth and nose, mixed with spittle, dribbled down

my face onto my chest. . . . Marx and Snyman now stood to the left and right of Siebert, facing me, and Nieuwoudt started delivering fast and heavy blows to my head with the hosepipe, which was excruciating in the kind of shocks it sent through my body.

Then Beneke started hitting me with his fist in my stomach and I started to stumble. Marx got a boot to my right leg as a warning to stand still. Beneke left and from a drawer of a filing cabinet took another hosepipe, black this time. Marx shouted: "Give him both—black power and green power!" Beneke took up his position again, on my left, and from then on he and Nieuwoudt hit me mainly on the head with hosepipes while Siebert carried on smacking my face. Snyman and Marx delivered kicks to my shins whenever I moved out of the way.

Every time I tried to defend my head with my hands the pipes would move to the back, the kidney area, or attack the hands. I found it impossible to cope with all the immense pain and I turned and faced the wall and, closing my eyes, hoping for oblivion, which never came, as blows rained down on my head and back.

After some time this assault stopped, with everybody panting for breath. I was just able to swallow the groans wanting to escape my mouth. When spoken to I couldn't reply. My mouth was very cut and swollen and I would just nod a reply.[85]

Among the evidence displayed at the Biko inquest were other photographs made by policemen: autopsy photos and another kind, ostensibly forensic, but not technically since they were taken weeks after Biko died and include actors oddly reenacting positions in which Biko was found by police officers in the days between September 7 and 11 (Figures 2.12–2.14). The photographs also recorded spaces that Biko had occupied: room 619 of the Sanlam Building where he was interrogated and received the injuries that proved fatal; a cell at Walmer Police Station where he was kept before and after the interrogation; a cell in the Port Elizabeth jail where he was held pending a medical examination; and the back of the Land Rover in which he rode 1,100 kilometers (about 685 miles) from Port Elizabeth to Pretoria in the last twenty-four hours of his life. The popular press printed these photographs and in doing so produced "evidence" of quite another kind.

Cameras have always been used to gather information and attest to facts. Although Alphonse Bertillon is now known as the father of the mug shot, police used photographs to identify suspects as early as 1839. Twenty years later, photographs were submitted as evidence in an American court of law. In 1888, Bertillon instituted standards for photographing "the scene of the crime."[86]

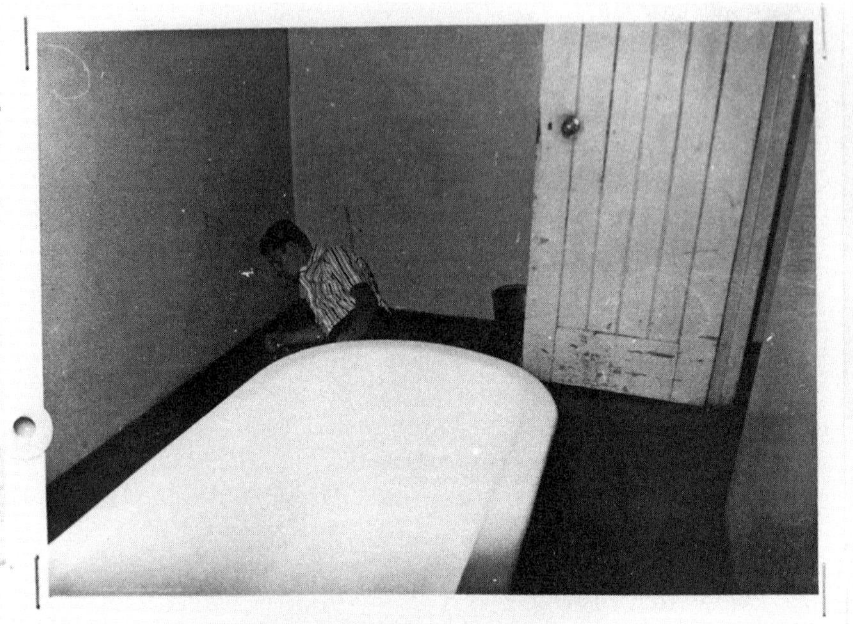

FIGURE 2.12. An actor in the role of Biko, slumped beside a tub, inquest evidence photograph 19, with original caption. Police photograph. Mayibuye Centre Archive, University of the Western Cape.

Institutional guides encourage police photographers to realize certain objectives: neutrality, straightforwardness, a complete perspective of record, a "legal quality" that retains "objectivity and accuracy," and a caution against dramatic effects.[87] As S. G. Ehrlich explains in his book about the use of photography in legal cases, "Any drama in the picture should emanate from the subject matter alone. . . . [but tellingly] this is not to say that photographers making photographs should dispense with the elements of imagination and artistry, but only that they should strive for accuracy rather than effect." In the printing process, police photographers should avoid an appearance of undo expense or slickness, "lest jurors come to believe that the preparation is being overdone." Once in the

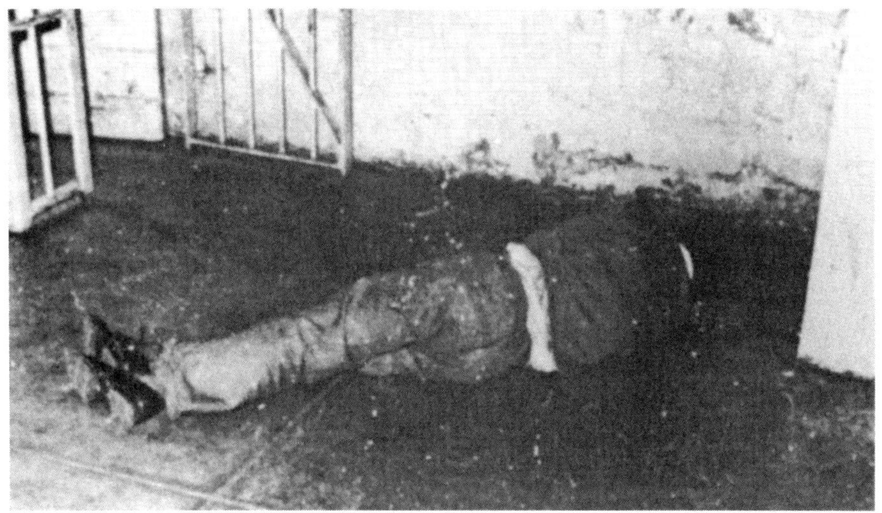

FIGURE 2.13. An actor playing Biko lying on the floor, inquest evidence photograph 14. Police photograph. Mayibuye Centre Archive, University of the Western Cape.

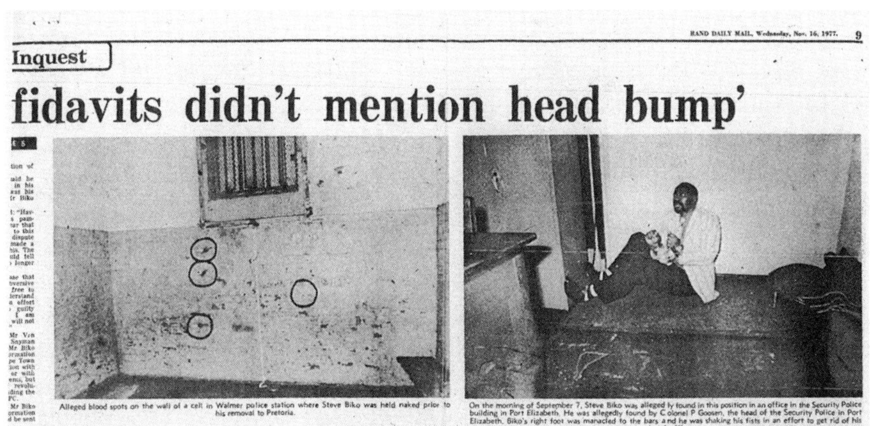

FIGURE 2.14. "Inquest: Affidavits didn't mention head bump." On November 16, 1977, the *Rand Daily Mail* printed two photographs submitted as evidence at the inquest, page 9.

courtroom, photographs should create within viewers a sense of having "observed the subject directly."

Although legal photographs assume an authority that other types may not, they are subject to the ambivalent semiotic cycles common to all imagery. The codes of forensic imaging and development of film allow for manipulations and distortions, interventions that ultimately create a "reality" for viewers, some of whom act as jurors and thus render judgment based on what they see and hear about the photographs admitted as evidence. But the history of that evidence—how it was made, by whom, of what, and for what purpose—is often unquestioned. John Tagg cautions that police photographs are "no less a construction than the montage, and no less artificial than the expressively 'transformed' experimental photograph."[88] Inherent to that construction is a power relation often ignored. He summarizes the problem at hand: "It is the product that is stressed, and production that is repressed."[89]

In the case of Steve Biko, police officers made the photographs in mid-October for presentation at the November inquest. Some of these images record actors assigned to reenact positions in which police officers found Biko in the last days of his life (there were five such photographs, two of which are reprinted here). The state had assigned General J. F. Kleinhaus to investigate matters, and the police who had interrogated Biko deemed which places and which postures were relevant.[90] These photographs astonish. This response arises in both contexts in which they appeared—at the inquest and circulated within the popular press—but to different effects.

The photographs were made in mid-October, just when the official autopsy report became available to the press after weeks of speculation about its conclusions. The police made these images, this narrative, to counter that of the pathologists, whose report typically "acquires a centrifugal status around which all other narratives revolve."[91] Mimicry and visual quotations of this kind are a form of what Richard Brilliant calls "living portraiture."[92] Thus by recreating the image of Biko alive and fearful (Figure 2.14) or disabled (Figures 2.12 and 2.13), the police photographs undercut portraits that were popularly disseminated—those that proclaim Biko's inherent pride and those of his body expired within the casket or interrogated anew on the autopsy table. Biko's daring and contempt for authority were well known; the collection of police-made photographs imagines him as vulnerable instead. The state's inquest visuals meant to diminish his stature and reduce police culpability in his death. Their captions indicate his humane treatment. He is "visited" repeatedly and found in the positions performed here. Captions to the photographs of cell spaces be-nignly cite the directional axis, call the circled blood spots on the wall "alleged," or draw attention to the comforts afforded to prisoners—bed, toilet, bathroom.

When printed in newspapers (e.g., Figure 2.14), these startling images inter-rupt the police narrative. The anonymity of the actors is readily sensed (as is, one hopes, the implausibility that these photographs could be useful as evi-dence), but their voice, or impact, is not unknown. Indeed, the familiarity of distress pictured here is understood and anchored by the captions. Readers who study the circled blood spots on the wall in Figure 2.14 are reminded that Biko was "naked" when held here. This descriptor was repeatedly used in this period, creating an image that is regrettably still evoked by journalists who report on annual commemorations held for Biko each September 12. The caption beneath the photograph at right describes what "Biko" is doing here, a gesture by now firmly associated with BC—"shaking his fists in an effort to get rid of his hand-cuffs." In this public context, the police-made photographs shift meaning. They heighten awareness of humanity, its lack in this context, and the resultant loss. When circulated in the press, these inquest photographs became what Jacques Rancière would call true art: images that educate readers about their own role in the communal body. In all of these ways they become emancipatory devices in that they "penetrate the police order . . . by implementing the universal pre-supposition of politics: we are all equal."[93]

In popular print, the inquest images become nothing less than a complete re-configuration of Rancière's distribution of the sensible. They disrupt the realm of experience that is determined by "the police," a trope Rancière uses to define an organizational system or law that divides into groups, functions, and social positions with or without access to what is visible, speakable, audible, and thus knowable. At the inquest, the images of actors performing the role of Biko were a kind of poetry in the Aristotelian sense. The photographs were what Rancière would call "fictions, that is to say, arrangements between actions" performed by the Port Elizabeth police.[94] Like poems, these dramatic reenactments-turned-inquest-documents blurred "the dividing line that separated the logic of facts from the logic of stories." They were "constructed necessities" of the police, made to recount, as poems do, "what could happen" rather than an empirical succession of events, or "what happened," the historical narrative that is cus-tomarily sought (if not realized) by forensic imagery.

The South African press overturned this version, this poetic performance as designed by the police. By printing these images and captioning them in ways that changed their function, the *Rand Daily Mail* (see Figure 2.14), *Die Transvaaler,* and other newspapers effectively engaged what Rancière calls "the aesthetic revolution(:) the honour acquired by the commonplace . . . the life of the anonymous."[95] Caption and photograph work together to evoke our shared humanity; attention is drawn to "blood spots" circled on the wall; we are encouraged to reenvision the absent Biko "naked" yet once more here, by the presence of actors, anonymous men at one with those readers who, as Rancière warns, "have no part in the perceptual coordinates of the [police-created] community."[96] Printed popularly, the "scene of the crime" becomes a "site of mourning."[97] Melancholy infuses the photographs. Unknowingly, the police created photographs akin to the Crucifixion pageant, thus the inquest reenactments and documented spaces became Stations of the Cross, captured moments in a prolonged death to come. Biko inquest photographs—autopsy and "forensic"—found a home in the visual culture of martyrdom ever after. Their currency weaves through the years, with examples shared in these pages (e.g., Figures 3.4–3.6, 5.2, and 6.8), but their role as Stations is readily realized in Willie Bester's *Homage to B.* of 1992 (Plate 14). In a path that spirals outward from its saintly subject, inquest moments narrated through word and image tell of Biko's suffering over the last weeks of his life.

Counsel for the Biko family wrote that the inquest images evidence little more than the state's "desire to conceal the true circumstances in which injuries were received . . . [because] amid the host of irrelevant photographs of places 'pointed out' to the police photographer, the one thing that was never pointed out was any place where Biko might have bumped his head in the struggle."[98] Snyman replied that Kleinhaus, who investigated the case, had not asked for this particular photograph to be taken.[99] Kentridge noted that it would not have been, given that neither police nor doctors even mentioned Biko bumping his head in any of the twenty-eight affidavits made following his death. (It had, however, been noted in the Occurrence Book on September 8, a record begun after Biko's health began to rapidly decline.) Amazingly, and despite an autopsy report that listed numerous fresh wounds to the skin, all imaged on film, at the inquest all police officers and doctors maintained that they did not see evidence of external injuries save for a cut and swollen lip. Lieutenant Winston Wilken was the only exception here. Stationed as Biko's guard over the night of September 6–7, Wilken said that while he sat "killing time" as Biko slept, he noticed a mark on the left side of Biko's forehead, which he took to be a birthmark.

Much has been made of the police's contention that Biko was "shamming" his injuries. They said his four years of medical training and ability with yoga (which his family said he did not practice) enabled him to feign illness. "Yoga people can turn themselves off from the world," Siebert said.[100] The police repeatedly told state medical professionals that they suspected Biko of falsifying bodily functions that were in fact by-products of a severely injured person. After the morning of September 7, he was found variously frothing at the mouth, ashen gray, mumbling incoherently, soaked in urine, sweating profusely, and breathing in a highly irregular manner. On the day before his death, Biko was found fully clothed but soaking wet, slumped beside a large porcelain bathtub (reenacted in Figure 2.12). Rather than regarding this as evidence of his increasing disorientation, Goosen absurdly claimed that he thought Biko had tried to drown himself and passed out as a result. He also theorized that Biko likely bumped his head on the bathtub.[101] He believed that "the deceased was clearly set upon self-destruction, even with his method of breathing."[102] Goosen went on to describe hyperventilation as a dangerous technique willfully practiced by deep-sea divers, of all things, despite "medical books [that] indicate . . . [it] can even give rise to death."[103] The implication: Biko was to blame for his death. Despite all evidence to the contrary, including a lumbar puncture performed September 9 that revealed red blood cells in Biko's cerebrospinal fluid, the police and attending district surgeons conspired to create a false medical certificate that identified their prisoner as wholly well. Kentridge insisted that the document was made to safeguard any future claim that Biko might make about the assaults he had suffered: "If Biko had lived and later claimed his lip had been injured, this certificate would have been produced to denounce Biko as a liar."[104]

As Colin Richards has said, somehow Biko could not existentially *be* himself.[105] In response to a question that exposed the inhumanity of withholding information from Biko's family as their beloved declined toward death, Goosen said, "The circumstances were quite special. We were trying to prove that Biko was somebody quite different from what he had seemed to be. Had we known he was ill the family would have been told."[106] Yet to his captors Biko could not verify his suffering; his physical symptoms could not embody truth. His incoherent speech and lapses in consciousness were cast off as "stubborn" evidence of his willful disregard of authority. He could not be human to these men. The police, organizers of Rancière's distribution of the sensible, knew that Biko possessed commonalities, but his differences—those "delimitations" that prompted the police to view him as a wild animal prone to shamming—were their chief concern.

The physicians who attended Steve Biko in his last days were profoundly negligible, thus they are as culpable as the police in his death. Benjamin Tucker was the first district surgeon to examine Biko, and he did so at the request of Goosen on September 7. At the inquest, Ivor Lang, the chief district surgeon, attempted to distance himself and other medical professionals from the security police by suggesting that Goosen, who pushed the notion that Biko was falsifying his illness, had misled him. "We had to assume they were right," he said.[107] But this merely testifies to Tucker's personal failures—his lack of fortitude and lapsed ethics—since the tests he administered to Biko evidenced that Biko was in dire straits. Most notably, a scratch to the sole of Biko's left foot (an extensor plantar reflex test) resulted in an upward-turned toe rather than a downward curl. Biko's response was abnormal, and Tucker admitted it was "virtually impossible to sham this symptom."[108] Biko also showed echolalia, a condition that prompts a person to repeat words again and again. Although Tucker issued a certificate on September 7 that said he found "no evidence of abnormality or pathology on the detainee," he admitted at the inquest that, prior to issuing this certificate he had seen the above abnormalities and Biko's swollen lip, bruised chest, swollen hands, feet and ankles, and he had witnessed Biko stagger while walking and slur his speech.

Lang was called in to examine Biko the next day. Tucker and Lang agreed that a lumbar puncture should be taken, so Colin Hersch performed the test on September 9. Test results were submitted under a false name, Steven Njelo, thus hiding the fact that Biko was detained and had been injured.[109] Red blood cells were found in Biko's spinal fluid, an abnormality that Hersch otherwise reported as "no pathology except with regard to reflex and apparent loss of sensation of lower limbs."[110] At the inquest, Hersch said his report was not false so much as incorrect: "There was an omission of one word. It should have read gross pathology . . . . there was no indication of gross pathology."[111] Hereafter Lang advised Goosen of "this non-perturbing picture" and said that Biko need not be moved to a hospital.[112] Notably, Biko went without any medical observation for at least a full day thereafter. Although doctors in 1977 were trained to run hourly checks on patients with head injuries, the Port Elizabeth district surgeons opted to examine Biko just twice each day. Not even his temperature and pulse were taken.

Pathologists, neuropathologists, and neurosurgeons testified in the last ten days of November 1977. Models, charts, and autopsy photographs were displayed during this period. Johan Loubser, chief state pathologist, had conducted the

September 12 autopsy on Biko's body. Present on behalf of the Biko family was Dr. Jonathan Gluckman, although he was notified late and rushed to Pretoria, arriving while the autopsy was already in progress. He felt he had missed nothing of importance, but the Inquest Act of 1959 had been violated.[113] Both pathologists took samples, and tests were run over the next four weeks. Both doctors agreed that Steve Biko's brain showed five distinct lesions and that which proved fatal was likely on the right partial frontal temporal lobe, where an injury of 8 x 4 cm was found. They concurred (and specialists agreed) that a contrecoup blow to the left side of Biko's head had caused his brain to shift in relation to his skull, thus causing the tear. Kidney failure often results from such an injury, thus Biko did not have this preexisting ailment, as Kruger had once claimed. Although all agreed that a contrecoup shock had ultimately caused Biko's death, they did not agree on the number of blows required to sustain the five lesions. Loubser believed a single blow could be the cause, whereafter the impact "fanned out" causing the other lesions.[114] Neville Proctor, who examined Biko's brain, believed at least three blows were necessary, and four was more likely.[115] Several medical professionals who examined the evidence agreed. Even Loubser, who represented the state, said that evidence of the damage—the mark on the left side of Biko's head—must have been visible to the naked eye within twelve hours of the injury. Loubser and Proctor concurred that the injury originated sometime between four and eight days prior to autopsy. Disturbingly, two of the five lesions extended into the white matter of Biko's brain, and one was "adjacent to the burn at the base of the skull."[116] Loubser testified that most contusions (bruises) were three to five days old by September 12, and that some came from a source of "mechanical origin."

That Bantu Stephen Biko had been tortured during his interrogation on September 6 and 7, 1977, is without question. Though the related hearings of the Truth and Reconciliation Commission twenty years later disappointed many, they did at least establish this fact (see chapter 6). What happened to Biko was well understood by black South Africans in 1977 since his torture and his death in detention were not the first instances of such for people subjected to laws that left policemen unaccountable for their actions. Many people have cautioned me to remember that Biko's suffering was not unique. As Lindy Wilson once wrote, "What happened in police room 619 happened countless times."[117] One can reasonably venture that corporal abuse of detainees was so pervasive, so part of the police psyche, that Goosen's infamous gaffe at the inquest was more than just a slip of the tongue. When Kentridge asked if assault charges had ever been filed against members of Biko's interrogation team, Goosen replied, "The assaulting team never assaulted anyone," then he quickly corrected himself.[118] At the inquest's eleventh hour, a telex sent by Goosen to security headquarters in Pretoria surfaced. Goosen, who had previously denied the existence of any telex from his office, was re-called to the stand. The document, dated September 16, said that Biko had appeared to be in a "semi-coma" before being transferred to Pretoria and that his injury "was inflicted" at 07:00 on September 7.[119] This, Goosen said at the inquest, was simply "an inference [to the] scuffle." The telex said that Biko's condition required an "urgent" response and made no mention of the belief that he was "shamming."

The South African inquest into Steve Biko's death concluded on December 1, 1977, nearly one year to the day that the SASO–BPC trial ended in convictions of all nine defendants in the same building. After thirteen long days of hearing and seeing evidence, of considering testimony and response under cross-examination, Magistrate Marthinus Prins gave his finding the next morning. It took just three minutes to impart his verdict:

> This is my finding in terms of the Inquest Act, No. 58 of 1959:
>
> The identity of the deceased is Steven *[sic]* Bantu Biko, Black man, approximately 30 years old;
>
> Date of death: 12 September 1977;
>
> Cause or likely cause of death: Head injury with associated brain injury, contusion of blood circulation, disseminated intravascular coagulation as well as renal failure with uraemia. The head injury was probably sustained during the morning of Wednesday, the seventh of September 1977, when the deceased was involved in a scuffle with members of the Security Branch of the South African Police at Port Elizabeth.
>
> The available evidence does not prove that the death was brought about by any act or omission involving or amounting to an offence on the part of any person. That completes this inquest.[120]

A Conclusion That Would Not Rest

The inquest verdict shocked people worldwide. Governments on all continents expressed disbelief, unease, and the desire to gain distance from South Africa. Editorial "attacks flowed in," as newspapers worldwide carried the verdict and related stories on the front page or just inside it over the following days.[121] In the United States, President Jimmy Carter's administration found it "inconceivable on the evidence presented at the inquest that no one was responsible,"[122] and *New York Times* columnist Anthony Lewis called it right: "The inquest showed that police sadism was officially condoned in South Africa."[123] Within South Africa, editorials in both English and Afrikaans newspapers carried conflicting responses to the verdict; in both languages one finds a mixture of disquietude toward and support for the state. Since the preeminent black paper *The World* was banned the previous October, the *Rand Daily Mail* stood out among others during these months in expressing the outrage most South Africans felt about the verdict.[124] Generally, papers agreed on the need to reform Section Six of the Terrorism Act so that detainees could secure the right to receive visitors and care from parties other than the state.[125] Although legal reform on this score was not to pass, indefinite detention under Section Six became less frequent.[126]

If Magistrate Prins disappointed by offering no reason for his ruling, then Sir David Napley pleased many by his scathing review of the Port Elizabeth Security Police testimony and State Police investigation of the case.[127] The Association of Law Societies of South Africa invited Napley, a distinguished member of the British Law Society, to the inquest as an independent observer. As to Prins's finding, Napley believed that Section Sixteen of the Inquest Act was read in too limited a fashion, and persons ought to have been held accountable. Napley wrote, "I was left in no doubt that Mr. Biko died as a result of brain injury inflicted on him by one or more unidentified members of the Security Police at some time prior to and reasonably proximate to 0715 hours on the morning of 7 September 1977." Further, Prins was "demonstrably wrong in adding the rider that the head injuries which resulted in death were probably sustained in a 'scuffle' with the police." Napley was heavily influenced here by the unanimous opinion among highly regarded medical witnesses—particularly that of Sir Charles Symons, "one of the greatest neurologists to have practiced in the United Kingdom in this century"—that Biko would have been unconscious for a lengthy period following his injury. Napley believed that, combined with Goosen's "urgent" telex that an injury had been "inflicted" on Biko that morning, Biko's "violence at the time of the so called scuffle was not the occasion of brain injury, but the result of one already sustained." Neither did he believe any real evidence could be disclosed by an internal investigation into a death in police custody, thus he urged the South African government to establish "some special branch . . . for the avowed purpose of monitoring the Force and thus ensuring the most diligent and searching enquiry where it is necessary."

Though a special branch was eventually created, it was not what Napley had in mind. A counterinsurgency unit called C-1 (popularly known as Vlakplaas) was formed in 1986, but its purpose was to hide evidence of police violence. Indeed, George Bizos, part of the Biko family inquest team, writes that by 1986 the government sought to avoid "Biko-type inquests" by murdering activists and disposing of their bodies (rather than detaining them at all), running political assassinations of better known antiapartheid figures, or poisoning those who were detained.[128]

Official bodies weighed in. The South African Medical and Dental Council undertook proceedings to censure Drs. Tucker and Lang for their mismanagement of Biko's physical care. The South African Council of Churches took up the same cause, as did the Black Sash, a historic women's antiapartheid collective. Discussed more fully in the notes to chapters 5 and 6, the effort took eight years, but eventually Tucker and Lang were found guilty of improper conduct; Tucker was also found guilty of disgraceful conduct. Legal scholars throughout the commonwealth pressed for a full judicial commission into the inquest findings. This did not come to pass.

Cultural and social functionaries have picked up the cause. Since 1977, the inquest has been reenacted in varied forms: Hilda Bernstein recorded it in detail in her book *No. 46–Steve Biko* (1978); theater productions were cast and played in London (1978) and Durban, and in parts of India. The London version, titled *The Biko Inquest,* was later filmed as a theatrical production and broadcast on television with Albert Finney directing and starring as Sydney Kentridge (1984). It has since been performed onstage many times, most recently with Patrick Stewart in this role (2007).[129] In September 1978, the inquest transcript was read in lieu of the regular evening service by actors at a London church; Westminister Cathedral paid tribute to Biko and other men "who played important roles in the struggle for human rights";[130] Kenya issued a commemorative stamp picturing Biko's face and grave; and the city of Amsterdam did what many cities have done since—it renamed a popular public square in Biko's honor.

September 12 marks an important date in South African history, and every year the nation honors Biko anew on this day. Before the first democratic elections of 1994, the Azanian People's Organization coordinated business and school closures annually on this day, and commemorative gatherings were held in churches and secular meeting halls throughout the nation. Sometimes these gatherings were banned in terms of the Riotous Assemblies Act (1956). And varied international bodies have marked the date annually. A United Nations committee commemorated Biko every September 12 until at least 1980; the Institute of Race Relations chose this day in 1978 to close its London office. In 1979, visitors to Trafalgar Square in London witnessed a twenty-two-meter banner bearing the names of the forty-six South Africans who died in detention, and in downtown San Francisco a mountaineer climbed Grace Cathedral's steep spire and for eleven hours held a long banner unfurled uniting Biko's name with Elmer "Geronimo" Pratt, an imprisoned Black Panther leader.[131]

Though internationally Steve Biko became a symbol of apartheid abuse in the years following his death, for the BC-minded (wherever they live) he has always been remembered for the life he led and the ethos he inspired among millions. And for his family and friends, he was much more: a husband, a father, a son, a brother, a confidant, a self-described freedom fighter. Since the Inquest Act allowed no provision for appeal, Biko's survivors quickly followed the inquest decision by filing for civil damages against the state, but their lawyers encouraged settlement for two reasons. According to George Bizos, "We were convinced the government would not fight the merits of the case and thus a judicial finding against the police and the doctors was not likely to come about. . . . [And the state aimed to] persuade the judge that Steve Biko's future was such that he was unlikely to earn much. The road he had chosen . . . would have led him to terms of imprisonment rather than improved earnings as time went on."[132] The state first offered a paltry 30,000 rand to Biko's mother, wife, and children for the loss of support they sustained. They rejected it. Eventually, a payment of 65,000 rand was accepted, but Nontsikelelo Biko made it clear that the money did not signal any resolution:

> It was declared that nobody was to blame for the fatal lesions on Steve's brain. . . . Nobody was to blame for the vegetable-like condition that he was in when he breathed his last. Nobody was to blame for his death. . . . We and the black people of South Africa will not rest until we know how Steve Biko came to meet his death.[133]

At some point in the inquest proceedings, the well-known photographer Peter Magubane captured a rare moment in which Nontsikelelo Biko let down her guard (Figure 2.15).[134] In every other photograph from this period available in print, she maintains the poise that is demanded of political widows despite the enormity of their grief. For such women, "the agency of the biologically dead man is located within the body of the living woman and is indivisible from it. The woman's body is the site of empowerment."[135] The responsibility that begins with a political activist's death (borne most often by mothers and wives) is

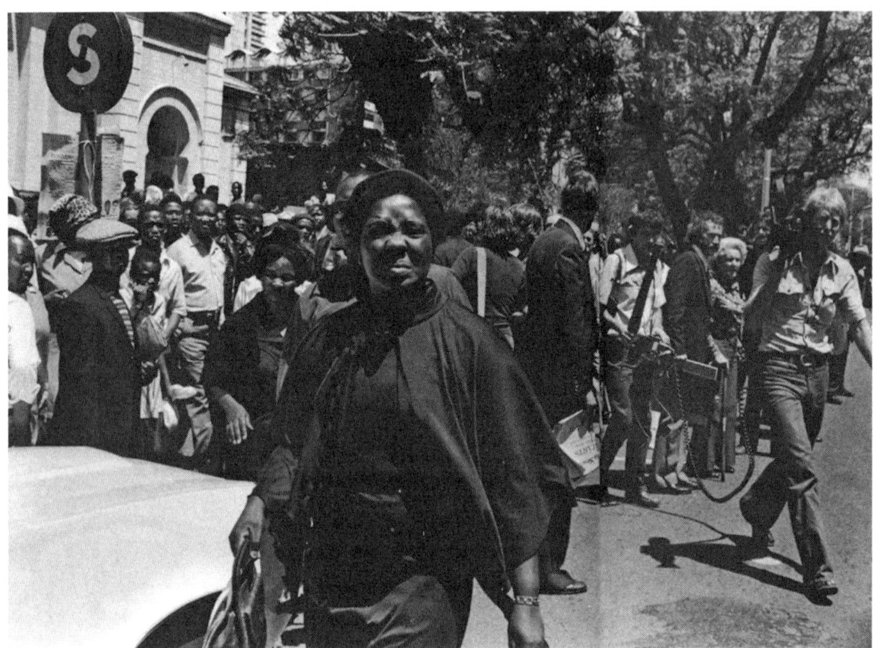

FIGURE 2.15. Peter Magubane, *Nontsikelelo Biko Leaving the Inquest into Her Husband's Death, November 1977,* 1977. Courtesy of Peter Magubane.

"carefully nurtured and managed" by the activist's colleagues to such an extent that a widow endures "public ownership" of her person.[136] Magubane's photograph is significant because it evidences a moment in which Nontsikelelo Biko reclaimed herself during a period of tremendous loss. She cast the mourning veil aside. Her expression—a pinched scowl that conveys complete dissatisfaction— reveals the extent to which her agency as woman, wife, mother, and professional (she was a nurse) had been constrained but not eliminated by her new role as widow. Here she renegotiates, even briefly, the terms of her space as public figure. The photograph also glimpses a moment in which the pained response to the proceedings stems almost entirely from the crowd of black South Africans at left. All eyes are on the family; all sympathies are with them. The mostly white crowd opposite is otherwise engaged.

Taking leave at the inquest's conclusion on December 2, 1977, Nontsikelelo Biko got into her car and was seen to have raised her fist high.

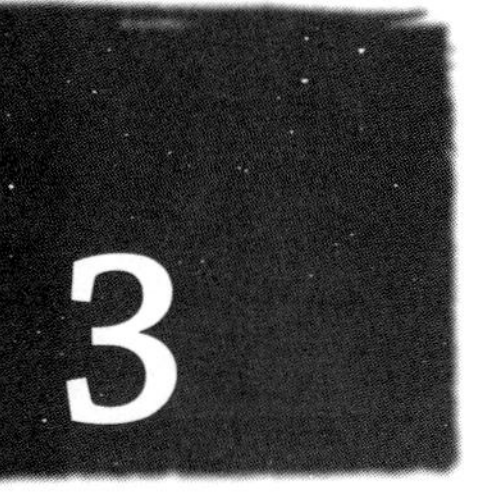

3 Contemplating Death

Artists and Abjection

> The writer, fascinated by the abject, imagines its logic, projects himself into it, introjects it, and as a consequence perverts language—style and content. . . . And yet, such texts call for a softening of the superego. Writing them implies an ability to imagine the abject, that is, to see oneself in its place and to thrust it aside only by means of the displacements of verbal play.
>
> — Julia Kristeva, *Powers of Horror: An Essay on Abjection*

AS CHANCE WOULD HAVE IT, STEVE BIKO'S DEATH COINCIDED WITH THE FIRST art exhibition about torture in detention that was shown in South Africa. The works were by Paul Stopforth, then senior lecturer in fine art at the University of the Witwatersrand in Johannesburg. Just one week after Biko's death, the exhibition opened at the Market Theatre Complex, a now historic not-for-profit arts venue. The art on display immediately became linked to Biko's particular history, even though the artist repeatedly insisted that he worked to raise consciousness about the larger problem of detainee death and torture. In South African art history, these works, simply called *Figures,* eventually gained independence from the shocking incidence of Biko's death, but in the popular press during the last quarter of 1977, they were inevitably linked.

With the exception of Sam Nhlengethwa's *It Left Him Cold—The Death of Steve Biko* (Plate 13), the best-known artworks about Biko to date were made in the years immediately following his death. Although *Figures* gained extra attention by chance, Stopforth's subsequent works derived from this specific history, as did those of Ezrom Legae, a renowned sculptor and draftsman. Both artists created emotionally moving bodies of work that have become canonical pieces in their own right. Interestingly, their respective forms illustrate how South Africa's varied populace understood Biko's death, and the vastly different realities that artists of dissimilar skin color faced. But regardless of these inequities, the key to interpreting these artists' works around Biko rests in their visceral responses to his death. Contemplating Biko, they shared a common impulse to exhume themselves from apartheid history and the brutal practices used to secure its future.

Both Stopforth and Legae supported Black Consciousness, both were interested in boundaries, either conceptual or metaphorical, and both evoked BC's humanism in their art. Both artists' works from this period also remain clouded in the literature, which consistently emphasizes their relationship to Biko's specific history rather than to the larger social contexts that Stopforth and Legae addressed.[1] Although both artists exorcized aspects of personal identity through their works, their responses to Biko's death advanced different objectives: Stopforth emphasized the prevalent abuse of detainees; Legae focused on spiritual renewal despite this violence. This distinction is determined in large part by the artists' skin colors, with Stopforth eager to educate fellow white South Africans about violence against detainees, and Legae, whose people needed no such education, expressing his response through metaphor, a tactic that alleviated suspicion and met commercial expectations of black artists.

Though racial ideas created very different realities for these artists (observable in their styles and the titles they chose), both labored beyond the confines of skin color to develop works that explore pain as a metaphoric index of their nation's sociopolitical conditions. By emphasizing the sensation of pain, Stopforth provoked viewers to reflect on their bodily experiences, and ultimately on their own mortality. In three separate bodies of work that express anguish, he hoped to promote opposition to a nation that inflicted pain to control its populace. Legae, on the other hand, emphasized the transformative state of being that accompanies pain, and finally death. His brilliant work projects a triumph realized through commitment to a greater common good.

One week after Biko's death and amid the frenzied reporting that accompanied it, the Market Theatre Gallery in Johannesburg opened an exhibition called *Figures,* a collection of life-size plaster-cast bodies modeled to look like detainees. Their maker, Paul Stopforth (b. 1945), had been investigating deaths in detention since 1971. *Figures* (Figure 3.1) was based on descriptions of inter-

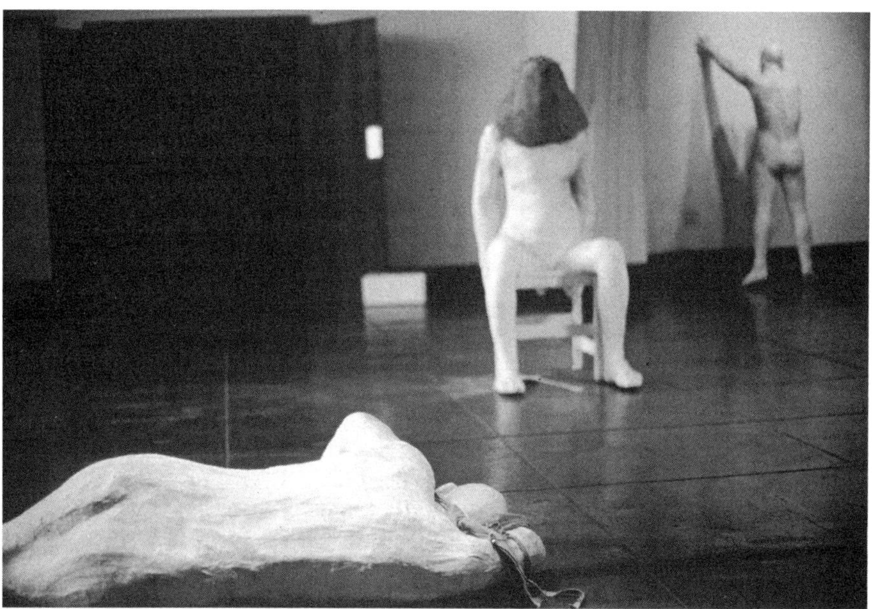

FIGURE 3.1. Paul Stopforth, installation view of *Figures: Torture and Deaths in Detention,* Market Theatre Gallery, September 1977. Mixed media. Courtesy of Paul Stopforth.

rogation methods he read about in *The World* and on explanations the South African police offered for deaths of detainees under their care, all termed accidental or self-inflicted. There were six figures in the exhibit: one seated with a bag over his head, another lying on the floor, one knotted and hanging from a bar, one falling down the stairs, another standing with palms on a wall and legs spread, and one falling from the roof of the Market Theatre Complex.[2] Their positions were frighteningly close to reality. Men who had been detained told Stopforth that his figures correctly reflected their experiences.[3] The sparseness of the exhibition space, which lacked the carpeting, soft lighting, and piped music of some commercial galleries, contributed to the figures' effectiveness. The gallery, founded by Stopforth, Rolf Finner, and Michael Goldberg in 1977, catered to a diverse downtown audience and profiled work that was "not viable within the commercial market," that is, politically engaged art.[4]

Each work in *Figures* was made of the same base material: layered bandages set in plaster of Paris. Their surfaces are uneven, with lumps in areas. All of the works are life-size; all depict adult males.[5] Some pieces include found objects, such as the sack placed over the seated figure's head or the torn clothing around the neck of the body on the floor. Stopforth experimented with a wax covering to create a better sense of skin and thereby enable a more intimate response from viewers. His intention seems to have worked. Anne Pogrund of the *Rand Daily Mail* found the surfaces effectively conveyed a "raw suggestion of nakedness."[6] The finished works produced what Jill Bennett calls "empathic unsettlement" in viewers: a doubled experience of the art in which we feel *for* another person and are aware that our response is sensory-based.[7] This "embodied perception" is the meat of critical inquiry, the response to Stopforth's call for our concerted action.[8] The figures' arrangement—isolated, each set at a distance from the others—heightened viewers' affective engagement and lent the bodies in duress a "positive strength" that, in Peter Fourie's analysis, enabled the "retention of dignity."[9]

Although Stopforth's *Figures* were based on a long history of state abuse, the exhibit's appearance concurrent with reports about Biko's death linked *Figures* to Biko's history. *The World* published installation photographs from the exhibition to illustrate articles about Biko's death. It also reprinted these shots in a two-page photo spread on other deaths in detention. Similarly, *Speak* illustrated its Stopforth interview with a photographic portrait of Biko. The exhibition received press coverage from September to December 1977, the same period in which Biko's death and the inquest it sparked were reported. In December, Stopforth reflected on the relationship his *Figures* had to public interest in Biko's death:

> Until the exhibit commenced, the figures had an historical connection. They were not related to any specific death but to deaths over the last years. But when the Biko death was published they became quite frightening because their relevance was no longer in a past historical framework. People who may never have seen these figures had been faced with a tremendous amount of information the week before the exhibition opened.[10]

Although Stopforth's exhibit received heightened attention due to its timing with Biko's death, the continued impact of the works is due to their evident timelessness. *Figures* was the first exhibition that explicitly portrayed the horrors of South African detention, thus making Stopforth one of the originators of what has been called "resistance art." He retains an important place in history because of his vital influence, as artist and instructor, in this time and place.

The full impact of his work would not be realized for a few years, however, as local critics generally analyzed the art based on its formal qualities alone. Only Anne Pogrund of the *Rand Daily Mail* and Joyce Ozynski of *Sunday Express* acknowledged that *Figures* focused on interrogation methods.[11] While some reviewers likely feared that explicit reference to Stopforth's criticism of the state would inflame readers or the Bureau of Information, others simply doubted the place of sociopolitical commentary in art.[12] Stopforth believes that the latter relied too much on art trends in Europe and the United States that emphasized abstraction or pop culture. They were disengaged from events in South Africa, realities that the artist could not ignore. He regularly emphasized the need for artists to become "involved with being inside of an African framework, along with all the complexities, problems and hassles that that entails."[13] As a lecturer at the University of the Witwatersrand in Johannesburg, he influenced many students. Among these is the talented Jane Alexander, who credits him for her own artistic development. She made the famed *Butcher Boys* for her 1986 MFA exhibition, and it bears Stopforth's influence. Although Alexander is less explicit about her intentions than is her mentor, Stopforth firmly believed that artists could best challenge South Africa's political realities through figurative means. In 1977, he said, "I want to make and spread an image as real as possible for the time now. . . . I want to bring the facts home to those willing to look. My figures parallel something that we [the majority of whites] can't be witness to. We can't refuse to accept that these things happen."[14]

As a child, Stopforth became aware of South Africa's inequality when he regularly accompanied his father, a supervisor for a bus company, on a route that serviced black passengers living in Alexandra. This historic township abuts Johannesburg's wealthy suburbs in the northeast. With training under his belt, Stopforth moved to Durban in 1969 to teach art at Natal Technical College. Durban was, as Stopforth describes it, "much more culturally fluent than Johannesburg" because he found greater social connections there among the officially segregated. Durban is also where Black Consciousness began to take shape, its roots developed in the life experiences of those who helped found the South African Students' Organization and later the Black Peoples' Convention.

Interested in mixed-race cultural and political events, Stopforth became involved with the Theatre Council of Natal, organized and overseen by Strini Moodley and Saths Cooper, leaders who were among the accused in the SASO–BPC trial of 1976. Through them, Stopforth met Steve Biko in 1970 and visited him and his colleagues on occasion at the Natal Medical School. At the time, Stopforth was aware that Biko was becoming an important influence in student politics. The artist recalled that he "had an awareness . . . as did obviously many of the students involved in politics at Durban University . . . of the enormous power and presence and potential importance that this man had as a leader. . . . There was a kind of gravity about him, a kind of seriousness about him, and a depth, which was, I felt, really extraordinary." In that Stopforth increasingly challenged his (inevitably white) audience to grapple with apartheid and their own place within it, he fulfilled what BC dictated for liberals. He worked to convince those to whom he had ready access: South African voters of varied political persuasion. (Remember that one had to be classified white in order to vote.) In 2000, he told me, in heavy tone, "I felt that if I wanted to make a difference, I wanted to do so as an artist. . . . So that's what I did, from then on out. I tried to make work that reflected what I understood to be the reality of the South African situation. And I mean it was top to bottom, through and through, sickening, repulsive, and essentially evil." Few South African artists had begun to frame their work in such politically charged ways, so Stopforth's inspirations were outside of his discipline but within South Africa. He identified with "the intense humanism" of playwright Athol Fugard, photographer David Goldblatt, and Market Theatre director Barney Simon. *Figures* was Stopforth's first step toward forming a visual dialogue about apartheid's dehumanizing nature. The works he made during the three years that followed Biko's death more fully explored the nature of humanity and, through the use of an entirely new technique, marked Stopforth as an artist of considerable talent.

In October 1979, he opened another solo show at the Market Theatre Gallery. Originally part of an installation, the most powerful of the eight works displayed is called *The Interrogators* (Figure 3.2). This well-known large vertical triptych represents three of the men implicated in Biko's death: at top, Colonel Pieter Johannes Goosen, then divisional commander of the Eastern Province Security Police; midway, Lieutenant Winston Wilken, the presiding night squad officer in Port Elizabeth's detention center while Biko was held; and at bottom, Major Harold Snyman, who oversaw Biko's interrogation during the day. Opposite *The Interrogators,* seven panels lay on the floor at an angle of about forty-five degrees. The panels, collectively called *Detainees* (Figure 3.3), figure, in flat, black silhouette, a naked male body spotlighted against a white background. All of the panels, including the three that make up the triptych of interrogators, are the same size: 60 x 33 cm. The comparative scale of the images, however, is drastically different. While the detainees are fully figured in the

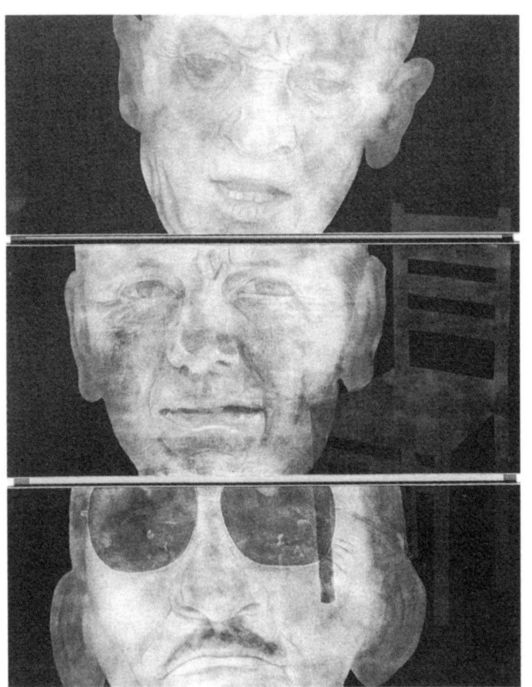

FIGURE 3.2. Paul Stopforth, *The Interrogators,* 1979. Mixed media on paper, on panel. Each panel 60 x 33 cm. Courtesy of Paul Stopforth.

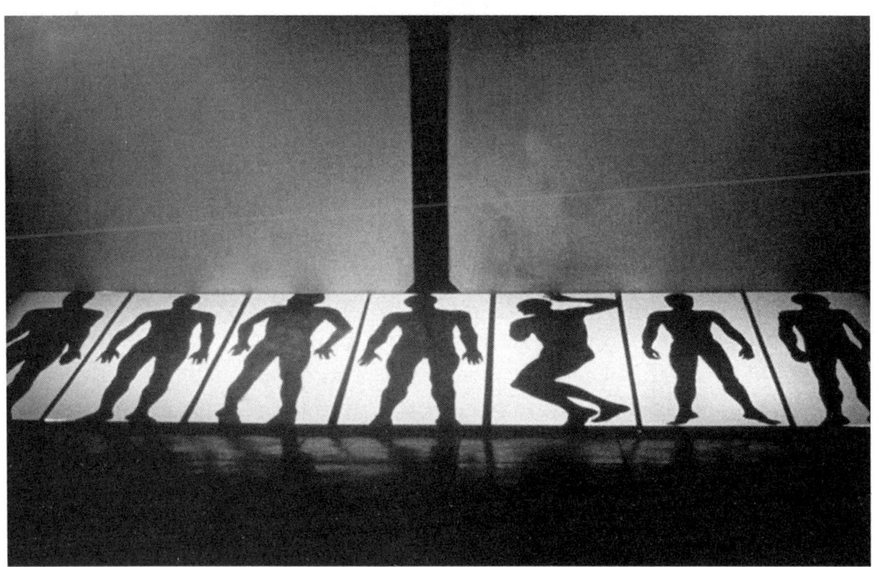

FIGURE 3.3. Paul Stopforth, *Detainees,* 1979. Mixed media on panel, 60 x 33 cm each. Courtesy of Paul Stopforth.

space, the interrogators' faces are gigantically enlarged beyond the dimensions of each panel. This difference in scale contributed to viewers' unease as they stood between the installation's respective parts.

The Interrogators is commonly understood as a representation of Big Brother, the Orwellian icon of social surveillance and constraint. Critics originally read its now forgotten companion, *Detainees,* either as corpses laid out on mortuary slabs or as living bodies reacting to tortures that are inflicted on them. Such "rites of defilement" created an abject space between the installation's respective parts. On one side: evil, impurity, even demonic forces rendered in detail and larger than life. On the other side: holiness, purity, an elevated otherness realized through comparative lack of detail. So purified, its filth—the torture once rendered—is extracted and the "collective existence" of these men is no longer of the secular world but, as Kristeva sees it, is one with the sacred.[15] Significantly, in 1979, *Rand Daily Mail* critic Sydney Duval understood all six *Detainees* to be portraits of Biko.[16] In the larger scope, they serve as premonition to Stopforth's *Elegy* of 1981 (Plate 3), a life-size painting based on an autopsy photograph of Biko. In this work, the figure of Biko is also clean, without wound or scar, and decidedly elevated.

The evil of *The Interrogators* stands in direct ratio to the holiness of the *Detainees* that defines it as such. Stopforth intended the trio to be read as typical Afrikaners, with the exception of Snyman in the lowest register, whose aviator glasses identify him as a security officer. These "terribly ordinary" men have come to embody evil for most who see them.[17] The reading has expanded: curators of the 1999 New York exhibition *Liberated Voices: Contemporary Art from South Africa* installed *The Interrogators* at the entrance. Here it represented a host of sociopolitical evils from which South Africa had been presumably liberated.[18] The evil depicted here is, as Hannah Arendt coined, "banal."[19] It is not obviously monstrous; rather, it is sickeningly commonplace in the social landscape. Though evil itself is incomprehensible, thus in part alluring, it "can be precisely anticipated" because it is "natural." Paul Oppenheimer writes, "Evil makes its appeal just because one has little trouble in identifying with it."[20] Motifs and representational devices such as fragmentation (in space or in time), darkened spaces, silence, lavishness, fantasy mixed with naturalism, and, crucially, redundancy are all culturally recognizable as eerie and, as Oppenheimer maintains, evil. Several of these devices exist within *The Interrogators* or are manifest in its relationship to *Detainees.*

After *The Interrogators,* lone wooden chairs became symbols of torture in

South African visual culture. This otherwise mundane object embodies the ghosts of detainees, and in this particular work it represents Steve Biko. Its frame stretches onto all three registers of the triptych to implicate each officer in the history of its use. During the inquest, police maintained that Biko hurled himself "like a wild man" from his chair and onto his interrogators, suddenly and unprovoked.[21] The fatal blow, they said, happened during the scuffle that followed.[22] Anchored in Biko's history, the chair evokes the final moments of consciousness. Its color and modeling are like those of figures in *Detainees* adjacent to this work in Stopforth's installation, thus the chair links Biko's specific history to those of men who died under similarly questionable circumstances.

While the fully figured panels represent many men who have suffered detention, the identities of the policemen are specific and were known to the many people who followed coverage of the Biko inquest. Each of the three men represented in this piece testified in court and their images appeared in the news often.[23] Stopforth re-created their likenesses from photographs that appeared in the *Rand Daily Mail*. The artist had a compelling interest in the Biko case, but his use of its inquest imagery was meant to question the multiple deaths that had occurred among detainees and broaden public awareness of such abuses. Stopforth said:

> The shock of Biko's death led me to become increasingly involved with the fact of these deaths—and that's what [*Interrogators* and *Detainees* are] about. I am trying to communicate the fact that certain people are vulnerable and that this kind of situation is in a sense the essential reality of the country. It's very important to recognize this destruction of human life.[24]

Although the artist's larger political objective and humanist concern remained consistently clear, *The Interrogators* and a series of works that followed in 1980 are firmly rooted in Biko's history. The trio within *The Interrogators* is interesting because it simultaneously fed the public's general perceptions of state abuse and displaced this important reality in favor of a specific history of one man's fate.

All of the works in this exhibition were made with a technique of Stopforth's own creation. He began by painting translucent liquid wax floor polish onto paper attached to boards. He then floated powdered graphite over the wax, and after it dried he engraved the minute details. This process was repeated ten to fifteen times in each piece, thereby working the graphite into the pitted surfaces. A strange metallic gleam resulted, one that unfortunately does not transfer to reproductions. The process is highly labor intensive, a fact that makes the resultant work more than an object for contemplation, more than a remnant of self-expression. The works testify to Stopforth's desire to communicate an issue of profound personal and social import through the medium that he understood best: art. In making *The Interrogators* and *Detainees,* Stopforth realizes what Gilles Deleuze calls "the encountered sign."[25] That is, the intensity of his process and his project—a commitment to end state torture—may be felt upon viewing the works, particularly so when seen installed together.

In mapping out the enormous heads of *The Interrogators,* Stopforth found himself "reflecting on my own race." This statement, together with his decision to change the title of a later work about detainees to *We Do It* (Figure 3.4), informs my understanding of *The Interrogators* and all of Stopforth's subsequent Biko-related works as meditations on the artist's sense of self within a political structure he opposed. The collective "we" of *We Do It* identifies Stopforth with his target audience and insists that all who benefit from apartheid's laws are responsible for the measures used to uphold them. (Black Consciousness advocates agreed.) The title also pays honor to Francisco Goya, whose famed *Disasters of War* series (circa 1810–20) includes a drawing of this title.

Stopforth's ruminations, then, caused him to feel at once outside South Africa and firmly within it. Throughout the 1970s, he made art that aimed to educate those who doubted, as Julia Kristeva sees it, "this truth of horror and sickness, of weakness and downfall. . . . [by realizing] its confrontation with the other term—the powerful, rich, and feared: 'There are two of you together.'"[26] The artist felt aligned with the corpses, the *Detainees,* by confronting what he called his "own race." Here is the longer passage from Kristeva:

> But when one's weak, the thing that gives one strength is stripping those one fears of the slightest prestige that one may still tend to accord them. One must teach oneself to see them as they are, as worse than they are, that is. One should look at them from all points of view. This detaches you, sets you free and is much more of a protection than you can possibly imagine. It gives you another self, so that there are two of you together.[27]

Having completed two exhibitions about torture and death in detention, Stopforth's mission was established. People strongly identified his interests with Biko's history. At a social event in 1979, Stopforth met Shun Chetty, a lawyer who had worked on behalf of the Biko family during the 1977 inquest. Through Chetty, Stopforth gained access to the photographs used in court, both forensic

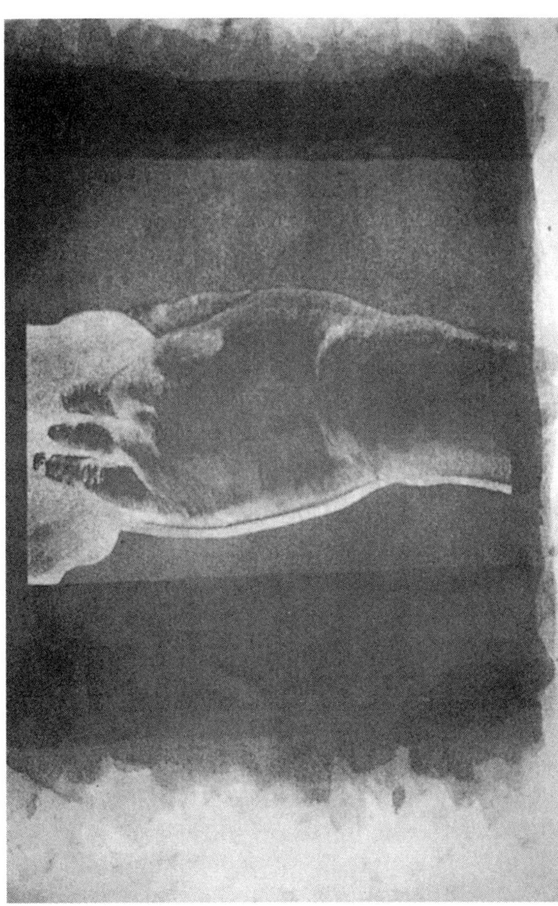

FIGURE 3.4. Paul Stopforth, *Biko Series* (originally *Untitled*, briefly changed to *We Do It*, then *Requiem for Allende I* in 1980), 1980. Mixed media on paper, 76.2 x 55.9 cm. Courtesy of Paul Stopforth.

and autopsy. He photographed a number of the images and used them as source material for a series of twenty engravings (e.g., Figures 3.4–3.6), one of which became canonical (Figure 3.6).[28] The series was first shown at the Johannesburg Art Gallery in September 1980, three years after Biko's death. At the time, Stopforth left them untitled because he intended to continue questioning abuse of all detainees in South African custody rather than spotlight Biko's death. Still, the works were immediately identified within the art world as representations of Biko's corpse.[29] The series focused on the postmortem examination of Biko's body, emphasizing the lower portions of his limbs. Each work frames a small part of the body, allowing close inspection of fresh scars. On the wrists one sees bruises where handcuffs bore into the flesh; discolored patches of skin blot the forearms (Figure 3.5); cuts and scrapes are evidenced on the ankles and toes (Figure 3.6); and the right hand is grossly swollen (Figure 3.4). Stopforth intimately examined Biko's photographed flesh for signs of trauma inflicted on his body. Because wounds are ready signs of pain, his series was essentially about pain and, in a larger sense, an appeal to South Africans who either supported or ignored its infliction. The distortions on the flesh register immediately, causing us to identify with the subject and experience a kind of secondary trauma because the works mimic a sensation that is familiar though not felt. Imagery that promotes empathic imitation within viewers has a long history. As Jill Bennett reminds us, "The operative element in the medieval devotional image is not the narrative framework but the affective detail," or the wound.[30]

Response to this series depends on its affective abilities, which it smartly actualizes by tapping our familiarity with pain, and with skin. Skin is a surface all viewers know, a place where "everything is immediate, bounded, instantaneous, and *sharp*"; James Elkins locates it as the place where "pain, irritability and sensation all reach their apex."[31] Though skin is often conceived of as an exterior boundary, a viewpoint that privileges sight, Elkins details a more nuanced historical understanding of skin as "both dividing and divided, at one and the same time inside and outside, inbetween." He argues that skin is more than a barrier that marks different realms; rather, skin's "attachment, its near identity" is with the inside.[32] Stopforth's *Biko Series* fosters the reading that the person imaged is being examined for internal injuries. The translucence of these works, a product of the same engraved wax technique he used earlier, compels us closer so that we might better decipher the boundary we thought we knew. Everything around this boundary, skin, becomes blurred. Despite the formal precision evident in all of Stopforth's wax-engraved works, the effect is ultimately one that prompts us to question boundaries and personal subjectivity within violent systems of governance.

Each work required great delicacy and precision; Stopforth's method was in effect an attempt to control the horror of the image he copied. Kristeva discusses authors (particularly poets) giving themselves over to "a language that gives up, a structure within the body, a non-assimilable alien, a monster, a tumor, a cancer that the listening devices of the unconscious do not hear." In so doing, "the abject permeates . . . . I become abject." But by naming that which seeps into them, that is, "through sublimation," the artist makes it possible to "keep [the abject] under control." Here, the abject is "edged with the sublime."[33] Thus each

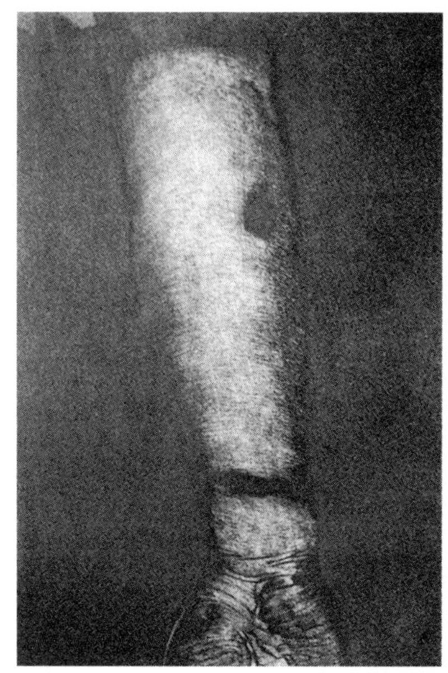

FIGURE 3.5. Paul Stopforth, *Biko Series* (originally *Untitled,* briefly changed to *We Do It,* then *Requiem for Allende I* in 1980), 1980. Mixed media on paper, 76.2 x 55.9 cm. Courtesy of Paul Stopforth.

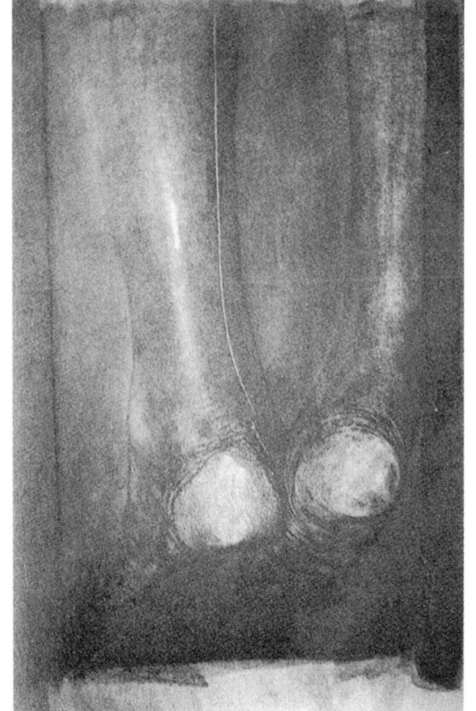

FIGURE 3.6. Paul Stopforth, *Biko Series* (originally *Untitled,* briefly changed to *We Do It,* then *Requiem for Allende I* in 1980), 1980. Mixed media on paper, 76.2 x 55.9 cm. Courtesy of Paul Stopforth.

time Stopforth's sharp instrument cut the wax to remove it from the template, he incised his own release. Imagining him at work over the year that he made the *Biko Series,* one thinks through the intensity of his focus and his sustained commitment to ending torture of detainees in South Africa. As he labored over these works, each of small scale, he created what he called "a more intimate, more personal kind of space." The images that result visually rise above the dark backgrounds; metaphorically, the body, fractured into parts, emerges from a murky depth, one clouded by questionable testimony.

His technique achieves a visual quality that differs from the photographic prints seen at the 1977 inquest. The layered graphite produces glimmering, metallic-like surfaces. Together with the compositional arrangements, this creates the sense that we are looking at something more like X-rays than photographs. Used to reveal inner ailments, X-rays find sources for troubles manifested on the exterior. Though used for scientific purposes, they are among the most intimate documents as they reveal that most private place: a body's interior. Colin Richards reflected on this intimacy in terms of a humanistic inquiry. In a fascinating analysis of works in this series, he suggests that Stopforth's method, which creates "identity through absence," might fulfill "[Biko's] brand of humanism" insofar as the interplay between exterior/surface and interior/self suits the sort of "self-inspired reflection [that] enables rather than cripples agency."[34] He also notes Stopforth's "unfaltering interest in humanism," which remains apparent all these years after he made this series.[35] Richards believes that Stopforth

> sought to give his articulation of . . . trauma a specifically human dimension and tenor. . . . he would want us perhaps, in spite of and through the image he produced, to read not simply spectacular surface, but begin imaging inside out. He would want us to see not only a body broken by others, but Biko's identity as a sentient, generous human being, as an activist committed to enabling agency and self-possession.[36]

This frame of analysis allows interpretation beyond what Njabulo Ndebele has famously called "the culture of spectacle" that dominated South African aesthetics beginning in the mid-1970s and throughout the 1980s.[37] The X-ray-like works in Stopforth's series seem to insist on an inquiry that delves beneath the surface, one that moves beyond the spectacular, riveted, as it is, on the seeable. The *Biko Series* critiques its source—evidentiary photographs—as inherently insufficient. Stopforth probes his audience to reexamine such evidence as it endeavors to find a more complete picture of what (and ultimately who) precisely caused Steve Biko's death.

One could also argue that Biko believed that spectacularly violent events (and perhaps images that linger thereafter) could be politically useful. One of his most often quoted statements was made just months before he died. In a 1976 interview with the British Broadcasting Corporation, he said, "You are either alive and proud of it or you are dead, and when you are dead you can't care anyway. And your method of death can be itself a politicizing thing."[38] Stopforth's *Biko Series* was, and remains, "a politicizing thing." Its history includes a well-known event that illustrates its political power. In 1981, two works in the series were selected to travel to Chile for the Valparaiso Biennial. Stopforth renamed them *Steve Biko* (Figure 3.6) and *We Do It* (Figure 3.4) so a Chilean audience would understand that South Africa was culpable for deaths in detention.[39] These titles were too explicit for the South African Department of Education (SADE), which was to fund Stopforth's inclusion in the Biennial, and he was asked to change them. He obliged, choosing the titles *Requiem for Allende I* and *II*, thereby commemorating Chile's popularly elected president, Salvador Allende, who was murdered in the brutal coup of 1973 that brought General Augusto Pinochet to power. Rather than risk offending its host, the SADE rejected these titles and withdrew Stopforth's work from inclusion in the Biennial, just as he had predicted. This event further confirmed the artist's commitment to fighting human rights violations and was in itself "a politicizing thing."

Stopforth created one last work from the autopsy images that Shun Chetty loaned him. Titled *Elegy*, the work was made by the same scratched-wax technique, but it stirs an entirely different response from that of the smaller autopsy images. *Elegy* (Plate 3) depicts Biko larger than life. The intimate scale of those in the *Biko Series* is replaced by a work of comparatively monumental proportion. A bright red field surrounds the corpse, dislocating it from any common referent. The tray beneath it appears to float in space. We sense that Biko is more than dead; indeed, there are no wounds visible at all. Instead, he appears risen, otherworldly. This is *Elegy*'s most important feature. For the body to abstain from abjection, "it must," Kristeva advises, "be clean and proper in order to be fully symbolic. In order to confirm that, it should endure no gash other than that of circumcision. . . . Any other mark would be the sign of belonging to the impure, the non-separate, the non-symbolic, the non-holy."[40]

Because it depicts Biko fully nude, *Elegy* has provoked some distaste among viewers who find this disrespectful.[41] Abjection, in the minds of some, attends nudity more than death. Viewer unease may be due to the sense of our own mortality and uncertainty about how to respond to a likeness that is akin to our own but free of all obstruction. All nude images convey some desire, but it is superseded here by another sensation: conversion. For those viewers who sense an inkling of what Stopforth must have experienced as he made *Elegy,* "the object of desire," explains Kristeva, "bursts with the shattered mirror where the ego gives up its image in order to contemplate itself as Other, [and herein] there is nothing either objective or objectal to the abject."[42] In other words, Kristeva believes that some works beckon us to fall away from ourselves, to become more than what we are. *Elegy*'s internal message is part political, part religious. As a light underneath gives form to Biko's body—it shimmers below his legs and shoulder, it shines brightly behind his chin and beneath his torso—he appears to lift skyward from the tray. The metaphoric parallels between a risen Christ and this martyr, Steve Biko, are uncomfortably close. One then wonders: He died for me. What have I done so as to assure that his death was not in vain?

As Paul Stopforth made *Elegy,* he regarded death fully, laboring to fill the media's gaps on the resounding prevalence of detainee abuse in his country. By closely observing death, "such a fearsome object," he realized what philosopher Michael Mendelson calls the "Mirror of Death," which does precisely what all mirrors do: it offers us a commuted image of ourselves.[43] *Elegy* is elsewhere regarded as an homage to Biko,[44] but I say it is something else entirely. It is a moral self-portrait. Mendelson writes:

> When the darkness of Death becomes a mirror, and when one gazes into the Mirror of Death, one cannot help but *draw a portrait of oneself.* And: in one of the curious yet almost predictable ironies of moral topography, the attempt to plot a terrain of the darkness off in the peripheral distance becomes instead a transfigured portrait of something far closer to hand yet, at times, seemingly every bit as inaccessible. One sets out to draw a landscape far off in the distance, and in so doing, *one is obliged to gaze deep* into the Mirror of Death and to construct a portrait of what is close to hand in a manner that is more revealing than any deliberate act of portraiture ever could be.[45]

Viewers may squirm before *Elegy,* but for Stopforth and those who attempt to join him in gazing deeply into death rather than getting stuck on its surface, a significant message unfolds. The work draws us in and compels us to do as its subject did: combat racism. Since the function of all elegies is to heal, *Elegy* is a visual poem to South Africa's greatest political martyr, much as is Jacques-Louis David's *The Death of Marat* (1793) to that liberator of France. As with the portrait of Jean-Paul Marat, in *Elegy* we are called to take up Steve Biko's cause because it is, or should be, our own.[46]

The field of bright red that surrounds the tray suggests the beginnings of ascent. It evokes bloodshed and thus violence, an appropriate reading to tales of martyrdom. In *Elegy* the nation to become is embodied by the figure in transcendence/transition at center. The threat comes from without, in the field (or land) that surrounds him. Kristeva records biblical forewarning of bloodshed; Stopforth similarly visualizes its cautions for those who, in 1981, brought suffering to South Africa's majority: "Whoso sheddeth man's blood, by man shall his blood be shed (Genesis 9:6); So ye shall not pollute the land wherein ye are: for blood it defileth the land: and the land cannot be cleansed of the blood that is shed therein, but by the blood of him that shed it (Numbers 35:33)."[47] Upon viewing *Elegy*, one is not soon to forget it. All who know its subject realize that it records a painful death for the man who experienced it. Through *Elegy* his pain extends outward, onto us. Veena Das's research into suffering gives us this: death is not experienced, that is, made palpable, *except among those who live and embody the pain* that caused it.[48] Biko's trauma and death did not leave his nation unchanged.

Though Stopforth's interest always concerned publicizing abuse of detainees, which fixed whites as his target audience, critics and historians consistently focus on Biko as subject in all of the works discussed here. Given the degree of reporting on Biko, the circulation of his image, and the previous critiques of Stopforth's art from this period (and indeed his altered titles for the Valparaiso Biennial), reading works like *Elegy* as Stopforth's "homage to Biko" is understandable. But this collective body of works is best seen as a meditation on pain and an understated interest in evil. Indeed, pain is a word that gives meaning to the very conception of martyr. By laboring to register that pain visible, Stopforth embraced and communicated what Kristeva would call his most "intimate subjectivity into being for (us); and this act of judgment and supreme freedom [for art is surely these], if it authenticates me, also delivers me over from death."[49]

In 1964, the Polly Street Art Centre was one of the very few places where adult black artists could train as such. Mission schools, such as that at Rorke's Drift in Natal, ran courses, but within Johannesburg there was no other option. The city's Council for Non-European Affairs was persuaded to open the Polly Street Art Centre in 1948 in the belief that it would keep black youth off the streets and out of the unions. Art classes were first held the next year. By the time it closed, Polly Street instructors had trained a whole generation of leading South African artists.[50]

Ezrom Legae's early training at Polly Street proved formative as it was here that he developed his abstract style and interest in monumental forms for which he became so well known. Originally schooled in three-dimensional art making, he began to draw with vigor after 1964 since drawing would enhance his sculpting and his new work as a teacher at the Jubilee Art Centre (Polly Street's new incarnation on Eloff Street as of 1960).[51] His drawings and sculpture adhered to the same aesthetic preferences. Forms were organic and abstracted; without context, they appeared to float freely in space. Further, Legae was interested in revealing interior structures in different mediums. For instance, like his Biko-related drawings, his sculpture *Head of a Wise Man* (1965–66) exposes vertebrae within an ovular form and is like other works described as "egg-shaped." Works such as *Carcass* (1966) and the award-winning *Embrace* (1967) evidence violence in subject and technique, the latter having been deeply scored by a hacksaw blade. Such forms and their violent treatment reappeared in works from the series *Chicken* and *Death of Freedom,* Legae's quiet tributes to Stephen Biko.[52]

Biko's death created some uncertainty within the world of South African censorship and its effects on artists and their aesthetic choices. Provisions of the 1950 Suppression of Communism Act enabled the banning of an individual, which prohibited the reproduction of their words and likeness, among other things. The question then became whether this law still applied to a person once banned, now dead. From 1977 until 1990, when the original act was overturned, most black artists deemed outright representation of Biko too dangerous, so they cloaked their visions of this famous leader in abstraction. Legae is best known among them. Among those who understood his veiled expression was Linda Givon, owner of Johannesburg's Goodman Gallery while it represented Legae from 1978 until his death in 1999. She reports that he "communicated his way around those dangers with intelligence," most particularly within "*Chicken,* [which] for all its covertness, is a profound piece of political work."[53]

Legae's ambiguous titles—*Chicken* and *Death of Freedom,* for example— suited the hybrid imagery he drew to reconcile contradictory feelings he experienced after Biko's death: tremendous sadness over the loss of an influential leader, and a renewed determination to express his own experience of black consciousness. In these works the artist becomes melded with the activist in a kind of self-portraiture that expresses in the most visible way Veena Das's notion that another's trauma can only be comprehended if it comes to rest in [or is translated by] the body of another. She writes, "In the register of the imaginary the pain of the other not only asks for a home in language but also seeks a home in the body."[54] By merging his own likeness with that of Biko (and to an extent, his own history), the works within *Chicken* and *Death of Freedom* adhere to what Kristeva calls "a crying-out theme" expressed with "maximal stylistic intensity."[55] In these works, Legae is the "I" that is so central to Kristeva's influential *Powers of Horror.* Within their historical context, works in *Chicken* and *Death of Freedom* respond specifically to Biko's death, but their larger allegorical meaning asserts the artist's own black consciousness. As Legae explained it, Biko's death inspired him to work after a period of lapsed creative desire between 1967 and 1977: "In that period I hibernated. . . . I needed some kind of explosion to rock me out of my inherent laziness as an artist and also the kind of lethargy and lack of incentive and confidence in my own work that I was suffering from at this time. . . . The explosion came with the death of Steve Biko."[56]

The artist's description of self here, coupled with his choice of metaphoric motifs—fragmented parts of birds and humans, and a glowing orb that is typically read as either sun or egg—compels us to consider the primacy that Kristeva affords "the inaugural *loss* that laid the foundations" of our being: loss of the womb.[57] Ambiguity, abstraction, and hybridity confounded viewers as Legae ruminated on his chosen motifs over five years, overlaying their forms and bursting the material boundaries they would otherwise impose. Contained within the orb/sun/egg, "the sperm does its work much too quietly, too intimately, and the whole thing escapes us."[58] Indeed, were Kristeva aware of Legae, she could have written this about his response to Biko's death:

> Discomfort, unease, dizziness stemming from an ambiguity that, through the violence of a revolt *against,* demarcates a space out of which signs and objects arise. Thus braided, woven, ambivalent, a heterogeneous flux marks out a territory that I can call my own because the Other, having dwelt in me as *alter ego,* points it out to me through loathing.[59]

Metaphor abounds through the recurrence of Legae's chosen motifs within these series. With broken bones and matted or swollen features, the chickens and humans become tortured victims sacrificed for a greater communal good, be it religious or political. The orb motif, whether sun or egg, symbolizes regeneration or renewal from the defilement that attends sacrifice. And since sacrifice is necessarily abject, Legae's embrace of Biko's death/martyrdom enabled "a series of good rebirths" that led to the artist "finding salvation."[60] Collectively, Legae's metaphors for torture, sacrifice, and regeneration become allegories for the strength of Black Consciousness and its renewal in an ever-wider sphere of influence. Consider his description of primary motifs in these series:

> I used the chicken as a symbol of the black people of this country, because the chicken is a domestic bird. Now, one can maim a chicken by pulling out his feathers; one can crucify him and even kill him; but beware—There will always be another egg and always another chicken. If you remember in all these drawings with the symbolism of the domestic fowl, the spirit of Biko hovered and emerged even in the shadows, sometimes behind bars and sometimes free. And then watch out because that chicken suddenly became a vulture and the aggressor.[61]

Legae's artistic ambivalence registers quite differently from Stopforth's concretized pain. While both artists suggest that violated bodies have lost wholeness, with Legae one finds that such figures insist on formlessness. In other words, pain cannot be represented, thus we naturally embark on a restless search for metaphorical meaning. So, too, did pain compel Legae as he drew each suite. As Kristeva's "deviser of territories, languages, works, [a] *deject,*" he could not stop "demarcating his universe." He was impelled, as we are, "to start afresh" with each version of *Chicken* and *Death of Freedom,* but more than most, the artist is a "tireless builder . . . a sort of *stray . . . .* And the more he strays the more he is saved."[62] Biko's death, in Legae's own estimation, renewed his purpose in the world, reinvigorated his life, propelled his own sense of black consciousness into mark making. The result was two utterly fascinating bodies of work.

In the first suite (Figures 3.7–3.12, Plate 4), the motifs exist in fairly distinguished realms. Bird and orb are clearly delineated, as is the solid borderline, or wall, between them. The first shadowy representation of what Legae called the "spirit of Biko," or Black Consciousness, appears in Figure 3.7: his head is depicted upright and in three-quarter perspective just above that of the bird, which partially obscures it. Their common destiny as sacrificed beings is evoked through their placement on an overturned crucifix. Crosshatched lines weather the wood, which is broken at the bottom. These are repeated, to similar effect, in the bird's body. All are contained by their placement within an oval that

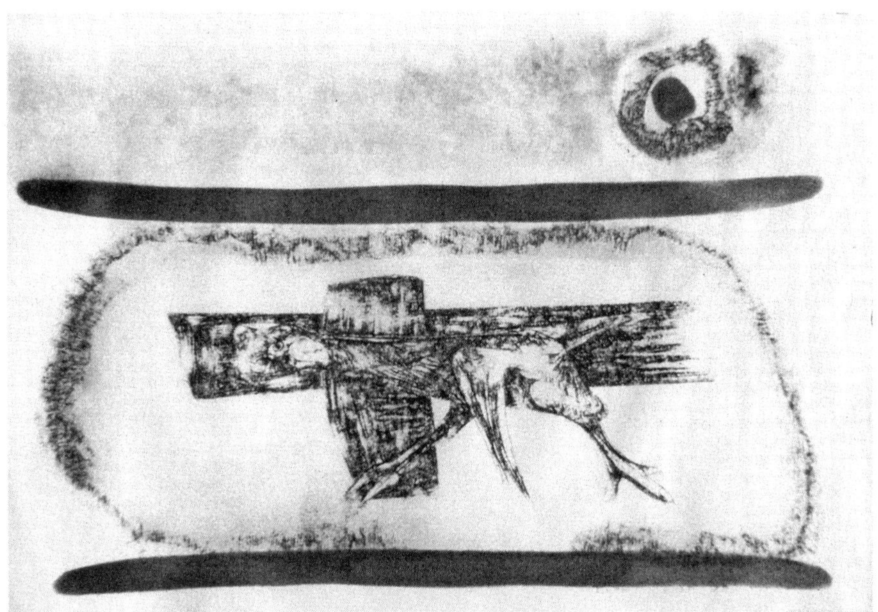

FIGURE 3.7. Ezrom Legae, *Chicken*, 1977–78. Conté and pencil on paper, 25.5 x 43 cm. Collection unknown.

is lightly painted and shaped by short lines that mimic those around the orb. This oval is further confined by broadly painted lines above and below. Such containment obscures the regenerative effects of the orb above, barring Black Consciousness from rejuvenation.

This barrier becomes lighter in Plate 4, where the orb rests on the line's thinnest end, right above a reclining figure, whose bound hands (knuckle to knuckle) and feet extend right to left. Two phallic forms are correctly positioned within an otherwise distorted body, one projecting toward the paper's lower edge, and the other, more carefully modeled, pointing up toward the gray orb. A pale pink wash with three semicircular contours encompasses the full body and space below and left of the feet. The rope/chain that binds the figure's feet breaks the oval at left. In keeping with other works in the series, the shape and pale color of the wash may be read as eggs, which, given the presence of phalluses and closeness of the orb above, imagines a second life for Black Consciousness, embodied by the tortured figure within. Two renderings of human heads are visible at right. A small face with a large nose, positioned frontally, is drawn just right of the hands. This face is enclosed within a much larger form that fills the space at right and balances the broken pink egg at left. This larger form appears to be the outline of a front-facing head, its hairline and skull shape delineated by the color change from dark to light. Read as such, the tortured figure within flows out of the face of Biko, whose shadowy presence is thus evoked in all representations of bound detainees. One may consider, too, that Biko's memory is bound within Legae and that this work, like others in the series, visualizes his cry: "The dead . . . says, I am the one who guffaws in horror inside the lungs of the live one. Get me out of there at once."[63]

Figure 3.8 of 1977–78 is an early example of merged human and avian forms that Legae repeated throughout this series and in works from *Death of Freedom*. The largest, and thus dominant, element occupies the lower third of the composition; it evokes Biko's autopsy portrait. An organic dark mass outlines a lighter form, within which one can discern swollen facial features at left: forehead, eyelids, and mouth appear to bulge outward by the dark lines that provide contour. The lighter mass that extends right—read as a distorted body, perhaps—is too small for the head and swaddled in what could represent either a funeral cloak or an embryonic sack. Thus the figure, representing Biko's spirit, is marked at once by the violence of his death and by the continued rebirth of his ideas. A bird's talons pierce the cloak/sack from above, and a hybrid figure, more bird than human, rises toward a barred window in the upper third of the composition. This figure is complexly rendered: it is an assemblage of bones, claws, legs, feathers, beaks, and eyes, all set at odd angles. Its complexity prompts further study, as does its proximity to the window, the bars of which match the darkened diagonal lines atop the form's head, read as such from the presence of an eye that looks directly out at the viewer. It is a sorry bird. With broken bones and matted feathers, one imagines that its life is nearly over. Yet its determined gaze and amorphous shape suggest another outcome: it may slip through the window, carrying the spirit of Biko with it, on to a new existence beyond the confined and limited space of one man's cell.

It is not yet known how many works comprise the *Chicken Series*; indeed, there is more than one such sequence. Bird and human are more distinctly separated in many works, but each is defined in some way by a shell/cell. The last two discussed here share this feature.

This fascinating version (1977–78) within the early *Chicken Series* encom-

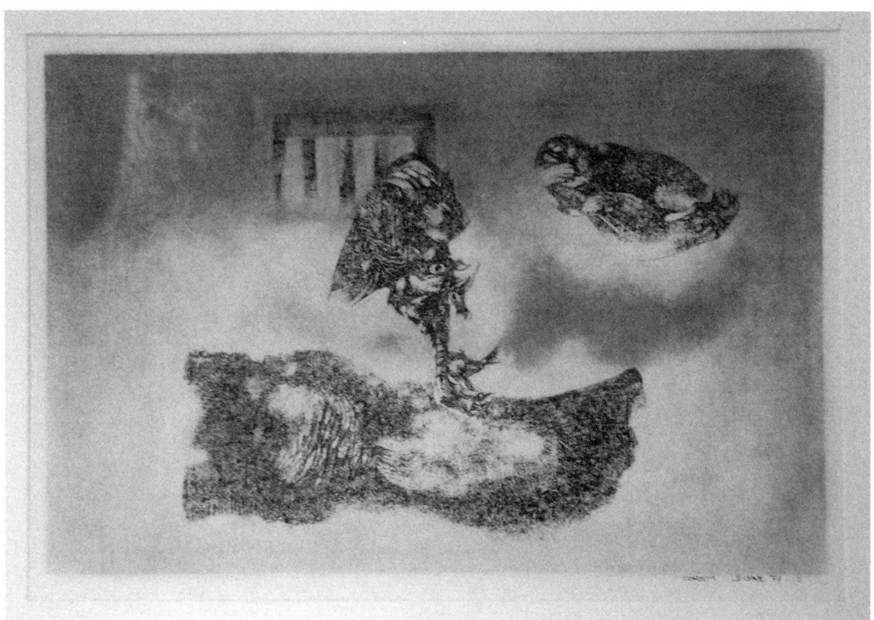

FIGURE 3.8. Ezrom Legae, *Chicken,* 1977–78. Conté and pencil on paper, 27.3 x 41.8 cm. Iziko South African National Gallery.

passes the full range of metaphoric possibilities. The reference to autopsy speci-fies Biko's death as a subject, and the rising spirit constitutes a kind of "fainting away" that engulfed Legae as he undertook the work. Thus, it also exemplifies how Black Consciousness reinvigorated him as an artist. Once "deprived of the world," that is, deprived of his artistic energy, Legae heard of Biko's death and he "[fell] *in a faint,*" as Kristeva predicts.[64] Witnessing the publication of Biko's postmortem portrait in the press ("that compelling, raw, insolent thing in the morgue's full sunlight"), Legae beheld "the breaking down of a world that [had] erased its borders: fainting away." Subsequently, and after ten years of lethargy, this magnificent artist began to create anew.

Also from 1977, *Chicken* (Figure 3.9) depicts a bird breaking free from its original container, forcefully pushing away a portion of its fragile side. The bird's neck and head are distorted. An elongated eyeball, phallic in shape, ex-tends downward toward the center of the egg to emphasize the bird's origin. The other eye looks upward toward a black mass of crosshatched lines that take the

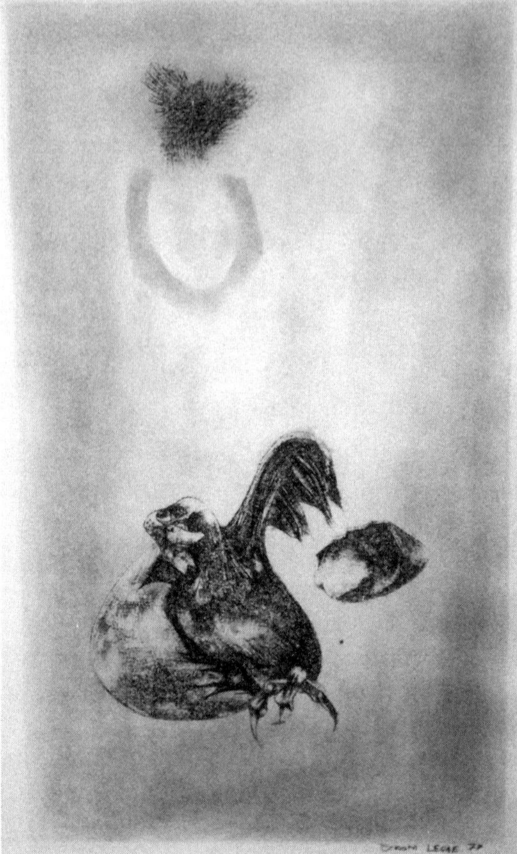

FIGURE 3.9. Ezrom Legae, *Chicken*, 1977. Conté and pencil on paper. 39.4 x 22.9 cm. Courtesy of John Stremlau, the Carter Center.

vague form of another bird in flight. The strain on the primary figure is evident: great tension registers at the nape of its neck as an unfurled wing holds taut. These parts mirror the horseshoe shape at top, lightly painted with the same pale pink wash Legae used elsewhere in the series. The vertical pairing of forms suggests a path: this bird, who freed itself from its cell, dependent on no one, begins to rise toward one of its own.

Other works within the *Chicken Series* evidence Legae's "insistence on a precise, forensic literalness,"[65] thus they depart from the more abstracted visions of autopsy imaging. In these and in others from his series *Death of Freedom* (1979–82), we still find composite creatures but also closely observed renderings

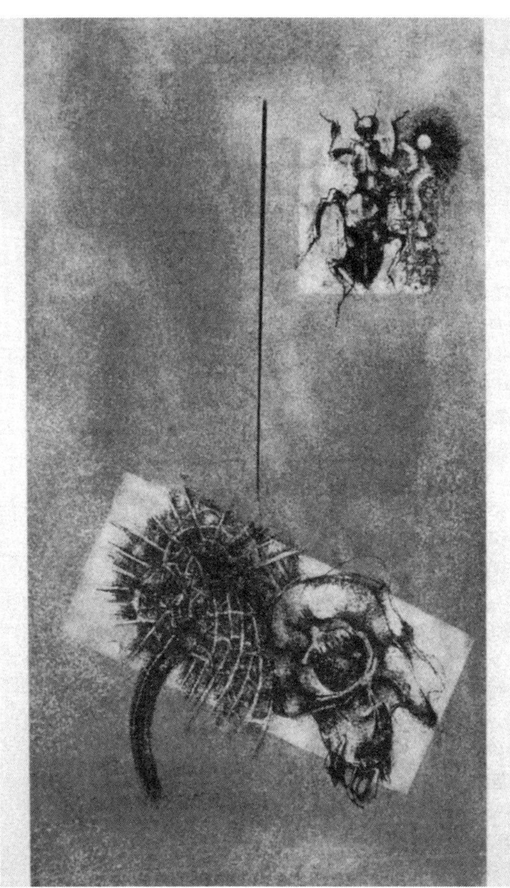

FIGURE 3.10. Ezrom Legae, *Death of Freedom (No. 2)*, 1979. Also once called *Statement for 1980*. Conté and pencil on paper, Johannesburg Art Gallery.

of predatory insects like locusts and buzzards. Forensic literalness is particularly evident in Figure 3.10, which won an honorable mention at Chile's 1979 Valparaiso Biennial, though the work traveled there under the name *Statement for 1980.*[66] Here the insect at upper right, laid out like a specimen against a colored slide, resembles a queen termite, which presides over large communities and produces thousands of eggs each year. Thus it bears a positive reading, particularly as it is positioned close to the glowing orb/sun/egg, which is formed by the same series of short splayed lines seen in earlier works and also evokes regeneration. A dark line vertically divides the top half of the composition and tapers near a diagonally positioned box in the lower half.

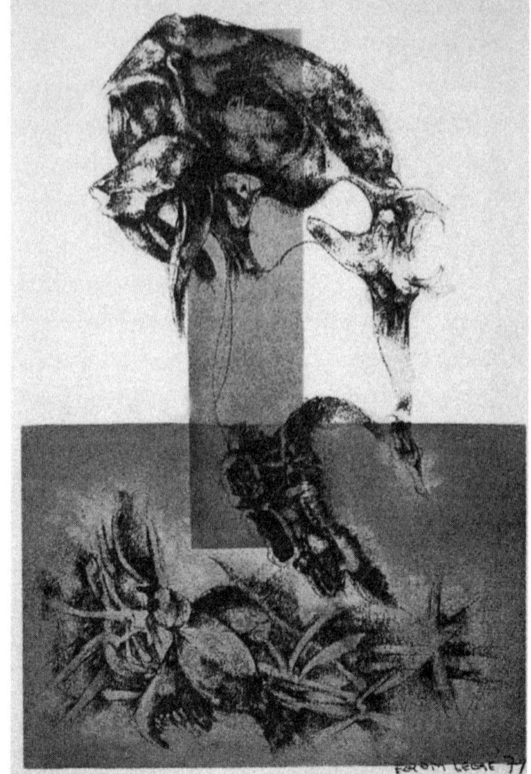

FIGURE 3.11. Ezrom Legae, *Chicken Series*, 1979. Conté and wash on paper, 47.5 x 34.5 cm. Gencor Collection (lettered *A* by Gencor curators).

Within the box are more specimens: a cross-section of tendons and a composite skull of bird and human. The light and thus pronounced amorphous shape atop the latter mimics a queen termite's body as it becomes gigantically distended during pregnancy, adding extra ovaries to accommodate its growing family. In light of its historical context, this version of *Death of Freedom* (1979) uses the termite as a metaphor for a kind of quiet industriousness that would dismantle an adverse political structure and replace it with the towering presence of Black Consciousness.

Legae also made the work in Figure 3.11 in 1979. Like others in this collection, this work features a composite skull shape, the addition of bright color fields or bars, and it lacks an orb.[67] The golden rectangle at bottom hosts a mass of taut double lines that allude to a cross between body parts (ligaments or tendons) and architectural parts (prison bars). Elements of a human head (two eyes and one ear) are just barely discernible beneath the tendons/bars near the composition's left edge. The eyes are open and fearful. Resting on top of the tendons/bars is a fully figured dove-shaped bird with wings spread wide as it works to free the human below. Above them is another abstracted form that resembles a human face in three-quarter perspective, mouth open unnaturally wide, as though it is shouting directions at the dove, urging it to make haste. A vertical gray color bar and tripartite tangle of lines connect the form to the skull that dominates the upper register. As the lines and colors unify significant parts of this composition (note the lightened brush that surrounds each sharp, piercing element within the bottom golden rectangle), there exists a call for our mindful response. The skull's cavity for the brain links to the "crying out" figure at center who directs his gaze toward the human whom the bird works to free. Close observers of this work (indeed, of all works that Legae repeatedly made during this period) realize the significance of Legae's encountered sign. His cloaked yet vibrantly drawn expressions of pain touch us viscerally. Kristeva theorizes that we respond because the pain that demands formlessness, or denies representation, is nonetheless familiar to our subconsciousness because we share the experience of birth.[68]

The last two works considered here are also from the series *Death of Freedom*. The version from 1979 (Figure 3.12) offers the most ready example of birth imagery: at right a fetal head, still pressed against the sheer sack of its mother's womb, emerges from tight confines that double as a bird's broken wing. Barbara Buntman also sees a bird's face and a seed within it, complementing her reading of the form as one of hope and rebirth.[69] Opposite this is one of Legae's more fully realized human faces: a bearded man, injured with a swollen left eye and distorted skull, is figured beneath a crosshatch of thick lines that, due to their pointed ends, evoke a kind of Crown of Thorns. Made over the same period that Paul Stopforth made the Biko series, this is among the first of many works that connect Biko's death to that of Jesus; indeed, his sacrifice was quickly elevated to saintly scale. Connected to this image is the familiar orb near the top center of the page. One thorn pierces the orb at left. Another line extends from below the orb in a near vertical manner to emit a shaft of light across the center of the composition. These, too, evoke regeneration.

In what appears to be Legae's final work on this subject, he explicitly portrayed himself in flight.[70] In 1982, he made the work in Figure 3.13. It is called

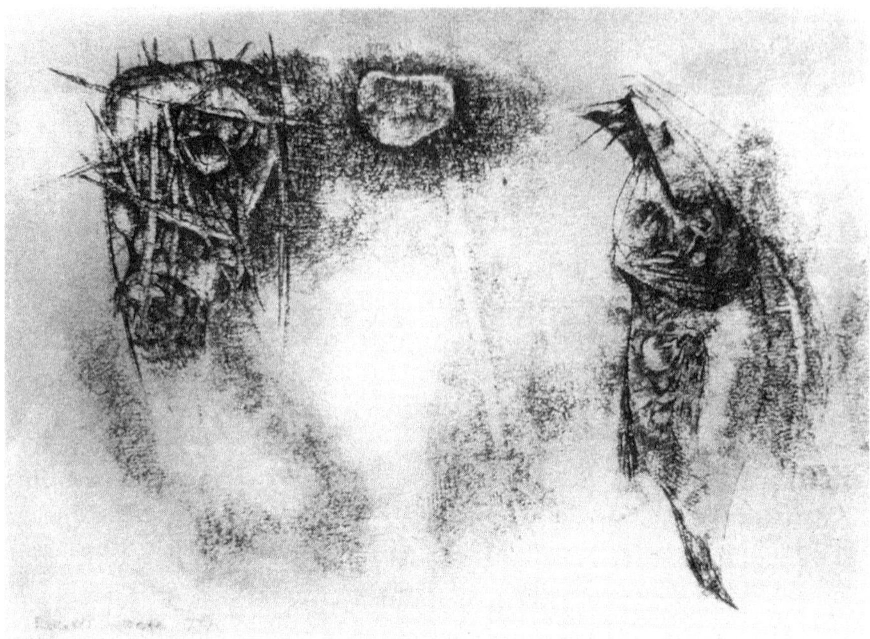

FIGURE 3.12. Ezrom Legae, *Death of Freedom,* 1979. Conté and pencil on paper. Collection unknown.

Death of Freedom, but the face beneath the wing is alive and alert and free of the mangled tendons, bars, and thorns that formerly obscured it. Here the "I" of the artist is pronounced. His project complete, confident in the strength of his own black consciousness, Legae rendered and thus released himself across the sky beneath a radiant sun.

> The corpse, the most sickening of wastes, is a border that has encroached upon everything. It is no longer I who expel, "I" is expelled. The border has become an object. How can I be without border? That elsewhere I imagine beyond the present, or that I hallucinate so that I might, in present time, speak to you, conceive of you—it is here now, jetted, abjected in "my" world.[71]

In these varied ways, Stopforth and Legae responded to the horror of Biko's death by claiming the pain it registered and, cutting and drawing in turn, repossessed life through their work.

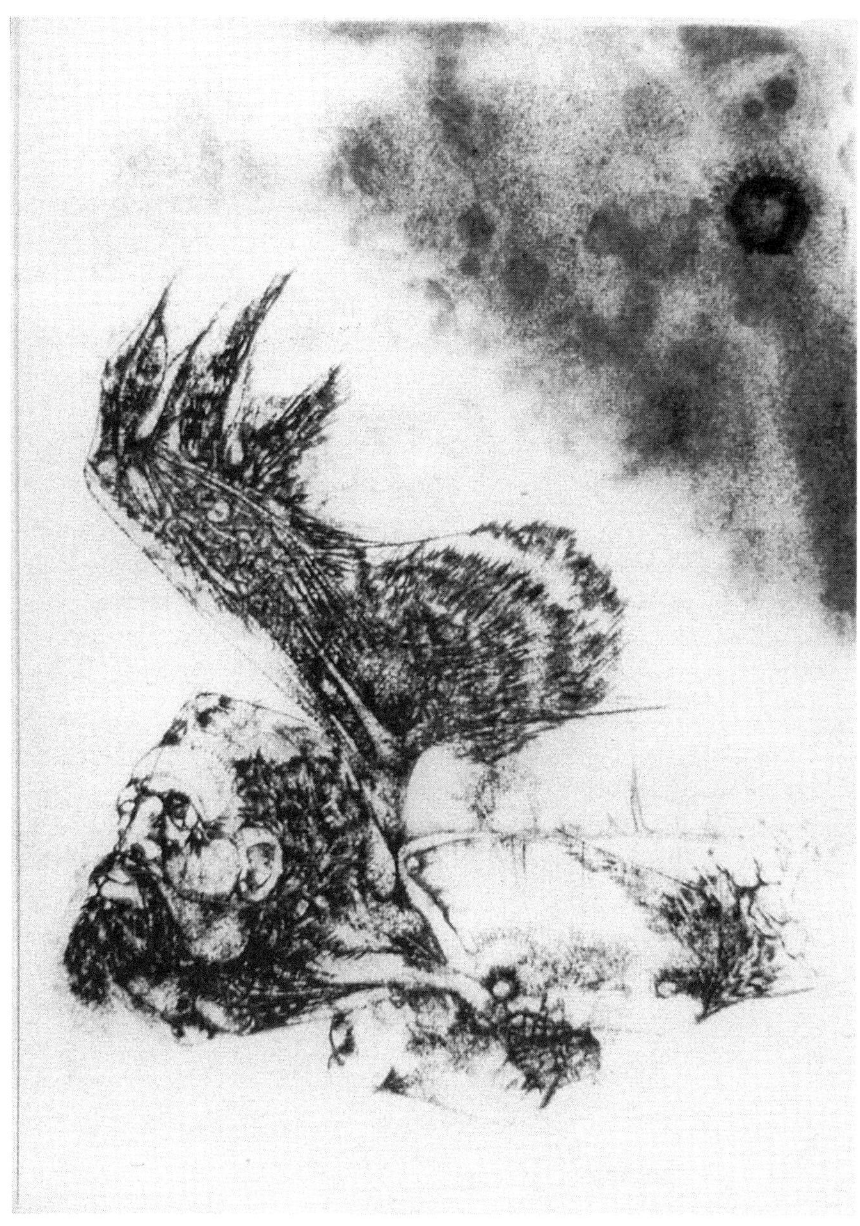

FIGURE 3.13. Ezrom Legae, *Death of Freedom,* 1982. Conté and pencil on paper, 21 x 29 cm. Collection unknown.

The art discussed in this chapter remains the best known of all works that explore Steve Biko's death and its lasting impact for South Africans. By visualizing their responses to this national tragedy in the years immediately following it, Paul Stopforth and Ezrom Legae initiated modes of visualization that would continue throughout the decades that followed: approaching extreme pain and the horror that attends it; expressing the ongoing impact of Black Consciousness despite attempts to squelch it by both the state and lead antiapartheid parties. For both artists, addressing Biko's specific death was a means by which to counter a prevalent issue in South Africa. For Stopforth, that issue was the torture of detainees. For Legae, it was the belief that one could not stymie, and certainly not smother, the great sense of pride and self-worth that Black Consciousness engenders. As Veena Das argues, pain depends on an external witness to make it known. And as Julia Kristeva envisions, the poet best translates that experience so that we feel it, too. The poet, now artist,

> speaks from the very seat of that horror, he is implicated in it, he is inside of it. Through his scription he causes it to exist and although he comes far short of clearing it up, he throws over the lacework of his text: a frail netting that is also a latticework, which, without protecting us from anything whatsoever, imprints itself within us, implicating us fully.[72]

Thus although the works discussed here discomfort because they image the state of radical alienation that necessarily attends a corpse, our understanding of this vital period in South African history is richer for them. We are richer for Stopforth's and Legae's endurance. For art is always this: a working through, a process before it becomes a product.

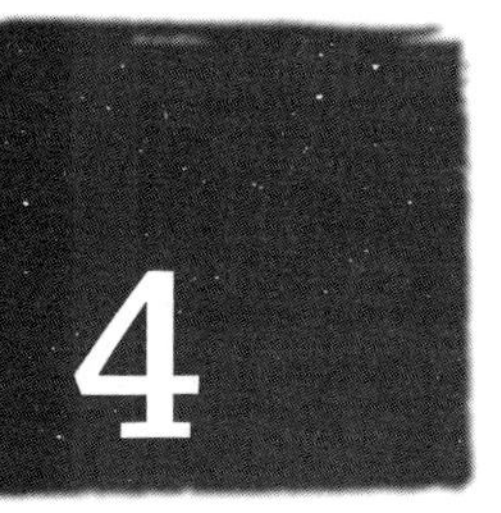

Creating a Culture of Resistance

Rising
from a bed
of aberration
and coir
I greet
the
blinding white dawn
with pride

far deeper
than
the pores
of
my skin
saying
I
am a Black man

— Christopher van Wyk, "Coming Home"

ON OCTOBER 19, 1977, A LITTLE MORE THAN ONE MONTH AFTER STEVE BIKO died at the hands of Port Elizabeth police, the South African government banned nineteen Black Consciousness (BC) organizations and began detaining BC adherents.[1] Although the movement had faced intense suppression since 1973, it was seriously damaged by the state in the last quarter of 1977. Since then, the widespread assumption has been that Black Consciousness became ineffectual. Some say that it waned in influence; others believe that it "evolved" to embrace a nonracialist position in which all people who sought the end of apartheid could participate, regardless of skin color.[2] Yet the visual culture of South African political iconography assures otherwise. This analysis of BC's portrait—its fist in action, either thrusting upward (SASO) or breaking chains (BPC)—accepts that icons are fluid, not fixed, since they always already re-present an idea. Thus Black Consciousness remained vibrant within the individuals who adopted it in the 1970s even as they chose different paths and methods of combating Pretoria. Crucially, I suspect that the term *nonracial* supplanted *Charterist* in the 1980s to describe the position of apartheid resisters who upheld the tenets of the Freedom Charter that was adopted in 1955 by four political parties: the African National Congress, the South African Indian Congress, the South African Congress of Democrats, and the Coloured People's Congress. The new descriptor subtly challenged Black Consciousness by typecasting it as fundamentally racial in orientation when in fact it was about the power of voice not race. In this way, Black Consciousness was cast as an outdated outlook, ineffectual for the struggle ahead.

Black Consciousness has always been a philosophy of being. It has always insisted on the right to determine one's own path, and with that the right to be heard. As such, it could neither be banned nor contained. In the swell of non-racialism that postdated 1977, BC was seen as necessarily abandoned in what Judy Seidman calls a "shift away from the racial divisions previously entrenched" within it.[3] John Peffer first limits BC's "essential combination of elements" to signs of woe and bursting rage, then anticipates its future by reading an abstract rendering of mother and child that Thami Mnyele made in 1972 as "a sign that even the mothers of the future revolution had not yet been fully formed."[4] His evolutionary perspective of the history unfolds: "Black Consciousness *evolved* from the activism of the South African Students' Organization (SASO). . . . from the racially exclusive ideology of Black Consciousness. . . . [with its] racially separatist perspective. . . . [to] become more aligned with the nonracialist principles of the ANC."[5] But why is the history written this way? Must the BC-inclined have given up anything at all? Rather, might it be that white apartheid resisters finally learned to hear and respect black voices, values, and visions? Might whites, be they self-described liberals or progressives, have shifted their viewpoint rather than the reverse? After all, Steve Biko once described this shift as inevitable.[6] What if we regarded Black Consciousness as the essential ingredient to the nonracial stew, the one that gave it substance, made it hearty?[7]

The state's actions in 1977 and 1978 did not kill the movement, but it did splinter Black Consciousness into different camps. In this chapter, I analyze the BC-inflected iconography of political organizations that either publicly claimed the mantle of Black Consciousness in the 1980s or derided it as a thing of the past, irrelevant to their own methods and mission. After analyzing odes to Biko that appeared in *Staffrider,* a literary journal with BC roots, I study examples of graphics issued by four political bodies—the African National Congress (ANC), the United Democratic Front (UDF), the Mass Democratic Movement (MDM), and the Azanian People's Organization (AZAPO)—each of which borrowed BC iconography and language to assert their own agenda.[8] Thus we find evidence of BC's ongoing impact in liberation history, an influence frequently diminished or denied. The resurfacing of Black Consciousness in the 1990s is not surprising given the undercurrents of the previous decade that were sometimes quiet but often not.

The argument I develop here is somewhat contentious given the politics of race that have developed in South Africa, particularly in the last decades of the twentieth century. I remind readers that Black Consciousness was fundamentally about the power of voice, also called self-agency, within representation. At its beginning in 1969, Black Consciousness became a politics of race in the minds of white liberals who could not abide their exclusion; since their voice dominated antiapartheid activism within South Africa at the time, their position of power mirrored that of the state. Crucially, Black Consciousness did not concern itself with whiteness. By the middle of the 1970s, and amid a series of attempts by the state to ban, arrest, detain, prosecute, and imprison BC leaders, race became a key element of Black Consciousness for a younger generation who ascribed to it. But even as the pressures of apartheid law prompted Soweto students to organize themselves in 1976, Biko reminded them, from his stand at the SASO–BPC trial, that although "protest talk about the situation of oppression . . . . always contained what I would call a round condemnation of White society. Often in very, very tough language," Black Consciousness sought to realize a democracy in which "both Black and White . . . shall continue to live together."[9] He described BC's admonition of "violent White society" as a form of ridicule that produced laughter when handled right. "Down with White society" was not the response BC sought. Instead, BC realized an "inner peace" among its audience since it encouraged them "to feel somehow that they have got a psychological ascendancy over White society."

Still, race-centeredness has come to define Black Consciousness for most who did not fully hear its message. The ANC, which continued to dominate struggles against apartheid from locations outside of South Africa, gained from this misinterpretation in the 1980s and began to call its membership *nonracial* in scope, even while it restricted its Executive Committee to black South Africans until 1984, as Paul Landau discovered.[10] Biko used the term to identify a variety of bodies at work against apartheid, and it appears that the organization from which he and others broke in 1967, the National Union of South African Students (NUSAS), was the first to formally adopt it. Although NUSAS is credited with the term's reactivation, the ANC benefited from its use in the 1980s, but in doing so it buried the influence of Black Consciousness. My aim, in part, is to recover that history here. The argument is important because nonracialism came to define "the struggle" for liberation in the 1980s, and it was the keystone to rhetoric of a new "rainbow nation" post-1994.

The ANC had little use for culture before Black Consciousness identified it as a medium of struggle. As BC-affiliated bodies like SASO and BPC had operated aboveboard and without armament, they relied heavily on culture to promote their cause. Theater, music, poetry, and literature were best known, but visual art was also part of the BC picture in the 1970s, as shown in chapter 1. Biko, who once edited a literary journal for the BPC called *Black Review,* often spoke and wrote of "culture" and "resistance" working in tandem.[11] In the 1980s, innumerable artists within Southern Africa were committed to creating a "culture of resistance," and most of those recorded thus far adopted nonracialism as their guiding approach. Many were inspired by the important Culture and Resistance Festival hosted by the Medu Art Ensemble (1977–86) in Gaborone, Botswana, in July 1982. Medu was founded by Black Consciousness adherents who sought and gained ANC affiliation in 1980. This fact has caused scholars to credit this party and its platform with the rise of resistance aesthetics in South Africa,[12] but the ANC, the most powerful of nonracial bodies, only established an official policy on culture in 1987.[13] I suggest that we linger with Medu's origins and consider the founders' use of culture as resistance. All were well known to promote BC; all had founded arts centers in South Africa before choosing exile in Botswana (see chapter 1). This study underscores the continuous register of visual culture throughout the life of this influential organization, which spawned numerous graphic production and arts centers in South Africa. Race has no place in my examination of BC iconography. My point is to illustrate its use by political organizations that advocated a nonracialist approach and those that did not do so. In this I show that BC held sway over artists and activists who adopted varied political affiliations despite the state's intensified suppression of BC in 1977.

Such is the confusion about BC's trajectory post-1977 that a poster, likely a state-issued example of what's called "black propaganda," surrounds Biko's iconic portrait with layers of logos adopted by organizations of varied interest (Figure 4.1). Propaganda of this kind is fundamentally false: it misidentifies and misrepresents the supposed maker. The central question of Figure 4.1 is posed in heavy text across three rows: WHAT IS OUR DESTINY? WITH ALL THIS CONFUSION! The query amplifies the bewildered space in between where numerous bodies are "revealed" here as fundamentally BC-oriented since they share Biko at heart. They include all the major political bodies of the 1980s and many of the best-known student, worker, and religious organizations committed to change in South Africa. The artist drew Biko's likeness and other revolutionary fare, including a forearm and fist in rotation at center right. The open palm of the Pan Africanist Congress (PAC) gradually becomes the clenched fist of Black

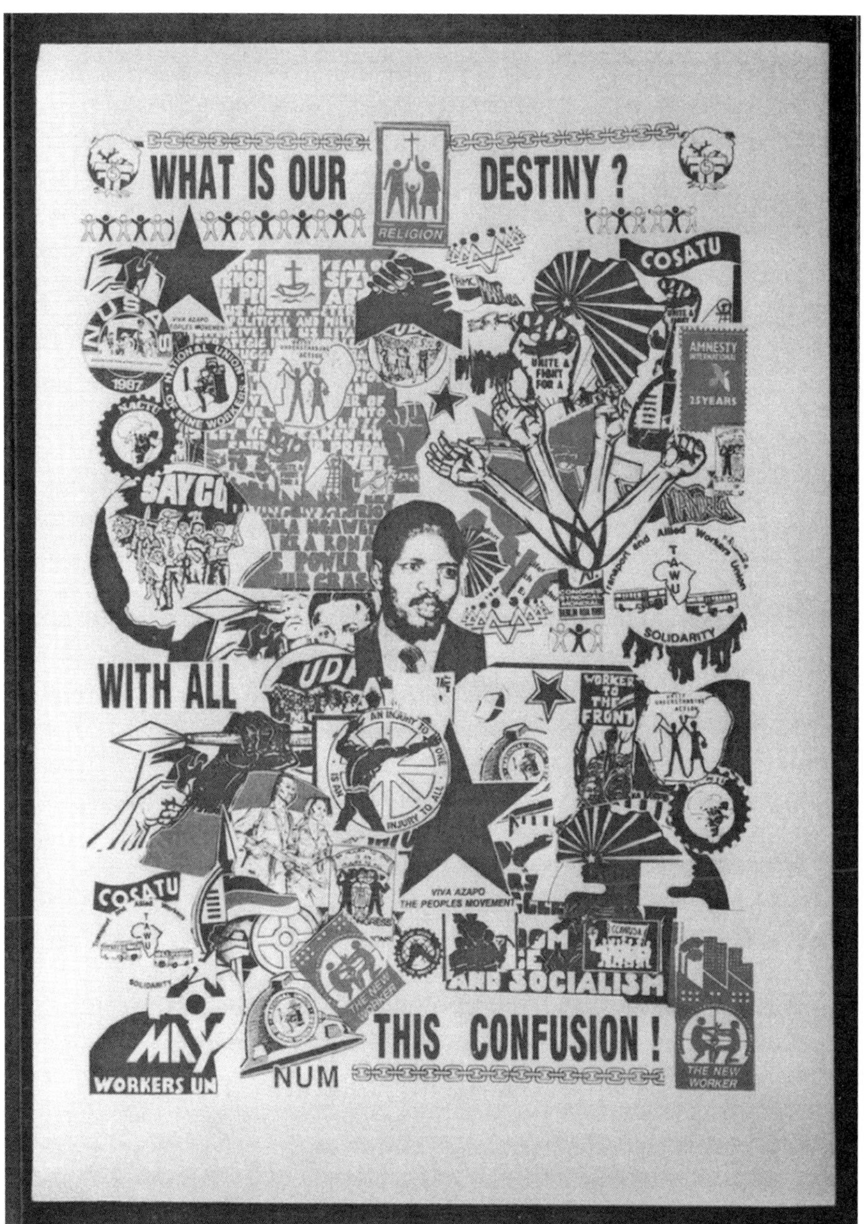

FIGURE 4.1. *WHAT IS OUR DESTINY? WITH ALL THIS CONFUSION!* Unrecorded artist, likely antipropaganda issued by the state. Approximately 25 x 19 inches. South African History Archive, University of the Witwatersrand.

Consciousness. I add that by this time ANC members also widely used it, but many also still favored the party's original salute: a raised fist, palm forward, with thumb extended upward. Documentary photographs of the period are well known for many things, among them protesters on the march or gathered collectively. A close look at their hands shows the widespread adoption of varied gestures with roots that once distinguished political affiliation now side by side, in unison. Such diffuse occurrence made the task of this false propagandist much easier. The poster's graphics confound us. Their concentrated density oppresses the eye; their contradictions confuse and tire. To achieve its aim, this piece of state-issued propaganda had to convince the viewer that the antiapartheid movement of the mid- to late 1980s was fractious, ill-suited to govern, and that its participants and parts were fundamentally the same. Their likeness was Biko's own, anchored in an activism construed here as centered on race, thus in all cases destructive to national interest.

Early Odes to Biko in Popular Graphics

The dramatically intensified state suppression of Black Consciousness in the last quarter of 1977 hardly ended its spread. Indeed, by early 1978 new cultural and political groups were created in the wake of the historic October 19 banning of BC organizations and detentions. Among them was *Staffrider,* a literary journal created to "feature the work of community-based projects" and "resist officially sanctioned culture and its concomitant aims of domination."[14] Among its initiators was Mothobi Mutloatse, a writer with a strong sense of black consciousness "without whom," Mike Kirkwood insists, "there would have been no *Staffrider.*"[15] The journal ultimately became one of the most successful of its kind in the country, and although debates about the degree to which it promoted Black Consciousness have circulated almost from the start, BC has a place in the work of a good many contributors whose own black consciousness is either quietly asserted or overtly manifest.[16] Rather than query whether or not *Staffrider* provided evidence of Black Consciousness, I suggest that we regard the journal as a forum in which BC was able to continue bearing fruitful impact and response.[17] Of interest here are artworks reproduced within the journal's earliest issues that paid tribute to Steve Biko.

Staffrider printed the drawings of Nkoana Harry Moyaga (b. 1954) several times. He made *Time Has Run Out* (Figure 4.2) in response to a poem of the same title

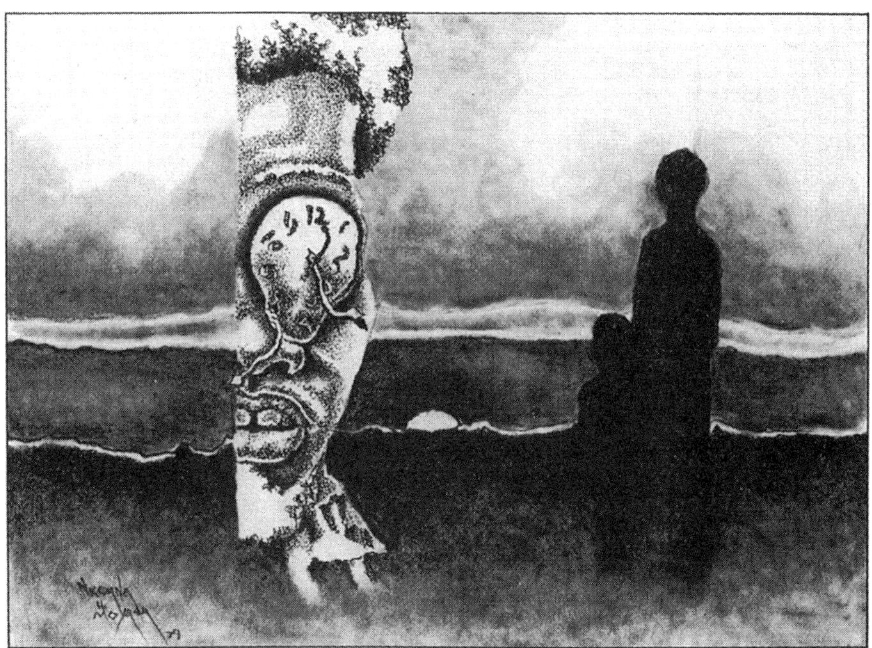

FIGURE 4.2. Nkoane Harry Moyaga, *Time Has Run Out*. Printed in *Staffrider* (November/December 1979): 5.

by Mongane Wally Serote; they were printed together in the journal's winter issue of 1979.[18] In the poem, the protagonist walks alone beneath distant stars that "keep whistling and whistling" in response to the night's "bright eye [that] keeps whispering and whispering." They tell of Biko's last days. "Listen," Serote tells us,

> these fucking stars
> whistled like this once long ago
> when one man
> walked like all of us do
> and then he was naked
> and then he was chained on the leg
> and then he was on the floor covered with a blanket
> in a landrover

> destined to make 1,000 km in that state
> to another cell
> where he woke up one morning
> naked
> chained
> alone
> with brain damage, his blanket wet
> his eyes strange as they said;
> and i dare say
> his damaged memory told him now, that he was going to die. . . .

In drawing the poem, Moyaga turned to Fraser MacLean's photograph of Biko for a template (see Figures 6.1 and 6.4) but cut away the right side of his face. The portrait floats in a space in between, half here, half not, distinguished from his surroundings by the fine point of the pen that defines his features. Nearby, people from two generations look to the horizon where a sunset creates waves of color across the sky. The line that crosses this bright star—creating its horizon, moving the land toward black—stems from Biko's mouth. Serote writes that the "bright eye-ball" of night "eats away into the bone of the distance of my life" and creates a noise that keeps "throbbing on my memory about the distances we made." Those "milestones" of progress are the lives sacrificed so that liberation will come. They weigh heavily, are felt everywhere, these

> broken droplets of blood which are now splashed
> and are scattered in the streets
> on fences
> and on walls of houses we live in
> on ceilings
> on floors and on desks
> even on floors of land-rovers.

The clock that melts away from Biko's left eye recalls Salvador Dali's well-known *Persistence of Memory* (1931), a work Moyaga surely discussed with fellow artists around Pretoria in the early seventies (see chapter 1). But it is Serote who secures the meaning of the clock in this context. It is "the heart of our country," which "when it makes its pulse, ticking time, wounds us." Pulling away from Biko's face, its hands pointing to both the sun and the voice-wave of Black Consciousness that covers it, the clock reminds that time has run out:

> too much blood has been spilled. . . . blood, no matter how little of it,
> when it spills, spills on the brain—on the memory of a nation—it is
> as if the sea floods the earth. . . . can someone, teach us how to mount
> the wound, and fight.

time has run out—

period.

Serote captured the thoughts of many when he wrote that the violent deaths of
BC adherents

> float like a rotting corpse would on
>
> > water
> on the memory of the people; . . .
> [who know] that the chain must be broken . . .
> yet,
> that isn't enough
> memories don't break chains. . . .

People break chains. *Time Has Run Out* is a call to act. Recalling the inspirational youth of 1976 who evidenced their own black consciousness, Serote wrote,

> and soweto will answer
> that:

school children took to the street one day. there will never be another soweto.
nor, south africa. there are many kinds of death and soweto knows them all,
south africa, too, and southern africa. you cannot kill children like cattle and
then hope that guns are a monopoly. we were born like everybody else, and
like everybody else, we know when it is too late or, to put it another way, when
there is nothing any longer to lose. we made love in strange places: ghettoes.
that is, we gave birth in these holes. we learnt from the pain and sorrow of
having lost our children to so many and such cruel deaths as malnutrition or
murder or sadness even dying while throwing spears or stones and being shot
dead. we can now say, while we claim our land and die in the process: *our
history is a culture of resistance.* [emphasis added]

The notion that a single "culture of resistance" brought about the fall of apartheid prevails in rhetoric that reduces varied ideologies to a single monolith called "the struggle" of the 1980s. My singular aim here is to dispel this notion by excavating BC iconography from varied organs—literary, political, and artistic (sometimes all at once). Although the modes of expression in publications like *Staffrider* and *Frank Talk* differed (literary/artistic on the one hand, and opinion/organization on the other), their language of origin is the same: their home is Black Consciousness. Individuals who read one publication might not have read the other, but that editors at both presses appeal to a like audience is evidenced in that both chose to highlight Moyaga's untitled tribute to Steve Biko shown in Figure 4.3. *Staffrider* made the same portrait available in poster form in 1979. It was the first in a poster series of influential South Africans, suggesting that the journal's readers were readily responsive to Black Consciousness. The series was printed in sepia, an aesthetic choice that prompts familial connection by way of old photographs more than it does political document. Five years on, editors at *Frank Talk,* media organ of the Azanian People's Organization (AZAPO), printed it on the September/October 1984 cover. Readers had a glossy, small-scale version of the portrait that could be torn out and hung up, and indeed Moyaga's artistry encouraged this. Thus we find that Black Consciousness appeals across the spectrum of ideological approaches—nonracial on one hand, antiethnic and cast as racial on the other—as advanced by the journals in question.

Harry Moyaga's drawing recalls his *Time Has Run Out* in that both blend realistic forms with imaginary ones. Biko's head is given in three-quarter perspective with eyes cast toward a vow: "I will only vote for a free Azania"—this, too, in response to the state's attempt to divide the nation through its new tricameral parliament. Stylistically, Moyaga's work is similar to that of the better-known Fikile Magadlela. Both trained in townships along the Johannesburg–Pretoria nexus in the early 1970s to create works steeped in the BC ideal of honoring ancestors. Here Biko is one with the rocky land that surrounds him. The terrain seems incapable of yielding fruit, yet a tree has sprouted from a fissure at right and grown sturdy through time. Its branches stretch outward toward a blazing sun and the full-winged bird at top whose legs echo the rippled bark below. The bird is sacrificed—its head is missing—but its life force gushes forth and radiates downward to bathe Azania with the strength of its ancestors. Biko, who knew his own strength well, gazes toward text that takes a figural form. The combination of gaze, a vow configured as a bust, and the personal pronoun *I* solidify the power of generations that Moyaga envisioned in enumerable drawings of the period.

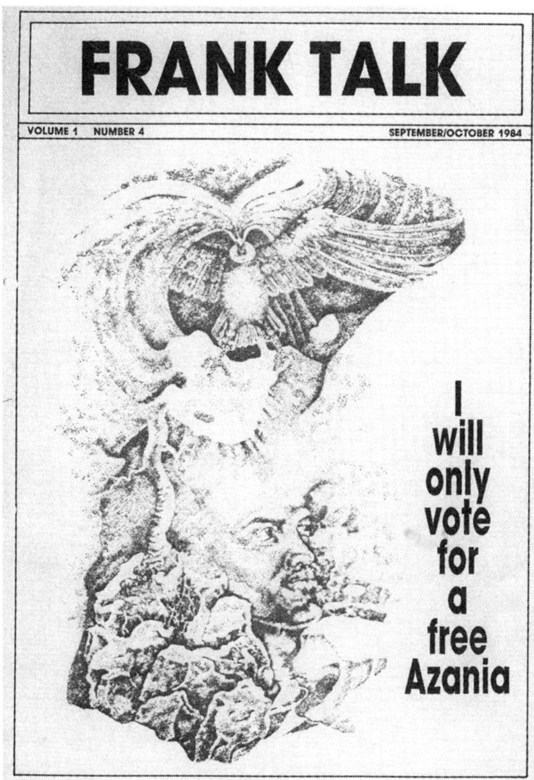

FIGURE 4.3. Nkoana Harry Moyaga, *Bantu Steve Biko*, 1979. Cover of *Frank Talk* 1, no. 4 (September/October 1984): 459. Also issued as a poster printed in sepia and sold as No. 1 in the *Staffrider* Poster Series, 70 x 50 cm.

Founded in 1978, AZAPO quickly became the best-known supporter of Black Consciousness because it publically claimed this mantle. Indeed, today AZAPO still garners the attention of reporters when they seek an "authentic" BC voice. The images it printed in newsletters and posters convey the agency and self-possession of its founders, albeit on a smaller scale and with fewer material options (thus aesthetic variability) than its better-funded counterparts in "the struggle" against apartheid. AZAPO issued fewer posters in the 1980s than did the better-funded United Democratic Front, and often it pooled resources with other bodies that laid claim to Black Consciousness post-1977 when the South African Students' Organization and the Black Peoples' Convention were banned. The poster in Figure 4.4 is a case in point. It unites AZAPO with the Azanian Students' Movement (AZASM), the members of which were

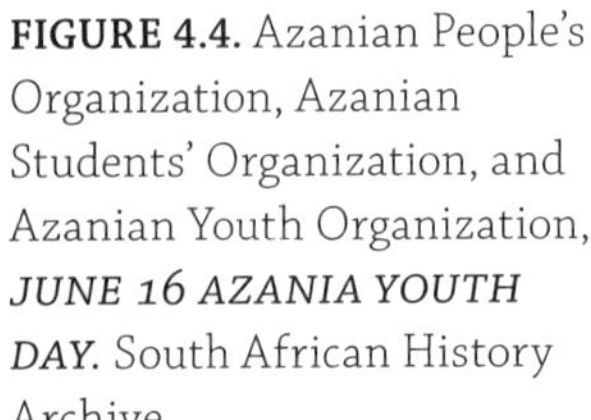

FIGURE 4.4. Azanian People's Organization, Azanian Students' Organization, and Azanian Youth Organization, *JUNE 16 AZANIA YOUTH DAY.* South African History Archive.

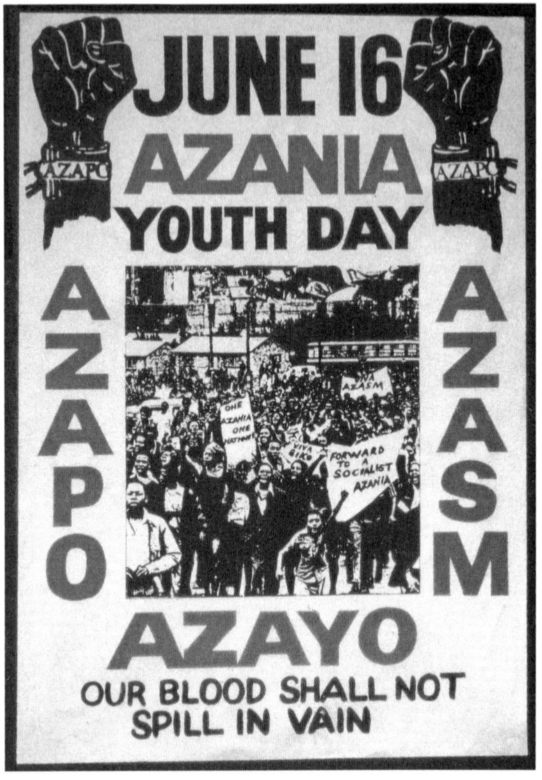

at university, and the Azanian Youth Organization (AZAYO), which attracted secondary students. Like the poster in Plate 5, *JUNE 16 AZANIA YOUTH DAY* also celebrates the 1976 uprisings. But here the BC lifeline is firm (acronyms are given in red), and it extends into the future: "OUR BLOOD SHALL NOT SPILL IN VAIN." Firmly clenched fists tug free of chains. At center a photographic montage of youth assembled in protest hold white banners with black lettering. The BPC's old motto, "One Azania One Nation," appears here, as does "Viva Biko." The format of this poster is in keeping with most others that AZAPO issued, as is the insistent use of the possessive.

It is harder to locate expressions of Black Consciousness within organs that promoted a nonracialist approach, but they surface in the images many promoted. The editorial direction of *Staffrider,* for instance, shifted its mandate soon after it was formed to include voices and visions of contributors regard-

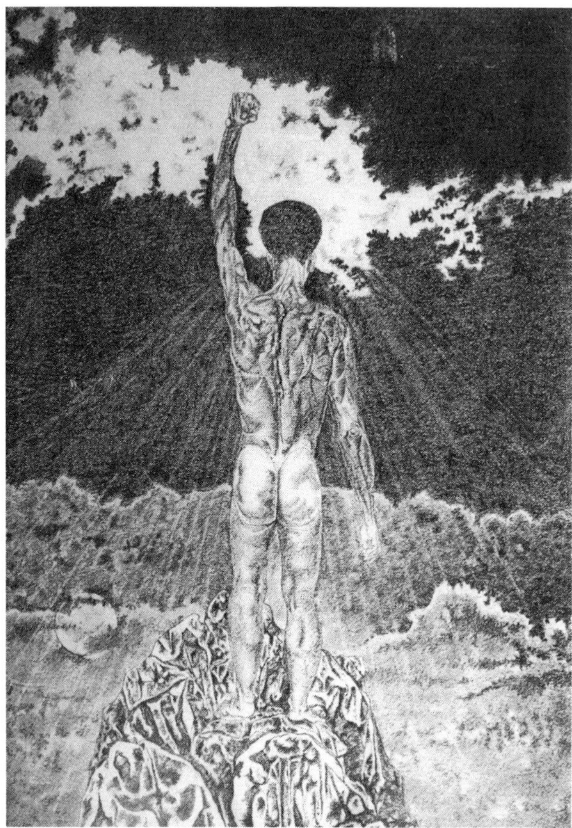

FIGURE 4.5. Dikobé Martins, *Untitled*. Back cover of *Staffrider* 4 (April/May 1981): 1.

less of skin color. But this in itself did not necessitate that BC be abandoned in any way. For instance, Dikobé Martins, who is unquestionably rooted in BC, contributed several drawings to *Staffrider*. Recalling the poem by Christopher van Wyk that opens this chapter, the man Martins drew in Figure 4.5 has risen to confront the streams of white light that shower upon his body, disrobed to reveal the strength and beauty of blackness. The one item that he wears is attached to his wrist: the round face of a watch is visible beneath his raised clenched fist. Steve Biko was known to have worn a large watch and, like Biko, this man represents Everyman. Muscles drawn taut, he responds not to the hazy orb veiled by clouds at lower left but to a second light, one that emerges from a frayed white field that fights to claim space within a predominantly black sky.

The man's body is like the landscape on which he stands: muscles, tendons, and veins define him, their ridges and shadows echoed in the rocks and cracks of the mountain's peak. He cedes no terrain. Indeed, with the sky darkening over the bright fissure, black appears to actively claim the space that white has taken. Although *Staffrider* did not include the title of this work, editors chose it as the departing image in the April/May 1981 issue. Placed on the back cover, this work by Martins salutes the magazine's many readers and contributors.

A Culture of Resistance: Black Consciousness in Popular Graphics of the 1980s

Highlighted within the same 1981 issue of *Staffrider* is an interview with Mongane Wally Serote, who said of his own artistic roots, "there was no doubt: I was clearly associated with black consciousness."[19] Born in Sophiatown and raised in Alexandra, this notable poet chose exile in Gaborone, Botswana, in late 1977. There he worked to "revive the spirit of Mihloti," the Alexandra-based performance troupe of BC-oriented artists he helped found in 1971 (with Thami Mnyele, among others).[20] The arts collective he eventually helped create in Gaborone, the Medu Art Ensemble, included visual arts and became for Serote the thing "I value . . . most" due to its emphasis on training, critique, and its commitment to "disseminating political awareness."[21] With the guidance of Black Consciousness artists (who were also leaders in this context), Medu became the most influential producer of political graphics in southern Africa.

The South Africans who founded the Medu Art Ensemble in 1977 held Black Consciousness close. Today Serote remains the best known among these founders; the others were Pethu Serote, Mandla Langa, and Tim Williams.[22] Medu was similar in profile to South African arts organizations in which these people once held significant roles. It was planned as and became a training facility for music, film, theater, photography, graphic art, and design. It also housed units in research and publishing. *Medu,* a SePedi word meaning roots, followed a line of BC-oriented cultural bodies organized in South Africa in the early to mid-1970s. The Dashiki MDALI, Mpumalanga Arts Ensemble, Malopoets, Bayajula Arts Group, Madi, Allah Poets, and the Creative Youth Association all come to mind.[23] The creation of another BC-oriented troupe beyond South Africa's borders made sense for artists who had gone into exile. Other BC artists joined the collective: Jonas Gwangwa gave to Medu's music unit; Mike Khan ran photography; Bachana Mokwena, once of Dashiki, headed the theater unit.[24]

Medu originally followed BC's antiethnic approach to membership. Like its antecedents, it excluded whites from joining. And, like earlier BC bodies, from the beginning Medu members debated the ongoing necessity of restricted membership. By 1979, they decided to include all Botswana residents as students and members, and they hired Thami Mnyele to teach graphic arts.[25] Scholars tend to identify Medu's first "white" members as Albio Gonzalez and Theresa Devant,[26] but given Medu's investment in tricontinental liberation, I wonder whether the descriptor *white* does justice. After all, Gonzalez was born in Cuba to Catalonians, and Devant was born in Spain.[27] As Catalonians were on the verge of winning independence from Spain, and Medu newsletters compared this impending change with Cuba's own,[28] I suggest that racial descriptors of the kind applied in this history are too limiting since they fail to capture the more nuanced, common objectives of tricontinential awareness.

Eventually, Medu worked to formalize relationships with the National Museum and Art Gallery and the ANC. Medu's founders convinced ANC leaders that culture could be used to mobilize support for its cause; it could be a weapon of struggle. As a direct result of Medu, the ANC established a Department of Arts and Culture and, as Elizabeth Morton wrote, "began to fund the arts for the first time in its long history."[29] As we write the history of Medu, and that of a well-known "culture of resistance" in South Africa of the 1980s, we must remember the vital role that Black Consciousness played within both.

It is important to emphasize that Medu's decision to open its doors to all people did not mean that Black Consciousness no longer swayed its operations and output, as has been suggested so frequently as to assume the commonplace.[30] Medu's acceptance of white members indicates that by 1982, the Serotes, Williams, Langa, Mnyele, and others who had joined agreed that some white people actually listened to their voices. They heard, they listened, and they learned. BC had created the very atmosphere in which Medu *could* exist, even thrive, and Medu artists adopted its values regardless of their own skin color. The three "basic principles" to which Medu members pledged "unswerving loyalty" in 1980 were also BC principles: "ANTI-RACISM, NATIONAL DEMOCRACY AND SELF-DETERMINATION."[31] By this time, the "Year of People's Unity," Black Consciousness had achieved its central aim. It had empowered once-marginalized people to fashion their own future without ceding territory to the voiced visions of liberal activists.

Education was Medu's purpose. Botswana registered it as a cultural society structured to teach a wide variety of arts—graphic, filmed, written, performed, and played—and to provide printed graphics for local community organizations, but it also devoted considerable energy to antiapartheid campaigns across the border. Medu's three units, Publications and Research, Theater, and Coordinating Committee, were further subdivided and specialized. Over Medu's eight years of existence and among a good many projects diverse in scope, its graphic arts and design team created at least eighteen political posters annually in its bid to end apartheid.[32] They regularly printed up to five thousand posters per edition.[33] This is exceptional since the unit was small (between two and ten members) and its mandate was large. The team also ran seminars and workshops, published, created murals, and undertook commercial work with an eye toward facilitating sponsorship of particular projects. The artists in this unit—Albio Gonzalez, Heinz Klugg, Gordon Metz, Thami Mnyele, Judy Seidman, and Tim Williams among them—committed themselves to cause-driven work that was "articulate but simple . . . with clear political insight . . . and firm revolutionary sentiment."[34] They thus promoted the creation of what has been called "political art," with the distinction that "it is not the subject of the picture, but the comment on the subject that makes [a] work of art 'political.' *Political art must not only record a situation, it must criticise it.*"[35] This call to make art active—to forge culture into a weapon against apartheid—recalls the early BC belief that to know oppression is not enough. As Biko put it in 1976, "One must, if conscious, be committed to the idea of getting himself out of the morass. . . . conscientization implies a desire to engage people in an emancipatory process."[36] Members of the Medu Art Ensemble committed themselves to this task precisely. Aware of their own agency as artists, they worked to educate and cultivate collective action against South Africa's oppressive apartheid state.

Black Consciousness iconography is present in many of the posters that Medu issued during its eight years of existence.[37] For instance, Judy Seidman adopted the broken chain motif in 1982 when she made *You Have Struck a Rock* in celebration of Women's Day (Figure 4.6). The woman figured here knows the strength of her own agency. She has freed herself from bondage and strides forward ready to crush any attempt to dislodge the substantive might of sisterhood. Her thumb extends outward from her fist to signify her allegiance to the ANC. Through such pictorial subtleties we find two principal actors—the ANC and BC—unified in vision and newly invigorated in their common objective: ending apartheid. The ANC came to dominate resistance discourse, and Seidman's poster reflects this edge. The colors she used, which shift gradually from black to yellow to green, are those of the ANC, and the phrase she chose

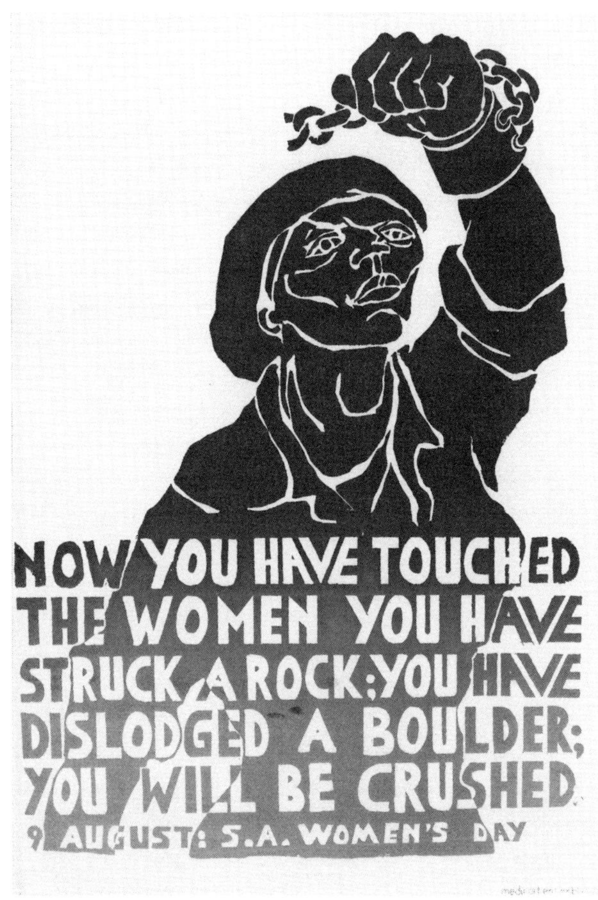

FIGURE 4.6. Judy Seidman for Medu, *You Have Struck a Rock*, 1982. Silkscreen by Medu Art Ensemble, Gaborone. South African History Archive, University of the Witwatersrand, No. 2618. Courtesy of Judy Seidman.

comes from an infamous event organized by the Federation of South African Women (FedSAW), which was linked to the ANC in important ways but included women who affiliated otherwise, too. The words that span this woman's torso come from a song sung by women who joined together on August 9, 1956, to protest a change to the Urban Areas Act that would require black women to carry an identity passbook. Twenty-six thousand in number, the marchers accompanied leaders of FedSAW who presented Prime Minister J. G. Strijdom with a petition against the amendment that was signed by tens of thousands of people.[38] Ever since, the well-known phrase "You have struck a rock" has symbolized the strength of women in concert.

Seidman (b. 1950) created some of Medu's most interesting posters, as did her friend Thami Mnyele. In 1979, Mnyele moved to Gaborone to join friends he had made in years prior while working with Milhoti Black Theatre. He quickly became the voice of Medu's graphic arts program through interviews published in its quarterly newsletter, a publication that periodically held posters tucked into its folds that were then carried to subscribers over the border into South Africa.[39] There they would be photocopied and further distributed. Dikobé Martins, also involved in Medu programs, described them as "treasured objects" (and often banned ones) that South Africans shared and handled with care.[40] The fact that Mnyele later joined the ANC does not mean he renounced Black Consciousness.[41] Indeed, he rejoiced that through Medu's projects, "we . . . have been able to make our voice heard."[42] Although South African agents murdered Mnyele in a raid on Medu on June 14, 1985, his voice and vision continued to resonate since both were well preserved through print.[43]

December 16 marked Heroes' Day for both the ANC and SASO, to which Mnyele once belonged. While with Medu, he celebrated this occasion by creating a poster in 1983 in honor of African leaders (Figure 4.7). He drew the image from an unattributed photograph found in a new book about mural art in Mozambique.[44] Attention is directed to a soldier who carries a rifle slung over his shoulder. Back turned to us as though he is ready to move deeper into the underbrush at his feet, he bids farewell to the child and adult who regard him with awe and appreciation. The text excerpts a speech given in 1972 by ANC President Oliver Tambo provocatively titled "Mobilise Our Black Power."[45] In it Tambo urges all to resist apartheid by taking up arms in the manner of Shaka, Moshoeshoe, and Maqoma, and to take up the pen, as did Plaatjie.[46] Although Mnyele quoted Tambo, he surely recalled the emphasis BC had placed on such leaders, since honoring them was also stressed by bodies in which Mnyele previously worked. Recall, too, that Steve Biko testified at length about the need to revise the teaching of black history at the SASO–BPC trial of 1976, which Mnyele had attended.[47] Further, Biko's words on this matter were well-known and readily available in print despite restrictions. Banned in 1973, he published the following in two articles written under the pen name "Frank Talk," which had been reprinted several times before Mnyele made this poster. Biko wrote:

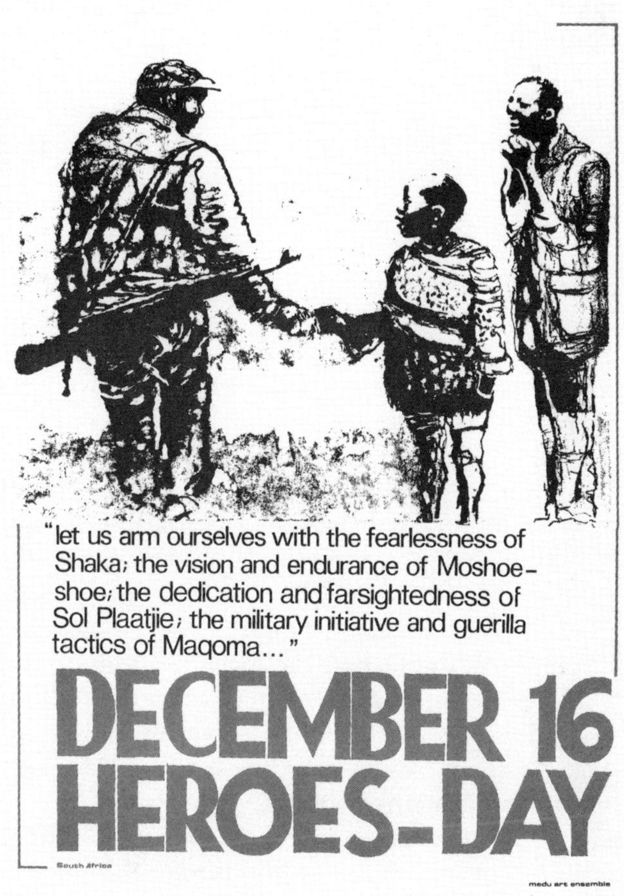

FIGURE 4.7. Thami Mnyele for Medu, *December 16 Heroes-Day*, 1983. Offset litho by Medu Art Ensemble, Gaborone, No. 1556. South African History Archive 1556.

[A] lot of attention has to be paid to our history if we as blacks want to aid each other in our coming into consciousness. We have to rewrite our history and describe in it the heroes that formed the core of resistance to the white invaders. More has to be revealed and stress has to be laid on the successful nation-building attempts by people like Shaka, Moshoeshoe and Hintsa.

Our culture must be defined in concrete terms. We must relate the past to the present and demonstrate an historical evolution of the modern African.[48]

In discussing Mnyele's work today, we must situate the powerful influence of Black Consciousness in his life. We see it, too, in the very fabric of resistance aesthetics that he promoted heart and soul. Within two months of joining Medu, he described an urgent need he felt to "say something" with his art, to speak through visual form.[49] His voice and vision were always fueled by an awareness of his own power to persuade.

Mnyele had a significant role in the famed Culture and Resistance symposium and festival that Medu hosted at the University of Botswana on July 5–9, 1982. He was also key to an exhibition at the National Museum and Art Gallery in Gaborone that ran concurrently, *Art toward Social Development,* for which he teamed with Gordon Metz to create a poster that fulfilled Medu's objectives (Figure 4.8). It has a clear message and is artistically compelling. A man clad in white walks on a rope of heavy twine. His cap, a beret, suggests he is a man of years. He is also a man of skill: he walks blindfolded and steadies himself with a balancing bar. He is used to this performance since he undertakes it most days, negotiating the well-worn line between suburban and periurban realities. To the right, his place of employ—lush gardens, refreshing pools, sunshine. To the left, his place of rest and perhaps also home—dry, crowded, beset by pollution. But his journey will be disrupted this day. *Art toward Social Development* is a knife that alters the operational boundaries. The coupling of culture and resistance expands the zone of awareness on all fronts. It "conscientizes," a word frequently used by both Mnyele and Medu.[50] The conference built on the work of Black Consciousness in that it helped create a "conscientised cultural worker" to further its objective: freedom for South Africa.[51]

The political awareness of many conference participants was rooted in Black Consciousness. Mnyele's public remarks emphasized the fundamental importance of process—art making as collaboration, thus art that is responsive to others' needs—and they equated vision with "voice" as he urged "cultural workers and artists" to embrace their role in "the struggle for national liberation and self-determination."[52] Like Mnyele, Gavin Jantjes and Dikobé Martins offered papers that, among other things, reinforced the social function of art for Africa's people. Jantjes saw the creative embrace of new techniques as inherently African, evidenced in African art, itself made "in the service of man."[53] Martins spoke of artists' "ethical responsibility" to critique social realities through their work; in this they would fulfill their "historical role" since their work would "become a process—a living, growing thing that people can relate to, identify with, be part of, understand."[54] In a final example, journalist Cynthia Kross of

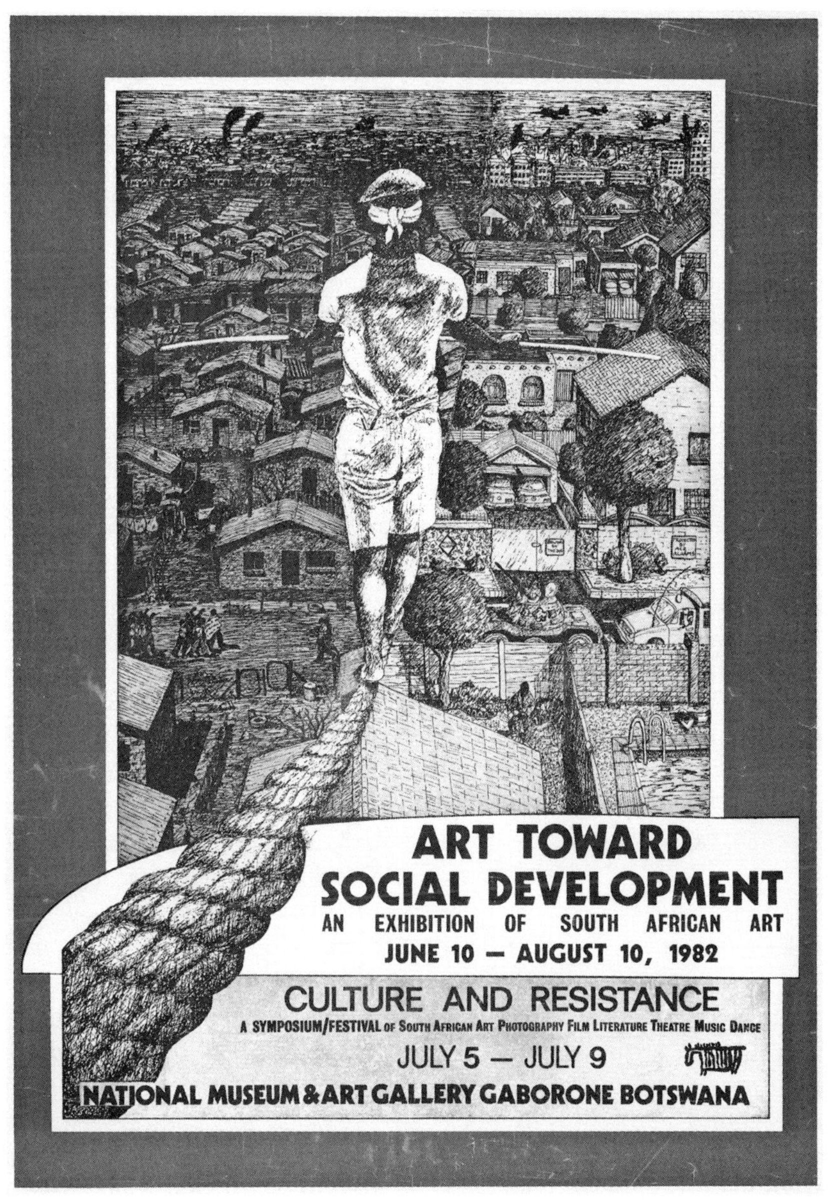

FIGURE 4.8. Thami Mnyele and Gorden Metz for Medu, *Art toward Social Development*, 1982. Offset lithograph from the Culture and Resistance festival in Gaborone, Botswana. Courtesy of South African History Archive, University of the Witwatersrand.

Staffrider reported that piano great Abdullah Ibrahim (aka Dollar Brand) described the private realization of self as "necessary for each individual . . . before society as a whole can be transformed. 'After all,' he maintained, 'it's no good shooting if you shoot in the wrong direction.'"[55] It should be said, too, that the conference offered a glimpse at a question that South Africans began publically debating in 1979 and continued to question in the decade to come, but which is given less emphasis here. The question concerned whether to commit one's work to the common cause of ending apartheid, and if so how.[56]

People from Africa, the Americas, and Europe attended the Culture and Resistance festival; several were South African, both in exile and not.[57] John Berndt and Lionel Davis were among the South Africans who returned home inspired by its message. Already connected to Cape Town's Community Arts Project (CAP), in 1983 they added a media unit that trained members of local organizations in the specialized field of poster making.[58] CAP Media and another body, the Screen Training Project (STP) in Johannesburg, subsequently played a significant part in the use of protest graphics by grassroots organizations, which had become widespread by the early part of the decade.[59] In 1983, a good many of these people-powered organizations (more than six hundred in all) gathered behind the United Democratic Front (UDF), an umbrella body for organizations committed to political freedoms.[60] The UDF readily embraced culture as a "weapon of resistance" and sent affiliates to the STP and CAP Media to produce posters and T-shirts, thereby generating a swell in resistance graphics in this period. The UDF has been explicitly tied to the Culture and Resistance festival.[61] Indeed, John Peffer calls Medu "a model, in exile, of UDF cultural operations inside South Africa" and rightly says that "the look and temperament of 'the people's culture' were already fully formed at the time of the launching of the UDF movement in 1983."[62] The problem, however, is in a persistent recounting of events that links Medu, its festival, and the UDF to the politics of nonracialism so that Black Consciousness is wiped out of the picture. It is as though these three elements move history forward without any precedent. The record is much more complex. The historical narrative as written is too clean. In what follows, I trace BC iconography in graphics produced by organizations that adopted different modes of combating apartheid. Some promoted their tract as nonracial, a choice that implied that others were "racial" at heart. Ironically, this tactic silenced the presence of Black Consciousness, which is fundamentally about voice.

Charterists and the Spirit of Nonracialism
at Work against Black Consciousness

In his compelling history of the United Democratic Front, Jeremy Seekings notes that Steve Biko "proposed some kind of a united front" well before the UDF was launched in 1983.[63] Seekings also calls the period between 1977 and 1979 one of "strategic ferment" for the exiled ANC, which "began to reassess their assumption that armed incursions alone would ignite a mass revolutionary movement."[64] In other words, the ANC was learning from Black Consciousness. BC bodies of the 1970s had successfully organized aid for and protest marches by township residents. They had also emphasized culture as an important vehicle for protest politics. These successes are seldom noted in narratives that herald the ANC, its promotion of the Freedom Charter, and its abiding belief in nonracialism as victors in South Africa's civil war. The historical record, visual and otherwise, implores us to revise the dominant narrative.

Seekings reveals that the ANC encouraged members in South Africa to seek leadership roles in organizations that were formally aligned with Black Consciousness, but to do so without revealing their Charterist inclinations. In this way, the exiled ANC could both build broad support *within* South Africa, and bring what it called "a third force" (BC) into line. Thus men like Popo Molefe and Curtis Nkondo, "clandestine" Charterists, became officers in the newly formed Azanian People's Organization and the Azanian Students' Organization in 1978 and 1979. Seekings describes others who also "sought to strengthen anti-apartheid forces whilst building the Charterists presence within them." By 1979, covert operatives followed recommendations of the ANC's newly appointed Politico-Military Strategy Commission. In the commission's words, its agents were to not "shun any organisation" that worked against apartheid, even if "it did not embrace [the ANC's] long-term revolutionary aims or criticized part of [the ANC's] strategy" and despite their likely eventual "parting of ways." Nonetheless, and despite Nkondo's expulsion from AZASO in 1980, Charterists had so thoroughly infiltrated the group that they "gained control" of it one year later and derided BC at AZASO's national conference and other events that it sponsored. By the end of 1981, "Charterists had planted their flag at the head of resistance politics," says Seekings. To see this metaphoric flag through popular graphics is to wonder anew over what became of Black Consciousness in the 1980s.

"This view of front politics," Seekings writes, was "endorsed in the ANC's

Strategic Review [and was thereafter] reflected in repeated efforts over the following three years, culminating in the formation of the United Democratic Front."[65] Yet somehow we keep forgetting that "this view" was Biko's own. To be sure, UDF graphics are as varied in character as were the organizations that joined forces behind it. As a front for bodies working to end apartheid, the UDF coordinated the efforts of affiliates more than it dictated direction, so it is not unusual that organizations with different strategies made use of its services.[66] Although the UDF promoted Charterist aims and was nonracial in character, this could not be said of all UDF affiliates. I believe that the dominant narrative of nonracialism—and its casting of Black Consciousness as fundamentally racial—has caused us to overlook the many ways in which Black Consciousness provided the basis for a heightened level of resistance in the decade. Here I devote analysis to the ways that nonracial bodies borrowed BC motifs and ideas; they are present in the graphics of the UDF and in those of its successor, the Mass Democratic Movement (MDM).

Publicity was the UDF's main thrust, and its affiliates benefited from technologies that were new.[67] The photocopier and printing methods like silkscreening eased the production of posters, pamphlets, and newsletters that typically included imagery, be it a familiar logo or something more evocative. T-shirts became ready vehicles for graphic arts that moved and matched the expressiveness of the people who wore them. Soon after its launch in August 1983, the UDF began sending affiliates to two facilities for production of posters and the like: the STP in Johannesburg and CAP Media in Cape Town.[68] Although some UDF affiliates produced graphics in-house, poster producers adopted common criteria for effective communication.[69] They searched for iconic images that were easily recognizable and carried meaning within a tradition of resistance; the raised clenched fist was foremost among them. Text was to be minimal and memorable, and colors necessarily complemented the message at hand. Photographs of jubilant activists were more commonly used than were those that recorded violence, but both have a significant place in media of this period. Portraits of fallen comrades were worn on T-shirts in ever-greater frequency since funerals became important sites of protest.

At CAP Media and the STP, posters were almost always designed through collective effort. Those running the programs worked with those who needed the poster, and its elements were chosen through consultation. When time was less pressing, they trained activists in the art of poster making. The idea was to build a new visual language that could be used repeatedly to build cohesiveness.[70]

In this way, local struggles would be seen as part of a broad movement. As described in 1983 by the UDF secretary for the Transvaal region (which included Johannesburg and Pretoria and much else besides), posters and other media drew people "into a movement that was both increasingly coherent and more clearly purposive."[71] In words that resonate strongly with Black Consciousness, Judy Seidman described the common objective that drove the choice of images:

> "Our art should speak to the immediate community, to the people who brought us up, who speak to us, who are living through what has made us as we are." The arts should build "self-awareness and self-image, link our people's experiences, create new understandings of our lives, and pass on these understandings." From this should come a vision of "how to take our community forward."[72]

Two STP posters made for UDF affiliates are discussed here; the first borrows a prominent BC motif and the second claims BC history as its own. The image used in *Resist Bantustan Violence* (Figure 4.9) recalls the logo of the banned Black Peoples' Convention, but the hands break a rifle rather than a chain. Coupled with minimal text, this motif exemplifies effective communication in poster design. Its BC undercurrent would have also resonated with members of the South African Allied Workers Union (SAAWU) who worked at STP to create it. After all, their union was established in March 1979 in East London following the split of another BC-inspired body, the Black Allied Workers' Union.[73] Some twenty thousand in number, SAAWU members refused to work with the state's puppet leaders in the "Border Region" of Ciskei, the so-called homeland of Xhosa people that was given "independence" from South Africa in 1981.[74] The government of Lennox Sebe, self-proclaimed Life President of Ciskei, had little patience for unions since, as he put it, "Ciskei itself is a trade union looking after workers' interests."[75] He thus authorized the use of force, often executed in extreme forms, to crush SAAWU, which actively opposed the creation of Bantustans, let alone their administration. *Resist Bantustan Violence* urges viewers to support SAAWU members in their peaceful approach to combating the forces that conspired to limit their livelihoods, rights, and dignity: South Africa, big business, and Sebe.[76]

Black Consciousness is recalled in a 1986 UDF poster that revises history in order to take credit for the student uprisings of 1976 (Plate 5). *10 Fighting Years 1976–1986* extends the life of the UDF by seven years; in reality, the organization was founded in 1983. That rhetorical gesture—reaching back into history

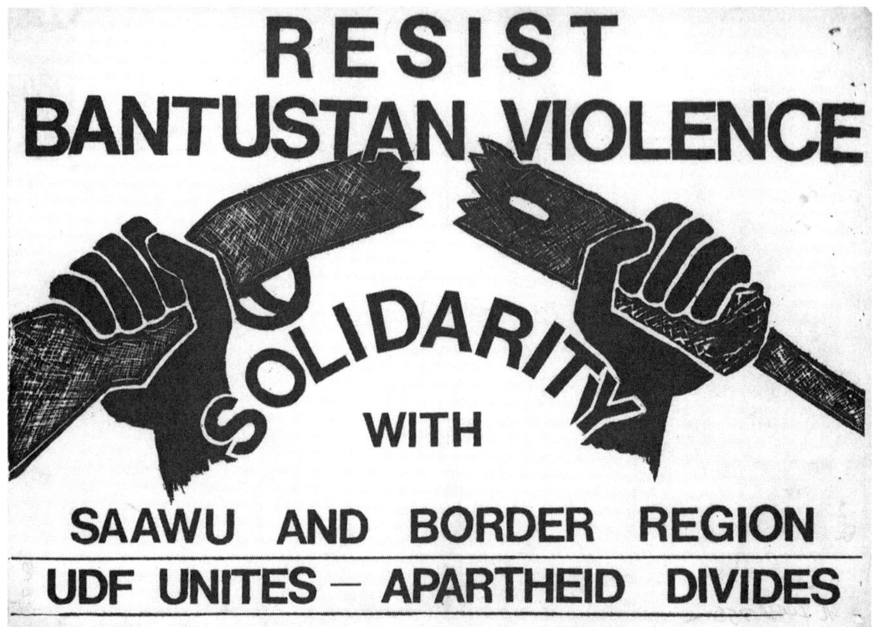

FIGURE 4.9. Screen Training Project for United Democratic Front, *Resist Bantustan Violence*. Artists not recorded. South African History Archive 756.

and sweeping it up alongside the present—suggests that nonracialism fueled the uprisings of June 1976. The BC that energized the students to resist changes at school is muted here. From design to print, the poster was fully created by the STP, which chose to bathe the decade in UDF colors of red, yellow, and black. Those gathered to honor the heroes of June 1976 are not students; they lack uniforms and almost invariably appear beyond their teenage years. Indeed, this generation became politically aware in the 1970s when Black Consciousness was at its height of influence. The UDF appealed to people of this generation by representing them here in assembled photographs and by prominently placing an icon of their times—the pietà of Hector Pieterson, among the first fallen in Soweto on June 16, 1976—on the blazing yellow shirt of the poster's dominant figure. The pietà trio casts a shadow, but it is covered, or absorbed, by the UDF logo. In ways both subtle and not, this poster evidences how the UDF used imagery (and explicitly rewrote its own history) to align its mission with that of Black Consciousness and overshadowed its legacy in the process.

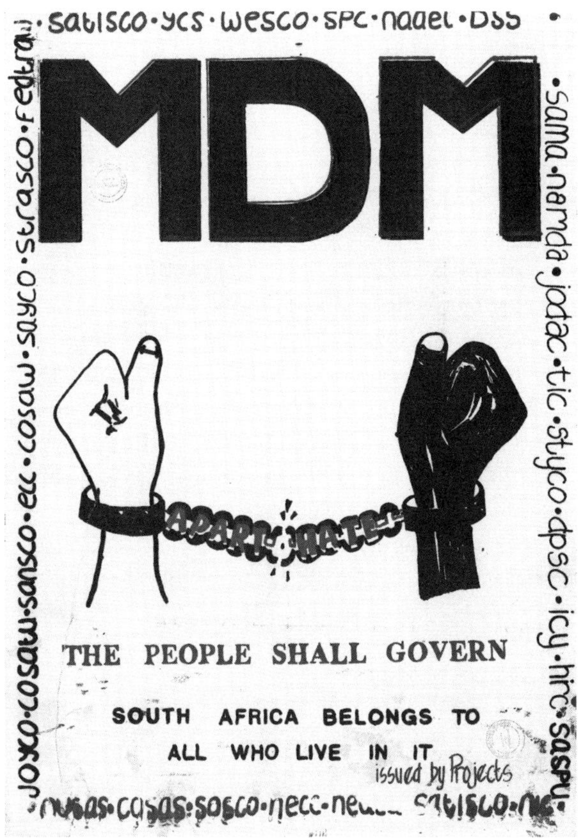

FIGURE 4.10. Mass Democratic Movement, *The People Shall Govern,* circa late 1980s. Issued by Projects. South African History Archive.

The UDF was effectively banned in February 1988.[77] In its place the Mass Democratic Movement (MDM) took shape with Murphy Morobe, once imprisoned for his role in Soweto's 1976 uprising, later a UDF publicity secretary, among key leaders. A poster supporting the MDM (Figure 4.10) explicitly uses BC's best-known motif in service of a Charterist clause that effectively "belongs" to the ANC by this time: "The people shall govern. South Africa belongs to all who live in it." The ANC's traditional salute, curled fingers with projected thumb, centers the organizations listed on the periphery, former UDF affiliates that now embrace the MDM's message.[78] Whether brazenly or unwittingly, here the MDM recorded the transmission of BC ideology through its ranks. Beneath the organization's weighty black acronym, white and black together break the oppressor's chain. Each adopts the ANC's recognizable salute. This poster is more than a record of BC iconography in the late 1980s: it effectively records the degree to which Black Consciousness influenced nonracial alignment in the period, and it directly communicates that bond. Black forearms originally broke the chains that bound them in the logo of the BPC. It also appeared on all official SASO documents between 1969 and 1977. The design is so firmly rooted in Black Consciousness that it became Steve Biko's departing gesture in the poster that mourners carried at his funeral (see Figure 2.6). The gesture's meaning became less certain after 1977 when, once forced to disband, BC adherents adopted varying approaches to dismantling apartheid. Innumerable photographs of political rallies and funerals from the 1980s witness a variety of salutes—it is not uncommon to see the ANC's classic curled fingers with thumb extended alongside BC's full fist with thumb laid over fingers—but the subtle change in thumb placement goes unremarked. The open palm salute of the also-banned Pan Africanist Congress is notable and rare. This suggests two things: one, BC's influence is certainly present through generations, but its location is not easily traced; two, we need a more critical engagement with the history and politics of nonracialism.

Conclusion

The South African state issued a state of emergency on July 21, 1985, and renewed it on June 12, 1986. In response, Sipho Hlati, then a student at Cape Town's Community Arts Project, made *Biko's Ghost Haunts Them . . .* (Figure 4.11).[79] The work is compelling because it directs attention to the presence of BC in both the UDF and AZAPO. A child at center immediately captures our interest. His bright shirt is the focal point for all parties. It names the painting, captures our eye, and draws the attention of the two large policemen who point their rifles at the person who wears it. This child's raised arm and clenched fist align with the spiraling fire behind.

Given the painting's structure, one assumes the armed men are the "them" of this child's shirt, but perhaps they are not. Hlati's use of color draws our eye to the object of this shirt, and elsewhere to a more compelling object within the painting. Conditions in the lower right are free of the smoke that spills out in other places across the landscape, but in the far distant corner at the end of this road are members of the UDF and AZAPO, holding their banners high, visible but veiled by the clouds of war. Might it be that Biko's ghost also haunts them?

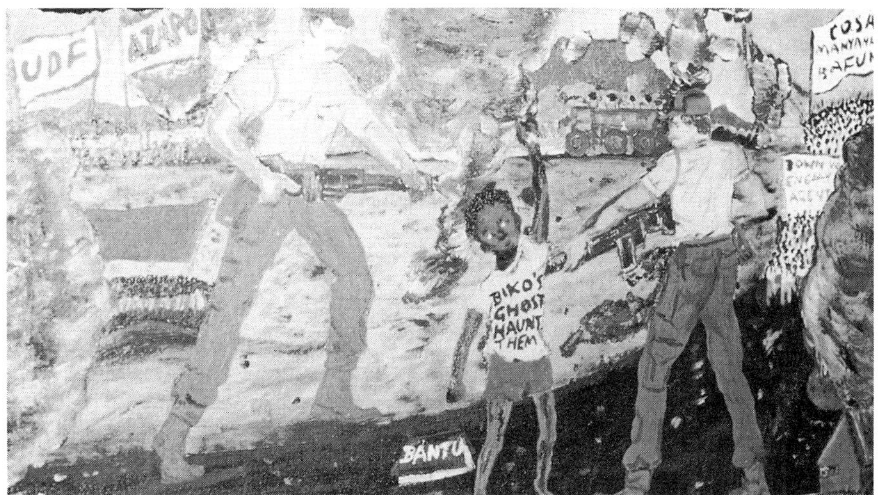

FIGURE 4.11. Sipho Hlati, *Biko's Ghost Haunts Them . . .*, 1985. Poster paint on paper. Location unknown; it was stolen in 1985.

After all, we have seen that BC is found in both parties and in others, besides. In Hlati's work it fills the townships outside Cape Town, its famed Table Mountain on the horizon. The throngs of people who march toward us from the right also embrace his message. The banners name their associations, all of which benefited from BC. Their energy builds in the fumes that engulf the landscape, and us with it, since Hlati framed the scene with the fires of Black Consciousness.

Certainly "Black Power" of the 1970s became "People's Power" in the 1980s, but this was more than mere rhetorical change. Those schooled in Black Consciousness of the 1970s refused the state's insistent analogy between Black Consciousness (out of South Africa) and Black Power (out of the United States). Although common in mission and mind, they argued that, unlike their American counterparts, South Africans did not operate from a position of power, because they lacked representational voice in the halls of government.[80] Rather, BC advocates insisted that their primary challenge was to instill a sense of pride through self-agency so that all South Africans would subsequently feel empowered to direct change in their own lives. Undoubtedly, Black Consciousness organizations achieved this aim. But in the troubling and still dominant discourse of nonracialism, People's Power of the 1980s supposedly arose without influence from the most persuasive political movement of the previous decade, Black Consciousness.

Although the record shows that members of SASO, BC's first visible force, labored to improve the physical lives, education, health, and well-being of township residents prior to 1977, the overriding message still renders them ineffectual. Thus, early in the twenty-first century, we still credit nonracialist organizations like the UDF, vehicles of People's Power, with creating the conditions through which apartheid would fall. As Seekings put it, "In South Africa people's power would involve people taking political and administrative control over their own lives in townships, schools, and factories, despite the state's military superiority."[81] He is right that "people's power was . . . unambiguously about power" by mid-1986, since a "discourse of power had conclusively replaced discourses of rights" previously advocated by Charterists and others.[82] Now let us recognize this: Black Consciousness created this reality since by then its agents understood the value of their own voice, and they had put it to use. Vitally, many whites had also learned to listen.

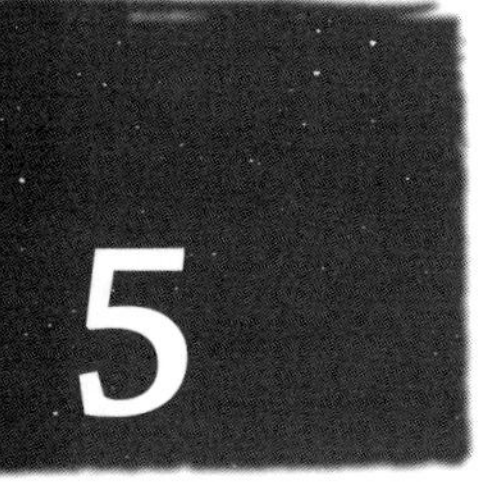

Silencing the Censors

Black Consciousness between the Lines in the 1980s

It was the Culture of Silence
For centuries we lived
In the shadows of oppression
And exploitation
We believed it was our lot
. . .
The seeds of freedom planted
By the will of our people
Was strengthened by the blood
Of workers murdered.

. . .

We shattered the lies
The road was spelt out
A united working class cannot be defeated
. . .
The children took to the streets
Workers striked
Women marched
Organizations were born
Guerillas sprouted
The Culture of Silence broken.

— Abduraghiem Johnstone

ALTHOUGH SOUTH AFRICA LONG MAINTAINED A CULTURE OF SILENCE, ITS "culture of censorship," as Christopher Merrett calls it, reached a highpoint in the mid-1980s just at the full flourish of its "culture of resistance," a favored phrase on the ground.[1] In the early 1970s, Black Consciousness advocates argued that culture should be used to resist dominance of all sorts, and through the mid-1970s some among them created spaces for artists to learn and exhibit their work. The spaces were physical and conceptual. Best known among them today is the Mihloti Black Theatre Troupe, a BC body that mostly performed in the Transvaal. Visual artists also embraced BC by creating and teaching art classes for the next generation of artists, and by taking their own work on the road to be exhibited in venues of their own making. Despite the state's massive suppression of BC bodies in 1977, the culture of resistance that had budded by then fully blossomed in the decade ahead. As voices and visions against apartheid resonated ever more powerfully, the state worked to control them through increasingly drastic measures. Silencing was their aim; censorship, faulty (or "black") propaganda, corporal violence, and murder were among their tactics. Indeed, the esteemed attorney George Bizos wrote that the attention garnered by Steve Biko's death in detention caused the Security Branch to do away with political activists without ever jailing or charging them.[2] But even murder did not silence the message. The majority would be heard: apartheid was nearing its end.

Southern Africa was on fire in the 1980s. This was a zone where the so-called Cold War ran hot. The exiled African National Congress and the Pan Africanist Congress had gained recruits in the late 1970s as thousands of BC-inspired youth fled their country to take up arms against Pretoria and apartheid.[3] Of these, the ANC's military branch, Umkhonto we Sizwe (Spear of the Nation), proved to be effective at orchestrating targeted attacks within South Africa that prompted Pretoria and its allies to brand it as terrorist. So, too, did the state multiply its repression: violent suppression of activists became widespread; successive states of emergency began in 1985 and were renewed annually until 1989; detention increased, as did the covert murder of activists; townships were declared enemy territory. But these were countered by swells of revolutionary certainty—some from within, others from without; some economically driven, others racially bound—that combined ultimately brought real change. Invigorated by the liberation of neighboring nations from colonial rule, inspired by Black Consciousness, and instructed by members of varied parties, township residents made themselves ungovernable during this period. New forms of combat were developed on all fronts.

Censorship, or the will to silence, frames the works discussed in this chapter, which date between 1978 and 1989. I am chiefly interested in the cultural combat that took place in the 1980s and, more specifically, in locating expressions of Black Consciousness during a period in which it is said to have waned in influence, even becoming noneffectual.[4] While the previous chapter examined Black Consciousness within print media of two kinds (that privately subscribed and that publicly posted), this chapter locates BC in the profession of art making.

After offering the reader some insight into South Africa's culture of censorship, I look at the state's efforts to control cultural expression of BC by censoring its vision. Next I analyze the well-known debates among artists at this time about responsibility and commitment to a larger community.

Although I analyze the works in relation to censorship, there is another kind of silencing afoot about these works in the present day. As evidenced in chapter 4, historians have erred by unduly crediting the ideology of nonracialism too much force behind South Africa's liberation. I argue that the descriptor *nonracial* gained greater currency in the early 1970s as exiled ANC leaders used it to supplant an orientation previously called *Charterist*.[5] By doing so, the ANC and others subtly cast Black Consciousness as racial, thereby silencing its real focus: the power of voice.[6] As historians today continue to adopt the dominant narrative, they perpetuate a kind of censorship over the quieter accounts. We must redraw the boundaries of South Africa's liberation story in order to access, and hopefully understand, a more nuanced, challenging history that began with a fight for voice. I begin with Black Consciousness, which worked to dissolve segregation by refusing ethnic identifiers of any kind. Thus, I ask that we read between the lines of history and images to realize a more complex picture.

A Culture of Censorship

Although the state had long restrained ideas by jailing or banning the people who held them, the 1980s witnessed a period of intensified state censorship in South Africa. In response to the groundswell in township activism in the late 1970s, the South African state increasingly restricted the flow of information over the years, reaching a high point in 1985 that carried straight through the rest of the decade. In 1980, parliament began to adopt President P. W. Botha's "reform" strategy with regard to dissemination of information, a kind of heavy-handed repression from above.[7] That same year limitations on the press were imposed making it an offense to disclose information about detainees arrested under the Terrorism Act.[8] Relating the conditions of detention was similarly proscribed.[9] Press access to sites of unrest was curbed with the declaration of a partial state of emergency on July 21, 1985 (renewed annually through 1989); thereafter journalists had an even tougher time reporting from townships wherein residents had taken up the call to make their communities ungovernable. The Soweto Uprisings of 1976 had prompted the state to ban all outdoor meetings save for those in the name of religion or sport. Apartheid resisters focused on funerals as sites of demonstration, but by 1985 these too were banned.[10] They became historic sites of contestation thereafter.

In its effort to suppress voices and visions, parliament "specifically targeted communication" when it renewed the state of emergency on June 12, 1986, and increased its parameters to "full scale."[11] The Publications Control Board (PCB) judged which works would be censored and based its decisions on whether a work ridiculed any part of the population, harmed relations among its sectors, or prejudiced the safety of the state.[12] PCB Chair Kobus Van Rooyen admitted that a "harsher view was taken of . . . the more accessible forms of communication," including the kinds of graphics discussed in chapter 4: posters, pamphlets, T-shirts, stickers, graffiti, murals, and the like. Further, "strong candidates for banning" were objects that promoted "the opposition's heroes, actions and principles" or illustrated police methods of suppression "in townships and prison cells [or illuminated] black and liberation theology."[13] In South Africa, readers who were attuned to these measures will recall seeing large swaths of text blackened out in papers like *The Rand Daily Mail,* at least until this resistance strategy was also banned. These measures illustrate that the culture of resistance that BC adherents began was achieving its aim.

Van Rooyen was considered more liberal than his predecessors; under his guidance the ban on the Freedom Charter of 1955 was lifted. Bans were similarly lifted on some books by progressive white writers, including Wessel Ebersohn's *Store Up the Anger* (1980), which is based on Steve Biko's final days and death in detention, and André Brink's *A Dry White Season* (1980), also devoted to detainee abuse.[14] Although Van Rooyen's PCB deemed acceptable such white views of black life, black viewpoints were more likely to be proscribed.[15] Indeed, such visions brought the state's heaviest hand: in the visual arts, one must cite raids on graphic arts centers in which works were confiscated, materials destroyed, and leaders were detained or murdered. The 1985 destruction of the Medu Art Ensemble and murder of Thami Mnyele, among others, are well known.[16] Consider, too, the Lesedi (Light) Silkscreen Workshop in the distant Northern Cape town of Huhudi, which was blown up and ceased operating.[17] When the busier Screen Training Project in Johannesburg was ransacked in 1986, its director, Morice Smithers, was detained and jailed for one year.[18]

Despite such measures, apartheid resisters of all stripes daringly navigated between the lines to make their visions seen and voices heard. In what follows I consider but one strand of resistance that garnered the state's attention, that expressive of Black Consciousness, but the will to speak was pervasive. Although the 1980s was a time of certain depravity in South Africa, it is also remembered as a decade in which committed individuals organized themselves to withstand the state's multiple traumas and ultimately bring apartheid to its end.

State Censorship of Biko and Black Consciousness

From March 1973 until his death in September 1977, Biko was banned to the magisterial district of King William's Town, which included his hometown of Ginsberg. Banning orders grossly limited one's life. His orders followed a standard common to all banned people. Among other things, he could not converse with more than one person at a time, which meant that he could not be in the same room with two people at any given time, immediate family excepted. He could not work within organizations he had helped found. He could not communicate with any other banned person, and neither his image nor words could be reproduced, a rule he subverted by publishing his opinions under the inspiring pseudonym Frank Talk. But friends like Asha Moodley told me that Biko "broke his banning orders all the time" since he would not be limited by the state.[19]

After Biko's death, some confusion remained over whether restrictions issued to banned persons—such as those that forbade printing their words or likeness—still applied should the person die while banned. Although it was no longer unlawful to represent his voice or visage, black artists typically masked tributes to Biko by technique (e.g., abstraction) or method (e.g., title). They had good cause: three years after Biko's death there was still a "perceived need by the police to attack the Biko image" as evidenced by the banning of books, plays, songs, and films about him.[20] Donald Woods's well-known biography *BIKO* was restricted because Woods himself was under banning orders, and others by Hilda Bernstein, Aelred Stubbs, and Millard Arnold were banned because they reprint Biko's voice and likeness. In the 1980s, films produced by the British Broadcasting Corporation and by Albert Finney and Richard Attenborough were restricted as well, as was a song by their countryman Peter Gabriel. A play called *The Biko Inquest* by a Durban-based writer was also banned. Ultimately, according to a *Daily Dispatch* reporter in 1980, "the government's ham-handed actions to suppress the Biko image inside South Africa [did] almost as much to bolster the man as the books, articles and plays outside the country; they added credibility to the reasons for remembering what he stood for."[21]

The best example of police attacking Biko's image occurred within the township of Mohlakeng near Randfontein in late 1985. A monument to Biko was erected here (Figure 5.1), one of several People's Parks that grew in response to the state of emergency issued earlier that year. Steven Sack describes a kind of "euphoric production" that arose within townships across the Transvaal in response to the collapse of municipal services as the "struggle for control of townships reached an unprecedented level."[22] In response to mounting garbage that remained uncollected, entire communities worked to beautify their neighborhoods by recycling and refashioning discarded materials. Inspired by younger residents who cleared common areas to create gardens of remembrance that honored fallen or imprisoned heroes (e.g., Mandela Park) or violated communities (e.g., Crossroads Park) or were named for an ideal (e.g., Democratic Park), People's Parks situated local struggles in tricontinental terms. For instance, images of Africa were painted on walls or assembled with stones on the ground and placed near images of cannons that Sack said, "looked exactly like those at the Union Buildings" in Pretoria.[23] Composite materials were fashioned to represent the guns and rifles of exiled apartheid resisters, and painted signs expressed the desires and dismays of their makers (e.g., "Only Poor Men Feel It"). Locals picked up on the energy and beauty of these parks, and soon whole blocks were transformed by festive color, and "house after house had some form of painted rocks, painted signs, or signs made up of small painted pebbles. Some assembled sculptures of a purely abstract nature lined the streets."[24]

Mohlakeng's residents were not the only ones to create a park in honor of Steve Biko—the people of Mamelodi did so as well—but the visual record seems to hold Mohlakeng's version alone.[25] This Biko Park was a bit different from other documented People's Parks. The space had a single focal point that was reinforced by an inner circle of rocks placed side by side and accented at the corners by four striped poles. The effect suggests a sacred site. The inner sanctuary resembles a grave with soil mounded on the ground; a portrait bust of Biko was erected where a headstone would sit. Triangular motifs and two signs (indecipherable in this photograph) were placed at the foot. The sculpted bust strengthens the visual currency of Biko's funeral portrait (Figures 2.6 and 2.9), reinforcing my interpretation of this People's Park as a mock gravesite.[26]

By early 1986, the state's security forces began destroying People's Parks. They bulldozed the parks ostensibly in the belief that they housed hidden arsenals, but it is more likely that the visual content of People's Parks was the real target.[27] Indeed, People's Parks were of a kind with "the more accessible forms of communication" that the director of the Publications Control Board had iden-

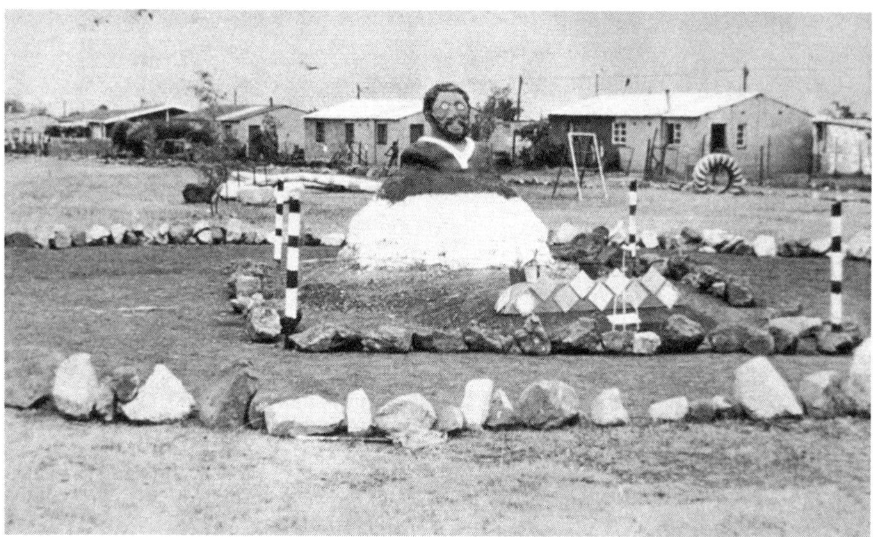

FIGURE 5.1. Residents of Mohlakeng, Peace Park for Steve Biko, 1985. Photographer not known.

tified as likely to be banned.[28] Biko's image at Mohlakeng certainly roused the ire of the police, who fired their weapons at the portrait before bulldozing it.[29]

It seems that the entire enterprise of People's Parks threatened the state. The parks were grassroots attempts to reclaim the land and mark it with inspiring words and icons, and the heroes and victims they commemorated notably contrasted the people and events honored by state-sponsored parks and monuments. People's Parks restored dignity to neglected neighborhoods because each one was made and shared by its surrounding community. Self-empowering in both process and purpose, the parks represented popular understanding of Black Consciousness, which Sack rightly (and refreshingly) identified as the "dominant ideological undercurrent" of the time.[30] Crucially, People's Parks directly challenged the state's attempts to control visual communication through censorship. Though short-lived, this movement represents a vital sense of political commitment, cultural ownership, and communal engagement that permeated Transvaal townships during South Africa's state of emergency.

Like several other artists discussed in this book (Bongiwe Dhlomo-Mautloa, Gavin Jantjes, David Koloane, Ezrom Legae, Fikile Magadlela, Dikobé Martins,

Thami Mnyele, Charles Nkosi, Judy Seidman, Durant Sihlali, and Paul Stopforth), Sue Williamson (b. 1941) was also included in the historic 1982 exhibition *Art toward Social Development* in Gaborone, Botswana.[31] Her distinguished career as an artist began with a series devoted to recovering histories that remained submerged in apartheid's version of events. Frustrated over "what was *not* in the media, a dark hole in available information," she made *A Few South Africans* (1983–85), now a well-known series of seventeen prints.[32] These portraits are restorative in that each portrays a woman who played an important part in resisting apartheid law but whose history was, in many cases, largely censored from public consumption. Williamson managed to secure banned books about them through Pretoria's bureaucracy because she held requisite institutional affiliation with the University of Cape Town at the time.

One work in the series is dedicated to Mamphela Ramphele, a physician whose own black consciousness is resolute and inspiring (Plate 6). Ramphele's portrait is like most in the series: she regards us directly, fills three-quarters of the frame around her, and is shown in a space that recalls her own history of protest. The landscape behind her is one of banishment. The hot sun that bears down on Ramphele, casting her face in shade, blankets the Naphuno district in the northern Transvaal, the place to which she was banished from April 1977 to 1983.[33] Banishment differed from banning. To receive an order of banishment was to be cast, as she put it, into a "'non-space'—unknown and amongst people with whom one has no real contact." Ramphele made the best of being made to live in what Donald Woods called, "the back of beyond."

In early 1978, soon after the death of Steve Biko and the birth of her son by him, Ramphele expanded the medical clinic she had established the previous year in Lenyenye, a township in Naphuno.[34] Local women with nursing backgrounds helped her provide medical services to residents of the many villages that surround it. Their work included travel to outstations on the hills around Lenyenye until the government disallowed this practice and confined Ramphele to the township alone. So great was the regional need that her practice thrived nonetheless. In another attempt to disrupt its success, the state sent an undercover agent to encourage her to flee into exile. Ramphele's response: "I needed to make one point very clear. I was going to be a pain in the neck of the security police and their masters, and was not going anywhere. This was my country and I was going to help liberate it."[35]

These facets of Ramphele's early biography are represented through repeated motifs within the diagonal, colored bars of Williamson's composition.[36] In the upper registers, stethoscopes and medicine jars reflect Ramphele's medical training while plant life reflects the traditional practices of many patients, modes that she honored and respected while treating up to eighty patients a day. At bottom, against a field of orange, we see the Ithuseng Community Health Centre that she established in Lenyenye in 1981, and a wheelbarrow and bricks reference a brickmaking project Ramphele initiated.[37] Only the darkened field records the negative forces that brought her to Lenyenye. Here we see police vehicles and handcuffs, and at lower left an image of Ramphele standing at the doorway to Ithuseng inviting us in. Positioned here, laid over the patterned objects of oppression, we see the evident truth of Ramphele's mission. She is South African and dedicates her life to her country's health and well-being.[38]

A Few South Africans marked Williamson's debut as an artist of note, but it was not her first project as activist. Her earliest ambitions were in journalism, and she worked for a time reporting for the Durban-based newspaper the *Daily News*. This experience in researching, interviewing, recording "people's exact words and precise narratives" resonates strongly in all of Williamson's art, itself smart in concept and technique.[39] While studying art and raising her children, she also dedicated great energy to activist work in and around Cape Town. She combined art and activism as early as 1973 when she joined the Graphic Workshop and the Women's Movement for Peace, eventually chairing the latter from 1978 to 1980.[40] At this early stage she began to explore uses of access; that is, she has long made art that is accessible to a broad audience and brings unrecognized histories to the fore.[41] For instance, original to the project, *A Few South Africans* was reprinted as posters and postcards, art made affordable on the whole. Later known as "Women's postcards," they were collected and translated into other media. Williamson recalls that they "popped up stuck to walls and pin boards in the most unlikely places," and some were exhibited overseas.[42]

Politicized expression constitutes the essence of Williamson's work. As an artist, she calls it her "responsibility to illuminate" vital issues of the day.[43] Narrative acts are always political acts. In her long and distinguished career, Williamson has consistently and expertly restored narratives that have been submerged or are at risk of being overlooked and forgotten. "One of my concerns," she says, "has always been the recovery of our history, and the ways in which the study of the past illuminates the present."[44] Made in the early 1980s, *A Few South Africans* shed light on buried histories and was a thumb in the eye toward the state's banning of some of the women portrayed. Her use of photography, decision to title by naming individuals portrayed, and her use of reproducible media all challenged the state in their own way. So, too, did the title of the series as a whole, since by 1983 the state had cast many of the women represented herein by its own brand of ethnic otherness. A number of the black South African women portrayed were said to properly belong to tribes in recently created Bantustans (homelands), therefore their South African citizenship was denied. In recording their lives to reassert their broad significance, Williamson also *reclaimed their nationality as South Africans.*

Derek Bauer (1955–2001) was a close friend of Sue Williamson and a well-known cartoonist whose works were frequently printed in the liberal-leaning *Weekly Mail* during this period.[45] In 1987, Bauer portrayed Biko as a battered being in an image respectfully titled *Steve Biko—In Memoriam* (Figure 5.2). By the tenth anniversary of Biko's death, which Bauer commemorated here, violence had intensified with the state of emergency first called on July 20, 1985. The image that Bauer drew to remember Biko—one that borrows from the police archive (Figure 2.13) but aggressively adds the stains of violence done to him—was the outcome of this artist's outrage over the continuing bloodshed that typified the age. As Susan de Villiers recalls, "violence begat violence begat violence."[46] In Bauer's rendition, the brutal suppression of Biko (or, more accurately by 1987, the continued suppression of those who supported his voice) marked the period in which the state's measures to uphold apartheid became extreme. So, too, did resistance against these measures, and it took many forms. For instance, by 1987, fratricide, such as that between rival liberation groups (some covertly backed by the state) and that against presumed police informers, exceeded deaths in the war on apartheid.[47] Bauer condemns it all. In its graphic aftermath, *Steve Biko—In Memoriam* is like another of Bauer's drawings, *For Ashley Kriel Who They Killed at Hazendal,* in that both replace significant portions of the body with dark stains of splattered blood. Such pictorial distortions simplify. These works are exceptional for a cartoonist who often conveyed his message through caricature that, though of grim content, conjured a laugh in response. But no humor can be had from *Steve Biko—In Memoriam.*

As a political cartoonist, Bauer faced certain public scrutiny since his art was to comment on current affairs and would have been read in conjunction with other newsworthy items. Political cartoonists are journalists, but the expectations that they must balance are at odds: the nonpartisanship of a reporter and the strong views of an editor. The nature of the medium is one that seeks

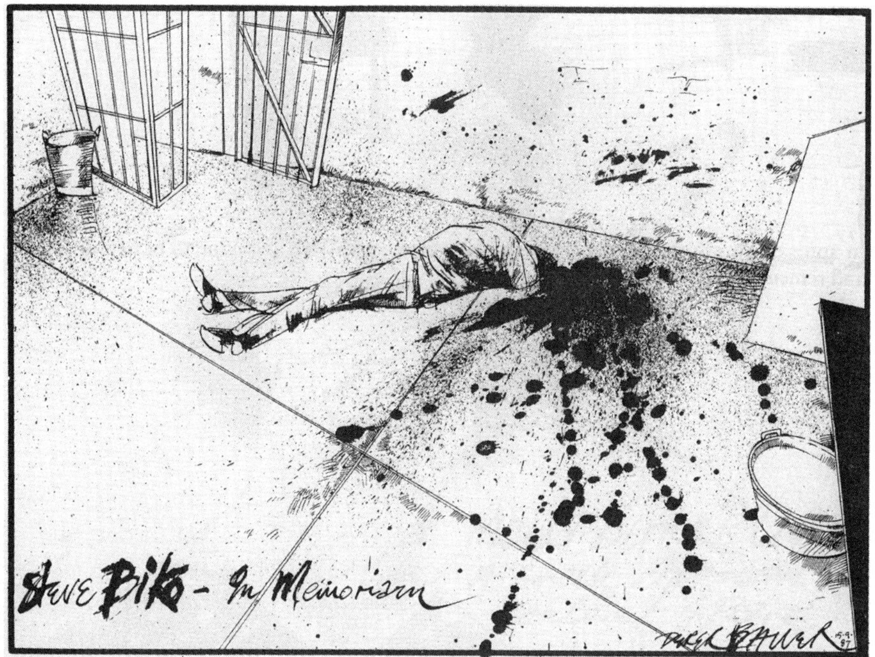

FIGURE 5.2. Derek Bauer, *Steve Biko—In Memoriam (Thorns in the Flesh)*, 1987.

a response, and Bauer, whose style recalls the work of British cartoonist Ralph Steadman, summoned both hilarity and offense in his art. In J. M. Coetzee's view, to feel offended is to also feel some measure of disgust, shame, hurt, anxiety, or another emotion that jars one's sense of soundness.[48] Such offense typically also brings resentment against the person who created the emotion. Moral indignation (offense, outrage) is said to be a "sister emotion" to another complex response called anger-revenge; both have the same origin—the retributive emotion of resentment. *Steve Biko—In Memoriam* surely offends, but it also manages to direct our response, resentment, toward the original maker of the photograph on which Bauer based his drawing: the South African state. He enlarged the space from the original, adding a bucket and basin for scale and spots of deep black ink that offset the darkened letters of Biko's name at lower left. The figure he translated without embellishment. Two rectangular shapes span the right side of the drawing. These may be seen as blank canvases viewed from both sides, or perhaps a partition and door. They suggest stories untold or obscured, waiting to be found out or realized.

Although Bauer made his living through popular graphics, he never supported the idea that images must be of a particular kind in order to be accessible to a large audience. Unlike those who pushed artists to show relevance and commitment through imagery directed toward "the people" or "the community," he was compelled to draw for other reasons. In 1988 he said, "Your only responsibility is to your artwork, subject and yourself. If it's anything else it stops being art and becomes propaganda or advertizing."[49] Although the other artists discussed here felt pulled in more directions, they all responded to the struggles of their day, both political and artistic.

Cry Freedom (1986), a flawed but at times compelling film by Richard Attenborough (1923–2014), provides an interesting case study in the contradictions of apartheid rule.[50] In November 1987, it passed muster with the state's arbiter of censorship, the Publications Control Board, which found it suitable for release. Board members reasoned that the facts about Biko's death were widely known and Black Consciousness was an "outdated political concept" that no longer threatened the state.[51] They found the scenes of police brutality relatively short, and the representation of police absurd thus easily recognizable as caricature. They judged the film's "emotive force" incapable of inciting either violence or revolution, and even believed that the film "will lead to greater 'awareness' and improved race relations," a position likely adopted in response to its "buddy film" structure, which I critique shortly. Keenly aware of the growing international condemnation of apartheid, the board reasoned that "far more will be achieved [by the film's screening] in creating a climate of hope, openness, tolerance and objectivity in the minds of the world outside of South Africa."

Four days before the film's opening, Minister of Information Stoffel van der Merwe recommended that the board's decision be reviewed, thus implying that he expected it to be overturned. It would appear that he and others in the State Security Council feared the effects of "the Biko story" on a population still under a state of emergency.[52] But in July 1988, the Publications Appeal Board upheld the original decision. Thirty-five cinemas received copies and the film opened nationwide on July 29, 1988. It ran just five hours before the police confiscated all copies on the authority of Emergency Media Regulation 9(2) of the Internal Security Act.[53] Police Commissioner General Hendrik de Wit ordered the film's seizure on the grounds that it "endangers the safety of the public, the maintenance of public order and will delay the termination of the State of Emergency."[54] Van der Merwe said that the Publications Appeal Board did not have the capacity to "judge the situation on the streets," the revolutionary character of which might be fueled by the film. He said, "We don't need that sort of internal disturbance and excitement from people like Richard Attenborough."[55] Tellingly, he also suggested that the state objected to the film's content: "Whites are typified as privileged and surrounded by wealth as opposed to blacks living in great poverty and subjected to exploitation and repression. This is in sharp contrast with the opening message that the film is based on truth."[56]

Bomb threats were received at some of the theaters where *Cry Freedom* was briefly screened, and in three cases small explosions occurred.[57] The culprits were never found. An estimated one thousand South Africans saw *Cry Freedom* before it was seized.[58] Thousands more saw it when it was rereleased in the country in 1990.

The state's actions against *Cry Freedom* indicate that it effectively portrayed certain truths about South Africa, a perception bolstered by Attenborough's regular use of a documentary aesthetic. Throughout the film, scenes are identified by captions that are typed out for viewers by an unseen reporter; the sound of typewriter keys clicking enhances the effect. A photojournalist's camera is evoked in the film's opening sequence, which depicts the state's 1975 raid on Crossroads, an informal settlement outside of Cape Town. Viewers become the photographer: we look through the camera's lens, frame and focus shots, and hear the shutter click as black-and-white images of police violence are momentarily stilled. These documentary photographs are spliced into color action footage of residents fleeing violence. Later, two other large-set sequences also evoke the documentary aesthetic. Biko's funeral was re-created with great attention to the visual matter recorded in photographs of the actual event. The poster, clothing, banner, clenched fist salute, and carvings on Biko's coffin are all shown in close-up. The scene ends with a closely cropped focus on the words *One Nation*, which are written in gold leaf on the top of Biko's coffin. The words appear to glow in an unearthly way, an aesthetic in keeping with Attenborough's saint-like representation of Biko earlier in the film. Several scenes in the Soweto sequence (which Attenborough places at the end of the film, thereby taking great liberty with history's chronology) mimic photographs by Peter Magubane, one of Africa's most famous photographers.[59] Another scene in the film highlights the documentary aesthetic and again Attenborough's willingness to fiddle with history: after Biko's death, Donald Woods accompanies Nontsikelelo to identify her husband's corpse. A photojournalist at the *Daily Dispatch* also joins them.

When the state's representative leaves the room, Woods instructs the journalist to quickly take pictures of Biko's battered body "from every angle." Woods is later found with the photographs and is banned as a consequence, but not before he has sent fourteen copies to overseas press members. This is pure fiction.

From the outset, the documentary aesthetic creates problems for the film's narrative since the tools that document—cameras, typewriters—are controlled by white people. After the opening sequence at Crossroads, the white photojournalist shows his pictures of violated black bodies to the editor of the *Daily Dispatch,* Donald Woods, played by Kevin Kline. Woods is our guide throughout the film, and we see nearly everyone and everything through his eyes. This follows the narrative mode of the buddy film, wherein a black protagonist can neither speak nor be seen in his own right. In this genre, he needs a white cohort to serve as middleman to convey his concerns to the audience, which studios bank on being mostly white. Mbulelo Mzamane takes care to point out that although this is a Hollywood convention, it merely responds to "a long tradition of racism [that] demands almost that you look through the eyes of a white star, a white hero."[60] Several critics of *Cry Freedom* rightly complained that Biko's story was hijacked by the Woods character, "the white disciple," in a "serious case of displaced heroism."[61] American film critic Roger Ebert put it best: "The problem with this movie is similar to the dilemma in South Africa: Whites occupy the foreground and establish the terms of the discussion, while the eighty percent nonwhite majority remains a shadowy, half-seen presence in the background."[62] The principal "shadowy" figure in the film is Steve Biko, played here by Denzel Washington.

When we meet Biko, we do so through the eyes of Woods. He is standing outdoors in King William's Town, his figure defined by light that filters through a tree, shimmers from a reflected surface, and haloes him from behind. Woods strains his eyes and shields the glare generated by this saintly apparition. Later, in the courtroom scene based on the SASO–BPC trial of 1976, Biko is again haloed by light as he explains Black Consciousness (Figure 5.3). It is cast as infinitely reasonable and just, as illustrated by this exchange from the trial's transcript:

> STATE PROSECUTOR: Your answer to this so-called "naked terrorism" [of the state] is to promote violence in the black community.
>
> BIKO: No, our movement seeks to avoid violence.
>
> PROSECUTOR: (agitated) But your own words call for direct confrontation!
>
> BIKO: (calm) That's right. We demand confrontation.

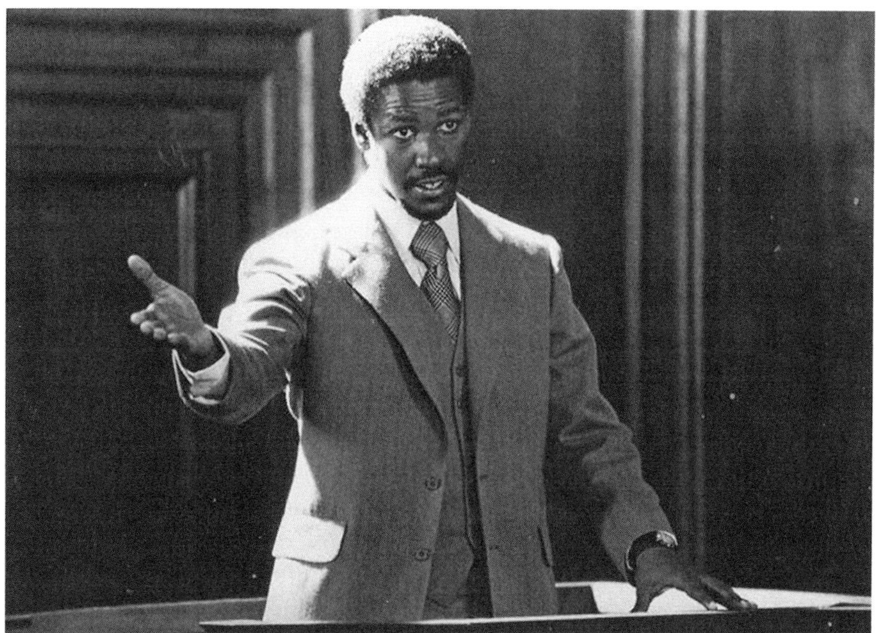

FIGURE 5.3. Denzel Washington as Steve Biko in *Cry Freedom,* a film by Richard Attenborough, released 1987.

PROSECUTOR: But isn't that a demand for violence?

BIKO: Well you and I are now in confrontation, but I see no violence.

The tenor of this exchange is consistent in every scene that includes the character of Steve Biko. Throughout *Cry Freedom,* he is cast as a patient teacher who instructs the audience about black values, realities, and history. Even after death, which occurs midway in the film, he continues to educate through flashbacks, memories that are new scenes, voice-overs, and ghostly apparitions visited upon Woods. The Woods character literally assumes Biko's role, supplanting black for white, in the last half of the film as he struggles to free himself and his family from South Africa in order to bear Biko's message abroad.[63] But that message, and Biko's role in the film, would have been different had Attenborough and Universal Studios envisioned the audience to be anything like that sought by Black Consciousness—that is, if the audience were seen as black in the antiethnic, tricontinental terms that BC embraced. Instead they relied on a white narrator and in doing so they enacted another kind of silencing, less direct than that of the South African state, but no less important.

Still, the director remained adamant that he had no interest in "preaching to the converted."[64] He was clear about what kind of person he aimed to reach with this film and the effects he hoped it would have: "I wanted to reach people who were indifferent, who didn't know what was going on and didn't care. . . . Most important of all, of course, I wanted to reach an American audience because it was, I thought, in the United States that fundamental change of attitude towards the administration of South Africa was likely to be the most influential."[65] In this respect, Attenborough achieved his aim; *Cry Freedom* certainly educated people outside of South Africa about apartheid. But troublingly, what he called "the strong, dramatic Biko story" that compelled him to make the film was one of death, not life. Like so many people who became aware of Biko after his death, Attenborough failed to explore just who the man was and what he stood for, shortcomings that remain evident in the film. He glosses over distinctions in black politics, so that Biko is represented as one with Nelson Mandela and Robert Sobukwe, leaders who advocated very different paths to the end of apartheid.[66] And the African National Congress is represented uncritically in a film that was ostensibly about Black Consciousness. The image in Figure 5.4 makes this explicit. Attenborough poses beneath a poster of Denzel Washington as Steve Biko (based on the watercolor by Donald Kenyon, Figure 2.4) that includes the words "Black Consciousness" within its frame. That Attenborough failed to understand the full power of this discourse is evident in statements like the following: "What had developed, due to the publication of Donald's book *[BIKO]*, was that Steve's life became an inspirational rallying point for black people, not only in his country but throughout the whole of the African continent."[67] Woods's book must be credited with educating readers in countries beyond Africa's borders, but to claim that his efforts brought blacks together is outlandish. Black Consciousness achieved this.

Attenborough's film was not the first work of art to convey the Biko story through a narrative that treats the death of this man over the life of his ideas. The famed Gerard Sekoto (1913–1993) was the first artist to publically pay tribute to Steve Biko; he was able to do so since he lived in France, far from South Africa's culture of silence.[68] Although *Homage to Steve Biko* of 1978 (Plate 7) seems unique within Sekoto's long and distinguished career (no other political leaders were so honored), the public reaction to it was regrettably common. It was unveiled in a solo exhibition at Guy Piazzinini's Galerie Art Premier in

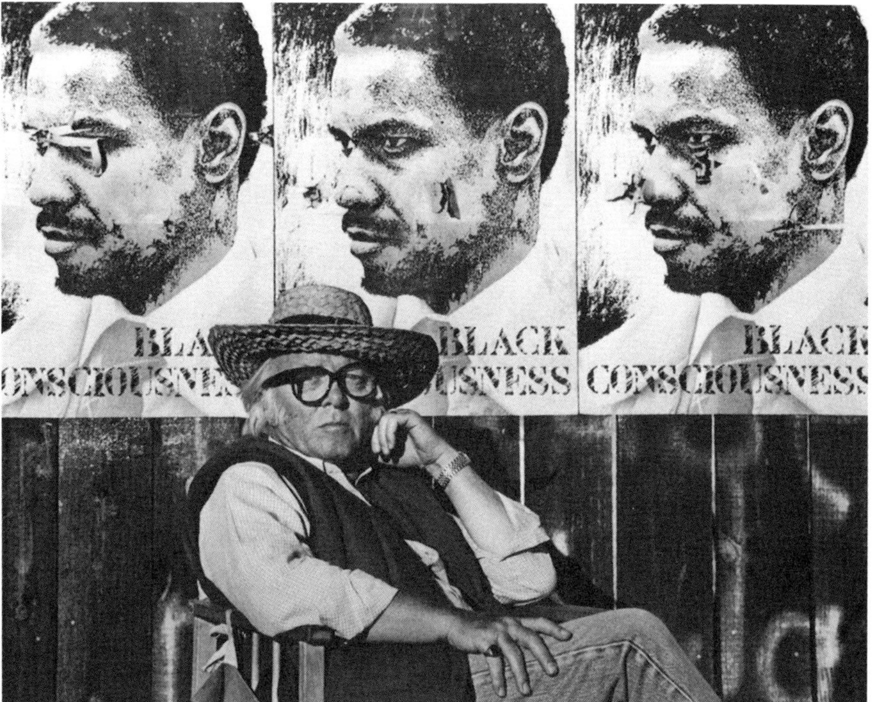

FIGURE 5.4. Richard Attenborough before a poster advertising his film *Cry Freedom*, 1987.

December 1978. Parisian art critics praised the work and it got more attention than others on display.[69] The name Biko had become known worldwide, and those unfamiliar with much of South Africa's history accessed it through his death. Regrettably, the story still stops there for so many people.

Sekoto surely had something else in mind when he made *Homage to Steve Biko*. He followed the Biko inquest in the Parisian news with care and used a press photograph as a template for his own portrait.[70] The hypericon so readily reproduced following Biko's death likely served as such, but Sekoto elected to shift Biko's gaze into a confrontational stare.[71] Such a probing presence effectively alters the relationship between those who see and those being seen. Biko is not a passive presence here. Unique for Sekoto in this way, the artist directly challenges us to contemplate the world as we make it.

The mosaic patterning is also unusual for Sekoto, as are the disembodied heads (hidden presences, really) in the form of collective memory, or ghostly weight.[72] These engage us directly, rather odd for Sekoto's subjects; only the central figure is lost to the moment.[73] She weighs burdensome thoughts—racially motivated violence on one hand (Biko's likeness is defined by equal measures of black and white) and a personal matter on the other (the woman silhouetted at left either embraces or restrains a male figure)—and she feels the pull of the African continent, a kind of body for Biko, that takes shape from the shadows. N. Chabani Manganyi described the effect of Biko's torture on Sekoto: "It was the kind of death that haunted him, raised many perplexing questions and left him helpless and depressed."[74]

The central figure of *Homage to Steve Biko* embodies the artist's own sensibility since he too entered a period of reflection, and reclusion, while the painting was made. The deaths of two women dear to him had preceded Biko's own. His mother, Anne Sekoto, a woman whom he called "serene" and was inclined to "always keep her inner thoughts to herself," died in November 1968.[75] Then another beloved passed in April 1976: Marthe Baillon, a woman with whom he had "at long last found a home in Paris . . . [within] a curious and enduring 'marriage' of sorts."[76] Sekoto was by all accounts steeped in grief in the period that followed and faced the added worry of potentially losing his residence.[77] It helped to return to painting after a lengthy period in which he cared for Baillon as she slowly succumbed to cancer. As he painted over the next two years, other deaths haunted. The Soweto Uprisings and Biko's death in detention weighed on Sekoto, too. Manganyi explains that "there were times when [Sekoto] was so depressed that he could not paint for days on end."[78] Ultimately, *Homage to Steve Biko* became the centerpiece of his work at this time. The critical acclaim it generated is in large part due to fascination with the inquest and Biko as a "magnifying glass [through which] . . . the structure of a whole nation . . . comes sharply into focus."[79] But the work also stood out for its unique features. In other words, Sekoto made it special. Through this work, that is, in its making, Sekoto came to terms with the deaths of loved ones and of those whose strength he admired.[80]

South Africa of the late 1970s to the late 1980s was riddled with violence enacted by multiple agents and in varied forms. It was a time wherein information was guarded, disinformation spread, and voices and visions deemed threatening were commonly suppressed. Censors come in two stripes. There are those that prohibit access to information deemed too sensitive or unlawful, or too richly sensual. And there are censors who collect information through a process of enumeration or counting. These two would come into conflict in the decade ahead when the Truth and Reconciliation Commission heard testimony in an effort to properly account for politically motivated bodily abuse that had been censored. The stories revealed there—for testimony is a vision realized through voice—provoked an ached response. It was experienced; it was sensed. This realm of visualized revelation, receptive experience, and censorial suppression is worthy of pursuit. My interest turns, however, to locating Black Consciousness in the central cultural debates of the period that have heretofore been accredited to an ideology of nonracial activism.

Relevance and Commitment: Locating Black Consciousness

The dominant debates among South African artists in the 1980s concerned how to best locate political viewpoint within one's work, and how, or whether, to represent the voice of another person. One camp, called "social revolutionaries" by Neville Dubow and "social realists" by Gary Van Wyk, advocated for the exclusive use of figurative imagery that supported an urgent cause: the end of apartheid.[81] There was but one audience of relevance: "the people" whose cause was expressed in popular forms. They formed "the community" in which some members of this camp were raised and to which all remained committed.[82] In visual art, its central protagonist was Thami Mnyele who, along with Dikobé Martins, registered their BC influence. The graphic in Figure 5.5, printed in *Staffrider* in 1979, captures the sentiment of these "cultural workers," as they preferred to be called. Accompanying an article about a Berlin-based event, "Horizonte 79—World Festival of African Arts," the image of four raised fists urges artists to take up their pens and paint brushes, the instruments of culture, and to use them as weapons of struggle. It also converts the well-known hands-breaking-chains motif of the banned Black Peoples' Convention to picture its cause.[83]

The other camp in the debate over representational voice, Dubow's "formal radicals," supported political cause but refused restrictions to method, medium, mode of expression, and potential viewer.[84] Their audience was unlimited, but "the community" that they addressed was not. The viewers that mattered, that had relevance, were within the professional community of artists. Note that positioning oneself in this camp expressed an objective that was no less political. In fact it was acutely so for black artists who conceived themselves as such and, amid the extreme inequity of apartheid education, worked for equal training

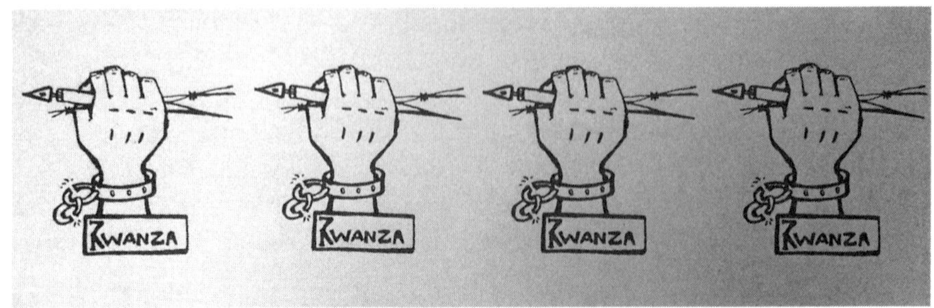

FIGURE 5.5. Logo for "Horizonte 79—World Festival of African Arts," *Staffrider,* July/August 1979.

to realize this profession. Since they experimented freely with abstraction and enjoyed the rare opportunity to use materials (thanks to patrons) that were too expensive to buy, their interests were misconstrued as advocating "art for art's sake." This regrettable phrase maintained a presence in the debate even though it was a bit of a ghost, called up now and then by the populace camp to attack the relevancy of their counterparts.[85] But what happens when we consider the objectives of Dubow's "formal radicals" in accord with Black Consciousness? BC artists of the 1970s endorsed technical and aesthetic experimentation as inherently black; critics and historians have called many of them "African Surrealists," a label far too confining to hold much meaning.[86]

Black Consciousness played a subtle but persistent part in the response to these debates, and it framed their central, challenging questions. This is not to say that BC was the sole originator; innumerable influences come to bear on the outlook that tempers any given image, the by-product of the maker's interests, methods, and skill. I mean to say that BC was embedded in the debates themselves. Indeed, it is omnipresent in speeches that historians now cite as key to the development of a "culture of resistance" in the period, but it remains woefully unacknowledged. For instance, Black Consciousness was a driving force in the keynote address that Nadine Gordimer gave to an almost all-white audience in 1979 at the State of the Art conference at the University of Cape Town. As evidenced in the last chapter, it was readily manifest in the papers that Thami Mnyele and Dikobé Martins offered at the Culture and Resistance symposium in Gaborone, Botswana, in 1982, for which Gordimer also gave the keynote. These meetings argued that combating apartheid was imperative in the arts, thereby making relevancy dependent on commitment. So regular is the cadence of BC-infused meaning in Gordimer's 1979 address that near the end she said, in a way that embodies the tautness of interpreting BC at the time, "I suppose I shall be accused of using the schema of Black Consciousness philosophy." Then she quickly defended the relevance of this "kick-me political label":

> It is an indication of the rethinking, remaking, needed in South African cultural contexts in which for years no-one, not even blacks, ever questioned the exclusive use of white cultural analyses. In my view, this conference should not be afraid of having kick-me political labels pinned on its back; it should assert the urgent need and right to use whatever ideas, from whatever source, that may reflect the facts of life here and penetrate the cataract of preconceptions grown over our vision.

She credits Black Consciousness with enabling her to see again. Next she makes use of it to call white artists into action: "This is consistent with an abandonment of the old positions of white and black in culture and the scrapping of the assumption that white-based culture is the mean, for white as well as black."[87]

Thus my argument: whatever the skin color of the protagonist, Black Consciousness continued to register, albeit more subtly, in much of the subsequent published record of the central questions of the time. How to best evidence commitment to change in South Africa *and* remain relevant? And how to respond to challenges that BC initially presented—of white artists, the challenge to listen to blacks and not speak for, or represent, them; of black artists, the necessity, culturally based, to work for and within one's own community, itself evidence of black agency, dignity, and pride.

In three years' time, another important conference took place that greatly influenced the debates of the 1980s. The Medu Art Ensemble organized the Culture and Resistance symposium in Gaborone, Botswana; Medu spearheaded an exhibition along with it at the National Museum and Art Gallery called Art toward Social Development.[88] The paper that Thami Mnyele gave at the Culture and Resistance symposium evidences the degree to which BC continued to sway him even as he welcomed white artists to work alongside him. This suggests that BC was about voice for Mnyele, not race, and it shows that the adoption of a nonracial approach to combating apartheid did not necessitate the abandonment of BC. Mnyele had by this time committed himself to Medu's mission and success, so he encouraged artists to create readable works that challenged apartheid norms. Realism was favored, as was popular media that could be reproduced and distributed widely, like posters, T-shirts, banners, and illustrated newsletters and pamphlets. Scholars have laid great emphasis on this aspect of Mnyele's vision, but they have neglected the portions of his Gaborone paper that welcomed other forms of address. In doing so, historians have propagated the dominant narrative, one that tints BC, even discolors it, by placing race at its center when in fact BC was (and is) a struggle over voice, a fight to be heard. Understanding that social demands on black artists created "a serious conflict" within them about how to engage with the "social, political and economic interests" of the day, Mnyele said that "the historical elements of distortion, mysticism, religiousness, abstraction, romanticism, are not necessarily negative in themselves. They can be employed with consciousness and supreme purposefulness."[89] Seconds later, he contextualized the problem as one of media and suggested that artists and historians reject the hierarchy in which it had been placed: "I am not of the opinion that artworks must be sacrificed for political posters, but in the same breath would demand to know the reason for the undesirability of political propaganda. In fact, our communities will restore us with the respect we have lost, the moment we utilize every form of art at our disposal, along with the political poster." In other words, the poster, which I considered in chapter 4, was but one medium for political expression. Medu aside, Mnyele continued to embrace other mediums, too.

It would thus seem that Mnyele, a man committed to popular, ephemeral media but who nonetheless invested in creating "art for posterity,"[90] supported the efforts of fellow South Africans who combined political critique with abstraction, like Ezrom Legae or Motlhabane Mashiangwako or David Koloane, for instance. And although the poles of the debate under way suggested spheres that were distinct and unyielding to interplay, they were far grayer in practice. For instance, Mnyele deplored South Africa's segregated educational system that left a "gap between intellectual and practical labour." He suggested that "there seems to be no hope that the education [of black South Africans] can deal even with the fundamentals of production: it is through a polytechnic system of self-reliance that the general impotence in this education can be overcome."[91] As John Peffer has proposed, the Thupelo Art Project, an important venue for training (mostly) black artists that emphasized experimentation with materials and technique over content, was created in response to this message, which a Thupelo founder and its best-known spokesman, Koloane, took home from the Culture and Resistance symposium.[92] For two weeks annually, Thupelo offered artists without other means a chance to work in a manner readily afforded to white students at universities. They enjoyed expansive space in which to work instead of the cramped domestic contexts that were customary; they worked in large scale and with materials unavailable to them otherwise; they were given a brief respite from the violence of the occupied townships in which most Thupelo participants lived; and, importantly, they were able to build a community of artists that subsequently claimed space in their profession.[93]

In his illuminating study of Thupelo, Peffer discusses all of these benefits, but he errs in restricting Thupelo's success to nonracialism, an ideology that gained widespread currency in response to Black Consciousness. He views non-racialism as "both cause and effect of the Thupelo Project," but one could just as easily regard BC as such. After all, BC overrode apartheid's limits in learning, refused to listen to well-meaning white patrons and critics, and enabled black artists to gain confidence within a profession that, with its prescriptive view of black art, left them feeling, as Koloane once put it, "inadequate."[94] The sense was one that Mnyele acknowledged in his Culture and Resistance address. He described the frustration of some members in Mihloti Black Theatre, an early BC cultural troupe, who experienced difficulty articulating their views due to poor attention within Bantu education to "technical skills and intellectual education" combined. Thus they "vowed to improve our techniques and knowledge in art" by pursing both on their own, with white artists like Bill Ainslie who were eager to help. Koloane, similarly prompted, decided to "go and learn— and come back and impart [professional skills] effectively." Although these artists eventually realized change within different "communities," broadly writ as "the people" on one hand, and "the profession" on the other, both Mnyele and Koloane exercised Black Consciousness in that they were their own agents, working to upend segregationist structures that inhibited their lives.

Jump back to July 1979 and the State of the Art conference at University of Cape Town. Any black artist, Nadine Gordimer reminded, inevitably faced "false consciousness" (reinforced since youth by whites) as a "point of departure towards his true selfhood."[95] Further, for him

> relevance is the supreme criterion. It is that by which his work will be judged *by his own people,* and *they* are the supreme authority since it is only through them that he can break his alienation. . . . The external reality to which relevance paces out the measure of this work is not a step away from him: another writer, Njabulo Ndebele, says "blacks are operating" from within "a crushing intellectual and educational environment."[96]

For some jurors in this debate, an artist's relevancy hinged on how well his or her images communicated a sanctioned social concern. They relied on what Gordimer called "a kit of reliable emotive phrases for writers, a ready-made aesthetic for painters and sculptors, an unwritten index of subjects for playwrights and list of approved images for photographers." Such agitprop, she remarked, "binds the artist with the means by which it aims to clear the minds of people." Instead, she promoted what were known BC objectives: expanded opportunities in learning and "the right" to find one's own voice of expression. She said that the black artist

> is aware that he is committed, not only as a voluntary act, but in the survival of his own being and personality, to black liberation. It is at this point that, as an artist, commitment takes over, from within, from relevance, and the black artist has to assert the right to search out his own demotic artistic vocabulary with which to breathe new life and courage into his people. His commitment is the point at which inner and outer worlds fuse; his purpose to master his art and his purpose to change the nature of art, create new norms and forms out of and for a people recreating themselves, become one aim.[97]

In the decade that followed, many black artists experimented with materials and forms unfamiliar to "the supreme authority" that judged relevancy in their work. Although the examples I provide in this chapter mesh abstraction with a stated political point, this was not always the case, nor is it necessary to an expression of Black Consciousness. Recall that when Lefifi Tladi celebrated experimentation and abstraction in the early 1970s, he did so in defiance of market expectations, a professional decision that was driven by BC. Even without the clear politicized expression encouraged by those in the cultural worker camp, artists made determined, directed choices to secure access to methods, materials, and subject matter long denied them. This, too, exemplifies Black Consciousness at work.

In the previous chapter I argued that Black Consciousness could not be claimed, or owned, by any single organization, thus its influences register among several. Here I show how artists whose work was meaningful to Dubow's "cultural worker" also responded to or embodied BC outside the perimeters of their frame. Whatever the sphere in which one sought relevancy—in organizing people for protest campaigns (his social revolutionaries), or in securing the freedom of voice and vision and the right to equal opportunity at the workplace (his formal radicals)—artists who engaged in the biggest debates of the decade were responding to challenges that Black Consciousness posed.

To limit the free expression of ideas among any public, for any audience, is to engage in *censorship.* The word describes oppression but not necessarily aggressively so. This is the context in which I engage the topic because my principle concern—locating the persuasive voice of Black Consciousness within visual expression—continues to be excluded from the dominant narrative of South African history in the 1980s. I ask that we look at the choices of artists discussed next as expressions of Black Consciousness. Surely now, more than three decades on, one need not fear that "kick-me label" anymore.

Black Consciousness through Realism

The distinguished career of Bongiwe Dhlomo-Mautloa (b. 1956) might best exemplify Black Consciousness at work in both camps because she has carried its assertive energy throughout, from her first experiments as an artist in the 1970s, through her accomplished turns as administrator, curator, and director since then. Her earliest works were biblical in theme and thus in keeping with the curriculum typically covered at the famous Swedish mission where she earned a certificate in fine art in 1979, the Evangelical Lutheran Art and Craft Center at Rorke's Drift.[98] But Dhlomo-Mautloa's figures were black, and the passages she chose to picture resonate with BC history in real time. Later works were included in the historic *Art toward Social Development* exhibition in Gaborone, Botswana, in July 1982. Three years later, exiled artist Thami Mnyele heralded these same works, plus a few others, as testimony to the refreshingly meaningful work his fellow South Africans were making within the repressive state: politically astute and easy to comprehend.[99] Mnyele, a vital voice among social revolutionaries, derided abstraction without an overt political mission. Yet Dhlomo-Mautloa herself embraced it when she helped organize the Thupelo Art Project. Later Dhlomo-Mautloa would defend the nuanced politics of artists who were inclined toward experimentation and thus rejected the censorious objections of the first camp. She said of her counterparts, "The images they are using are not always *overtly* political. It's difficult to identify the 'nature' of political art, especially in the case of black artists."[100] To see black consciousness in Dhlomo-Mautloa's life and work is to see how fluidly its effects were manifested across this decade of debate.

Like the artists who shared studio space at the home of Geoff and Maokaneng Mphakati, those at Rorke's Drift engaged in open exchange, and their conversations moved beyond the technical and artistic. Dhlomo-Mautloa is said to have gained great political awareness through discussions with classmates at Rorke's Drift.[101] Classmate Sam Nhlengethwa, who began studies one year before she, steered her toward a Black Consciousness aesthetic in her very first assignment, a linoleum cut print called *Adam and Eve.* The artist recalled:

> I'm from a church background, and I made Adam and Eve white in the lino
> that I worked on. My printmaking teacher was pleased with my first effort—he
> was white, and he was only commenting on the execution of the print. But Sam
> Nhlengethwa called me and told me in a very nice way that I did not have to
> make Eve white. He was really saying: there is nothing wrong with using black
> people as your subject. But I hadn't been exposed to that, because I hadn't
> grown up with that kind of *consciousness*—for me Adam was white! I began
> to understand how art could be used to record, inform and document, so that
> when you see an image, it says something; it speaks to you in the manner the
> artist intended or in the manner in which you read it.[102]

After *Adam and Eve,* Dhlomo-Mautloa made a work called *Untitled (Female Crucifixion),* which figures a black woman suspended from a tree and two make-shift poles. Rorke's Drift was like other art training centers for artists at the time in that conversations took place among classmates about things beyond the walls around them. For instance, Nhlengethwa's best-known work from this period emphasized the brutal conditions in which miners worked. The center offered technical training and the space for artists to work through ideas and come to know one another over the period of a two-year residency. As Philippa Hobbs and Elizabeth Rankin see it, Rorke's Drift "laid a strong foundation for the future" in that through its graduates it was "able to fashion a diaspora of social consciousness."[103] I propose that the art center achieved much in technical training, but that the students themselves, many already equipped with a "foundation" in BC when they enrolled at Rorke's Drift, continued to rely on its principles after they left it. Recall that Patrick Mautloa, among the best known of Rorke's Drift alumni, created a T-shirt for the South African Students' Organization in the early 1970s (see chapter 1). I see the artists as agents of change in this regard rather than their instructors, since many had working knowledge of BC before they arrived.

Dhlomo-Mautloa's *Tower of Babel* of 1978 (Figure 5.6) is important to this

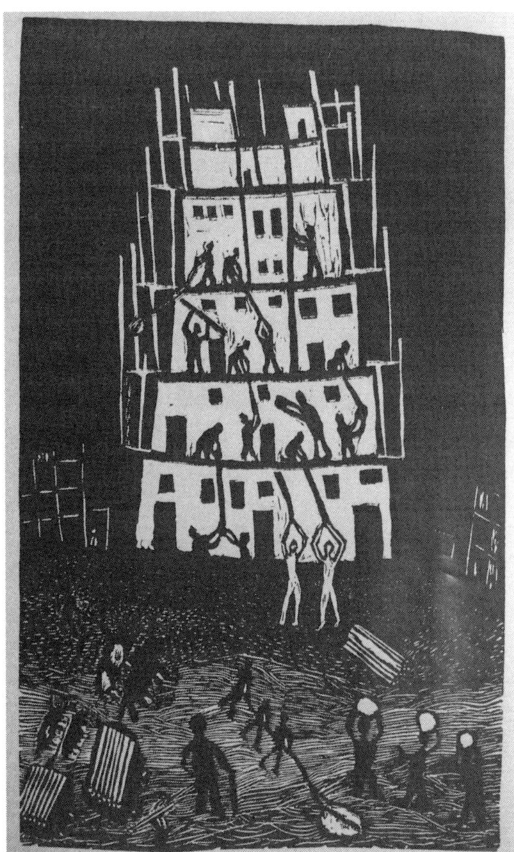

FIGURE 5.6. Bongiwe Dhlomo-Mautloa, *Tower of Babel,* 1978. Linoleum cut print, 390 x 235 cm. Collection of Sam Nhlengethwa. Courtesy of Bongiwe Dhlomo-Mautloa.

study because it agitates against Bantustans, an issue that enflamed the BC-minded for much of the decade. It illustrates Genesis 11:1–9, The City and Its Tower, a story popularly known by the title she chose. In the telling, humans, having learned a lesson from the Great Flood, resolve to unify in purpose and speak in one language. In honor of their newfound sense of harmony, they begin to build a tower of unprecedented height. God is offended by their pride and responds to it by scattering them, literally and figuratively, across the globe. Babel is from the Hebrew word *babal,* meaning to confuse or confound. God's action disabled human ability to understand one another's speech; indeed, some were left with no voice at all. It also disabled their ability to meet or see one another by casting them into distant places.

At the time that Dhlomo-Mautloa made *Tower of Babel,* BC's central organizations were recently banned, their leaders detained, arrested, or killed, and thousands had fled into exile since 1976. Bantustans, the state-determined Homelands of black people based on presumed ethnicity, remained very contentious in the period, but especially so in Natal, the eastern province in which Rorke's Drift was located and to which Zulu nationalists laid claim. Lionel Davis recalls a tension between "the Soweto guys" at the art center who "had been involved in the '76 uprising" and thus had a BC, antiethnic outlook (akin to his own), and members of the Inkatha Freedom Party, Zulus who agitated for an independent nation-state wherein ethnicity mattered. He said, remembering the BC attitudes of his contemporaries at Rorke's Drift: "But this was Inkatha territory. Inkatha would have meetings in the hall above our dormitory. We were invited but we never went. We were advocating anti-Inkatha. We stirred it up. We'd have discussions amongst us but we'd have to keep it quiet."[104]

Several of Dhlomo-Mautloa's works were shown in the *Art toward Social Development* exhibition in Gaborone in July 1982. *Adam and Eve* (1978) was among them, as were three works in a series of six called *Removals* of 1981–82.[105] *Removals III: Resettlement* (Figure 5.7) records the violent relocation of people from so-called "black spots," urban areas that the state recently restricted for white use only. We are invited into the work by a stippled path at bottom center that is braced by two figures of opposing interests: a police officer at right and a woman carrying her belongings at left. As we wind through the road, we are surrounded by chaos on all fronts. The people who rush to and fro carrying their children and property are not the only ones being removed from this place. Two bulldozers, one at right and the other near the print's upper edge, begin to level the buildings in which these people made their homes. In the next moment, *Removals IV: Against Our Will,* we see the result: rubble flattened across a landscape that fills half the frame, and displaced residents standing front and center looking back on the neighborhood that is theirs no more.

Direct political defiance at Rorke's Drift was rare before the 1980s, but that changed early in the decade.[106] An instructor there, Gabriele Ellertson, remembered seeing her "share of clenched fisted, shackled wrists and other staples of liberation art" in the works of students, which she regarded as "cliché" but feared any criticism of it might "sound like censorship."[107] But defiance at Rorke's Drift did not depend on pat motifs, and indeed one finds a range of resistance imagery in works by artists while in residence there. In addition to Dhlomo-Mautloa,

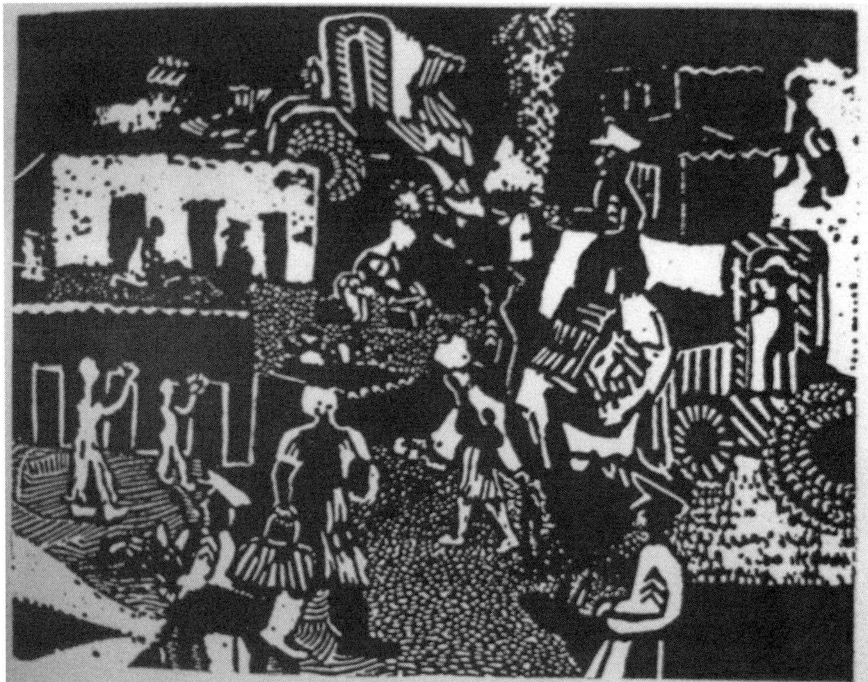

FIGURE 5.7. Bongiwe Dhlomo-Mautloa, *Removals III: Resettlement*, 1982. Linocut, 19 x 24½ cm. Standard Bank African Art Collection, Wits Art Museum. Courtesy of Bongiwe Dhlomo-Mautloa.

Nhlengethwa, and Nkosi, talents like Thami Jali, Patrick Mautloa, Anthony Nkotsi, and Paul Sibisi come to mind.

Next I highlight one of the quieter works, *Portrait of a Man (Biko),* which Anthony Molebatsi Nkotsi (b. 1955) made in 1982 (Figure 5.8). In Tony Nkotsi's vision, Biko is both cast as commoner (merely "a man" of the title) and as saint since he bears the keys to a new Republic of South Africa, thus an end to apartheid and the toiled existence it caused. He appears to be engaged in debate, mouth slightly open and right hand gesturing reasonably, thus he actively works to convince us to take his path, that of Black Consciousness.

Nkotsi copied his visage from the photograph that became hypericonic (Figure 2.1) once Dikobé Martins chose it for Biko's funeral poster (Figure 2.6), but he makes an essential change: he cloaked Biko in a garment that signals Black

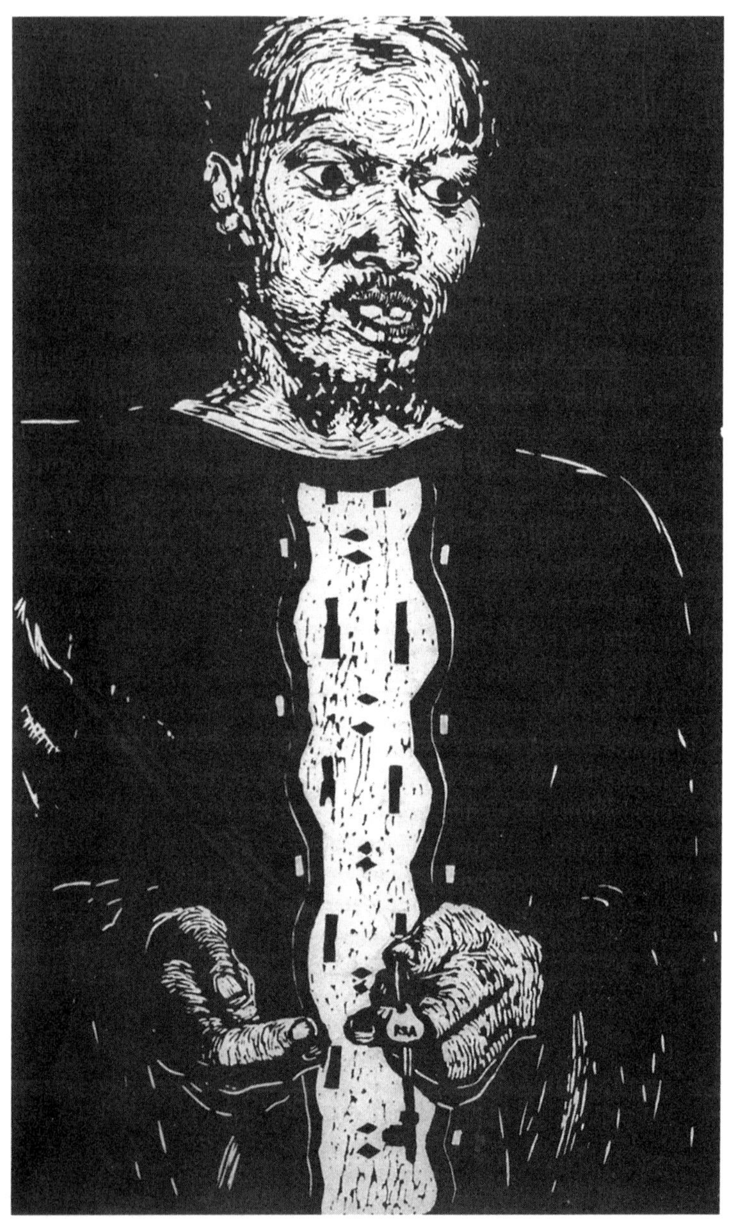

FIGURE 5.8. Tony Nkotsi, *Portrait of a Man,* 1982. Linocut, 593 x 357. Artist's collection.

Consciousness. It is a dashiki of the kind that Biko was buried in and that many BC-minded men wore to show pride in their heritage. Recall that Mohlakeng residents selected this identifier for their People's Park to Biko (Figure 5.1), in essence a monument, in late 1985. The combination of an everlasting death mask as cast by the poster and the "moment of reality" pictured in *DRUM* (Figure 2.10) translates into this saintly rendering of a martyr who not only lives but also holds the keys to a peaceful future.

Interestingly, Nkotsi copied Martins's poster image another time, in 1979, while at Rorke's Drift, but he only imaged the head against a dark backdrop and he left the work untitled. The fact that the work was copied but left untitled is important to my interests here, and I suspect that the *Portrait of a Man* originally had no identifier either.[108] Nkotsi, who took part in the Soweto Uprisings that began June 16, 1976, and was among the hundreds of students detained at that time,[109] likely paid tribute to Biko without explicitly identifying him for two reasons: one, violence in this period made one want to avoid the attention of the state; and two, Nkotsi imaged Biko for those who would recognize him, and them alone. If so, then *Portrait of a Man* is evidence of how Black Consciousness continued to be embraced despite the state's efforts to suppress its adherents, like Nkotsi, and curtail its impact.

Among BC artists, Fikile Magadlela created the most angered response to the state's violent crackdown on all forms of resistance. In a daring work within his undated series of drawings titled *Roots* (circa 1980), Magadlela imaged a black man, scarred by racial violence, overcoming a hooded member of the Ku Klux Klan whose death is marked by the blood that pools beside his head (Figure 5.9). Flames from a burning cross light the middle ground and expel soot into a darkening sky. They cast a thin stream of light across a hard, rough landscape and onto the back of the man, who is of African descent. He slumps over his dead enemy, exhausted, chest heaving and strong muscles taut. The series was made in response to Alex Haley's phenomenally popular novel and film of the same title. Published in 1976 and televised in much of the world as a twelve-hour miniseries in 1977, *Roots* was a landmark in American literature and in serial filmmaking. It resonated widely in the tricontinental world and a fourteen-hour sequel followed in 1979.

Although promptly banned within South Africa, Haley's novel was in the library of Geoff and Maokaneng Mphakati, art patrons in Mamelodi West who made studio space for Magadlela and other artists in their home. Both Haley and *Roots* inspired the artist in project and purpose. Haley sought out his family's

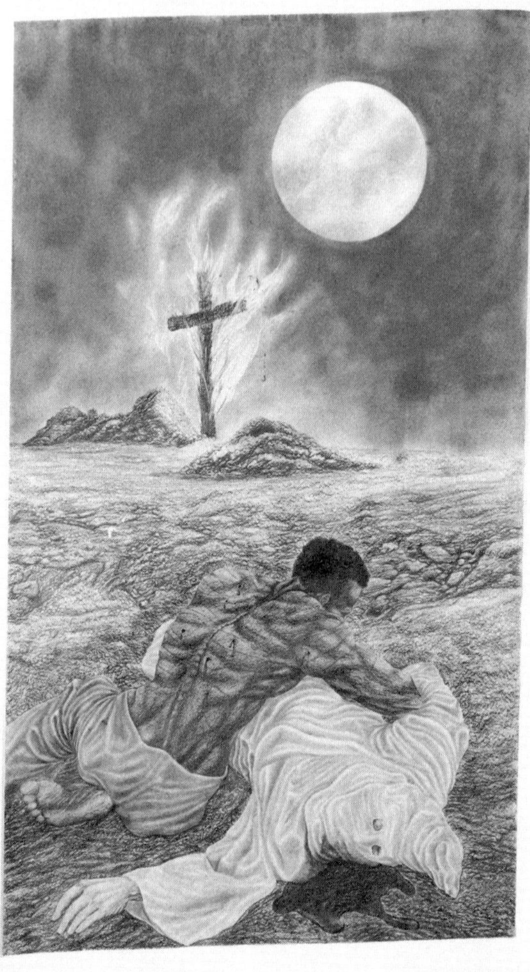

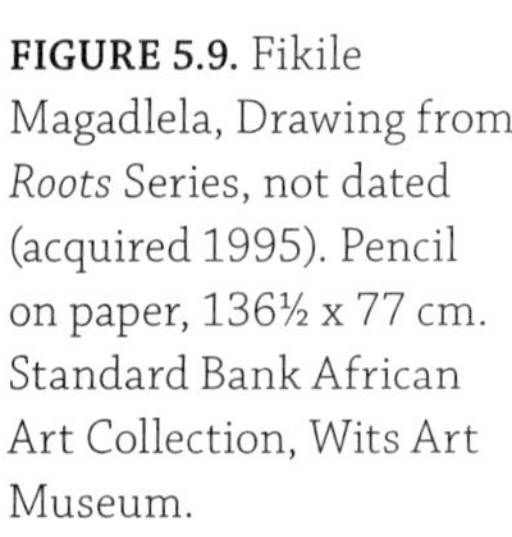

FIGURE 5.9. Fikile Magadlela, Drawing from *Roots* Series, not dated (acquired 1995). Pencil on paper, 136½ x 77 cm. Standard Bank African Art Collection, Wits Art Museum.

lineage and then brought it to the world in grand scale, a forceful retelling of history wrested from the dominant narrative. Magadlela evidenced like boldness in his own *Roots* series; it is a brave, forthright rendering of self-liberation at a time when such content brought the state's unwelcome attention. BC's message is most explicitly stated here, but Magadlela's sense of modern black culture—its audience, causes, and himself within it—infuses all his work of this period.

Black Consciousness through Experimentation

Realism was the most important criteria for advocates in the cultural worker camp, the "social revolutionaries" who supported the kind of binding agitprop that Medu and other graphic centers produced to combat apartheid. They argued that images must register immediately in order to be effective, thus they believed that those culled from real-life experiences would best suit their cause. Too frequently this prompted some among them to dismiss abstraction out of hand as an elitist product, one without relevance to any cause beyond itself. But the art-for-art's-sake argument of old did not adequately represent the objectives of many artists who found meaning in abstraction; indeed, their finished works always represented a political struggle of one kind or another. Those who favored this mode ultimately found the work more meaningful since such work prompts viewers to explore beneath the surface, pulled in by components that prompt wonder more than mystery.[110] Remember that these artists, Nadine Gordimer argued, must "assert the right to search out [their] own demotic artistic vocabulary with which to breathe new life and courage into [their] people."[111] Their purpose, she said, was singular: to master both the medium and to change the very nature of their field, to create "new norms and forms out of and for a people recreating themselves." The artists I study here found purpose in this mission since it describes the kind of self-agency with communal purpose implicit to Black Consciousness.

Motlhabane Mashiangwako (1945–2010) created *To Be Born, to Live, to Die, and to Continue Living* in 1979 (Figure 5.10), a work that recalls the deaths of BC advocates over the previous three years and uses these to propel history forward. Indeed, he embraces his role in the revolution by transforming the spear of *Time Past, Present, and Future* (see Figure 1.9) into a painter's sharp brush. Two arms that have grown too large and powerful for containment pierce the sphere-like form at center. They burst outward, each fueled by a feminized fluid mutating at the core. That at left bears an offering, and the lightly drawn traces of a winded current suggest a response. The hand at right grasps an artist's weapon that pierces the flesh and feeds from the blood in its veins. Art is urgently meaningful. It has a message. Here that message unites people along a continuum toward liberation and it advocates imagery's lasting power.

The efficacy of this image for Mashiangwako is apparent in that he adopted it, with some variation, as his signature. The form at lower left here is repeated, and further adapted, in future works. This signature honors the primacy of

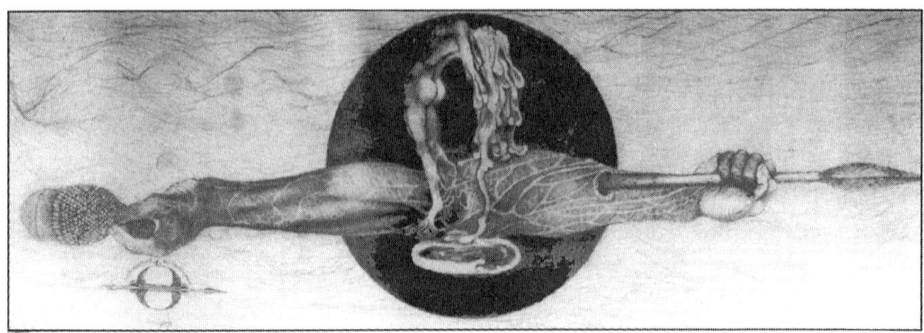

FIGURE 5.10. Motlhabane Mashiangwako, *To Be Born, to Live, to Die, and to Continue Living,* 1979. Pencil on paper, 33 x 100 cm. Collection of Geoff Mphakati. Courtesy of the Mashiangwako Estate.

African languages because it represents his name: Motlhabane means "warrior" in Sesotho, and Mashiangwako means "he who has left his dwelling."[112] His *Leokotsane: For Steve Biko* (1980) is a tricolor ink wash on paper scarred with bleach (Plate 8). Figures and forms are barely discernible; their contours are defined by delicately drawn lines and slight color variations in the free-flowing ink. Biko's likeness partially emerges from the blue field at center. His left eye, nose, and mouth are drawn frontally in black. His face appears again above the blue vertical strip, reclined and in profile as though he is dead. Mourners advance toward the corpse in a line that weaves down the left side of the paper and ends with a lean female figure. In cloak and cap at the bottom left, she turns her back on viewers, a compositional device that makes us part of the procession. Her extraordinary height signifies her might; for Mashiangwako, women, particularly mothers, are pillars of strength.[113] Her headwrap is like the elaborately drawn textile at upper right that dresses, or bandages, the point of fatal impact: the left side of Biko's head. Readers will recall that Biko's family chose to cover this wound in velvet when guests viewed their loved one's body in a procession on September 24, one day before burial.

The Sesotho word *leokotsane* may be translated in two ways that are meaningful to the reading of Mashiangwako's tribute. Frieda Hattingh translates it as a "colony of ants moving in single file," a reading that suggests communal progress toward a common goal, a key tenant of Black Consciousness.[114] Mashiangwako's procession, in which veiled mourners quietly advance and recede within the layers of washed color, implies that Black Consciousness will eventually emerge from the shadowy depths of repression. This message is also conveyed by the color green that spills forth toward the composition's upper edges. The artist chose this color to signify the fertile ground that is Black Consciousness. Mourners skirt the edge of blue, used to symbolize pain, and largely occupy the red field, which evokes blood, death, and sacrifice.[115] Mottled but vast, the field and its figures wrap around the blue center to heal Biko's pain in the afterlife.

Translating *leokotsane* as "a skimming off the top," Daniel Kunene believes that Mashiangwako might not be "saying all that there is to be said."[116] In this context the title implies that Biko's legacy is so far-reaching that visual tributes merely hint at his lasting impact. It also reflects Mashiangwako's method. With a deep breath, he blew the colored ink across the paper so that it skimmed the surface. This gesture left the artist's personal mark, his breath, upon the page. He also pressed his thumbs and hands into the ink, leaving his prints behind. Finally, he blew bleach across the composition to create the lighter tones and contours. This process inscribes Mashiangwako's presence onto *Leokotsane* and registers life in a work that records death.

The artist found himself through Black Consciousness in the early 1970s. As discussed in chapter 1, he gained much from the dialogue that regularly took place with peers who gathered at the Mphakati home in Mamelodi West. He distinctly situated himself within an African continuum and cited only African artists and writers as inspirations. His mother, Elisa, provided the earliest examples of artistic creativity when she expanded her mural painting practice by carving designs into the walls on which she worked.[117] She shared with him customary color theory as Northern Sotho artists have practiced it for as long as can be remembered. In this conceptual system, colors are gendered and affect the space in which they are used in ways that cannot be seen. That is, they have a spiritual dimension. Mashiangwako would not have described *Leokotsane: For Steve Biko* as an abstract work; instead, it is an efficacious one. He once said, "I don't believe in abstract work like Joan Miro's. I don't think I have roots in Abstraction. I deal with untouchable concepts and make [them] visible, unabstract, concrete."[118] From his earliest exposure to art making, he has engaged African-centered modes of creating. It is no wonder that he was predisposed to the aesthetics of Black Consciousness when he first took up drawing at the Mphakati residence in 1974. Its insistence on self-agency made sense. As he put it, "Only when you know who you are, can you do something."[119]

Mashiangwako's activism was tricontinental in reach and aspiration. Also of 1980, *A Dedication to the People of Biafra: Four Meditations on the Biafran*

War (Plate 9) precisely captures concerns that center the artist's work in this period. Made in honor of the people of southeast Nigeria ten years after the end of a civil war (1967–70) that they effectively lost, the drawing offers a kind of prayer set in four-part harmony across the paper. This energetic, deeply layered composition conjoins numerous figures and faces at varied angles to the viewer, at least three palms flexed open in protest, and lushly textured fabrics that flow with the colored ink. The images that converge here comprise a tribute to people who suffered and starved from hunger, or died of illness and infection in a humanitarian crisis that captured worldwide attention and has in many ways since come to define the Biafran War. In the end some three million (mostly Igbo) civilians lost their lives in the last of the wars that followed independence from Britain and shaped the political landscape of Nigeria.

The Niger Delta is well known today for its rich oil reserve, and for the civil and environmental injustices the business of extracting it has wrought upon the people of this region. Mashiangwako's method—he used a straw to blow colored ink across paper and followed this with a thin layer of bleach similarly applied—created an effect wherein variations in the wash give rise to more figures turning this way and that, grouped and alone, always expressive. Circular shapes float in the background. At once they recall the bounty found in the delta's depths and the oil slicks that now sit on the water's surface. Mashiangwako was particular in his brand of bleach; he preferred a South African product called Javel because the name symbolized destruction.[120] As an artist, he wielded his own Javel of sorts in the form of a pen, a straw, ink, breath, and bleach. He described his drive: "It is important that I live now and that I register what I witness during my time."[121] *A Dedication to the People of Biafra* thus testifies to the efficacy of BC within Mashiangwako, an artist whose libratory vision reached across borders and boundaries.

Motivated by the ideas of Steve Biko, Julius Nyerere, and Ngũgĩ wa Thiong'o, among others, Mashiangwako embraced a philosophy of life that placed the common interests shared among humans at heart.[122] He upheld Nyerere's conviction that "Man is the centre, so everything we do is done in the interest of man."[123] In Mashiangwako's vision, the people of Biafra had survived decades of violent destruction wrought by ethnic notions. But a spirit to live exists within this tribute to Biafrans, *A Dedication to Life* one might call it. Although the figures within this incredible work issue a range of emotions—sorrow, fear, refusal, fatigue, perhaps perseverance—we see no joy. Still, beneath a breast heavy with milk at center, and near a rib cage that descends from it, ghostly figures of all ages gather around a fetus within the womb. A swollen phallus points upward right to center. This collective running vertically along the central axis ignites wonder over human resilience amid the stains of war and continued exploitation. Always complexly negotiated and ripe with dispute, ethnicity was critically tested by both South Africans and Nigerians at this point in time.

Mashiangwako's work from this period is the most politically charged of his career. Every element appears inflected with his adoption of BC. He even chose an abstract manner of expression as an act against racial bias, once describing it as a means for him to "stand up against injustice" and counter the art market's expectations of black artists.[124] He described "township art [as] proof of an art trapped in the oppressor's context. Its inferiority is based on the fact that it is subscribed to a debased human situation."[125] Choosing to work outside expectations, Mashiangwako pursued Pan African aesthetics, and to him this meant an expansive, experimental, dynamic art of resistance. His subjects belie a commitment to tricontinental liberation; his methods and vision refused to engage with an art market that oppressed free expression. Black Consciousness held his attention in this period and certainly enabled him to say, "I am an African artist. I was initiated in an African environment rather than the four-walled structure of western culture."[126]

The art of Lefifi Tladi (b. 1949) in this period shares his friend Mashiangwako's appreciation for BC's tricontinental appeal, and for its fundamental support of self-expression. Some of their works evidence shared technical knowledge as well. Tladi's small drawing *Untitled* of 1979 (Plate 10) is a case in point. Drawn on a paper marked with red ink, bleach, and breath are figures with enlarged heads, a flag, rifles and ammunition, and a darkened orb. By the time he made it, Tladi had practiced (and taught intermittently) almost twenty years, combining his loves of visual art, music, poetry, and philosophy that are natural to him. Tladi met Geoff Mphakati in 1966, and he was the first of many artists that Mphakati mentored in Ga-Rankuwa and Mamelodi West; indeed, Tladi is credited with having introduced Mphakati to these men in the early 1970s.[127] Tladi, an eclectic talent, played drums for Dashiki and met Fikile Magadlela at an arts festival hosted by the South African Students' Organization (SASO) at Soweto's Mofolo Hall in 1972 where Dashiki performed along with others.[128] In turn, Magadlela met the others who frequented the Mphakati home, thereby bringing artists based near Johannesburg into the mix. It must be said that Tladi was fostering his own black consciousness in the years that Durban-based students were creating SASO. He was key to BC's infusion in the highly populated province known as Gauteng, but like so many others in this history he has received far too little attention.[129] No doubt this is due in part to his exile; forced to flee to Gaborone, Botswana, after the Soweto Uprisings of 1976, four years later he moved farther north to Sweden. The work selected to illustrate Tladi's BC leanings was made in Gaborone in 1979.

Of the published work Tladi made in this period, many are untitled and combine tightly drawn figures in spaces that defy identification. Frieda Hattingh believes his preference for enlarged heads indicates a swelling consciousness. I find the work illustrated here fascinating for its subtle suggestions of tricontinental teamwork that register in two arenas. First, the flag that freedom fighters carry at left suggests a national identity beyond borders defined by passport. Second, the facial features of these armed men are alike but different from those in the collective at right. Like the majority of figures in Tladi's work of this period, shaded lines define features and provide a sense of skin color as well. The body of people configured at right (a mass of many that stretches to eternity) looks to these soldiers for leadership. Luckily, the flag they hold testifies that the masses are welcome; indeed, the flag of transnational blackness bears a hole that only they, by virtue of the black orb above, can fill.

Tladi's art making was necessarily what Hattingh called "guerrilla vanguard."[130] I view this identifier as Hattingh does, that of a call to revolt issued by pictorial content, but I add that Tladi's verve to create as he chose was a "guerrilla" tactic and assured his place in the "vanguard." Committed though he has been to creating venues in which art of all kinds can be experienced, his insistence on defining the terms of his aesthetic explorations is itself an expression of Black Consciousness. In this way, Tladi's professional decisions have been in keeping with those of the better-known David Koloane. So, too, have their common commitment to artistic developments been long-standing and intellectually profitable.

In this same period, the great David Koloane (b. 1938) was also experimenting with abstraction. Koloane's embrace of Black Consciousness was exemplified in 1977 when he applied for funds from Black Community Programmes to open a gallery in downtown Johannesburg that was run by and for black artists and their communities. His *Made in South Africa* of 1979 (Plate 11) visualizes BC in several ways. Its size resembles that of its source, a *dompas* or passbook that black people alone were required to carry each time they ventured beyond their place of residence. Although the region has a long history of legislating movement on the land and ownership of it, in technique and title Koloane's work reflects a BC response to the Black Homelands Citizenship Act (1970).[131] Homelands, also called Bantustans, were a sharp focus of BC critique throughout the 1970s as proponents worked to counter the act's effects. It essentially stripped all black South Africans of citizenship and imposed a new "nation," in the act's words, based on presumed ethnicity. It is no wonder that BC advocates took up their cause. Anthony Marx found that more than 327,000 families were forcibly relocated from urban areas to Bantustans in the 1960s. By 1972, another 171,000 families were scheduled for removal.[132] Regarding pass laws, he calculates that one in four black adults were arrested at least once by the mid-1970s for transgressions. Given a whole host of edicts regulating movement and rights by skin color, it would seem that he is right to suggest that "in South Africa it was illegal simply to be black."[133] Despite the vocal opposition of BC proponents, three Bantustans claimed nominal "independence" from South Africa before Koloane made this work—Transkei in 1976, Bophuthatswana in 1977, and Venda in 1979—and Ciskei followed soon after in 1981.[134] At this time of contested citizenship, *Made in South Africa* reminded that Koloane, his passbook photo pasted at lower right, would not be told that his home was elsewhere. He was already there.[135]

To make the work, Koloane first tore his photograph from his *dompas* and pasted it onto board. He did the same with a ledger page; entries are visible beneath heavily laid paint, particularly above his photograph. This bold act effectively destroyed a document of the state that he was forced to carry. Koloane then applied layers of acrylic paint over the prepared surface in varying sweeps, sometimes brushed, other times dripped. He highlighted his own image by circling it in red. John Peffer describes the resulting work as "a sort of soft iconoclasm, a metaphorical erasure" of ethnic identity by a man who had lived in Alexandra since birth but had been identified as a citizen of Bophuthatswana by the state.[136] True enough, but the process of creating *Made in South Africa* was anything but soft. It was assertive, risky, and driven by Koloane's own sense of black consciousness. By actively claiming his rights as a citizen of South Africa in such a compelling way, he enacted modern black culture at a time when BC had defined its essence.

Koloane had by this time left studies at Ainslie Studios and was teaching with the Federated Union of Black Artists (FUBA) in Johannesburg.[137] As he described it, the directors at both venues shared a belief that BC was of fundamental import. Kolonae recalls that Bill Ainslie, a white South African who mentored him after his first teacher, Louis Maqubela, left the country in 1974, "had the right approach to BC ideology. He didn't have conflict with it. . . . He wasn't threatened. [He] actually had more BC than some of the people who professed to be more BC than others."[138] Ainslie challenged segregation directly by establishing the foundation at his home in Parkview, a Johannesburg suburb that was zoned for white use.[139] He taught black students and hired black teachers. He "was actually amenable to a lot of ideas" from black artists who studied with him. And he provided something scarce—space—and encouraged artists to "operate freely to free themselves of the many inhibitions and obstacles that were placed before them."[140]

While at FUBA in the early 1980s, Koloane took in the strongly BC-infused proclamations of its director, the writer Sipho Sepamla. FUBA's staff and patrons included people who varied in color (including white) but shared a common vision and understanding: "[They] did not negate what the institution was all about: it is the black child first who had to be taught."[141] In this way, FUBA was a bit like the Medu Art Ensemble, founded the same year in Gaborone, Botswana. BC was vividly expressed in the missions of both bodies, and the presence of whites within them merely means that these people were willing to first listen and learn, and then teach.

Save for that by Matsemela Manaka's *Echoes of African Art,* studies of FUBA tend to emphasize the role of Bill Ainslie. I wish to draw attention to the people who had an equal, if not greater part, in realizing FUBA and endeavors like The Gallery and the Thupelo Art Project. For instance, John Peffer cites 1978 as the year that Ainslie and colleagues sought to create an interdisciplinary school of the arts, so they "merged with a similar [initiative] headed by Gibson Kente in Soweto, and the Federated Union of Black Artists was begun."[142] Now let us note that Kente's vision was significant here and driven by Black Consciousness; indeed, the Soweto-based gallery had been granted funding from Black Community Programmes (BCP), but these were curtailed when the government banned BCP on October 19, 1977.[143] Although Ainslie was instrumental to FUBA and Thupelo, one could easily conceive of these as vital to the "life's work" of David Koloane.[144] These efforts were preceded by The Gallery, for which Koloane applied to the BCP for funding in 1977 together with Hugh Nolutshungu and Zulu Bidi.[145] Ainslie joined the effort in 1978.[146]

We see Koloane's continued effort in community building today: the Bag Factory/Fordsburg Artists' Studios in Johannesburg (founded 1991), a famed artists' space complete with international residencies, approaches its twenty-fifth year in operation. I do not mean to diminish Ainslie's role in any way. Rather, I aim to enhance our understanding of FUBA, Thupelo, and even Ainslie's studio by underscoring that Black Consciousness was present within its instigators. The dominant view is similar to Peffer's: "Multiculturalism, or more accurately a 'Freedom Charter' policy of nonracialism, was both cause and effect of the Thupelo Project."[147] But as I argued in the previous chapter, such ideas have gained currency because the ANC has largely controlled the rainbow-inflected narrative to date, and it conveniently situated Black Consciousness as racial when in fact BC was about the power of voice, not race. Thupelo's insistence that black artists receive training and materials afforded to white artists, albeit in comparatively modest scale, is an expression of Black Consciousness.

Throughout its seven-year run, the Thupelo Art Project funded invited artists to a two-week period of training, discussion, and experimentation.[148] Thupelo was for people who were largely denied access to formal lessons, but some white artists attended.[149] Also included was an international guest. Thupelo gave South African artists of color a few precious things that were not customarily part of their lives: imported materials far too costly to purchase privately; large open spaces in which to create instead of the cluttered environments in which many worked; a chance to experiment with new media and incorporate new techniques (like the use of found and handmade objects); and, importantly, a sense of community. In return, workshop participants were to take their new insights home again and share them at the art centers formed in townships the previous decade in response to BC. In this way, they exercised *thupelo,* a Southern Sotho word meaning "to teach by example." Such a choice reflects the swell in accountability that had struck artists in this period, one that spilled over from cultural activists of the 1970s whose BC alignment was clearer than those of the next decade.

Several artists within this study participated in Thupelo workshops over the years, and usually multiple times: Peter Clarke, Lionel Davis, Garth Erasmus, David Koloane, Bongiwe Dhlomo-Mautloa, Sam Nhlengethwa, and Tony Nkotsi.[150] I choose to focus attention here on works by one artist not yet mentioned, the world-renowned Durant Silhali, who attended every Thupelo workshop but one. Silhali is heralded for his mastery of watercolor and his record of intimate, human scenes he "documented" through art. Scholarship tends to focus on such figural works presumably because they are more accessible and thus more explicitly "political." They enable an answer to the ever-present question that Colin Richards wryly observed, "What does it mean?"[151] But Silhali's experiments at Thupelo prompted him to shift from humans in public to studies of their public mark making. Because of Thupelo, Silhali stepped up close to the walls that define townships and detailed their cracked plaster and flaked paint, the pealing posters on them that whisper behind the graffiti that shouts out. In the late 1980s, the pressing needs scrawled on public walls became the subject of Silhali's work. His *Reminders of Past Apartheid* of 1987 (Plate 12) is one example.

Across a space layered with color and line, Silhali recorded the words and forms of generations by painting and scratching acrylic on paper. Political slogans and personalities of our time share space with forms of lighter hue that evoke cave paintings of the distant past. By virtue of color, two words rise quickly to meet our eye: *Mandela* in black and *Amandla* (a familiar shout-out meaning Power) in white. They nudge out *Azania,* repeated in red and gray at right, the name Black Consciousness advocates chose for South Africa. Peffer suggests that Sihlali "predicted . . . a more fully integrated national culture to come," but for me it was meaningful the year it was made, 1987.[152] Thanks to Silhali's careful observation of his world, competing voices for liberation are recorded in one space: Mandela represents the ANC and its supporters within South Africa; Azania represents AZAPO; Amandla was used across parties. Its deeply marked acrylic surface, so different from the quick brush required of watercolor, is, as Colin Richards put it, "violent, bloody and vicious. The pigment embalms the anger, the bitterness and the rage of life" that engulfed people who expressed themselves so urgently on public walls.[153] But the violence is not bodily, nor does it follow a neat trajectory of state to people, as Peffer proposes. To my eye, Silhali records the less public battle between the ANC and AZAPO, a division less visible but no less vocal.

Although Silhali did not speak on record about Black Consciousness, his actions and description of his wall-based works reverberate with a sense of modern black culture not far afield from that which Biko espoused. Consider what he told Richards in 1995. Reflecting on pictures made by *Idlozi,* a complex lineage set, he said:

There was no other art except the wall. *I'll do the wall, say what I have to say, but it will remain the wall.* At one stage they were saying that the wall is not art, hence my sticking to the wall because I need to celebrate the wall. *It is the symbol of the nation.* The first impression that man made was on the wall in a cave and so for me that is the beginning of art.[154]

Call it sensibility or awareness or consciousness, Silhali allied himself with ancestors within a rubric that transnational blackness defined. Coming out of the Thupelo Art Project, itself resounding with Black Consciousness in its insistence to work in the manner of one's choice ("hence my sticking to the wall"; to "say what I have to say"), Silhali lived modern black culture as the younger generation defined it.

The visual culture gathered in this chapter has been the most elusive to analyze. I only understood its relation by researching across disciplines to discover pertinent nuggets (representations) of Black Consciousness history and values/voice/vision tucked away in studies of nonracialist histories and the political parties that promoted them. Fascinated by a general dismissiveness that occasionally contradicted itself within my own field of art history, I came to understand this mode as another form of silencing. I hasten to add that which is passed down through scholarship ought not be compared to that rendered by the state through successive years of emergencies, and I mean no direct corollary. But I do mean to challenge the dominant vision of visual culture and racial theory as we record it because historic documents like those linked here illustrate the need. Interviews and other primary research confirmed it.

Black Consciousness was alive and flourishing in the 1980s, detectable in multiple spheres, some more evident than others. Although its currency necessarily divided in the 1980s (most significantly as the BC-inclined joined different political parties after organizations that formed their own "party in the making" were banned October 19, 1977), it registered strongly within the nation's visual culture of the decade, a world of representation imag(in)ed through what we read and sense (primarily see and hear, but not exclusively so). We see it in popular media, and not just coverage of a Hollywood film, or annual commemorations of Biko in which narratives of death regrettably still share space with discussion of BC's relevance today. I believe that we must see it, too, in the more reified realm of art making and the debates sparked by self-described "cultural workers" who contested its value. One need not be as steeped in this debate as was Nadine Gordimer, but as she explicitly stated the value and necessity of BC in keynotes at conferences that scholars prize (also keeping in mind that she was a Nobel laureate), we might listen.

Denying Gordimer's vision, or David Koloane's, or those of others who expressed their own black consciousness by insisting to create as they liked, is no different from denying those early BC artists their right to self-identify as they might. Gavin Jantjes, Fikile Magadlela, Motlhabane Mashiangwako, and Lefifi Tladi all spoke out about BC's importance in their lives, but rarely did they find a writer willing to consider it righteous, thus the failure to dislodge preconceptions about it. Just as those invested in overturning apartheid debated roles in shaping culture as resistance, I aim to foster debate about BC's centrality in creating this ideology. As Annie Coombes rightly assessed, South Africans are accustomed to rigorous debate given the broad-based political education that knew no walls.[155] In the best interest of traditions like these, I look forward to our discussions ahead.

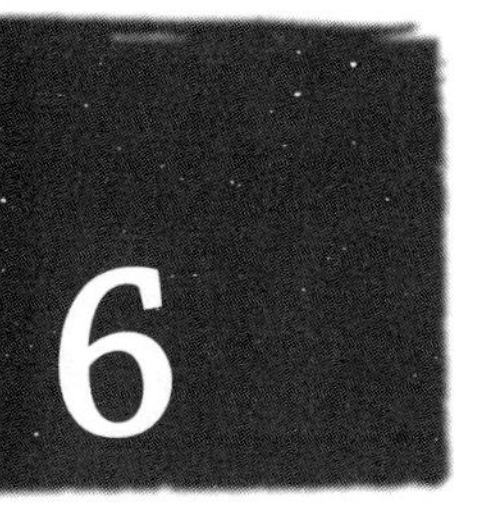

6 Transitions and Truths in a New Democracy

SOUTH AFRICA'S TRANSITION FROM APARTHEID TO DEMOCRACY WAS LONG IN coming. When the doors of a new era publically opened on February 2, 1990, South Africans began an intensive period of negotiation at all levels, public and private. In one sphere, former rivals—the National Party (NP) and the African National Congress (ANC), newly unbanned—undertook talks toward a settlement of interests. These were derailed by intensified violence and proof of the NP's collusion in fueling it, but eventually negotiations brought change.[1] Negotiations in the public arena, for instance, took place among interest groups of wide range and affiliation that were invited to the Convention for a Democratic South Africa (CODESA) to help formulate the start of a new constitution. Though the process was difficult, hampered by disagreements and eventually cut short due to ongoing violence in the country, it sustained a growing sense of support for a new democracy.[2]

In other, highly personalized spheres, individuals were rethinking themselves within the context of change around them. Oral history—a space of autonomous recovery—gained sway in several contexts. Historians emphasized it as method;[3] autobiography held new importance for artists of all kinds; memory became, in Colin Richards's words, "a veritable industry" as personal recollection, and self-reflection, took shape in daily reports about hearings before the Truth and Reconciliation Commission (TRC).[4]

The TRC's most visible work took place before its committees on human rights and amnesty wherein victims and perpetrators recounted their roles in the gross violation of bodily human rights that met two criteria: they were politically motivated, and they took place within a specified period of a bit more than thirty-four years.[5] The act that defined the TRC's mandate (Promotion of National Unity and Reconciliation Act, Number 34) described the nation's "need for understanding but not for vengeance, a need for reparation but not retaliation, a need for *ubuntu* but not victimization."[6] The Truth and Reconciliation Commission was tasked with realizing these needs.

Ubuntu, an Nguni word that roughly translates to "humanity," has come to characterize South Africa's utmost aspiration. The word embodies an ethical stance within human interaction, one that recognizes commonality and thus assures humane engagement among people. To possess ubuntu is to be generous in spirit and practice, and to be compassionate and forgiving. To practice ubuntu is to respect a Zulu maxim: *umuntu ngumuntu ngabantu,* "a person is a person through persons."[7] Nelson Mandela has described ubuntu as a practice from "the old days, when we were young," and Desmond Tutu has noted the "proper self-assurance that comes from knowing that [one] belongs in a greater whole."[8] Ubuntu honors human relations as central to being and, although this social value is understood to be of Africa, it is also of Black Consciousness.

In several respects, Steve Biko in this period came to represent the ideal of ubuntu, what his friend and colleague N. Barney Pityana has called "a renewal of African moral values" that inspired the "African Renaissance" then unfolding.[9] *Holy Stephen* (see Figure 6.5) captures this currency quite well as the advice unfurled from this saint's hands *enables* a return to what is deemed in essence African custom. Philosophers like Hennie Lötter stressed Biko's own position and in so doing followed the academic trend. In 1992, Lötter quoted Biko's speech of 1971 when assessing his "intellectual legacy" for South Africa. Here Biko expressed the need to "restore (to the black man) the great importance we used to give to human relations, the high regard for people and their property and for life in general; to reduce the triumph of technology over man and the materialistic element that is slowly creeping into our society."[10]

Moreover, since race has no part in ubuntu, Biko's legacy was seen by many to transcend a boundary of their own creation, blackness. To project such ideals, this "martyr of hope" was seen to have died for unity.[11] Indeed, since 1990 the press has often characterized unity as his dying wish, since on the last journey of his own choosing he had traveled to Cape Town intent on getting different organs of common interest but conflicting methods—the BPC, the ANC, and the PAC (the latter two then in exile)—to meet; he proposed a funeral in Gaborone, Botswana, as the opportune site.[12] The meeting took place but without Biko.[13] En route back to Ginsberg, Biko and Peter Jones were stopped at a police roadblock outside of Port Elizabeth. Biko lived another twenty-five days; Jones was held another 533 days, without trial, under Section Six of the Terrorism Act. Nonetheless, Biko's last project was one of bridge building among adversaries, an image that suited a new "rainbow nation" at work in South Africa in the years of transition from apartheid.

As much as BC was bent in this period, through Biko's iconographic sanctification, to highlight a humanistic, nonracial future, it was also rather paradoxically skewed by the press to favor two race-based parties as registrars of BC opinion: the Azanian People's Organization (AZAPO) and the Black Consciousness Movement of Azania (BCMA). Both were among early organizational responses to the state's banning of BPC and other BC bodies in October 1977. In the 1990s, the South African press commonly reported on Biko commemorations through AZAPO's voice, citing either party statements or interviews, and largely neglected other BC voices. Although the legacies of Biko and Black Consciousness had been cast wide (and publically honored as such at an important 1990 Harare conference), tensions continued as to how race effected meaning and, with this, how Biko and Black Consciousness would further influence South Africa's future.[14]

For instance, Dikobé Martins designed the cover of *Bounds of Possibility: The Legacy of Steve Biko & Black Consciousness* (Figure 6.1) by quoting a 1978 drawing he made called *Biko and Solidarity—One Nation* (see Figure 2.7). Both works depict a mass of demonstrators at Biko's funeral where a poster, designed by Martins no less, is prominent. Recall that the photograph cited in the funeral poster showed Biko in suit and tie (see Figure 2.1); in the 1978 drawing, Martins borrowed this photograph but omitted all clothing. With two earlier referents, the book cover for *Bounds of Possibility* is Martins's third version of Biko in memoriam, and in this 1991 incarnation Biko reappears, is made "real" once more, through photograph rather than drawing. Vitally, the photograph (by Fraser MacLean) differs from the funeral icon: Biko has shed the diplomat's necktie for a workman's shirt in a photograph that gained iconic weight in this period, even surpassing the funeral icon, always heavy, as it is, with death. All text has been removed from this version of the poster (most conspicuously absent is "One Azania—One Nation") and it is now edged in green, common to several political parties, but not among the colors of any political organization Biko supported through membership. Refashioning Biko as a man of the people suited the editors' objective: to underscore BC's expansive, influential reach into realms that are harder to "book," or categorize, such as party memberships. Instead, *Bounds of Possibility* explores BC's effects in South African cultural, legal, gendered, theological, and political spheres, and it historicizes BC after more than twenty years of practice.

What follows is a study of two realms in which Steve Biko factored significantly in the life of the nation in this time of transitions and truths. In the first he figures among a few heroes whom artists honor in the effort to recollect

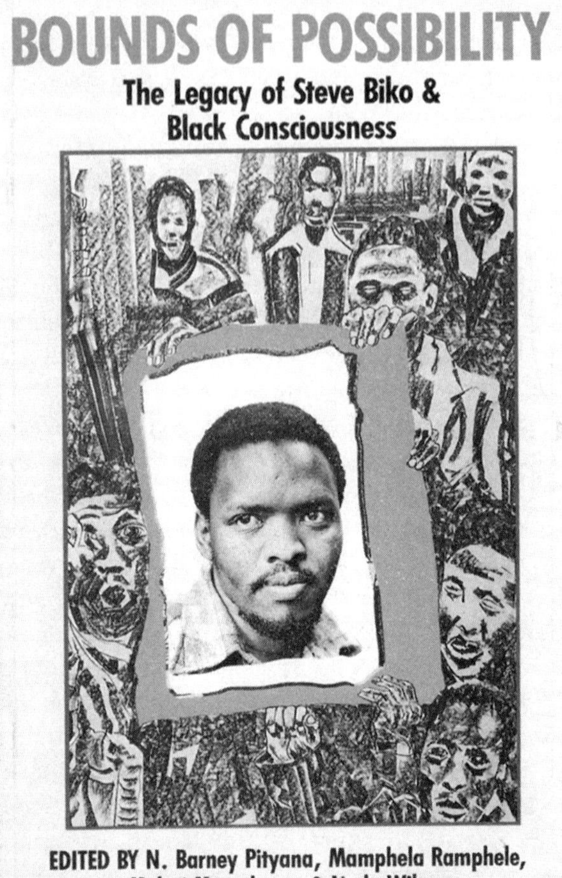

FIGURE 6.1. Dikobé Martins, *Bounds of Possibility*, 1991. Book cover for N. Barney Pityana, Mamphela Ramphele, Malusi Mpumlwana, and Lindy Wilson, eds., *Bounds of Possibility: The Legacy of Steve Biko & Black Consciousness* (Claremont and London: David Philip and Zed Books, 1991).

history after decades of silencing. His prominence in this unfolding story was matched by another, the casting of Biko as a saint of sorts, the embodiment of ubuntu. As a martyr for black liberation whose death has been narrated in South Africa more than any other, Biko and his humanism represented the ultimate olive branch. It reinforced the very "respect for human life and dignity and [the] revival of *ubuntu*" that the Truth and Reconciliation Commission sought.[15] The TRC is thus the second realm of this chapter. Biko's case history was heard before amnesty and medical ethics committees, and it flashes across two covers of the TRC's five-volume report, unmatched by any other. Here I describe that case history alongside the TRC's evolution and mission, and critiques of these. Then I undertake a close study of three rather complex artworks that the Biko hearings inspired.

Imag(in)e a History Once Censored

A good many factors brought about the eventual end of apartheid in South Africa. Pressures within the nation and without combined to create significant economic decline, with unemployment and inflation running high by the late 1980s. From within, grassroots tactics like work stay-away days had borne results. The UDF had brought together over six hundred organizations that carried greater influence over national campaigns as a result. Consecutive states of emergency from 1985 to 1989 fanned resentments; censored reporting on the civil war did the same. Ongoing international sanctions in materials trade and official boycotts in sports and culture were at their height in the 1980s. So, too, had pressures mounted on international corporations to cease business in South Africa as campaigns to end apartheid gained greater focus in European capitals and on American university campuses. The fall of the Berlin Wall in 1989 and gradual easing of Cold War tensions among its principles created further difficulties for Pretoria. The ANC, with which F. W. de Klerk and NP members had begun secret negotiations in 1988, could no longer be cast as terrorist as it had in the previous decade. And with a technological revolution under way worldwide, apartheid would not insulate South Africans from change, but it would further isolate them from economic progress.

February 2, 1990, marks the public beginning of apartheid's end, since on this day de Klerk, elected Prime Minister five months prior, stood before Parliament and lifted restrictions on thirty-three opposition groups and put a moratorium on the death penalty. Clearly, concrete change was afoot. Nine days later, several of South Africa's best-known political prisoners were released, including Nelson Mandela, who had by then spent twenty-seven years of his life sentence behind bars on the finding that he had violated the Suppression of Communism Act (1950). The changes sparked violent response. On the far right, parties like the Afrikaner Weerstandsbeweging (AWB, Afrikaner Brotherhood) and Witwolwe (White Wolves) launched a "counterrevolution" through a series of violent tactics like bombing ports of transit and schools, posting explosive parcels, and committing random killings.[16] Attuned to ethnic pride, the newly created Inkatha Freedom Party (IFP) targeted ANC and UDF members and, as eventually shown, was paid by the NP to be violent.[17]

Negotiations between parties, principally the ANC and the NP, progressed in fits and starts, hampered by ongoing violence and revelations that caused mistrust. But by October a systemic repeal of apartheid laws had begun in earnest. In February 1991, Parliament opened the year by abolishing such key pieces of legislation as the Land Acts (1913, 1936, amended post-1948), Group Areas Act (1950), and the cornerstone of apartheid, the Population Registration Act (1950).[18] All South Africans were now free to own land in the place of their choice and free to live without segregation, whether in urban, periurban, or rural locations. Most crucially, they were now free of the demand to be divided and classified first by faulty notions of race and then by equally problematic notions of ethnicity.

The historic reforms of 1990 prompted many artists to create tributes honoring men and women who helped bring about apartheid's end. Most of their subjects had been banned, so any citation (in word or image) was illegal until de Klerk lifted this restriction on February 2. Although artists had both quietly circumvented such laws and boldly challenged them in prior decades, one senses in South African art an urgent need to narrate a new nation at this time, one that followed the beliefs and lives of resistance history. Three such works that honor Steve Biko are considered here.

Sam Nhlengethwa (b. 1955) works in varied materials and is South Africa's most accomplished collage artist. He first began exploring with this medium in 1977 while studying with Bill Ainslie on an informal basis at his home in Parktown, a suburb of Johannesburg.[19] It was here that he remembers first making works collaged with images clipped from the news.[20] They were tributary works: *Winnie in Brandfort,* in honor of Mrs. Mandela, then banished to this small town north of Bloemfontein; and another called *My Heroes,* which included Biko, Nelson Mandela, Muhammad Ali, and John F. Kennedy each playing an instrument in an orchestra.[21] After seeing these, Ainslie gave him a book about Romare Bearden, the famed American master of collage. For Nhlengethwa, the medium appealed because it combined the familiar with the hidden. Culled from black magazines like *DRUM, Pace, Style, Bona,* and *Cosmopolitan,* the images he clipped maintain the immediacy of their source but are configured anew.[22] At this time in Nhlengethwa's career, they testify to truths denied and histories untold. Collage distorts. One disjuncture upon the next, its troubling juxtapositions enabled Nhlengethwa to visualize lives "disorganized by the apartheid system."[23] Coming out of the 1980s, a period of heightened censorship, the artist felt a "duty [to record] the truth" of township lives, full as they are with ubuntu, insistently residing alongside the violence that secured apartheid.

Nhlengethwa's best-known work, also a tribute, is the ironically titled *It Left Him Cold—The Death of Steve Biko* of 1990 (Plate 13).[24] Nhlengethwa resolved to make the piece soon after de Klerk repealed laws that restricted the imaging of banned people. Immediately, he said, "I knew what I wanted to do with the Biko portrait." His vision of death in isolation, reaffirming "what the public knew" by visualizing its extremes, resulted in this now iconic work. Collage, pencil, and charcoal on paper, it sits in a shallow recess from the glass above and is boxed in by a dark frame. All were original to Nhlengethwa's concept to capture a sense of suffering within a confined space. He focused on the head, a composite of six autopsy photographs that together make up the work's central focus point. Enlarged beyond measure to anything else in the composition, the portrait conveys several messages at once. By magnifying attention to the point of fatal impact—Nhlengethwa twice clipped and pasted the same photograph (note the common lighting on the eyelids), a gesture in tune with an aesthetics of repetition that confronts loss—the artist underscores the brutality suffered by a man who remains larger than life.[25] His torso, broken legs, and nakedness register uncomfortably, reminding us of the vulnerabilities of the state in this time of transition.

Elsewhere, conflicting patterns and textures set at odd angles confuse the eye. The jumble forms a gray, dank interior that contrasts with the day's intense light outside. Activity abounds there amid several clippings showing police and their vehicles. At lower left a pile of objects recalls their presence inside. The empty chair, an object synonymous with detainee abuse, is broken but upright. The very imaging of a jail cell was outlawed prior to 1990; so too were sketches or photographs of prisons and police headquarters.[26] Nhlengethwa's decision to picture a man and a space soon after they were no longer censored suggests an urgent need to imag(in)e both.

It Left Him Cold—The Death of Steve Biko was first shown in a solo exhibition Nhlengethwa called *Today, Yesterday and Tomorrow* that traveled within South Africa in 1993. The representation of violence within several works generated heated response in the press, for the artist too. On display were the collages *Very Ugly, Funeral in Alexandria, Sharpeville Shooting, Sophiatown, District Six, Hospital Scene, Police Action,* and *Aftermath,* among others. Also shown were tributes like that to Bearden, a series to jazz musicians, and other celebratory scenes like weddings and church gatherings, but these generated little attention.[27] *It Left Him Cold* is part of this highly praised collection, but unlike its partners it registers stillness amid the chaos.[28] Nhlengethwa reasoned that his own "wounds were too itchy to be ignored," so he created works that vividly recall the suffering that violence wrought for decades, thereby enabling himself to feel "healed."[29]

Several works in the series are a cluster of images, tightly intertwined and heavily layered with paint or drawn over. The artist uses photographs clipped from news sources to reveal "facts" or "truths" about black life in South Africa. The collected works in *Today, Yesterday and Tomorrow* image a history denied by the state, which had censored news of violence upon township residents.[30] When laws were lifted early in 1990, Nhlengethwa created this body of work in order to "put all those things together, about our life . . . our history," in order to secure truths before they were lost in the transition to democracy.

Willie Bester (b. 1956) has supported Black Consciousness since his youth. As a self-described teenage "young rebel" of the mid-1970s, he wore an army jacket embroidered with a peace sign and the popular slogan "Black Is Beautiful."[31] Today he locates his desire for a more humane South Africa in Black Consciousness and attributes his own self-awareness and agency to the movement's earliest leaders. Okwui Enwezor finds Bester "able to speak, to threaten, to be angry" about the innumerable social injustices he has witnessed.[32] With vision and wit, Bester has made use of this anger by creating art that sparks debate about the things that trouble him most: poverty, violence, and racism.[33] He is best known for the large-scale compositions (high relief and sculptural) that combine his own photographs and paintings with objects discarded by township residents in and around Cape Town that he collects for reuse.

Bester's *Homage to B.* of 1992 (Plate 14) is the first in a six-part series called *Heroes* made to honor people whose efforts helped bring about apartheid's end.[34] By then he had mastered collage, even brought it to new heights. Michael Godby and Sandra Klopper found the technique particularly apt for the period, in that it "facilitates interesting notions of memory, history and narrative as the juxtaposition of elements and varying depth of field enable readings that are at once layered and simultaneous."[35] His ever more complex combination of found objects, photographs, and bright paint were timely in this transitional period when the past, present, and future all competed for attention.

In *Homage to B.,* a narrative of torture (or Stations of the Cross) surrounds a painted portrait of Biko that derives from a photograph of him in a light-hearted moment.[36] Bester uses tones of gray here in order to retain the aesthetic of newsprint; indeed, three distinct areas in the composition include newspaper copy that tells of Biko's leadership within the Black Peoples' Convention and his detention and interrogation. Primary colors overlaying the gray zones unite the portrait and text with other parts of the composition in which multiple stories are told. Biko's image blends with the materials, images, and words that immediately abut his likeness. A reused matchbox reminds us that he is a "Lion" who lives within and asserts his pride; he is the very embodiment of "Super Black" identity. A traffic sign extends leftward to begin a narrative of imprisonment and torture that spins clockwise from his portrait. The roadblock outside of Port Elizabeth is painted beneath the stop sign. Just above, Minister of Justice James Kruger appears in profile beneath the window of a jail cell numbered 619. Violence within detention is referenced in several ways. The closed door of a jail cell is suggested at the upper right by the attachment of a door handle and lock to an airvent plate. Wire mesh elsewhere in the composition—at the right center edge, in the far upper-left corner, and again slightly below it—reiterates confinement, as does the barbed wire that frames the composition on three sides. Torture devices are evoked by tightly coiled metal springs. Two images denote Biko's cross-country transport in his final hours: a brightly painted yellow Land Rover moves in the direction of Pretoria as indicated by the green sign above. Finally, a doctor's torso, cloaked in scrubs and labcoat, appears above a pair of feet that are toe-tagged for the morgue. On the whole, *Homage to B.* isolates the story of Biko's death to this relatively small spiral.[37]

The rest is given over to a more generalized study of violence that apartheid enforced and that lingered, even grew in some places, during the nation's transition to democracy. A target above Biko's left shoulder encircles a photograph of township residents. The state's anti–Black Consciousness crusade that led to Biko's death in 1977 registers across time and space to include all black South Africans since all are still targeted by abuse.[38] Found objects collected in townships are reconfigured here into metaphoric indices that link Biko's particular history to that of millions, but, Bester emphasized, they are "more than a connection of events." Racially motivated violence is Bester's subject—both that explicitly enforced during apartheid and that committed in the years of apartheid's long fall. Included are military boots painted with the words "woman rapers," "woman killers," "why are you afraid?" and "BAT 32" (a battalion that warred in

Namibia). Affixed below Biko's portrait is a shiny piece of old corrugated metal, once used to roof or side a home. It is painted with icons of governmental control: SC300 (Section 300), which denotes the address assigned a neighborhood of so-called shacks, and a blue-eyed policeman, masked to enter a township at night. The makeshift stringed instrument at bottom is a common motif in Bester's work that connotes conflicting meanings: the need for social harmony and the Afrikaans command to "dance as the music dictates."[39] Resistance to this dictate registers in the slingshots at the lower-right and left edges, and again in the bullet shells strung across the work's lower half. Finally, the numbers painted on discarded tin cans connote the randomness of apartheid's system of racial classification. Bester particularly abhorred the Population Registration Act because it divided his childhood home into three racial categories.[40]

Like others in the series that it sparked, *Homage to B.* critiques racial violence by exposing its varied forms. Histories of individuals and collectives are complexly intertwined. The narrative of Biko's last days records physical violence, a story Bester rendered mostly in paint. Economic violence registers most strongly in the objects Bester collected from townships, places where material deprivation was "instrumental in defining a sense of reduced humanity amongst the majority of South Africans."[41] As Godby and Klopper relate, apartheid's "institutionalized poverty and systematic degradation created an entire population of oppressed people; and, in a similar way, the South African security apparatus effectively constructed people's leaders as villains."[42] With the *Hero* series, Bester both corrects this narrative and, by creating radical disjunctions with material, encourages us to read racial violence as multifaceted and meaningful across space and time. Godby and Klopper find:

> Most significant is Bester's quietly stated but insistent endeavor to restore the quality of human dignity to the population that institutionalized racism had worked to degrade. His figure subjects are emphatically alive, active, and expressive, in contrast to the reduced level of existence accorded them by apartheid statistics. This sense is confirmed in the medium of oil painting itself, with its connotations of the human tradition of portrait painting and its ability to communicate a virtually abstract sense of human dignity and worth. In fact, Bester's intention to reclaim and restore the very language of art, and the human condition that is its principal subject, is apparent even in his techniques, for in choosing to communicate this vision in society's discards, he is demanding that even this material be looked at again and revalued.[43]

The works discussed here honor Steve Biko for his fearlessness; he paid the ultimate sacrifice for standing strong in his beliefs. Although each narrates moments of passing (gradually in Bester's work, and complete in Nhlengethwa's), each contributes to Biko's rebirth in a new era. In this way, their efforts were similar to those of politicians who recognized Biko's symbolic potential as they also engaged newly in narrating the past in order to guide the future.

Political parties began claiming Biko as a posthumous member soon after his death, but on the eve of democracy the debate about which party he would call "home" (a debate about the tenor of Black Consciousness at the time) had become vitriolic. AZAPO claimed to own BC, a stance it holds today. In 1990, Strini Moodley, among AZAPO's best-known members since he went to prison as one of the so-called SASO Nine, described the Black Consciousness beliefs of ANC members as "a betrayal" to the movement.[44] People who found BC relevant in their own lives regardless of the political parties to which they belong have consistently countered AZAPO's position. Khotso Makhule, an Anglican archbishop and president of the World Council of Churches, captured this spirit in 1990 when he said that BC adherents "have gone to different political homes without relinquishing the BC philosophy." An attempt to unify members of AZAPO, the ANC, and the PAC early in the decade did not work, and the press continued to favor AZAPO and related organs as torchbearer of "the movement" in this period.[45] As such, AZAPO's position on negotiations, transitional governance, and constitutional reform were seen to be Biko's own. "Biko Would Have Fought This Sell-Out," headlines a *South* editorial by Jimmy Yekiso, AZAPO publicity secretary.[46] In his 1993 "Focus on Steve Biko," *Sowetan* writer Themba Molefe both adopted AZAPO's position as representative of Biko's (it alone provides "the context" in which Biko can be translated) and cast Black Consciousness as illicit. He reported on the black consciousness of leaders outside of AZAPO, particularly that of Tokyo Sexwale of the ANC:

> ANC and the PAC leadership today *admit* that their political grooming is rooted in BC and Biko's beliefs.
>
> Many of them were his close *confidants.* Tokyo Sexwale, a political powerhouse in his own right, *admits* he is intrinsically black conscious, and *does not apologize for it.*
>
> To him BC is a teaching. "BC has made me, but what I am involved in right now is political and real," he once *confided.*[47]

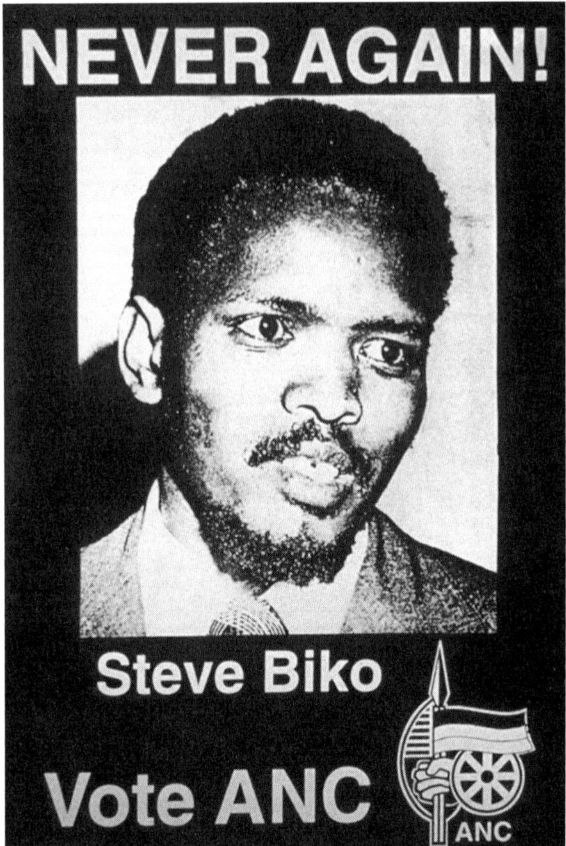

FIGURE 6.2. *Never Again!* ANC election poster, 1994. South African History Archive, University of the Witwatersrand.

Molefe translates Black Consciousness as somehow unacceptable for public airing. And he condones Sexwale's typecasting of BC as something of the past, no longer "real" in any efficacious way. Is Molefe aware that he and other journalists largely set the context in which Biko and BC may be remembered? Tokyo Sexwale had nothing to hide. The ANC claimed Steve Biko as a member in an election poster the next year (Figure 6.2). Borrowing the command of World War II's holocaust survivors, *Never Again!* titles a series that followed a common form, all presented in shades of gray: series title at top; portrait photograph of a murdered activist; name of the fallen; and "Vote ANC" beside the party's logo at bottom. That Biko was never an ANC member was not relevant to the

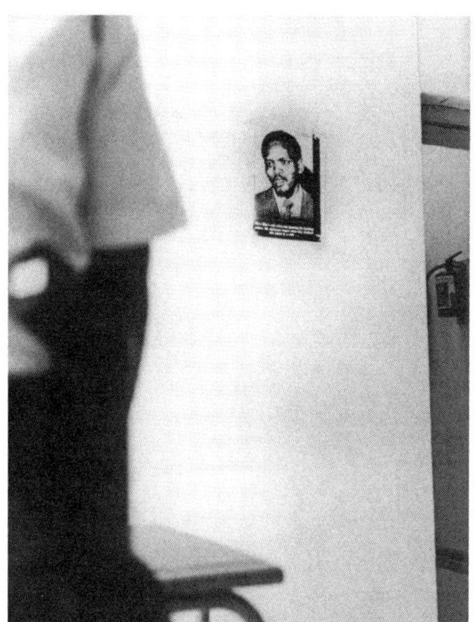

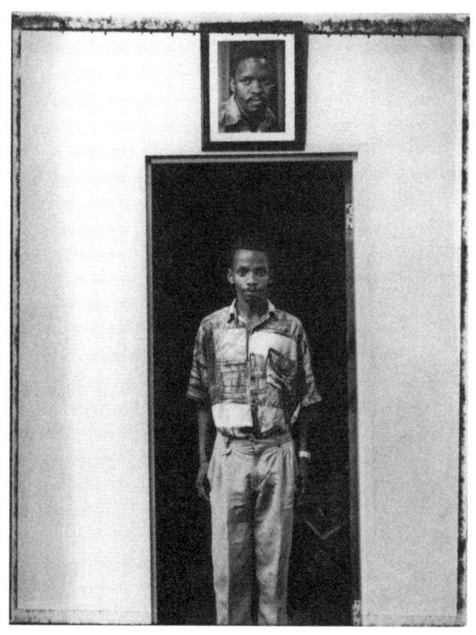

FIGURE 6.3. Jillian Edelstein, poster of Biko at a hearing of the Truth and Reconciliation Commission, 1997. Courtesy of Jillian Edelstein.

FIGURE 6.4. Jillian Edelstein, Belgium Biko standing beneath a portrait of Biko captured by Fraser MacLean, at home in Ginsberg, 1997. Courtesy of Jillian Edelstein.

project. Indeed, all martyrs in this series share this factor: all were killed by the state. More important are its understated impacts. Given its use on the poster issued for Biko's funeral (see Figure 2.6), the photograph forever registers as a portrait of death. In using this "death mask" (recall the same image that was carved and affixed to the top of Biko's coffin), *Never Again!* doubles its impact: It is a portrait of torture. Finally, its use here unknowingly signaled an end in public preference for this iconic image of Steve Biko. It has seldom been used since 1997, when the Truth and Reconciliation Commission held amnesty hearings for the five men previously implicated in Biko's death; Figure 6.3 shows a poster at one of the hearings. More commonly seen now is Fraser MacLean's photograph of Biko taken around 1972 (Figure 6.4).

AZAPO continued to reject any part in a negotiated settlement, and it chose not to participate in the nation's first democratic election in April 1994. Ultimately, Saths Cooper (also accused as one of the SASO-Nine) and others persuaded AZAPO to work toward its goals from an elected post; AZAPO participated in local elections the following year.[48] Also in 1995, well-known Black Consciousness leader and ANC member Mamphela Ramphele seized the moment to defend her own vision of BC, no less influential in her life at that time than it was twenty-five years prior. Further, she honored the work of Cyril Ramaphosa, Cheryl Carolus, Barney Pityana, Thenjiwe Mthintso, and Frank Chikane, all "products" of Black Consciousness who were then putting its lessons to use in public posts.[49] And in Pretoria, AZAPO marked September 12, the eighteenth anniversary of Biko's death, with the words, "Today as South Africa stands on the shores of liberation, the stamp of Biko's impact and influence is everywhere. In every political venture we find footprints of comrade Steve Biko—the leading light, the revolutionary, the hero and the martyr."[50] Still, debates about the role of Black Consciousness in South Africa's past, present, and future persisted.

The nation's election of April 1994 included nearly twenty million voters, a bit less than 87 percent of the population.[51] The ANC won decisively in national and regional races, garnering 62.2 percent of the vote and seven of nine provinces. The National Party surprised many by taking 20.39 percent, including a substantial win in the Western Cape. The Inkatha Freedom Party, which decided to participate in the elections just weeks before they took place, won 10.43 percent and the province of KwaZulu-Natal, as expected. The remaining 5.6 percent was divided among the Freedom Front, Democratic Party, the Pan Africanist Congress, and the African Christian Democratic Party.[52] On May 10, when Nelson Mandela was inaugurated as president of South Africa, he used words that would resonate with proponents of Black Consciousness and Black Theology, among others: "We enter into a covenant that we shall build a society in which all South Africans, both black and white, will be able to walk tall, without any fear in their hearts, assured of their inalienable right to human dignity—a rainbow nation at peace with itself and the world."[53]

By 1990, there was no longer any need to disguise tributes through titles, and the difficulties of transitioning from apartheid to democracy required a role model with no party affiliation who bore great influence among people of varied outlook. This section explores the theme of a sanctified Biko that emerged post-1990 wherein humanism was popularly conceived as his guiding principle. In this period Black Consciousness was bent to fit the rainbow-nation ideal that flourished in accord with the nation's new aspirations.[54] In this decade, cultural production of various kinds in and out of South Africa advanced the image of

Biko as "an apostle of hope, a man whose philosophy has the power to liberate blacks psychologically and whites from prejudice and fear."[55] The characterization of Biko as holy figure was readily exemplified in a 1992 opera first performed in London. Librettist Richard Fawkes made this analogy:

> The thing about Biko that appealed to me is that he doesn't conform to the standard freedom fighter image. Mandela might have been more topical but . . . he is very much in the tradition of [Jomo] Kenyatta or [Julius] Nyerere, leaders of political movements. Steve Biko was much more of a philosopher, more in the [Mahatma] Gandhi tradition: what he wanted was not to replace white rule with black rule, but for people to learn to live together as equals. It's the same sort of message Christ was teaching, and we know what happened to him.[56]

The dominant South African narrative at this time required, and still does to a large extent, that Biko be similarly represented. The times suggested that no other vision would do.

Saint Biko the Radiant: Apostle of Hope

On December 9, 1993, this excerpt from Rian Malan's book *My Traitor's Heart* (1990) appeared in the widely read newspaper *Sowetan*:

> I remember Steve Biko. I never met him, nor saw him speak, but he towered over my White youth like a colossus, a figure who inspired awe. . . . He seemed to be saying, First this, first black healing, and then we can talk, when we are all fully men. I don't know, my friend, I am not sure that Steve Biko was a political figure. I think he transcended politics. I could scarcely believe, in my secret racist heart, that a black could be so wise and perceptive, and the awe I felt for him had almost religious overtones. I am not mocking when I call him Saint Biko the Radiant.[57]

Steve Biko is widely recognized as South Africa's most influential martyr for a just and free society. Since his death in 1977, religious metaphor has often been invoked to describe his life, beliefs, and manner of death. This is most evident around September 12 each year, as events are organized and articles are printed in his honor. We are reminded of his sacrifice on the date of his death rather than that of his birth. So persuasive was this narrative of sacrifice that in 1982 Anglicans nominated him for canonization.[58] Artists, too, have regularly envisioned Biko in a saintly state by drawing on Christian iconography in works that position him centrally. Remember Paul Stopforth's influential works of 1980 (Figures 3.4–3.6) that recall the long-standing tradition of imaging the torments suffered by Jesus of Nazareth in miniature; focused studies of the stigmata historically used to affect a response.[59] Recall, too, that Biko holds the key to a better, or more heavenly, tomorrow in Tony Nkotsi's *Portrait of a Man* (Figure 5.8).

Created by Brother Robert Lentz (b. 1946) about 1985, the work in Figure 6.5 was reproduced on cardstock and glued to the front of small wooden plaque.[60] As such it served as a devotional icon made to focus prayer.[61] Here a dramatically flattened Biko stands before prison bars and holds a scroll that reads "Begin to look upon yourself as a human being." The Greek script to either side of his halo reads "Holy Stephen." On the reverse side, text briefly describes Biko's objectives—"instilling pride and a sense of identity in fellow Blacks"— and likens apartheid to Nazism. Biko, it reads, "laid down his life for Christ" in order to promote the message on the scroll. His torture and death remind readers of Matthew 25:40, which Lentz cites: "Whatsoever you did to the least of my brothers and sisters, you did to me." The plaque was sold by at least one Catholic Church in South Africa as early as 1986.[62] A popularly available devotional tool that is light and small enough to carry, it is well grounded in post-iconoclastic Byzantine traditions that continue in Orthodox churches today.[63] Centuries of Christian martyrs are recalled through Biko's features, gesture, the flattened halo, the folds of the fabric he wears, and the use of text to either side of his head. His elongated hands and fingers, almond-shaped eyes, and narrowly drawn nose stress his close association with the Divine since they indicate that Biko is holy, or no longer of this world. The halo confirms fellowship with the sacred. It breaks through the border at the top to suggest that his ideas did not die within the cell that contained him but live on despite his physical demise. The uniform striations of his shirt align him with other Christian martyrs who, like Biko, no longer possess a body that would otherwise define its shape. Its collar indicates contemporary design; this allies Biko with would-be owners of the votive icon, thus extending the reach of his message. And in keeping with tradition, this sacred subject has pictorial attributes that are his alone: the prison bars (an instrument of torture) and the scroll, which bears his own words. The scroll gradually unrolls to evoke the passage of time between Biko's martyrdom in 1977 and the present day. Its command to "begin" self-possession—to claim agency for oneself in the face of forces that deny it—underscores the continued need for Black Consciousness in our time. "Holy Stephen" still urges enlightenment when the laws of apartheid are gone, but its effects continue to linger.[64]

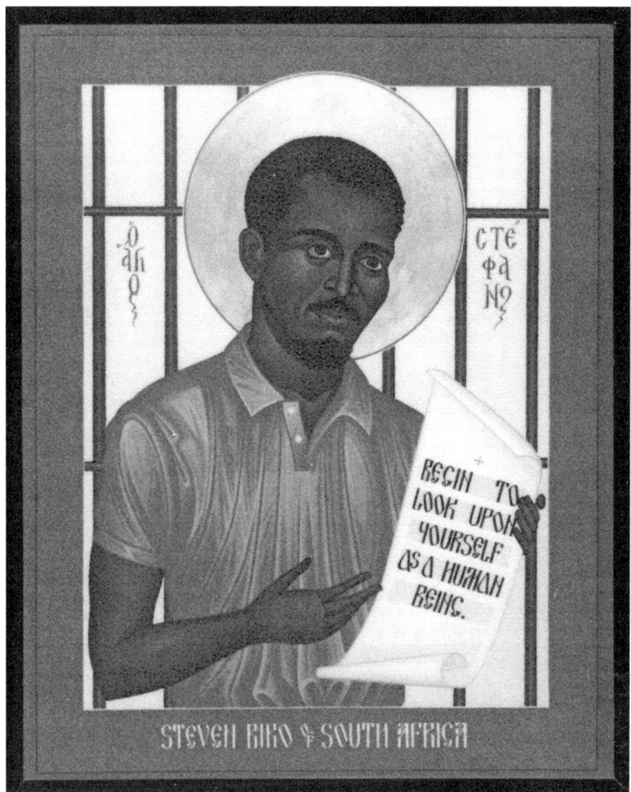

FIGURE 6.5. Brother Robert Lentz, *Holy Stephen*, before 1986. Portable icon of wood, paper, ink, and glue. 13.3 x 11.4 cm. Courtesy of Brother Robert Lentz.

Jane Alexander (b. 1959) has made only two tributary works during her distinguished career. In 1993, she made *Beauty in a landscape: Born Aliwal North 19–?, Died Boksburg 1992* to honor a woman called Beauty whose influence on Alexander was great.[65] Two years later, she made *Portrait of a man with landscape and procession (Bantu Stephen Biko 1946–1977)* (Figure 6.6). Alexander is well known as a sculptor who brings new life to her three-dimensional pieces through montage. *Portrait of a man* was made by the predigital cut-and-paste method; this project was then photographed and sold as such. It incorporates three separate works to manifest its own meaning, but the histories encoded in the originals bear significance here, too. The trio before the billboard at left was incorporated from a small sculpture called *something's going down* (1994); Biko's portrait (1989) was originally painted as a gift to a friend, a woman who

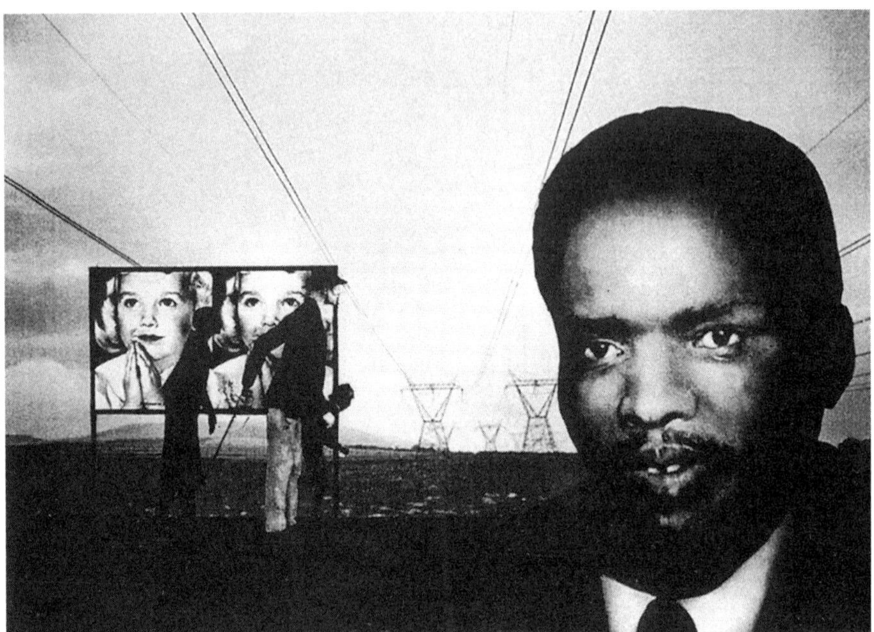

FIGURE 6.6. Jane Alexander, *Portrait of a man with landscape and procession (Bantu Stephen Biko 1946–1977)*, 1995. Photographs and glue on paper, 178 x 225 cm. Art copyright Jane Alexander/DALRO, Johannesburg. Licensed by VAGA, New York, NY.

knew Biko and is mother to the artist's playmates when she was a girl; the photographed landscape first formed the backdrop to *Beauty in a landscape,* a mixed-media work. Ivor Powell rightly calls Biko the composition's "psychic register."[66] He offers solace to those who seek it and answers those who ask.

The billboard at left bears a repeated image of a blonde, fair-skinned girl who holds her hands in prayer. In *something's going down,* text on the billboard's reverse side recounts a sign the artist saw at a police roadblock.[67] Biko's final detention began at just such a site, which makes *something's going down* an interesting component of *Portrait of a man,* albeit for rather obscure reasons. More compelling is the girl's youth, placement, posture, and the sense that the light behind enhances her glow. Indeed, she recalls the artist's own biography in two respects. First, Alexander was roughly the same age when she played with the children of her friend and experienced what she called her "first political encounter"—a visit to a segregated aquarium in which she could not sit with them. Second, the girl suits the Aryan ideal promoted by the Third Reich through popular media, thus she represents the racist ideology that Alexander's father fled when he left Germany for South Africa. Her "Radiance of Faith" (as the text at her wrists reads) effectively makes the group before her—a young activist wearing a balaclava, a pale man who drags a bundle behind him, and a person dressed in a green coat—less readable. They crane their necks to get a glimpse of what lies beyond.

The landscape that they seek recalls the vast, depopulated spaces imagined by such painters as Jacobus Hendrik Pierneef, celebrated for the way he captured Afrikaner nationalist sentiment in his rendering of vast outdoor space. But Alexander's version populates—indeed, it magnifies the absurdity of any space being ready for the taking—by the presence of three electrical pylons, their power lines stretched to the outer limits of vision, seemingly out of reach to most. Taken from *Beauty in a landscape,* the photograph reminds us there, as it does here, that electricity is still a luxury in South Africa. In her varied incantations within Alexander's oeuvre, Beauty embodies the displacement endured by generations who were either uprooted from their homes or who migrated cross-country in search of work. The trio on the move before the billboard also recalls such painful histories in a place where land rights have always troubled and assert multiple visions of national identity. The man of Alexander's title, Bantu Stephen Biko, responds to their history of displacement and omission.

His likeness dominates the composition as it sits close to the picture plane and is dramatically lit by two sources: an unseen light that emphasizes his forehead and alludes to mindfulness; and the light that streams from the distance and renders him otherworldly. Flattened against the picture plane, he is effectively haloed, or sainted, by blunt contrasts. Other elements provoke the reading of Biko as saint: the girl's display of reverence and the distant pylons, modern equivalents of the crosses of Calvary.

A third element, less evident, also registers his martyrdom: the portrait recalls the photograph that became iconic through its display at Biko's funeral.[68] Recall that the original was a painting Alexander made for her friend. Seen not for what it is (a photograph of a painting) but as a photograph of Biko while he breathed, the image carries with it that intense longing created by what Roland Barthes called "flat death."[69] Theorizing that photographs give the illusion of being "distractedly alive," we look on Biko's photograph with the thought, as Barthes described another, "He is dead and he is going to die." The idea that "this will be and this has been" accompanies all photographs, particularly historical ones, but the punctum of this equation—that which pierces us and causes images to be remembered—is perhaps most acutely felt when the person imaged is dead. The impact is even greater when the person is mourned by so many.[70]

Alexander's pictorial disruptions are consistently read as reflections of social discord. Alienation, marginalization, vulnerability, and disquietude frequently describe her work.[71] But unlike others who have analyzed this fascinating piece, I believe that *Portrait of a man* suggests something else. Ivor Powell sees the procession at left "moving . . . confusedly, displacedly, pathetically into a wasted future."[72] Kathy Grundlingh views Biko and child as kindred spirits, equally "unaware of . . . the impending danger" that looms beyond in "the distant background."[73] An honorific work of solemn title, *Portrait of a man* surely beckons a more positive interpretation. As I see it, Alexander's ode is masterful. The trio, an intergenerational collective of uncertain gender and race, moves determinedly toward the promising future that glows on the horizon. The girl, a propagandistic image of Afrikaner nationalism, is reduced to but two screens. She cannot shield the rising light of Black Consciousness as it bathes the landscape of their birth. The landscape is a metaphor for history, and Biko, once tortured but now risen, is the site on which history is played out. As the inspiration sought by the trio at left, Biko embodies the spirit of a new nation. The work recalls a now commonly excerpted passage from Biko's "Quest for a True Humanity" of 1973:

> We have set out on the quest for true humanity, and somewhere on the distant horizon we can see the glittering prize. Let us march forth with courage and determination, drawing strength from our common plight and our brotherhood. In time we shall be able to bestow upon South Africa the greatest gift possible—a more human face.[74]

Pictured as holy, Biko and his guiding ideology are considered essential to South Africa's future. Archbishop Desmond Tutu, then chairperson of the Truth and Reconciliation Commission, described the seed, the root, the branch, and the blossom when he wrote, in 1996:

> Reconciliation needed Black Consciousness to succeed because reconciliation is a deeply personal thing happening between those who acknowledge their unique personhood and who have it acknowledged by others. . . . the inspired words of Steve Biko . . . could just spark a black renaissance.[75]

The seed is Black Consciousness. The root it spawns is a sense of unique person-hood. The branch is reconciliation. The blossom is a black renaissance.

A More Precise Picture: Biko and the TRC

South Africa's Truth and Reconciliation Commission (TRC) aimed to facilitate national unity through public testimony of gross human rights violations that occurred within or outside of the nation between March 1, 1960, and May 10, 1994. The dates roughly correspond to a period of heightened physical violence in South Africa's apartheid-era history: from the Sharpeville Massacre on March 21, 1960, to the days soon after the nation's first democratic elections on April 27, 1994. The TRC's mandate was clearly defined in the Promotion of National Unity and Reconciliation Act (1995) that gave structure to previous negotiations between the African National Congress and the National Party over amnesty for perpetrators and reparations for victims of apartheid-era abuses. In the process of discussing, editing, and ultimately passing the act, parliament held public hearings in which South Africans argued that national investigations should be held in a public forum.[76]

The TRC faced a mind-boggling challenge, as it was formed to facilitate unity and understanding in order to eventually transcend apartheid's divisions. It was to provide "as complete a picture as possible" of the causes, nature, and extent of politically motivated gross violations of human rights committed during the designated period.[77] In order to do so, the TRC sought testimony from all parties in their home language, of which South Africa now officially recognizes eleven. Perpetrators of human rights violations, their victims, and victims' survivors told their stories of violation in public forums—a first for truth commissions of this kind. The commission granted amnesty whenever perpetrators were shown to have revealed all facts relevant to their case, and it recommended reparations for the dead, the abused, and their families. Finally, the TRC made a full report of its investigations, proceedings, and findings, including recommendations the state should take to prevent future violations of human rights.

Though international organizations had long condemned apartheid as a "crime against humanity,"[78] the TRC was not designed to examine institutional or structural violence that ensured blacks' poverty, limited education and employment, and restricted their movements and residence. Instead, the commission focused on violations of "bodily integrity rights" such as those now ensured by South Africa's constitution: the right to life; the right to be free from torture and cruel, inhuman, or degrading treatment or punishment; and the right to freedom and security of the person, including freedom from abduction and arbitrary or prolonged detention.

The TRC adopted a "victim-centered approach" in pursuing its aims.[79] By providing a forum in which victims could publicly share their stories, the TRC hoped to validate victims' pain and help to restore self-confidence, self-esteem, and personal dignity. The restoration of dignity was also reflected in the fact that submissions were investigated on a case-by-case basis, as were perpetrators' applications for amnesty. Initially, it was thought that most people would share their stories in public hearings. In the end, faced with more than fifty thousand individual cases of human rights violations, the commission needed to select "window cases" for public proceedings that were "representative of broader patterns of abuse."[80] This emphasis on listening to and collecting personal stories was motivated by the desire to facilitate the speaker's restoration of dignity—a theme repeatedly cited in the commission's final report. Promoted by apartheid resisters for many decades, personal dignity was at last recognized as vital to the health of the nation.

The TRC's emphasis on recording victims' stories was one of a few characteristics that distinguished it from truth commissions elsewhere in the world. Other distinctive features were its transparent proceedings and public testimony; its power to grant or deny amnesty for crimes (it was the first of its kind to hold this responsibility); its stronger powers to subpoena those implicated and to search for and seize evidence. Also unusual were the TRC's special hearings on business and health sectors that benefited from apartheid policy: the legal system, women, youth, prisons, compulsory national service, biological and chemical warfare, media, and faith communities. It established a witness protection program, and it had a budget and staff that far exceeded those of truth commissions elsewhere.[81]

The TRC's mandate received criticism before and during the two years that victims and perpetrators told their stories. Some people believed that the public nature of the proceedings prevented South Africa from embracing a more positive future. Others felt that the violent past must be confronted head on lest their wounds remain forever fresh. The commission's defenders argued that public confrontation could heal *and* empower both victims and perpetrators. It was particularly necessary, they said, in cases of large-scale violence such as that done by a state to its citizens. Archbishop Desmond Tutu, who chaired the

TRC and gave it a face and rhetorical force, was of this opinion: "There are erroneous notions of what reconciliation is all about. Reconciliation is not about being cosy; it is not about pretending that things were other than they were. Reconciliation based on falsehood, on not facing up to reality, is not true reconciliation and will not last."[82]

More compelling criticisms centered on questions of amnesty and justice and whether these fundamentally collide. The principal concern here was that trading justice for truth would hinder the nation's ability to heal. But in the end amnesty was not easily earned, neither in process nor in fact. When the commission's report was published in October 1998, only about one hundred and fifty applicants out of seven thousand had received amnesty for their crimes. Judgments had not yet been rendered on a further two thousand.[83] Between 1990 and 1994, the limits on amnesty and how it was to be achieved were a matter of much dispute. The NP wanted blanket amnesty for political offenses, particularly those committed by security forces. The ANC, backed by international opinion, insisted on accountability for human rights violations. The compromise became the operating framework of the TRC.

Though amnesty feels to many inherently unjust, it is unlikely that South Africa's democracy would have been realized if not for a provision for such in the nation's interim constitution. Or if democracy had come without this concession, the cost in lives lost and damaged would have been greater. Nuremberg-like trials, a standard favored by those who sought retributive justice, would likely not have worked in South Africa. For one thing, the NP had negotiated its own demise as parliament's majority. Its active participation was acknowledged internationally as other nations did not call for a tribunal like Nuremberg. Secondly, the NP maintained control over the nation's arms and security forces until the 1994 elections. Its military power far exceeded that of opposition parties, and it used this leverage to ensure an avenue to amnesty for people who had enforced apartheid laws. The compromise—a qualified amnesty requiring truthful public accountability—provided justice of a kind.

The commission's foremost task was to promote reconciliation and national unity, and this could not be achieved, it argued, if the nation sought retribution for apartheid crimes. Thus South Africa sought something else: restorative justice. Restorative justice is concerned with publicly communicating experiences and perspectives in an effort to rectify wrongs. Public hearings were a vital part of the process. By fully disclosing their crimes before victims, the survivors of victims, their own families and communities, and the nation, perpetrators would be punished and would cleanse their conscience at once. Only this way, the TRC reasoned, could the wounds of South Africans possibly heal. As one supporter put it:

> The truth always goes hand in hand with justice. We do not tell our stories only to release the dammed up tears that have waited years to be shed. It is in order that truth should be uncovered and justice seen to be done. . . . The [Amnesty Committee] may . . . refuse amnesty. That rightly demonstrates that truth can be tough. The refusal to grant amnesty is a sign that [the TRC] is not a body setting out simply to show leniency, but, more especially, that it requires justice before there can be reconciliation. Reconciliation is not taking the least line of resistance; reconciliation is profoundly costly.[84]

For some of apartheid's victims, it must be said that amnesty through truth was too high a price to pay for their pain. The TRC acknowledged this but hoped that some solace might be found in knowing the truth, which is more likely given in amnesty processes than in trials. Thus victims heard what motivated their assailants, and many surviving relatives learned what happened to their loved ones. And as memories of apartheid crimes took center stage, the nation underwent a period of meaningful reflection.

What of truth? Like justice, debates about truth proved that there are many kinds. The commission ultimately relied on four types of truth: factual or forensic truth, social or dialogic truth, personal or narrative truth, and healing or restorative truth.[85] The first of these figured largely in the commission's methodology. The TRC's Investigation Unit led an extensive program to verify and corroborate evidence. In the end, this effort dispelled misinformation long circulated and accepted as truth among South Africans. Personal or narrative truth was revealed through individual accounts of traumas experienced or rendered. As people told their stories before the Human Rights Violations Committee, a complex understanding of truth through perspective unfolded. The commission believed that these collected stories offered "history lessons" of such power that they would certainly affect the future. Social or dialogic truth was pursued by encouraging and considering equally the perspectives of all those who testified. The resultant "truth" reflects social relations among speakers and among South Africans who shared the speakers' perspectives or experiences. Finally, healing or restorative truth placed "facts and what they mean within the context of human relationships."[86] The full and public acknowledgment of facts and experiences fueled the restoration of personal dignity as the nation began its "Long Night's Journey into Day."[87]

The Biko family opposed the Truth and Reconciliation Commission in court on the grounds that it would violate their rights to justice and redress if amnesty was granted to those who admitted culpability for their loved one's death.[88] In 1996, the Constitutional Court, the nation's highest, recognized the truth of their complaint but ruled unanimously against the petition, deciding that the constitution's epilogue effectively curtailed individual's rights in its amnesty provisions. The decision cleared the way for the Truth and Reconciliation Commission to proceed. For the Biko family, this meant that the case of their loved one would be heard in two types of TRC hearings: that in which five police officers—Harold Snyman, Gideon Nieuwoudt, Ruben Marx, Daantjie Siebert, and Johan Beneke—applied for amnesty, and that concerning the culpability of medical professionals—in this case, Benjamin Tucker and Ivor Lang—who colluded with the state and reneged their Hippocratic oath.[89]

The amnesty hearing took place in Port Elizabeth on the twentieth anniversary of Steve Biko's death and coincided with the unveiling of monuments to him in East London and Ginsberg (see chapter 7). The TRC's judgments were rendered in December 1998 and February 1999. All five policemen were refused amnesty. The commission found that Biko's death was not associated with a political objective and that his attackers were motivated by "ill-will or spite towards him."[90] Further, his death was "wholly disproportionate to any possible objective" as stated by the applicants, such as extracting information or an admission of illegal political activity. Quite important to the commission's decision was its belief that the facts were not fully disclosed—indeed, the TRC believed the applicants were not truthful because their respective testimony was "so improbable and contradictory that it had to be rejected as false."

The TRC's Health Sector hearing gave great weight to Biko's death while in detention.[91] (This was one of several institutional and special hearings that spotlighted how gross violations of human rights pervaded institutions and sectors of society.) As a case study in the history of medical misconduct, the report highlights the depraved conditions in which Biko was kept during his last days. The narrative makes much of Biko's nudity, confinement, and neglect. His inhumane treatment still resonates powerfully as an emblem of shameful state abuse.[92] The Truth and Reconciliation Commission heard testimony for a little more than two years.

During that time, South African artists created enumerable works that stemmed from TRC proceedings and revelations. In what follows I examine Biko narratives within the works of three artists by integrating three of the TRC's four types of truth. The TRC's Investigation Unit led an extensive program to verify and corroborate evidence, thereby establishing the factual or forensic truth of a case. Questioning authenticity is a crucial feature of *Veils,* a fascinating 1997 multipart installation by Colin Richards. The work is partly autobiographical and questions forensic truths within narratives that include the state's 1977 inquest into Biko's death, its 1975 invasion of Angola, the artist's childhood, and his abiding fascination with Samuel Beckett, trauma, "life in dead thing," and slow, meditative processes.[93] Social or dialogic truth was elemental to the methods of the Human Rights Violations Committee, bound as it was to equally encourage and weigh all perspectives before rendering a decision. Sue Williamson's *Truth Games* of 1998 is discussed in this context, with focus on one piece in the series. In a place where oral traditions run strong, the commission acknowledged personal truth: "Stories [of trauma] provided unique insights into the pain of South Africa's past."[94] Victims used their home language to tell their stories, a process that helped uncover facts, validate the voices of people previously silenced, and create a narrative truth that acknowledged "perceptions, stories, myths, and experiences" as persuasively present.[95] Trauma is the centerpiece of David Koloane's *The Journey* (1998), a suite of nineteen paintings in which Steve Biko's last four days form the substantive part. Of the many works made in response to the TRC's mission, Koloane's translation is in some ways the most daring attempt "to recover parts of the national memory that had hitherto been officially ignored."[96] As a longtime proponent of Black Consciousness, he felt a need to visualize the testimony of 1997. Although his narrative spans just five days, it records a violence well known to the men and women of Koloane's generation, the whole of which stood witness to a history long denied.

Geb nodrap: A Layered Look at *Veils,* by Colin Richards

A 1996 exhibition called *Faultlines—Inquiries into Truth and Reconciliation* was the first to stage an artistic response to the TRC and the histories that it was actively recovering.[97] Presented within Cape Town's Castle of Good Hope, *Faultlines* included the work of many South African artists within a fortress that is a relic of European imperialist enterprise. Built by settlers in 1666, the fortress is the oldest building still in use in South Africa. Though it still partially operates as a military base, in recent years the building has housed cultural events, some of which critically examine the violent legacies of colonialism once enforced by the castle's administrators. As such, it was the perfect venue for an exhibition that explored the histories revealed daily through the TRC. For *Faultlines,* Colin Richards (1954–2012) staged an installation titled *Veils* that suited its site better than most (Plate 15).[98] It was placed in the castle's basement, a space that accommodates his long-standing interest in relics since it evokes death and its memorials (crypts and tombs historically reside there) as well as a sense of foundation, the historical structure of which was reconsidered by the TRC.

Relics and the many desires they convey—mourning, transcendence, truth of existence—were at the heart of Richards's installation, which incorporated objects found, made, and once owned by the artist, each of which questioned the power of a relic. Repetition and its partner, ritual, were also vital to the installation and enacted in varied ways. Through these a kind of healing surfaced, at least for its maker, as the histories that converged in this darkened space were lightened through the ritualized process of making the works, installing them at this site, and nurturing elements among them through performance.

Key to this installation was the re-presentation, or modified duplication, of photographic images first used in the 1977 inquest into Biko's death. At that time, Richards worked as a medical illustrator at the University of the Witwatersrand and in this capacity he was asked to prepare photographs of Biko's autopsy for display at the state's inquest into his death. His was an intimate form of looking as he labored to label "swellings, contusions, abrasions and cuts which were not always clearly visible" against varied fields of shifting tone, shape, and light.[99] By revisiting that experience nearly twenty years later, Richards achieved what he calls recovery, a personal trial that involves both resurrection of truths (rediscovery) and transcendence of the suffering they cause (a covering over). *Veils* is a complex and fascinating installation with multiple intersections among the three avenues of inquiry—relics, repetition, and recovery—all of which were emphasized by the TRC. It contains within it revelations from 1976 when Richards saw army combat in Angola, from 1977 when he first saw autopsy photographs that later proved to be Steve Biko's, and from the mid-1980s when he first became entranced by a particular motif on which he continued to meditate, the Veil of Veronica.

Relics: Truth and the Crisis of the Real

Relics are objects that may serve diverse functions, but they always testify to some truth. Popularly understood as the remains of a person or culture, relics are more than keepsakes from a bygone time; rather, they are venerable, thus authoritative. Understood to embody the spirit of the person they represent or the values and ideals of the culture that produced them, relics are preserved in the belief that they embody spiritual or cultural certainties. Yet despite their testifying to truths, relics also convey an element of doubt since bodily remains are either too widely attributed or the translation of their historical meaning relies too heavily on the subjectivity of memory. Richards's installation situated this duality within the proceedings of the TRC, which relied heavily on objects and memory. Though several scholars have reflected on the vital role of memory for the TRC, fewer have considered the commission's reliance on factual or forensic truth, the search for objects, which figured largely in the methodology of its Investigative Unit. Through *Veils* we are compelled toward both aspects of the TRC's mission.

Multiple types of material fragments from Richards's life came together for the installation: objects that he gathered while serving as a South African soldier in the war on Angola; broken funerary sculpture he found in cemeteries near his home; a collection of spent ink cartridges he used when copying the Bible by hand; and the Biko Inquest photographs, here reproduced by laser print on bed sheets that once folded around Richards while he slept. Trauma binds them together, and recovery was their aim. For Richards, these are deeply realized in both intellectual and emotional capacities. Ever questioning, he seemed intent on "keeping immutable truth and contingency in play simultaneously."[100]

Richards regularly returned to a particular motif in his work (indeed, a particular *arrangement*) that is based on what one might call the first relic, which by name purports to be true: the Veil of Veronica.[101] The object is said to have miraculously recorded the face of Jesus of Nazareth when a woman of that name wiped sweat, tears, and blood from his face as he carried the cross to Calvary. Thus it predates the better-known Shroud of Turin. *The True Image (Vera Iconica),* the title of Richards's 1994 watercolor (Figure 6.7), is a Latin-Greek hybrid; the Veil of Veronica is considered by some to be a species of photograph because it instantaneously captured an imprint of Christ's face without the mediation of the human hand.[102] Thus the Veronica is an ideal framework for an inquiry into the power of relics, the truths to which they seemingly attest,

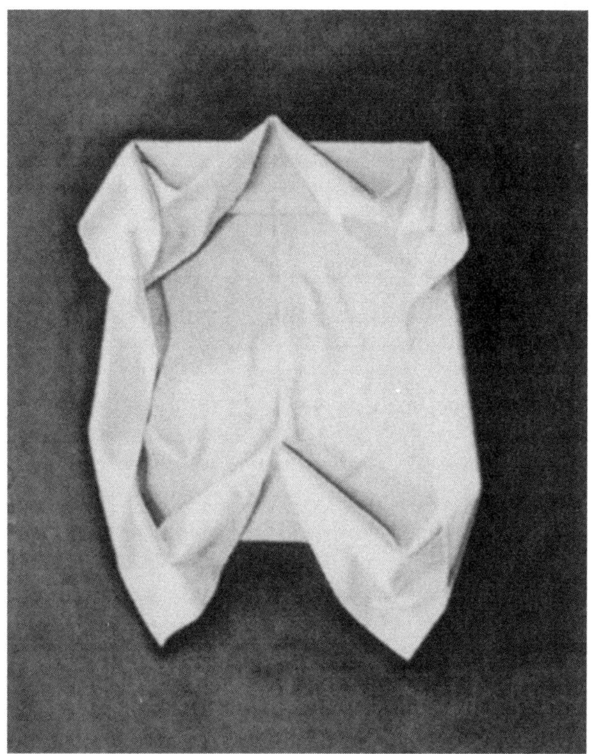

FIGURE 6.7. Colin Richards, *The True Image (Vera Iconica)*, 1994. Watercolor, 32.2 x 24 cm. Iziko South African National Gallery, 96/61. Courtesy of Penny Siopis.

and to the presumption that forensic photographs likewise represent certain truths. As a type of photograph heavy with the weight of human longing and, presumably, the blood, sweat, and tears of the world's most famous martyr, the Veil of Veronica perfectly frames a 1996 reconsideration of photographs first used as forensic exhibits nearly twenty years prior during the state's inquiry into Biko's death.

For *Veils,* Richards arranged eight cloths as the Veronica on blackened boards. Most of these were imprinted with inquest photographs of the spaces that Biko occupied in his last five days. Retaining their history was important, thus Richards included the punch holes, staples, and misspellings in the captions of the originals. The captions are descriptive and do not reveal Biko as a subject, but viewers mindful of such details as dates and names will recognize the source of the images. For instance, the caption to *Veil I* (Figure 6.8) reads: "Possision

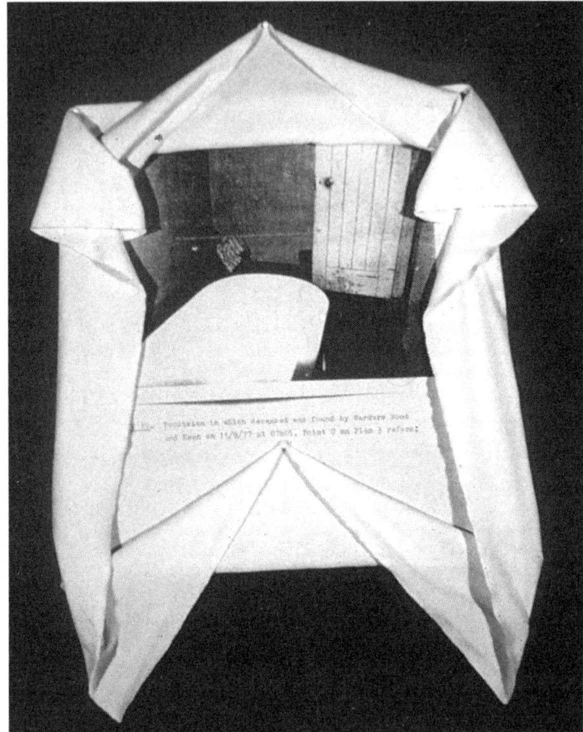

FIGURE 6.8. Colin Richards, *Veil I,* 1996. Laser-printed image on bed sheet, pins, board. 89.5 cm x 73.5 cm. Courtesy of Penny Siopis.

in which deceased was found by Warders Wood and Koen on 11/9/77 at 07h05. Point C on Plan 3 refers." The image records a staged reenactment of a position in which Biko was found the day before his death, slumped in the far-left corner beside a bathtub, unable to move (see Figure 2.12). Other veils reproduce photographs of (and inquest text about) the cell's stained, dirty, chipped walls, dark corners, bars, and locks.

Veil VII (Figure 6.9 and installed in Plate 15) and *Veil VIII* (Plate 16) are different from the others. Most important, they image Biko's body, though it is so decontextualized that this is not evident. The image in *Veil VII* records a dissection of Biko's hemorrhaged brain and that in *Veil VIII* details cut skin seen so close that individual cells seem distinguishable.[103] Richards added color to their reproduction (yellow and blue, respectively) to mark the aesthetic discomfort that accompanies a shift from viewing architectural to human interiors. Installed in their own spaces rather than in sequence, these veiled body images

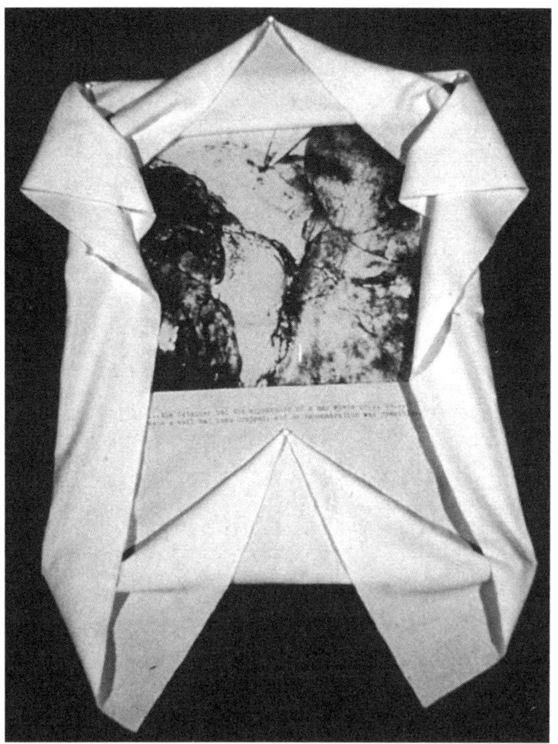

FIGURE 6.9. Colin Richards, *Veil VII*. Laser-printed image on bed sheet, pins, board. 89.5 cm x 73.5 cm. Courtesy of Penny Siopis.

achieved sanctity that was distinct from the veiled cell images. Finally, *Veil VII* and *VIII* differ from others in that their captions are not original to their use as inquest exhibits; rather, both address the manifest obligations and inconsistencies of the TRC. The caption to *Veil VII*, an excerpt from Karl Marx's *18th Brumaire of Napoleon Bonaparte* (1852), reads: "The tradition of all the dead generations weighs like a nightmare on the brain of the living."[104] This hints at the image's source, but more important it reflects on the great difficulty of reconstructing historical narratives, or "tradition," which was part of the TRC's project. The words in the caption to *Veil VIII*, first spoken at the 1977 inquest by police counsel Retief van Rooyen, read: "The detainee had the appearance of a man where uh . . . um . . . where a veil had been dropped, and no communication was possible." This suggests that Biko had agency (he dropped a veil, purportedly fueling the state's belief that he was "shamming" his injuries) and, as Richards put it, "could not somehow existentially 'be' the truth."[105] The caption foregrounds the presumption that objects, which inherently lack agency, testify to truths, while evidence writ on the body is always susceptible to its mutations, whether feigned or physical.

Holding cells, brain cells, skin cells: the composite effect of *Veils*, which positioned cell as both space and substance, encourages the viewer to interpret Biko, albeit a veiled subject, as a relic of state abuse. More than this, the images—and particularly those of Biko's corpse—brilliantly intersect with the artist's personal history (his own skin, one might say) through the use of domestic bed sheets, which once acted as membranes of a sort, enfolding and protecting the artist much as the membranous tissue of skin enfolds and protects us. The bed sheets thus act as skin metaphors, and their folds, varied from veil to veil, yet more or less the same, are in keeping with a surface that "we expect . . . to be moderately complex, with a numerable set of kinds of invaginations and out-foldings."[106] Historically, the body's interior has been considered too painful to represent because it is such a powerful sign of death. Wounds such as those imaged in *Veil VII* and *Veil VIII* reveal a lack of skin, the cure for which is, James Elkins proscribes, "an excess of skin."[107] The layers of cloth that enfold Biko's autopsy images work as a curative device both in terms of excess and in their replication of an icon embedded in the hope for transcendence and humane gestures. While the inquest photographs retained a moral distance required of forensic illustration, their duplication on bed sheets, folded in the manner of the Veil of Veronica, instills once more an intimate sense of personhood. For though images of the dead are widely held to signify absence rather than presence,[108] Richards's work *reconstructs presence* and with it "a meaningful self."[109]

Repetition: To Awaken to the Real

The tinted yellow and blue of *Veil VII* and *Veil VIII* match two watercolor portraits hung to either side of *The True Image: Vera Iconica*. Titled *Sleeping Dogs Lie I* and *Sleeping Dogs Lie II* (Figure 6.10), these 1996 paintings remind us of the need to not leave well enough alone, not let sleeping dogs lie.[110] Their sources were two starving dogs that Richards saw in India; children were stoning one dog, and the other lay still beside the rotting corpse of her pup while nursing its siblings.[111] As I see it, positioned as they are within *Veils*, the three watercolors recall the tradition of *transi,* or decomposing corpses, responding to Christ at center. Historically, such macabre iconography was used where the face of the

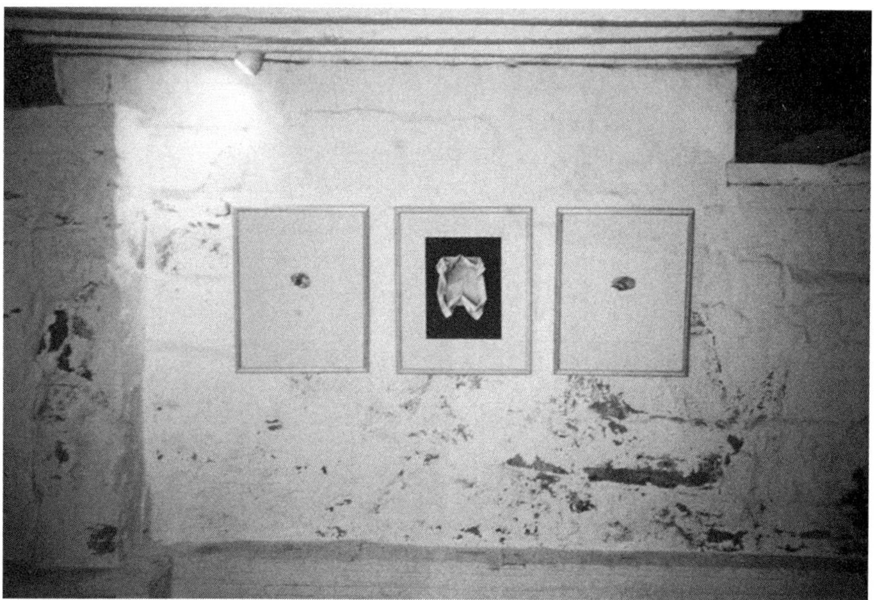

FIGURE 6.10. Colin Richards, *Sleeping Dogs Lie I*, *The True Image (Vera Iconica)*, and *Sleeping Dogs Lie II*, installed at the Castle of Good Hope, Cape Town, 1996. *Faultlines* exhibition. Courtesy of Penny Siopis.

deceased was concealed, much as *The True Image* records no likeness.[112] I draw attention to the dogs' doubling: more than simply a pair, they share multiple links with the veils that image Biko's body.

Starving dogs, the Veil of Veronica, and the colors yellow and blue all surface in Samuel Beckett's *Watt* of 1953. Watt is a keeper of sorts who attends a man always outside the frame: Mr. Knott. Over the course of the book, Watt is repeatedly instructed to give Knott's leftover food, his "remains," to a dog. Since Knott owns no dog, Watt must employ one from the neighborhood for the task. There are many dogs to choose from since all here are nearly starved, and as one expires, another is easily found. But Watt is often uncertain, so employs two starving dogs at a time, indefinitely, so that Knott's remains are always attended. The dogs take different colors: "Red, bluer, yellowish, that old dream has ended, half ended, ended. Again."[113] Earlier, Watt had contemplated truths—what he can and cannot know—as he watched a dog named Kate feast on leftovers:

Not for a moment Watt supposed that he had penetrated the forces at play, in this particular instance, or even perceived the forms that they upheaved, or obtained the least useful information concerning himself, or Mr. Knott, for he did not. But he had turned, little by little, a disturbance into words, and he had made a pillow of old words, for the head. Kate eating from her dish, for example, with the dwarfs standing by, how he had laboured to know what that was, to know which the doer, and what the doing, and which the sufferer, and what the sufferer, and what the suffering, and what those shapes, that were not rooted to the ground, like the Veronica, but melted away, into the dark, after a while.[114]

Repetition, doubling, duplicity, doubting, uncertainty are all encompassed here, as they are in Watt's most common phrase, uttered with increasing confusion in the book: "Geb nodrap, nodrap, geb nodrap"—an inversion of "beg pardon." Watt recalls, "These were sounds that at first . . . were so much Irish to me. . . . Thus I missed I suppose much I presume of great interest."[115] For Beckett, and for Richards, truth and meaning are illusive things. What meaning can be found from life's experiences usually escapes us in the moment. This is particularly so with trauma, which can only be realized—or fully awakened to—through repetition. Traumatic experiences require revisiting to understand their impact. Thus to awaken to trauma, as the slumbering angels in the installation might (Figure 6.11), is to accept a larger responsibility, an "*ethical* relation to the real."[116] The real, or the true, is not so simple that it can be recounted from a sequence of events and narrated on stage before a commission. Instead, it depends on *understanding what it means to not see,* or even recognize, the unthinkable.

Recovery: Art and Ritual

How to respond to trauma once awakened is the question at hand. Geb nodrap. How, and for what, did Richards beg pardon? Autobiography bore significant weight in the *Veils* installation as it was here that he addressed a series of events from the mid-1970s that had troubled him ever since. In 1977, he had readied Biko's autopsy photographs for the state's inquest. He described their impact:

> The pictures, my initial professional and subsequent personal reaction to them (first distanced and later disturbed), came at some point since to mark one important stage in a continuum in which I felt confused, compromised, implicated, and ultimately angry about what in shorthand I must call

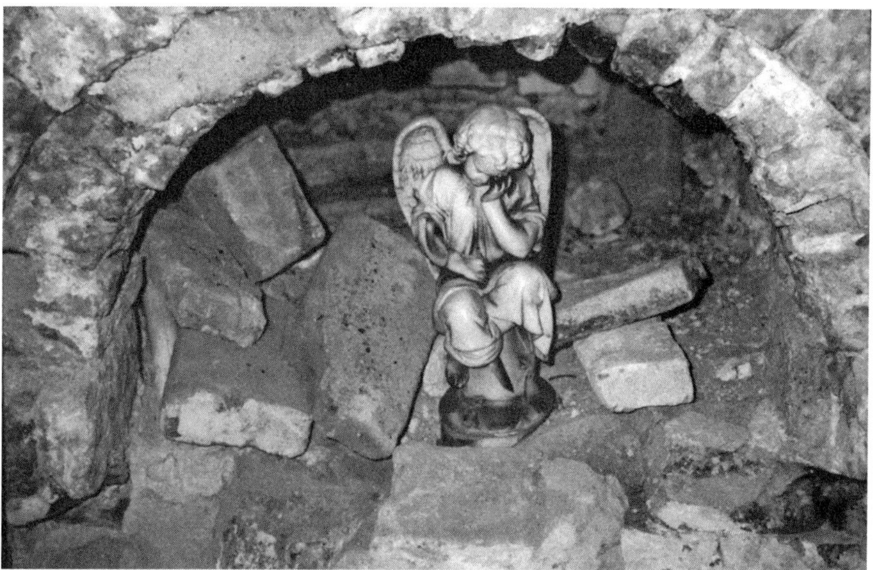

FIGURE 6.11. Colin Richards, *Angel,* installed at the Castle of Good Hope, Cape Town, 1996. *Faultlines* exhibition. Courtesy of Penny Siopis.

"Apartheid" and its baleful effect on my private and public sense of reality, and indeed truth.[117]

His work as a medical illustrator had followed close on the heels of the artist's compulsory military service in an artillery unit.[118] He found himself in Angola for several months in 1975 and 1976 even though the South African state denied its presence there, lying even to its soldiers about where they were headed.[119] He has called those years in the military "the single most traumatic experience publically I've ever had to go through."[120] This trauma—a composite of violent acts witnessed and a sense of masculinity as it is defined by and lived within the military—is linked with Biko's death in time. So, too, were a third and fourth disturbance: one of the artist's brothers died, and an autopsy was performed on his body; his father unexpectedly died soon after.[121] The bind with his father, what Richards described as "his authority; his lack of authority," seems to have been elemental to his practice.[122]

The process of art making was therapeutic for this artist, and he preferred methods that are labor intensive.[123] Illusionistic watercolors take time and precision. He described the medium's appeal in that its "slow motion opens up a space for the active presence of artistic identity, fulfilling precisely . . . [the] dual need to be understood as a documenter and an artist."[124] For Richards, painting was a ritual, one that served his stated need to "spend time, quietly, every evening, doing this kind of thing. That's really really important. . . . The process is real, even though the result is an illusion."[125] Within *Veils,* he staged other rituals (one past, one current), suggestive of a kind of quiet act of penitence.

Two works, *Angola 1976* and *Invalid Cup Series* (Figure 6.12), occupied a nook adjacent to the trio *Sleeping Dog I, The True Image (Vera Iconica),* and *Sleeping Dog II. Angola 1976* is a small tableau of objects set before a photograph of the castle wall on which it is hung. It is made from collected objects: a medal Richards received for active military service; a metal flame taken from a Catholic relic found in Venice; and spent ammunition cartridges of Cuban manufacture picked up in Angola. The last of these were among several objects that Richards stole away from the war.[126] He recalled:

> I remember desperately collecting and concealing objects taken in Angola and the operational area. We were explicitly forbidden by the military to take any material which might be linked to our activities in Angola. Amongst the items I eventually managed to smuggle out were a Cuban army jacket, two shotgun rounds stamped as made in Luanda, the clasp of bullets . . . and a pair of leather ammunition pouches. Many of my compatriots also collected material. . . . It was very important then to some of us to secure physical proof of having been in Angola. . . . I simply wore the jacket, putting some live rounds in my water bottle and sewing some in the lining of the poncho I wore over my jacket.[127]

At the castle, *Invalid Cup Series* sat below *Angola 1976.* As Jennifer Law has discussed, invalid cups are used to aid the less well among us—the infirm, the helpless, the bedridden, the weak—and the word *invalid* means defective, but also erroneous or untrue.[128] Richards filled each cup with mielie meal seed in cotton wool and water taken from the castle's moat. In the above register, bottles were filled with different materials: in one, soil and water, referring to land and fertility; in another, urine, smoke, and mirrored glass to reference deceitful practices; a third bottle contained milk and honey, allusions to the Promised Land described by early Dutch settlers in southern Africa; the last bottle held tar and feathers, a trope for informers, collaborators, and complicity.[129] In a daily ritual, Richards carefully nurtured the seeds at first to bring about their germination. He then abandoned this practice to assure that the budding plants

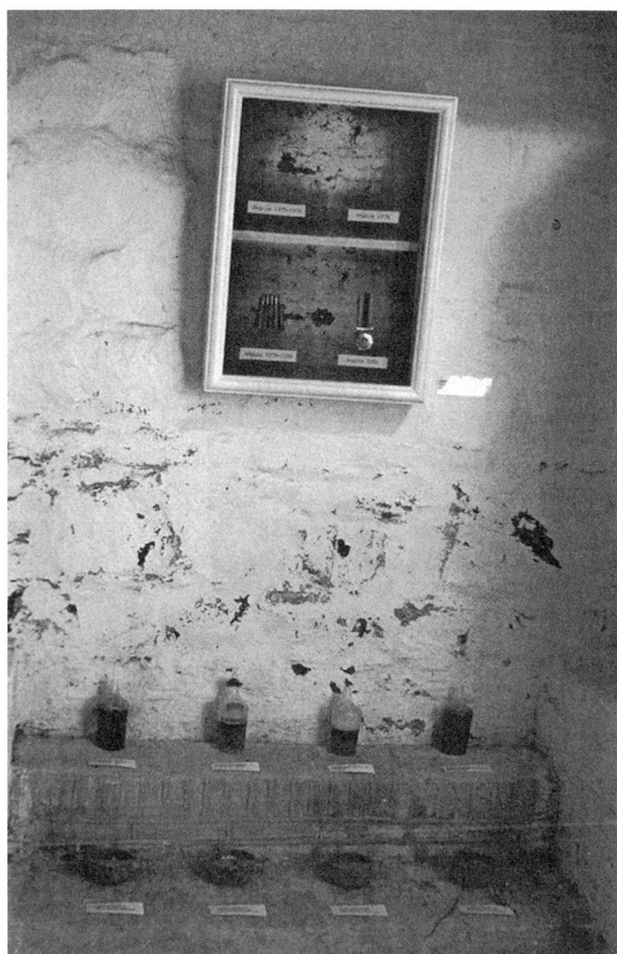

FIGURE 6.12. Colin Richards, installation of *Angola 1976* (above) and *Invalid Cup Series*, 1997. Installed at the Castle of Good Hope, Cape Town, Faultlines exhibition, 1997. Courtesy of Penny Siopis.

would wither and die. So, too, did the milk sour, the tar harden, and the urine putrefy. This quiet performance extended over days but was enacted without fanfare. Its tone was of a ritual compelled by and for the artist alone.

The remains of an earlier private ritual undertaken daily were staged on the floor nearby beside a well from which water was once drawn. *Oath II (The Good Book)* of 1996 (Figure 6.13) consists of a stack of paper on a cloth table of sorts (stacked duplicates of the *Veil* works hung nearby) and a collection of spent cartridges—of ink this time rather than ammunition as in *Angola 1976*. The papers

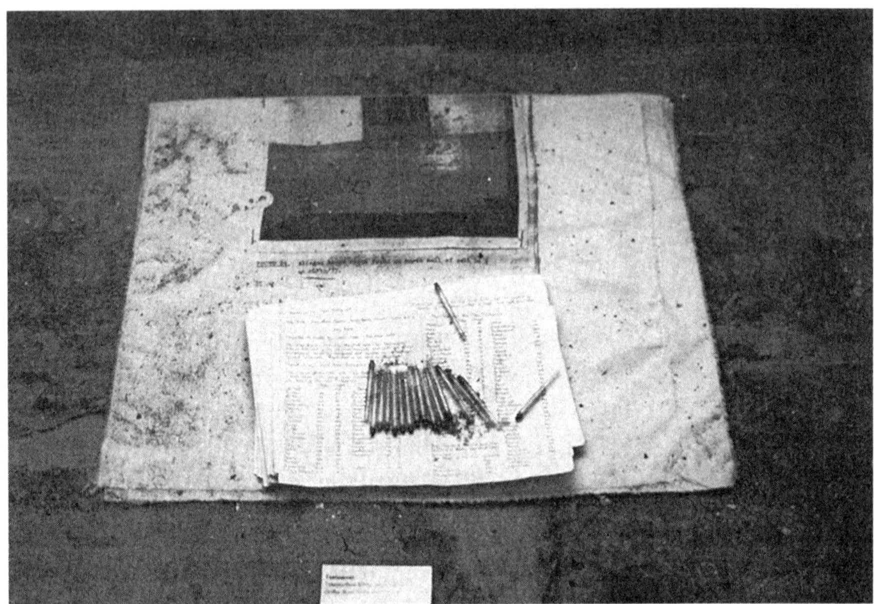

FIGURE 6.13. Colin Richards, *Oath II (The Good Book)*, 1996. Paper and ink cartridges on bed sheet. Installed at Castle of Good Hope, Cape Town, 1996. *Faultlines* exhibition. Courtesy of Penny Siopis.

record the artist's handwritten copy of the Bible; the ink cartridges are those he used for this draining task. Although it is tempting to read this tedious undertaking as emblematic of a desire for purification, as does Law,[130] I believe *Oath II* suggests something else. As part of the *Veils* installation, this piece stands as witness to the gap between the infliction of trauma and its later experience.

If *Veils* was essentially about Richards's own trauma, then Christianity was necessarily a part. Its relation to *Angola 1976* rests in more than the commonality of cartridges. It rests in deceit. Richards remembers his realization that the church colluded with the state, which left him, at the age of nineteen, in "a state of shock."[131] In text written for the exhibition *Memórius—Intimas—Marcas,* the artist recalled a conversation with his father, who worried that his son would be sent to war.[132] Young Richards replied:

> We are not in Angola. Anyway, I've heard only volunteers go. Citizen force conscripts sign a form. . . . I won't go. I won't sign anything. It will be alright.

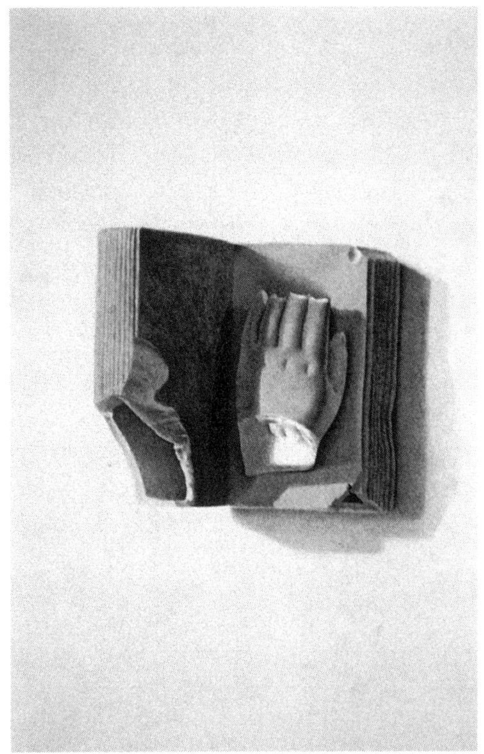

FIGURE 6.14. Colin Richards, *Oath I,* 1994. Watercolor. Courtesy of Penny Siopis.

The minister has just said, "There are no South African troops in Angola." They would not lie to us. Not blatantly. Skeptical silence. I was angry at my father's doubt. It sapped my frail confidence.[133]

Expecting to be deployed in South-West Africa (now Namibia), his artillery unit wound up in Angola instead. He gradually understood the deceit to which he was subject as the tattered road signs read from the back of the truck in which he traveled changed from familiar (English and Afrikaans) to expected (German, anglicized Owambo), and then to surprising (Portuguese). "On we churned. Bush is bush. Road-signs were infrequent. The first sign shocked. . . . We had not stopped. I had not signed anything."[134]

Although Richards's installation within the *Faultlines* exhibition included other works not discussed here, one more must be mentioned. *Oath I* of 1994 (Figure 6.14) embodies the manifold tensions at play for Richards, whether among deceits realized or concepts studied. This watercolor copy of a cemetery relic shows a maimed hand resting on a chipped and broken Bible. Its pages are worn. Multiple shadows cast by the original have been recorded with care. An oath is a vow, a signature of sorts, that upholds a series of truths: truth in testimony, honest endeavor, belief in the power of the body to which one swears. *Oath I* is on some level about broken delusions, but its target is fundamentally truth itself. The Bible on which this hand rests yields authority by way of the Veronica, which Richards once theorized as "perhaps the only 'true' image, the first 'photograph' of the first cause."[135] As a watercolor—a fugitive medium that wants to run—*Oath I* responded to its conceptual source: *The True Image—Vera Iconica,* a veil without an imprint, without authority—without truth—at all.

Removing the Blinds: Biko in Sue Williamson's *Truth Games*

Among South Africa's most accomplished artists, Sue Williamson is distinguished for her ability to convey personal narratives of political importance. With *Truth Games: The Series* (1998), she staged a central objective of the Truth and Reconciliation Commission: enacting and enabling dialogic truth. The TRC's deputy chairman, Alex Boraine, described it: "Dialogic truth . . . is social truth, truth of experience that is established through interaction, discussion and debate. . . . The process of dialogue involved transparency, democracy, participation as the basis of affirming human dignity and integrity."[136] The process of exchange is central to this series, an ensemble of thirteen cases that were heard before the TRC. One piece within the suite is considered here, *Nkosinathi Biko—false medical certificate—Dr. Benjamin Tucker* (Plate 17).

The composition and material elements of this work are like others in the series. A triptych frames the subject of each case (a person who died or a scene where violence was done) between a surviving victim or loved one at left and perpetrator at right. All images and text originally appeared in press accounts of the TRC proceedings, which Williamson clipped and enlarged on a photocopier. These she bleached and stretched into varying scales and fonts and altered their hues to fit the confines of large-scale triptychs.[137] Nine horizontal registers cross the three images and contain quotes from the hearings, etched into Perspex that slides and is color-coded to match the muted tones that bathe the parties to either side. (In Plate 17, those colors are sepia for Biko and gray for Tucker.) Viewers can manipulate the testimonies by sliding the Perspex quotes

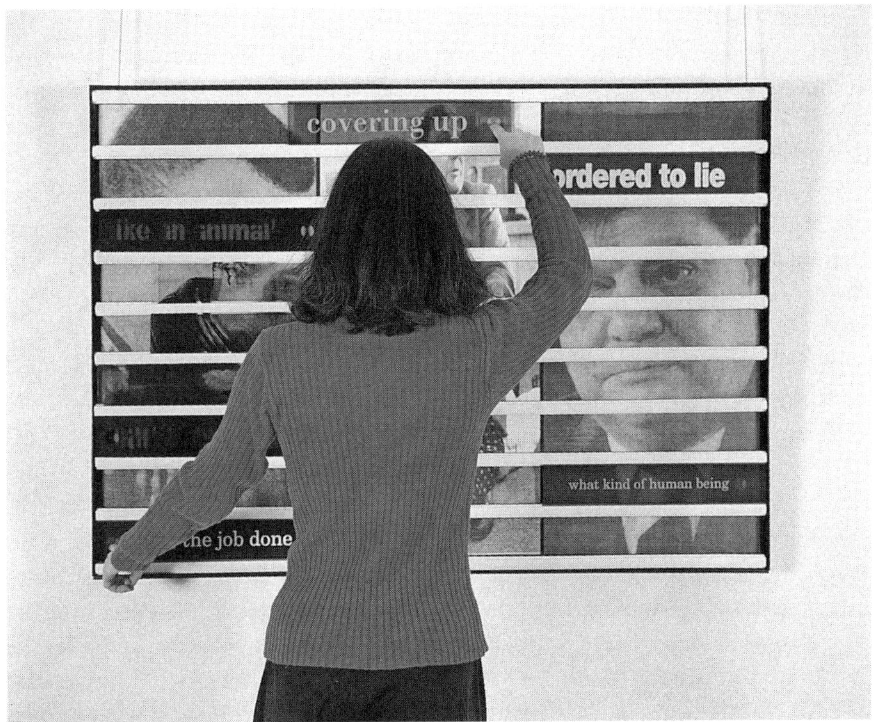

FIGURE 6.15. Sue Williamson, *Tony Yengeni—"wet bag" torture—Jeff Benzien*, 1998. *Truth Games* series. Installation view. Laminated color laser prints, wood, metal, plastic, Perspex. 800 x 1200 x 60 mm. Copyright Sue Williamson. Courtesy of The Goodman Gallery.

on their white plastic supports, thereby obscuring portions of an image while revealing others (Figure 6.15).

When *Truth Games* first opened in 1998 at Johannesburg's Goodman Gallery, Lloyd Pollack wrote, rather problematically:

You can superimpose the victim's accusation on the defendant and the defendant's justification on his victim. You can displace the image of the crime and attribute it to either. You can exchange features so as to erase identity. By exploiting the work's interactive potential, you shift the meaning of words and images. . . . No unilateral reading is possible.[138]

Too much has been made of the "play" that *Truth Games* invites. Although interactivity may prompt critical awareness of "contradictory interpretations" displayed before the TRC, it does not "universalize the guilt of a diseased society," as Pollack would have it.[139] As the translucent Perspex is slid and the image beneath it varies, one senses the shifting complexity of dialogue—what's said, what's heard, what's offered, what's not—but one does not sense that apartheid history is morally opaque. It has not been this for Williamson herself, in any case, whose excellent work over the decades (both as artist and activist) has consistently enlivened viewers to critically engage with South Africa's sociopolitical realities.

All thirteen works in the series are the same large size; Williamson conceived of them as windows that separate the viewer on the outside from the TRC proceedings on the inside.[140] This analogy is enhanced by the white vertical slats, which resemble opened Venetian blinds. Multiple boundaries are suggested: apartheid's divisive and dividing legacy (as the artist once put it, "That's what apartheid does, it cuts people off from each other");[141] the ways that documentary images offer small windows into lived experience, but always incomplete ones; the abject voyeurism that attends tales of violence; and the propensity of many white South Africans to disregard, or stand outside, the substantive proceedings of the TRC. *Truth Games* shakes us. The large scale of each work and their familiar aspects—mass-produced images, well-known stories, window coverings—invite us in but require caution. The ghosts at center are without color, violated, the lost but present subjects of each hearing. They cause an uneasy ripple up the spine.

The ghost at the center of *Nkosinathi Biko—false medical certificate—Dr. Benjamin Tucker* lingers in an uncertain space. The name Bantu Stephen Biko on this headstone (itself a portrait) is enlarged and echoes out, in this arrangement, onto the Perspex above it. The photograph's foreground captures the hazy brush of high grass at the foot of his grave, which obscures, even destabilizes, the flat concrete tomb above his coffin. The headstone reaches toward Biko's eldest son at left, who bows his head to meet and complete the curve. Biko is personalized in this work of art like no other. He is identified by one aspect: his role as father. The third register, just above that which echoes his name, reads "father's brain haemorrhage." Color-coded to match Nkosinathi at left, the words resonate with sadness over the loss of father to son.

The other excerpts from media reports on this TRC hearing on medical ethics all respond to the central question, also etched into orange Perspex: "What happened in room 619?"[142] Though this question was never adequately answered by those who failed to aid Biko, the first words of each phrase chosen by the artist sum up certainties: death, false, disgraceful, and examined. Although the last of these is attributed to Dr. Tucker, his claim falls flat. Rather, the case that has been "examined repeatedly" seeks a perpetrator who caused Biko's death: first in the 1977 inquest, then through the years up until 1985 as medical organizations questioned the ethics of district surgeons, and ultimately twice before the TRC. Read top to bottom, the narrative of the work flows logically from the reason for the investigation (death in detention) to an inadequate conclusion (disgraceful conduct). That key question is followed by fragmented images of the doctor, including his left hand. Thus Williamson makes clear the doctor's complicity—or the hand he had in Biko's death. The title and composition align to secure this reading: Biko's grave was dug in part because of Tucker's "false medical certificate." This central finding of the Biko medical ethics hearing is given center place in the composition, laid immediately over Biko's headstone.

By visualizing causality, *Nkosinathi Biko—false medical certificate—Dr. Benjamin Tucker* differs from most other works in *Truth Games*. Indeed, there is only one other that finds an explanation for the human rights violation under study *(Linda Biehl—understand the context—Mongezi Manqina)*, and in this case causality was found in the testimony itself, not through Williamson's placement of text with image and select narration.[143] This work also differs in the degree of balanced testimony Williamson chose. It stands alone in *Truth Games* in that the perpetrator's testimony is restricted to but one phrase and his voice is replaced elsewhere with the findings of TRC commissioners. Tucker was found to have signed a "false medical certificate" in 1977, and he was maligned for his "disgraceful conduct."[144]

The Biko case had likely received more attention prior to the TRC hearings than any other Williamson chose to study, an indication that through the TRC South Africans hoped to confirm what was long suspected and to publically correct the spurious record about what happened to Steve Biko in his final days. The Biko family, however, doubted new evidence would come to light.[145] They would prove to be right as once again public desire for truth in this case went unmet. In all of the Biko hearings—two for amnesty and another regarding medical ethics—dialogic truth did not result.[146] Transparency was not offered; dignity and integrity were not honored. Elsewhere in *Truth Games*, Williamson leaves resolution to the viewer; here one finds that she corrects those errors and apportions blame appropriately.

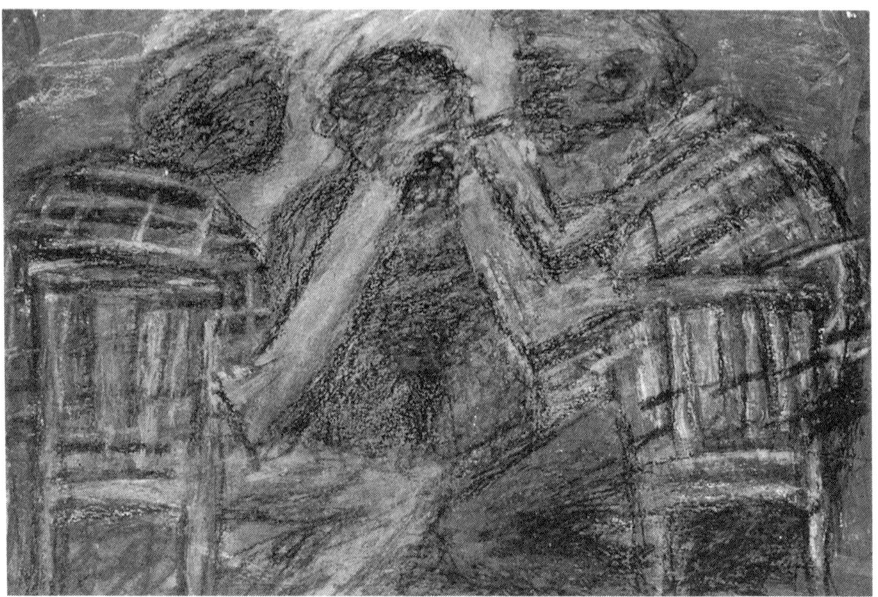

FIGURE 6.16. David Koloane, *The Journey, no. 4,* 1998. Acrylic and oil pastel on paper, 29 x 42 cm framed. Courtesy of David Koloane.

David Koloane, Timely Attendant

David Koloane is an ideal translator (Kristeva's "attendant") of Steve Biko's last days because he has long exemplified Black Consciousness. He is the one individual whose work spans the breadth of this book. The TRC amnesty hearings into Biko's death prompted him to make two works: a series titled *The Journey* (1998) and a mural-sized mixed-media work called *Passage* (1999). I focus on *The Journey,* a suite of nineteen paintings in acrylic and oil pastel on paper that narrates Biko's capture, interrogation, detention, and death (Figures 6.16–6.18 and Plate 18).[147] Koloane's narrative isolates suffering and thus visually represents a horror commonly sensed in response to Biko's death. The artist records successive moments that many people have imagined by concentrating attention on a lone figure, bound and naked, twisting and turning in a small space. Such intimate scenes, which comprise more than half of the total narrative (eleven of nineteen works), personalize the experience of living through a slowly debilitating death. The focus on suffering rivets viewers' attention on time and offers a painful response to a question Biko once posed. Threatened

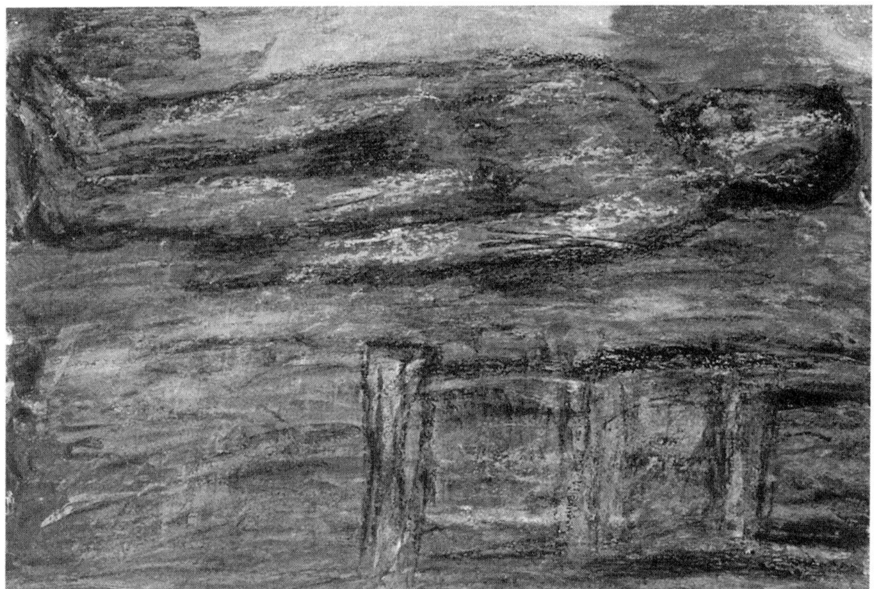

FIGURE 6.17. David Koloane, *The Journey, no. 19,* 1998. Acrylic and oil pastel on paper, 29 x 42 cm framed. Courtesy of David Koloane.

by a police officer with the words "I will kill you," Biko cracked, "How long is it going to take you?"[148] In Koloane's episodic vision, the time from torture, inflicted in scene four (Figure 6.16), to death, realized in scene nineteen (Figure 6.17), passed slowly.

The narrative begins with three scenes at the roadblock outside of Port Elizabeth where Steve Biko and Peter Jones were taken into custody. The search is paramount here as bright yellow headlights flood the scene and drown out any representation of the passengers. Thus begins the dehumanizing process realized within the narrative. Police officers, abstractly rendered in black to either side of the car, shine their flashlights into the automobile. This first sequence defines the palette for the series in shades of black, yellow, white, purple, blue, and red. Koloane layered the paint, a method he has perfected over decades of notable work, in order to reach a desired luminosity—one that captures what was for Biko yet another interrogation.[149] Further, the artist scratched the surface of each piece, an act that enhances the effect of layered coloring and connotes both wounding and healing. For Koloane the TRC hearings gnawed, itched, and ached, sensations that beg a response. But the method of scratching, according to Mike Kili, evokes the TRC's attempts to heal: "Sometimes a wound must be scratched to be cleaned."[150]

From the roadblock in Port Elizabeth, Koloane next envisioned Biko's torture in a sequence of five works wherein violence is explicit just once and is otherwise obscured behind a row of plainclothes police officers gathered as witnesses or metaphorically present in empty chairs. The lone chair motif, which Paul Stopforth first used to signify detainees' duress (see Figure 3.2), is carried through ten of the eleven scenes devoted to Biko's captivity and death. Set upright, skewed in relation to the picture plane, toppled over on its side, the chair's twisting and turning parallel the figure's tortured struggle, until at last in the final frame it lays at rest alongside Biko's corpse (Figure 6.17).

At the TRC, it was revealed that Biko's refusal to rise from his chair and stand as directed drove amnesty applicant Daantjie Siebert to "unbridled action against a black man who did not know his place."[151] Koloane's deep translation of Biko's suffering (emotionally, pictorially) is a defiant response to Siebert's brand of racism. He described the personal impact of Biko before the TRC: "It was also a journey . . . for me."[152] In Julia Kristeva's classic treatment of abjection, she writes that in its most extreme, that "journey to the end of the night," by which she means those hours before death, an attendant is required "to accompany as far as possible the speaking subject on that journey."[153] In 1998, David Koloane was this attendant. With *The Journey* we may access pain because its "whole narrative stance seems controlled by the necessity of going through abjection, whose intimate side is suffering and horror is its public feature."[154]

It is fitting somehow that Koloane would feel most compelled by Biko's case since they share a generation. Recall that he is a longtime proponent of Black Consciousness who worked with Black Community Programmes before its banning in 1977. He attended the historic *Culture and Resistance* conference in Gaborone, Botswana, in 1982, and lent his art to the accompanying exhibition, *Art toward Social Development*. His always vigorous defense of black professionals brought about the Thupelo Art Project in 1985 and the Fordsburg (aka Bag Factory) Artists' Studios in 1991. All of these decisions were fundamentally informed by Black Consciousness. So, too, were his dramatic experiments with paint in the late 1980s. Thus as much as *The Journey* depicts Biko's life at its end, so too does it engage an aspect of Koloane's being—what Kristeva would call an "unbearable identity" that demands voice, or vision.[155]

The final and largest sequence within the series imagines Biko's bodily suf-

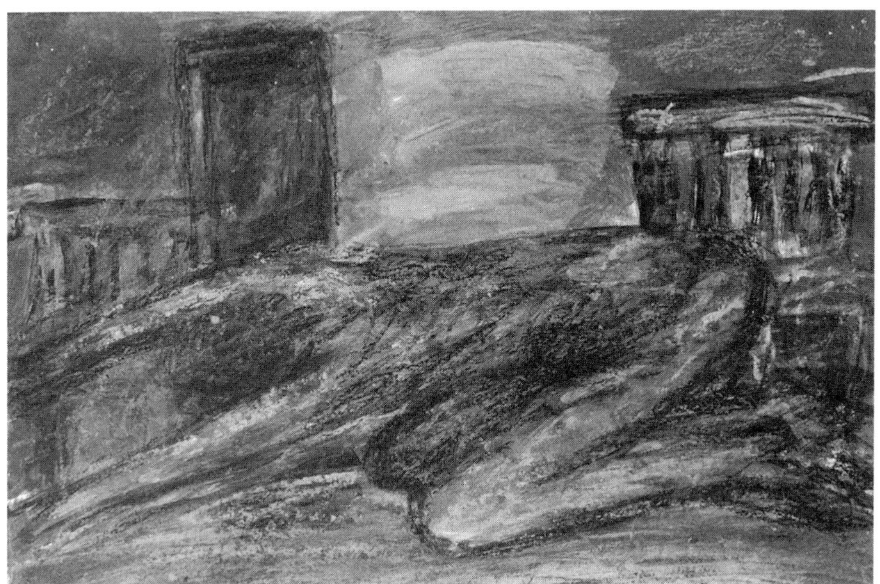

FIGURE 6.18. David Koloane, *The Journey, no. 16,* 1998. Acrylic and oil pastel on paper, 29 x 42 cm framed. Courtesy of David Koloane.

fering. His features are rendered abstractly, with emphasis on limbs and torso in motion (Figure 6.18 and Plate 18). His is not an ideal body; he is in decline. Koloane demystifies Biko's final days by representing his pain and neglect. He is shown as Everyman from his first appearance in scene four (Figure 6.16) in that his face, his individuality, is entirely obscured by the fists of police officers who batter him from either side. The officers' faces are yellow to match the glaring searchlights of the narrative's first sequence, and the features of the figure at right are clearly depicted. Such elements set the abusers apart from the abused. Rendered as Everyman, Biko's suffering stretches outward to call, Kristeva suggests, "upon what, within us, deludes defenses, trainings, and words, or else struggles against them. A nakedness, a forlornness, a sense of having had it; discomfort, a downfall, a wound. What people do not acknowledge but know they have in common; a base, a mass, an anthropological commonality."[156] He moves through states of consciousness, isolated, save for once: crouching on knees and centered within a stream of yellow light cast from an open door, he looks at us from an even plane (Plate 18). We look death squarely in the eyes. Echoing

Ludwig Wittgenstein, and, in turn, Kristeva, Veena Das regards pain as only realized—only made real—through our response to its call, what Kristeva calls our own "crying-out." Language, visual or otherwise, is "hooked rather inadequately to the world of pain," thus Das urges us to abandon "simplified images of healing . . . [and instead] think of healing as a kind of relationship to death."[157] *The Journey* is a most fitting exercise in this, precisely. After its completion, very few works have imag(in)ed Biko's "journey to the end of the night." Nor has he been cast much again as Everyman.[158]

Koloane's determination to work in any style he wished, with whatever materials he needed, has made him a role model for succeeding generations of artists. Some colleagues now affectionately call him "The Old Man" to suggest there is no other.[159] For most, the effect of earlier drives toward self-definition is readily seen in postapartheid art. But it is worth remembering that while the nation was negotiating its transition in 1992, Koloane said, "Fortunately the artists are becoming more and more impertinent, and they want to do what other artists, and whites in particular have always been able to do: say what they want, with all the materials they could want, in any size, in any way."[160] His thoughts here bear the imprint of Biko's:

> Not only have [whites] kicked the black but they have also told him how to react to the kick. For a long time the black has been listening with patience to the advice he has been receiving. . . . With painful slowness he is now beginning to show signs that it is his right and duty to respond to the kick *in the way he sees fit.*[161]

Black Consciousness has infused David Koloane's voice and vision for as long as it has been recorded, whether by journalists or historians or his own hand. We need only shift our own perception of BC to better hear, and thus better understand, this great artist's work. In my opinion, he could not have been better suited to translate Biko's last days.

Public contestation over the legacies of Steve Biko and Black Consciousness became pronounced in the 1990s as South Africa transitioned from apartheid to democracy. Freshly empowered early in the decade, both the Azanian People's Organization and the African National Congress claimed to represent Biko's ideals. Each promotes Biko as the spirit of ubuntu so that he remains suspended between advocacy of a nonracial, neoliberal, capitalist political economy on the one hand, and a nonethnic, African-centered, socialist platform on the other.

The production of Biko as unifier, a saint of sorts who died so that we might be human(e), gained greatest currency in the early 1990s, as for most South Africans the drive to be free of apartheid and reconcile with its past was fast and strong. This continued through the rhetorical force of the Truth and Reconciliation Commission, whereafter representations of Biko's death—whether in decline, deceased, or under inquiry—largely ceased to be made after twenty years of meaningful artistic meditation on this subject. Although the TRC amnesty hearings did not satisfy public desire for honesty in the Biko case, it did reach an interesting conclusion of sorts by signaling the end of this particular stream of representation.

Yet this singular aspect of Biko's history, his death, is like that of too many others who died at the hands of the state in that it continues to register in the lives of those whom he loved. South Africa's Truth and Reconciliation Commission enabled translators to share their versions of history, which are also visions of the past, in order to create the nation anew. But as an unnamed mother potently conveyed, translation is never complete, and we cannot expect conclusion from it. Reading her words reminds us of the need to listen closely now and after: "It's an everlasting pain. It will stop never in my heart. It always comes back. It eats me apart. Sonnyboy, rest well, my child. I've translated you from the dead."[162]

7 Museum, Monument, Marking

Black Consciousness in the New Millennium

AS THE TRUTH AND RECONCILIATION COMMISSION ENABLED PUBLIC WITNESS of apartheid era violations of the body, which are always profoundly personal and deeply experienced over time for those who suffer them, other discourses developed in the 1990s that sought to heal the larger body politic as it embraced democracy. The need to narrate was distinct. One such story shared a unifying, pluralistic vision with the nation cast as a rainbow, wherein eleven distinct bands (one for each of South Africa's constitutionally recognized languages) enjoyed equal status. Lines between were a bit blurred, as one would expect of a nation newly emerging from the strict divisions of Bantustans and the ethnic stripes cast by apartheid law. Early in the decade, South Africa was celebrated worldwide as the Rainbow Nation, but in reality it remained more divided than this beatific rhetoric allowed. Among the ripples reflective of disharmony below the surface was the sense that the African National Congress had hijacked the narrative of liberation, and the certainty that its socialist coloring had turned from deep red to rather pink.

In this period the ANC again adopted a new symbol of national unity: the raised clenched fist of the mid-1980s transformed into a multib(r)anded rainbow of respectable plurality. And in the very best tradition of the nation, questions quickly fermented and a rigorous debate ensued. Annie Coombes attributes such vital, vibrant exchange to its popular struggle for representation. "This tradition," she notes, "is not confined to the academic sphere alone, possibly as a result of the political education for liberation that sometimes had the capacity to cut across class and ethnic boundaries and that provided rigorous intellectual training."[1] Thus the discordant voices recorded in this chapter show the rainbow-infused identity advanced by their government to be but a shallow veneer covering the much more complex reality of slow change.

"Biko Belongs to All of Us": President Nelson Mandela, 1997

Since the transition to democracy in 1994, South Africans have created many monuments and memorials to individuals and events that helped bring about the end of apartheid. Healing gestures all, their presence reminds that dismantling this beast was difficult; all battles were hard won. Sabine Marschall's research into commemorations of struggle illustrates that they too have been hotly contested.[2] East London, Eastern Cape, is home to the best-known public sculptural tribute to Steve Biko (Figure 7.1), and it is no exception to this trend, but it adds to those debates in at least two important ways. First, it was unlike most public monuments in that it was privately commissioned and funded, thus created without the benefit of a competition that would have included varied visions of how to best commemorate its subject. Second, its unveiling on the twentieth anniversary of Biko's death displayed more than a monument; it also became a contest of political will as supporters of varied parties used the event to promote their versions of how Biko and Black Consciousness should be remembered and, indeed, which among them held the right to narrate these histories.

The monument was troubled from the start since an individual, Donald Woods, commissioned it rather than a collective. He also arranged for private financing.[3] Operating without knowledge of customary procedures for monument making, he approached his neighbor Naomi Jacobson (b. 1925) to make the work. Jacobson was well known for her portraits of black leaders, most of which were busts rather than larger-than-life representations such as that of Biko.[4] At the time, both resided in the upscale suburb of Parkview just north of downtown Johannesburg. Although Jacobson's credentials must have seemed appropriate, her lifestyle and skill set ought to have deterred Woods as he acted as a jury of one. Her marriage to a former district surgeon ought to have also given him pause, particularly with the culpability of such physicians in supporting apartheid.

Cast in bronze, the monument sits outside the front door of city hall in East London with a sculpture that commemorates British soldiers who died in the South African War (1899–1902) opposite. Jacobson based her portrayal on Woods's memory; they sat in the evenings over wine and discussed such particulars as Biko's watch, clothing, and how he would have typically stood.[5] She aimed to create an image of self-confidence but, she cautioned, one that was "not aggressive" in appearance and would not make anyone "upset."[6] Such statements

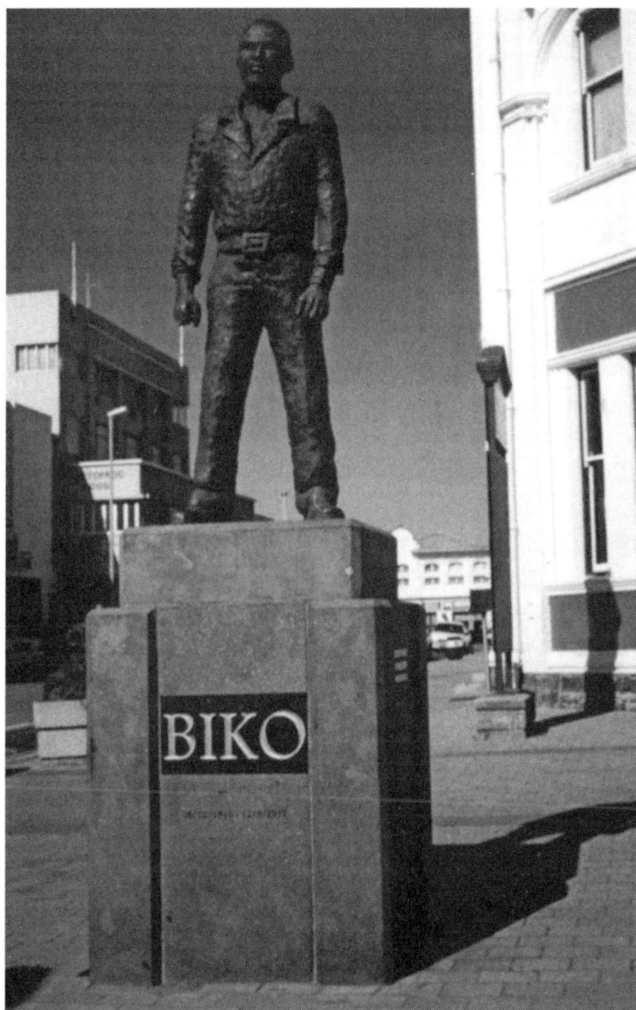

FIGURE 7.1. Naomi Jacobson, *Biko Monument*, 1997. East London.

belie a lack of understanding about Black Consciousness and the reasons why a monument to Steve Biko was much needed in the immediate postapartheid years. She was keen to represent him as "a common man on the streets" and thus chose to clothe him in a flannel shirt with sleeves rolled up, ready to work for his beliefs. The monument has been justly criticized for its formal faults (it is ill proportioned and stiff with no sense of a body beneath the cloth),[7] but these are less important than the failure to organize a competition that would have allowed artists with vested interest in Black Consciousness to submit proposals. Given the limited resources available for such commemorative projects, it is doubtful that another monument will be built. Woods acted prematurely to honor his friend in this way since the Biko Foundation (launched September 1997, the same week as Jacobson's statue) has flourished these past decades and would have been an ideal partner to help realize his mission.

More than ten thousand people gathered to witness the unveiling of the monument on September 12, 1997.[8] Among them were "several thousand passionate supporters" of the Azanian People's Organization who protested the "hijacking" of Biko's memory by other political parties.[9] After waiting for more than an hour for the noise to subside, President Nelson Mandela took the stage and chastised protesters.[10] "Biko belongs to all of us," he said in Xhosa, "not just AZAPO."[11] He then called for unity among political parties and asked the leaders of AZAPO, the Pan Africanist Congress, and the Inkatha Freedom Party to join him onstage before the monument was revealed (Figure 7.2).[12] He described his mission to "unite the country before I step down," implying that unity was at the core of Biko's vision as well.[13] Indeed, that same day the *Sowetan* ran an article in which Biko was said to have regarded "the differences between the Black Consciousness Movement, PAC and ANC [as] merely historical."[14] Mandela's prepared remarks echoed this belief, and they maintained the ongoing relevance of Black Consciousness to all South Africans:

> The driving thrust of black consciousness was to forge pride and unity amongst all the oppressed, to foil the strategy of divide-and-rule, to engender pride amongst the mass of our people and confidence in their ability to throw off their oppression. . . . A new attitude of mind and way of life are required in our efforts to change the human condition. But they can only thrive if we succeed in that common effort to build a better life. They are required as we strive to bring all power into the hands of the people; as we seek to shape a new media that appreciates the conditions and aspirations of the majority; as we change the structure of ownership of wealth; as we build a new ethos in our ideals, and yet at the same time, the specificity of our own concrete conditions.
>
> While Steve Biko espoused, inspired, and promoted black pride, he never made blackness a fetish. At the end of the day, as he himself pointed out, accepting one's blackness is a critical starting point: an important foundation for engaging in struggle. Today, it must be a foundation for reconstruction

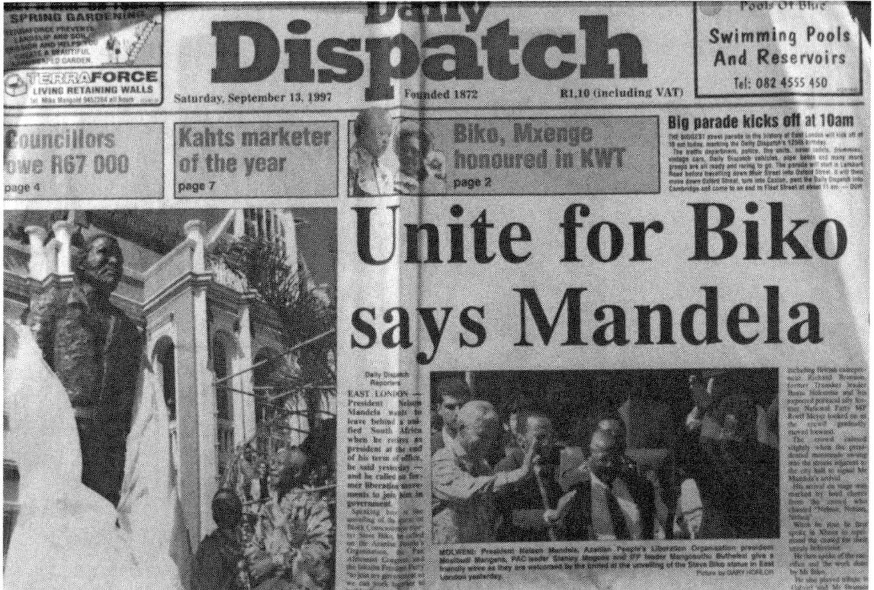

FIGURE 7.2. Cover of the *Daily Dispatch,* an East London daily, September 13, 1997.

and development, for a common human effort to end war, poverty, ignorance and disease.[15]

Now, nearly eighteen years on, Mandela's revitalization of Black Consciousness as an engine of reconstruction and development seems only partially fulfilled. Intense economic disparity still exists in South Africa. Although all adult citizens can now vote, power has hardly filtered beyond the ANC's grip since it has held a majority in all chambers of federal government since 1994. The nation has accepted the global expectation that it broker an end to conflicts elsewhere on the continent, but it has proven ineffective in ending the despotic, ruinous reign of Robert Mugabe in neighboring Zimbabwe. And while Mandela himself embraced commonly accepted modes of treating HIV-AIDS, his successor, Thabo Mbeki, famously refused them. This effectively perpetuated poverty and disease due to ignorance and arrogance.

Monumental public sculptures of the kind in East London can be used to promote interest in current social needs. They suffer a loss of attention rather soon after their unveiling, but they are reanimated through performances or rituals staged within their radius. Annie Coombes attributes their visibility entirely to "debates concerning the reinterpretation of history that take place at moments of social and political transition."[16] In this way, the ideals imparted by a given monument actively mutate as the past enters into conversation with the present. The Biko Monument has been used by activists for the disabled, among others, who chained themselves to it in order to protest social security laws that disqualified former recipients of funds.[17] Their signs, which read "Taking my grant has stripped me of my dignity," emphasized Biko's legacy as spokesman for the downtrodden, restorer of self-esteem, and, in the context of a protest against ANC policy, it recalled BC's socialist bent.

But other, destructive performances at the Biko Monument have received more attention than those that glean positive messages from BC. Most notable is the acronym AWB (for the far-right Afrikaner Weerstandsbeweging), which was painted on the monument's plinth the night after it was unveiled.[18] The letters were promptly cleaned off, but white paint was thrown over the statue two weeks later. Such actions illustrate the degree to which an image is what W. J. T. Mitchell calls a "vital sign." Pictures, he writes, are "not merely signs for living things but signs as living things."[19] Figural images are perhaps riper in this sense because their apparent vitality is linked to those who view it. Iconoclastic acts like the AWB's are attempts to disable the revolutionary ideals represented by figural monuments, but equally so they are attacks on the body of the person represented. There is a sense in which the image holds on to its animated, living counterpart, that it is "an object with feelings, intentions, desires and agency."[20] To see Biko whole in East London was to upend the dominant narrative in which his broken, tortured body eventually died. Those who performed secreted acts of destruction meant to offend precisely because their target image embodied a worldview of national unity that countered their own.

The AWB is a marginalized fringe party that loudly contested post-1994 attempts to commemorate antiapartheid activists and events. In the period that South Africa reconsidered its past through such highly visible forums as the Truth and Reconciliation Commission and the National Monument Council, members of the AWB and other conservative parties worked to destabilize their efforts to reconfigure the landscape by representing heroes and histories long neglected. This was the case even as South Africans opted not to topple public sculptures to figures whose influence was no longer dominant. In these years of transition, monuments both old and new prompted great debate as purveyors of a national consciousness in flux. These debates were visibly present through such actions as the defacement of Biko's likeness with white paint and a protest it sparked: the October 1997 covering of Pretoria's apartheid-era heroes in black shrouds. Those who cast dark cloaks on "public art works that mean nothing to the vast majority of people" saw their act as more accessible than most. They "transformed" the statues in city center into what they called "billboards of visual justice."[21]

By equating their guerrilla tactic to the world of billboards—prominent sites of desire within capitalist economies like South Africa—those who shrouded figures of colonial conquest described their intervention in terms that critique capitalism itself. Indeed, this mode of socioeconomic production was embedded in the figures they cloaked since it largely drove their interest to claim the mineral wealth of the land beneath. This desire fed a history that was particularly unjust to the nation's majority, most of whom still saw little material gain despite the transition to democracy. Further, Pretoria's anonymous activists critiqued the state's conception of its public. Ignored by those who funded public projects for decades, they demanded a visual representation of history that was truer to their own experience of it. The intervention of the guerilla artists around Pretoria was brief. In that it was a public critique of histories the state continued to sanction through the art it creates, exhibits, and maintains, it is of a kind with a better-known project that also fused art, political demonstration, and, literally, commercially owned billboards. Mounted in Cape Town in response to its rainbow-esque One City Festival of September 2000, *Returning the Gaze,* discussed below, drew starker lines than a rainbow allows. After a decade of continued strain, the rainbow was bound to dissolve.

Of Museums and Markets

Whatever their variety, museums are like monuments in that both are typically founded as sites that aim to foster nationalism. Thus the tales they tell through the objects they possess narrate the nation's past and their stories are reconfigured, or take new form, through curatorial vision. In the last third of the 1990s, two museums in Cape Town approached blackness in ways that are meaningful to Black Consciousness. In 1997, the District Six Museum was home to an exhibition named for Steve Biko and organized by the Twenty Years Later Collective, a tag chosen to recognize the efficacy of BC over the decades since Biko's death. The BLACK ARTS COLLECTIVE (BLAC) was formed the next year on an explicitly

BC platform. Black Consciousness shaped BLAC's response to an art market that effectively continued to sideline black perspectives in favor of what Julie McGee calls its particular "canon underclass with its own set of meanings, values, and expectations."[22] In BLAC's case, the institutional interests of the South African National Gallery (SANG) best represent those in need of critique.[23] The locations and collections of these two museums are dramatically different, but their mission to educate is the same, and their respective responses to Black Consciousness are instructive.

The District Six Museum was just two years old when it hosted *The Legacy of Steve Biko Twenty Years Later* exhibition, a bold but woefully underappreciated decision. Named for the historic Municipal District Six established in 1867, the larger site near which the museum stands today starkly visualizes the Group Areas Act of 1950 essentially in action. Claimed as a whites-only location in 1966, District Six saw the deportation of families to places in the distant Cape Flats and the demolition of buildings in which they had worked and lived. Since 1982, the land has sat scarred in the same state. On the near outskirts of Cape Town's City Bowl, as it is called, the District Six Museum receives visitors, but far fewer than those nestled within the Company Gardens that run down the city's old spine. This is where the South African National Gallery has sat since 1930 alongside several other cultural institutions that share its colonial origins.[24]

More Eurocentric in method than not, SANG's efforts to transform its collections, staff, and definitions of art have been under critical eye since apartheid's end. By the mid-1990s it had spawned more than a few controversies in its efforts to redress past transgressions.[25] Yet these have registered little impact on SANG's sway within an international market eager for South African art during the same period. As an arbiter of art from within, neither SANG's curatorial nor staffing decisions garnered much change for black arts professionals. Thus this influential museum found itself under fire from the fringe, most notably from BLAC. When it at last started to listen, new voices and visions began to register.

Twenty Years and Counting

When the Twenty Years Later Collective staged the exhibition *The Legacy of Steve Biko Twenty Years Later* at the District Six Museum, several had long known one another through arts work undertaken outside Cape Town's city center; they organized under this title and disbanded after the exhibit to make a point. The nation's message of harmonious unity had discolored truths still evident to many South Africans in this nascent democracy, and it had mutated Biko's legacy into a rainbow-striped humanism devoid of blackness. As scores of people from abroad visited South Africa eager to learn more about its history—one that relied on a consistent narrative of unity and reconciliation after a time of extreme adversity and brutality—artists in the collective sought to remind visitors that the transition was not so seamless. Twenty years after Biko's death and concurrent with the Truth and Reconciliation Commission's hearings about it, another story was on view in Cape Town.

The exhibition (held September 12 to October 24, 1997) was the first of its kind; no other had focused solely on Steve Biko. Instigators Paul Hendricks and Donovan Ward approached the owners of Agency Africa, Olav Hector and Nicky Beele, to realize an exhibition that showcased works by artists who remained outside the institutions that make careers—the circuit that relies on university training, gallery representation, and international exhibitions and patronage. Tyrone Appollis, Jane Duncan, Achmat Esau, Albert Hess, Craig Masters, Mustafa Maluka, Selvin November, and Alvin Mark Schroeder were among them; Hendricks and Ward also displayed works. Poets performed at the opening, Appollis and Mavis Smallberg included.

From the start, the exhibition faced resistance from different art sectors within Cape Town. Ward sensed that many critics were not interested in promoting artists whose explorations of identity were different from their own even though the unified vision captured by such televised slogans as Simunye: We Are One were by then under fire. Although he understood the need for such mantras, he was driven to critique them since they failed to capture reality, which was far more fragmented and increasingly defined by class. Paul Hendricks believes that some critics remained hedged by a negative interpretation of BC, thus their project was believed to be "not in their interest or, rather, one should say, viable for business."[26] The professional art circuit promoted certain stars, including some without university training, but its celebration "of the ordinary" was without a "connection to it," Ward said.[27] It would appear that a conception of race defined by skin color continued to dominate popular perception of BC, thus the exhibition was not widely welcomed because, as Hendricks believes, it "threatened to disrupt the euphoria of . . . a new 'non-racial' South Africa."[28] Cape Town's artists and administrators with international attention, and thus access, were largely silent on the subject. No reviews were printed in South Africa. The *Cape Times* printed a picture of Schroeder beside Biko's portrait, but that was all.

The talented Donovan Ward (b. 1962) made *Biko* in 1997 for the exhibition (Plate 19). The artist engages a wide range of materials, practices, and topics, so attempting to locate his work conceptually is a bit futile, but *Biko* perpetuates two elements that have long intrigued him: a worn, wall-like background that evokes derelict surroundings replete with torn posters and graffiti, and the commoditization of Africa in the capitalist marketplace. In this period he embraced the idea of a palimpsest (paper with writing that has been scraped away and replaced) and worked with cement, acrylic, dust, collage, silt, rust, Perspex, and found objects in order to weather the surface of his works. The effect is one of layered images on a neglected, dilapidated wall. Viewers must seek meaning among the juxtaposition of disparate images, and in this they may find what Ward calls "the hybrid, changing, contested, and sometimes ambiguous nature of Black Consciousness."[29]

The mottled and rust-stained surface of *Biko* includes torn paper fragments that roughly form the raised, clenched fist of the Black Peoples' Convention at center, and a portion of the red star favored in socialist propaganda. Located close to his heart, the bursting star offsets the sun motif on his left temporal lobe, site of the wound that adversely affected Biko's speech and vision and eventually proved fatal. The letters *B.P.C.* are seen on the paper below, and the artist coupled this with the same letters scratched onto the surface just at the end of lines that radiate rightward from the sun. Although worn over the years on this wall of public space, their resonance remains.

This sun motif, among the more popular "graphic violators" used in advertising, is one Ward favors; he has used it in several works to shift its meaning. Its visual punch grabs attention, but rather than drawing us toward an item that is "FREE!" or "NEW!" or "IMPROVED!" its appearance here operates to "wound" BC even as it codes the "spark of ideas" that Biko engendered. The tension between a crippled sense of agency and one filled with positive intellectual energy results in a crossroads wherein the stylized sun is emptied of meaning. Merged in a work made to consider Biko's legacy, this graphic violator calls up what Ward described as "the changing nature of BC, as represented by those who use BC rhetoric whilst furthering their own individualistic interests."[30] Solidly configured within a space that seems to disintegrate (only the family photograph remains similarly pristine), this corporate-like logo in Perspex suggests that capitalist enterprise has claimed territory once enhanced by the communalist and socialist motifs printed on poster paper.[31] It is manufactured and slick; it appears "false." But the stenciled fist and star, now torn with age, epitomizes low-tech, popular graphics, thus they signify the "true" expression of antiapartheid activists.

Biko is otherwise filled with graffiti-like markings, most visibly the drawing of Biko's face and hands gesturing with enthusiasm. Ward chose to copy this image from among the few photographs of Biko, since he once heard biographer Lindy Wilson describe him as an animated man. Other photographs fail to record this warm trait. Unlike the torn-fist form above, the hands retain the expressiveness of their bearer. They radiate faint lines that suggest lively motion. Sprayed in bluish gray, we see an American dollar above Biko's hand at left and the outlines of a wrench beside several steel washes at upper right. These combine with the graphic violator emblazoned on Biko's likeness to suggest distaste for the commoditization of his image, devoid, as it often is, of his ideas. The logo of a key company in colonial era trade, the Dutch East India Company or VOC (Vereenigde Oost Indische Compagnie), is engraved above the wrench, thus casting the interests of their representatives—the capitalist profiteer versus the socialist worker—into conflict. In a state that now ascribes to the same economic principles that the VOC once did, Biko's vision of "a more human face" for his nation appears to wither like the paper affixed at bottom right. Here Ward repeated the passage from Biko's "Black Consciousness and the Quest for a True Humanity" that has been quoted perhaps most often postapartheid (see discussion in chapter 6). But here "true humanity . . . [that] greatest gift possible" to future generations, that "glittering prize on the distant horizon," no longer inspires united action. Rather, in Ward's hands the passage appears frayed and worn down, lost amid commitments to more self-interested pursuits.

Ward comes from a middle-class mixed heritage and was "conscientized," as he put it, in his Claremont high school where much of the staff was highly politicized. Some had been banned; many belonged to the New Unity Movement.[32] After graduating in 1980, he started graphic design studies at the Ruth Prowse School of Art and Design and found at least a few other like-minded activists (David Brown, Jonathan Comerford, Lionel Davis, Graham Goddard) among the largely conservative student body. He worked designing graphics for the Western Cape Youth League, the United Democratic Front, the ANC, and several unions that came calling. Contrary to the notion that "the ANC tradition would replace Black Consciousness as the dominant ideology" among so-called coloured students at this time, Ward was "exposed more to BC" through some of these outlets and says, "I found an ideological home there." (He feels differently today and describes notions of blackness as more polarized.) Ward understood BC in its tricontinental form and cites this larger world of influence, including "BC in London and in the United States" as important to his formative thinking on the subject. He embraced the BC that Biko expounded and recalled, in 2011: "We are not just oppressed because of our skin pigmentation, but for other reasons as well." Note that he used the present tense.

Today Mustafa Maluka (b. 1976) is the best known among those who took part in the Twenty Years Collective. For the *Legacy of Steve Biko* exhibition he made a small enameled piece with found objects stuck to it. Titled *BLACK MAN U R ON YOUR OWN,* the work translated a keystone of Black Consciousness into a street scrawl in tune with Maluka's larger professional purpose. Artist, musician, writer, hip-hop producer, Maluka has long intertwined these interests. At this time he was also instrumental to the Black Fist Art Movement, a collective of aerosol artists in the Cape Town area who reclaimed historic spaces in the mid-1990s.[33] Regrettably now lost, *BLACK MAN U R ON YOUR OWN* was darkly hued and spoke a language Maluka knew well from childhood.[34] The phrase, with a photograph of Biko above, appeared on a poster in his parents' Bishop Lavis home in the Cape Flats. Thus the mixed-media work made in honor of Biko is a kind of tribute to the artist's parents, too.[35]

The Twenty Years Collective named itself for a momentous turn in political activism in South African history. By marking the stark changes of late 1977, they made use of Biko and Black Consciousness in the present tense, as a vehicle by which to parse out the rhetoric of equality realized through liberation from the reality of politics realized through capitalism. All of the artists who gathered in 1997 to proclaim BC's usefulness in their lives worked outside the mainstream and challenged its hesitant glance their way; nearly all still do. Although some works in this exhibition echoed the popular vision of Biko as unifier—Tyrone Appollis's *The Man Who Loved Us All* translates the famed death mask into a rainbow of colors and replaces its active hands-breaking-chains motif with small figures dancing (to democracy, perhaps)—but I focus on works that challenge this view. That the historical record bears so little about this exhibition and the works within it (even as some of its participants have become terrifically well known) suggests a discomfort with the principles around which it was organized. That discomfort needs to be revealed, discussed, and addressed. Artists in the Twenty Years Collective managed to make their ongoing exclusion clear.

Isintu, not Ubuntu

Isintu—Ceremony, Identity, and Community, A South–South Dialogue was the name of an exhibition organized around Black Consciousness principles that the South African National Gallery hosted in 1999. Curated by Zayd Minty and Tumelo Mosaka, the exhibit responded directly to the mainstream adoption of ubuntu (the idea that we are only realized through our relations to others) to serve nationalist objectives sometimes at odds with the concept itself. As Mosaka put it:

> Unlike Ubuntu, which is concerned with respect for the individual, Isintu frames cultural practises and thoughts within an African Perspective promoting a black consciousness. A consciousness that realizes the need for black people to rally together and rid themselves from oppression and to infuse their communities with pride in themselves, their value systems, culture, religion and their outlook on life. Isintu embodies all these experiences and through cultural manifestations tries to move beyond the present into the future.[36]

The curators recalled *Isintu* because they wanted to express BC fundamentals. I read their exhibit's subtitle, *Ceremony, Identity, and Community* as a current translation of action, ancestry, and unity, or modern black culture at work. The title's *South–South Dialogue* underscores the presence of these values across the southern hemisphere, thus it builds on the tricontinental activism from which BC drew inspiration and to which it later lent shape.[37] Their common "African Perspective" is one of uplift, of pride in a heritage distinct from an oppressor's. It derives from struggle and uses this as a basis to improve the future. Crucially, Mosaka envisioned *Isintu* as "Africanness. . . . [an] identity . . . shaped by an experience of disempowerment rather than a racial divide."[38] He and Minty chose artists who were not well known, an act of stewardship that also bears the mark of Black Consciousness. One among them, Berni Searle, is now internationally esteemed. Although her *Traces* (1999), created for this exhibition, is much discussed, its BC beginnings are all but forgotten.[39] This suggests an ongoing discomfort with BC within art criticism and history, one that needs to be faced head on.

Going Public: BLAC Looks Back

In 1998, Zayd Minty established the BLACK ARTS COLLECTIVE (BLAC) because he was frustrated by the lack of space available to artists of notable talent who were outside the mainstream. BLAC, based in Cape Town and operative until

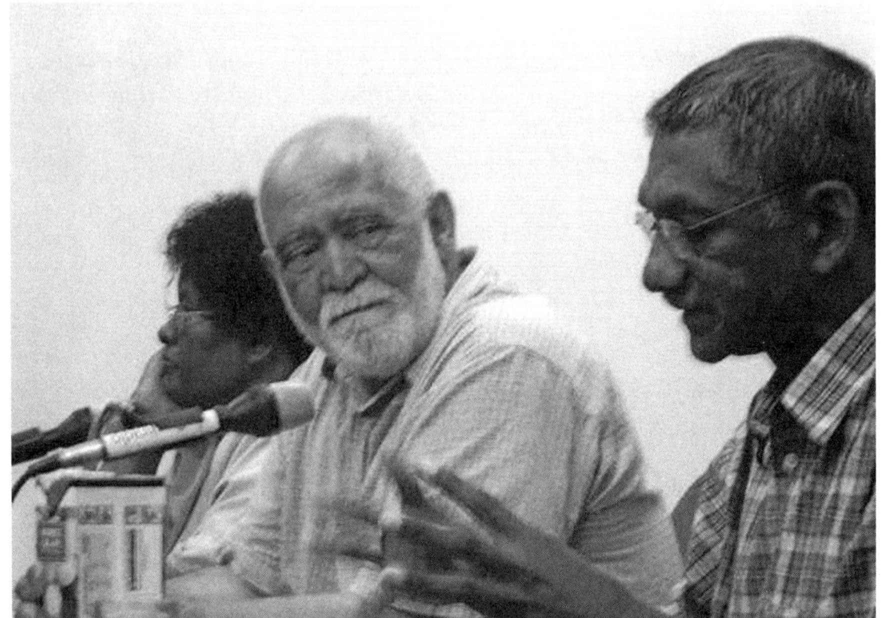

FIGURE 7.3. Three participants in a roundtable discussion during BLAC's Liberating Zones event (man at center identified as Joseph Marks), Cape Town, 2002. Archive of Zayd Minty.

2003, was founded on "principles of positivity, proactivity, nurturance and respect," and members cited Black Consciousness as the engine behind its mission.[40] In its first year, it limited members to those "people who have, as a result of Apartheid, been marginalized on the basis of race," a position that prompted some concern among white artists who now found themselves excluded. But BLAC's early members felt the need to make space for open discussion that would not be drowned out by white artists with ready access to a global art market a bit too eager for South African work emblematic of the "nonracial" glow it preferred.[41] BLAC achieved many things in its short life. It held numerous seminars that addressed intersections of heritage, identity, and art, topics of considerable interest to the state, its tourist industry, and the academy, forums from which BLAC members felt excluded (Figure 7.3).

It established BLACONLINE (www.blac.co.za) to create space for artists' work beyond those conventionally used at the time and, it must be said, limited to

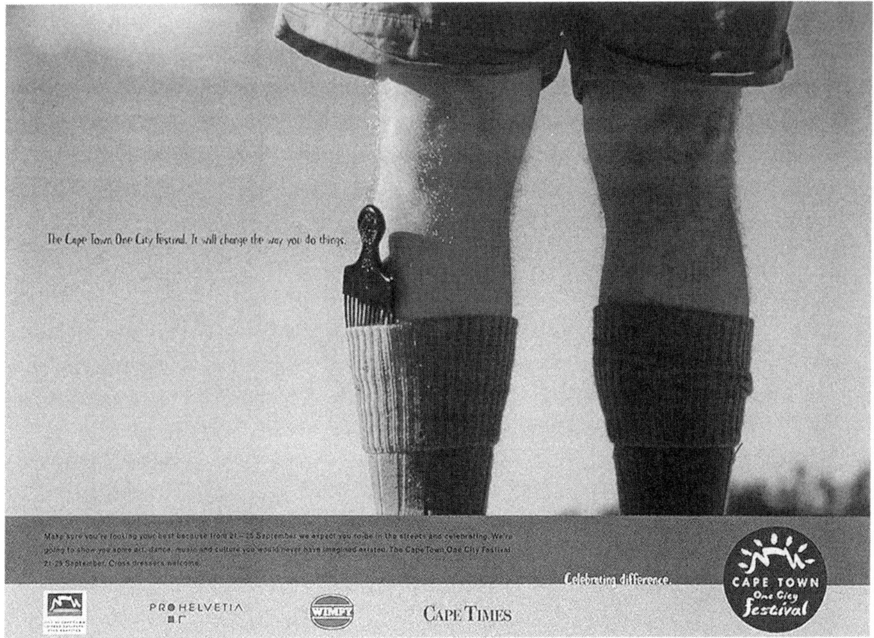

FIGURE 7.4. Advertisement for Cape Town's One City Festival of September 2000.

those with Internet access. Its chat feature assured ongoing debate; its columns featured important viewpoints; it welcomed new and emerging black arts professionals alongside those who had practiced for decades but were frequently overlooked by dominant streams. It achieved these and much more, but its best-known accomplishment was a public display of art made in response to Cape Town's highly touted One City Festival of September 2000, a project BLAC called *Returning the Gaze.*

The One City Festival implicitly endorsed the idea that Cape Town had overcome apartheid's many divisions, but *Returning the Gaze* explicitly stated that it had not. While the advertisement promoting the festival evokes a vast, sundrenched, exotic land of (containable) mystery just beyond our gaze, works in BLAC's outdoor exhibition challenged "the gaze" of tourists and South Africans alike who imagine equal opportunity even as they ignore the poverty witnessed across the Cape Flats (Figure 7.4). To counter this tendency, BLAC organized bus tours that offered another way to look at things, including that captured by

Antonio Coetzee (aka Ice) and Evaron Orange (aka Sky 189), creators of *Township 2000*, a mural along Klipfontein Road, which connects Guguletu to Athone to Cape Town (Plate 20). Equally so, the exhibit returned the gaze that ethnographers and other scholars have historically cast on their subjects, people who are seen as Other to themselves. Through BLAC, artists challenged these viewpoints in an array of works that were accessible to all; billboards, murals, postcards and performance pieces could be viewed without the admission price of institutions that joined the One City chorus.

Tourists arriving in Cape Town had the chance to see Donovan Ward's *Leisure Time* just off the N2 highway in the township of Langa (Plate 21). Many viewers, at least in Langa, were well familiar with the then-new movement to enhance Black Economic Empowerment (BEE) that later gave shape to the Broad-Based Black Economic Empowerment Act of 2003. Among other things, this act sought to increase black-owned businesses and black management and access to financing for these to be realized; improve mentoring of would-be business owners and managers; increase community-owned and -operated enterprises; and, interestingly, specifically named black women as a sector of the population in need of attention in this regard. The degree to which these objectives have been realized is debatable, but there is little disagreement that the ANC, the party that promoted BEE objectives, is now capitalist in orientation. In this it seems to have all but shed its earlier ideals of economic liberation for all.

Classic theories of national democratic revolution such as South Africa's rely on two stages in which capitalism leads to socialism. But this mode has been questioned given the fall of the state socialist model of the former Soviet Union, thus "allowing the ANC," a longtime ally of the South African Communist Party and the Congress of South African Trade Unions "to quietly abandon 'the second stage' of the revolution as an historical goal," writes Roger Southall.[42] Even still

> the National Democratic Revolution (NDR) continues to frame the official discourse whereby the ANC and its Alliance partners discuss South Africa's long term strategy. . . . The continuing formal commitment to the NDR has also the advantage that the conception's inherent ambiguities allow for the *papering over* of recurrent differences between the ANC and its partners about economic policy.

This passage strikes me as particularly apt for a discussion of Ward's *Leisure Time,* a work that culls imagery from varied sources that are layered into a large-scale critique of the economic injustice that continues to pervade South Africa.

Regard *Leisure Time* and see that three-quarters of the work was gleaned from commercial advertising that promotes tourist pleasures to be had in an exotic Africa that also meets expectations of comfort. This photograph of Ward's installation emphasizes something others cannot: the billboard's computer-generated features contrast the hand-painted signboards of businesses common to townships, to remind the viewer that making it in a globalized marketplace requires ready access to new technology. The woman pictured at center is lit by the stylized sun she holds in her hand; its color matches the daybreak behind Table Mountain. (Recall that this "graphic violator" also appears in Ward's *Biko*.) Her dress resembles that worn by bourgeois women who can afford finely tailored fabrics that are beautiful and colorful, and always identified with Africa even if they are made elsewhere. Her long, honey-toned neck supports a head and face with elongated features that are historically identified as Western despite that deeply problematic designation. This "empowered" black woman is paired with the fit woman at right who skirts the wind by surfing toward her counterpart. The landscape she rides over is effectively Langa itself, darkened compared to the lights of commerce that speckle the city center at the edges of Table Mountain. She embodies the leisure of the work's title and has come to Cape Town, as so many do, simply to play. Together these women and the text that unites them suggest that a new age has truly dawned on South Africa.

But Ward has another perspective to share, and the torn edge of this slick ad suggests that it covers an older reality or, more accurately, veils a present one. The mother and child at left are pictured in black and white, an aesthetic choice that evokes a bygone era and a documented reality. She is suited in workers' clothes; the child is likely her employers' offspring, as her own children are necessarily raised by extended family elsewhere. Ward suggests the presence of graffiti artists who have encircled her head with spray paint, a choice that counters the stylized sun at center and undercuts the shallow superficiality that attends its design. The mark makes her holy, but Langa residents would also recognize it as the sign of a gang called 26 that is ubiquitous in the Cape Flats where it often appears with the words *son op* (sunup, or sunrise), the time most members of 26 prefer to work. While gangs tend to fuel informal economies among people who have little access to state support, they also claim the lives of the poor, holding them hostage to a criminal ethos. Working in a market that depends on her labor to succeed, and resident in a place that permits little freedom, the holy mother of *Leisure Time* remains "disempowered" in a society that Ward says, "is still highly fragmented, sometimes I think even more so [than during apartheid], especially along class lines. The inequalities have become even more glaring, especially in Cape Town, but throughout the country really."[43] If a single line can be drawn among the multifarious work of this artist, it is his distaste for consumerism and the dis/ease it has spread in his country. It resonates within the word emblazoned here: di$EMPOWERED.

Closer to city center, visitors to Cape Town's One City Festival could see an early work by Berni Searle, now among Africa's best-known artists. She made the billboard *Not Quite White* (Figure 7.5) for BLAC's *Returning the Gaze* intervention; it was mounted above the Community Arts Project and seen by thousands as they drove along a major highway that links Cape Town's city center with roads heading south and east. Although this work has been frequently reproduced along with others Searle made in this period, neither BLAC nor its BC origins are mentioned.

Not Quite White reflects on many aspects of Searle's family history and, like all of her work to date, records her own performance. Her likeness was gigantically enlarged, laid out across the billboard through a series of four sequential photographs, their disjunction visible at the edge. Above and below, tape measures suggest that her identity, or sense of self, can be known somehow through calculations of her body. Of course, the West's long history of measuring and classifying people who are "not quite white" is challenged here as neither the tape measure nor the photograph, seemingly whole, indicates anything other than European fascination with taxonomy. Searle lies covered in pea flour; piles are most visible across her brow, on her feet, and on the ground around her. The flour enhances the natural variability of skin color on any single body, casting longer shadows and greater contrasts than typically seen.

At this point in Searle's career, she frequently used food as a medium because it significantly informs her memories of childhood and family heritage. Flour and spices, in particular, were favored mediums that recalled the food preserved and made at home by Searle's mother and grandmothers, each of them from a sector of South Africa's population known as Cape Malay. They are descendants of people who were taken from the Dutch colony of Malacca (Indonesia) and enslaved in the Western Cape. Her maternal great-grandfather was a cook who hailed from Mauritius, and his descendants, particularly the women, have shared his expertise with their families down the line.[44] By using substances that her family once used to preserve food and feed one another, the artist both preserves her heritage and feeds our knowledge of a history more complex than any single identifier can capture.

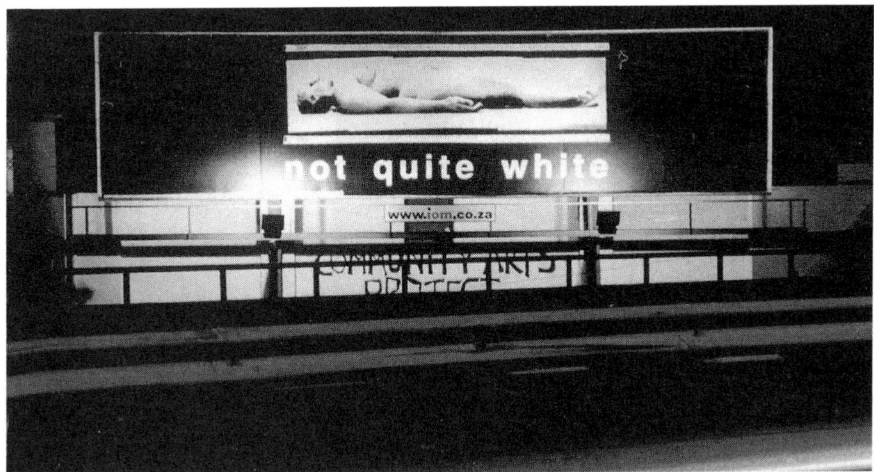

FIGURE 7.5. Berni Searle, *Not Quite White*, 2000. Courtesy of Berni Searle.

Indeed, her family comes from many parts of the world, with Germany, Saudi Arabia, South Africa, and England in the mix. These were reduced to Coloured by way of the Population Registration Act (1950). This is a term that Searle uses cautiously and always to resist the notion that such fixed identities exist. Annie Coombes made the excellent point that interventions such as Searle's are quite important in this period, "when various constituencies are making competing claims to originary status" and can often overlook the "necessarily messy and complicated mixings that have produced all contemporary societies."[45] *Not Quite White* boldly projects the problems of assigning identity from without and contradicts new forms of classification taking place postapartheid.

While artists like Thembinkosi Goniwe created a billboard in which he quite literally "returned the gaze" of viewers, Searle's eyes project upward, and it appears that her entire countenance is that of mere object.[46] But the very act of choosing to picture oneself nude in this context reclaims the self that others have objectified. African women have been exoticized in photographic histories of varied strains since the advent of the medium. Searle responds to these histories, most particularly that deemed scientific as the measuring instruments above and below suggest, but her choice to appear nude on a large-scale billboard is akin to a history of greater resonance. Coombes rightly points out its relation to a powerful mode of resistance undertaken by African women

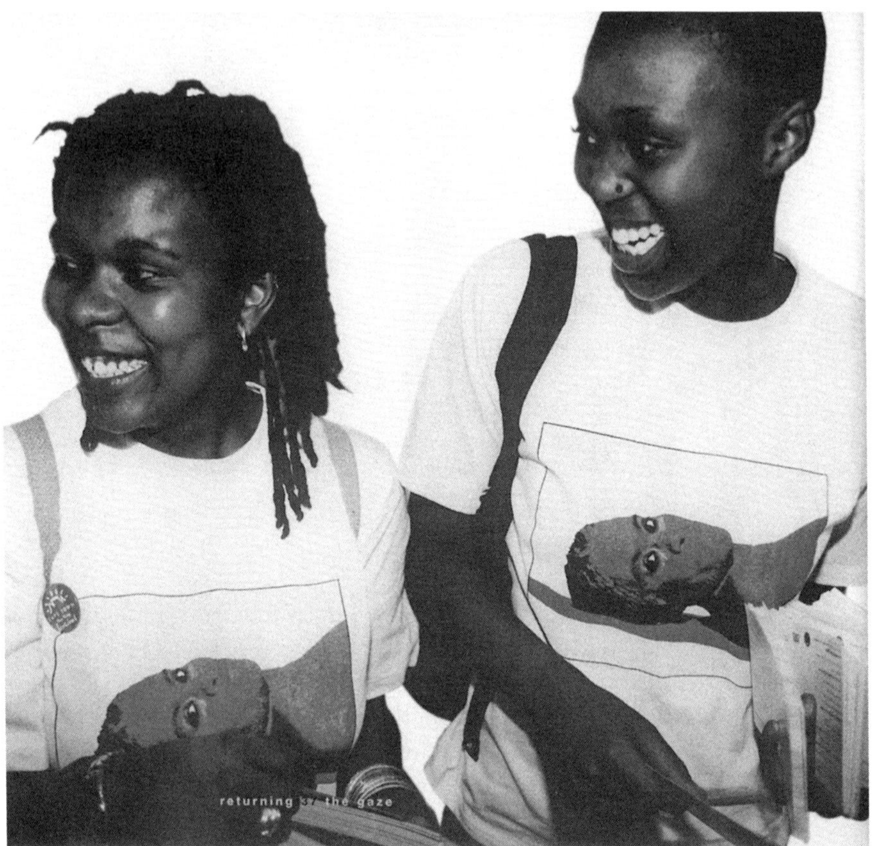

FIGURE 7.6. Art students distributed postcards by artists made for BLAC's *Returning the Gaze* outdoor exhibit, September 2000. Their T-shirts reproduce a work titled *Looking Back* from Berni Searle's series *Colour Me* (1998). Archive of Zayd Minty.

in several nations that explicitly rejects attempts to undercut their authority.[47] Within South Africa, the best-known act of this kind occurred in Dobsonville, Soweto, in 1990 when a group of women living in informal settlements stripped naked during a confrontation with police who tried to bulldoze their only means of shelter. Captured in the film *Uku Hamba 'ze—To Walk Naked,* these women succeeded in stopping armed men from destroying their makeshift homes by using their own bodies, unclothed but utterly dignified in action.[48]

BLAC advanced its message by new modes of combat as well. It hired Uni-

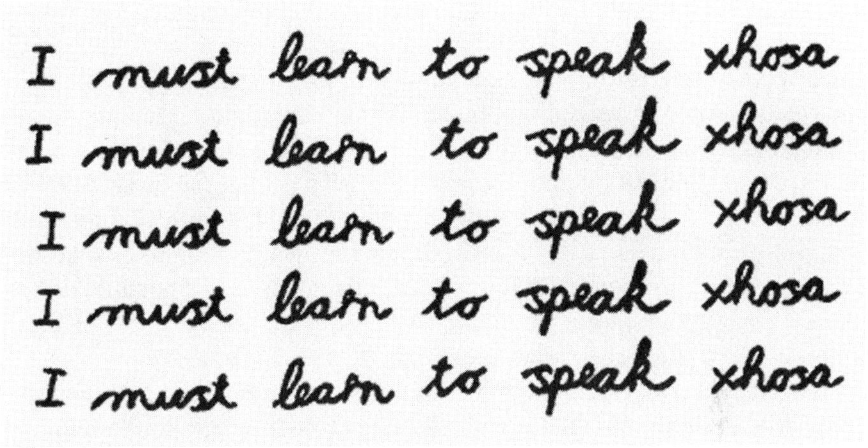

FIGURE 7.7. Brett Murray, *Mantra*, postcard made for *Returning the Gaze* exhibit, 2000. Courtesy of Brett Murray.

versity of Cape Town art students to wear T-shirts promoting their exhibition while they distributed postcards that challenged the veneer of a rainbow nation (Figure 7.6). Among the seven types on offer were Selvin November's telescopic landscape *Returning the Gaze* (Plate 22) and Brett Murray's satirical *Mantra* (Figure 7.7).[49] Both cards rivet attention on the bearer. In November's vision, three figures confront us, each with a marked identity that seeks to differentiate: a targeted gay man at left, a card holding "coloured," and an artwork, a painting of an Africanized female sculpture. Collectively challenging our gaze, these three figures render useless. In thick script, the word BLACK covers a state-issued card thereby asserting this self-selected identity above others issued from without. They are pasted over a backdrop that collapses the whole of the nation east to west—from the jagged Drakensburg Mountains in the foreground to the purple silhouette of Cape Mountain on the horizon—into foreign terrain. Claimed for "WHITES ONLY," the landscape is visible only through a lens that skews color and mines the golden underbelly within.

Meanwhile, by lampooning white South Africans who publically and repeatedly self-flagellate, Murray's *Mantra* betrays anxieties and bursts funny bones, depending on one's viewpoint. A personal admonishment that looks like chalk on a blackboard, this handwriting appears identical one row to the next and, expressed in English, is a sure sign that this would-be Xhosa speaker has made little progress. In the world of "posts" that fuels academic curiosity, Murray's ready use of satire to evidence sociopolitical mores in conflict exemplifies a postracial (in this case postwhite) position. Although such identifiers are usually vacuous, they can also enable us; they can produce meaning. We see in Murray's mantra both outward resolve and inner hesitancy. Ever in motion, they are both "a question and a search"; they signal what Liese van der Watt would call "a departure, but no arrival."[50] As I see it, that Murray consistently presses our awareness of this gap illustrates his own arrival. So too did this project evidence his understanding of BLAC's foundations and mission. Having joined the collective once it admitted people privileged by apartheid, he chose, in this context, to address the audience that BC mandated: his own.

Whether covering billboards, walls, or the palms of people, the images BLAC generated for *Returning the Gaze* all challenged (ad)vantages in the very best tradition of Black Consciousness. And although the project remains the best known of BLAC's many endeavors, others were equally insistent on a public airing of views. They all relied on the lively intersection of word, text, and image, in civic spheres of circulation to share their vision: one that questioned and contested the serene scene of a racial rainbow promoted by national and local institutions. Other projects in the life of this arts collective include *Liberating Zones: Cultural Movements of the 80's in Cape Town,* a drive to combine and promote the city's rich archives of popular history, and BLAC's (almost) monthly seminar series and commissioning of articles for its website, BLACONLINE, which Minty recalls "boasted a substantial database for emerging black talent in Cape Town and South Africa."[51] BLAC's members looked to "the old Black Consciousness movement" of the early 1970s when they needed to challenge the center from the margin decades later, and they enacted its principles through richly varied initiatives that empowered people, registered their visions, and challenged others to do the same. This history needs more of our attention.

Marking

In their efforts to overturn apartheid, South Africans have long marked city spaces by painting slogans of defiance and uplift on walls that scores of people pass daily. In the early 1980s, graffiti of a different genre, hip-hop art, appeared alongside more overt political messages, and it shared much of the same intent.[52] Whether painting words or pictures, the act of public marking is inherently transgressive. Graffiti reclaims space in the face of forces that deny access;

aerosol artists are masters of the quick work, a method typically counter to that of artists who make a living through commercial markets; and in their parlance, they "bomb" urban sites by acting outside the law at personal risk.[53] The Cape Flats, a collection of neighborhoods that stretch eastward out of Cape Town, is home to some of the best aerosol artists in South Africa, and it is base point to a thriving hip-hop culture that has always found potent visual expression on the streets.[54] Graffiti artists remain anonymous to most who see their work, but this is part of their point. They rely on what Sandra Klopper calls "sheer hard work and determination, rather than money (or patronage of more privileged individuals or communities)" to gain recognition from people who share their concerns, locally and well beyond it in our age of globalized networks.[55]

Indeed, self-worth can be expressed by denying access to people who question their concerns. Wealz130, founder of a group called YMB (Your Millennium's Best), told Klopper that he learned "all that BC stuff" through transgressive acts of self-expression from the first generation of graffiti artists in the Cape Flats.[56] One might say that the kind of battles that hip-hop music undertakes today—Weamm Williams describes racism, gangsters, violence, and drug trafficking as key among them[57]—are akin to those that Black Consciousness advocates took up in the 1970s as they sought to improve conditions within black neighborhoods through programs that provided medical and educational aid, architectural revitalization, and financial assistance while breaking down the racist tribalism promoted by the state. Although not all graffiti can lay claim to artistry, much graffiti is artfully expressed. Figures 7.8 and 7.9 picture text and a mural that sat on opposite ends of a pedestrian underpass at the University of Cape Town. Although the text was painted over soon after it was written, the mural has remained on display, unaltered, since it was made in the early 1990s.[58] This busy walkway is one of two that enable safe passage beneath a major highway that splits the campus in two.

More common than graffiti are colorful murals and pasted leaflets that take turns here, as they often do in Africa's prosperous cities, promoting cultural events and contemporary sociopolitical causes. Over many years, I have seen those that endorse HIV-AIDS awareness and treatment, gender equality, and local community projects as well as campaigns for public office or those to promote social justice, among others. Messages that rely on text alone are rare. Given that the mural in Figure 7.9 has remained untouched for at least twenty years, it has gained a kind of sanctified aura that no other wall in its vicinity holds. Might this be due to the iconic centerpiece, a re-creation of Dikobé

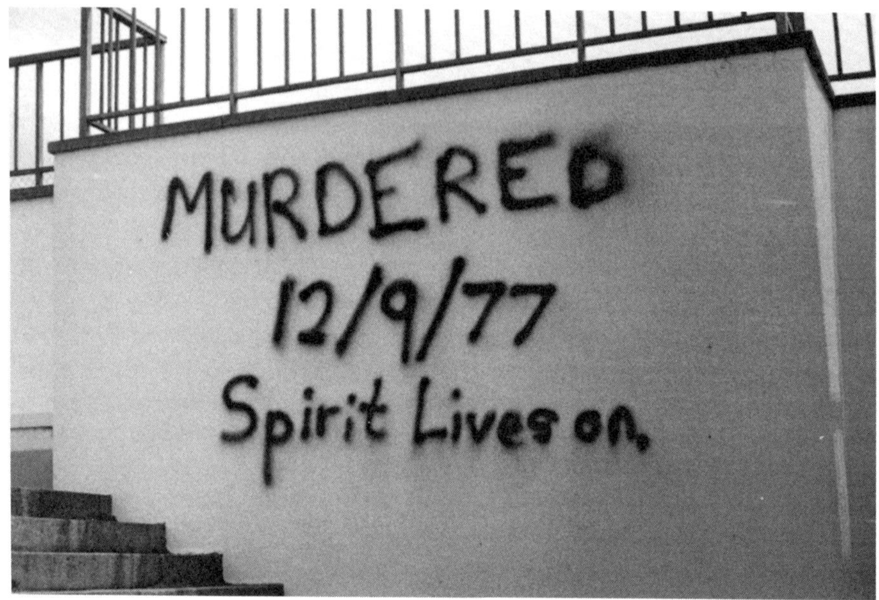

FIGURE 7.8. *Murdered / Spirit Lives On,* graffiti at the University of Cape Town, September 1999.

Martins's funeral portrait? Here the icon rests on top of the African continent. Rendered in black and gold, the colors of the Black Peoples' Convention, Biko's unifying message radiates outward across the continent from Cape Town, landing point for the Dutch in 1647. The mural resounds with BC's impact, booming across the continent, itself icon of a tricontinental world.

Biko's portrait shares space with that of Marcus Garvey at left and an embodied African continent at right. The effects of their inclusion here are twofold: viewers reflect on Black Consciousness as a Pan African ideology and on Africa as the cradle of civilization. Garvey's Universal Negro Improvement Association is best known for its dictum to create a United States of Africa governed by and for Africans. He encouraged Africa's diasporic peoples to make the journey Back to Africa to establish governments independent of colonial rule. Biko advocated similar conditions in South Africa when he wrote, "As much as black people live in Europe on terms laid down by Europeans, whites shall be subjected to the same conditions."[59] The embodied continent at right— surrounded by the hair of a primate—makes clear that humans originated in

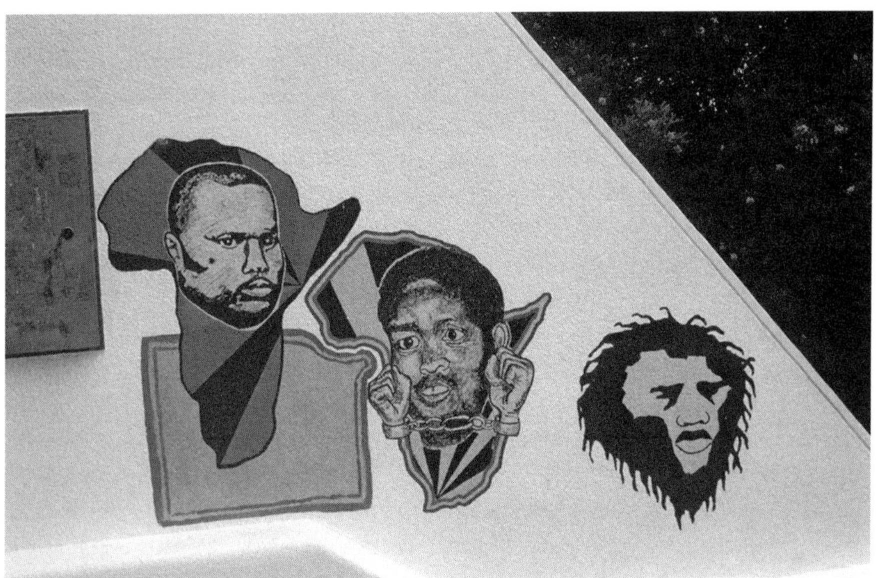

FIGURE 7.9. Unknown artist(s), *Marcus Garvey, Steve Biko, and Portrait of Africa,* campus of University of Cape Town. Recorded 1997, on view into 2012.

Africa, thus emphasizing the continent's *humanist foundations.* Placed beside Biko, it reminds viewers of how in 1971 he described a key concept of modern black culture—that Africans are above all human-centered:

> In all we do we always place Man first and hence all our action is usually joint community oriented action rather than the individualism which is the hallmark of the capitalist approach. . . . I cannot help feeling that more time also should be spent in teaching man and man to live together and that perhaps the African personality with its attitude of laying less stress on power and more stress on man is well on the way to solving our confrontational problems.[60]

Although the essentialism expressed here is not without its difficulties, Biko's purpose here was to ease confrontation by promoting education and respect.

In *Self Love* (1998), a work that readily brings the aesthetics of the street into a white-walled gallery space, Mustafa Maluka (b. 1976) disrupts another narrative of master to slave (Plate 23). Pasted at center is a photocopy of a Biko photograph, fantastically enlarged to reveal the original's pixilated page and the creases it had accumulated over time. The artist reversed the original before copying it (a highly evocative word, *sense,* appears backward beneath Biko's name), and then he laid paint over the paper affixed to canvas.[61] Significantly, the artist chose an image that captures Biko's serious side; he listens intently with eyes firmly set. The portrait is like those published on the cover of *Black Review,* the BPC literary publication that Biko edited (Figure 1.12), and drawn by Dikobé Martins (Figures 1.10 and 1.11). The layered, colorful paint that fills the space is akin to that Maluka used when he painted murals and graffiti as a member of the Black Fist Art Movement a few years prior.

Made in residence at the Thami Mnyele Foundation in Amsterdam, *Self Love* combines several elements of Maluka's life. He describes his "background" as a place in which "ignorance is the main weapon that the previous system used to teach people to hate themselves. People are still mental slaves."[62] Although *Self Love* challenges this notion directly, Maluka appears to adopt BC's method of overturning the oppressor's "most potent weapon . . . the mind of the oppressed" in every work he makes.[63] Here the text most firmly conveys his message. Viewers are encouraged to insert themselves into the narrative as a series of ellipses invites self-identification with Biko's resonant message of self-love. The artist used black paint again to define Biko's form. The halo at top, rendered in the mode of Jean-Michel Basquiat, does not set this prophet of positive thought apart so much as it unifies him with the text at right.[64] All are of the same width—apparently painted with the same brush—an affect that unifies viewers with Biko, bringing this radiant saint, as Rian Malan once described him, back into our midst.[65]

The combination of popular imagery, text, and layered, colorful paint evokes a graffiti aesthetic for which Maluka is now well known. As a genre, graffiti art encourages viewers' direct involvement with its message because it is so readily accessible, and it often engages the politics of identity. Maluka's best-known work—large-scale bust portraits of anonymous urbanites whose skin is configured by a wide range of colors—explicitly challenges fixed notions of who we are and where we come from.[66] These are citizens of the world, figures modeled on those Maluka finds in popular media. Each levels a direct stare at the viewer and shows no warmth. Although their clothing and hair are sometimes painted in even, heavy swaths of color, their skin is always composed of mixed hue. One by one, these fashionable people sit before a patterned backdrop of bright colors, each different from the next, but all compete for attention with the person portrayed.

In 2003 at the Michael Stevenson Gallery in Cape Town, works such as these accompanied a series that had raised, clenched fists at their base. The exhibition was called *Accented Living (A Rough Guide)* and included the work in Plate 24. Like the faces in the better-known works that surrounded it, *The Realness* (2002) is also a portrait. In Maluka's hands, it is not, as Kim Gurney would have it, an "overused stylistic device . . . [that] has a tendency to become repetitive."[67] Rather, it is the source of the varied, loud expression of defiance that fills the large canvas above and around it. (See chapters 2 and 4 for further discussion of salute as portrait.) The same hand, bearing the same shimmering pinkie ring, appears on several canvases, moving the raised clenched fist that Black Consciousness brought to South Africa into contemporary times. Such shine, favored by rap artists and the hip-hop culture that infuses Maluka's art and life with so much energy, gives rise to a graffiti-like bubble of popping colors, ever ascending as it spreads powerfully over a pale-skinned base hue on the margins.[68] The forms inside the bubble, organic and geometric, some cellular in character, match those behind the bust portraits that have brought Maluka so much praise. His description of these people suits the patterned fields of his raised-clenched-fist works:

> There is a certain aura I am trying to capture, of the things that go on beyond just the simple face. The entire picture plane is covered with markings and patterns that speak about the layers of the subject's personality. This aura is very important to the composition of my portraits in that it frames the subject and gives an idea of the complex layers that make up the individual. I am inventing personalities with each portrait because I am using images of people in magazines—fake, posed images—and transforming them into something that speaks to you on a completely different level—images that speak louder than the photographs they were based on. I am inventing personalities as well in that I am translating the photograph into a completely different language, a more complicated language, the language of complex national and cultural entanglements that combine to make up the individual.[69]

The "individual" in *The Realness* is the raised, clenched fist, a symbol of self-empowerment that has been condemned by some critics as a tired, overused motif. Here Maluka is "translating the photograph" that first gained popularity through Black Consciousness (e.g., see Figures 1.5, 1.16, and 2.11) to show that it retains real power, real meaning, in a world that increasingly embraces blackness in all its great variety in so many cultural spheres. The titles of other works in the same series (such as *Occasional Harassment*; *Diamonds Aren't Forever*; and *Keeping the Faith*) suggest that other arenas still lack such appreciation and are in need of reform.

Maluka's portraits are profitably compared to those by Nontsikelelo (Lolo) Veleko (b. 1977), a Johannesburg-based artist whose love of its distinctly urban appeals also underscores the variety of color that is blackness. The dynamic *Sibu VIII* (Plate 25) of 2007 forms part of *Beauty Is in the Eye of the Beholder*, a series of large-scale photographic portraits of fashionable young folk in and around her hometown. Veleko approaches (some of) her sitters on the street, which lends an air of authenticity to works that fundamentally challenge this tired dictate of "African art(ist)" from the global art market.[70] Those that Veleko chose for this beauty contest tend toward bright colors and vibrant patterns that contrast the spaces in which they stand, be they industrialized cityscapes, barren landscapes, or crumbling walls. That behind Sibu was once painted white, but it now appears weathered, its flakes and chips accumulated alongside debris from passersby. His sunglasses reflect shadows across a dirt road beneath a blue sky and a white car that may have transported artist and sitter to this site. The absence of skyscrapers in his lenses indicates Sibu was photographed outside the city center.

The dark band around Sibu's arm is a mark of affiliation or mourning that matches the heroic portrait behind him, a stenciled copy of Fraser MacLean's photograph of Steve Biko. Below the stencil and behind Sibu we see the markings of other artists that came before, letters in blue and a form spray-painted beneath Biko's likeness. The stencil looks like a geometric figure toy-toying (a historic, distinctive dance step that energizes revolutionary songs and chants of protesters in South Africa), and it bears one word, *Homecoming*. Read together with Sibu's black band and Biko's portrait, the figure and its song suggest not death but rejuvenation. In this vision, where queer identity attends several aspects (Sibu's sartorial style, his framing gesture, and the "Queen" that inevitably follows "Homecoming" in our mind's eye), Black Consciousness is needed in a nation where lesbian, gay, bisexual, and transgendered people must still toy-toy since their constitutional rights remain denied by many. Sibu revives BC in this context just as he recalls the period of its origins through his retro 1970s dress. His collar is so large that it appears like wings extended beyond his shoulders, but his own sense of agency and pride take flight in our time. Like others in this series, Sibu undoubtedly expresses empowerment through wonderfully stylish, eye-catching, even flamboyant dress.

In *Snap Judgments,* Okwui Enwezor describes the need for such portraits to undercut colonial photographs with their fixed notions of Africa. Veleko and her sitters embrace an indeterminate identity, thus they are among the "bodies without limits" that Enwezor describes as essential to African photography.[71] Veleko combats what Enwezor and others call an "Afro-pessimism" promoted by photographers who visit the continent and then publish images that are almost uniformly abject: poverty, misery, disease, famine, and warfare are its essential ingredients. But insofar as Veleko's is a generation that, as Mark Sealy says, "demands to be seen as living in the moment," the men and women of *Beauty Is in the Eye of the Beholder* "claim a new kind of assertive cultural pattern that reclaims the street" from photographers who have historically positioned black subjects as objects rather than individuals with character, intelligence, wit, and flare.[72] Alongside Biko, Sibu refuses to be regarded as anything other than his authentic self. He is not alienated from Africa but shows us that Africa is in and of the world, gloriously multifarious and complex.[73]

Regard Plate 25 once more. When we finally wrest our eyes from Sibu's allure, we spend more time with Biko. Looking closely, we see layers of paint and scratch marks on his stenciled portrait, repeated, as it is, in the mutated sameness that iconography bears. Marks once red, now pink, cascade downward; another hand crossed out Biko's face with a giant X. Here is evidence of a counterargument where one might locate his legacy: nowhere. Those who defaced his icon constitute one opinion among many, but they are not alone, as the marks on the Biko Monument attest. Michael Godby recounts hearing that the words "Biko was a rat" were scrawled on a wall in the Cape Flats in the early 1990s; we speculated as to what drove the writer's discontent, the perception that Biko united people or divided them.[74] Surely neither the incident nor the sentiment it expressed were unique, as both the man and the ideology he embodies, Black Consciousness, have been borrowed, amended, denied, contested, championed, and, vitally, hotly represented in South African visual culture for more than forty years.

In May 2012, Brett Murray included *Killed Twice* when he unveiled new work in his *Hail to the Thief* exhibition at Johannesburg's Goodman Gallery.[75] *Killed Twice* is a painting of words that shout "BIKO IS DEAD" in a font that recalls the 1970s; yellow letters leave red tracks to one side as the words rush out of brown space. What might this mean in 2012? I find significance in its relation to the larger body of works, nearly all neglected in the press save for one, *The*

Spear, a painting at the heart of an uproar because it portrays President Jacob Zuma's genitals, flaccid at that.[76] Of course, the portrait depicted the "thief" of Murray's larger project, lampooned twice over: first for the contradictions between his party's rhetoric and its practice (Zuma's stance is based on that of Vladimir Lenin—figuratively, thus politically); second to undercut Zuma's projected sense of virility. Through humor, Murray critiques the ANC's "party of the people" rhetoric amid other works that send up its capitalist thirst and the troubling rise in ethnic divisions that Zuma embodies when he excuses bad (sexual) behavior as essentially Zulu and not within his control. *Killed Twice* is best understood in this context. "BIKO IS DEAD" is still newsworthy, just as it was on September 13, 1977 (Figure 2.2), but this second occurrence is notable because the embrace of Steve Biko after 1990, as healer, as humanist saint, always antiethnic/antiracial in viewpoint, has, in Murray's eyes, died out by 2012. Zuma's nonracialist party and his ethnic nationalism do not mix. Within the larger body of works that comprise *Hail to the Thief,* the rise in ethnic nationalism and evident embrace of capitalism is of a kind Biko explicitly scorned. Considered within Murray's larger vision, the message of *Killed Twice* is not that BC remains ineffectual, but that it must not be allowed/aloud to be so in the future. The work shouted a need, not a fact, in the context of its original display. I have repeatedly been told that Black Consciousness is needed to heal the economic wounds of our time (xenophobia, stagnation, a forgotten class), or to contest ideals of beauty that prompt some to change their hair and eye color or bleach their skin. Let us consider *Killed Twice* in this light before assuming that this news is not newsworthy; let us question the narrative of BC's efficacy.

As the explosive colors of these most recent works suggest, Black Consciousness in our time can and should be seen as richly varied in expression, audience, and use. Although the slogan Black Is Beautiful has been commonly understood as such by most who have embraced it since the 1970s, others opted to view it as a polarizing proclamation that erased all distinctions, rendering beauty impossible to behold. Although most artists discussed in this chapter regularly remind us of identity's many blends (and shapes), they do so through the variability that Black Consciousness has always encouraged. Such mixing is seen here: in the contests to claim Biko's legacy or deny it; in the interplay between word and image that is visual culture; in the self-assertion that style can afford (at least for those who can afford). Black Consciousness has long held that self-expression as a means of empowerment enables restoration of dignity.

South Africans' need to publically narrate lives lost and altered was profound postapartheid, and to be sure, scholarly inquiry into memory was widespread in the 1990s. If that decade witnessed the recovery of histories denied, and their validation through the proceedings of the Truth and Reconciliation Commission, then the first decades of the twenty-first century must project a vision of greater inclusion amid diversity, of equity despite difference, and, most important, recognition that Black Consciousness readily enhances our ability to realize these.

Epilogue
"After Such a Long Time His Life Is Still Dug Out"

After such a long time *ube ubomi bom bakhe busombiwa*
[his life is still dug out]

— Mrs. Alice "Mamcete" Biko

WHEN STEVE BIKO'S MOTHER, A WOMAN KNOWN AS MAMCETE TO HER FAMILY, combined English and Xhosa to describe the world's lasting interest in her son, her words captured the often difficult work of translation. Digging out the full register of Biko's influence and that of Black Consciousness is a tremendous task, and this book only partially fills one of several holes, that of the visual. As Black Consciousness is an ideology with lasting impact, taken up by individuals through time to underscore their beliefs, its history will stretch beyond our time, beyond any single generation. Mrs. Biko's words reflect on the past and present but project into the future as well, anticipating that more holes will be dug. It is vital that we do the difficult work of giving attention to these holes and help to fill them with our findings.

Paul Stopforth's *Round-Up* of 2009 (Plate 26) likewise anticipates a positive, regenerative future for his country, one that will balance "up" in the end. Its history and features also offer the best conclusion to this book. Through motif, method, and concept, this small-scale work reminds those who study it closely of a body and land suppressed, or pinned down, but only superficially. It was made soon after the artist's three-week residency on Robben Island, that historic place of banishment off Cape Town that is now a UNESCO World Heritage Site. The motifs reference particular people, places, and practices, but their power registers across the citizens of this nation who struggle toward a brighter future.

The top-left quadrant bears a hand whose print is known to many. Given Stopforth's translation of Biko's autopsy photographs in 1980 (see Figures 3.4–3.6,

Plate 3), the print is curiously Biko's and Stopforth's at the same time. It extends downward across a gray field toward a safety pin laid out horizontally. The pin replicates one that Stopforth found in the island's prison, famous for its holding of political activists. The original pin was handcrafted, a delicate material bent into a useful, sharp object. As such, it bore the trace of an unknown prisoner's hand and mind, elements that appealed to the artist as he reflected on how to make meaning from his residency at this historic site, and after so much time exiled from his country of birth. He ultimately translated that pin into a large-scale work called *Monument* (2005).[1] Thus a rudimentary object gained magnificent status, and the hand of an unknown prisoner was marked with significance.

The central motif in green resembles a duct that Stopforth found on the island, one of many that provided air to bunkers deep within the earth. It is repeated three times in a 2005 triptych called *Transformer #2: Breath,* also made postresidency. As the island's lungs, the duct keeps its history alive, its breath released from the pipe at right. The air flows toward an intercom, a device that spreads words beyond firm boundaries. Brilliantly, this work records another means by which words were spread: Stopforth chose a milk-based paint because prisoners once communicated by writing in milk on paper. The combination dried quickly and could be read only when sprayed with a solvent cleaner routinely distributed by guards.[2] The censors' rules were thus undone, and the prisoners continued to fuel liberation from within, feed ideas, expand breath, live on within a nation that remembers all its heroes, large and small.

It is commonly held that Bantu Stephen Biko lives on through many people who remain inspired by the ideas he held dear and actively practiced. Although the South African state worked to smother Black Consciousness as early as 1971, many individuals and organizations would not allow it. The heart of this anticolonial ideology—that individuals committed to promoting ancestry, unity, and action can overcome oppression—continues to be enacted daily by the people who ascribe to it. Visual culture has played an enormous role in the ongoing life of Black Consciousness. Through images conjured by word and picture, or voice and vision, Biko and Black Consciousness have been conflated in many ways yet retain distinct entities nonetheless. In South Africa, they are most visibly united annually in mid-September as numerous press outlets report on several organizations throughout the nation that honor Biko's life on the anniversary of his death. Every year since that discussed in chapter 2, full weeks have been blocked out for the celebration of Biko and Black Consciousness and named for them. At the time of this book's printing, South Africans have been regularly reminded of BC's ongoing vitality for thirty-eight years. Visual culture disabled the state's efforts to wipe it from memory.

And it will continue to be so. While activists, artists, and other image makers have long directed us toward Black Consciousness, scholars of visual histories within South Africa are now doing the same. I note with interest that the four-volume compendium *Visual Century: South African Art in Context, 1907–2007* has several chapters that register BC's influence in its last two volumes.[3] In recent years, academics in history, literature, philosophy, politics, religion, sociology, and women's studies have published articles and books that reshape our awareness of BC's broad efficacy.[4] Visitors to several museums will find permanent displays dedicated to (regrettably) Biko's death or (promisingly) Black Consciousness, and one senses that the latter has an ever-greater prominence in displays that narrate the nation's history.[5] And the Steve Biko Foundation, created and directed by Biko's eldest son, Nkosinathi, invests great energy in many arenas dedicated to social justice. Based in Johannesburg, the foundation opened the Steve Biko Centre in King William's Town in 2012, thus dramatically expanding the influence of its satellite office in the Eastern Cape, a province long known for its activism if not its resources.[6]

To dig is to move something in order to create or reveal something else. Because it is associated with soil, it evidences a loosening of matter, and the concentrated labor this requires. In slang, it means to enjoy something or understand it. Let us joyfully continue to locate a deeper, more meaningful understanding of liberation, despite the hard work it requires. For many people die and suffer to register their beliefs in the face of oppression; their voices and visions must also be dug out.

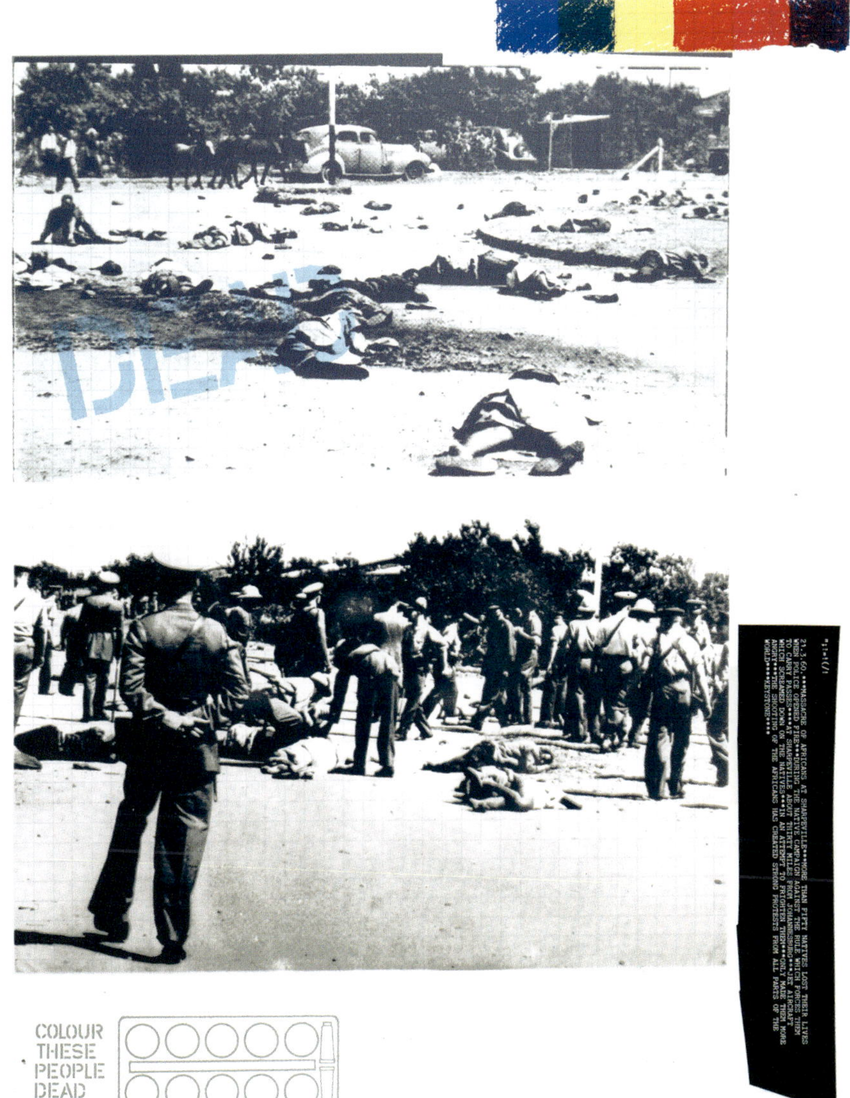

PLATE 1. Gavin Jantjes, "Colour These People Dead," in *A South African Colouring Book* (a suite of eleven prints), 1974–75. Screen print on paper with mixed media, 60 x 45 cm (23⅝ x 17¹¹⁄₁₆ inches). Museum purchase, 2003-16-1.11. Photograph by Franko Khoury. Courtesy of Gavin Jantjes and the National Museum of African Art, Smithsonian Institution.

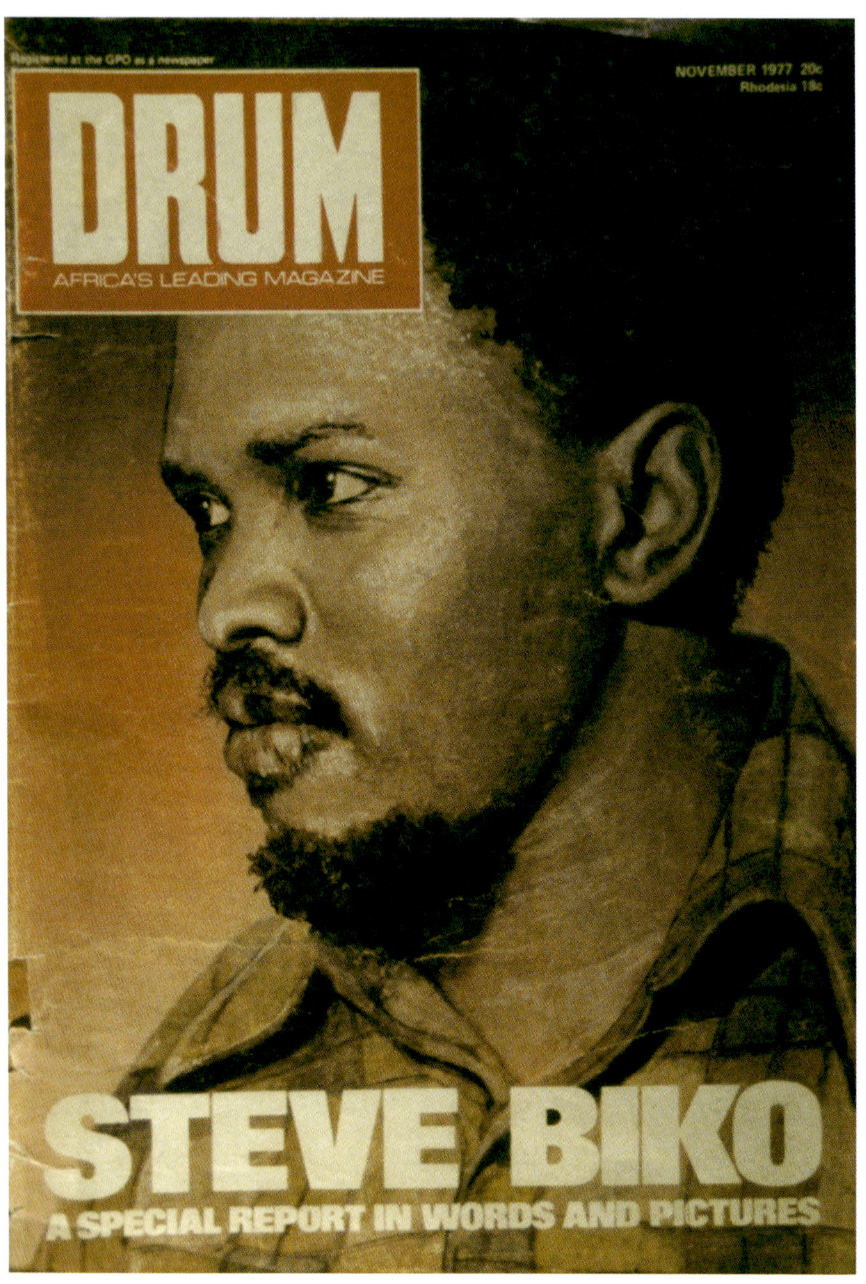

PLATE 2. Tributary cover to Steve Biko, *DRUM*, November 1977. Copyright Bailey's African History Archives. Photograph by BAHA Drum Photographer.

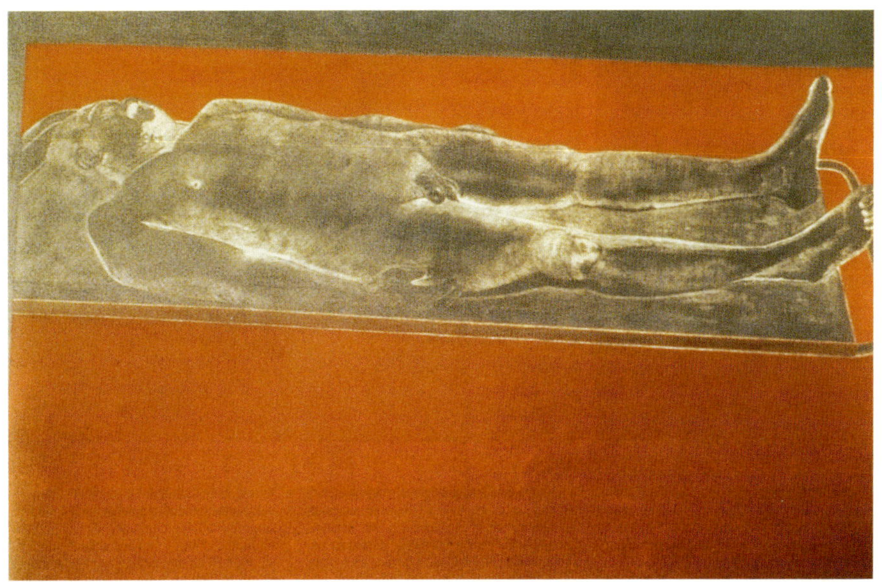

PLATE 3. Paul Stopforth, *Elegy,* 1981. Mixed media on paper on panel, 60 x 96 inches. Courtesy of Paul Stopforth.

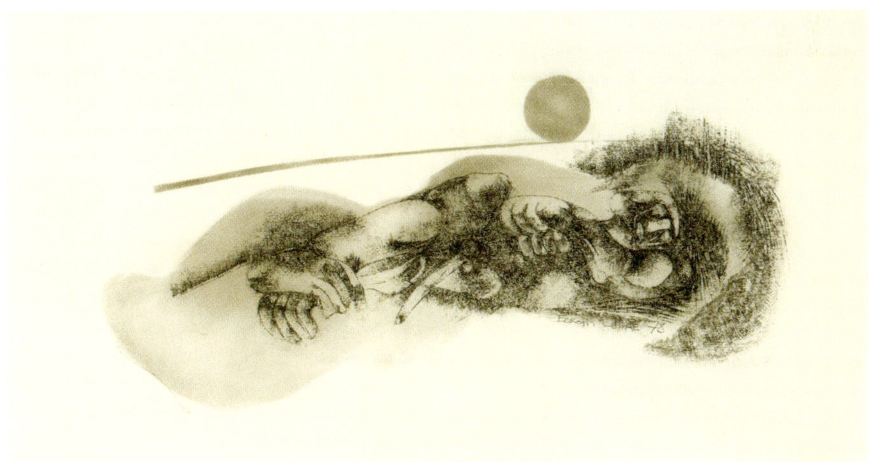

PLATE 4. Ezrom Legae, *Chicken,* 1977–78. Corporate collection.

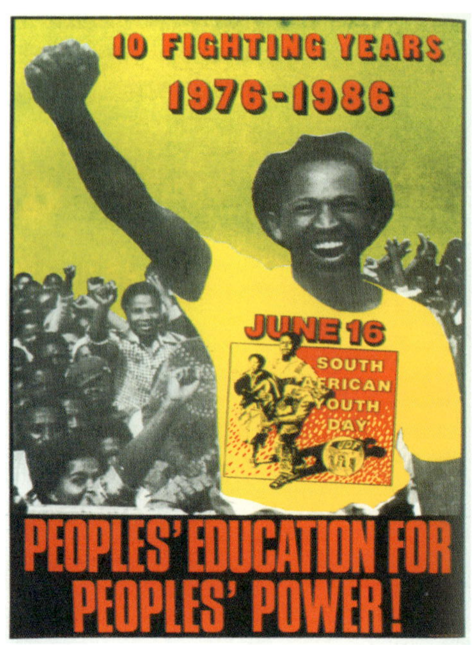

PLATE 5. Artist unrecorded, printed at Screen Training Project for the United Democratic Front. *UDF: 10 Fighting Years: 1976–1986*, 1986. Offset lithograph. South African History Archive.

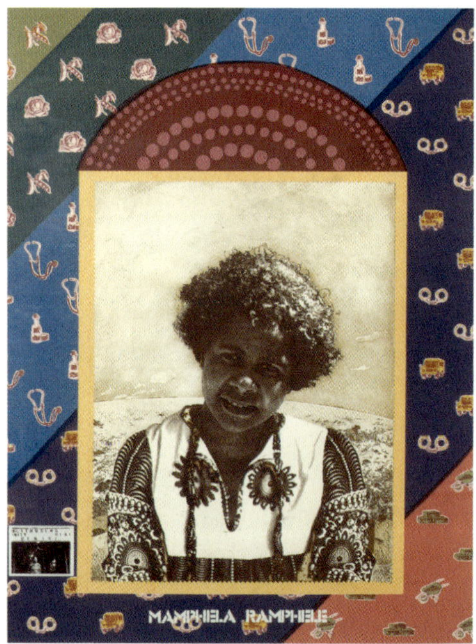

PLATE 6. Sue Williamson, *Mamphela Ramphele*, 1985. *A Few South Africans* series. Photo etching and screenprint collage, 1000 x 700 mm. Copyright Sue Williamson. Courtesy The Goodman Gallery.

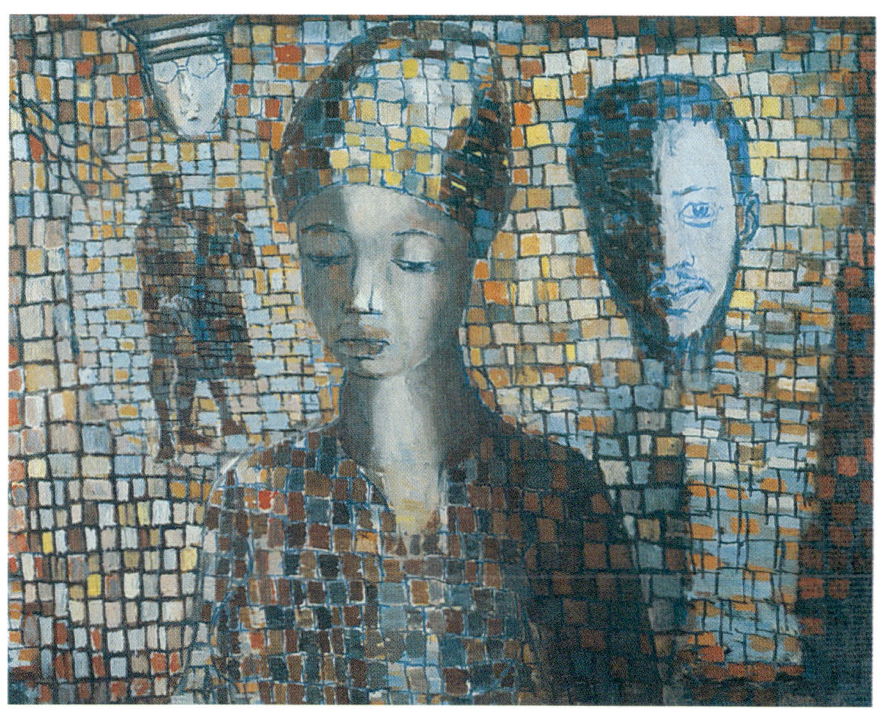

PLATE 7. Gerard Sekoto, *Homage to Steve Biko*, 1978. Signed, oil on canvas, 130 x 163 cm. Copyright the Gerard Sekoto Foundation, 1978. Reproduced with permission of the Gerard Sekoto Foundation.

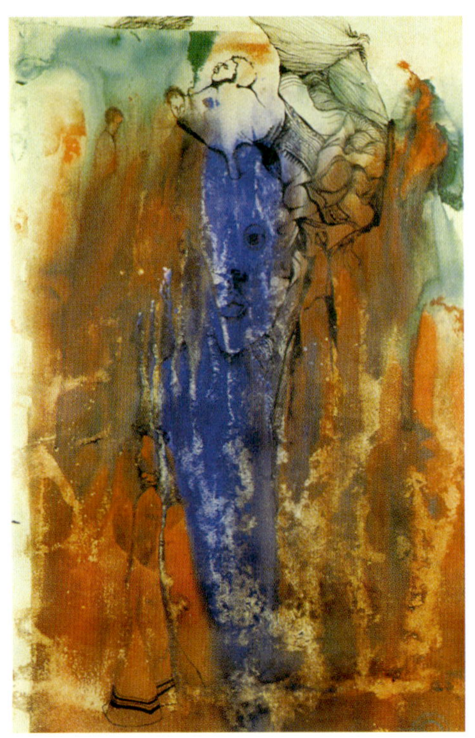

PLATE 8. Motlhabane Mashiangwako, *Leokotsane: For Steve Biko,* 1980. Ink on paper, 70.5 x 44 cm. Art Gallery, University of South Africa. Photograph by Fritz van Rensburg. Courtesy of the Mashiangwako estate.

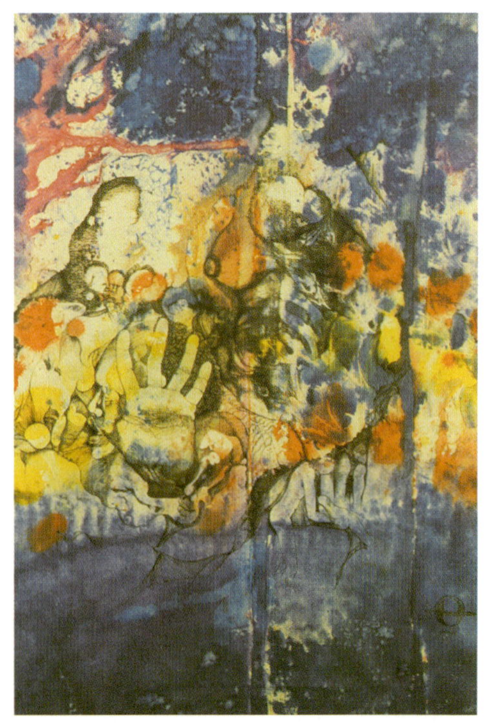

PLATE 9. Motlhabane Mashiangwako, *A Dedication to the People of Biafra: Four Meditations on the Biafran War,* 1980. Ink on paper, 101 x 83 cm. Art Gallery, University of South Africa. Courtesy of the Mashiangwako estate.

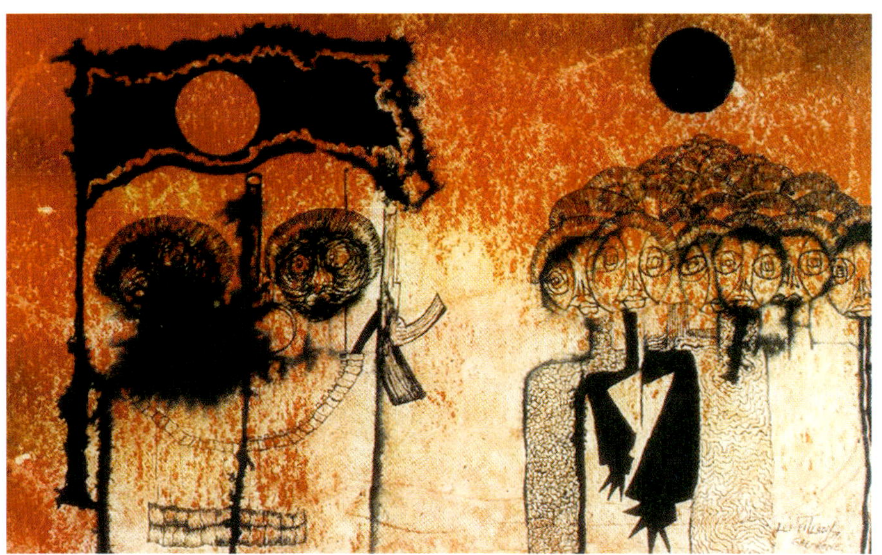

PLATE 10. Lefifi Tladi, *Untitled,* 1979. Ink on paper, 18.5 x 30 cm. Courtesy of Lefifi Tladi.

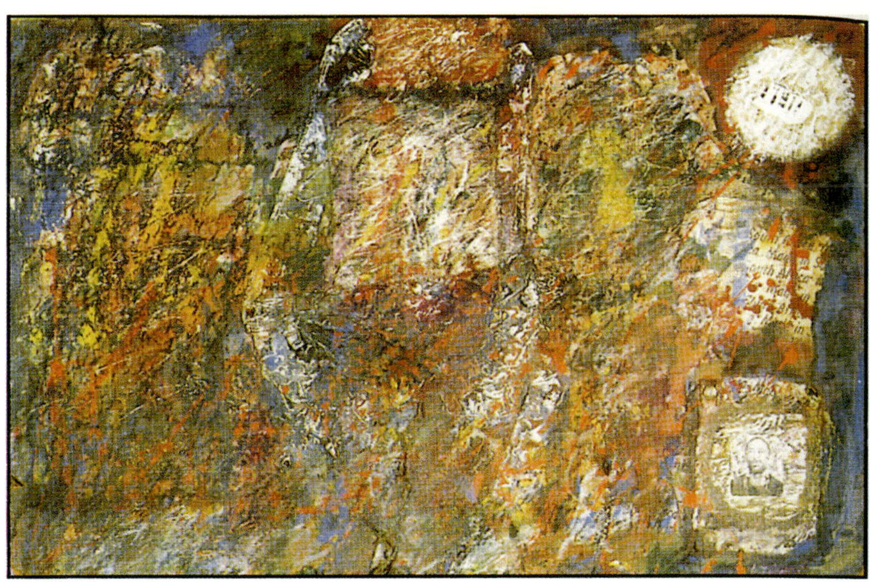

PLATE 11. David Koloane, *Made in South Africa,* 1979. Acrylic on canvas, 145 x 184 cm. Courtesy of David Koloane.

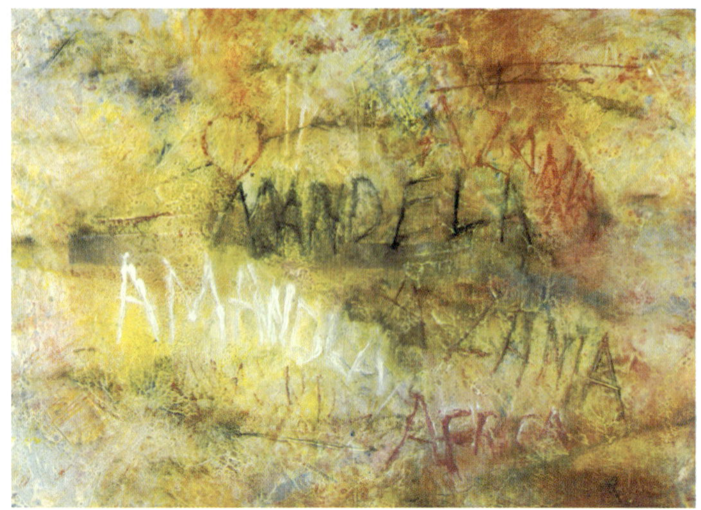

PLATE 12. Durant Silhali, *Reminders of Past Apartheid*, 1987. Acrylic on paper, 9 x 56.7 cm.

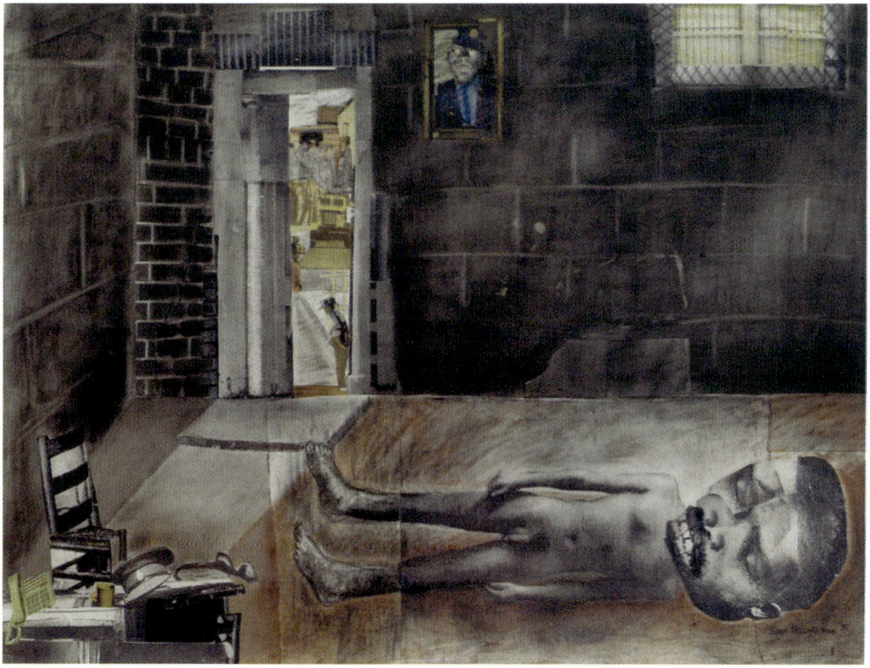

PLATE 13. Sam Nhlengethwa, *It Left Him Cold—The Death of Steve Biko*, 1990. Collage, pencil, and paper, 69 x 93 cm. STD Bank Collection, Wits University. Courtesy of Sam Nhlengethwa.

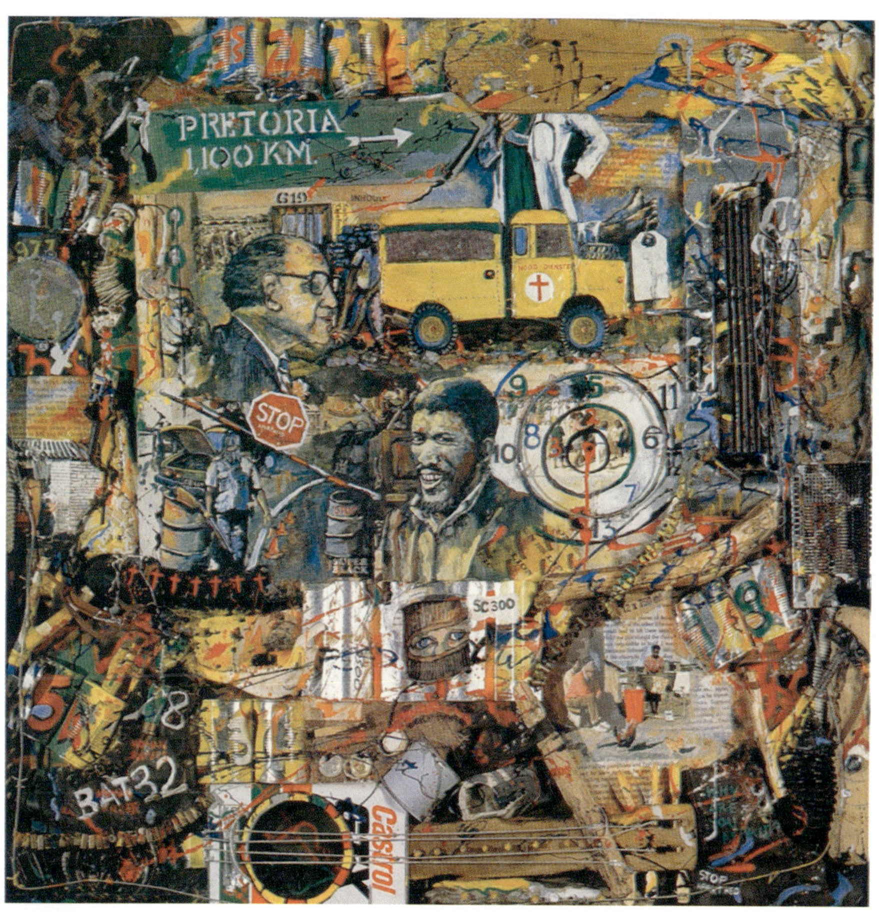

PLATE 14. Willie Bester, *Homage to B.,* 1992. Oil, enamel paint, photographs, and found objects on board, 126 x 126 cm. Collection of Jean Pigozzi. Courtesy of Willie Bester.

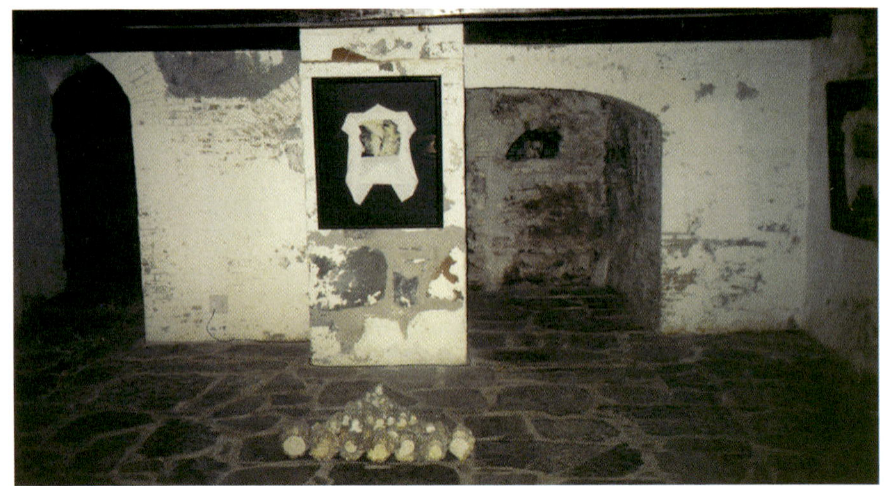

PLATE 15. Colin Richards, *Veil VII* and *Angels,* installed at the Castle of Good Hope, Cape Town, 1996. Courtesy of Penny Siopis.

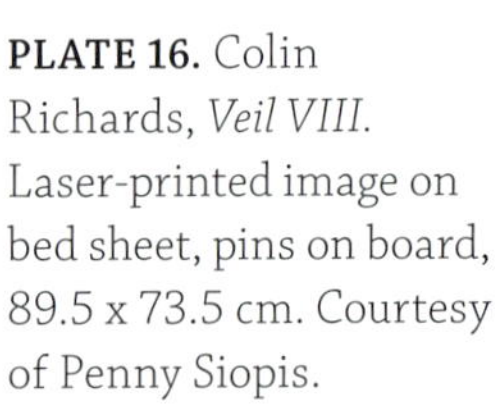

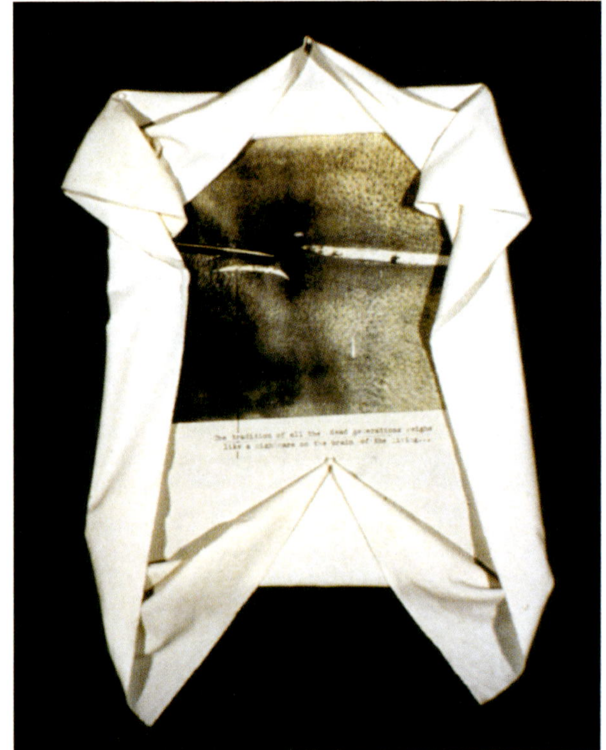

PLATE 16. Colin Richards, *Veil VIII.* Laser-printed image on bed sheet, pins on board, 89.5 x 73.5 cm. Courtesy of Penny Siopis.

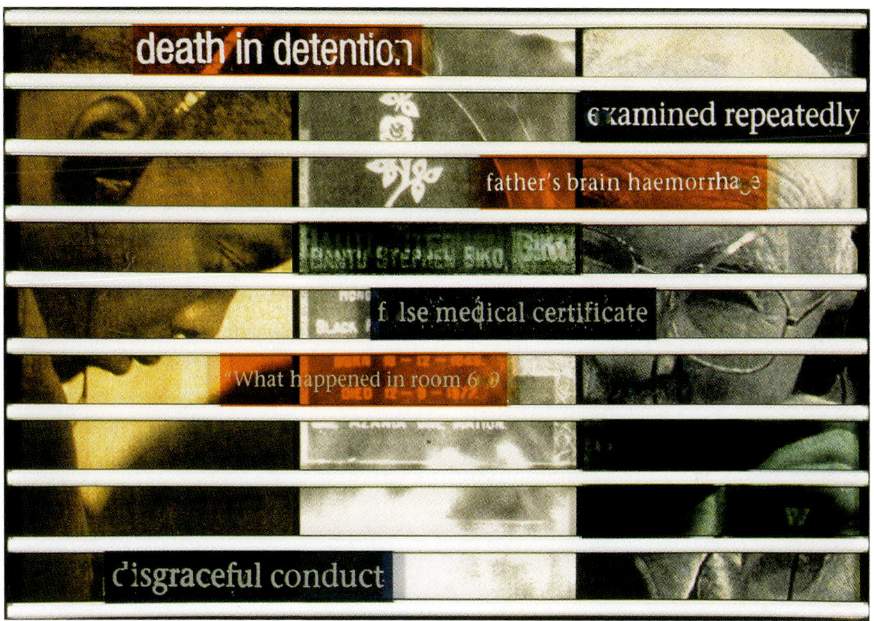

PLATE 17. Sue Williamson, *Nkosinathi Biko—false medical certificate—Dr. Benjamin Tucker*, 1998. *Truth Games* series. Laminated color laser prints, wood, metal, plastic, Perspex, 800 x 1200 x 60 mm. Copyright Sue Williamson. Courtesy The Goodman Gallery.

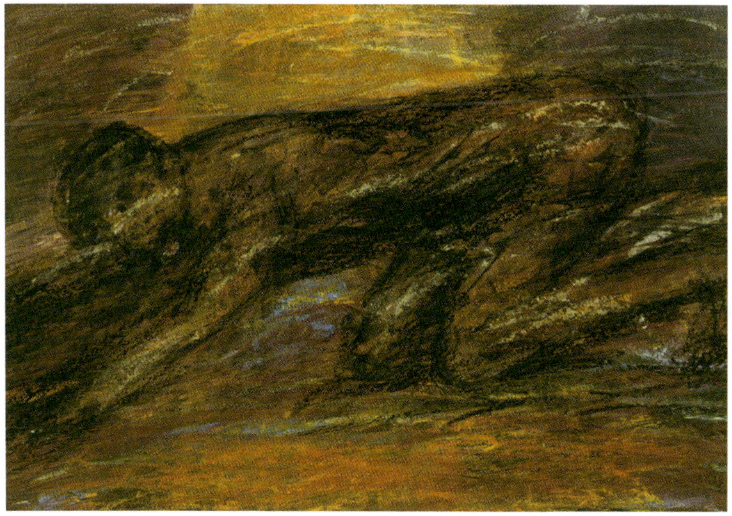

PLATE 18. David Koloane, *The Journey, no. 13 (crouched down, engaging the viewer)*, 1998. Acrylic and oil pastel on paper, 29 x 42 cm framed. Courtesy of David Koloane.

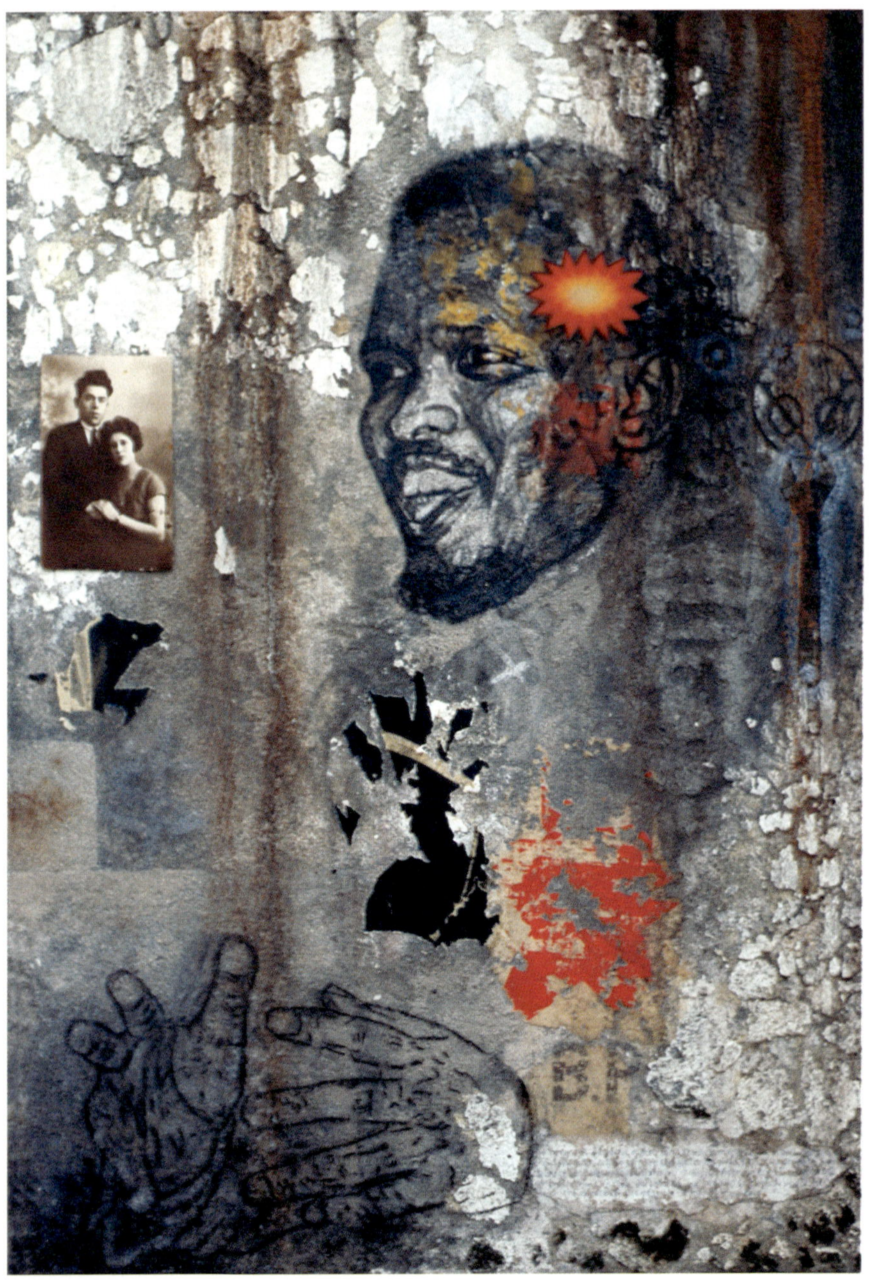

PLATE 19. Donovan Ward, *Biko,* 1997. Cement, paint flakes, acrylic, bone ash, rust stains, Perspex, lichen, dust, décollage and photograph on Masonite, 82 x 58 cm. Private collection. Courtesy of Donovan Ward.

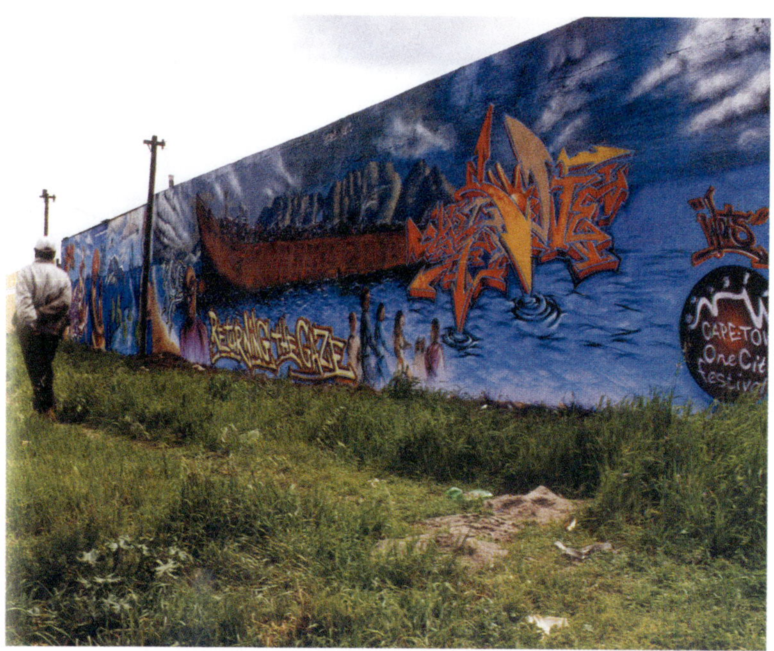

PLATE 20. Sky 189 and Ice (aka Evaron Orange and Antonio Coetzee), *Township 2000*. Mural along Klipfontein Road, Cape Town, September 2000.

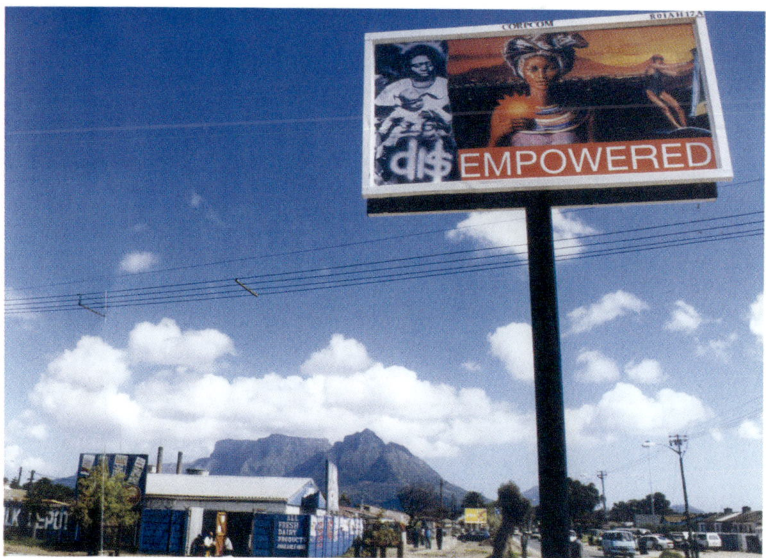

PLATE 21. Donovan Ward, *Leisure Time*, 2000. Billboard installed in Langa, Cape Flats. Photograph by Nic Aldridge. Courtesy of Donovan Ward.

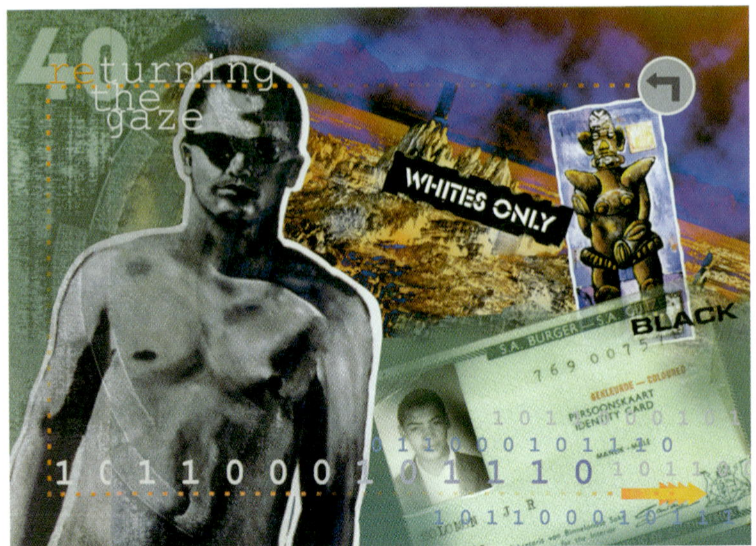

PLATE 22. Selvin November, *Returning the Gaze,* 2000. Postcard, 10.5 x 14.8 cm. Courtesy of Selvin November.

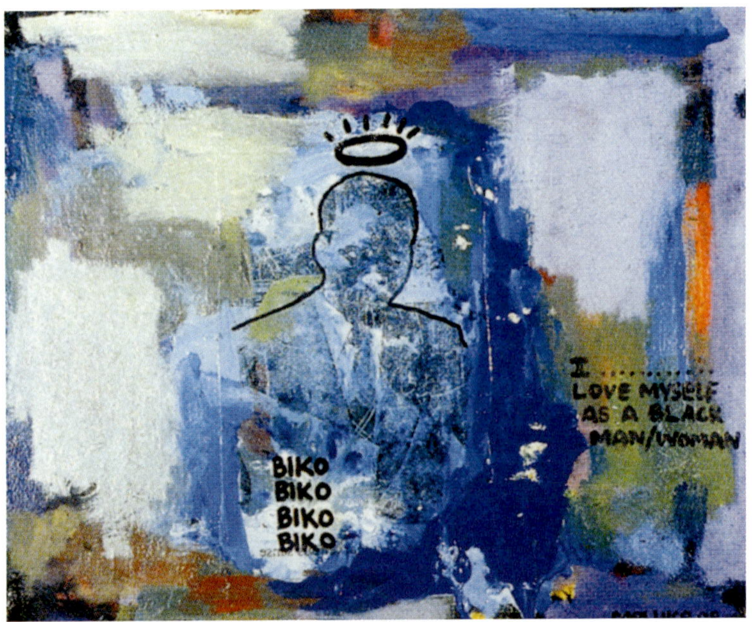

PLATE 23. Mustafa Maluka, *Self Love,* 1998. Oil, household oil paint, marker, photocopy on acetate on board, approximately 25.4 x 33 cm. Private collection. Courtesy of Mustafa Maluka.

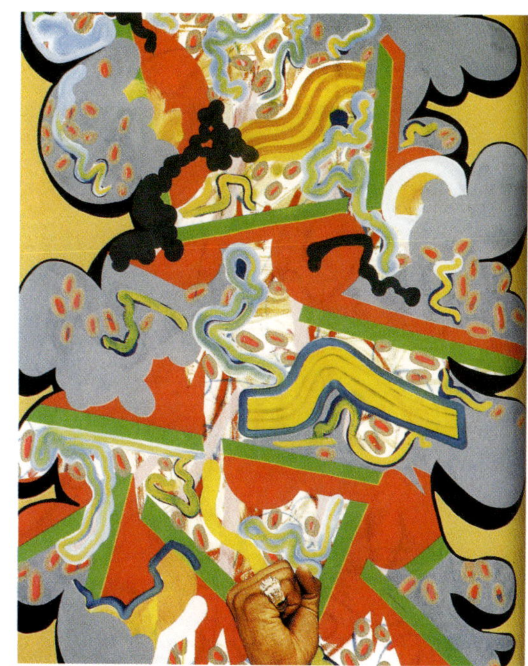

PLATE 24. Mustafa Maluka, *The Realness,* 2002. Oil and collage on canvas, 183 x 133 cm. Courtesy of Mustafa Maluka.

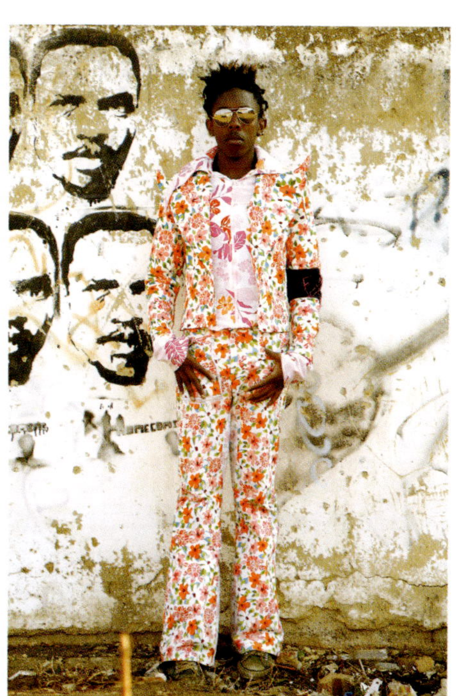

PLATE 25. Nontsikelelo Veleko, *Sibu VIII,* 2007. Pigment print on cotton rag paper, edition of 10. Reproduced courtesy of The Goodman Gallery.

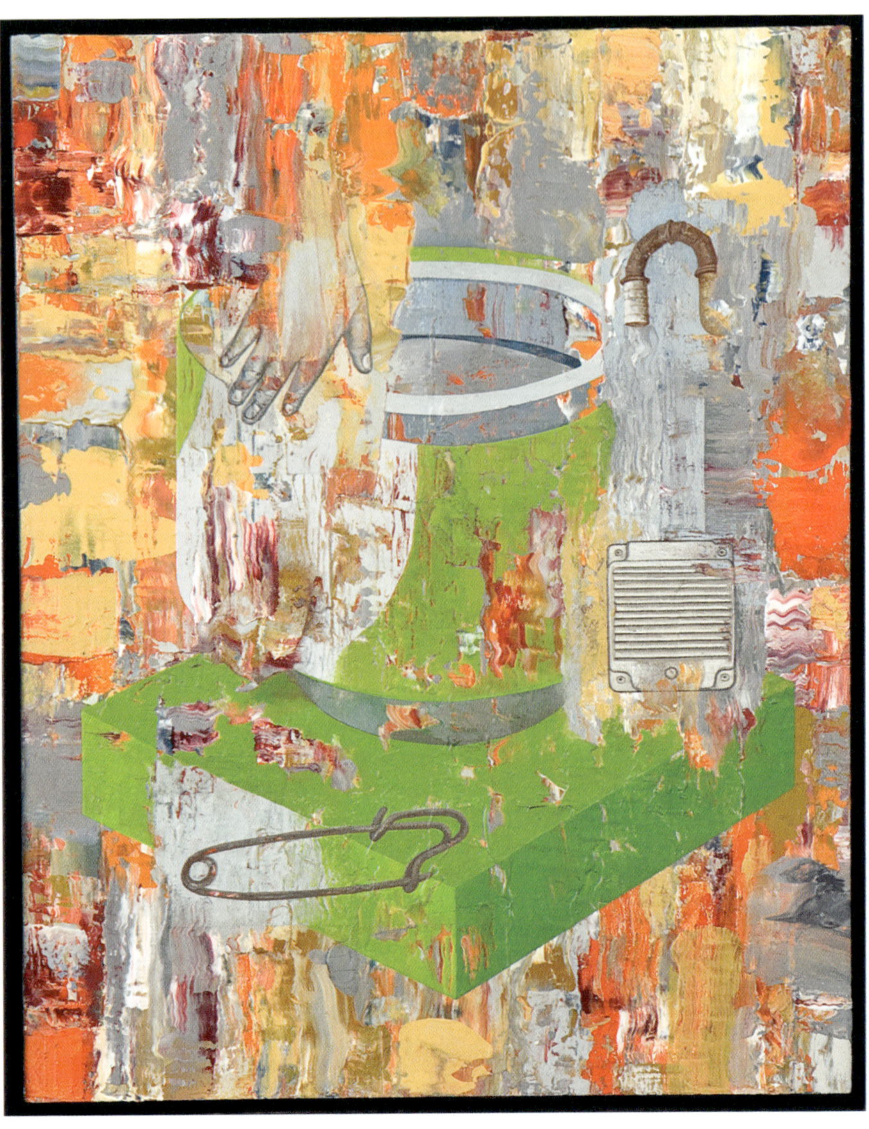

PLATE 26. Paul Stopforth, *Round-Up*, 2009. Gouache on panel, 20 x 16 inches. Courtesy of Paul Stopforth.

Acknowledgments
I Write What I Must

AT THE HEART OF BLACK CONSCIOUSNESS ARE UNITY, ANCESTRY, AND AGENCY (or action) against oppressive forces that reaffirm the importance of race within global systems of exchange. Originally combating a racist state apparatus built on the notion of "separateness," Black Consciousness remains relevant today.[1] Recent rhetorical twists on nonracialism obscure the importance of blackness and black agents in history. Black Consciousness, an important feature of tricontinental activism, is still largely regarded as too limiting in scope to be of much lasting historical import to South Africa's liberation narrative. Thus I write what I must: a book that challenges this view.

When, in 1978, Random House published select writings by Steve Biko in a book called *I Write What I Like,* editors chose a title that reflected the keystone to any discussion of Black Consciousness (BC) then and now. That is, agency is more than self-determination: it requires action of the mind and the body to build a better society. As the famed poet and activist Mongane Wally Serote once put it, "There is an intense need for self-expression among the oppressed in our country. When I say self-expression I don't mean people saying something about themselves. I mean people making history consciously."[2] In writing this book I have accepted Serote's charge. In listening to BC's many voices, I have learned to trust my own.

The path that led me to write this book has no single point of departure. James Baldwin's epigraph is one that captures some of my earliest memories. I was raised in an American military family; my brother and I went to college and quite happily on to graduate studies. My undergraduate years ran concurrent with antiapartheid activism on university campuses. I earned a BA in political science and vividly recall divestment demonstrations at the University of Puget Sound and elsewhere in the late 1980s. This set within me a desire to learn more about people elsewhere in the world whose visions were also circumscribed.

At the University of Wisconsin–Madison, I earned graduate degrees in art history and in African studies. I have profound respect for varied ways of thinking, and artistry offers us access to this precisely. I marvel before a musician who masters many instruments or who writes to combine their varied tunes. Oral performers—storytellers, poets, comedians—capture thoughts and images that make us sway. Writers of all genres broaden our capacity for empathy and understanding. The physical stamina of stage actors and dancers can stagger. All of these humanistic endeavors compel me, but the visual captivates most fully, from idea to process to realization to viewership to idea once more, altered (or maybe not), and so forth, through time. And historicized: this compels most of all.

I have spent more than three years living and working in South Africa, with half that period devoted to researching the visual culture of Biko and Black Consciousness. I have made friends and met many people while driving so many roads, large and small, across its nine provinces; the roads' insights are profound. South Africa is surely a home for me. Its people have offered help time and again; I warmly and frequently recall the generosity of friends, colleagues, and strangers I have encountered there. Hundreds of people lent time and energy to this book's realization, nine years in the making. I am deeply grateful to all who assisted and offer apologies to those whom I may inadvertently omit here.

Brenda Schmahmann, Paul Mills, Anitra Nettleton, Sue Webb, Lewis Ashwal, Fiona Rankin-Smith, Sandra Klopper, Michael Godby, Barbara Buntman, Bongiwe Dhlomo-Mautloa, Louisa Potter, Ian Alexander, and Julia Charlton hosted me on occasions too numerous to recount. Their advice and encouragement were wonderful; my gratitude is everlasting. I give special thanks to the artists and activists whose work appears in this book and to those whom I interviewed but, regrettably, could not include here. All are cited in the bibliography. I thank scholars, archivists, and curators at the universities of Cape Town, Durban–Westville, Fort Hare, Natal, Rhodes, Western Cape, Witwatersrand, the University of South Africa, and at the Durban Art Gallery, Goodman Gallery, Iziko–South African National Gallery, Market Theatre Gallery, Michael Stevenson Gallery, and the Johannesburg Art Gallery. Special among them are Neil Dundas, Jacob Leboko, Sipho Mokwena, Ramila Patel, and Michelle Pickover.

I thank the scholars in my writing group—Cynthia Becker, Amanda Carlson, Andrea Frohne, and Carol Magee—for their suggestions as the book was being written. I thank an anonymous reader whose comments were helpful, encouraging, and kind in a context that does not assure this will be so. Thanks to Henry Drewal for his continued wisdom, and to Federico Freshi, Joanna Grabski, Allen Roberts, and Zoë Strother for their ongoing support. Many thanks to colleagues who offered meaningful feedback at conferences and meetings in South Africa and the United States; these are a joy in all forms.

I thank the J. Paul Getty Foundation for sponsoring one year of writing, and the University of Denver, which also funded time spent in this manner. I am especially grateful to Richard Morrison and Erin Warholm-Wohlenhaus at the University of Minnesota Press for their direction, vision, and labor. Thanks also to Laura Westlund and Louisa Castner for shepherding the book through to its final form. The Margaret S. Harding Memorial Endowment at the Press enabled us to reproduce artworks in color. Jessica Williams I thank for help with image rights.

Finally, I thank my good friends and family for their steady support. My parents, Cecille and Wayne Hill, and my brother, Doug, have always encouraged. My beloved, Peter Burkholder, made this book possible in ways that cannot be accredited. To him I am eternally grateful. Our sons, Jonah and Linus, came to this world, and to South Africa, during the years that I researched and wrote this book; I love them to no end.

Notes

Introduction

1. Quoted in Anthony Marx, *Lessons of Struggle*, 45. The previous sentence paraphrases Marx. Beginning in 1971, Khoapa was executive director of Black Community Programmes, a BC organization that ran a variety of social initiatives (e.g., literacy, crèches, construction, medicine, auto repair) in townships, for the most part.

2. *I Write What I Like* (1978) is the most popular collection of essays by Biko. The 1972 essay cited here contests the thinking behind the Bantu Homelands Citizen Act (1970) and the Bantu Homelands Constitution Act (1971).

3. "SASO Policy Manifesto," July 1971. (SASO stands for the South African Students' Organization.) Quoted in Mublele Vizikhungo Mzamane, Bavusile Maaba, and Nkosinathi Biko, "The Black Consciousness Movement," 116.

4. Throughout this book, I use capital letters to identify Black Consciousness when discussing the ideology as such and lowercase letters when describing an individual's own sense of black consciousness.

5. The Suppression of Communism Act (1950) enabled the state to ban people it deemed a threat to security. People held under this act faced the same consequences, which included, among others, the restriction to location, limited access to conversation outside one's immediate family, and the denied right to have their opinions aired or visage printed in any form.

6. I adopt the term *tricontinental* in keeping with Robert Young's conception of its geographic, political, and cultural pulse. He favors it over *Third World* since it is without the negative implication and inconsistencies of that term. It was the term endorsed (along with *three continents*) by Anouar Abdel-Malek after the first conference of the Peoples of Africa, Asia, and Latin America at Havana in 1966. "Above all," Young writes, "the tri-continental marks an identification with the great Havana Tri-continental of 1966, which initiated the first global alliance of the peoples of three continents against imperialism, and the founding moment of postcolonial theory in its journal, the *Tri-continental*" (*Postcolonialism: An Historical Introduction*, 5).

7. Portuguese slaving vessels recorded not the number of people held in chains below but their value as units of labor, or *pieza de India*. A full *pieza de India* was the ideal capture: a male of good health aged fifteen to twenty-five years. All other people were fractions of this unit. (See Philip D. Curtin, *The Atlantic Slave Trade: A Census*, 1969.)

8. Cited in Millard Arnold, *Steve Biko*, 141.

9. Derrida, "Racism's Last Word," 331.

10. Michael MacDonald, *Why Race Matters in South Africa*, 92.

11. In its early years, "communalism" publically named the socioeconomic structure favored by BC organs, but privately members debated how (and whether) to "modernize" it. By May 1976, Biko began to publically identify BC as "African Socialist" in orientation. This occurred at the SASO-BPC trial (Arnold, *Steve Biko*, 64) and again in a July 1976 interview with the British Broadcasting Corporation (Biko, *I Write What I Like*, 147–49).

12. Black Consciousness activists were not the first in South Africa to promote affiliation based on common oppression. The Non-European Unity Movement had done so in 1943. The next year, the ANC's Youth League advocated a kind of cultural nationalism that resurfaced, altered, in BC (Mzamane, Maaba, and N. Biko, "The Black Consciousness Movement," 126). BC's ideology is most commonly compared to that of the PAC, but the PAC admitted only people with full African ancestry, so it was less generous in membership. (That said, PAC founder Robert Sobukwe was greatly admired by BC leaders.)

13. A. J. Christopher, *The Atlas of Apartheid*, 2.

14. Marx, *Lessons of Struggle*, 82; Biko, *I Write What I Like*, 89.

15. Resolution 45c of the General Students' Council of SASO. Cited in Mzamane, Maaba, and N. Biko, "The Black Consciousness Movement," 124–25. This passage closely matches its source, *Black Power: The Politics of Liberation in America* (1967) by Stokely Carmichael and Charles Hamilton. The book is described as a "seminal work in the evolution of Black Consciousness in South Africa" (ibid., 126).

16. MacDonald, *Why Race Matters in South Africa*, 92–123.

17. Ibid., 96.

18. Ibid., 95–96. I note that voting rights were still conditioned by European standards. Whiteness regulated, thus centered, progress.

19. Ibid., 97; italics original.

20. Ibid., 101.

21. Records show that the question of white participation was debated with some regularity over the life of SASO and the BPC. Membership did not allow white activists, but supportive liberal organizations and individuals participated heavily in BC's cause. Mamphela Ramphele, one of BC's best known advocates, credits Anne Hope as an "important resource" in SASO's leadership training seminars. She was, Ramphele writes, among the "truly good white people" (*A Life*, 65). Among those who financed BPC undertakings were the theologian Beyers Naudé, and Helen Suzman, member of Parliament and its sole liberal voice. See Marx, *Lessons of Struggle*, for more about the ongoing debate within BC organs, and its contradictions, particularly pages 78–79.

22. MacDonald, *Why Race Matters*, 102–6.

23. Marx, *Lessons*, 79; Julie Frederikse, *The Unbreakable Thread*, 162.

24. Among those who disavow BC's influence: NUSAS, *A People's History: Resistance in South Africa*, 28; Terry Bell, *Unfinished Business: South Africa Apartheid and Truth*, 128. Marx sees SASO as mostly ineffectual with community-based initiatives and credits the BPC with a more action-oriented agenda (*Lessons of Struggle*, 46, 51–54, 59). Among those

who credit SASO's abilities to organize and lead: Ramphele, "Empowerment and Symbols of Hope," 154–78; and Mzamane et al., "Black Consciousness Movement," 100.

25. Some BC leaders were banned from public speaking as early as 1971 (Marx, *Lessons of Struggle,* 53). Many BC leaders were banned and jailed beginning in 1973, and a parcel bomb murdered one, Abram Onkgopotse Tiro, in 1974. SASO was banned in 1975, and nineteen other BC organizations were banned on October 19, 1977, a little more than one month after Steve Biko died at the hands of security police.

26. See, for example, John Peffer, *Art and the End of Apartheid*; Diana Wylie, *Art + Revolution*; Judy Seidman, *Red on Black*; the Poster Book Collective, *Images of Defiance*; Sue Williamson, *Resistance Art in South Africa.*

27. There are just two biographies of Steve Biko, both published recently: Xolela Mangcu, *Biko: A Life* (2013); and Lindy Wilson, *Steve Biko* (2011). All information in this section is gleaned from these sources unless otherwise noted.

28. Wilson, *Steve Biko,* 23.

29. Gail Gerhart, *Black Power in South Africa: The Evolution of an Ideology,* 21.

30. Wilson, *Steve Biko,* 22–23.

31. Ibid., 44.

32. Ibid., 15.

33. Jantjes is quoted in Caroline Collier, "To Go and Come Back," 6.

34. Shannen Hill, "Iconic Autopsy: Postmortem Portraits of Bantu Stephen Biko."

35. I admire Dan Magaziner's recent tribute, "We Write What We Like about Steve Biko," offered on what would have been his sixty-sixth birthday, December 18, 2012.

36. Private conversation with author, September 1997.

37. At a July 1996 hearing of the Truth and Reconciliation Commission, Elias Molatseli testified that he was made to report daily to the Bloemfontein police for more than a year because a photograph of Biko was found during a raid on his home. Booker T. Washington's autobiography, *Up from Slavery* (1901), was also found ("Old Man Arrested for Biko Photo, Truth Body Told").

1. Shaping Modern Black Culture in the 1970s

1. Several sources recount the night in July 1967 when Steve Biko and Barney Pityana led a black exit from the annual conference of the National Union of South African Students (NUSAS), held that year at Rhodes University in Grahamstown (Arnold's *Steve Biko* offers the best account). I place emphasis elsewhere: though the event marked a public demonstration of pride and agency, it was but one among many exerted by BC-oriented individuals. For Biko, Pityana, and many others, evident tensions preexisted that night at Rhodes.

2. Bell, *Unfinished Business,* 126.

3. Mzamane et al., "Black Consciousness Movement," 122.

4. Marx, *Lessons of Struggle,* 42. Mamphela Ramphele recalls listening to the speeches of Malcolm X and Martin Luther King Jr. on tape while living at the Alan Taylor Residence at the University of Natal in 1969. The picture she describes is one of debate and good humor,

smoke and drink, music and dancing (*A Life*, 58). Diana Wylie lists Kohinoor Records on Diagonal Street in Johannesburg as one vendor that sold banned recordings of their kind (*Art + Revolution*, 51).

5. Compiled from Mzamane et al., "Black Consciousness Movement," 126; C. R. D. Halisi, *Black Political Thought in the Making of South African Democracy*, 119–21; Kogila Moodley, "The Continued Impact of Black Consciousness," 146–47.

6. Marx, *Lessons of Struggle*, 42; Bell, *Unfinished Business*, 131.

7. Mzamane et al., "Black Consciousness Movement," 126. The most thorough list of influences is given in this source. Anthony Marx argues that BC adherents in South Africa learned about Black Panther strategy in the United States through informal means and were thus not fully familiar with corollaries between them (*Lessons of Struggle*, 43). George Frederickson drew multiple parallels between these two in "Black Power in the United States and Black Consciousness in South Africa: Connections and Comparisons."

8. Halisi, "Rethinking Steve Biko and Black Consciousness."

9. Bell, *Unfinished Business*, 121.

10. Graffiti enjoys a large audience by boldly changing the landscape, and when the sentiment is political it seemingly represents a widespread concern given its public placement. To those with few resources, graffiti in the period was a medium often used to educate, unify, and mobilize. See Mzamane, "The Impact of Black Consciousness on Culture," 186.

11. "Some African Cultural Concepts," in Biko, *I Write What I Like*, 40–47.

12. Ibid., 46.

13. Ibid., 43.

14. Hendrik Verwoerd (1954), quoted in Nancy L. Clarke and William H. Worger, *South Africa: The Rise and Fall of Apartheid*, 51.

15. Arnold, *Steve Biko*, 153.

16. Interview with author, 2011; and Frieda Hattingh, *Oto La Dimo: Joint Retrospective Exhibition of Lefifi Tladi and Motlhabane Mashiangwako*, 46.

17. Biko, "Black Souls in White Skins?" in *I Write What I Like*, 23.

18. John Peffer brings this world of black cultural commerce to life in *Art and the End of Apartheid*, 50–53, 184–88.

19. Ramphele, *A Life*, 57.

20. Arnold, *Steve Biko*, 25.

21. Bester's jacket eventually led to his arrest in Milnerton outside of Cape Town. There he was made to sign a statement that he would not promote the phrase again, and his jacket was confiscated. Interview with author, 1999.

22. Ramphele, *A Life*, 57–58. Other notable BC women of this period include Nomisis Kraai, Deborah Matshoba, Vuyelwa Mashalaba, and Thenjiwe Mthintso. Mthintso is given special praise in Ellen Kuzwayo's *Call Me Woman* (1985) for her self-assured demeanor despite numerous and varied kinds of detentions, one of which they shared. "Thenjiwe was cool, calm, composed and very unruffled by the appearance or even the presence of the most officious wardress. Not once did she verbally indoctrinate me, but her actions spoke much louder than words, and their message was loud and clear" (211).

23. K. Moodley, "Continued Impact of Black Consciousness," 147.

24. Ramphele, *A Life*, 71.

25. Biko, "The Definition of Black Consciousness" and "Some African Cultural Concepts" in *I Write What I Like*, 49, 46. Unless otherwise stated, the attributes of modern black culture are gleaned from these two documents. Both papers were written in 1971. The first was prepared for a SASO leadership training session; the second was given at a Natal conference cohosted by the Interdenominational African Ministers Association of South Africa (IDAMASA) and the Association for the Educational and Cultural Development of the African People (ASSECA). See also Arnold, *Steve Biko*, 64, 66.

26. Quoted in George Bizos, *No One to Blame?* 42.

27. Temba Sono, "Black Consciousness: Its Significance and Role in the Life of the Community," 4–5.

28. Arnold, *Steve Biko*, 20.

29. Biko, "Black Consciousness and the Quest for a True Humanity," in *I Write What I Like*, 95.

30. Arnold, *Steve Biko*, 179, 201.

31. Ibid., 206.

32. W. J. T. Mitchell, *Picture Theory: Essays on Verbal and Visual Representation*, 285–89.

33. Seidman, *Red on Black*, 51. Between 1969 and 1973, SPRO-CAS produced a series of reports on apartheid for the Christian Institute and the South African Council of Churches. Ben Khoapa was invited to join SPRO-CAS but proposed to develop Black Community Programmes (BCP) instead. See Arnold, *Steve Biko*, 161. SPRO-CAS and BCP shared a common sensibility and purpose, but it is unlikely that SPRO-CAS was "structured into a Black Community Programme by Bennie Khoapa and Steve Biko," per G. E. de Villiers (see Seidman, *Red on Black*, 51), because its target audience and inclusion of white members would have made public affiliation with BC impossible. Rather, SPRO-CAS exemplified a quiet support for BC and its agents.

34. They also worked together illustrating textbooks at the South African Committee for Higher Education, an organization founded by European charities to fill the gaps left by discriminatory Bantu education laws. See Seidman, *Red on Black*, 51. See also Wylie, *Art + Revolution*, 53–54.

35. See Seidman, *Red on Black*, 50, for reproduction of the other posters described here.

36. The distinction is not minor. Innumerable photographs of ANC and PAC members record these salutes. The ANC's salute became increasingly blurred in the 1980s, particularly as a large number of the BC-minded joined the party in exile. Still, the extended thumb salute of the ANC is readily seen in this period, and it continues among an older generation today. See Peter Magubane, *Women of South Africa*, 34, for a 1987 image of Winnie Mandela and others in this mode. In 1989, the ANC relied on the fully clenched fist in a poster that repeats the motif against bands of color. (Reproduced in the Poster Book Collective, *Images of Defiance*, 22.) Photographs of United Democratic Front (UDF) events bear witness to both ANC and BC gestures within the crowd, but fists in UDF graphics consistently follow the BC form. Less repeated is the broken chain motif. I note its inclusion in Fikile

Magadlela's drawing of 1978 *Remind Me Not* (reprinted in E. J. de Jager, *Images of Man*, 167; and Hill, "Creating Consciousness: Black Art in 1970s South Africa") and in a poster by Medu-aligned artist Judy Seidman, who connects it with a history of women's activism in South Africa (Figure 4.6).

37. Voyiya, interview with author, 2011.

38. Quoted in Marx, *Lessons of Struggle*, 52. Emphasis added.

39. Gail M. Gerhart, *Black Power in South Africa*, 295, n. 41.

40. Arnold, *Steve Biko* reprints the trial transcript. For an excellent summary of these distinctions, see Frederickson, "Black Power in the United States and Black Consciousness in South Africa."

41. Wylie, *Art + Revolution*, 52.

42. Peffer, *Art at the End of Apartheid*, 51, 53.

43. Ibid., 103. Peffer moves from the uprisings of 1976 to the formation of the nonracial United Democratic Front in 1983 in just three sentences.

44. Ibid., 74.

45. Jantjes earned a BFA at the University of Cape Town's Michaelis School of Fine Art in 1969. After teaching for a time, he moved to Hamburg, Germany, and in 1972 earned an MFA at the Hochschule für bildende Künste. Here he began to make the kind of work for which he became well known: collaged prints that urge action in response to South Africa's violent oppression of liberty at home and abroad.

46. Araeen, "Art and Black Consciousness," 36–41.

47. Araeen, "The Emergence of Black Consciousness in Contemporary Art in Britain," 5. Eddie Chambers first used the term *black art* here in 1981 in relation to an exhibition he curated at the Wolverhampton Art Gallery. Statements by Chambers and Keith Piper "emphasized the radical critical function of 'black art' in the context of black struggle, both at home and abroad" (ibid., 6). I note that South African Fikile Magadlela used the term the same year to locate his work within Black Consciousness.

48. The series is reproduced in full in Elizabeth Harney, "Word Play," 220–24. See also Jean Kennedy, *New Currents, Ancient Rivers*, 180–83; Okwui Enwezor, *The Short Century*, 110–13; and Pep Subirós, *Apartheid: The South African Mirror*, 135.

49. South Africa regulated the movement of people by issuing several pass laws over decades. Relevant to Jantjes's work is the Native Urban Areas Act of 1923, which deemed urban areas "white" and required all black South Africans to carry a pass indicating their right to temporarily reside there. Also, the Pass Law Act of 1952, which required all "Bantu" over the age of sixteen to carry a pass at all times. Under this law, only whites could verify the authenticity of a pass holder's claim to rightfully be in any given location.

50. The text reads as follows:

RE: The Population Registration Act (Act No. 30 of 1950)

The Population Registration Act defines three main racial groups—"WHITE" "COLOURED" and "NATIVE" (or "Bantu"). The "Coloured" group has seven sub-divisions viz. "Cape Coloured" "Cape Malay" "Griqua" "Chinese" "Indian" "Other Coloured" and "Other

Asiatics." The "Bantu" group is sub-divided into either "national units" viz. Zulu Xhosa Swazi North-Sotho South-Sotho Tswana Shangaan and Venda.

The general practice is to distinguish between the people in four categories—"white" "coloured" "Bantu" and "Asiatic."

The racial label put on a non-white child at birth is not only a badge of race, it is a permanent brand of inferiority, the brand of class distinction. Throughout his life his race label will warn all concerned which doors are open to him, and which are closed. In addition to the political and social taboos attached to his race identity card, it will proclaim what sort of education he may receive and the limits on his choice of employment.

If he is classified as "Coloured" he will be excluded from certain occupations reserved for "Whites," his trade union and other rights will be inferior to those of his "White" fellow workers. In many occupations his pay is likely to be lower. If he is classified as a "Bantu" he is in every way made inferior both to "Whites" and "Coloureds"—in education, employment, earnings, trade union rights and everything else concerned with making a living.

51. Jantjes, "Art and Cultural Reciprocity," 44.

52. Ibid.

53. Arnold, *Steve Biko*, 22; Bizos, *No One to Blame?* 43.

54. Bizos, *No One to Blame?* 42.

55. Jantjes as quoted in Kennedy, *New Currents, Ancient Rivers*, 182–83.

56. Sack, *The Neglected Tradition*, 17. Peffer thoughtfully addresses this history in *Art and the End of Apartheid*, 41–59, but the dominant method of locating individuals by style remains unexamined.

57. Wylie, *Art + Revolution*, 68. Before 1974, Mnyele's work conforms to Wylie's description, but such penchant for evoking sorrow, sacrifice, and alienation through imagery and verse is anomalous among Black Consciousness artists of this time. His work matured greatly after 1974. BC evidently altered his aesthetic.

58. Magadlela, "Staffrider Profile," 24–25. Also quoted in Sack, *Neglected Tradition*, 18.

59. Biko, "Black Consciousness and the Quest for a True Humanity," in *I Write What I Like*, 91. For more on BC's rejection of black imagery without agency, see Ramphele, *A Life*, 67.

60. Quoted in Hattingh, *Oto La Dimo*, 20.

61. Sack, *Neglected Tradition*, 17. Percy Mabandu, author of a forthcoming book on Fikile Magadlela, drops the boundary-laden identifier and simply calls him "surrealist" (see Themba Ka Mathe, "An Obituary").

62. Sack, *Neglected Tradition*, 17.

63. Magadlela, "Staffrider Profile," 25.

64. Ibid. For a limited reading of BC in Magadlela's art, see Peffer, *Art and the End of Apartheid*, 52–53. The artist attended one SASO conference (at the University of the North, better known as Turfloop) and took part in SASO's cultural committee. (Magadlela, interview with author, 1999; Wylie, *Art + Revolution*, 77.)

65. Joyce Ozynski, cited in *Black Art Today*, n.p.

66. Ka Mathe, "An Obituary."

67. E. J. de Jager, *Images of Man,* 167.

68. Hattingh, "Lefifi Tladi and Mothlabane Mashiangwa Notes"; Magadlela, *Staffrider Profile,* 25. See also Ka Mathe, "An Obituary."

69. His *Floating Spirits* (n.d.) is a beautiful example of figures in flight. It is reproduced in de Jager, *Images of Man,* 168.

70. Hattingh, *Oto La Dimo,* 9. Ka Mathe names Leonard Matsoso, Andrew Motjuoadi, Vincent Baloyi, Percy Sedumedi, and Thami Mnyele as among Magadlela's contemporaries ("An Obituary").

71. The following is a sample cited in Hattingh, *Oto La Dimo,* 69: James Baldwin: *Go Tell It on the Mountain, The Fire Next Time,* and *Blues for Mr. Charlie*; Eldridge Cleaver, *Soul on Ice* and *Post Prison Writings*; W. E. B. Du Bois, *Black Folks Then and Now*; Frantz Fanon, *The Wretched of the Earth* and *Black Skin White Masks*; Malcolm X and Alex Haley, *The Autobiography of Malcolm X*; Okot P' Bitek, *African Religions in Western Scholarship* and *Song of Lawino*; Ngũgĩ wa Thiong'o, *Home Coming*; Richard Wright, *Black Boy* and *Native Son*; John A. Williams and Charles F. Harris, *Amistad I* and *II, Writings on Black History and Culture.*

72. Aryan Kaganof, "Geoff Matlherane Mphakati."

73. Two people discussed below, Mongane Wally Serote and Thami Mnyele, performed with Mihloti. Serote later helped found the Medu Art Ensemble, which Mnyele joined. Both Mihloti and Medu were BC-influenced in origin. As Peffer writes of Mihloti, "their experiences with the collective later informed their collaborative work and their interest in integrating performance and visual art after they went into exile" (*Art and the End of Apartheid,* 73).

74. Lefifi Tladi, interview with author, 2011.

75. Wylie, *Art + Revolution,* 49–50.

76. Kaganof, "Geoff Matlherane Mphakati."

77. In 2005, two Australian patrons of the period, Diana Johnstone and Bruce Haigh, donated forty-seven pieces to the newly created Ifa Lethu Foundation, which works to repatriate South African art from abroad and thereby restore this crucial history at home. Ifa Lethu has since received more than one hundred artworks from donors worldwide. See Brown Maaba, "Challenges to Repatriation and Preservation," 505.

78. Hattingh, *Oto La Dimo,* 10.

79. Tladi, interview with author, 2011.

80. Hattingh, *Oto La Dimo,* 12.

81. Ibid., 18.

82. Hattingh mentions Dan Mogale, Tau Mokoka, Moss Tshikane, and Colin Maaga among those who also regularly attended Pretoria hearings (ibid., 12).

83. See Hill, "Creating Consciousness" for more information about and a reproduction of *Soul of a Dying Black Man.* Mashiangwako also paid tribute to the musicians Mbizo Johnny Dyani and Hugh Masekela. The photographer Ernest Cole is honored with a three-part series from 1993. These are in keeping with praise poetry (*izibongo* or *lithoko*), practiced for centuries in this part of Africa. See Hattingh's *Oto La Dimo* for images.

84. Ibid., 23.

85. Biko as quoted in Bizos, *No One to Blame?* 42.

86. Hattingh, *Oto La Dimo,* 10, 11, 44.

87. Ibid., 13. The next quote comes from the same source.

88. Ibid., 15, 16.

89. The artist's name is given differently in print. Publications in the 1970s use Dikobe wa Mogale. Some confusion arose after Steven Sack's influential exhibition and catalog *The Neglected Tradition: Towards a New History of South African Art (1930–1988).* In a February 1996 letter to Julia Charlton, then a curator at the Johannesburg Art Gallery, the artist wrote: "The biographical information from the *Neglected Tradition* catalogue (1991) fused my Biographical information with that of Modikwe Dikobe and consequently created a fictional third person." In this book I follow the spelling given on stationery from his office in parliament: Ben Dikobé Martins; he signs letters "D. B. Martins."

90. Martins, "The Necessity of Art for National Liberation."

91. Martins endured seven months of solitary confinement before being transferred to Robben Island. He was later transferred to Diepkloof prison in Gauteng. He was released in late 1990 due to a negotiated settlement between the ANC and National Party.

92. Martins, "Corn in a Court of Chickens," 43.

93. Hattingh, *Oto La Dimo,* 10; Sack, *Neglected Tradition,* 112.

94. Peffer, *Art at the End of Apartheid,* 137–38.

95. That above is based on a photograph of Serote on the back cover of his epic poem *No Baby Must Weep* (1975). This poem and artwork based on it are analyzed in Hill, "Creating Consciousness."

96. Serote, *Selected Poems,* 24–25.

97. Martins, "Corn in a Court of Chickens," 44.

98. The book's jacket lists Dikobe wa Mogale as artist, but this is a misidentification. See note 89 above.

99. Biko had evident interest in the arts and even contributed to them as the founding editor of *Black Review,* a literary journal published by SASO from 1972 to 1976. Copies are available at www.disa.ukzn.ac.za, but the journal is incorrectly listed as a Black Community Programmes publication. As chairman of SASO publications in 1972, Biko initiated studies on politics, economics, theology, poetry, aesthetics, and culture. These were printed in the books *Creativity and Development* and *Essays on Black Theology,* and in the journals *Black Viewpoint* and *Black Review.* See Mzamane et al., "Black Consciousness Movement," 123.

100. Diana Wylie's *Art + Revolution: The Life and Death of Thami Mnyele, South African Artist* is a welcome biography in a field that has too few. She reports that he attended the SASO–BPC trial (93) discussed near the end of this chapter, and Steve Biko's funeral (109), which is discussed in the next.

101. Ibid., 34.

102. The first cover is reproduced in ibid., 45; and Peffer, *Art and the End of Apartheid,* 52. The second cover is also in Wylie, *Art + Revolution,* 80.

103. Mnyele and Fikile Magadlela enjoyed a close friendship that began when they met through SASO's cultural committee. (Wylie, *Art + Revolution,* 77.)

104. Peffer, *Art and the End of Apartheid,* 74. In chapter 3, I compare the exhibition to another that opened that night, Paul Stopforth's *Figures.* Both opened amid reporting about Steve Biko's death three days prior and both bore unexpected influence because of this coincidence.

105. See Wylie, *Art + Revolution* for reproductions of both. See also Hill, "Creating Consciousness," for analysis of that in the Standard Bank Collection.

106. The tendency thus far is to divide Mnyele's art into distinct periods of political engagement, black-centered in the 1970s and nonracial in the 1980s (Peffer's *Art and the End of Apartheid,* 74, which I quote here, and Wylie, *Art + Revolution,* chapters 4–6). I propose that we see the artist's professional decisions, be they in a finished work or in the context in which they were made, as affected by his internalization of Black Consciousness.

107. Several works in the series were reprinted in the November/December 1979 issue of the journal *Staffrider.* This publication gives the title *Black Crucifixion* to the series, while another titles it *Pain on the Cross.* See Philippa Hobbs and Elizabeth Rankin, *Rorke's Drift,* 186.

108. Hobbs and Rankin, *Rorke's Drift,* 186.

109. Steve Biko saw photographs of works in Nkosi's *Black Crucifixion* series and is said to have expressed a wish to purchase one for his own collection. Ibid., 188.

110. Bernstein, *No. 46–Steve Biko,* 16.

111. Aelred Stubbs, editor's note to Biko's "The Righteousness of Our Strength," 120. A "shebeen" is a bar.

112. Franklin Thomas, *South Africa: Time Running Out,* 185.

113. Marx, *Lessons of Struggle,* 53.

114. FRELIMO had been ten years at war with Portugal, Mozambique's colonizer since 1505. Freedom was ultimately won through a tripartite guerrilla campaign to oust Portugal from Africa, with wars in Angola and Portuguese Guinea as well. With independence gained on June 25, 1975, the People's Republic of Mozambique would face another fifteen years of war (fostered and financed by other nations, but called a "civil war" nonetheless), starting in 1977. The nation adopted the name *Mozambique* in 1992.

115. While the state issued special bans on all pro-FRELIMO rallies, it permitted an anti-FRELIMO rally to take place in Johannesburg on the same day as the Durban and Turfloop events. See editor's note (A. Stubbs) to Biko, "What Is Black Consciousness," in *I Write What I Like,* 99.

116. Arnold, *Steve Biko,* xxiii.

117. Ibid., xiv.

118. Bernstein, *No. 46,* 16.

119. Bernstein reports that six defendants were sentenced to six years of imprisonment and three received three to five years (ibid., 16); Arnold writes that the sentence for all nine was five to six years (*Steve Biko,* xxiii).

120. Bernstein, *No. 46,* 16.

121. Arnold's *Steve Biko* reprints the testimony in its entirety.

122. Ibid., 35–36.

123. Quoted in ibid., 227.

124. *Art + Revolution,* 93–94. In this biography of Thami Mnyele, Wylie misinterprets Biko. Indeed, at trial he referenced several other political parties and modes of struggle, but Wylie does not read these as "implicitly endorsing" them; rather, this she keeps for non-racialism. In fact, over the previous three years Biko had tried to reconcile divergent opinion on how to best combat apartheid. He sought to unify the ANC and the Pan Africanist Congress, a desire consistent with BC's own attempts to unify people classified by ethnicity. See chapter 4 for critique of scholarly methods that unduly favor nonracialism.

125. Quoted in Arnold, *Steve Biko,* 158. By the end of its first year, BPC had forty branches nationwide and more than three thousand members. Marx, *Lessons of Struggle,* 54.

126. Arnold, *Steve Biko,* xiii.

127. Ibid., 167.

128. Quoted in ibid., 147–49.

129. The following quoted passages in this paragraph are from ibid., 290–91, 296.

130. Quoted in ibid., 248.

131. They were found not guilty on counts three through thirteen because SASO and BPC were not shown to be revolutionary groups (ibid., xxxvi).

132. Bernstein, *No. 46,* 17.

133. Marx, *Lessons of Struggle,* 73.

134. Unidentified newspaper clipping of September 15, 1977, filed with Biko papers in the South African History Archive, University of the Witwatersrand. Marx writes that the ANC was "effectively extinct internally" at this time, though it later claimed influence in Soweto by calling Black Consciousness "one of its subsidiaries." (ibid., 67.)

135. SASM grew out of the African Students' Movement, which began in 1968, and changed its name in 1972 when members decided to formally align with SASO, its counterpart in postsecondary education. See www.africanhistory.about.com for more on this piece of history.

136. Interview with author, 2012.

137. Gerhart, *Black Power in South Africa,* 297.

138. Marx, *Lessons of Struggle,* 66.

139. Ibid. Marx writes that people in rural areas did not respond as readily as those in urban ones. One reason, he suggests, was the misrepresentation of BC by homeland leaders who presented themselves as BC-minded even while they enforced "continued submission" to state laws (70).

140. Ibid., 69. The next quotation is from the same source.

141. Pieterson was among the first schoolchildren shot that day in Soweto. Sam Nzima's famous photograph of Pieterson became the iconic image of this event. It shows Mbuyisa Makhubo carrying the injured child with Hector's sister, Antoinette, running beside him. Both hurry to save the boy's life. Following June 16 and often since, newspapers worldwide have printed the picture in reports about the bloodshed.

142. In Moore, *Black Theology,* 43. The book includes several papers given in 1973 as the conference moved among urban and rural locations in at least two provinces. The following quotes in this paragraph are on the same page of this source.

143. More recent studies include Daniel Magaziner, *The Law and the Prophets: Black Consciousness in South Africa, 1968–1977* (2010); Mcebisi Ndletyana, *African Intellectuals in 19th and 20th Century South Africa* (2008); Bennie Khoapa, *The Legacy of Stephen Bantu Biko: Theological Challenges* (2008).

144. Marx, *Lessons of Struggle,* 53.

145. Following the nationwide discussions of 1971, the steering committee met first in Lenasia, outside of Johannesburg, on January 13, 1972. The IDAMASA hosted a prelaunch meeting in Pietermaritzburg July 8–10 that welcomed more than one hundred delegates representing a range of interests—religion, poverty, education, and sport among them. When the BPC was officially launched in Hammanskraal at the December 16–17 conference, 1,400 delegates representing 145 groups were there to cast votes. This history underscores the efficacy of SASO's leadership training programs, and the rapid response that BC adherents received among oppressed peoples, still mostly youth at this point, but intergenerational to some degree (Mzamane et al., "Black Consciousness Movement," 133–35).

146. Bell, *Unfinished Business,* 69–70, 78, 85. Bell details Operation Daisy, initiated and overseen by the Bureau of State Security (BOSS). Agents focused on BC adherents and their supporters at Fort Hare, Rhodes, Witwatersrand, and Cape Town. They operated out of either the Education Research Trust or the Prisoner Support Trust, posts that brought undercover agents access to families of political prisoners. As Bell writes, "In this way the police were able to seize control of most of the BC networks" (ibid., 85). They attempted less to infiltrate BC bodies at black campuses, where targets were "mainly dealt with by repression" (ibid., 70).

147. Given at the University of the North (Turfloop) graduation exercises in 1972, Tiro's speech publically declared one of the divisive issues among BC adherents. Mzamane et al. reveal that the degree to which BPC should adopt a militant versus moderate approach was debated, mostly along generational lines, at a December 1971 foundational meeting in Orlando East, Soweto. A vote favored what Gail Gerhart called "the 'gloves off' militance of SASO" (quoted in "Black Consciousness Movement," 133). Fissures like this one were there from the beginning.

148. Ibid., 137. Koka attended the first BPC organizational meeting in April 1971 in Bloemfontein. He represented IDAMASA as its president in Transvaal. He was also on the steering committee that met in January 1972. Mafuna had decades of experience in union organizing that he put to use for BPC by going door to door in recruitment campaigns launched in Port Elizabeth and Durban (ibid., 133, 137). Interesting for this study, Wylie reports that Mafuna was a photographer and journalist who contributed to the "black edition" of the *Rand Daily Mail* (*Art + Revolution,* 34).

149. Wylie places the banning of Mafuna, whom she calls by the familiar "Bokwe," together with those of early 1973 (ibid., 70). Also banned: Strini Moodley, Drake Koka, Jerry Modisane, and Saths Cooper (Daniel Magaziner, *The Law and the Prophets,* 164).

150. Tiro was expelled by the state to Botswana following his Turfloop address in 1972. BC leaders met with exiled ANC leaders at his funeral in 1974 (Marx, *Lessons of Struggle,* 54).

151. Ibid., 53.

152. Ibid., 61. In the mid-1970s, South Africa was fifteen years into a significant recession.

Marx details the effects of this plight on black South Africans and demonstrates that material deprivation combined with empowerment through BC led to widespread anger among youth (see 61–63 for statistics).

153. Mzamane et al., "Black Consciousness Movement," 136.

154. Ibid., 138.

155. Koloane, interview with author, 2011.

156. Mzamane et al., "Black Consciousness Movement," 100.

2. Of Icons and Inquests

1. Mitchell, *Picture Theory: Essays on Verbal and Visual Representation*, 490.

2. Ibid., 285; Carol Shloss, *In Visible Light: Photography and the American Writer: 1840–1940*, 182.

3. Mitchell, *Picture Theory*, 287.

4. "We Do Not Use Force—Col Goosen," *The Citizen*, November 19, 1977.

5. Barthes, *Camera Lucida: Reflections on Photography*, 88–97.

6. Tagg, *The Burden of Representation: Essays on Photographies and Histories*, 3.

7. The Biko family strongly favored an inquest over a trial because their lawyers would be allowed to pose questions ("South Africa Orders Inquest into Biko's Death in Jail"). This points to a sense of collusion between the policemen who could be accused and the prosecutor, in this case the South African state.

8. Bernstein, *No. 46–Steve Biko*, 20–21. The laughter that rang through the assembly that day had an edge. Three members of the Black Sash, a white women's organization that protested a variety of apartheid laws, walked silently into the room and laid a commemorative wreath bearing the name Steve Biko on the floor up front. The wreath was torn to shreds within seconds. See "A Wreath for Steve."

9. Elders in the Grahamstown Cathedral put out a call for South Africans to collectively fast for eight and a half days to prove that people do not expire without food in such a short time. This act of protest ended on September 25, the day that Biko was buried. The fast undertaken by Graham and Santie McIntosh of Cape Town was the most publicized among several others.

10. "A Wreath for Steve."

11. Several Afrikaans newspapers initially denounced the English press as "venomous" toward the police, and *Die Vaderland* dismissed this reporting as "hysterical." *Rapport, Die Transvaler, Oggendblad,* and *Die Burger* "were quick to express grave disquiet over the incident and call for a searching inquiry" (Nadere Kennis, "Soul-Searching over Biko"), but George Bizos, an advocate for the Biko family at the inquest, contends that this was mostly because they sought to clear the National Party of any wrongdoing (*No One to Blame?* 48). Letters to editors at *The Star* and the *Rand Daily Mail* indicate that not all readers supported the papers' suspicion of the police.

12. John Patten, "Biko: Hot Issue for Cabinet."

13. The causes of death in all cases were recorded as self-inflicted, accidental, or natural (Bernstein, *No. 46*, 148–50). Few attracted attention. Biko's death was the first to spark

widespread concern among South Africans and international interest into police interrogation methods and prison conditions.

14. Hugh Murray, "Biko's Brain Injured."

15. The final medical report filed with Attorney General of Transvaal J. E. Nothling on October 25, 1977, states that the head injury caused extensive brain damage. A reduction of circulation to other organs followed, complicated by widespread "intravascular coagulation . . . [and] acute renal failure and uremia." It also listed twelve abrasions and bruises on Biko's body, including injuries to his ribs. Pathologists determined that all injuries were sustained within eight days to twelve hours before Biko's death (*The Star*, October 26, 1977). The autopsy report notes an injury to the left thigh that "has the appearances of a healing burn," and multiple fresh, pink scars in the process of healing. "All these abrasions . . . are covered with crusts and suggest macroscopically that they are more or less of the same age" (Johan Loubser, *Report on Autopsy of Steven Biko,* 4.9).

16. "Kruger Denial and a Tape Transcript."

17. Meyer Feldberg, quoted in Terry MacDonough, "Why SA Has Lost Some of Its US Credit Rating."

18. The pamphlet was dated August 18, 1977, the same date that Biko and Jones were detained at the roadblock outside of Port Elizabeth. If nothing else, it was impossible for these men to have authored and published material on the very day that they were caught traveling from Cape Town to King William's Town. By October 6, Kruger claimed that he never said Biko had authored this material; rather, he said Biko had been detained in connection with it ("Kruger Quotes Biko Pamphlet"). It is well known, however, that Biko was detained because he broke his banning order.

19. "Prime Minister Must Sack Mr. Kruger."

20. Ike Motsapi, "BPC Chief Speaks Out."

21. There was some debate as to whether the law banning reproduction of one's likeness or words was still in effect if the subject died while the ban was still in effect. It was common to err on the side of caution.

22. Donald Woods, "A Great Man Dies."

23. The *New York Times* interview was conducted by John Burns in 1976. See also "Biko Predicted Violence—Report."

24. Munich TV taped an interview with Biko shortly before his final arrest that is well known. It runs on a continuous loop at the Apartheid Museum near Johannesburg. The British Broadcasting Corporation (BBC) aired it in 1977.

25. "After Biko's Death."

26. Jennifer Hyman, "Steve Biko."

27. Tomaselli and Louw, "The South African Progressive Press under Emergency, 1986–1989," 23, 99. *The World* was originally founded as *Bantu World* in 1932. It changed its name in 1955. It was among those nineteen BC-influenced organizations banned by the state on October 19, 1977.

28. "Death of a Martyr."

29. Little has been recorded about Donald Kenyon; sadly, such is the history of many

artists who devote themselves principally to cartooning. He was born in the Transkei and spoke Xhosa as well as his native English. He was once a magistrate but left this profession to draw full time. He joined the *Daily Dispatch* in November 1964 and primarily drew political cartoons and caricatures over more than two decades. He gifted the portrait discussed here to the Woods family.

30. Richard Brilliant, "Portraits: A Recurrent Genre in World Art," 20.

31. The painting was reproduced at least one more time, in *The Sowetan,* January 29, 1991, 7.

32. Since at least the mid-nineteenth century, wreaths have been made as funeral objects to "soften the remembrance [of the deceased] by only indirectly referring to death" (Jay Ruby, *Secure the Shadow: Death and Photography in America,* 137). Kgware's choice of a watercolor portrait of Biko rather than a photograph is in line with this aesthetic. In addition to the wreaths mentioned here, others were displayed in varied locations throughout the country.

33. Bizos, *No One to Blame?* 54.

34. David Kunzle, *Che Guevara: Icon, Myth, and Message,* 22.

35. Quoted in Nunka Mkhalipe, "Motlana Blames Govt for Biko Death."

36. "Prime Minister Must Sack Mr. Kruger."

37. Small, "Steve Biko," 23, 27.

38. The Afrikaans newspaper *Die Beeld* reported that the police began investigating select South African newspapers after they printed photographs of Biko in his coffin ("Biko foto's ondersoek").

39. Veena Das, "Language and Body," 78.

40. Ramphele, "Political Widowhood in South Africa," 102.

41. Though the work's physical prominence was certainly overstated in the film *Cry Freedom* in which a sea of posters consumes the crowd (see chapter 5), the footage reflects the overwhelming influence this hypericon has had on Biko's legacy.

42. Brilliant, "Portraits," 14. For a discussion of how emblems can become portraits, Brilliant also writes, "Like the emblem, the 'what' represented by the attribute contributes to the viewer's knowledge of the 'who' portrayed" (ibid.). The conflation of emblem and person occurred in South African debates in the weeks following Biko's death. Once again, Kruger stirred controversy by repeatedly using the phrase *Black Power* to describe the emblem and the ideology of those people who used it—"Marxist conspirators," he claimed, who aimed to overthrow the state. Thereafter, newspapers with largely white readerships continued to use this term *(New Mercury, Sunday Express)* and even called Biko a "Black Power activist" ("Ondersoek na Biko"). Major Harold Snyman also used the words at the inquest to describe Kruger's understanding of Biko (Carol Steyn and Helen Zille, title unavailable). Conversely, BPC president Hlaku Kenneth Rachidi issued a statement in September 1977 that rejected the equation of Black Consciousness with Black Power and emphasized the BPC's promotion of nonviolent protest, among other things. He said that the organization viewed communism and capitalism as equally abhorrent (M. Duff, "BPC Case for Black Consciousness").

43. Funerals became important sites of political protest because they were not subject to the Riotous Assemblies Act (1956), which penalized public protest of the South African government and its laws.

44. Bernstein, *No. 46*, 25. Among others, eight thousand people reportedly came to services at Soweto's historic Regina Mundi Church. Thousands more attended commemorations in Durban's Emmanuel Cathedral. At St. Paul's Cathedral in London, dignitaries from Australia, Belgium, Britain, Brazil, Canada, France, Italy, the United States, and West Germany attended a service in Biko's honor. While no official of the South African government attended, at least two notable politicians did: Helen Suzman and Zac de Beer, both of the Progressive Federal Party ("Police Will Protect Town—in Case").

45. Other clergy included Reverends Pat Ncaca, Leo Rakale, Drake Tahenkeng, Geoffrey Moselane, and Mcebisi Xundu.

46. This and other bible verses are taken from the *King James Version*.

47. Emphasis mine. Until 1997, the cemetery where Biko is buried was called Leighton-ville Cemetery. It was renamed in his honor in September 1997 along with a bridge in East London. It is now called the Garden of Remembrance.

48. Included were Hlaku Rachidi and Thandisiwe Mazikbuko, both of BPC; Ntato Motlana, BCP; Faouk Meer, Natal Indian Congress; Fikile Bam, Zimelle Trust Fund; and a representative of SWAPO.

49. Rachidi, "Tribute to Steve Biko—King William's Town," 8. The quotations that follow are also from this source.

50. Philippe Ariés, *The Hour of Our Death*, 118.

51. I have chosen to discuss Mr. Biko as a subject body—that is, a person who retains his identity despite his death. Although a corpse (the material remains of a death) is regarded as "the utmost of abjection" (Julia Kristeva, *Powers of Horror: An Essay on Abjection*, 4), it is not an object body for the people entrusted with its last presentation. Kristeva does distinguish between contexts of viewing: "Rites are *acts* rather than *symbols*. In other words, rites would not be limited to their signifying dimension, they would also have a material, active, translinguistic, magical impact" (73–74).

52. Elizabeth Hallam, Jenny Hockey, and Glennys Howarth, *Beyond the Body: Death and Social Identity*, 31.

53. Ibid., 32.

54. Kristeva, *Powers of Horror*, 126.

55. Ariés, *Hour of Our Death*, 260.

56. Quoted in Mandla Ndlazi, "'Hundreds of Bikos Around.'"

57. There is precedent for this, but it is rare. Ariés records a custom enacted for Polish lords of the seventeenth and eighteenth centuries wherein their features were carved on their coffins. These were visible during the funeral proceedings and then naturally buried afterward (*Hour of Our Death*, 171).

58. "Death Not in Vain—BPC."

59. Hallam, Hockey, and Howarth, *Beyond the Body*, 93.

60. Little research has been published concerning associative effects of forensic imagery,

and within that field autopsy is hardly discussed. See ibid.; James Elkins, *Pictures of the Body: Pain and Metamorphosis*; Sandra S. Phillips, Mark Haworth-Booth, and Carol Squiers, *Police Pictures: The Photograph as Evidence*; Ralph Rugoff, *Scene of the Crime*; John Tagg, *The Burden of Representation*; and Shannen Hill, "Iconic Autopsy: Postmortem Portraits of Bantu Stephen Biko."

61. Rugoff, *Scene of the Crime*, 91.

62. Hallam, Hockey, and Howarth, *Beyond the Body*, 88.

63. A selection of forensic imagery originally prepared for the November 1977 inquest is on file at the Mayibuye Centre at the University of the Western Cape. The autopsy report prepared by Johan Loubser is available at the South African History Archive at the University of the Witwatersrand. Most of the police reports regarding Biko's last detention cannot be found. They are likely among the state documents that were destroyed between 1990 and 1994 (Michelle Pickover, personal correspondence, 1999). The Truth and Reconciliation Commission studied this method of concealing gross human rights violations.

64. The films and photographs of Nontsikelelo Biko during this period convey dignity and restraint despite the enormity of her loss. So, too, do the images of other members of Steve Biko's larger family. At the time of the inquest, Biko's widow told *DRUM*, "I am not bitter, nor even amazed—but I was not officially informed of Steve's death or even his detention this time. I learned of his detention through newspapers and heard about his death from my sister-in-law, Nobandile. Up to now I still have not been officially informed" (Stan Motjuwadi, "Ntsiki Biko: The Last Time I Saw My Husband Alive"). For an interesting study of how female survivors of political leaders—particularly mothers and wives—must alter their mourning to suit the needs of the parties to which their beloved belonged, see Ramphele, "Political Widowhood in South Africa."

65. For images contained within the *DRUM* article, see Hill, "Iconic Autopsy: Postmortem Portraits of Bantu Stephen Biko."

66. James Elkins reflects on death as the ultimate reality by calling it "the state without distortion" (*Pictures of the Body*, 22). Distortion, he argues, is the very essence of representation, and it is dependent on motion. The dead cannot move, thus representations of the dead somehow seem beyond the representable and thus "without distortion."

67. Small, "Steve Biko," 27. Emphasis in original.

68. Hallam, Hockey, and Howarth, *Beyond the Body*, 98.

69. "South Africa Orders Inquest into Biko's Death in Jail."

70. This location has a fascinating history. Founded in 1898 as the first Jewish place of worship in Pretoria, in 1952 it was expropriated by the government to house the nation's Supreme Court. Soon after, the state decided to use it for hearings related to security matters alone. The infamous Treason Trial of 156 activists ran here between 1958 and 1961. All were found innocent and acquitted. Equally important, the Rivonia Trial was also heard here in 1962. The judgment herein led to the long imprisonment of leaders within the African National Congress, including Nelson Mandela and Walter Sisulu. In a 1967 trial, Eliaser Tuhadeleni and thirty-six other Namibian patriots were charged—in this foreign South African court—to life imprisonment under the Terrorism Act of 1967. Winnie Mandela

and twenty-one other activists were also tried here under this act, acquitted, and immediately redetained in 1969. The 1976 trial of the SASO Nine was conducted in this building (see chapter 1). After the Biko inquest in 1977, the Old Synagogue witnessed other hearings through the years.

71. Sir Sydney Kentridge, father of the artist William Kentridge, was knighted by Britain in 1999 in recognition of his work as a leading advocate for black South Africans in several famous cases.

72. John Ryan, "Hot Time in the Old Temple."

73. Twenty years later, when Peter Jones testified before the Truth and Reconciliation Commission about his experiences as a person detained with Steve Biko, he named Siebert as the person most likely to have dealt the blow that eventually killed him. This belief was based on Jones's abuse at the hands of the same men who had interrogated Biko and Siebert's propensity to target the head when assaulting people. Jones said, "He is an ideologue, a holy man who believes passionately in his cause. He is a much more substantial person in terms of his knowledge, his depth, his viciousness and his capacity for violence" (quoted in Bizos, *No One to Blame?* 95).

74. Bernstein, *No. 46*, 45.

75. Ibid., 45, 46.

76. Quoted in Bernardi Wessels and Helen Zille, "Biko Chained for 48 Hours 'To Protect Him'"; and in Wilson, "Bantu Stephen Biko: A Life," 71.

77. Ryan, "Hot Time in the Old Temple."

78. Quoted in Bernstein, *No. 46*, 53.

79. "'No Evidence Biko Was Beaten Up.'"

80. Bizos, *No One to Blame?* 68.

81. Kentridge quoted in "Police Had Conspiracy of Silence—Kentridge."

82. Ibid.

83. Van Rooyen then countered that Biko was not shown the statements but had been told about them. Magistrate Prins disallowed the "evidence" of the document. Oddly, the decision was reversed two days later and the statements were admitted as evidence—not as a testament to truth but simply to show that they existed. The alleged authors, Titi and Jones, were held under Section Six of the Terrorism Act and could not be called to verify their signatures (Carol Steyn, Bernardi Wessels, and Helen Zille, "Our Technique—by Security Colonel").

84. Bizos, *No One to Blame?* 58.

85. Jones is quoted in Wilson, "Bantu Stephen Biko: A Life," 69–71.

86. Vicki Goldberg, *The Power of Photography: How Photographs Changed Our Lives*, 59–61.

87. Tagg, *The Burden of Representation*, 96–102. The longer quotes that follow are from S. G. Ehrlich, *Photographic Evidence: The Preparation and Use of Photography in Civil and Criminal Cases* (1967), cited by Tagg.

88. Tagg, *Burden of Representation*, 2.

89. Ibid., 99.

90. Kleinhaus merely asked a series of predetermined questions given on a form with multiple answers, a "multiple-choice test." Colonel Goosen was never questioned. Kleinhaus did not conduct searches, nor did he request supportive documents. He belatedly interviewed the district surgeons (one of which was Benjamin Tucker, in the dialogue below) and, like his fellow police officers had done in early September, prompted the use of damning descriptors. These were revealed at the inquest: "KENTRIDGE: 'Aggressive.' That is how General Kleinhaus put it to you. / TUCKER: Yes. / KENTRIDGE: So General Kleinhaus put the words in your mouth. / TUCKER: I wouldn't say he put the words in my mouth, he asked the questions and I answered them" (quoted in Saunders, "The Agony and the Allegory," 245).

91. Hallem, Hockey, and Howarth, *Beyond the Body,* 95.

92. Brilliant, "Portraits," 12, 15.

93. Rockhill, "Translator's Introduction: Jacques Rancière's *Politics of Perception,*" 3.

94. Rancière, *The Politics of Aesthetics,* 36–38.

95. Ibid., 32.

96. Rockhill, "Translator's Introduction," 3.

97. Rugoff, *Scene of the Crime,* 98.

98. Kentridge et al., *Magistrate's Court for the District of Pretoria; Inquest No. 573/1977.*

99. Steyn, Carol, and Helen Zille, title unavailable.

100. Ibid.

101. Bernstein, *No. 46,* 56.

102. Quoted in "Security Man Suspects Biko Suicide Attempt."

103. Helen Zille, "Biko Was Bent on Suicide—Colonel."

104. Bernardi Wessels and Helen Zille, "Biko Chained for 48 Hours 'To Protect Him.'" Not even such a minor wound as a swollen lip was listed on the certificate.

105. Richards, "Drawing a Veil," 9.

106. Bernstein, *No 46,* 59.

107. Carol Steyn, Bernardi Wessels, and Helen Zille, "Medical Certificate Incorrect, Says Doctor."

108. Ibid.

109. Carol Steyn, Melanie Yap, and Helen Zille, "Point of No Return for Biko 'Soon after Injury.'"

110. Carol Steyn, "Bed Letter Wrong, Biko Doctor Admits."

111. Ibid. Of Hersch's written report on the lumbar puncture, Dr. Jonathan Gluckman said it was "nonsense . . . only fit for the wastepaper basket" (Steyn, Yap, and Zille, "Point of No Return for Biko") Oddly, the South African Medical and Dental Council did not censure Hersch for his part in falsifying Biko's records, as it eventually did Lang and Tucker.

112. Steyn, "Bed Letter Wrong."

113. Bizos, *No One to Blame?* 48. This act establishes that only three people can attend an autopsy: the State pathologist, a medical doctor with an abiding interest in the outcome, and a police officer (Brian Bamford, "What's in an Inquest?"). In the case of Steve Biko, it appears that several people were in the room, and Dr. Gluckman was not informed of the autopsy until it was already under way.

114. Helen Zille, "On Seven Foot Chain."

115. "How Many Impacts Caused the Fatal Brain Injuries?"

116. Melanie Yap and Helen Zille, "Injury '4 to 8 Days Old.'" The next quote is also from this source.

117. Wilson, "Bantu Stephen Biko: A Life," 72.

118. Quoted in "No Kruger File, Rules Biko Magistrate."

119. Carol Steyn, "Biko 'Confession Story Fabricated.'" The following quotes are also from this source.

120. Bizos, *No One to Blame?* 70–71.

121. "Finding Disgusts World's Press"; "Outcry in Overseas Press over Decision."

122. Bizos, *No One to Blame?* 71.

123. Quoted in ". . . In Biko Finding."

124. In his review of the inquest, Sir David Napley, an independent observer from London, cited the *Rand Daily Mail* for its "high degree of accuracy, comprehensiveness and objectivity" (cited in Bernstein, *No. 46*, 137).

125. Ibid., 137.

126. Bizos, *No One to Blame?* 74.

127. For Napley's full report, "Stephen Biko Inquest," see Bernstein, *No. 46*, 137–47. The quotes that follow come from this report.

128. Bizos, *No One to Blame?* 5, 84.

129. Also in 2007, the Finney production cycled a regular broadcast on Showtime, an American cable station. This underscores a persistent international interest in the reading of Biko as victim of state abuse. It also shows that Finney's performance as Kentridge endures; he was roundly praised in that role.

130. "Tribute to Biko, Luthuli."

131. "The World Mourns"; "Biko Banner Held High by Cathedral Protester."

132. Bizos, *No One to Blame?* 74.

133. Quoted in ibid., 80.

134. Although this image's original caption suggests it was taken just after the verdict on December 2, 1977, (Magubane, *Women of South Africa: Their Fight for Freedom*), this cannot be true. Steve Biko's mother, Mrs. Alice Duna Biko, is also imaged here, just beyond her daughter-in-law. But Biko's mother did not come to hear the verdict read on the last day. Reasonably, she did not feel well enough to attend.

135. Hallam, Hockey, and Howarth, *Beyond the Body*, 151.

136. Ramphele, "Political Widowhood in South Africa," 110.

3. Contemplating Death

1. An exception is Colin Richards's thought-provoking conference paper titled "Drawing a Veil: Art in the Age of Emergency."

2. All figures were intended to reference detainees generally, but two recalled specific people. One recalled the death of Ahmed Timol, who died as a result of injuries sustained after he was thrown from a window on the tenth floor of John Vorster Square, a place re-

nowned for police abuse of detainees. Installed on the roof, this work was visible from the jail located to the south. Another work recalled the death of George Botha. This was the only titled work within *Figures,* and in 1999 Stopforth asked that its title be changed from *George Botha* to *Detainee,* thereby enabling the work to speak beyond a specific case of torture in detention (Stopforth, email correspondence).

3. Peter Fourie, "Paul Stopforth Speaks to Peter Fourie," 41.

4. Paul Stopforth, interview with author. Unless otherwise cited, such recollections and information about Stopforth's art came from this interview.

5. At the time he made the series, Stopforth did not realize the large number of women and children who were also subjected to torture in South Africa.

6. Pogrund, "Statement of Torture."

7. Bennett, *Empathic Vision: Affect, Trauma, and Contemporary Art,* 8.

8. Ibid., 48.

9. Fourie, "Paul Stopforth Speaks with Peter Fourie," 41.

10. Ibid., 40.

11. Pogrund, "Statement of Torture"; Ozynski, "Three Views of Local Sculpture."

12. Stopforth said that Pogrund had difficulty getting the *Rand Daily Mail* to publish her review because it acknowledged his criticism of the state.

13. Stopforth, "Stopforth: Art as a Political Statement."

14. Fourie, "Paul Stopforth Speaks with Peter Fourie," 40.

15. Kristeva, *Powers of Horror,* 64–65.

16. Duval, "Biko as Martyr."

17. Williamson, *Resistance Art in South Africa,* 112.

18. See Herreman and D'Amato, *Liberated Voices,* for the exhibition catalog.

19. Arendt, *Eichmann in Jerusalem: A Report on the Banality of Evil.*

20. Oppenheimer, *Evil and the Demonic,* 3.

21. See Bernstein, *No. 46* for lengthy inquest transcripts.

22. Amnesty applicants described the chair differently twenty years later before the Truth and Reconciliation Commission. It was Biko's insistence to sit on a chair rather than stand as directed that propelled the onslaught of interrogators. See chapter 6 for more details, particularly discussion of David Koloane's nineteen-part series *The Journey.*

23. Still, when the acquisition committee at the South African National Gallery (now Iziko–South African National Gallery) discussed this work prior to purchase, nothing was said about the violence it represents. Neither the subject nor Stopforth's larger project on detention abuses was discussed at all. Instead, the committee focused on the artist's technique, which was entirely new (Bedford, *Contemporary South African Art, 1985–1995 from the South African National Gallery Permanent Collection,* 27). This history aligns with the culture of censorship that frames chapter 5.

24. Quoted in Duval, "Biko as Martyr."

25. Deleuze is quoted in Bennett, *Empathic Vision,* 36.

26. Kristeva, *Powers of Horror,* 143.

27. Ibid., 44, quoting Louis-Ferdinand Céline, *Journey to the End of the Night* (1934), 59.

28. Figure 3.6 was even reproduced in the press to accompany reporting on the Truth and Reconciliation Commission in 1998. The article was not about Biko, thus this series of engravings now represents a much larger history of bodily abuse in South Africa. One thinks that Stopforth's mission was at last accomplished.

29. For additional reproductions of works in this series, see Deliss, *Seven Stories about Modern Art in Africa*; and Hill, "Iconic Autopsy," among others. Stopforth now asks that the works be titled *Biko Series* (interview with author).

30. Bennett, *Empathic Vision*, 36.

31. Elkins, *Pictures of the Body*, 36, 51 (emphasis in original).

32. Ibid., 43.

33. Kristeva, *Powers of Horror*, 11.

34. Richards, "Drawing a Veil," 16.

35. Ibid., 46.

36. Ibid., 17.

37. Ndebele, *South African Literature and Culture: Rediscovery of the Ordinary*.

38. Quoted in Matsemela Manaka, *Steve Biko: Journey of the Spirit*; see chapter 6 for longer excerpt.

39. The renamed works are given different titles in the literature—called *Biko I* and *Biko II* (Richards, "Drawing a Veil," 11)—but here I use titles that Stopforth cited in our February 2000 interview.

40. Kristeva, *Powers of Horror*, 102.

41. Musa Mncwabe, personal communication.

42. Kristeva, *Powers of Horror*, 9.

43. Mendelson, "The Body in the Next Room," 195.

44. Williamson, *Resistance Art*, 112.

45. Mendelson, "Body in the Next Room," 197–98. Emphasis mine.

46. David's masterpiece is an icon of the French Revolution. Jean-Paul Marat was, like Biko, trained in medicine, a well-known activist, and an outspoken populist journalist. He was aligned with Montegnard, and Paris deputy to the National Convention in September 1792 together with David. He was stabbed to death by Marie-Anne Charlotte Corday of Caen, a Girondin sympathizer, on the evening of July 13, 1793, while bathing. David, who was friend to Marat and had seen him in the tub on a visit the previous day, was quickly commissioned to paint his portrait. He chose to capture Marat at the moment of his final breath thereby depicting, in Aristotelian terms, his soul. David's version "represents a single moment of suspense. . . . [It] is a laconic transparent work, a history painting and an icon whose power to fascinate has hardly diminished since the day of its first exhibition" (Vaughn and Weston, *Jacques-Louis David's Marat*, 7–8). Arthur Danto, among others, has analyzed David's *The Death of Marat* as paralleling Christ's body as it was removed from the cross ("Painting and Politics").

47. Kristeva, *Powers of Horror*, 112.

48. Das, "Language and Body: Transaction in the Construction of Pain."

49. Kristeva, *Powers of Horror,* 129.

50. Elsa Miles clears up confusion among historians about the chronology of Polly Street tutelage in *Polly Street: The Story of an Art Centre* (14–16, 36, 136). The Polly Street Art Centre was established in 1949. It moved units (beginning with music) to the Bantu Men's Social Centre (also called the Jubilee Social Centre) on Eloff Street between 1957 and 1960 but was still sometimes called Polly Street. It moved once more to Mofolo Art Centre in 1969.

51. Ibid., 16.

52. Legae called this series *Death of Freedom* (Linda Goodman [now Givon], unpublished interview with Ezrom Legae, 1984), as does Barbara Buntman (*Ezrom Legae, 1976-1986,* 25–27), but most publications record it as *Freedom Is Dead.* Legae's chosen title is used here. E. J. de Jager reports that the series *Chicken* was also known as the *Jail Series* (*Images of Man,* 115), but perhaps this name was only spoken aloud since my research uncovered no other published reference of this title.

53. Quoted in Friedman, "It's a Privilege to Remember Legae."

54. Das, "Language and Body," 88.

55. Kristeva, *Powers of Horror,* 141.

56. Goodman, unpublished interview with Ezrom Legae, 1–2.

57. Kristeva, *Powers of Horror,* 5. Emphasis in original.

58. Louis-Ferdinand Céline, quoted in Kristeva, *Powers of Horror,* 155.

59. Kristeva, *Powers of Horror,* 10. Emphasis in original.

60. Ibid., 76.

61. Goodman, unpublished interview, 2.

62. Kristeva, *Powers of Horror,* 8. Emphasis in original.

63. Antonin Artaud, quoted in Kristeva, *Powers of Horror,* 25.

64. Ibid, 4. Emphasis in original. The next quotation comes from the same source.

65. Richards, "Drawing a Veil," 10.

66. Both Barbara Buntman ("Ezrom Legae") and Colin Richards ("Drawing a Veil") call the work *Freedom Is Dead,* but the title I use is more common. They suggest that the title may have prompted the funding government agency, South Africa's Department of Information, to pull the work from inclusion. Richards argues that the decision was motivated by the belief that "the threat of Black Consciousness culture and the death of one of its foremost activists might infiltrate and contaminate the avian metaphor" (Richards, "Drawing a Veil," 9–10).

67. See Geers, *Contemporary South African Art: The Gencor Collection,* for more illustrations.

68. See Kristeva, *Powers of Horror,* 6–7, for a theory of the conditions that link abjection and its ultimate rejection of representation to a common experience, birth, which is inevitably gendered through the mother, purveyor of desire and its refusal.

69. Buntman, "Ezrom Legae, 1976–1986," 26.

70. Ibid., 27.

71. Kristeva, *Powers of Horror,* 3.

72. Ibid., 156.

4. Creating a Culture of Resistance

1. The epigraph above is courtesy of Christopher van Wyk. Christopher van Wyk founded *Staffrider,* a literary journal that printed the writings and art of black South Africans, for the most part. This important journal was fundamentally a product of Black Consciousness.

2. For example, see Peffer, *Art and the End of Apartheid,* 50; and *Medu Art Ensemble Newsletter* 3, no. 1.

3. Seidman, *Red on Black,* 90.

4. Peffer, *Art and the End of Apartheid,* 51–52.

5. Ibid., 50, 74, 85. Deeply invested in political history and visual culture, I cannot help but see such threads popping up as I read scholarly interpretations that do not invest equal energy in both. These signs are troublingly just below surface. In writing across disciplines we cannot take one or the other for granted.

6. At the trial of the SASO–BPC Nine in May 1976, Biko said, "We believe that there is a way of getting across to where we want to go through peaceful means. And the very fact that we decided to actually form an aboveboard movement implies that we accepted certain legal limitations to our operations. We accepted that we are going to take this particular course. We know that the road to that particular truth is fraught with danger. Some of us get banned, like I am. Others get arrested, like these men who are here. But inevitably the process drives toward what we believe history also drives to: an attainment of a situation where Whites first have to listen. I don't believe that Whites will be deaf all of the time" (quoted in Arnold, *Steve Biko: Black Consciousness in South Africa,* 70).

7. In my 1997 interview with him, Paul Stewart, who worked with Progress Press, described the influence of Black Consciousness as widespread but "suffuse" within organizations of the 1980s. He said BC was "like salt you throw in a pot. Now it has taste. It's flavored." It was BC, he said, that "helped white liberals develop their own consciousness." At the time I was researching a different topic, but this comment stuck with me. I thank him for the insight.

8. Innumerable political bodies benefited from the state's banning of Black Consciousness affiliates in October 1977; just a few are studied here. In April 1978, BC activists exiled in London formed the Black Consciousness Movement of South Africa. The organization changed its name to the Black Consciousness Movement of Azania (BCMA) in April 1980. It remained operative in exile until 1994, when it relocated its base to South Africa and joined forces with Azanian People's Organization (AZAPO) in national and regional elections that year. Also in April 1978, AZAPO took root near Johannesburg as the first political party in South Africa to adopt BC ideology as part of its platform. In November 1979, the Azanian Students' Organization (AZASO) formed. Exiled but active apartheid resistance organizations also benefited from the state's intensified suppression of BC. The African National Congress is the most obvious of these.

9. This and following quotes come from Arnold, *Steve Biko,* 32, 47, 206.

10. The ANC promoted multiracialism, itself an acceptance of difference, until the early 1970s when it opted for nonracialist terminology that sought to diminish it. Crucially, Black

Consciousness and Black Theology had started to take root in this period. The term *non-racial* dates to the mid- to late nineteenth century, but as it gained widespread currency in the 1980s (and was frequently described as a "conscientized" position), I see it as a response to Black Consciousness, one reflective of a demand that whiteness be present.

11. The most readily available sources include his "Quest for a True Humanity," 70, 95–96; and "Black Souls in White Skins," 24, in *I Write What I Like*; and Arnold, *Steve Biko*, 219–20.

12. Peffer, *Art and the End of Apartheid*, 74–81; Gary Van Wyk, "Reflecting Democracy," 5; Wylie, *Art + Revolution*, 110, 129. Judy Seidman handles this history with care in a section called ". . . Distancing Black Consciousness," *Red on Black*, 90–91.

13. Elizabeth Morton [Gron], "Exchange and Impact of South African Exiles in Botswana," 75.

14. A. W. Oliphant and Ivan Vladislavić, *Ten Years of Staffrider 1978–1988*, preface (n.p.).

15. Kirkwood, "Remembering *Staffrider*," 5. In the collected volume of *Staffrider*'s best, editors chose to include Mutloatse's "Ngwana wa Azania: A Film Concept." It follows a "recalcitrant Azanian child" from age two to seventeen when "this child of bastardized society and bastard people-in-high-office and colour-obsessed and paranoid of communism and humanism, shall break through and *snap the chain of repression* with its bare hands, and this child, with its rotten background and slightly bleak future shall however liberate this nuclear crazy world with *Nkulunkulu's greatest gift to man: Ubuntu*" (61). Recalling that Biko wished to "bestow upon South Africa the greatest gift possible: a more human face," we see that BC is woven into the language of ubuntu that was later widely promoted by the South African state beginning in the early 1990s. This element of Black Consciousness is discussed in greater detail in chapter 6.

16. See Oliphant and Vladislavić, *Ten Years of Staffrider*, for primary voices in this debate, especially *Staffrider* and Christopher van Wyk in conversation, 165–70.

17. Christopher van Wyk, *Staffrider* editor for six years, had this to say in response to whether the skin color of contributors provided evidence of BC: "This . . . is a typical response of someone conditioned by Apartheid. On the other hand, the relationship between a cultural magazine like *Staffrider* and broader political thinking is a very complicated matter, especially when contending ideologies and political positions make claims to a magazine on the grounds of what they see, or imagine they see reflected in it. However, what remains crucial for me with regard to the establishment of *Staffrider* as well as *Wietie* [a BC-oriented journal founded in 1980] is that the notion of magazines controlled by blacks was the direct result of the self-reliant philosophy of BC. This philosophy, which was by no means a form of racial exclusivity was, I think, operative for only a brief phase in the (editorial) history of the magazine and certainly gave way to the openly declared non-racial position of the eighties" (van Wyk, "CHRISTOPHER VAN WYK: *Staffrider* and the Politics of Culture," 168).

18. Serote, "Time Has Run Out." The following excerpts are all from this single poem, which is lengthy. The September 16–22, 1977 issue of *Variety* erroneously attributes a portion of this poem to another author, Mandlenkosi Mandla.

19. Quoted in Jaki Seroke, "Poet in Exile: An Interview with Mongane Serote," 32. The interview is among the features highlighted on the issue's cover. Subsequent quotes in this paragraph are also from this source.

20. Wylie, *Art + Revolution,* 111.

21. Ibid., 121.

22. Morton [Gron], "Exchange and Impact," 14.

23. Mbulelo Mzamane is the best source for Black Consciousness writers of all kinds. See his *New Poets of the Soweto Era: Van Wyk, Johennesse, and Madingoane*; and "The Impact of Black Consciousness on Culture."

24. Morton [Gron], "Exchange and Impact," 20–21.

25. Seidman, *Red on Black,* 91.

26. Morton [Gron], "Exchange and Impact," 21; Wylie, *Art + Revolution,* 123.

27. Gonzalez worked at a Swedish aid mission in Gaborone, and Devant, his wife, trained in progressive theater in Barcelona and Sweden (Wylie, *Art + Revolution,* 123).

28. Mandla Langa, "Cultural Invasion," 24.

29. Morton [Gron], "Exchange and Impact," 16. Morton cites an interview with Tim Williams here. Morton's master's thesis is exhaustively researched and cites valuable primary and rare secondary sources. In a 1998 interview, Judy Seidman told me that Medu saw "itself as the ANC cultural wing, prior to the existence of an ANC cultural wing."

30. Wylie, *Art + Revolution,* 110; Peffer, *Art and the End of Apartheid,* 74; G. Van Wyk, "Reflecting Democracy," 5.

31. "Editorial," *Medu Art Ensemble Newsletter.*

32. Mongane Serote, "Ngwedi Graphic Art Unit," 26.

33. Judy Seidman, 1999 interview with author.

34. Thami Mnyele, "Thoughts for Bongiwe," 299.

35. "Fine Art and Political Reality," 16. Emphasis in original.

36. Quoted in Arnold, *Steve Biko,* 140–41.

37. Judy Seidman, a member of Medu for most of this time, reports that the collective made more than fifty posters. Her book *Red on Black: The Story of the South African Poster Movement* records the history of this medium and is richly illustrated. See also *Images of Defiance: South African Resistance Posters of the 1980s* by the Poster Book Collective.

38. Worden, *The Making of Modern South Africa: Conquest, Apartheid, Democracy,* 111; and Clarke and Worger, *South Africa: The Rise and Fall of Apartheid,* 57.

39. Wylie, *Art + Revolution,* 128. Mnyele drew the cover design for at least two of the collective's earliest newsletters. In its second year, the newsletter featured his work several times in an interview with, images by, and articles about Mnyele (vol. 2, nos. 1 and 2). His work is featured again in vol. 5, no. 2. I thank Judy Seidman for sharing her archive with me.

40. Ibid., 129.

41. In a valued biography that emphasizes the politics of nonracialism, Wylie writes that Mnyele's choice reflected a concomitant reversal of BC ideals since this ideology was one that Medu members "knew barely anything about" (ibid., 124). She is mistaken.

42. Mnyele, opening remarks, *Art toward Social Development—An Exhibition of South African Art*, National Museum and Gallery of Art, Botswana, July 1982.

43. After Mnyele's death, Christopher van Wyk wrote the following poem called "We Can't Meet Here, Brother (for Thami Mnyele)": "We can't meet here, brother. / We can't talk here in this cold stone world / where whites buy time on credit cards. // I can't hear you, brother! / for the noise of the theorists / and the clanging machinery of the liberal Press! // I want to smell the warmth of your friendship, Thami / Not the pollution of gunsmoke and white suicides. // We can't meet here, brother. / Let's go to your home / Where we can stroll in the underbrush of your paintings / Discuss colour / Hone assegais on the edges of serrated tongues." Courtesy of Christopher van Wyk. Cited in Oliphant and Vladislavić, *Ten Years of Staffrider*, 186.

44. Seidman, 1998 interview with author. The image appears in Albie Sachs, *Images of a Revolution: Mural Art in Mozambique*.

45. Tambo, "Mobilise Our Black Power," www.nelsonmandela.org/omalley/index.php/site/q/03lv02424/04lv02730/05lv02918/06lv02977.htm.

46. He thus respectively honored Zulu, Basotho, Xhosa, and ANC leaders.

47. Wylie, *Art + Revolution*, 93. For Biko's testimony on this topic, see Arnold, *Steve Biko*, especially days one and three.

48. See Biko's "White Racism and Black Consciousness" and "The Quest for a True Humanity," both in *I Write What I Like* (70, 94, respectively).

49. See Mneyle 1980 interview by Timothy Williams, *Medu Art Ensemble Newsletter*.

50. For documented examples, see, among others, from the *Medu Art Ensemble Newsletter*: Thami Mnyele, "Interview with Tim Williams"; the Medu Women, "Women and Culture"; Mongane Serote, "Ngwedi Graphic Art Unit." For reference of this term's use at the Culture and Resistance festival, see Dikobé Martins, "The Necessity of a National Art for Liberation"; Cynthia Kross, "Culture and Resistance." For general use, see Jaki Seroke, "Poet in Exile: An Interview with Mongane Serote." I have noted that white South Africans use the word to describe their own ambitions vis-à-vis political printmaking in the 1980s: Morice Smithers, interview with author; Paul Stewart, interview with author; Mario Pissarra in conversation with author. Artist and scholar Gary Van Wyk infers that it informed his work as well, "Reflecting Democracy," 5.

51. Kross, "Culture and Resistance," 11.

52. Mnyele, "Opening Remarks," 3.

53. Gavin Jantjes is quoted in Peffer, *Art and the End of Apartheid*, 86.

54. Martins, "Necessity of a National Art for Liberation."

55. Abdullah Ibrahim is quoted in Kross, "Culture and Resistance," 11. John Peffer correctly notes that Ibrahim's words "resonated with the fundamental Black Consciousness goal of unlearning the ingrained psychology of apartheid by resisting despair and negativity," but Peffer errs in summarizing BC as a "racially separatist perspective" (*Art and the End of Apartheid*, 85).

56. See, among others, *State of the Art* (conference proceedings); Peffer, *Art and the End of*

Apartheid, chapter 3; Van Wyk, "Reflecting Democracy"; Seidman, *Red on Black*; Seidman, "Finding Community Voice." This list is hardly exhaustive.

57. Peffer, *Art and the End of Apartheid*, 97.

58. John Berndt, 1997 interview with author; Lionel Davis, 2011 interview with author. Seidman identifies the addition a "Production Unit," *Red on Black*, 111.

59. Morice Smithers, who founded the STP together with Jon Campbell in November 1983, did not attend the Gaborone festival since he was banned at the time. STP's roots were laid in 1979 when Smithers and Campbell began producing posters in support of trade unions on strike. By 1981 they started the graphics workshop Raw Materials Project, but their work was violently disrupted when the police raided and "smashed up" the site. Smithers and Campbell were detained for some months thereafter and banned on release (Smithers, 1999 interview with author).

60. Seidman, *Red on Black*, 127.

61. Peffer, *Art and the End of Apartheid*, 88–92; Judy Seidman, 1998 interview with author. Seidman traveled under cover from Gaborone to Cape Town to attend the UDF's launch. She then reported on it through the *Medu Art Ensemble Newsletter* under the name "Linda."

62. Peffer, *Art and the End of Apartheid*, 88, 91.

63. Seekings, *The UDF: A History of the United Democratic Front in South Africa 1983–1991*, 30. Chapter 2 of this book is my source for the present discussion, particularly 29–38.

64. Ibid., 33.

65. Ibid., 34.

66. The UDF was a federation of regional bodies, each of which matched the character of its resident organizations. It was not a political party that one could join, thus it never had members. Its affiliates were independent and autonomous in relation to it. Seekings details UDF structures and cautions that despite intent they intruded on affiliates' activities nonetheless. He supports Tom Lodge's view that the UDF functioned "more in the fashion of a social movement than a deliberately contrived political machine" (cited in ibid., 15.)

67. Ibid., 92.

68. Smithers, interview with author.

69. Between 1997 and 1999, I interviewed Smithers and Addison Nxele of STP, Seidman of Medu, John Berndt and Lionel Davis of CAP Media, Marlene Powell and Charlotte Sheer of the Congress of South African Trade Unions, Paul Stewart and Jean de la Harpe of Progress Press, and Chris de Villiers of the End Conscription Campaign. Each described effective imagery in roughly the same way. Steven Sack, a well-known arts activist, scholar, and curator, shared their views in our interview of 1998.

70. Seidman, *Red on Black*, 74.

71. Report to UDF Regional General Council, cited in Seekings, *The UDF*, 93.

72. Seidman, *Red on Black*, 72. Although Seidman does not cite her source, the words are like those generally published by Medu.

73. Denis MacShane, Martin Plaut, and David Ward, *Power! Black Workers, Their Unions and the Struggle for Freedom in South Africa*, 43.

74. The Bantu Self-Government Act (1959) enabled the creation of ten homelands or "Bantustans" that were ostensibly independent of South Africa and designated territory for Africans based on lineage or tribe. Transkei, the first Bantustan, was designated in 1976; others followed in close succession.

75. Quoted in MacShane et al., *Power!* 45.

76. This region of South Africa, known as the "cradle of black resistance" (Julie Frederikse, *South Africa: A Different Kind of War*, 111), includes the Biko family home of Ginsberg. In this interesting turn, Lieutenant General Xhanti Charles Sebe, who directed security for the Ciskei, had been assigned to spy on Biko when he worked for the South African police in the mid-1970s (Clarke and Worger, *South Africa: The Rise and Fall of Apartheid*, 68).

77. Seekings, *UDF*, 20. The Screen Training Project had been banned in 1986, and Morice Smithers was detained for several months yet again. But he and others continued to produce protest graphics upon release by working in whatever space was available. Steven Sack recalls posters being made in the hallways of row houses that were occupied by like-minded activists, musicians, artists, and lawyers who lived in cooperatives (1998 interview with author). Seekings similarly reports, "Political education and media were nationally based activities. . . . these activities had gone semi-underground during the State of Emergency, and stayed there after the Emergency was lifted" (*UDF*, 189).

78. Most of the acronyms on this poster are those of student and/or youth organizations, or those with relevance to youth (e.g., the End Conscription Campaign, the ECC). Many are also worker-led organizations.

79. Gavin Younge, *Art of the South African Townships*, 19.

80. Hlaku Rachidi, last president of the Black Peoples' Convention, repeatedly emphasized this to the press in the last quarter of 1977. See George Frederickson, "Black Power in the United States and Black Consciousness in South Africa," for further analysis.

81. Seekings, *UDF*, 173. For discussion of SASO's community initiatives, see Mamphela Ramphele, "Empowerment and Symbols of Hope"; and Mzamane et al., "The Black Consciousness Movement."

82. Seekings, *UDF*, 173.

5. Silencing the Censors

1. Merrett, *A Culture of Censorship*.

2. Bizos contends that the Bureau of State Security (BOSS) began interrogating and killing political activists without arresting them in the 1980s because the state didn't want "another Biko" on its hands (*No One to Blame?* 84). Detainee deaths were certainly curtailed post-1977.

3. Recruits waged war against South Africa beyond its borders as the nation assumed significant roles in the wars that created Namibia, Angola, Zimbabwe, and Mozambique. See Phyllis Johnson and David Martin, *Apartheid Terrorism*; and William Minter, *Apartheid's Contras*.

4. In the visual arts, only Matsemela Manaka, in *Echoes of African Art*, and Steven Sack, in *The Neglected Tradition*, saw BC as operative in the works of artists they consider. More

recently, John Peffer, in *Art and the End of Apartheid,* nods toward BC's impact (159) in a book that otherwise views BC as racially determined (50, 74).

5. Although the National Union of South African Students used *non-racial* to describe its constitution in the 1960s, the effect of the term within black communities was marginal. Until about 1971, the ANC cited the Freedom Charter of 1955, a document signed by four parties—itself (then with black members only), the South African Indian Congress, the Coloured Peoples' Congress, and the Congress of Democrats (with white members only)—to describe its makeup as the Congress Alliance. The Charter is significant to most because it showed that people of different parties shared common goals. Of primary interest to me in this context is that these signatories belonged to parties that were segregated by the very racial boundaries mandated by the state.

6. By emphasizing that BC centered on voice, I do not mean to diminish the experiences of people who have been subject to race-based hatred in the name of BC. Racism is regrettably present in our lives. I believe racial interpretations of BC to be the least productive since they are short-sighted. They close doors, effectively silencing their target, instead of opening them in order to educate.

7. Merrett, *Culture of Censorship,* 80.

8. Marian Shinn, "Steve Biko's Death Could Have Been Kept a Secret."

9. Tyson, "Can You Bear Those Cries?"

10. Merrett, *Culture of Censorship,* 95.

11. Ibid., 114; Susan de Villiers, *Derek Bauer,* 1.

12. Hill, "South African Street Arts," 2298.

13. Van Rooyen is quoted in Merrett, *Culture of Censorship,* 81, 83.

14. Ebersohn included a disclaimer: "This story is not derived from a knowledge of actual incidents or real people" (*Store Up the Anger,* 6), but many details in his narrative suggest otherwise. The novel unfolds through the perspective of its central character, Sam Bhengu, an activist who is already injured and dying when we meet him. Time is woven between the present—in which Bhengu's health deteriorates after repeated blows from his interrogators that left "his brain . . . like a ping-pong ball inside his head" (111)—and the past. Bhengu remembers, among other things, his days as a leader in student politics, his work with "the Convention" [short for Black Peoples' Convention] (132), and his brand of activism, which promoted "self-respect" (89), nonviolence (97), and was symbolized by "the black power salute" (78). Further allusions to Biko's death in detention are made through dates (Bhengu is arrested for a pamphlet written August 18, the date that Biko was taken into custody), the belief that Bhengu might be shamming symptoms since he "studied medicine for three years" (40), and the name of a police officer, van Rooyen, which was the name of the state's lead counsel at the 1977 inquest. Bhengu eventually dies of "brain damage" (122). Several other parallels are drawn between Bhengu and Biko.

15. Merrett, *A Culture of Censorship,* 80.

16. Poster Book Collective, *Images of Defiance*; Jon Berndt, *From Weapon to Ornament*; Judy Seidman, *Red on Black*; John Peffer, *Art and the End of Apartheid*; Clive Kellner and Sergio-Albio González, *Thami Mnyele + MEDU.*

17. Poster Book Collective, *Images of Defiance*, 2.

18. Smithers, interview with author.

19. Asha Moodley, interview with author. In the years before his death, Biko was detained six times. In 1975, he was held for 137 days without charge or trial. In 1976, he spent 101 days in solitary confinement. On those occasions when charges were laid, they included breaking banning orders, defeating the ends of justice, and conspiring to commit sabotage. He was never found guilty of any charge (Bernstein, *No. 46*, 9–10).

20. Barry Streek, "Biko Image Goes on Growing."

21. Ibid. For the biographies, see Bernstein, *No. 46*; Stubbs edited *I Write What I Like*, a collection of Biko's writings that are universally cited under the surname Biko; and Arnold, *Steve Biko*. For banned films, see Peter Davis, *In Darkest Hollywood: Exploring the Jungles of Cinema's South Africa*. The banned play, *The Biko Inquest*, was by Jon Blair and Norman Fenton (Streek, "Biko Image Goes on Growing").

22. Sack, "Garden of Eden or Political Landscape?" 194; Sack, "Work by Collectives," 80. In several articles from 1986 to 1990, Sack discusses People's Parks, which Sue Williamson calls Peace Parks in her well-known book *Resistance Art in South Africa* (88–89). Of these, Mamelodi's parks are best documented.

23. Sack, interview with author.

24. Sack, "Garden of Eden or Political Landscape?" 208.

25. Ibid., 209. In fact, few People's Parks were photographed because regulations effected under the state of emergency forbade journalists from entering sites of unrest (ibid., 250; Merrett, *Culture of Censorship*, 119).

26. Portraiture appears to have been rare in this genre. Since the photograph used for Biko's funeral portrait was reproduced more often than any other of him at this time (making it a hypericon: see chapter 2), the makers of this monument in Mohlakeng likely used it as a template.

27. Sack, "Work by Collectives," 81; Williamson, *Resistance Art in South Africa*, 72.

28. Merrett, *Culture of Censorship*, 81. Van Rooyen identified these as pamphlets, but such popular media as T-shirts, posters, and murals were likewise banned on this premise.

29. Soon after, "the shadow of Steve Biko" registered in other realms of police misconduct (Wendy Orr, *From Biko to Basson*, 8). In September, Dr. Wendy Orr, a district surgeon in Port Elizabeth, filed forty-four affidavits with the province's supreme court following an investigation she led into the injuries detainees sustained while being interrogated by local security police since July 21, the date that a state of emergency was declared nationwide. The evidence amassed was so overwhelming that the presiding judge granted a temporary interdict against the Port Elizabeth police (ibid., 5, 14). The next month, and after an eight-year campaign that was regularly reported on in the press, the Transvaal Supreme Court found the so-called Biko doctors, Ivor Lang and Benjamin Tucker (district surgeons who oversaw his care in 1977), guilty of improper conduct, with Tucker also guilty of disgraceful conduct. Their sentences, however, were not severe. Tucker was suspended for three months, though the penalty was postponed for two years on condition that he would not commit a similar offense. During that time he retired with full benefits. Lang was suspended for three years,

but "this suspension was conditionally suspended for two years," so his practice continued; indeed, the Department of Health promoted him to Tucker's former position as Port Elizabeth's chief district surgeon (ibid., 15).

30. Sack, "Garden of Eden or Political Landscape?" 200. In our 1998 interview, Sack made the important distinction between posters and other graphics of the kind discussed in chapter 4 as being made "in the name of the people," and People's Parks, which were "made by the people."

31. Her contributions were *Monument I* and *Monument II,* and *Farmers' Weekly,* all silkscreen prints. Others who contributed art to the exhibition and are also mentioned in this book include Bill Ainslie, Lionel Davis, Garth Erasmus, Emile Maurice, Gordon Metz, Steven Sack, and Paul Sibisi (*Art toward Social Development—An Exhibition of South African Art,* 2–5).

32. Williamson, "Art as Media: Filling the Gap," 27 (emphasis in original).

33. Ramphele's autobiography *A Life* (1995) recounts her time in this distant place in a chapter called "Surviving in the Wilderness" (122–52). All biographical information given here is from this source, as are quotations unless otherwise cited.

34. Ramphele named their son Hlumelo, which means "the shoot that grew from a dead tree trunk" (ibid., 137).

35. Ibid., 141.

36. The patterned backdrops within *A Few South Africans* are based on homemade frames that Williamson observed while conducting research for the series in townships and rural environs. In this artist's hands, one will find the voices and visions of her subjects translated even in the smallest of details.

37. Williamson, email correspondence with author.

38. Williamson honored Ramphele in another work, *Eighteen Women +* of 1990, an experiment with photojournalism and photocopy. Ramphele's portrait, twice given, is torn from newsprint with the bold title "Dr." and half of an *R* visible. See Williamson, "Art as Media," 39–40 for the image.

39. Barbara Pollack, "Profile: Sue Williamson."

40. Betty LaDuke, *Africa through the Eyes of Women Artists,* 106; Dale Lautenbach, "From Copywriter to Artist."

41. Williamson is well known for pursuing these interests throughout her career. In the 1980s she designed some T-shirts and graphics for political organizations to which she belonged. A longtime advocate of alternative media, she has authored numerous articles and books that have advanced knowledge of South African art, and she created the valued website www.artthrob.co.za, groundbreaking in its own way. Ever versatile, Williamson consistently taps into local concerns and skillfully negotiates the line of representing these to varied audiences.

42. Williamson, "Art as Media," 28.

43. Interviews with author, 1999.

44. Williamson, "Artist's Statement."

45. Williamson, email correspondence with author. Bauer first began to regularly pub-

lish his drawings in the *Weekly Mail* in 1985. He joined the paper's launch following the closures of its predecessors, two liberal papers called the *Rand Daily Mail* and *Sunday Express*. In 1988, the *Weekly Mail* was suspended for three months. Since 1990, the paper has been printed under the title the *Mail and Guardian*.

46. Susan de Villiers, *Derek Bauer*, 3.

47. Peffer, *Art and the End of Apartheid*, 130.

48. Coetzee, *Giving Offense*, 28.

49. Quoted in Mario Pissarra, "Prejudice and Potential in Political Cartooning," 140.

50. The screenplay of *Cry Freedom* was written by John Briley, who wrote a novel of the same title. Briley based the screenplay on two books by Donald Woods: a now well-known biography called *BIKO* and an autobiography titled *Asking for Trouble*. Several publications accompanied the film's release, and all were banned in South Africa: *Cry Freedom—A Pictorial Record*; *Filming with Attenborough: The Making of* Cry Freedom; and a sound track.

51. Jay Savage, "*Asking for Trouble*: The South African State and the *Cry Freedom* Saga," 19–20. All quotes in this paragraph are from this source.

52. John MacLennan and David Chapel, "Never a Chance for Biko Film."

53. Savage, "*Asking for Trouble*," 31.

54. Ibid., 32, quoting *Saturday Star*, July 30, 1988.

55. Ibid., 33, quoting *Natal Mercury*, July 30, 1988. Journalists followed Attenborough when he traveled in South Africa in 1984 to conduct research for the film. Peter Davis details their efforts "to inculpate him in 'terrorist activities'" of the then-banned ANC. Martin Spring, editor of *The Citizen*, used the occasion to claim the absurd: that Biko was once an agent of the U.S. Central Intelligence Agency and that Attenborough's film (which cost $21 million to make) would be financed by "the Anti-Apartheid Movement, the Defense and Aid Fund, the United Nations Committee Against Apartheid, or some other similarly disinterested party" (Davis, *In Darkest Hollywood*, 99–102).

56. Savage, "*Asking for Trouble*," 33, quoting *Natal Mercury*, July 30, 1988.

57. Mark Oleeson, "South African Government Planned to Stop 'Cry' from the Outset."

58. Scott Kraft, "*Cry Freedom* Gets New Release Date in South Africa."

59. Some viewers found the scenes of Crossroads and Soweto "brilliant simulation[s] of precisely the kind of footage that has been withheld from" audiences overseas (David Sterritt, "Review of *Cry Freedom*," *Christian Science Monitor*). *New York Times* reporter John Burns, whose account of Crossroads led to his expulsion from South Africa, wrote that Attenborough's depiction of the police raid "was [like] watching an eerie rerun" (Lynette Steenveld, *Representation and Meaning*, 1991, 73). Thus the film's documentary style was believed to have filled a gap left by censorship's restrictions. South Africa's *Sunday Times* ran a lead editorial that reads, "[The government] is not afraid of exposing us to the evident propaganda of the film but of confronting us with its considerable truth." (Scott Kraft, "*Cry Freedom* Viewed as a History Lesson").

60. Quoted in Davis, *In Darkest Hollywood*, 98.

61. Strini Moodley, "*Cry Freedom*—A Film about All of Us"; David Sterritt, "Review of *Cry Freedom*."

62. Ebert, "Review of the Film *Cry Freedom*."

63. The escape of the Woods family absorbs the last half of the film. Critics almost universally condemned this narrative structure since neither Woods nor his family's plight is as enthralling (or important) as Biko, his message, and the reasons for his death. And one remains aware that the Woods family leaves one comfortable home for another while South Africa's majority struggles amid great poverty and violence. Indeed, the final scene, or last word, splices footage of violence in Soweto with the Woods clan rising high above the earth at a safe remove. As one critic put it, *Cry Freedom* might have been better titled "The Brady Bunch Flees Apartheid" (Corliss, "Review of *Cry Freedom*").

64. Davis, *In Darkest Hollywood*, 104.

65. "Richard Attenborough," *UNESCO Courier*, 4.

66. Posters of all three leaders appear in the film, with that of Mandela hanging inside the Biko family home no less, but no attempt is made to untangle their differences of opinion and approach.

67. Quoted in Davis, *In Darkest Hollywood*, 99.

68. Sekoto lived more than half of his life in Paris, having moved there from South Africa in 1947 and never returned. He accepted the invitation to participate in the First World Festival of Negro Arts in Dakar in 1966, and spent a year traveling Senegal thereafter. For biographical details, see N. Chabani Manganyi, *I Am an African: The Life and Times of Gerard Sekoto*; Gerard Sekoto, *Gerard Sekoto: My Life and Work*; Leslie Spiro, *Gerard Sekoto: Unsevered Ties*; and Barbara Lindop, *Gerard Sekoto*.

69. Manganyi, *A Black Man Called Sekoto*, 124–25.

70. Ibid., 124.

71. Few photographs were taken of Biko while he lived. Among portraits, I know of six only, and in them Biko is shown alone.

72. *Woman with a Patterned Headscarf* (1973) partly shares this trait, and her likeness bears resemblance to the thinker in *Homage to Steve Biko*.

73. Joe Dolby, "Gerard Sekoto," 102.

74. Manganyi, *A Black Man Called Sekoto*, 124.

75. Quoted in Lindop, *Sekoto: The Art of Gérard Sekoto*, 45.

76. Manganyi, *A Black Man Called Sekoto*, 87. Other Sekoto biographers have not stressed the importance of Marthe Baillon in his life; indeed, they leave the nature of this relationship unexamined. Only Manganyi offers a reading of her life and influence (76–87 in particular). Oddly, others date Baillon's passing to 1982, including Sekoto himself (*Gerard Sekoto: My Life and Work*, 105), but Manganyi records otherwise. He alone has studied her life in depth and relates the impact of her death on Sekoto's life in 1976 (*A Black Man Called Sekoto*, 123–25).

77. Lindop (*Sekoto: The Art of Gérard Sekoto*) and Manganyi (*A Black Man Called Sekoto*) recount the same events but chronicle them as beginning at different times, 1982 and 1976, respectively.

78. Manganyi, *A Black Man Called Sekoto*, 124.

79. Bernstein, *No. 46*, 7.

80. This important artist rendered in oil some of the earliest images of black urban culture, and the subject pervaded his work whether set in South Africa, Senegal, or France.

81. Dubow, "Art and the State: Questions of Conformism, Censorship and State Control," 118; Van Wyk, "Reflecting Democracy," 6.

82. Although several members of the principal organization that pushed this line, the Medu Art Ensemble, were not born and raised in deprived communities, they nevertheless aligned with the interests of people who had been. They evidenced understanding that their counterparts' voices and visions would lead the way.

83. The word *Kwanza* appears beneath each raised fist. This names the organization to which the author of the article, Risimati j'Mathonsi, belonged. Kwanza was one of the many cultural organizations that sprang up in South Africa at this time in response to Black Consciousness. The word now names a transnational holiday and reaffirms principles common to transnational blackness: unity, self-determination, collective work and responsibility, cooperative economics, purpose, creativity, and faith (j'Mathonsi, "Kwanza," 2).

84. Dubow, "Art and the State," 118.

85. Art is always for someone or something exterior to itself. For instance, it is now well known that the U.S. government heralded American abstract expressionism, to which the phrase was first attached, as evidence of its own ideals: liberty, democracy, freedom of expression, and so forth. Art exists because people make it. This makes it political.

86. In "Creating Consciousness," I argue that this descriptor is unsuitable because Surrealists prize the subconscious and these artists purposefully created an awareness of Black Consciousness.

87. Gordimer, "Relevance and Commitment."

88. The symposium was held at the University of Botswana from July 5–9, 1982. The exhibition ran July 10–August 10, 1982. Artists from both camps described in this chapter showed work within the exhibition.

89. Mnyele, "Observations on the State of the Contemporary Visual Arts in South Africa," 7. I thank Judy Seidman for sharing her copy of Mnyele's paper with me. The following quotes are also from this source. Mnyele echoed this sentiment, using nearly the same words, in his article "Thoughts for Bongiwe."

90. Mnyele, "Observations," 5.

91. Ibid., 6.

92. Peffer, *Art and the End of Apartheid,* 151.

93. Ibid., 131–52.

94. Quoted in Ibid., 140. Following quotes are also from this source.

95. Gordimer, "Relevance and Commitment."

96. Ibid., 6; emphasis in original. Gordimer cited *Black Viewpoint,* a publication of the Black Peoples' Convention, as her source for the Ndebele quotes. She mentions *Black Review,* BPC's best-known literary journal, as enabling "the important cultural debate that was taking place, in the early and mid-70s," but was "cut off [I would say curtailed] by the banning of organizations and individuals concerned" (9).

97. Ibid., 7.

98. Dhlomo-Mautloa had worked as a teacher, nurse, and maid before she began training at Rorke's Drift in 1977. The center was divided into subsections that included crafts and domestic science courses, both of which were heavily enrolled with women, and fine arts courses, in which Dhlomo-Mautloa was one of few women to ever earn a degree (Hobbs and Rankin, *Rorke's Drift,* 181).

99. Mnyele, "Thoughts for Bongiwe," *Rixaka*; Mnyele, "Thoughts for Bongiwe and Revolutionary Art," *Staffrider* 7, nos. 3 & 4 (1988).

100. Quoted in Hobbs and Rankin, *Rorke's Drift,* 203. Emphasis in original.

101. Ibid., 204.

102. Emphasis mine. Dhlomo-Mautloa is quoted in Hobbs and Rankin, *Rorke's Drift,* 185.

103. Ibid., 203. In a similar misappropriation, Rorke's Drift is regarded as a "source for debate about political issues" (Artists' Press, "Tony Nkotsi"). The problem with such phrasing is that it implicitly credits those in a position of authority at Rorke's Drift (all white) with sponsoring, even advancing, a dialogue that largely took place among black students.

104. Davis is quoted in Hobbs and Rankin, *Rorke's Drift,* 202.

105. Hobbs and Rankin record the date of *Removals III: People Are Living There* as 1983. This cannot be correct since it was included in the 1982 Gaborone exhibition. My source is the exhibition brochure for *Art toward Social Development,* which includes a full checklist of all works shown. Further, the work that Hobbs and Rankin reproduce is given as *Removals VII* in Amanda Jephson, "Bongiwe Dhlomo," 38–39.

106. Hobbs and Rankin, *Rorke's Drift,* 166, 202.

107. Quoted in Hobbs and Rankin, *Rorke's Drift,* 199.

108. In September 1999, Philippa Hobbs showed me the untitled print in question and I told her that the portrait was of Biko. She and Elizabeth Rankin subsequently added a subtitle in parenthesis to this same print—*(Untitled Portrait of Steve Biko)*—when they reproduced it online (Hobbs and Rankin, "Imprinting Primitivism"). When their book *Rorke's Drift* was published, it included a different Nkotsi print, the same that I reprint here, but with the name "Biko" in parenthesis. I suspect that both Biko portraits did not originally identify their subject. The artist has not replied to my inquiry on this score. Interestingly, *Portrait of a Man (Biko)* is the only print reproduced across a full page in Hobbs and Rankin's lengthy book. This emphasis is yet another small indicator of Biko's ongoing historical significance.

109. Artists' Press, "Tony Nkotsi."

110. Gordimer, "Relevance and Commitment," 6. Cultural workers often used variations on the word *mystery* to condemn expressions that they sought to censor.

111. Ibid., 7. The following quote is from the same source.

112. Frieda Hattingh, *Oto La Dimo,* 39.

113. Ibid., 25.

114. Ibid., 71.

115. Ibid., 25.

116. Personal correspondence, 2003.

117. Hattingh, *Oto La Dimo,* 18–19. Although mothers are frequently cited as great influ-

ences on artists in this context, their names are rarely recorded. I thank Sipho Mokwena for providing this information.

118. Ibid., 32.

119. Ibid., 23.

120. Ibid., 25.

121. Ibid., 19.

122. Ibid., 18, 20, 19.

123. Ibid., 20.

124. Ibid.

125. Ibid., 21.

126. Ibid., 18.

127. Ibid., 42, 10.

128. Ibid., 53.

129. Frieda Hattingh must be credited with securing Tladi's record for posterity in the nicely illustrated *Oto La Dimo,* the catalog to an exhibit of the same name at the Art Gallery at the University of South Africa. For additional reproductions, see Hill, "Creating Consciousness."

130. Hattingh, *Oto La Dimo,* 47.

131. The following bear influence on my discussion of this work's title. In the late eighteenth century, Dutch settlers required "'Bastaard Hottentots' (the offspring of Khoikhoi and slaves or Khoikhoi and colonists)" to carry passes. The Native Land Act (1913) limited ownership of land to white people in all territory except reserves, which were also created with this act. The Native Affairs Act (1920) established councils to run the reserves and to advise Africans who lived in urban areas, but these were under the authority of the state's Native Affairs Department. The Native Trust and Land Act (1936) extended the land reserved for Africans to just 14 percent of the total within South Africa. Laws that required black men to carry passes were intensified in 1937 with the Native Laws Amendment Act. The Bantu Authorities Act (1951) enabled the government to select chiefs to serve their interests within the reserves. The Abolition of Passes and Coordination of Documents Act (1952), a great historical misnomer, added black women to the roll of those made to carry a passbook. Finally, the Bantu Self Government Act (1959) introduced ethnicity as the basis for segregation by creating eight "homelands" (later extended to ten) for Africans. It also enhanced the power of the co-opted chiefs and encouraged them to promote independence from South Africa (Worden, *The Making of Modern South Africa,* 11, 54, 66, 67, 82, 121).

132. Marx, *Lessons of Struggle,* 63.

133. Ibid., 63.

134. Although blacks could own land in Bantustans, their rights extended to just six feet below the surface. This condition reserved South Africa's right over any minerals that might be found in the future.

135. In 1992, amid the nation's transition from apartheid to democracy, Koloane made a series also called *Made in South Africa.*

136. Peffer, *Art and the End of Apartheid,* 176.

137. See chapter 5 of ibid., for a discussion of Ainslie Studios and FUBA's history.

138. Koloane, interview with author, 2011.

139. The foundation moved to Saxonwold, also a wealthy suburb of Johannesburg in 1982, when the Ainslies took up residence there (Peffer, *Art and the End of Apartheid,* 138).

140. Koloane, interview with author, 2011.

141. Ibid.

142. Peffer, *Art and the End of Apartheid,* 139.

143. Koloane, interview with author, 2011.

144. In his study of the Thupelo Art Project, an annual two-week workshop spearheaded by FUBA and the United States–South Africa Leadership Exchange Program that ran from 1985 to 1991, Peffer writes, "At the center of all of these interests was the life's work of Bill Ainslie" (*Art and the End of Apartheid,* 133). I urge us to rethink the directional axis.

145. Koloane, interview with author, 2011.

146. Peffer writes that Koloane "became a close collaborator with Bill Ainslie on a number of projects, including the Gallery, a black-run exhibition space" (*Art and the End of Apartheid,* 139). Coming at the end of several pages of praise for Ainslie (133–39), this suggests that Koloane joined the project when it was already under way.

147. Ibid.,151.

148. Workshops were held in the Magaliesberg Mountains northwest of Johannesburg. The first took place outdoors near Rustenberg and was called the FUBA-USSALEP Workshop. Subsequent annual gatherings were held at a hotel in Broederstroom, and the name Thupelo Art Project was adopted (ibid., 131, 133).

149. Very few venues had existed for students of color to train in the arts. Sites such as Rorke's Drift (Natal), the Polly Street Art Centre (Johannesburg), and the Community Arts Project (Cape Town) are discussed to varying degrees in this book. Readers should consult the following for in-depth consideration, mindful that this list is hardly exhaustive: De Jager, *Images of Man*; Hobbs and Rankin, *Rorke's Drift*; Hayden Proud, *Revisions: Expanding the Narrative of South African Art*; Peffer, *Art and the End of Apartheid*; Miles, *Polly Street*.

150. See Peffer, *Art and the End of Apartheid* (151–52) for a complete list of attendants.

151. Richards, "Cross Purposes: Durant Silhali's Art of Allegory," 82.

152. Peffer, *Art and the End of Apartheid,* 217.

153. Richards, "Cross Purposes," 95.

154. Quoted in ibid. Emphasis mine.

155. Coombes, *History after Apartheid,* 5.

6. Transitions and Truths in a New Democracy

1. In June 1991, Nico Basson, a colonel retired from the South African Defense Force, verified that the state had secretly supplied Inkatha Freedom Party supporters with assault weapons "in order to undermine and weaken the African National Congress" (Wendy Watson, *Brick by Brick: An Informal Guide to the History of South Africa,* 122). Police collu-

sion with Inkatha in Natal (now KwaZulu-Natal) and southeast of Johannesburg was known as scores of people were killed in so-called "black on black violence" in the first years of fighting between ANC and United Democratic Front (UDF) on one side, and Inkatha and the NP on the other.

2. After CODESA dissolved in mid-1992, a white referendum found that 68 percent of voters favored the transition in process (Nigel Worden, *The Making of Modern South Africa: Conquest, Apartheid, Democracy,* 153).

3. A history book based on interviews, Van Onselen's *The Seed Is Mine: The Life of Kas Maine, a South African Sharecropper, 1894–1985,* was among the most acclaimed in the 1990s.

4. Richards, "Drawing a Veil," 2. I am grateful to Richards for sharing this conference paper with me.

5. Commissioners chose to use the term *victim* for abused people rather than *survivor* since the state of mind and/or survival of the one who suffered violations were irrelevant to the TRC's purpose. They reasoned that the intentions and actions of *perpetrators* (a term also debated) create conditions wherein people are victimized. I adopt their terminology here.

6. Jennifer Law, "Performing on a Fault Line: The Making(s) of a South African Spy Novel and Other Stories," 155, 192.

7. Chi-Shona speakers recognize the saying as *munhu munhu nekuda kwevanhu.*

8. Nelson Mandela was interviewed by Tim Modise, "Interview with Nelson Mandela"; and Desmond Tutu, *No Future without Forgiveness,* 31.

9. Pityana, "The Renewal of African Moral Values," 138.

10. Quoted in Hennie Lötter, "The Intellectual Legacy of Stephen Bantu Biko (1946–1977)," 29. The parenthetical passage is in the original (Biko, "Black Consciousness and the Quest for a True Humanity," 45) and implied outside quotes in Lötter's accounting.

11. Oupa Ngwenya, "Saint Biko the Radiant."

12. See, for example, Sandile Memela and Shafa'ath-Ahmed Khan, "Hero Who Could Not Be Silenced"; Mathatha Tsedu, "Back to the Front"; Molatlhegi oa Thlale, "Where Would Biko Have Stood Today?"; and Mamphela Ramphele, "Can the Dead Act as Arbitrators?"

13. Marx, *Lessons of Struggle,* 53–54.

14. Many papers from the Harare conference are published in Pityana et al., *Bounds of Possibility.*

15. *Truth and Reconciliation Commission of South Africa Report, Volume I,* 126. Hereafter, given as *TRC Report,* followed by the specific volume number.

16. For example, Witwolwe members bombed a busy bus and taxi terminal in Johannesburg on July 6, 1990, injuring twenty-seven people. In October, Nic Cruise died when he opened a package sent to his employer, which serviced computers for various political parties objectionable to the six men charged in his death. In August 1991, an estimated two thousand AWB members came to Ventersdorp to disrupt an NP meeting. After violent confrontation with the police, nearly the entire AWB leadership was charged with public

violence and arrested. And in March 1994, about one month shy of national elections, AWB members invaded Bophuthatswana and killed forty-two residents of Mafikeng. See Watson, *Brick by Brick,* 120–30.

17. Ibid., 121.

18. For information about the Land Acts, see A. J. Christopher, *The Atlas of Apartheid,* 32–35; about the Group Areas Act, 105–21; about the Population Registration Act, 103–5.

19. David Koloane, "Sam Nhlengethwa," 4. Nhlengethwa was born in Payneville, Springs, and raised in Ratanda near Heidelberg. Art training was nonexistent in his youth, but he drew and developed skill nonetheless. Note Koloane names Cyrene as the place of Ainslie's residence (an oversight no doubt, since this is a place in Zimbabwe); Peffer cites it as Parktown (*Art and the End of Apartheid,* 136).

20. Nhlengethwa studied with Ainslie in 1976 and 1977. He followed this experience with two years at Rorke's Drift (Hobbs and Rankin, *Rorke's Drift*). He first combined paint and collage while at Rorke's Drift and earned his diploma here in 1979 (Koloane, "Sam Nhlengethwa," 13). He later taught at the Federated Union of Black Artists and held residencies in London and New York. Fellow collaborators at the Thupelo Arts Project in the mid-1980s influenced his style as well.

21. Nhlengethwa, interview with author, September 16, 1999. Information given here was obtained in this interview unless otherwise cited.

22. Koloane, "Sam Nhlengethwa," 14.

23. Ibid., 13.

24. The title plays on the well-remembered words of James Kruger, minister of justice in 1977, who described his reaction to Biko's death: "I am not glad and I am not sorry about Mr. Biko. It leaves me cold." The artist switches up the words and meaning: "It" becomes the state and "Him" becomes Biko. He also included Kruger's portrait on the wall near the door.

25. See Okwui Enwezor, "Remembrance of Things Past: Memory and the Archive" (23) for more on the use of repetition to realize paradox, melancholy, and loss.

26. Vicki Goldberg, *The Power of Photography,* 7.

27. Erina Botha, "If There's a Corpse at My Garden Gate." It is not surprising that the press largely ignored Nhlengethwa's inclusion of ubuntu in his narration of township truth. Peffer writes of early "imaginative explorations of the ordinary" among black artists that fell outside normative market strains in *Art and the End of Apartheid* (173–74). See especially his chapter on Durant Silhali.

28. Nhlengethwa won the coveted Standard Bank Young Artist Award in 1994, the year after *Today, Yesterday and Tomorrow* was shown in Johannesburg and Durban.

29. Nhlengethwa, "Artist's statement."

30. David Koloane notes the irony of using scissors to create when in the 1970s and 1980s they were "associated with censorship" in South Africa ("Sam Nhlengethwa," 3).

31. Bester was arrested for wearing the jacket and taken to the Milnerton Police Station, where he was forced to sign a statement that he would never promote the phrase again. His jacket was taken from him. (Interview with author. Unless otherwise noted, this interview is the source for my study of Bester's work.)

32. Quoted in Kendell Geers, "Contemporary Art from South Africa." (exhibition review), *The Star*, March 19, 1997.

33. The artist has challenged troubling social realities since he first began creating art as a student at Cape Town's Community Arts Project in 1986. His work of this period mostly depicts poverty by combining found objects with oil paint. By 1988, he developed the high-relief, mixed-media collage style for which he is now well known.

34. Honored within single works devoted to their histories are Oliver Tambo, Matthew Goniwe, Chris Hani, all well-known leaders, as well as the unknown, like a man named Semekazi whose story, in Bester's hands, comes to represent a common one shared by migrant laborers. Another work, *Cradock Four*, honored Goniwe, Fort Calata, Sicelo Mhlaudi, and Sparrow Mkhonto.

35. Godby and Klopper, "The Art of Willie Bester," 43.

36. As such, the composition of *Homage to B.* is like that of vita icons, which present the passions of Christ in a circular fashion around the martyr. Though this precise tradition was an unlikely influence, the result nonetheless lends to the history of a sanctified Biko that developed at this time.

37. Bester made another work about Biko in 1993. Simply titled *Steve Biko*, it is reproduced in Colin Richards, "In Human History: Pasts and Prospects in South African Art Today," 52.

38. Black figures appeared on targets in shooting ranges in apartheid South Africa. Michael Godby reports that "not too long ago [these figures] had exaggerated facial features indicating blackness" ("The Landscape of Slaughter," 30).

39. Godby and Klopper, "The Art of Willie Bester," 49. Sandra Klopper offers this rough translation of "Jy sal moet dans soos die musiek speel."

40. Bester's family history encapsulates the widespread problems caused by racial categorization. His parents were classified differently under apartheid law. His mother was called "Cape Coloured" and his father, a Xhosa man who migrated to the Western Cape for work, was called "Black." Since Bester was born before his parents wed, he was classified as "Other Coloured." His siblings, born to married parents, received the "Black" status of their father (ibid., 43). Such divisions within a single family were not uncommon. The resulting tensions caused Bester to be particularly upset by this law; he draws attention to it through scattered numbers in many of his compositions.

41. Godby, "The Landscape of Slaughter," 30.

42. Godby and Klopper, "The Art of Willie Bester," 49.

43. Ibid., 49.

44. Memela and Khan, "Hero Who Could Not Be Silenced." Next quotation is from the same source.

45. All three parties took part in a September 1990 meeting in Durban, likely called by the ANC (Tsedu, "Back to the Front").

46. Yekiso, "Biko Would Have Fought," 6.

47. Molefe, "Focus on Steve Biko." Emphasis mine.

48. Mdhlela, "Focus on Steve Biko."

49. Ramphele, "Can the Dead Act as Arbitrators?"

50. Tiyani Mabasa Lybon (AZAPO Gauteng Chair), "Biko's Legend Lives On."

51. International Institute for Democracy and Electoral Assistance, "Voter Turnout Data for South Africa." The following statistics are from the same source.

52. Watson, *Brick by Brick,* 131.

53. Ibid., 132.

54. Archbishop Desmond Tutu coined the term *rainbow nation.*

55. Mdhlela, "Focus on Steve Biko."

56. Quoted in Jackson, "Biko Finds His Way to Opera."

57. Cited in Ngwenya, "Saint Biko the Radiant."

58. "Biko Set in Line as Martyr."

59. In our February 2000 interview, Stopforth described his explicit intent to recall, and contribute to, an art history of martyrdom in this series and in *Elegy* (Plate 3). I thank Stephen Perkinson for consultation on the subject of efficacy in medieval miniatures and for translating Greek to English.

60. Through our correspondence, the artist, a Franciscan brother based in the United States, explained his desire to "adapt" Catholic iconography for our time by "changing models of holiness [in order to] plant seeds of change." Describing his life as one of prayer and work (art making and training), Lentz is deeply committed to using Byzantine aesthetic tradition to challenge Church conventional selection of mostly "celibate, white, and middle to upper class" people for canonization, for he finds Christ's very being in the world within "every human being, but especially the poor and oppressed." Lentz identifies most acutely with "all those marginalized by the Church" and recounted his own experience with prejudice in the 1940s and 1950s. He recalled cross burnings on the lawns of neighbors in the Colorado hometown of his youth, and his father's stories of "the violent struggle for justice of workers" that labor unions necessarily wage, his own among them. Having emigrated from Russia in the early 1900s, his parents "encountered terrible prejudice" in the United States, and their American born son too experienced a sense that his "country belonged more to others than it did to us." These experiences led Lentz toward the life he now leads, one driven by "reason to stand with the poor and oppressed" (email correspondence, April 23, 2010).

61. At the time of publication, the image was available for purchase upon a variety of objects, including T-shirts, bookmarks, and coffee mugs, at www.trinitystores.com.

62. I thank Steve de Gruchy and his friends for supplying information from Pietermaritzburg (email correspondence). The version I saw in 1999 was purchased at the Little Sisters of Jesus in nearby Edendale.

63. Lentz apprenticed as an iconographer in a Greek Orthodox monastery in 1977. The related information that follows derived from our email correspondence.

64. The artist misspelled his subject's name, a common error. It should be "Stephen" instead of "Steven."

65. Artist and muse met one another in Cape Town, where Beauty had migrated in search of domestic work. She has since figured in three of Alexander's works. In our 1999 interview,

the artist expressed awe of displaced people who regularly "transcend the pettiness of the day," and most particularly of Beauty, who was "incredibly powerful, hugely admirable. I learned an extra amount from her." This interview provided information shared here, unless otherwise cited.

66. Powell, *Jane Alexander: Sculpture and Photomontage*, 29.

67. The text reads: "WE ARE HERE TO: *Search for stolen property *Search for unlicensed firearms and ammunition *Identify suspects and arrest them. This is necessary to maintain law and order and to protec[t] you from troublemakers. You have no reason to fear us. Thank you for your co-operation" (ibid., 28).

68. Alexander's is not a direct translation—a slight tilt of the head, shift of the eyes, and part of the lips are visible—but the average viewer of *Portrait of a man* hardly recognizes these without the benefit of a comparative image. Such slight distortions are recognizable, naturalistic forms, which the artist described as inherently subconscious, and have long been part of her work.

69. Barthes, *Camera Lucida*, 92–97. The following quotes come from the same source.

70. Interestingly, Alexander's painted portrait of Biko has since been reproduced several times as a photograph. *Tribute* magazine and *DRUM* pictured it prominently in two collections, Nontsikelelo Biko's "Beating Their Own Drum" (in *Tribute*, see Charles Molele, "Beating Their Own Drum"); and Mamphela Ramphele's "She Fought for Our Freedom" (in *DRUM*, see Adélle Horler, "My Tragic Love for Steve Biko").

71. Powell, *Jane Alexander*; Marion Arnold, *Women and Art in South Africa*; Hazel Friedman, "Souring over Murky Terrain."

72. Powell, *Jane Alexander*, 29.

73. Grundlingh, "Portrait of a Man with Landscape and Procession," 9. (The title is in lowercase, which humbles overall. This small but significant detail has been lost in the literature; let us restore it.) The chief difficulty with Grundlingh's reading of this work is her reliance on another; her interpretation of "danger" is based on the text behind the screen in *something's going down*.

74. Quoted in Basil Moore, *Black Theology: The South African Voice*, 47.

75. Tutu, "Preface," vi.

76. *TRC Report Vol. I*, 52–53.

77. Ibid., 59.

78. "Appendix A," *TRC Report Vol. I* (94–102) lists the following: four resolutions of the United Nations General Assembly, eight resolutions of the United Nations Security Council (1970–1980), six statements of international conventions and court bodies (1968–91), draft articles of the International Law Commission (1976), and the International Court of Justice (1970–71).

79. *TRC Report Vol. I*, 53.

80. Ibid., 143, 147. The commission introduced new channels for statement taking within six months of beginning its work. Together with nongovernmental and community-based organizations, it trained statement takers, established more offices, and sent representatives to rural areas to record statements.

81. The World Court copied South Africa's method of public hearings for victims, their families, and perpetrators in investigating the genocides in Rwanda and Bosnia in the 1990s. Several other nations, including Chile and the Solomon Islands, have followed South Africa's model in their own efforts to address politically motivated human rights abuses of the past.

82. Quoted in *TRC Report Vol. I,* 17–18.

83. Ibid., 12. It remains difficult to locate the final statistics since authors cite close but not exact numbers of total amnesty applications, and their success or failure in winning amnesty. All report that the number of amnesties denied was much higher, by thousands, than the number granted.

84. Bishop David Beetge, quoted in ibid., 120.

85. Ibid., 110–14.

86. Ibid., 114.

87. I borrow the title of a 2000 documentary film by Frances Reid and Deborah Hoffman.

88. Others who took part in the same petition were the Azanian People's Organization, and the families of Fabian and Florence Riberio, and Griffiths and Victoria Mxenge.

89. The South African press questioned the compliance of district surgeons at regular intervals between 1977 and 1997, highlighting the Biko doctors as a case study. Individuals and organizations within South Africa and without actively sought to censure Tucker and Lang, and the case went through multiple appeals until 1985, when the Transvaal Supreme Court opted to find them guilty of improper conduct. Tucker was also found to have practiced disgraceful conduct (Orr, *From Biko to Basson,* 15). Throughout, Biko's image appeared alongside these news features. The long case of censure was publically rehashed again in 1988 when the film *Cry Freedom* was banned in South Africa (see, e.g., Sankey, "Forget the Film—These Are the Real Biko 'Stars'"). Galvanized by five medical doctors between 1978 and 1985—Frances Ams, B. M. Barker, Trevor Jenkins, L. Robertson, and Phillip Tobias—and covered so often in the press, Biko's case became historically quite important to questions of how medical professionals colluded with the police in the ongoing abuse of political detainees.

90. See the online source at www.justice.gov.za/trc/decisions/1999/99_snyman.html. Accessed November 12, 2014; the following quotes come from the same source.

91. Lapses in Biko's care practically defined the special hearing on the health sector. In the TRC report, the chapter on this hearing is introduced by photographs of the headstone on Biko's grave and of Dr. Wendy Orr, former district surgeon who blew the whistle on detainee abuse in the Eastern Cape (*TRC Report Vol. IV,* 107–8). In 1997, news media repeatedly printed Biko's portrait when reporting on the health sector hearings.

92. Regrettably, these continue to be recounted by the press every mid-September. I much prefer those articles that use the occasion of Biko's death to reconsider the relevancy of BC today. The Biko Foundation does just that through its annual Steve Biko Memorial Lecture.

93. Email correspondence with author.

94. *TRC Report, Vol. I,* 112.

95. Ibid.

96. Ibid., 113.

97. Jane Taylor curated the exhibition and organized a conference of the same name at the University of the Western Cape in July 1996. Portions of this study were first printed in Hill, "Iconic Autopsy."

98. I admire Dr. Richards, whose scholarship has proved profoundly influential. He was talented in many ways. He passed away too young, just days before I submitted this manuscript to the publisher. Rest in peace, Colin. You once wrote of "Our Giftedness." May we write more about your own.

99. Richards, "Drawing a Veil," 9.

100. Richards, "The Double Agent: Humanism, History and Allegory in the Art of Durant Sihlali (1939–2004)," 62. Though the citation comes from his study of another artist, the interest is shared.

101. Richards's version was inspired by Francisco de Zurbarán's painting *The Veil of Veronica* made around 1635 (see Hill, "Iconic Autopsy: Postmortem Portraits of Bantu Stephen Biko" 2004 for a color reproduction). The artist rendered its contours in a good many works over his career, beginning with a series of hand-painted dry etchings called *Endgame* (1984) that he made in graduate school. The title of this early series recalls the work of Samuel Beckett, another significant inspiration. Beckett's *Endgame* (1958) and *Watt* (1953) make rhetorical use of the Veil of Veronica. So, too, does J. M. Coetzee, another author Richards favored, in *Age of Iron* (1990).

102. Richards, "Drawing a Veil," 6.

103. See Hill, "Iconic Autopsy" for color reproductions of both *Veil VII* and *Veil VIII.*

104. A larger excerpt reads, "Hegel remarks somewhere that all facts and personages of great importance in world history occur, as it were, twice. He forgot to add: the first time as tragedy, the second as farce. . . . Men make their history, but they do not make it just as they please: they do not make it under circumstances chosen by themselves, but under circumstances directly encountered, given and transmitted from the past. The tradition of all the dead generations weighs like a nightmare on the brain of the living" (quoted in Richards, "Drawing a Veil," 10).

105. Ibid., 9.

106. James Elkins, *Pictures of the Body,* 59.

107. Ibid., 114–15.

108. See, for example, Barthes, *Camera Lucida*; Elkins, *Pictures of the Body*; Ernst van Alphen, "Deadly Historians: Boltanski's Intervention in Holocaust Historiography."

109. Richards, "Drawing a Veil," 7.

110. For color images of both sleeping dogs, as well as several numbered veils, see Emma Bedford, *A Decade of Democracy: South African Art 1994–2004,* 28–29, 140.

111. Richards, "Drawing a Veil," 12.

112. Philippe Ariés, *The Hour of Our Death,* 114.

113. Samuel Beckett, *Watt,* 148.

114. Ibid., 117.

115. Ibid., 169. I have long believed that scholars have also missed much of great interest by neglecting, to a large extent, Richards's artwork. It is every bit as intriguing as the writing for which he is better known.

116. Cathy Caruth, *Unclaimed Experience: Trauma, Narrative, and History*, 102. Emphasis in original.

117. Richards, "Drawing a Veil," 10.

118. Compulsory conscription in South Africa began in 1957. Though there were some conscientious objectors, draft resistance did not gain currency until 1983 when the End Conscription Campaign was launched. See *Out of Step: War Resistance in South Africa* for more information.

119. Richards, *Memórius—Intimas—Marcas*, 1.

120. Richards, "Drawing a Veil," 3.

121. Autopsies disturb because they are performed when the cause of death is questioned and they defile in some sense, thus troubling those who love the deceased. Additionally, in this particular case, the autopsy performed on the artist's brother bears relevance because it took place soon before Biko's; memory of it surely arose while Richards worked with the inquest autopsy photographs.

122. Email correspondence with author.

123. Before returning to Cape Town toward the end of his life, for decades Richards donated his considerable skills to an art therapy program he helped establish in Soweto.

124. Richards, "Cross Purposes: Durant Sihlali's Art of Allegory," 86.

125. Interview with author. Here Richards also discussed the practices of monks at St. Marcos in Florence, who have favored illusionism for centuries, as of a kind with his own— "this idea that you had to do something constructive with the conditions you are given and there are these beautiful paintings as a result."

126. For more on South Africa's role in this clandestine warfare, see Marga Holness, "Angola: The Struggle Continues"; William Minter, *Apartheid's Contras: An Inquiry into the Roots of War in Angola and Mozambique*; and Terry Bell, *Unfinished Business: South Africa Apartheid and Truth*.

127. Richards, "Drawing a Veil," 13.

128. Law, "Performing on a Fault Line," 179.

129. Ibid.

130. Ibid., 190.

131. Richards, email correspondence with author.

132. Richards, *Memórius—Intimas—Marcas* included Angolan, Cuban, and South African artists who reflected on the war in Angola. Curated by Fernando Alvim, the exhibition was first shown in Johannesburg in 1998 and toured in European cities thereafter.

133. Ibid., 1.

134. Ibid.

135. Richards, "Drawing a Veil," 6–7.

136. Boraine, *A Country Unmasked*, 290–91.

137. The method was employed in other works by Williamson that address the TRC such

as *Cold Turkey: Stories about Truth and Reconciliation* (1996) and *Can't Remember, Can't Forget* (1999). *Cold Turkey* includes differently scaled images that were photocopied and then hung side by side on a light board, like X-rays. The images were collected from the popular press, where they were "under the spotlight of judicial process." This series, for which Williamson made just two works, evolved into *Truth Games*.

Can't Remember, Can't Forget is an electronic work of art that resembles the grid format of *Truth Games* but couples the fragmented imagery with sound and motion. With the use of a mouse, viewers navigate through select TRC hearings and listen to recorded testimony as they choose among several audio and video selections. Like *Truth Games*, testimony can be made to obscure images, thus altering the viewer's understanding of how dialogic truth unfolds.

138. Lloyd Pollack, "Artist Universalises the Guilt That Emerges from Our Sick Society."

139. Ibid.

140. Interview with author, December 1, 1999. Unless otherwise noted, all discussion of this work's creation was gleaned from this interview or another conducted December 6, 1999.

141. Williamson is quoted in Betty LaDuke, *Africa through the Eyes of Women Artists*, 111.

142. Note that the work records images and excerpts from the TRC's special hearing on medical ethics, where Biko's case history was prominent. The man imaged at right, Benjamin Tucker (the medical doctor who signed his death certificate), did not apply for amnesty, nor did his colleague Ivor Lang.

143. There is one work in the series to which I do not have access. An obstructed installation view of this work (seemingly devoted to the Chris Hani amnesty hearing) appears briefly on the CD that accompanies the exhibition catalog *Sue Williamson: Selected Work*. The *Truth Games* exhibition brochure illustrates eleven of thirteen works in the series. One of these is featured on the CD.

144. Williamson told me that she set out only to include direct quotes from the persons represented in each work, but that she altered her objective in some cases. One TRC finding in this case echoed that of a 1985 inquiry into Biko's medical treatment conducted by the South African Medical and Dental Council. It concluded that Tucker and Lang were guilty of "improper and disgraceful conduct," a ruling that strongly suggests complicity in Biko's death (Katie Sankey, "Forget the Film—These Are the Real Biko 'Stars'").

145. Bizos, *No One to Blame?* 83.

146. Gideon Nieuwoudt filed his amnesty application separate from the four others. This resulted in two amnesty hearings.

147. Although the exhibition *Liberated Voices* at New York's Museum for African Art originally displayed twenty paintings as part of this series, Koloane told me that the last of these—an image of a vehicle—was not part of the series. Rather, it was made later and added to the original nineteen-part work titled *The Journey*. The fact that the nineteenth work in the series depicts Biko's corpse is important to my analysis of the series as a whole. For additional images of these paintings in color, see Hill, "Iconic Autopsy"; Herreman and D'Amato, *Liberated Voices: Contemporary Art from South Africa*.

148. Steve Biko, "On Death," in *I Write What I Like,* 152.

149. Color has almost always been key to Koloane's work. He favors layering acrylics and oil pastels because this enhances the work's luminosity. Allergies prevent him from working with oils that require cleaning solvents (interview with author, December 1999). Some works in *The Journey* were made with layered acrylics and oil pastels; for others, he used only the latter.

150. Gillian McAinsh, "Intriguing Display to Scratch Through." Together with Patrick Mautloa, in 1997 Koloane created an installation that emphasized the effects of the scratch technique in an exhibition appropriately titled *If You Scratch.* Township life was their subject, and it was rendered in a raw manner to jolt white viewers. Their technique was used to suggest excavation of neglected histories. Perhaps the purpose was less to heal than to provoke awareness of stories long denied or conditions long ignored.

The TRC publicity poster for the Biko hearings appeared on streets throughout the country during the first weeks of September 1997. Koloane and Mautloa later used the TRC's Biko poster in *If You Scratch* to connect what Brenda Atkinson called "disparate and desperate divisions" among South Africa's populace (Atkinson, "Hostel Witness").

151. Bizos, *No One to Blame?* 58.

152. Interview with the author, December 1999.

153. Kristeva, *Powers of Horror,* 58.

154. Ibid., 140.

155. Ibid., 141.

156. Ibid., 154.

157. Das, "Language and Body: Transaction in the Construction of Pain," 78.

158. Koloane returned to the subject in 2011. Vuyile Voyiya's *Black and Blue,* a linocut series from 2005 also suggests Biko's last days (see Judith Hecker, *Impressions from South Africa, 1965 to Now: Prints from the Museum of Modern Art,* for reproductions). Their existence points to new paths of inquiry ahead in the visual culture of Biko and Black Consciousness.

159. Thembinkosi Goniwe used this honorific in my presence on January 14, 2011, in Johannesburg.

160. Koloane is quoted in Pauline Burman, "Huge Contrasts and a Lot of Irony."

161. Biko, "White Racism and Black Consciousness," in *I Write What I Like,* 66. Emphasis in original.

162. A (regrettably) unnamed mother speaking about her child at a hearing of the Truth and Reconciliation Commission (quoted in Antjie Krog, *Country of My Skull,* 28).

7. Museum, Monument, Marking

1. Coombes, *History after Apartheid,* 5.

2. Marschall, *Landscape of Memory,* 2011.

3. It appears that Woods consulted with the East London council of the Ministry of Arts and Culture, but this is not confirmed (Tsedu, "Two Decades On," 11). The donors' names are carved into the monument's granite base on the right side. They include Richard

Attenborough, Richard Branson, Ken Follett, Peter Gabriel, Kevin Kline, Denzel Washington, and Donald Woods.

The controversy surrounding the Biko Monument recalled another of the same period: that by Danie de Jager of Mandela's fist rising out of a hillside near the Vortrekker Monument in Pretoria, which was never realized. Among other similarities, de Jager was not considered a "struggle artist" and the project was to be privately financed. Annie Coombes writes, "Many critics were particularly dismayed by the lack of transparency in the process of assessing the project. . . . They claimed that the commission had been undemocratically handled and lacked consultative mechanisms" (*History after Apartheid,* 23).

4. Jacobson was born in Namibia of European parents. She trained at the University of Cape Town's Michaelis School of Fine Art. Since the 1950s she has created bronze busts of many famous political figures including Hosea Kutako (a Herero leader in Namibia), Mangosuthu Buthelezi (of the Inkatha Freedom Party), King Sobhuza of Swaziland, and African National Party leaders Nelson Mandela, Walter Sisulu, and Oliver Tambo. Her life-size bronze sculpture of King Shaka stands outside the entrance of legislative buildings in KwaZulu Natal (Janet Smith, "Monument to Biko").

5. Interview with author. Other quotations of Jacobson are from this interview unless otherwise cited.

6. Quoted in Smith, "Monument to Steve Biko," 3.

7. "Art Critics Give Biko Statue Thumbs Down," 3.

8. Piet Meiring, *Chronicle of the Truth Commission,* 213; Bizos, *No One to Blame?* 92.

9. Robert Brand, "Mandela in Call for Black Unity as Biko Statue Unveiled," 5.

10. Pat Reber, "Race Rift Mars Ceremony for South African Activist."

11. Brand, "Mandela in Call for Black Unity." Similarly insistent AZAPO demonstrators caused the Biko family to walk out of a different commemoration held earlier that week in King William's Town when Jacobson's portrait bust of Biko was unveiled at his mother's former home.

12. George Bizos notes that representatives from "all political parties were there. Even some of those who had applied the apartheid policy wanted to be seen at the commemoration service" (*No One to Blame?* 93).

13. Brand, "Mandela in Call for Black Unity."

14. Renwedzi Nengwekhulu, "Biko Fought, Died for Black Unity," 11.

15. Mandela, "A More Human Face."

16. Coombes, *History after Apartheid,* 12. Okwui Enwezor concurs in "The Enigma of the Rainbow Nation," 30. In *Art and the End of Apartheid,* John Peffer offers a full chapter to postapartheid performances staged at monuments made before 1994.

17. Peter Dickson, "First You Lose Your Dignity."

18. "AWB Defaces Biko Statue"; Coombes, *History after Apartheid,* 14.

19. Mitchell, *What Do Pictures Want?* 6.

20. Ibid., 127.

21. Article in the *Star* (October 27, 1997), quoted in Coombes, *History after Apartheid,* 14.

22. McGee, "Canons Apart and Apartheid Canons," 290.

23. The museum is now part of a consortium of museums in Cape Town called Iziko, thus its name is now Iziko–South African National Gallery.

24. SANG grew out of the South African Fine Arts Association, established in 1871 (McGee, "Canons Apart and Apartheid Canons," 293).

25. The 1996 exhibition *MisCast: Negotiating Khoisan History and Material Culture* is well known in this capacity. Another case: SANG's 1991 decision to purchase a woodcut by a black woman whom they thought was Joyce Ntobe. In truth the work was by Beezy Bailey, a white man who purposely evoked an "African aesthetic" that has appealed to white audiences (and proscribed black artists) for decades.

26. Hendricks, email correspondence with author.

27. Ward, email correspondence with author, September 5, 2011.

28. Email correspondence with author, August 25, 2011.

29. Ward, email correspondence with author, September 5, 2011.

30. Ibid. Ward offered all of these meanings and mentioned Roy Lichtenstein as an influence.

31. Ward found the photo in a trade shop. With research, he found that it once belonged to a Lebanese family newly immigrated to South Africa.

32. Ward, interview with author. Other quotes come from this source unless otherwise cited.

33. Crain Soudien and Renate Meyer, *The District Six Public Sculpture Project,* 18.

34. Maluka, correspondence with author.

35. Maluka's paternal line comes from Zambia, his maternal line from Maori in New Zealand. They refused to change their surname during apartheid, even though doing so would have made life easier since some members could "pass for white," as it is often put. This pride is in keeping with what Maluka calls the "warrior" lineage on his mother's side (Sophie Perryer, "Mustafa Maluka").

36. Mosaka, "On *Isintu*," 1.

37. Minty and Mosaka were approached by Australians to co-curate an exhibition, and they found a common vision, one celebratory and critical, about transformation in national, indigenous, and transnational spheres. As Minty described it, "Seeing the 'black' and 'indigenous' as essentially contested terms, we decided to focus our attention on the dialogue aspect with particular emphasis on the issue of 'blackness' in the context of identity (re)formulation" (Minty, "South–South Dialogue Project," 4–5).

38. Mosaka, "On *Isintu*," 1.

39. Other artists were chosen from across the country, including Ezekiel Budeli, Isaac Nkosinathi (Nathi) Khanyile, Amanda Mji, Usha Prajapat, and Sandile Zulu.

40. Zayd Minty, "What Is BLAC?" The following quote is also from this source.

41. Among BLAC regulars were Shelley Barry, Anthea Carolus, Carol-Anne Davids, Roxanno Davids, Graham Falken, Gertrude Fester, Thembinkosi Goniwe, Valmont Layne, Emile Maurice, Zayd Minty, Roshila Nair, Ciraj Rassool, Berni Searle, Sabata Sessiu, Candice

Smith, and Crane Soudien. This list is gleaned from several sources in the archive of Zayd Minty, whom I thank.

42. Southall, "The ANC and Black Capitalism in South Africa." The next quoted passage is from the same source; emphasis mine.

43. Ward, interview with author.

44. Berni Searle, "Artist's Statement."

45. Coombes, *History after Apartheid,* 250.

46. Goniwe's billboard was installed near the city center and later purchased by the Iziko–South African National Gallery. It images two men (the artist and another, Malcom Payne) in white and black spaces, meeting and averting viewers' eyes, respectively. For reproductions, see Zayd Minty, "Finding the 'Post-Black' Position," 111; Hayden Proud, "Scratches on the Face," 63.

47. Coombes, "Skin Deep"; *History after Apartheid,* 254.

48. The film was made by Sheila Meintjes, Jacqueline Maingard, and Heather Thompson. I thank Penny Siopis for providing me with a copy of it.

49. Others were by Mustafa Maluka, Zen Marie, Cameron Platter, and Alexander Smith, and Selvin November created a second version as well. I thank Donovan Ward for the gift of a catalog, one of the last in print.

50. Liese van der Watt, "Towards an 'Adversarial Aesthetics,'" 47.

51. Minty, "BLAC Bows Outa."

52. Sandra Klopper, "Hip-Hop Graffiti Art," 180.

53. Ibid., 186.

54. Hip-hop originated in New York City in the early 1970s and quickly coupled with a graffiti scene that had gained popularity in the late 1960s (ibid., 180). Weamm Williams writes that Mitchell's Plain is the "Mecca of South African hip hop, with bands such as Black Noise, Brasse Vannie Kaap and some members of P.O.C. hailing from the area" (Williams, "Graffiti, Popular Culture's Most Potent Visual Representation?").

55. Klopper, "Hip-Hop Graffiti Art," 184.

56. Ibid., 185.

57. Weamm Williams, "Graffiti, Popular Culture's Most Potent Visual Representation?" I thank Zayd Minty for sharing BLAC materials with me.

58. When I first saw the mural in early 1997, Michael Godby told me that it had been up for some time.

59. Biko, "Some African Cultural Concepts," in *I Write What I Like,* 42.

60. Ibid., 44.

61. *Sense* is legible despite its reverse lettering, but the other words beneath Biko's name are difficult to decipher. One possibility is the popular reply to the state's initial explanation for Biko's death, "Starve? Nonsense."

62. Maluka, "Artist's Statement." Maluka also earned an MFA at De Atelierspe while in Amsterdam. Initially inspired by pop artists like Andy Warhol and Roy Lichtenstein, and by mentors like Tyrone Appollis, Willie Bester, Peter Clarke, and Lionel Davis, Maluka quickly

developed his own vision, and a remarkably fertile vision it is. He is well known today as a leading exponent of cultural cross-referencing that is everywhere present in our lives, but long denied by art world purists, particularly in Cape Town, who in the 1990s continued to hold segregationist expectations as they opened their doors just a little wider to black artists (email correspondence with author, 2011).

63. Steve Biko famously said, "The most potent weapon in the hands of the oppressor is the mind of the oppressed" ("The Quest for True Humanity," in *I Write What I Like,* 92).

64. Basquiat was an American artist of the 1980s famed, among other reasons, for his artistic beginnings in graffiti (and its persistent presence in his art), his love of music, and for the disturbance he created within New York's art world by being a black man who managed to work his way into its exclusive ranks. Like Basquiat, Maluka embraces graffiti outside of its usual context. The effect is to encourage direct, personal involvement in a space and with an aesthetic tradition that typically denies it.

65. Rian Malan, *My Traitor's Heart,* 248.

66. Works within the series are much published. For an example, see the cover of Sue Williamson's *South African Art Now.*

67. Kim Gurney, "Mustafa Maluka at the Michael Stevenson Contemporary."

68. Maluka was a rapper and graffiti writer before he began making visual art around 1994. Music fuels much of his creative energy. A cofounder of www.Africanhiphop.com, Maluka has long used the Internet to create, explore, and build networks within the worlds that interest him most. As he put it, "I've never felt like I was trapped, like I was only here [in South Africa]. I had a global passport because I had access to the net. People assume that because you come from a certain area, you are influenced by certain things only" (quoted in Perryer, "Mustafa Maluka").

69. Quoted in Tracy Murinik, "Mustafa Maluka," 91.

70. The literature makes much of these presumably spontaneous (thus documentary and authentic) interactions between artist and sitter. But the method cannot have been used in all cases, since Sibu appears in several works. Interestingly, the clothing he wears here is the same worn in three other photographs, with shoes and glasses changed.

71. Enwezor, *Snap Judgments,* 31.

72. Sealy, "The Canvases of Representation and the Photographs of Nontsikelelo Veleko," 174.

73. In this way, Veleko's work is aligned with that of Malik Sidibé, a Malian who captured the vibrancy of Bamakois life in the 1960s. Mark Sealy compares her sitters to those of photographers in Harlem in the 1920s (ibid., 174). Veleko herself cites Socichi Aoki, a Japanese photographer, as an inspiration for this series (Lauren Haynes, "Nontsikelelo Veleko," 101).

74. Godby, personal communication.

75. Find an image of this work at www.brettmurray.co.za/work/hail-to-the-thief-exhibition/killed_twice.jpg/.

76. Several thousand ANC supporters marched on the Goodman Gallery, where just four people stood guard, to demand that *The Spear* be removed from display. The gallery refused. Controversy ensued. On May 22, in a dramatic censorious act, two men defaced the work

by painting an X across the figure's face, and wide swaths of thick paint down the body and across its genitals. For more on this history, see Steven Dubin, *Spearheading Debate: Culture Wars and Uneasy Truces,* 176–87.

Epilogue

1. Leora Maltz-Leca compares *Monument* to *Elegy* (Plate 3) in her excellent essay "The Logic of the Relic."

2. Ibid., 57.

3. The most notable among these are Andries Oliphant, "Imagined Futures"; Colin Richards, "In Human History"; Ruth Simbao, "Self-Identification as Resistance"; and Roger Van Wyk, "The (Non)sense of Humour."

4. For example, *Biko Lives! Contesting the Legacies of Steve Biko,* edited by Andile Mngxitama, Amanda Alexander, and Nigel C. Gibson, is a great collection of essays on the topic from diverse viewpoints. Andile M-Afrika's *The Eyes That Lit Our Lives* is part memoir, part biography, as the author reflects on Biko in Ginsberg and beyond. And Daniel R. Magaziner's excellent *The Law and the Prophets* is a history of BC's intellectual might steeped, as it was, in liberation theology. Whereas scholars in fields such as these have built on previous studies (e.g., Themba Sono, *Reflections on the Origins of Black Consciousness in South Africa*; Robert Fatton Jr., *Black Consciousness in South Africa*), those of visual arts histories have sidelined BC until now.

5. Biko's death as visualized at Pretoria's Police Museum is atrocious. Thankfully, far more people visit the Apartheid Museum near Johannesburg and the Hector Pieterson Museum in Soweto, where displays about Biko and Black Consciousness are thoughtfully constructed.

6. See www.sbf.org.za for more information.

Acknowledgments

1. Cornell University and New York University convened the conference Global Black Consciousness in Dakar, Senegal, on May 11–12, 2014, as part of the biennale Dak'Art that ran through June 8. The conveners, Salah Hassan, Margo Natalie Crawford, and Manthia Diawara, will coedit an upcoming volume of the same title.

2. Quoted in Jaki Seroke, "Poet in Exile: An Interview with Mongane Serote," 31.

Bibliography

"After Biko's Death." *The Economist,* October 15, 1977, 9.

Araeen, Rasheed. "Art and Black Consciousness." Paper delivered at the First National Black Art Convention at Wolverhampton Polytechnic, 1982. Reprinted in Araeen, *The Essential Black Art,* 36–41.

———. "The Emergence of Black Consciousness in Contemporary Art in Britain: Seventeen Years of Neglected History." In Araeen, *The Essential Black Art.*

———. *The Essential Black Art.* Exhibition catalog. London: Chisenhale Gallery and Black Umbrella, 1988.

Arendt, Hannah. *Eichmann in Jerusalem: A Report on the Banality of Evil.* New York: Viking Press, 1963.

Ariés, Philippe. *The Hour of Our Death.* Translated by Helen Weaver. New York: Oxford University Press, 1981.

Arnold, Marion. *Women and Art in South Africa.* New York: St. Martin's Press, 1996.

Arnold, Millard, ed. *Steve Biko: Black Consciousness in South Africa.* New York: Vintage Books/Random House, 1978.

"Art Critics Give Biko Statue Thumbs Down." *Argus,* September 20, 1997, 3.

Art toward Social Development—An Exhibition of South African Art. Brochure. Gaborone, Botswana: National Museum and Gallery of Art, 1982. Archive of Judy Seidman.

Artists' Press. "Tony Nkotsi." www.artprintsa.com/tony-nkotsi.html (accessed July 19, 2010).

Atkinson, Brenda. "Hostel Witness." *Mail and Guardian,* October 17–23, 1997.

Attenbourgh, Richard (producer and director). *Cry Freedom.* Marble Arch Productions, Universal Studios, 1987.

———. *Cry Freedom—A Pictorial Record.* New York: Knopf, 1987.

"AWB Defaces Biko Statue." *Weekend Post* (Port Elizabeth), September 13, 1997, A1.

Bamford, Brian. "What's in an Inquest?" *Argus,* September 29, 1977.

Barthes, Roland. *Camera Lucida: Reflections on Photography.* Translated by Richard Howard. New York: Hill and Wang, 1981.

Beckett, Samuel. *Watt.* New York: Grove, 1953.

Bedford, Emma. *Contemporary South African Art, 1985–1995 from the South African National Gallery Permanent Collection.* Cape Town: South African National Gallery, 1997.

———, ed. *A Decade of Democracy: South African Art 1994–2004.* Cape Town: Double Storey Books and Iziko–South African National Gallery, 2004.

Bell, Terry. *Unfinished Business: South Africa Apartheid and Truth.* Observatory, South Africa: Redworks, 2001.

Bennett, Jill. *Empathic Vision: Affect, Trauma, and Contemporary Art.* Stanford, Calif.: Stanford University Press, 2005.

Berndt, Jon. *From Weapon to Ornament: The CAP Media Project Posters (1982 to 1994).* Cape Town: AMAC, 2007.

Bernstein, Hilda. *No. 46–Steve Biko.* London: International Defense and Aid Fund for Southern Africa, 1978.

Biko, Steve. *I Write What I Like: A Selection of His Writings.* Rev. ed. Edited by Aelred Stubbs. London: Bowerdean, 1996.

"Biko Banner Held High by Cathedral Protester." *The Star,* August 13, 1979.

"Biko foto's ondersoek." *Die Beeld,* October 17, 1977.

"Biko Predicted Violence—Report." *Cape Times,* October 11, 1977.

"Biko Set in Line as Martyr." *Rand Daily Mail,* September 4, 1982.

Bizos, George. *No One to Blame? In Pursuit of Justice in South Africa.* Cape Town: David Philip, 1998.

Black Art Today. Exhibition catalog. South Africa: Mofolo Art Centre, 1981.

Blair, Jon, and Norman Fenton. *The Biko Inquest.* London: Rex Collings, 1978.

Boraine, Alex. *A Country Unmasked.* Oxford: Oxford University Press, 2000.

Botha, Erina. "If There's a Corpse at My Garden Gate, the Flowers Will Have to Wait, Says the Artist Who Paints with the People in Mind." Source not recorded in archive (*Argus* or *Star*), December 21, 1996.

Brand, Robert. "Mandela in Call for Black Unity as Biko Statue Unveiled." *Mail and Guardian,* September 13, 1997.

Brilliant, Richard. "Portraits: A Recurrent Genre in World Art." In *Likeness and Beyond: Portraits from Africa and the World,* edited by Jean M. Borgatti and Richard Brilliant, 11–28. New York: Center for African Art, 1990.

Brink, André. *A Dry White Season.* New York: Morrow, 1980.

Buntman, Barbara. "Ezrom Legae, 1976–1986." BA honor's thesis, University of the Witwatersrand, 1987.

Burman, Pauline. "Huge Contrasts and a Lot of Irony." News source not recorded in Johannesburg Art Gallery Archive, 1992.

Carmichael, Stokely, and Charles V. Hamilton. *Black Power: The Politics of Liberation in America.* New York: Random House, 1967.

Caruth, Cathy. *Unclaimed Experience: Trauma, Narrative, and History.* Baltimore: Johns Hopkins University Press, 1996.

Christopher, A. J. *The Atlas of Apartheid.* London and New York: Routledge and University of the Witwatersrand, 1994.

Clarke, Nancy L., and William H. Worger. *South Africa: The Rise and Fall of Apartheid.* Harlow, England: Pearson Longman, 2004.

Coetzee, J. M. *Giving Offense: Essays on Censorship.* Chicago: University of Chicago Press, 1996.

Collier, Caroline. "To Go and Come Back." In *Korabra,* edited by Gavin Jantjes, 3–7. Exhibition catalog. London: Edward Totah Gallery, 1986.

Coombes, Annie. *History after Apartheid: Visual Culture and Public Memory in a Democratic South Africa.* Durham, N.C.: Duke University Press, 2003.

———. "Skin Deep/Bodies of Evidence. The Work of Berni Searle." In *Authentic/Ex-centric: African Conceptualism in a Global Context,* edited by Salah Hassan and Olu Oguibe, 178–99. Catalog for the 49th Venice Biannale Exhibition *Authen/Ex-centric: Africa in and Out of Africa.* New York: Ford Foundation, 2001.

Corliss, Richard. "Review of Cry Freedom." *TIME,* November 9, 1987.

Curtin, Philip D. *The Atlantic Slave Trade: A Census.* Madison: University of Wisconsin Press, 1969.

Danto, Arthur. "Painting and Politics." In *Unnatural Wonders: Essays on the Gap between Art and Life,* 348–54. New York: Farrar, 2005.

Das, Veena. "Language and Body: Transaction in the Construction of Pain." In *Social Suffering,* edited by Arthur Kleinman, Veena Das, and Margaret Lock, 67–91. Berkeley: University of California Press, 1997.

Davis, Peter. *In Darkest Hollywood: Exploring the Jungles of Cinema's South Africa.* Athens: Ohio University Press, 1996.

"Death Not in Vain—BPC." *Daily Dispatch,* September 15, 1977.

"Death of a Martyr." *Daily Dispatch,* September 14, 1977.

de Jager, E. J. *Images of Man: Contemporary South African Black Art and Artists.* Alice: University of Fort Hare Press, 1992.

Deliss, Clementine, ed. *Seven Stories about Modern Art in Africa.* Exhibition catalog. Whitechapel Gallery, London. Paris, New York: Flammarion, 1995.

Derrida, Jacques. "Racism's Last Word." In *"Race," Writing, and Difference,* edited by Henry Louis Gates Jr., 329–38. Chicago: University of Chicago Press, 1985.

de Villiers, Susan. *Derek Bauer: S. A. Flambé and Other Recipes for Disaster.* Cape Town: David Philip, 1989.

Dickson, Peter. "First You Lose Your Dignity. Then Your Life." *Mail and Guardian* (Johannesburg), August 27–September 2, 1997.

"Dikobé Ben Martins." www.sahistory.org.za (accessed August 17, 2009).

Dolby, Joe. "Gerard Sekoto." In *Revisions: Expanding the Narrative of South African Art,* edited by Hayden Proud, 102–9. Johannesburg: SA History Online and University of South Africa Press, 2006.

Dubin, Steven C. *Spearheading Debate: Culture Wars and Uneasy Truces.* Auckland Park/Johannesburg: Jacana Media, 2012.

Dubow, Neville. "Art and the State: Questions of Conformism, Censorship and State Control." In *The State of the Art,* 113–26. Conference proceedings, University of Cape Town, July 1979.

Duff, M. "BPC Case for Black Consciousness." *The Star,* September 16, 1977.

Duval, Sydney. "Biko as Martyr." *Rand Daily Mail,* February 16, 1979.

Ebersohn, Wessel. *Store Up the Anger.* Concord, Ontario: Irwin Publishing, 1980.

Ebert, Roger. "Review of the Film *Cry Freedom.*" *New York Post,* November 6, 1987.

"Editorial." *Medu Art Ensemble Newsletter* 2, no. 1 (March 1980): 3.

Elkins, James. *Pictures of the Body: Pain and Metamorphosis.* Stanford, Calif.: Stanford University Press, 1999.

Enwezor, Okwui. "The Enigma of the Rainbow Nation: Contemporary South African Art at the Crossroads of History." In *Personal Affects: Power and Poetics in Contemporary South African Art,* edited by Sophie Perryer, 23–43. New York: Museum for African Art, 2004.

———. "Remembrance of Things Past: Memory and the Archive." In *Democracies Images: Photography and Visual Art after Apartheid,* edited by Jan-Erik Lundstrom and Katarina Pierre, 18–27. Umea: BildMuseet, 1998.

———, ed. *The Short Century: Independence and Liberation Movements in Africa, 1945–1994.* New York, London: Prestel, 2001.

———. *Snap Judgments: New Positions in Contemporary African Photography.* New York: International Center for Photography, 2006.

Fatton, Robert, Jr. *Black Consciousness in South Africa: The Dialectics of Ideological Resistance to White Supremacy.* New York: State University of New York Press, 1986.

"Finding Disgusts World's Press." *Sunday Express,* December 4, 1977.

"Fine Art and Political Reality." *Medu Art Ensemble Newsletter* 3, no. 2 (n.d.: 1981?).

Fourie, Peter. "Paul Stopforth Speaks to Peter Fourie." *Speak,* December 1977, 40–41.

Frederickson, George. "Black Power in the United States and Black Consciousness in South Africa: Connections and Comparisons." In *Comparative Perspectives on South Africa,* edited by Ran Greenstein, 135–84. London: MacMillan, 1997.

Frederikse, Julie. *South Africa: A Different Kind of War.* Gweru: Mambo; and London: Currey, 1986.

———. *The Unbreakable Thread: Non-Racialism in South Africa.* Bloomington: Indiana University Press, 1990.

Freidman, Hazel. "It's a Privilege to Remember Legae." *Mail and Guardian,* May 28–June 3, 1999, 9.

———. "Souring over Murky Terrain." *Mail and Guardian,* September 29–October 5, 1995.

Geers, Kendell. "Contemporary Art from South Africa." Exhibition review. *The Star,* March 19, 1997.

———, ed. *Contemporary South African Art: The Gencor Collection.* Johannesburg: Jonathan Ball Publishers, 1997.

Gerhart, Gail M. *Black Power in South Africa: The Evolution of an Ideology.* Berkeley: UCLA Press, 1978.

Godby, Michael. "The Landscape of Slaughter: Bisho and Transition." *Ventilator,* no. 1, September 1994, 29–33.

Godby, Michael, and Sandra Klopper. "The Art of Willie Bester." *African Arts* 29, no. 1 (Winter 1996): 42–49.

Goldberg, Vicki. *The Power of Photography: How Photographs Changed Our Lives.* 2nd ed. New York, London, Paris: Abbeville Publishing Group, 1993.

Goodman, Linda [Givon]. Interview with Ezrom Legae, 1984. Unpublished. Archive of Barbara Buntman.

Gordimer, Nadine. "Relevance and Commitment." Keynote presented at *The State of the Art* conference, University of Cape Town, July 4–11, 1979. Published as "Art and the State in South Africa," in *The Nation,* December 24, 1983, 657–61.

Grantham, Tosha. *Darkroom: Photography and New Media in South Africa since 1950.* Exhibition catalog. Richmond: Virginia Museum of Fine Arts, 2009.

Grundlingh, Kathy. "Portrait of a Man with Landscape and Procession." Educational guide. Cape Town: South African National Gallery, n.d. (1996?).

Gurney, Kim. "Mustafa Maluka at the Michael Stevenson Contemporary." www.artthrob .co.za (accessed November 9, 2005).

Halisi, C. R. D. *Black Political Thought in the Making of South African Democracy.* Bloomington: Indiana University Press, 1999.

———. "Rethinking Steve Biko and Black Consciousness within the Context of the South African Liberation Tradition." Presented at the symposium *The Legacy of Bantu Steve Biko,* Ohio State University, October 8, 2009.

Hallam, Elizabeth, Jenny Hockey, and Glennys Howarth. *Beyond the Body: Death and Social Identity.* New York: Routledge, 1999.

Harney, Elizabeth. "Word Play: Text and Image in Contemporary African Art." In *Inscribing Meaning: Writing and Graphic Systems in African Art,* edited by Christine Mullen Kreamer, Mary Nooter Roberts, Elizabeth Harney, and Allyson Purpura, 201–38. Washington, D.C.: Smithsonian Institution, 2007.

Hattingh, Frieda. "Lefifi Tladi and Mothlabane Mashiangwako Notes." www.3rdearmusic .com (accessed October 9, 2009).

———. *Oto La Dimo: Joint Retrospective Exhibition of Lefifi Tladi and Motlhabane Mashiangwako.* Pretoria: University of South Africa, 1998.

Haynes, Lauren. "Nontsikelelo Veleko." In *FLOW,* edited by Christine Y. Kim, 100–101. New York: Studio Museum of Harlem, 2008.

Hecker, Judith. *Impressions from South Africa, 1965 to Now: Prints from the Museum of Modern Art.* New York: Museum of Modern Art, 2011.

Herreman, Frank, and Mark D'Amato, eds. *Liberated Voices: Contemporary Art from South Africa.* New York: Museum for African Art, 2000.

Hill, Shannen. "Creating Consciousness: Black Art in 1970s South Africa." In *Global Black Consciousness,* edited by Salah Hassan, Margo Crawford, and Manthia Diawara. Forthcoming 2016.

———. "Iconic Autopsy: Postmortem Portraits of Bantu Stephen Biko." *African Arts* 38, no. 3 (Autumn 2005): 15–25, 98.

———. "South African Street Arts." In *Censorship: A World Encyclopedia,* edited by Derek Jones, 2298. Chicago: Fitzroy Dearborn, 2001.

Hobbs, Philippa, and Elizabeth Rankin. "Imprinting Primitivism: Perceptions and Preconceptions in Printmaking at Rorke's Drift." www.motspluriels.arts.uwa.edu.au/ MP1299r&h.html (accessed July 19, 2010).

———. *Rorke's Drift: Empowering Prints.* Cape Town: Double Storey Books, 2003.

Holness, Marga. "Angola: The Struggle Continues." In *Destructive Engagement: Southern Africa at War,* edited by Phyllis Johnson and David Martin, 73–108. Harare: Zimbabwe Publishing House, 1986.

Horler, Adélle. "My Tragic Love for Steve Biko." *DRUM* 198 (October 1995): 22–35, 127–29, 137, 139.

"How Many Impacts Caused the Fatal Brain Injuries?" *Sunday Tribune,* November 27, 1977.

Hyman, Jennifer. "Steve Biko." *Sunday Express,* April 2, 1978.

". . . In Biko Finding." *The Star,* December 5, 1977. Archive copy missing full headline. South African History Archive, University of the Witwatersrand.

International Institute for Democracy and Electoral Assistance. "Voter Turnout Data for South Africa." www.idea.int/vt/country_view.cfm?CountryCode=ZA (accessed April 18, 2011).

Jackson, Kevin. "Biko Finds His Way to Opera." *Daily News,* June 3, 1992.

Jantjes, Gavin. "Art and Cultural Reciprocity." Presented at the East Midlands Art Conference, April 12, 1986, East Midlands. Published in Araeen, *The Essential Black Art,* 42–47.

Jephson, Amanda. "Bongiwe Dhlomo." *ADA* 5 (1988): 38–42.

j'Mathonsi, Risimati. "Kwanza." *Black World* 12, no. 14 (December 15, 1982): 2.

Johnson, Phyllis and David Martin. "Angola." In *Apartheid Terrorism: The Destabilization Report,* 122–49. London: James Currey; and Bloomington: Indiana University Press, 1989.

"June 16: Student Uprising." www.africanhistory.about.com (accessed January 6, 2010).

Kaganof, Aryan. "Geoff Matlherane Mphakati." www.kaganof.com (accessed October 20, 2009).

Ka Mathe, Themba. "An Obituary." www.facebook.com (accessed October 12, 2009).

Kellner, Clive, and Sergio-Albio González, eds. *Thami Mnyele + MEDU: Art Ensemble Retrospective.* Exhibition catalog. Johannesburg Art Gallery. Auckland Park: Jacana Media, 2009.

Kennedy, Jean. *New Currents, Ancient Rivers.* Washington, D.C.: Smithsonian Institution, 1992.

Kennis, Nadere, "Soul-Searching over Biko." *Sunday Express,* September 25, 1977.

Kentridge, Sidney, Georges Bizos, E. Wenzel. *Magistrate's Court for the District of Pretoria: Inquest No. 573/1977.* December 1, 1977. South African History Archive, University of the Witwatersrand.

Kirkwood, Mike, "Remembering *Staffrider.*" In *Ten Years of Staffrider 1978–1988,* edited by Andres Oliphant and Ivan Vladislavić. Athens: University of Ohio Press, 1988.

Klopper, Sandra. "Hip-Hop Graffiti Art." In *Senses of Culture,* edited by Sarah Nuttell and Cheryl-Ann Michael, 178–96. Oxford: Oxford University Press, 2000.

Koloane, David. "Sam Nhlengethwa: Standard Bank Young Artist Award." Exhibition pamphlet. Grahamstown, Standard Bank National Arts Festival, 1994.

Kraft, Scott. "*Cry Freedom* Gets New Release Date in South Africa." *Los Angeles Times,* February 20, 1990.

———. "*Cry Freedom* Viewed as a History Lesson: South African Critics Oppose Government Censorship of Film." *Los Angeles Times,* August 2, 1988.

Kristeva, Julia. *Powers of Horror: An Essay on Abjection.* New York: Columbia University Press, 1982.

Krog, Antjie. *Country of My Skull.* New York: Random House, 1998.

Kross, Cynthia. "Culture and Resistance." *Staffrider* 5, no. 2 (1982): 11.

"Kruger Denial and a Tape Transcript." *The Star,* November 11, 1977.

"Kruger Quotes Biko Pamphlet." *The Star,* October 6, 1977. Reprinted in *TIME,* October 3–10, 1977.

Kunzle, David. *Che Guevara: Icon, Myth, and Message.* Los Angeles: UCLA Fowler Museum of Cultural History, 1997.

Kuzwayo, Ellen. *Call Me Woman.* Randburg, South Africa: Raven Press, 1985.

LaDuke. Betty. *Africa through the Eyes of Women Artists.* Trenton, N.J.: Africa World Press, 1991.

Langa, Mandla. "Cultural Invasion." *Newsletter of the Medu Art Ensemble* 1, no. 4 (1979): 24. Archive of Judy Seidman.

Lautenbach, Dale. "From Copywriter to Artist." *Argus,* December 16, 1984.

Law, Jennifer. "Performing on a Fault Line: The Making(s) of a South African Spy Novel and Other Stories." In *Para-Sites: A Casebook against Cynical Reason,* edited by George E. Marcus, 151–94. Chicago: University of Chicago Press, 2000.

Lindop, Barbara. *Gerard Sekoto.* Randburg: Dictum, 1988.

———. *Sekoto: The Art of Gérard Sekoto.* London: Pavilion, 1995.

Lötter, Hennie. "The Intellectual Legacy of Stephen Bantu Biko (1946–1977)." *Acta Academica* 24, no. 3 (1992): 22–36.

Loubser, Johan. *Report on Autopsy of Stephen Biko.* South African History Archive, University of the Witwatersrand, 1977.

Maaba, Brown Bavusile. "Challenges to Repatriation and Preservation of Tangible Heritage in South Africa: Black Art and the Experiences of the Ifa Lethu Foundation." *South African History Journal* 60, no. 3 (2008): 500–513.

MacDonald, Michael. *Why Race Matters in South Africa.* Cambridge, Mass.: Harvard University Press, 2006.

MacDonough, Terry. "Why SA Has Lost Some of Its US Credit Rating." *Rand Daily Mail,* November 26, 1977.

MacLennan, John, and David Chapel. "Never a Chance for Biko Film." *Sunday Tribune,* July 30, 1988.

MacShane, Denis, Martin Plaut, and David Ward. *Power! Black Workers, Their Unions and the Struggle for Freedom in South Africa.* Nottingham: Spokesman, 1984.

M-Afrika, Andile. *The Eyes That Lit Our Lives: A Tribute to Steve Biko.* King William's Town: Eyeball Publishers, 2010.

Magadlela, Fikile. "*Staffrider* Profile." *Staffrider* 3, no. 2 (June 1980): 24–25.

Magaziner, Daniel R. *The Law and the Prophets: Black Consciousness in South Africa, 1968–1977.* Athens: University of Ohio Press, 2010.

———. "We Write What We Like about Steve Biko." www.Africaisacountry.com (accessed December 19, 2012).

Magubane, Peter. *Women of South Africa: Their Fight for Freedom.* Boston: Little, Brown, 1993.

Malan, Rian. *My Traitor's Heart: A South African Exile Returns to Face His Country, His Tribe, and His Conscience.* New York: Atlantic Monthly Press, 1990.

Maltz-Leca, Leora. "The Logic of the Relic: Traces of History in Stone and Milk." In *Paul Stopforth,* edited by Bronwyn Law-Viloen, 50–75. Cape Town: David Krut, 2010.

Maluka, Mustafa. "Artist's Statement." www.artthrob.co.za/july/fr-9807.htm (accessed 14 November 2014).

Manaka, Matsemela. *Echoes of African Art: A Century of Art in South Africa.* Johannesburg: Skotaville, 1987.

———. *Steve Biko: Journey of the Spirit.* Johannesburg: Ekhaya/Tent Production for SABC1, 1997.

Mandela, Nelson. "A More Human Face." Speech of September 12, 1997. www.soiuser .hyperchat.com/rainman/speech.htm (accessed November 12, 2014).

Manganyi, N. Chabani. *A Black Man Called Sekoto.* Johannesburg: University of the Witwatersrand Press, 1996.

———. *I Am an African: The Life and Times of Gerard Sekoto.* Johannesburg: University of Witwatersrand Press, 2004.

Mangcu, Xolela. *Biko: A Life.* London: I. B. Tauris, 2013.

Marschall, Sabine. *Landscape of Memory: Commemorative Monuments, Memorials and Public Statuary in a Post-Apartheid South Africa.* Leiden and Boston: Brill, 2010.

Martins, Dikobé. "Corn in a Court of Chickens." *African Communist* 1 (1991): 44. www.disa .ukzn.ac.za (accessed August 17, 2009).

———. Letter to Ms. Julia Charlton. February 13, 1996. Johannesburg Art Gallery Archive.

———. "The Necessity of a National Art for Liberation." Presented at Culture and Resistance festival, Gaborone, Botswana, June 1982. In "Dikobé Ben Martins." www. sahistory .org.za. Archive of Judy Seidman.

Marx, Anthony W. *Lessons of Struggle: South African Internal Opposition, 1960–1990.* New York: Oxford University Press, 1992.

McAinsh, Gillian. "Intriguing Display to Scratch Through." *Eastern Province Herald,* July 11, 1997.

McGee, Julie. "Canons Apart and Apartheid Canons: Interpellations beyond the Colonial in South African Art." In *Parisian Canons,* edited by Anna Brzyski, 289–308. Durham, N.C., and London: Duke University Press, 2007.

Mdhlela, Joe. "Focus on Steve Biko." *Sowetan,* September 14, 1994.

Medu Art Ensemble Newsletter 3, no. 1 (January 1981).

Medu Women. "Women and Culture." *Medu Art Ensemble Newsletter* 6, nos. 1 & 2 (n.d.): 25.

Meiring, Piet. *Chronicle of the Truth Commission.* Vanderbijlpark, South Africa: Carpe Diem Books, 1999.

Memela, Sandile, and Shafa'ath-Ahmed Khan. "Hero Who Could Not Be Silenced." *City Press,* September 9, 1990.

Mendelson, Michael. "The Body in the Next Room." In *Images of the Corpse,* edited by Elizabeth Klaver, 186–205. Madison: University of Wisconsin Press, 2004.

Merrett, Christopher. *A Culture of Censorship: Secrecy and Intellectual Repression in South Africa.* Cape Town: David Philip, 1994.

Miles, Elsa. *Polly Street: The Story of an Art Centre.* New York: Ampersand Foundation, 2004.

Minter, William. *Apartheid's Contras: An Inquiry into the Roots of War in Angola and Mozambique.* Johannesburg: University of the Witwatersrand Press; and London: Zed Books, 1994.

Minty, Zayd. "BLAC Bows Outa." www.artthrob.co.za/03feb/reviews/blac.html (accessed November 23, 2009).

———. "Finding the 'Post-Black' Position." In *A Decade of Democracy: South African Art 1994–2004,* edited by Emma Bedford, 110–19. Cape Town: Double Storey Books, 2004.

———. "South-South Dialogue Project." Archive of Zayd Minty.

———. *What Is BLAC?* Pamphlet produced by BLAC, c. 2000. Archive of Zayd Minty.

Mitchell, W. J. T. *Picture Theory: Essays on Verbal and Visual Representation.* Chicago: University of Chicago Press, 1994.

———. *What Do Pictures Want? The Lives and Loves of Images.* Chicago: University of Chicago Press, 2005.

Mkhalipe, Nunka. "Motlana Blames Govt for Biko Death." *The World,* September 19, 1977.

Mngxitama, Andile, Amanda Alexander, and Nigel C. Gibson, eds. *Biko Lives! Contesting the Legacies of Steve Biko.* New York: Palgrave Macmillan, 2008.

Mnyele, Thami. "Interview with Tim Williams." *Medu Art Ensemble Newsletter* 2, no. 1 (March 1980).

———. "Observations on the State of Contemporary Visual Arts in South Africa." Presented at the Culture and Resistance symposium, Gaborone, Botswana, July 1, 1981. Archive of Judy Seidman.

———. "Opening Remarks." *Art toward South Development* exhibition, National Museum and Art Gallery, Gaborone, Botswana, July 1981. Archive of Judy Seidman.

———. "Thoughts for Bongiwe." *Staffrider* 7, nos. 3 & 4 (1988): 297–302. Originally published in *Rixaka* 3 (1986).

Modise, Tim. "Interview with Nelson Mandela." http://en.wikipedia.org/wiki/File: Experience_ubuntu.ogg (accessed December 7, 2014).

Molefe, Themba. "Focus on Steve Biko." *Sowetan,* September 10, 1993.

Molele, Charles. "Beating Their Own Drum." *Tribute,* September 1995, 72–75.

Moodley, Kogila. "The Continued Impact of Black Consciousness." In Pityana et al., *Bounds of Possibility: The Legacy of Steve Biko and Black Consciousness,* 143–52.

Moodley, Strini. "*Cry Freedom*—A Film about All of Us." *Natal Witness,* July 30, 1988.

Moore, Basil, ed. *Black Theology: The South African Voice.* London: C. Hurst, 1973.

Morton, Elizabeth [Gron]. "Exchange and Impact of South African Exiles in Botswana through the Medu Art Ensemble from 1976 to 1985." Master's thesis, University of Botswana, 1992.

Mosaka, Tumelo. "On *Isintu.*" *Isintu Publication.* Archive of Zayd Minty.

Motjuwadi, Stan. "Ntsiki Biko: The Last Time I Saw My Husband Alive." *DRUM,* January 1978, 39.

Motsapi, Ike. "BPC Chief Speaks Out." *The World,* September 16, 1977.

Murinik, Tracy. "Mustafa Maluka." In *Personal Affects: Power and Poetics in Contemporary South African Art,* edited by Laurie Ann Farrell, 86–93. New York: Museum for African Art; Cape Town: Spier, 2004.

Murray, Hugh. "Biko's Brain Injured—Report." *Sunday Express,* September 25, 1977.

Mutloatse, Mothobi. "Ngwana wa Azania: A Film Concept." In Oliphant and Vladislavić, *Ten Years of Staffrider 1978–1988,* 58–61.

Mzamane, Mbulelo Vizikhungo. "The Impact of Black Consciousness on Culture." In Pityana et al., *Bounds of Possibility,* 179–93.

———. "New Poets of the Soweto Era: Van Wyk, Johennesse, and Madingoane." *Research in African Literatures* 19 no. 1 (Spring 1988): 3–11.

Mzamane, Mbulelo Vizikhungo, Bavusile Maaba, and Nkosinathi Biko. "The Black Consciousness Movement." In *The Road to Democracy in South Africa, 1970–1980. Vol. 2,* edited by South African Education Democracy Trust, 99–160. Pretoria: University of South Africa, 2006.

National Union of South African Students (NUSAS). *A People's History: Resistance in South Africa.* Cape Town: NUSAS, June 1980.

Ndebele, Njabulo S. *South African Literature and Culture: Rediscovery of the Ordinary.* Manchester: Manchester University Press, 1994.

Ndlazi, Mandla. "'Hundreds of Bikos Around.'" *Rand Daily Mail,* September 19, 1977.

Nengwekhulu, Renwedzi. "Biko Fought, Died for Black Unity." *Sowetan,* September 12, 1997, 11.

Ngwenya, Oupa. "Saint Biko the Radiant." *Sowetan,* December 9, 1993.

Nhlengethwa, Sam. "Artist's Statement." Johannesburg: Johannesburg Art Gallery, n.d.

"'No Evidence Biko Was Beaten Up.'" *The Star,* December 2, 1977.

"No Kruger File, Rules Biko Magistrate." *The Star,* November 18, 1977.

"Old Man Arrested for Biko Photo, Truth Body Told." www.doj.gov.za/trc/trc_frameset.htm (accessed July 3, 1998).

Oleeson, Mark. "South African Government Planned to Stop 'Cry' from the Outset." *Variety,* August 3, 1988.

Oliphant, Andries. "Imagined Futures: Some New Trends in South African Art." In *Visual Century: South African Art in Context, vol. 4, 1990–2007,* edited by Thembinkosi

Goniwe, Mario Pissarra, Mandisi Majavu, 176–93. Johannesburg: University of the Witwatersrand Press, 2011.

Oliphant, Andries Walter, and Ivan Vladislavić, eds. *Ten Years of Staffrider 1978–1988.* Athens: Ohio University Press, 1988.

"Ondersoek na Biko." *Die Burger,* October 10, 1977.

Oppenheimer, Paul. *Evil and the Demonic: A New Theory of Monstrous Behavior.* New York: New York University Press, 1996.

Orr, Wendy. *From Biko to Basson: Wendy Orr's Search for the Soul of South Africa as a Commissioner of the TRC.* Saxonwold, South Africa: Contra, 2000.

Out of Step: War Resistance in South Africa. London: Catholic Institute for International Relations, 1989.

"Outcry in Overseas Press over Decision." *The Post,* December 4, 1977.

Ozynski, Joyce. "Three Views of Local Sculpture." *Sunday Express,* October 2, 1977.

Patten, John. "Biko: Hot Issue for Cabinet." *The Star,* September 20, 1977.

Peffer, John. *Art and the End of Apartheid.* Minneapolis: University of Minnesota Press, 2009.

Perryer, Sophie. "Mustafa Maluka." In *Accented Living: A Rough Guide.* Johannesburg: Stevenson, 2005. Exhibition catalog.

Phillips, Sandra S., Mark Haworth-Booth, and Carol Squiers. *Police Pictures: The Photograph as Evidence.* San Francisco: San Francisco Museum of Modern Art, 1997.

Pissarra, Mario. "Prejudice and Potential in Political Cartooning." Proceedings of South African Association of Art Historians conference, July 17–19, 1989, University of Natal, Durban, 135–44.

Pityana, N. Barney. "The Renewal of African Moral Values." In *African Renaissance,* edited by Malegapuru William Makgoba, 137–48. Sandton and Cape Town: Mafube and Tafelberg, 1999.

Pityana, N. Barney, Mamphela Ramphele, Malusi Mpumlwana, and Lindy Wilson, eds. *Bounds of Possibility: The Legacy of Steve Biko & Black Consciousness.* Claremont, Cape Town: David Philip, 1991.

Pogrund, Anne. "Statement of Torture." *Rand Daily Mail,* October 6, 1977.

"Police Had Conspiracy of Silence—Kentridge." *The Star,* December 1, 1977.

"Police Will Protect Town—in Case." *Rand Daily Mail,* September 24, 1977.

Pollack, Barbara. "Profile: Sue Williamson." www.contemporary-magazines.com/profile86.htm (accessed December 7, 2014).

Pollack, Lloyd. "Artist Universalises the Guilt That Emerges from Our Sick Society." *Sunday Independent,* October 25, 1998.

Poster Book Collective. *Images of Defiance: South African Resistance Posters of the 1980s.* Johannesburg: Raven Press, 1991.

Powell, Ivor. *Jane Alexander: Sculpture and Photomontage.* Exhibition catalog. Johannesburg: Standard Bank, 1995.

"The Prime Minister Must Sack Mr. Kruger." *The World,* September 19, 1977.

Proud, Hayden, ed. *Revisions: Expanding the Narrative of South African Art.* Johannesburg: South African History Online and University of South Africa Press, 2006.

———. *Scratches on the Face: Antiquity and Contemporaneity in South African Works of Art from Iziko Museums of Cape Town.* Exhibition catalog. Cape Town: Iziko Museums of Cape Town, 2007.

Rachidi, Hlaku Kenneth. "Tribute to Steve Biko—King William's Town." In "Funeral Program for Bantu Stephen Biko." Black Peoples' Convention, September 25, 1977, 5–8. South African History Archive, University of the Witwatersrand.

Ramphele, Mamphela. "Can the Dead Act as Arbitrators?" *Mail and Guardian,* September 8–14, 1995.

———. "Empowerment and Symbols of Hope: Black Consciousness and Community Development." In Pityana et al., *Bounds of Possibility: The Legacy of Steve Biko and Black Consciousness,* 154–78.

———. *A Life.* Cape Town and Johannesburg: David Philip, 1995.

———. "Political Widowhood in South Africa." In *Social Suffering,* edited by Arthur Kleinman, Veena Das, and Margaret Lock, 99–117. Berkeley, Calif.: University of California Press, 1997.

Rancière, Jacques. *The Politics of Aesthetics.* Translated by Gabriel Rockhill. London and New York: Continuum, 2004.

Reber, Pat. "Race Rift Mars Ceremony for South African Activist." *Herald* (Glasgow, Scotland), September 13, 1997, 16A.

Reid, Frances, and Deborah Hoffman. *Long Night's Journey into Day.* Documentary film. USA/South Africa: Reid-Hoffman Productions, 2000.

"Richard Attenborough." *UNESCO Courier,* August 1989.

Richards, Colin. "Cross Purposes: Durant Silhali's Art of Allegory." In Geers, *Contemporary South African Art—The Genor Collection,* 81–97.

———. "The Double Agent: Humanism, History and Allegory in the Art of Durant Sihlali (1939-2004)." *African Arts* 39, no. 1 (Spring 2006): 60–69.

———. "Drawing a Veil: Art in the Age of Emergency." Presented at the conference *The TRC: Commissioning the Past,* University of the Witwatersrand, June 11–14, 1999.

———. "In Human History: Pasts and Prospects in South African Art Today." In *Visual Century: South African Art in Context, vol. 4, 1990–2007,* edited by Thembinkosi Goniwe, Mario Pissarra, and Mandisi Majavu, 46–73. Johannesburg: University of the Witwatersrand Press, 2011.

———. *"Memórius—Intimas—Marcas."* Unpublished autobiographical text, for European tour of exhibition of same name. Archive of Colin Richards.

———. "Our Giftedness." In *A Decade of Democracy: Witnessing South Africa,* edited by Gary Van Wyk, 17–21. Exhibition catalogue. Boston: South Africa Development Fund, 2004.

Rockhill, Gabriel. "Translator's Introduction: Jacques Rancière's *Politics of Perception.*" In Jacques Rancière, *The Politics of Aesthetics: The Distribution of the Sensible.* London and New York: Continuum, 2004.

Ruby, Jay. *Secure the Shadow: Death and Photography in America.* Cambridge, Mass., and London: MIT Press, 1995.

Rugoff, Ralph. *Scene of the Crime.* Exhibition catalog. Cambridge, Mass.: MIT Press, 1997.

Ryan, John. "Hot Time in the Old Temple." *Rand Daily Mail,* November 19, 1977.

Sachs, Albie. *Images of a Revolution: Mural Art in Mozambique.* Harare: Zimbabwe Publishing House, 1983.

Sack, Steven. "Garden of Eden or Political Landscape? Street Art in Mamelodi and Other Townships." In *African Art in Southern Africa: From Tradition to Township,* edited by Anitra Nettleton and David Hammond-Tooke, 191–210. Johannesburg: A. D. Donker, 1989.

———. *The Neglected Tradition: Towards a New History of South African Art (1930–1988).* Johannesburg: Johannesburg Art Gallery, 1988.

———. "Work by Collectives." In *Art from South Africa,* edited by David Elliott et al. Exhibition catalog. Museum of Modern Art. Oxford: England, 1990.

Sankey, Katie. "Forget the Film—These Are the Real Biko 'Stars.'" *Sunday Star,* August 7, 1988.

Saunders, Rebecca. "The Agony and the Allegory: The Concept of the Foreign, the Language of Apartheid, and the Fiction of J. M. Coetzee." *Cultural Critique* 47 (Winter 2001): 215–64.

Savage, Jay. "*Asking for Trouble*: The South African State and the *Cry Freedom* Saga." Unpublished paper, 1989. Archive of University of Durban–Natal.

Sealy, Mark. "The Canvases of Representation and the Photographs of Nontsikelelo Veleko." *Foam Magazine* 23 (2010): 171–74.

Searle, Berni. "Artist's Statement." In *Isintu—Ceremony, Identity, and Community, A South-South Dialogue.* Exhibition catalog. Cape Town: Iziko–South African Gallery, 1999. Archive of Zayd Minty.

"Security Man Suspects Biko Suicide Attempt." *The Star,* November 17, 1977.

Seekings, Jeremy. *The UDF: A History of the United Democratic Front in South Africa 1983–1991.* Cape Town: David Philip, 2000.

Seidman, Judy ["Linda"]. "Letter from South Africa." *Medu Art Ensemble Newsletter* 5, no. 2 (1983): 17–21.

———. *Red on Black: The Story of the South African Poster Movement.* Johannesburg: STE Publishers, 2007.

———. "Finding Community Voice." In *Visual Century: South African Art in Context, vol. 3: 1973–1992,* edited by Mario Pissarra, 104–27. Johannesburg: University of the Witswatersrand Press, 2011.

Sekoto, Gerard. *Gerard Sekoto: My Life and Work.* Text adapted by Karen Press. Kensington: Viva Books, 1995.

Seroke, Jaki. "Poet in Exile: An Interview with Mongane Serote." *Staffrider* (April/May 1981): 30–32.

Serote, Mongane Wally. "Ngwedi Graphic Art Unit." *Medu Art Ensemble Newsletter* 6, nos. 1 and 2 (n.d., 1984?): 26.

———. *No Baby Must Weep.* Johannesburg: Ad. Donker, 1975.

———. *Selected Poems.* Johannesburg: Ad. Donker, 1982.

———. "Time Has Run Out." *Staffrider* 2, no. 4 (November/December 1979): 4–5.

Shinn, Marian. "Steve Biko's Death Could Have Been Kept a Secret." *Sunday Express,* May 18, 1980.

Shloss, Carol. *In Visible Light: Photography and the American Writer: 1840–1940.* New York: Oxford University Press, 1987.

Simbao, Ruth. "Self-Identification as Resistance." In *Visual Century: South African Art in Context, vol. 3, 1973–1992,* edited by Mario Pissarra, 38–59. Johannesburg: University of the Witwatersrand Press, 2011.

Small, Adam. "Steve Biko." *DRUM* (November 1977): 20–27.

Smith, Janet. "Monument to Biko." *Mail and Guardian* (Johannesburg), September 5–11, 1997, 3.

Sono, Temba. "Black Consciousness: Its Significance and Role in the Life of the Community." Unpublished paper, 1971. Liberation Movement Archives at the University of Fort Hare, Alice.

———. *Reflections on the Origins of Black Consciousness in South Africa.* Pretoria: HSRC Publishers, 1993.

Soudien, Crain, and Renate Meyer, eds. *The District Six Public Sculpture Project.* Exhibition catalog. Cape Town: Business and Art, Art and Culture Trust, District Six Museum Foundation, Royal Netherlands Embassy, c. 1998.

"South Africa Orders Inquest into Biko's Death in Jail." *New York Times,* October 27, 1977.

"South African Students' Movement." www.africanhistory.about.com (accessed August 30, 2009).

Southall, Roger. "The ANC and Black Capitalism in South Africa." www.ccs.ukzn.ac.za (accessed August 16, 2011).

Spiro, Leslie. *Gerard Sekoto: Unsevered Ties.* Exhibition catalog. Johannesburg: Johannesburg Art Gallery, 1989.

Staffrider 2, no. 4 (November/December 1979).

State of the Art Conference Proceedings. Cape Town: University of Cape Town, 1979.

Sterritt, David. "Review of *Cry Freedom.*" *Christian Science Monitor,* November 6, 1987.

Steyn, Carol. "Bed Letter Wrong, Biko Doctor Admits." *Rand Daily Mail,* November 25, 1977.

———. "Biko 'Confession Story Fabricated.'" *Rand Daily Mail,* December 1, 1977.

Steyn, Carol, Bernardi Wessels, and Helen Zille. "Our Technique—by Security Colonel." *Rand Daily Mail,* November 19, 1977.

———. "Medical Certificate Incorrect, Says Doctor." *Rand Daily Mail,* November 22, 1977.

Steyn, Carol, Melanie Yap, and Helen Zille. "Point of No Return for Biko 'Soon after Injury.'" *Rand Daily Mail,* November 30, 1977.

Steyn, Carol, and Helen Zille. Title unavailable. *Rand Daily Mail,* November 16, 1977. Title clipped from archived copy. South African History Archive, University of the Witwatersrand.

Stopforth, Paul. "Stopforth: Art as a Political Statement." *WITS Student,* April 3, 1978, n.p.

Streek, Barry. "Biko Image Goes On Growing." *Daily Dispatch,* September 18, 1980.

Stubbs, Aelred. Editor's note to "The Righteousness of Our Strength." In Biko, *I Write What I Like.*

Subirós, Pep, ed. *Apartheid: The South African Mirror.* Barcelona: Centre de Culture Contemporània de Barcelona, 2007.

Tagg, John. *The Burden of Representation: Essays on Photographies and Histories.* London: Macmillian, 1988.

Tambo, Oliver. "Mobilise Our Black Power." www.nelsonmandela.org/omalley/index.php/site/q/03lv02424/04lv02730/05lv02918/06lv02977.htm (accessed November 22, 2014).

Thlale, Molatlhegi oa. "Where Would Biko Have Stood Today?" *City Press,* September 15, 1991.

Thomas, Franklin A. *South Africa: Time Running Out.* A Report of the Study Commission on U.S. Policy toward South Africa. Berkeley: University of California Press, 1981.

Tomaselli, Keyan, and P. Eric Louw. "The South African Progressive Press under Emergency, 1986–1989." In *The Alternative Press in South Africa,* edited by Keyan Tomaselli and P. Eric Louw, 175–90. Bellville, South Africa: Anthropos; and London: James Currey, 1991.

"Tribute to Biko, Luthuli." *Daily Dispatch,* July 1, 1978.

Truth and Reconciliation Commission of South Africa Report. Vol. I. Cape Town: CTP Book Printers, 1998.

———. Vol. IV. Cape Town: CTP Book Printers, 1998.

Tsedu, Mathatha. "Back to the Front." *Sowetan,* September 12, 1991.

———. "Two Decades On We Honour Noble Hero." *Sowetan,* September 12, 1997, 11.

Tutu, Desmond. *No Future without Forgiveness.* New York: Doubleday, 1999.

———. "Preface." In Biko, *I Write What I Like.*

Tyson, Harvey. "Can You Bear Those Cries?" *The Star,* August 1, 1988.

van Alphen, Ernst. "Deadly Historians: Boltanski's Intervention in Holocaust Historiography." In *Memory and Oblivion: Proceedings of the XXIXth International Congress of the History of Art, Amsterdam, 1–7 September 1996,* edited by Wessel Reinink and Jeroen Stumpel, 913–17. New York: Springer, 1999.

van der Watt, Liese. "Towards an 'Adversarial Aesthetics': A Personal Response to Personal Affects." In *Personal Affects: Power and Poetics in Contemporary South African Art,* edited by Sophie Perryer, 45–54. New York: Museum for African Art, 2004.

Van Onselen, Charles. *The Seed Is Mine: The Life of Kas Maine, a South African Sharecropper, 1894–1985.* New York: Hill and Wang, 1996.

van Wyk, Christopher. "CHRISTOPHER VAN WYK: *Staffrider* and the Politics of Culture." In Oliphant and Vladislavić, *Ten Years of Staffrider 1978–1988,* 165–70.

———. "Coming Home." *Staffrider* 2, no. 3 (July/August 1979): 54.

———. "We Can't Meet Here, Brother (for Thami Mnyele)." In Oliphant and Vladislavić, *Ten Years of Staffrider 1978–1988.*

Van Wyk, Gary. "Reflecting Democracy." In *A Decade of Democracy: Witnessing South Africa,* edited by Gary Van Wyk, 5–9. Johannesburg: Sondela, 2004.

Van Wyk, Roger. "The (Non)sense of Humour." In *Visual Century: South African Art in Context, vol. 3, 1973–1992,* edited by Mario Pissarra, 156–79. Johannesburg: University of the Witwatersrand Press, 2011.

Vaughan, William, and Helen Weston. "Introduction." In *Jacques-Louis David's Marat,* edited by William Vaughn and Helen Weston, 1–33. Cambridge and New York: Cambridge University Press, 2000.

Watson, Wendy. *Brick by Brick: An Informal Guide to the History of South Africa.* Claremont, South Africa: New Africa Books, 2007.

"We Do Not Use Force—Col Goosen." *The Citizen,* November 19, 1977.

Wessels, Bernardi, and Helen Zille. "Biko Chained for 48 Hours 'to Protect Him.'" *Rand Daily Mail,* November 17, 1977.

Williams, Weamm. "Graffiti, Popular Culture's Most Potent Visual Representation?" Presented at BLAC event, May 1, 2000. Archive of Zayd Minty.

Williamson, Sue. "Art as Media: Filling the Gap." c. 1987.

———. "Artist's Statement." Government tourist brochure. Goodman Gallery, c. 1992.

———. *Resistance Art in South Africa.* New York: St. Martin's Press, 1989.

———. *South African Art Now.* New York: Harper Collins, 2009.

———. *Sue Williamson: Selected Work.* Brussels: Centre d'Art Contemporain, 2003.

Wilson, Lindy. "Bantu Stephen Biko: A Life." In Pityana et al., *Bounds of Possibility: The Legacy of Steve Biko and Black Consciousness,* 15–77.

———. *Steve Biko.* Auckland Park: Jacana Media Ltd, 2011; Athens: Ohio University Press, 2012.

Woods, Donald. *Asking for Trouble.* New York: Atheneum, 1980.

———. *BIKO.* London: Paddington Books, 1978.

———. *Filming with Attenborough: The Making of* Cry Freedom. New York: Henry Holt, 1987

———. "A Great Man Dies." *Rand Daily Mail,* September 16, 1977.

Worden, Nigel. *The Making of Modern South Africa: Conquest, Apartheid, Democracy.* 4th ed. Malden, Mass.: Blackwell, 2007.

"The World Mourns." *The Post,* September 17, 1978.

"A Wreath for Steve." *The World,* September 15, 1977.

Wylie, Diana. *Art + Revolution: The Life and Death of Thami Mnyele, South African Artist.* Charlottesville: University of Virginia Press, 2008.

Yap, Melanie, and Helen Zille. "Injury '4 to 8 Days Old.'" *Rand Daily Mail,* November 25, 1977.

Yekiso, Jimmy. "Biko Would Have Fought This Sell-Out." *South,* September 10–14, 1992.

Young, Robert J. C. *Postcolonialism: An Historical Introduction.* Oxford: Blackwell, 2001.

Younge, Gavin. *Art of the South African Townships.* New York: Rizzoli, 1988.

Zille, Helen. "Biko Was Bent on Suicide—Colonel." *Rand Daily Mail,* November 17, 1977.

———. "On Seven Foot Chain." *Rand Daily Mail,* November 26, 1977.

Interviews and Personal Correspondence

Alexander, Jane. Interview with author, Gardens, Cape Town, December 2, 1999.

Berndt, Jon. Interview with author, Woodstock, Cape Town, April 12, 1997.

Bester, Willie. Interview with author, Kuilsriver, Cape Town, December 6, 1999.

Clarke, Peter. Interview with author, Ocean View, Cape Town, January 3, 2011.

Davis, Lionel. Interview with author, Gardens, Cape Town, May 8, 1997.

———. Interview with author, Muizenberg, Cape Town, January 3, 2011.

de Gruchy, Steve. Email correspondence, March 25–30, 2008.

de la Harpe, Jean. Interview with author, Johannesburg, July 9, 1998.

de Villiers, Chris. Interview with author, Braamfontein, Johannesburg, June 27, 1998.

Dhlomo-Mautloa, Bongiwe. Interview with author, Braamfontein, Johannesburg, January 10, 2011.

Erasmus, Garth and Emile Maurice. Interview with author, Woodstock, Cape Town, January 3, 2011.

Godby, Michael. Personal communication, November 1999.

Goniwe, Thembinkosi. Interview with author, Braamfontein, Johannesburg, January 14, 2011.

Hendricks, Paul. Email correspondence, August 25, 2011.

Hlati, Sipho. Interview with author, Gardens, Cape Town, January 5, 2011.

Jacobson, Naomi. Interview with author, Parkview, Johannesburg, September 8, 1999.

Koloane, David. Interview with author, Newtown, Johannesburg, December 13, 1999.

———. Interview with author, Braamfontaine, Johannesburg, January 14, 2011.

Kunene, Daniel. Personal correspondence, 2003.

Landau, Paul. Personal communication, February 21, 2015.

Lentz, Robert. Email correspondence, April 23, 2010.

Magadlela, Fikile. Interview with author, Orange Grove, Johannesburg, August 28, 1999.

Maluka, Mustafa. Email correspondence, April 14, 2003.

———. Email correspondence, August 14, 2011.

Manganyi, N. Chabani. Interview with author, Centurian, Pretoria, January 17, 2011.

Masters, Craig. Telephone interview, August 30, 2011.

Mautloa, Patrick. Interview with author, Newtown, Johannesburg, January 17, 2012.

Minty, Zayd. Interview with author, Greenpoint, Cape Town, January 5, 2011.

Mncwabe, Musa. Personal communication. Durban, November 1, 1999.

Moodley, Asha. Interview with author, Durban, November 9, 1999.

Moodley, Strini. Interview with author, Durban, November 3, 1999.

Nhlengethwa, Sam. Interview with author, Newtown, Johannesburg, September 16, 1999.

Nkosi, Charles. Interview with author, Diepkloof, Soweto, January 17, 2012.

Nxele, Addison. Interview with author, Johannesburg, July 1998.

Pickover, Michelle. Personal communication, September 20, 1999.

Pissarra, Mario. Personal communication, January 13, 2012.

Powell, Marlene. Email correspondence, September 1998.

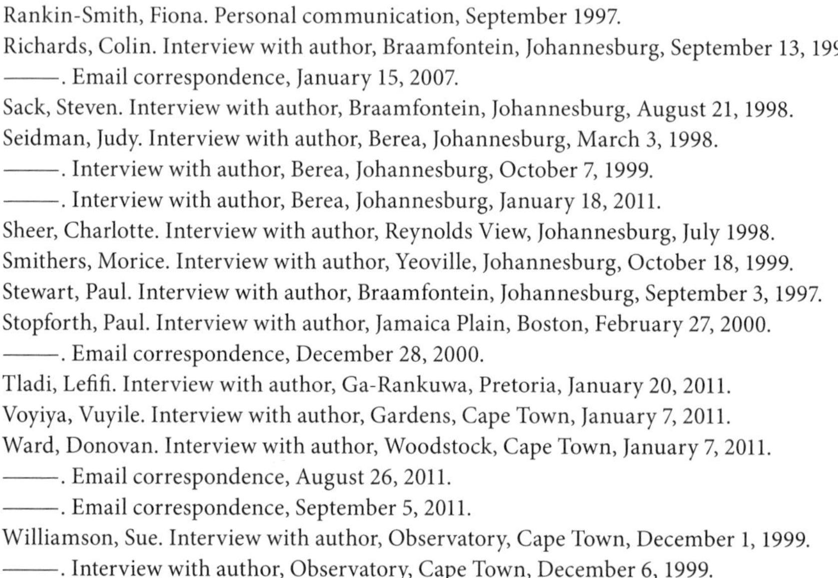

Rankin-Smith, Fiona. Personal communication, September 1997.

Richards, Colin. Interview with author, Braamfontein, Johannesburg, September 13, 1999.

———. Email correspondence, January 15, 2007.

Sack, Steven. Interview with author, Braamfontein, Johannesburg, August 21, 1998.

Seidman, Judy. Interview with author, Berea, Johannesburg, March 3, 1998.

———. Interview with author, Berea, Johannesburg, October 7, 1999.

———. Interview with author, Berea, Johannesburg, January 18, 2011.

Sheer, Charlotte. Interview with author, Reynolds View, Johannesburg, July 1998.

Smithers, Morice. Interview with author, Yeoville, Johannesburg, October 18, 1999.

Stewart, Paul. Interview with author, Braamfontein, Johannesburg, September 3, 1997.

Stopforth, Paul. Interview with author, Jamaica Plain, Boston, February 27, 2000.

———. Email correspondence, December 28, 2000.

Tladi, Lefifi. Interview with author, Ga-Rankuwa, Pretoria, January 20, 2011.

Voyiya, Vuyile. Interview with author, Gardens, Cape Town, January 7, 2011.

Ward, Donovan. Interview with author, Woodstock, Cape Town, January 7, 2011.

———. Email correspondence, August 26, 2011.

———. Email correspondence, September 5, 2011.

Williamson, Sue. Interview with author, Observatory, Cape Town, December 1, 1999.

———. Interview with author, Observatory, Cape Town, December 6, 1999.

———. Email correspondence, June 24, 2013.

Index

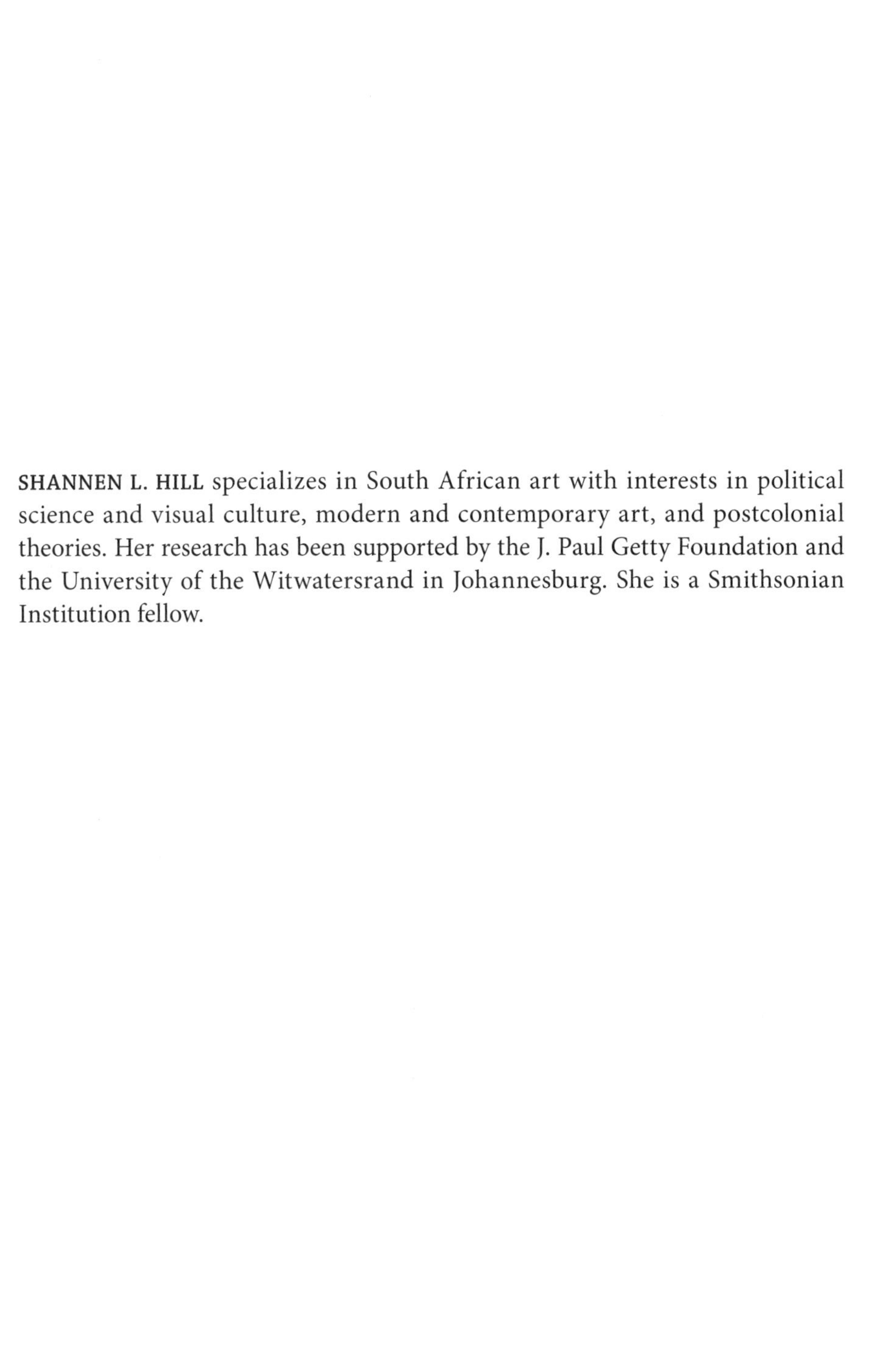

SHANNEN L. HILL specializes in South African art with interests in political science and visual culture, modern and contemporary art, and postcolonial theories. Her research has been supported by the J. Paul Getty Foundation and the University of the Witwatersrand in Johannesburg. She is a Smithsonian Institution fellow.